Management Information Systems

Management Information Systems:

Using Cases within an Industry Context to Solve Business Problems with Information Technology

Dr. David L. Anderson
Charles H. Kellstadt Graduate School of Business,
DePaul University, Chicago, Illinois

Prentice Hall, Upper Saddle River, New Jersey

Acquisitions Editor: *David Alexander*
Editor-in-Chief: *Mickey Cox*
Assistant Editor: *Lori Cerreto*
Editorial Assistant: *Erika Rusnak*
Associate Managing Editor: *Sondra Greenfield*
Senior Manufacturing Supervisor: *Paul Smolenski*
Manufacturing Manager: *Vincent Scelta*
Design Director: *Patricia Smythe*
Cover Design: *Richard Hannas*
Cover Image: *Artville*
Production Services: *Pre-Press Company, Inc.*

Copyright ©2000 by Prentice Hall, Inc.
Upper Saddle River, New Jersey 07458

Library of Congress Cataloging-in-Publication Data

Anderson, David L. (David Lee)
    Management information systems: using cases within an industry
context to solve business problems with information technology /
David L. Anderson.
        p. cm.
    "Chapters follow the textural material in the Post/Anderson
textbook, Management information systems: solving business problems
with information technology."
    Includes bibliographical references and index.
    ISBN 0-201-61176-7 (alk. paper)
    1. Management information systems.   I. Post, Gerald V.
Management information systems.   II. Title.
HD30.213.A525   1999
658.4'038—dc21   99-38662
                                                                 CIP

ISBN: 0-201-61176-7

Prentice Hall International (UK) Limited, *London*
Prentice Hall of Australia Pty, Limited, *Sydney*
Prentice Hall Canada, Inc., *Toronto*
Prentice Hall Hispanoamericana, S.A., *Mexico*
Prentice Hall of India Private Limited, *New Delhi*
Prentice-Hall of Japan, Inc., *Tokyo*
Prentice-Hall (*Singapore*) Pte, Ltd
Editora Prentice-Hall do Brasil, Ltda., *Rio de Janeiro*

Printed in the United States of America

10 9 8 7 6 5 4 3 2 1

BRIEF CONTENTS

CONTENTS

A UNIQUE APPROACH TO STUDYING WITH CASES

Learning technology is easier than ever before. Microsoft Suite enjoys nearly universal acceptance, including almost 85 percent of the personal computer marketplace. Learning to use this powerful tool is relatively easy. Help documents and tutorials are readily available online. CD-roms and videotapes promise to teach even the novice user how to use word processing, spreadsheets, and databases in a short period of time. Books ranging from *Word for Dummies* to *The Power User's Guide to Excel* provide everything from the first steps with the application to advanced programming capabilities.

In the midst of all of these resources, many college and university students as well as businesses have asked themselves how they can move beyond a technical knowledge of the tool to an applications-driven implementation of the technology. In many situations, they have used examples and problems to learn the full range of the tool's abilities. However, they have not been able to fully develop an understanding of how the tools can help them strengthen their personal decision making, enhance their business analysis, or improve their career capabilities.

This textbook focuses on using the technical understanding that you may have obtained in an Introduction to Management Information Systems class. Your class may have been a traditional course in which you learned what a computer was, how to distinguish between micro-, mini-, and mainframe computers, and how centralization and decentralization of technology are different. The textbook also seeks to build upon the knowledge you have developed in your efforts to learn to use Microsoft Word, Excel, Powerpoint, and Access. You may have obtained this knowledge through a course, in which you studied a textbook that taught these applications, or you may have obtained this knowledge on your own, through a book that you purchased in a bookstore.

With the base of your understanding of these tools, it is important to gain experience applying them to business decision making. That is the direction in which this case book is focused. By using real business cases and descriptions of actual situations, this book will help you apply your skills and understanding of the Microsoft Suite to actual business decision making.

The outline of the book is different from what you might be used to. However, it has a specific objective and focus. The chapters follow and reinforce the textual material in the Post and Anderson textbook, *Management Information Systems: Solving Business Problems with Information Technology*. The cases in each chapter will reinforce the concepts that you may have learned or may be learning in this textbook or another one like it. By stepping through each chapter, you should develop a progressive understanding of what is involved in the implementation of information systems in today's business environment.

An additional enhancement is the organization of the chapters by industry and by company within each industry. Many casebooks teach stand-alone cases; none has endeavored to develop a clear understanding of how a company operates within the context of its industry and the companies with which it competes. Organizing the cases by industry will help you to better understand the role that competition plays in business strategy and the impact it can have on the decision to computerize your business.

This casebook, however, is not just a collection of cases. Each chapter contains a progressively difficult collection of case examples and problems to expand your knowledge and understanding of statistical and quantitative analysis, particularly as it relates to financial and data analysis. The application/analysis sections of each case will include the following components:

1. *Internet Exercises*. Vast amounts of information about companies and industries are now available on the Internet that were never available before. No matter where you are working, you can obtain extensive information about the company itself from its own web page. This often includes the annual report, advertising material, and catalogs. As a result, information about each company in the casebook includes a link to its web site along with specific questions to help you focus on the best sources of information. Equally important are the links to the industry-relevant web pages. No company operates in a vacuum, particularly today. As a result, it has become increasingly important to determine the business that the company is in, the industry in which it competes, and the best source for information about that industry. Since each chapter is organized by industry, web sites and questions are included to assist you in examining the role that industry analysis plays in your understanding of the business objectives of each company.

2. *Excel Exercises*. The implementation of technology is costly. It is particularly so if the technology is to be used to enhance the strategic direction of the company. To help you see this, the most recent balance sheets and exercises related to them are cited for each case. Viewed individually, these balance sheets and their related exercises will help you "zero in" on the problems and opportunities that each of the corporations is facing. The balance sheets and income statements come from the Edgar database on the Securities and Exchange Commission home page or from a CD-rom source for financial information. The important thing to remember is that this information is readily available for free for your analysis. If you follow the exercises and study the cited financial information, you will develop the skills to analyze financial information no matter the company. You will have a stronger basis to make an investment decision, analyze a potential supplier or buyer, or even evaluate the financial

strength of a potential employer. Since the financial information is so readily available, you can accomplish this analysis wherever you are located.

3. *Access Exercises*. Increasingly, the most valuable commodities that a corporation owns are its data resources. The information that a corporation maintains on its customers can be crucial to its continued successful operation. Its linkage to its suppliers through Electronic Data Interchange and other data-gathering devices further strengthens the need to collect and maintain data on those parts of the organization that supply it with the products and services that it ultimately assembles, manipulates, or repackages to sell to its customers. As a result, each case includes a database with sections and questions relating to the particular business and market segment in which the company is operating.

4. *Microsoft Project Exercises*. Work is increasingly project-driven. This means that funding proposals, special projects, and development efforts have a measurable beginning and end. They do not just continue. As a result, it is important to know and understand a project management tool. Microsoft Project is a readily available, fairly inexpensive tool that charts time, duration, cost, and human resources. A clear understanding of these variables is important to manage technology and other projects in the future. As a result, each case includes a Microsoft Project Plan with sections and questions relating to a specific business project in the industry in which the company is operating.

This book is unique in its application of this combination of tools to your study of companies and the industries in which they operate. While other casebooks may include a series of technology cases, the inclusion and arrangement of the cases in this book will assist you in your efforts to examine and understand the core competencies, critical success factors, and change drivers that may impact each of these industries and corporations. This will give you experience asking the important questions regarding what ultimately impacts business decision-making processes in each of these areas. It will also give you experience working with the financial, statistical, and analytical data that is readily available in the marketplace. The goal, of course, is that you will develop the self-confidence needed to address these questions on your own when you are in the marketplace without the benefit of a textbook or professor.

Equally important, these cases are focused and straightforward. Although couched in a standard business context, each case includes a readily apparent technology impact and decision. Unique to this casebook, the decision scenario is not presented in a vacuum, but within the business constraints identified by the financial and other information that is provided with the excel and access data.

An extensive bibliography is provided with a listing of the most up-to-date books to provide additional references and supporting material.

THE IMPORTANCE OF STUDYING CASES

The case method is based on the belief that students in management education can significantly improve their analytical ability through studying, analyzing, and discussing actual business scenarios. Cases develop the skills of logical thinking, searching for relevant information, analyzing and evaluating facts, and drawing conclusions, all of which are needed for business decision making. Making a point in front of your peers improves your ability to communicate clearly, evaluate the opinions of others, react wisely, and reach conclusions that gain collective support.

By definition, a *case* is a description, using words and numbers, of an actual management situation. The case paints a picture of the setting of a business decision and takes the student to the brink of the decision without revealing what happened. A *case study* is a written story that serves as the basis for a group discussion. It can foster a classroom program of role-playing, simulation, question-answering, and discussion. The actual case is a description of a company within a particular context in time. A written case attempts to provide a synopsis of past events in the life of an organization. It sets the stage for making a decision by describing the context from a number of different perspectives. These include financial data about the assets of the organization, statistical information about the employees and markets that the company addresses, organizational information about reporting structure and decision making, technological information about the decisions to implement technology, and managerial information about competitors, internal operations, and the personalities of the individuals involved.

A good case will place you in the position of facing a managerial challenge and preparing an action plan. It will force you to determine what decisions need to be made, justify them, and make recommendations to the class. The financial aspects of a case will enable you to develop skills in analyzing and making financial decisions. Cases with marketing or production information will lead to decisions made by marketing or production managers. Cases that combine all of these issues result in the development of skills in strategic analysis.

The founder of the case-teaching method and its chief advocate is C. R. Christensen. In his book, *Teaching and the Case Method*, Professor Christensen asserts,

> The active intellectual and emotional involvement of the student is a hallmark of case teaching. That

involvement offers the most dramatic visible contrast with a stereotypical lecture class.[1]

Unlike case teaching in law school, which is bound by legal precedent, case teaching in business school is focused upon the stimulation of creative thinking. Business cases are "won" by the students who most accurately analyze the problems and opportunities facing an organization and make the most financially rewarding recommendations, given these constraints.

Case-based teaching is unique because it facilitates a dynamic interchange between the professor, the student, and the material. Rather than merely conveying facts or even ideas, the professor becomes an actor who uses descriptions to set the stage for the analysis of a company or its competition. Case-based teaching can be more effective than lecture teaching because it combines cognitive with motivational aims in the classroom.[2] The study of cases will provide you with hands-on practice in how to think inductively within the context of an actual situation. It combines theoretical concepts with real-life experience to provide practical decision-making experience. The cases in this book combine real-life experiences with those of companies to enhance your practical understanding of the real-life situation. By studying these cases, you will be able to develop rules that you can subsequently apply to business situations you currently face or will face in the future.

These management information systems cases have been written to merge substantive and procedural aspects of technology. Setting a technology decision within a case context helps to convey the complex aspects of these decisions. The successful application of technology to business involves not only the understanding of the substantive concepts, but also the ability to understand the procedures that often must be followed for technology to be implemented successfully.

A case class differs from a lecture situation since you, as the student, must shoulder more of the responsibility. In a lecture situation, you are primarily responsible for mastering the material that is presented to you. Cases present what is often the most difficult part of the learning process, the decision about what material on which to concentrate. As such, these decisions are more like real life choices.

In your class preparation, study your cases as a business practioner, not as a student. By addressing case questions as a team before class, you can use the

---

[1] C. R. Christensen and A. J. Hansen, *Teaching and the Case Method*, Harvard Business School Publishing Division, Cambridge, MA, 1987.

[2] Frank Bocker, "Is Case Teaching More Effective than Lecture Teaching in Business Administration? An Exploratory Analysis," *Interfaces* 17:5, September–October, 1987, pp. 64–71.

synergy of the group to develop better solutions than you could working alone. In doing so, you can use collective problem-solving and multiple role-playing to confront ineffective strategies and misconceptions.

Studying cases will assist you in your efforts to develop approaches or rules that you plan to apply to achieve success in business. Cases provide an easy, low-cost way to experiment with ideas and proposals. They give you experience in debugging incorrect hypotheses and making reasonable predictions in new situations. Your case preparation provides the opportunity to experiment with the best questions to ask, the best way to test a theory, and the best way to verbalize and defend rules or theories. Once these rules have been derived from the specific cases that you are studying, they can be extrapolated to other cases that you will study or situations in which you find yourself. You can use the progression of cases to refine and confirm the ideas that you are developing.

THE BEST WAY TO PREPARE A CASE

Cases are best addressed systematically, through a standard approach. Applying this standard framework will enable you to make sure that you have thoroughly researched the subject, examined the material, and are not missing any important issues. The standard framework frequently used in business cases is:

Student Case Analysis Outline

I. **Issue**
The issue is the essential question of the case. It is the single reason why the case was written. The answer to the issue is the main idea with which you should walk away from the case and the classroom discussion.

II. **Environmental Analysis**
The environmental analysis presents the events leading to the development of the issue. This includes the financial/stock/portfolio analysis as well as the governmental and other constraints in which the decision makers must operate. The environmental analysis includes the variables that the individual company cannot control.

III. **Problems and Opportunities**
The problems and opportunities section lists the strengths and weaknesses within which the business leaders must operate. While these factors are often received by the business managers, they are also the ones over which the manager has the most control.

IV. **Alternatives**
The alternatives are the three to four most likely next steps that the managers can take in their attempt to address the original business issue. These must be succinct and clearly thought out. They must be the most comprehensive steps that the managers can take, given the environment in which they are working and the problems and opportunities that they are facing.

V. **Recommendation**
The recommendation is the choice of the best alternative and the decision to follow that path in future efforts.

The Competitor Analysis should be different and should incorporate the Case Analysis with a particular focus on the identified competitor(s).

Student Competitor Analysis/Outline

Competitor Company Name

I. **Description of the Competitor Company**

II. **Financial Analysis/Portfolio Issue**

III. **Stock/Investment Outlook**

IV. **Potential/Prospective for Growth**

V. **Competitive Structure**

VI. **Role of Research and Development**

VII. **Technological Investment and Analysis**

VIII. **Recommendation for the Future**

Similarly, the Student Industry Analysis/Outline focuses upon the industry in which the company is operating and competing. You should keep in mind that the key to this analysis is not to allow yourself to fill in the blanks by writing down everything that is available. You must constantly keep in mind that the goal is to collect and present only information that will lead to the successful evaluation of the case.

Remember that extensive and complex material such as this should be collected and analyzed in small steps. This will enable you to more easily decide which information is important. Collecting the information in small steps will also enable you to more thoroughly organize it.

Student Industry Analysis/Outline

Industry Name

I. **Description of the Industry**

II. **Financial Analysis**

III. **Stock/Investment Outlook**

IV. **Potential/Prospective for Growth**

V. **Competitive Structure**

VI. **Role of Research and Development**

VII. **Technological Investment and Analysis**

VIII. **Recommendation for the Future**

To complete the industry analysis, the following steps should be helpful.

1. Identify the industry.

2. Seek general industry information.

3. Identify and search the industry's trade and consumer magazines.

4. Learn about the consumers of the product or service.

5. Examine the patent and trademark situation in the industry.

6. Determine the legal issues in the industry.

7. Find information about specific companies in the industry.

8. Define the type of competition in the industry.

9. Examine the geography of the industry.

10. Determine the impact of weather and climate on the industry.

11. Examine the international market.

12. Interview people from the industry.

13. Fill in the gaps with information from information providers.

Whenever lists of items to identify, research, and present are made, the temptation always exists to focus on the lists, not on the issue at hand. The cases in this book were included to enable you to "put yourself in the shoes" of the manager and make decisions as a manager would. Taking this approach will make case-teaching intrinsically motivating, including the elements of challenge, fantasy, and fun. Satisfaction can come from applying a standard process of analysis to the case and then succinctly presenting the results to the class. The goal, of course, is to recognize a unique point that no one else has identified.

The cases include personal descriptions of the major players in the cases so that you can make decisions from the framework they bring to the case. Remember, if the manager or company is extremely conservative financially, he, she, or it will be less likely to adopt and implement a cutting-edge management information system. Although personal nuances are not included in the thorough financial and quantitative analysis discussed previously, it is often these nuances and perspectives that lead to the difference between the successful and less-than-successful implementation of technology.

While you are putting yourself in the manager's shoes and making decisions from this perspective, it is also important to bring your own unique perspective to the decision making process. One danger in business, of course, is the temptation to become myopic and focus only on those things that make sense from your perspective. Managers and companies that have adhered strictly to this approach often get into trouble, since they miss new market segments, changing environments, or ways in which they can further mine their current customer lists for new sales and product opportunities.

As a result, after you have thoroughly analyzed the information, it is extremely important to bring your perspective to the final mix of business recommendations. Perhaps you have worked in the industry, can identify with a particular untapped market segment or group, or just have a tangential interest in the subject. All of these perspectives give you a unique viewpoint to include in your analysis. Breadth of exposure to the conventions, points of view, and practices of many industries is important to provide the depth required to understand the complexities involved in conducting business within each case setting. Particularly in technology, simple formulas for success are not readily available for easy application. Cases provide contextual understanding from which to make business judgments in a protected environment. Even the most quantitatively-oriented manager will agree that the emotion, attitudes, aspirations, and values he or she brings to the task will play an important role in managerial decision making.

Examining cases within the context of an industry helps to guard against grasping for the first comparison opportunity that exists and attempting to force-fit it to the next business problem. The memorization of rules, even the correct ones, are of minimal worth unless the rules can be applied at the right time and in the proper situation. Breadth of exposure to the conventions, points of view, and practices of many industries provides the wisdom necessary to identify subtleties in the organization and respond accordingly. Knowledge of the business environment, economies, or problems of specific industries or companies may never be explicitly used. However, they will provide the perspective or influence the imagination to discover a new innovation or apply an old one to a new situation.

Several approaches can be important keys to developing this perspective. Your final analysis should incorporate aspects of all five.

1. *Generalist.* The generalist approach advocates breadth of perspective rather than specialization. Focus is placed upon addressing the issue from a broad business perspective. Often the most difficult part of the problem is to identify in which discipline the problem lies. Thus, it is important to rise above your individual perspective or discipline to first determine in which area the problem resides.

2. *Practitioner.* The practitioner approach focuses on the importance of acting and the willingness to act. Courses of action must be chosen and decisions must be made even when there is incomplete information or the risk is high that subsequent information will prove the decision maker wrong.

3. *Professional.* The professional approach insures that the role of the manager includes and goes beyond the entrepreneurial function. Quality and clarity of the final purpose are important. The goal is long-term return-on-investment, not just short-term profit.

4. *Innovative.* The innovative approach stresses the implementation of new ideas rather than the maintenance of the status quo. Focusing policy upon changing circumstances is as important as developing innovation through new inventions and advancing technology. Profits can be maximized through the application of the company's long-established strengths to unexplored segments of the market through price, service, distribution, or advertising innovations.

5. *Communication.* The communication approach involves the effective communication of the decision to the rest of the organization.

THE BENEFITS OF USING CASES

Cases focus on the problems of strategy formulation, building the organization, and accomplishing assigned tasks. Utilized effectively, the case approach will maximize the benefit you will receive in the development of additional knowledge and skills. The increasing complexity, both financially and conceptually, of the cases in this book should lead to a deeper understanding and perspective of the business issues involved in management information systems.

Concentration on these cases will enable you to learn about the functions, roles, and skills of senior management from the perspective of the general manager. They help you develop techniques in setting goals, outlining the functions and activities that must be performed to achieve the goals, and determining the strategies needed to accomplish these objectives. They clearly demonstrate the role that risk plays in management. Cases will help you identify and deal successfully with uncertainty and rapidly learn to make decisions from limited information. Cases will provide experience in dividing the organization into logical, understandable assignments with limitations on authority and provisions for individual decision making. Cases provide practice with setting performance standards. These standards will assist you in the application of your skills to making leadership decisions through insight, self-confidence, and imagination. Finally, the cases will assist you with the anticipation and acceptance of responsibility for your actions and those of the organization as you someday relate to the organization's stakeholders, investors, employees, suppliers, communities, countries, and environment.

Learning from cases will also change the way you interact with your professor. By emphasizing student involvement and self-teaching, the use of case studies requires a substantial shift in the traditional roles played by you and your professor. Teaching with cases provides fundamental opportunities but also dilemmas and risks. For some professors, case-teaching can be an uncomfortable assignment[3] since it introduces an element of the unknown into the classroom equation. Many variables can be controlled in a well-written and delivered lecture. Well-prepared students and the professor can direct a case in many different directions, some of which were neither planned for nor even foreseen. The crafting of questions, careful listening, and constructive response are the key skill requirements for effective case interactions.

As a student, you can use cases to gain expertise in responding quickly to new situations and environments. The best decisions are made with perfect information. Unfortunately, few decisions have the luxury of being made with this background. Cases provide practice in "landing on one's feet" and responding quickly to a problem or opportunity given a limited amount of information and the time constraints under which you must operate.

---

[3] C. R. Christensen and A. J. Hansen, op. cit.

PREFACE TO THE INSTRUCTOR

TEACHING WITH CASES

Today's students enter college focused on timeliness, and with a great deal of impatience. They have a much clearer focus than previous generations on using their education to achieve their personal and professional goals. Computer games flash images and rapid change continuously before their eyes. Television has become a constant channel-surf with the remote control and picture-in-picture available to jump to whatever is most interesting or dynamic at the moment. The World Wide Web sends students surfing across the Internet driven by their own desire to find knowledge or action on a particular web site. When they become bored with a site or a topic, it is easy to move toward the next site or idea. All this is done without apology or consideration of what such rapid action may do for discipline or direction.

It is within this context that today's college professor must present and attempt to motivate. Television, including Mind Extension University, presents one-hour choreographed presentations complete with pictorial examples from industry and tours from manufacturing plants. Videotaped presentations are available from publishers that include one-on-one interviews with leaders in the industry.

Given these opportunities for learning, today's college professor must find new and more effective ways to communicate increasingly complex and technical information. As a result, this book takes a three-pronged approach to teaching management information:

1. Textual material

2. Cases (actual)

3. Hands-on exercises

Students enroll in management information systems classes both with business experience and with no business experience. For those with business experience, real business cases provide the spark that is often needed to enable the student to say, "I've experienced that," or "My company addresses that problem this way." For those without business experience, cases provide the first glimpse of business problems and the decision making structure that they require. For this reason, cases and examples have been included from companies that the students have experienced as customers and/or as employees and with which they would easily identify.

From a pedagogical perspective, teaching with cases provides a *framework* and serves as an *example*. The framework provides a structure upon which to build an approach to the analysis of a business problem. The example gives the student a context within which to place the business problem.

Preparing to bring cases to class includes the following four steps:

1. Individual analysis and preparation

2. Optional informal small-group discussion

3. Classroom discussion

4. End-of-class generalization about the learning process

The *individual analysis and preparation* step involves the student in the following activities before class begins:

1. Reading and analyzing the case to get a good understanding and contextual flavor for the facts of the case as they are presented

2. Researching the context in which the case was written. This could include the following factors:
   Historical context for the case
   Economic factors/indicators at the time of the case (inflation, employment rates, building, and expansion)

Technological impact for the case (state of technology and ability to implement change)

3. Analyzing the financial impact of the case. This could include:

    Financial reports from the case company

    Financial evaluation from services (Moody's or Standard and Poor's)

    Financial evaluation from online sources (Disclosure Global Access)

    Financial evaluation from Internet sources (SEC Edgar Web page)

4. Evaluating the industry of the case company. This could include:

    Choosing the industry in which the company operates (This step is often overlooked, but can be the most critical. For example, banks now compete with insurance companies and brokerage houses and vice versa.)

    Deciding what will be the change-drivers in the industry

    Analyzing the cost of entering or remaining in this industry given the costs of these change-drivers

    Evaluating the barriers to entry that the competition is constructing

5. Evaluating the competition of the case company. This would include:

    Determining who the competitors are, given the product line for the case company

    Identifying the strengths and weaknesses of the competitors

    Evaluating the financial ability of the competition to meet customer demand

    Analyzing brand and customer loyalty to the competitor's product

    Evaluating the research and development investment of the competitor

    Understanding the ability of the competition to use technology to identify and capture new market segments

6. Extending the conceptual framework of the case company. An extensive bibliography is included to provide additional sources of conceptual and industry information to research and incorporate into the class dicussion.

The written component of the *individual analysis and preparation* includes the following:

1. *Issue*

    The issue is a succinct question that asks why the case was written and what it is about. The issue is the single most important point that is to be examined in the case analysis.

2. *Environmental Analysis.*

    The environmental analysis incorporates the context, financial, industry, and competitor information into an assessment of the environment in which the case company operates.

3. *Problems and Opportunities* (Strengths and weaknesses)

    Problems include:

    a. Financial resources to maintain current product base or develop new or modified products.

    b. Engineering talent to develop new technological or machine-based innovations.

    c. Level of interest or ability in outsourcing functions or sections of the company.

    d. Age and depreciation status of the buildings, equipment, and property.

    Opportunities include:

    a. Unactualized or unrealized assets such as property that has substantially increased in value or patents that have appreciated

    b. A new or reorganized management team

    c. Patents and trademarks

    d. Public trust and good will in names or trademarks

    e. Underutilized or undeveloped products

4. *Alternatives.* This is a list and explanation of two to three realistic and comprehensive alternatives that are available to the case company. These alternatives need to be complete in their ability to incorporate the issue identified at the beginning of the case analysis as well as to actualize the problems and opportunities of the issue within the context of the problems and opportunities of the company in the environment in which they operate.

5. *Recommendation.* At this stage, the student chooses the best of the three alternatives previously presented. The recommendation includes the rationale or reason that this recommended course of action is the best to solve the business issue presented.

The following sources of information should be helpful to the case analysis process:

Internet:

    Web page for the company

    Web page for industry trade groups and associations

    SEC Edgar: 10K forms and annual reports

Online services:

    Computer Select

    ABI Inform

    Lexis/Nexis

Online financial analysis sources:

    Moody's

    Disclosure Global Access

    Morningstar (Mutual Fund Data)

Published sources:

    Standard and Poor's Industry Analysis

    U.S. Department of Commerce Industry Analysis (dated)

Moody's Industry Analysis
Gartner Group Industry/Technology Analysis/
Assessment

Government regulations for particular industries:
  Thomas: Legislative Information
  Federal Regulatory Information
  U.S. House of Representatives Law Library
  U.S. Code
  Code of Federal Regulations
  Federal Register
  Small Business Administration reports

Industry/Economic Analyses:
  Predicasts, an index of forecasts
  Predicasts F&S index, an index of business periodicals

Demographic information:
  Lifestyle Market Analyst
  Lifestyle Zipcode Analyst
  Simmons Study of Media and Markets
  Source Book of Zipcode Demographics
  County and City Data Book
  American Demographics magazine

Legal issues of the industry:
  Index to Legal Periodicals
  CD-Rom version of Index to Legal Periodicals
  American Legal Reports

EVALUATION OF WELL-WRITTEN CASES

Well-written cases present problems and choices that have consequences depending upon the direction that is taken. The situations presented must be realistic and the alternatives believable. The case must be able to be evaluated systematically. The case should spur an evaluation process that would enable students to reach a conclusion, rather than present the best choice and ask students to justify it. Over time, the classroom should help develop a systematic approach to business problems and business decision making. As a result, the student should leave the class not with the answers, but with an approach he or she can use to address problems faced at work. Finally, the class should be careful to focus on both successes and failures. No company does everything right; likewise, no company always does everything wrong. As a result, cases should be chosen which require the student to analyze the subtleties between the two. The best case, although most difficult to write and to obtain permission to use, is the one that presents a realistic description of a company in a difficult situation that was not necessarily solved successfully.

CASE UPDATES

Some professors prefer to teach cases as they are written. That is, they maintain the case in its historical con-text and present the case decision as if it were being made at the time. Other professors prefer to bring the case "up to date." This includes organizational information about the change in administrators or other persons in the company. It includes financial information about the resources, expenses, and profits that were incurred. It incorporates information about new technologies that are purchased, written, or implemented. Whatever approach is taken, it is important to remember that case analysis is accomplished under the following guidelines:

1. *Context*. Cases must fit into an historical context. Decisions are not made in isolation. They must be explained and incorporated in the context in which they actually occur and with the information available.

2. *Decision orientation*. Cases are about making a decision. Even if that decision is to do nothing, it is important to have decided to do that. Reaching a conclusion or taking a step by default is not a good response, particularly in the fast-moving world of technology.

3. *Dynamism*. Case analysis is dynamic. It is not possible to predict the outcome or to structure the class in a way that the same solution will always result. An important part of case-teaching is the ability to insert information from many different perspectives. The skill set is not the ability to come up with the right conclusion, but to incorporate a variety of ideas into the final conclusion.

4. *Process*. To a large extent, a case class teaches an approach or process to solving problems. The student can then take this process to the next case, or ultimately, business situation.

5. *Technology*. Technology is often the tool that is used to implement the dynamic change that organizations face. As a result, it is important to evaluate the company so that a reasonable technology solution can be presented to resolve the most important issues that are raised.

The interactive nature of the case class can be simulated by an expert system. Ultimately, however, technology cannot duplicate the dynamic interchange between the faculty and students and, it is hoped, between the students themselves. In a case class, there are just too many variables to track. The dynamics of the interaction are too complex.

This is what makes case-teaching exciting and dynamic. It enables a professor to interact directly with students, provide immediate feedback regarding performance, and simulate as closely as possible today's dynamic business environment.

ACKNOWLEDGMENTS

Technology, more than any other force, is changing the way we work, educate, and live. This book was written within the context of a rapidly changing environment. The textual and case materials were constantly updated, right to press time. The financial and economic information was constantly changing. The technology tips at the end of each chapter were always improving with software updates. Even the tools that were used to input and process the information were reaching new levels and versions throughout the process.

A casebook that relies on real cases and individuals is also constantly in development and change. This is particularly the situation in the rapidly expanding area of management information systems. As a result, I have worked to bring as much up-to-date information about the implementation of technology to the casebook as possible.

Given the complexity of the project, it would never have been completed without the committed assistance of a number of individuals. My research assistants worked with me writing, analyzing, and formatting information throughout the winter of 1998–99.

Todd James worked with me from the beginning and organized myriad details, sources, citations, and footnotes. He always had a clear understanding of the direction and the immensity of the project. I shall always be grateful for his ability to collect, organize, and track all the disks and backup files for the project.

Oscar Teran refined and rewrote the case materials, checked the sources, and integrated the very latest ma-terials into the project. When annual reports indicated changes, he researched and wrote the updates.

Richard Merced analyzed and developed the Technology Tips and worked to keep them up to date and focused on the latest version. He spent many hours understanding the components of the Microsoft Office Suite and sought ways to explain what could be accomplished with the suite in an understandable way.

Brian and Kassia Shaw provided invaluable technical and editing expertise. They clearly understood the requirements of case writing and were tireless in their contribution to insuring that the components were accurate and up to date.

The editors and managers at Prentice-Hall provided unique and valuable perspective as we brought the book to completion.

David Alexander applied his years of experience in technology crafting the book for the marketplace and making it relevant to the needs of professors and students.

Sondra Greenfield provided valuable feedback and perspective, always gracious and always striving to keep the book on a reasonable course to meet its goals.

Margaret Saunders and the staff at Pre-Press Company, Inc. took all the disks and written edits and produced a book. They kept track of the myriad changes and tracked down all the needed components to bring the book to completion. They worked tirelessly to make the book internally consistent and externally reliable.

DePaul University was always supportive of my efforts. In particular, the Quality of Instruction Council provided Competitive Instruction Grants to enable me to hire research assistants to assist in the completion of the case writing and analysis.

My students have always been valuable critics, analysts, and recommenders. In particular, the following students from my MIS classes contributed to the research and evaluation process: Eugenia Adeleye, Angela Alessandrini, David L. Anderson, Eric Baker, Ken Barber, Andrew Bauer, Jody Bender, Larry Brannow, Michael Brett Branson, A.A. Brooks, Dale Cabreira, Kimberly Cook, Erin Crothers, A. Cumpian, Cory Chottanapund, Keith Danly, Julie Day, Rose DeLuna, Ivana Drazic, Sascha Edge, Ron Fabbi, Kathy Featherstone, John Friel, M. Hendrickson, Mitch Hirt, Dan Hubicki, Martin Jahn, Paul Karageorge, David Kerwin, Jim Kinney, Anna Krishnaiah, George Lane, Rebekah Martinek, Angela Mazza, Kathryn McNamara, Marina Menard, Sean O'Connor, James Oswald, Frank Paganis, Kenneth Pearl, Robert Pecina, Bitchell Prosk, Brian Rady, Catherine Rice, Charles Sebaski, Brian Shaw, Jesse Sletteland, Mike Smith, Angela Sonders, Gardner Van Ness, G. Walent, Robert Wilshe, Jason Wolf, and Timothy Zellmer.

Years ago, even before technology, my parents stressed the importance of learning and exploration. That encouragement and foundation has served me well. For that, too, I am grateful.

David L. Anderson
Chicago, Illinois
October 1, 1999

ABOUT THE AUTHOR

Dr. David L. Anderson received his law degree from the George Washington University National Law Center in 1979. He is a member of the bars of the State of Ohio; District of Columbia; United States Court of Appeals, District of Columbia Circuit; United States District Court, Northern District of Ohio; and the United States Supreme Court. He received his Doctorate in Educational Administration from Harvard University in 1987. His doctoral thesis examined the innovative implementation of management information systems. His Master of Science in Computer Science and Electrical Engineering was from Northwestern University in 1992. His thesis examined computer security on the OS/2 workstation and LAN platform. His Master of Business Administration was from the University of Michigan in 1981.

Currently, Dr. Anderson is a technology executive at a major supplier of health insurance in the Chicago metropolitan area. In this role, he is responsible for the implementation of an internally-written, client-server-based, internet-delivered membership system. His responsibilities encompass network implementation, software distribution, application development, security identification, and web implementation. Previous to this position Dr. Anderson worked in strategic technology positions at Hewitt Associates, IBM, the Continental Bank, and Andersen Consulting.

Dr. Anderson's textbook, written with Jerry Post, is entitled *Management Information Systems: Solving Business Problems with Information Technology*. Published by McGraw-Hill/Irwin, it became available in a second edition in September, 1999. In conjunction with his textbooks, Dr. Anderson serves as an adjunct professor of management information systems at the Charles H. Kellstadt Graduate School of Business at DePaul University in Chicago, Illinois.

Management Information Systems

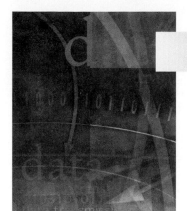

CHAPTER 1

STRATEGIC THINKING
INDUSTRY ANALYSIS: FAST-FOOD INDUSTRY

Strategic Thinking

Technology is rapidly changing what we do in society, in business, and at work. For years, the goal in employment was to fit into an organization and work up the organizational ladder. Organizations were successful because of their ability to develop rules and a hierarchy to set a process in place to accomplish a business objective.

Today, the goals are much different. Specific skill sets are rewarded rather than broad knowledge about a subject area. In technology, these skills can be measured and defined. The goal is to identify those areas where these skills can be specifically applied.

Technology change drivers are the technology innovations that enable technology to be implemented in the organization. Change drivers can include point-of-purchase displays, scanning devices, ATM machines, or voice-activated data entry. The change drivers are the tools that propel the implementation of technology to the next stage.

Technology has resulted in the identification and implementation of a number of trends. Understanding the role that these trends play in the industry is important. Recognizing them can assist you in your endeavors to position yourself for career growth and expansion.

Standardization is the conscious effort to make all jobs similar, routine, and interchangeable. It includes the economies saved because the components of the job are the same. One example of standardization is the rule set that McDonald's applies to all of its tasks, from making fries to ordering and tracking the inventory. By measuring everything from hours worked to wasted fries, McDonald's' management information system enforces the rule set required for standardization.

Leverage is the effort to move the responsibility for all tasks to the lowest possible level. Leverage requires tasks to be carefully evaluated and assigned based on the ability required. An example of leverage is the managerial structure set in place in the major consulting firms. The role and budgetary requirements of the partner, manager, senior, and staff levels force tasks to be accomplished at the level that most closely matches the required expertise. Using technology to direct the billing structure ensures that tasks are accomplished with this approach in mind.

Mass customization places the focus of all products and services on a specific customer. Using this approach, companies can market their products not just to specific market segments, but to specific individuals. An example of mass customization is the coupons that you receive in the grocery store that are specifically printed for you based on the products that you bought. Another example would be a specifically focused mailing that you might receive from a store based on previous purchases on a store credit or buyer's card.

A **franchise** is the organization of the corporation into a small central office with many autonomous, but identically structured units. Strict guidelines in terms of cost and output are set for each location. Information is required to be reported to headquarters in a structured format. This reduces the need for layers of middle management to evaluate and interpret the information that is received from the regional offices. Examples of franchises are most evident in the fast-food industry. Franchising has made possible the proliferation of identical restaurants with identical products around the world.

Methodology provides the user with a set of clear directives to use in the management process. A methodology is a step-by-step, almost cookbook-like approach that anyone with a minimum set of skills can pick up and use to deliver a product. Technology enables this methodology to be available across an organization. In strategic firms, the methodology defines and reinforces the overall approach used to manage the business. An example of the application of a methodology is in systems development. Following the methodology provides the programmers with clear directives on what the next steps are, the deliverables from each step, and what to do at each step of the process.

Modularization enables the finished product to be constructed using sections of code, rather than at the most granular level. The technological concept of object orientation enables modules to be constructed and applied. As long as the inputs and outputs are standard, these objects can be encapsulated and always addressed in the same way. It is much faster and more straightforward to put objects or modules together than to work with individual lines of code. An example of the technological application of modules is the ability of Word, Excel, Access, and PowerPoint to fit together in the Microsoft Office suite. Using the concept of modules, users can apply the components of the suite to their individual needs. On the World Wide Web, plug-ins are examples of inserting a module into your web application.

Liquid assets is the focus of organizations that try to reduce costs by reducing their reliance on fixed assets by using liquid assets instead. Changing costs from fixed to variable enables an organization to more directly link the individual costs of an item to an expenditure. Thus, costs can be broken down and only incurred when they are needed rather than purchased as part of a larger package. An example of the application of the liquid asset concept is the outsourcing of the human resources or even technology departments or the lease rather than purchase of fleet cars and office space.

Client/servers provide for the decentralization of the technology tools. This technology enables data to be stored at the enterprise-wide, group, and individual levels. Diversifying the data and the technology in this way enables information to be stored throughout the organization rather than concentrated in a single place. Applying a client/server approach enables the technology, applications, and data to be stored and accessed efficiently at the local level while being maintained across the organization.

Knowledge-driven workers are constantly reassembled to lend their expertise to a project rather than being restricted to working in a hierarchy. This constant reassembly keeps the workers fresh and focused. They must clearly understand that the sharpness of their expertise keeps them employed and focused rather their longevity in the organization. An example of the importance of knowledge-driven workers occurs when persons are organized into teams to accomplish specific project objectives. Set with a clear beginning and end, the project is organized to accomplish specific objectives using a cross-section of knowledge-driven skills.

These approaches will assist you in your effort to evaluate and implement technology in the cases in this book and in your career. This introduction can be used as a framework for your evaluation of the material in the cases. Some of these approaches can even be used as the foundation for your recommendations for the best way to approach the cases.

Word	W.1	Using a Wizard and a Template Additional Note	Using a Resume Wizard Using a Resume Template
Excel	E.1	Basics	
PowerPoint	P.1	Creating a Presentation	Using the AutoContent Wizard Using Presentation Layouts to Create a New Presentation Using a Blank Presentation
Access	A.1	What are Databases?	How are Databases Organized?
FrontPage	I.1	Understanding the Web and Getting Some Tools	The Internet Necessary Tools

Industry Analysis: Fast-Food Industry

Restaurant franchising is a system in which a producer or marketer of a service, the franchisor, sells others, the franchisees, the right to duplicate a concept and use the trade name. The franchisor provides sales and other support within a specific territory for an agreed period of time. A franchise can include the name, decor, menu, management system, accounting system, and usually the information system. Supplies are ordered from preapproved sources. Managers often receive training at corporate sponsored institutes.

Due to rapid growth during the 1970s and 1980s, franchise chains account for roughly 25 percent of restaurant outlets and 43 percent of industry sales. The introduction of restaurant alternatives is expected to slow new unit growth and sales through the 1990s. Restaurants that want to continue high-growth and above-average sales have already focused on the international markets. New domestic initiatives include operating units in nontraditional markets and dual-branding, in which several restaurant chains or services operate in the same location.

The simplest franchise type involves a contract between a supplier and a business owner. The business owner agrees to only sell one version of a particular product. For example, McDonald's sells only Coca-Cola soft drinks. Conversely, product-trade name franchising, which accounts for 52 percent of all franchise sales and 33 percent of all the franchise units in the United States, involves selling products to distributors who resell them.

The fastest growing type of franchise is the prototype or package franchise. In the franchise the business operations include the product or service, inventory system, sales and marketing methods, and record-keeping procedures. Package franchising has grown 10 times faster than product-trade name franchising, 11.1 percent compared to 1.1 percent per year.

Through franchising, a business can quickly grow and achieve higher market penetration than a single-owner business. Franchisees are often entrepreneurs who lack the knowledge to start a business. Franchising allows those individuals to adopt a business concept without starting from scratch. Franchisees also face less risk than that encountered when starting a business because the concept behind the franchise has already proven to be profitable on a limited scale. Thus, the five-year survival rate for franchises is much higher than that of start-up businesses (85.7 versus 23 percent).

The franchiser's revenues are in the form of a start-up fee, ranging from $10,000 to $600,000 depending on the size and market share of the franchise. This includes a license for the use of the trade name, managerial training and support, and royalties that amount to 3 to 8 percent of gross sales.

Start-Up Fees

McDonald's	$45,000
Subway	$10,000
Domino's Pizza	$1,000

Additional initial outlays include rent, inventory legal fees, equipment, insurance, and licenses. These can amount to 10 times the start-up fee. In the case of McDonald's they can reach $500,000. The average initial cost of $330,000 per franchise often limits an individual's ability to buy this type of franchise. Franchisers may also require that purchasers have experience in the particular franchise or in the segment represented.

FINANCIAL ANALYSIS OF FRANCHISE INDUSTRY

Franchise restaurants are an $800 billion industry employing more than 8 million people. One out of every three dollars spent in the United States on food services goes to franchise restaurants. In 1996, the industry showed a 1.7 percent increase in revenues, continuing a decade-long trend in which the industry benefited from a strong economy. Industry growth measured in terms of the increase of total domestic units, however, has been decreasing, from 7.9 percent in 1994 to 5.9 percent in 1995.

Profit levels for most fast food franchises averaged 14.6 percent in 1997. Pizza and chicken chains showed a faster growth rate than burger chains due to the more health-conscious consumer. Even though burgers are currently outpacing pizza and chicken, burger sales grew a healthy 7.2 percent in 1995.

STOCK/INVESTMENT OUTLOOK

The growth rate for the fast food industry is about 15 percent per year. Investment projections for the largest franchises are optimistic. Analysts project that sales for Wendy's and McDonald's will increase by 17 percent and 14 percent, respectively, during the next five years.

Investors can expect a continuation of the recent trend toward mergers and acquisitions. The early 1990s saw a large number of initial public offerings from small franchise chains. Many of the more successful mom-and-pop franchises are being acquired by corporate giants.

The long-term investment prospects are favorable. The national trend toward two-income households has been beneficial to the restaurant industry as a whole. Today's working parents eat out far more than their parents did. In 1996, 51.9 percent of all spending on food took place in restaurants, compared to 48.1 percent in grocery stores. Conversely, in 1972, only 38.2 percent of spending for food occurred in restaurants while 61.8 percent went to grocery stores.

With their targeted marketing and expanded menus, the larger restaurant franchises have positioned themselves to take advantage of the social trend toward dining out.

POTENTIAL FOR GROWTH OF FRANCHISE INDUSTRY

Growth in the entire franchise industry is expected to continue with expansion from 41 to 50 percent of all retail sales. Sales are expected to reach $2.5 trillion by the year 2010. Even though the domestic market for the fast-food restaurant industry has matured and competition is tight for consumer dollars, companies are continually searching for new areas for growth. These include the following:

Niche Marketing in the United States
Marketing toward children
Health-conscious and nutritionally balanced meals
Home meal replacement (traditionally family meals with the ease of fast food)

Mergers and Consolidations
Wendy's purchase of Tim Horton's, Hardee's, and Roy Rogers
Boston Market's purchase of Einstein Brothers Bagels

Dual-Branding (Several Restaurants Operate at the Same Location)
Taco Bell and KFC locations under one roof
Dunkin' Donuts and Baskin-Robbins
Arabya's and p.t. Noodles

Nontraditional Operations
McDonald's' operations in Wal-Mart stores and gas stations
Little Caesar's Pizza outlets in K-mart stores

International Development
Companies such as McDonald's, KFC, and Burger King continue aggressive development of markets in Asia and South America

Value Offerings
Consumers want value, so prices will be kept low; many restaurants will focus on combo value offerings or value menus
Wendy's 99¢ value menu
McDonald's combo menu, which offers standard combinations of popular items at a slightly reduced price

Franchise growth can be attributed to changing demographics. The elderly, seeking convenience, will be making up a bigger portion of the population than ever before. The 21 percent of the population over 55 has access to 50 percent of domestic income. By the year 2000, aging baby boomers' expenditures will increase by 90 percent.

COMPETITIVE STRUCTURE OF THE FRANCHISE INDUSTRY

The fast-food industry is highly competitive and fragmented. The largest 10 chains make up approximately 15 percent of all units and account for 23 percent of all sales. McDonald's remains the industry leader with more than $15.9 billion in sales and more than 11,000 units in the United States. Burger King, Hardee's, Pizza Hut, KFC, Wendy's, and Taco Bell follow (Figure 1.1).

Mergers have changed the competitive structure of the industry. In 1995, Wendy's merged with Tim Horton's, Canada's largest national chain of coffee and baked goods. In addition, Wendy's purchased 40 Roy Rogers restaurants in New York from Hardee's in 1995 and 35 Hardee's in the Detroit area in 1996. Wendy's also plans to purchase 37 Rax restaurants in Ohio and West Virginia. These stores will be converted into either Tim Horton's or Wendy's stores. Wendy's ended 1996 with approximately 5,000 Wendy's units and 1,300 Tim Horton's units.

In 1993 and 1994 Boston Market was one of the fastest growing restaurant chains with sales of approximately $384 million in 1994. This represented an almost 150 percent increase over 1993. It also more than doubled its unit growth between 1993 and 1994, jumping from 217 units to 534 units. Boston Market focuses on home-style entrees, vegetables and salads. As late as 1998 there were over 1,000 Boston Market units. However, Boston Market filed under Chapter 11 Bankruptcy restructuring on October 5, 1998.

A chief competitor to the franchise food industry is grocery stores. They have targeted busy students and working parents by offering more prepared foods, deli counters, and eat-in dining areas.

TECHNOLOGICAL INVESTMENT AND ANALYSIS IN THE FAST-FOOD INDUSTRY

Technology has impacted the growth of the franchise industry. Improvements have included electronic systems that track inventories and sales. These systems result in more efficient operations and ease in the transmission of information between the owner and franchisor. Electronic data interchange (EDI) is being used by some franchises such as car rentals and hotels to communicate regarding reservations and customers.

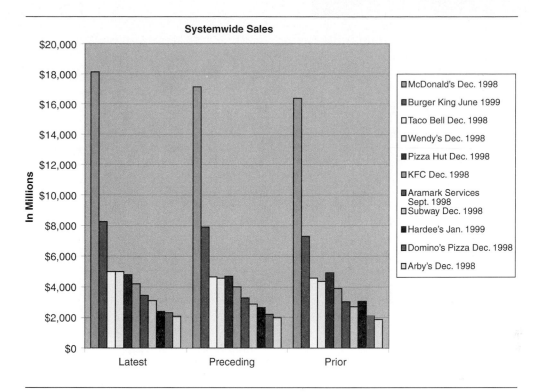

Figure 1.1 1995 U.S. sales (in millions) for the top 11 U.S. fast-food restaurant chains (1997–1999). (Sources: *Nation's Restaurant News, Restaurant Business*, and company reports.)

Prospective franchisers can also use the Internet to find key locations for their business by examing demographics and market research reports rapidly and at a low cost. Constructing web pages to advertise to prospective owners is another use of technology. Lastly, because starting a franchise network requires a lot of communication comprised of training and support, telecommunications technology has helped make the global exchange of information easier than ever. This development has allowed easier monitoring of the required uniformity of the franchisee.

The role of research and development in the fast-food industry is generally limited to the test marketing of new products and improvements in food taste, calories, and consistency. Fast-food companies constantly test the market acceptance of new menu items. Usually several restaurant locations serve as a test market to check the popularity of a new menu item. This type of market research helps keep the company ahead of the competition by adjusting to consumers' changing food tastes. Research also includes food science experimentation to improve the cost, taste, texture, shelf life, and fat content of menu items.

RECOMMENDATIONS FOR THE FUTURE OF THE FAST-FOOD INDUSTRY

The fast-food industry faces many challenges during the first five years of the 21st century. Although there is room for growth in the international market, sales will continue to lag in the United States. Companies will have to fight to increase or even keep their market share.

In an effort to increase domestic market share, companies must focus on nontraditional and niche markets. They must also focus on dual-branding. Careful attention must be given to delivery speed and customer service. As competition continues to tighten, the number of mergers between companies, such as that between Wendy's and Tim Horton's, will increase.

INDUSTRY WEB SITES

Franchise Restaurant Industry

www.olen.com/food/

http://dfwmusic.com/fastfood/

http://www.restaurant.org

McDONALD'S

Executive Summary

Case Name:	McDonald's Corporation
Case Industry:	Fast-food industry
Major Technology Issue:	Technology governing the distribution mechanism Technology to enable customer to input his/her own order Technology to decrease the cost of financial reporting and increase the efficiency of consolidated statements Method to track frequent customers
Major Financial Issue:	Saturation of marketplace, particularly in the United States Increasing competition between the three to five main fast-food chains Increasingly lower product margin
Major Strategic Issue:	Globalization of franchises Increasing price competition Reduced brand loyalty Market saturation Personnel reduction Integrated value chain
Major Players/Leaders:	Mac and Dick McDonald, initiators Ray Kroc, founder Jack Greenberg, chairman and CEO
Main Web Page:	www.mcdonalds.com
Case Conclusion/Recommendation:	Boost profits and market share Increase brand loyalty Increase market saturation Use technology to reduce employee costs

CASE ANALYSIS

INTRODUCTORY STORY

McDonald's has worked hard to be more than a restaurant chain. It has become a marketing icon and is part of the routines of millions of people. Its success is so far reaching that it has developed its own culture and identity. It has become a symbol of the success and desirability of American popular culture.

SHORT DESCRIPTION OF THE COMPANY

McDonald's operates more than 24,000 restaurants in 114 countries. It has a 21 percent share of the very competitive U.S. fast-food industry. Overseas restaurants now account for half of the company's profits. McDonald's plans to open 10,000 new restaurants by the year 2005. McDonald's has been a forerunner in the recent industry trend of co-branding and satellite locations.

SHORT HISTORY OF THE COMPANY

Since its incorporation in 1955, McDonald's has not only become the world's largest quick-service restaurant organization, it has changed America's eating habits. Seven percent of Americans eat at a McDonald's each day; 96 percent visit a McDonald's restaurant each year. The McDonald's brand name is second only to Coca-Cola in worldwide recognition.

In 1948, Mac and Dick McDonald converted their drive-in carhop into a self-serve operation. In doing so, they helped found the fast-food restaurant industry. The original restaurant had no sit-down tables, provided no waitresses, and offered only a limited menu. The McDonald brothers carefully streamlined their kitchens to ensure maximum efficiency. The reduction in preparation time increased volume and lowered costs.

This "assembly-line" approach to food preparation attracted Ray Kroc. Kroc felt the simplicity of the operating system made it ideal for duplication. He believed the McDonald's formula could be even more successful if it could be expanded through franchising. McDonald's now operates only about 30 percent of all McDonald's restaurants; franchisees control the rest.

Kroc's approach was to first establish the restaurants and then franchise them. This enabled him to expand while controlling the uniformity of the stores. In 1955, Kroc had 14 restaurants; two years later this number increased to 100 restaurants. The steady growth of the automobile and the expansion of the suburbs led to the early success of McDonald's. In 1961, Kroc was able to buy out the McDonald brothers for $2.7 million; in 1965 the company went public.

The company's continuing success during the 1970s and 1980s was due largely to excellent marketing and the willingness to adapt to customer demand. In 1969 McDonald's launched the Big Mac and the hugely successful "You Deserve a Break Today" advertising campaign to all 50 states. In the 1970s, McDonald's pioneered breakfast fast-food with the introduction of the Egg McMuffin. By 1987, one-fourth of all breakfasts eaten out in the United States came from McDonald's.

In 1975 the company's goal was to provide service in 50 seconds or less. To meet this challenge McDonald's installed its first drive-thru window. Drive-thru sales later accounted for more than half of McDonald's sales.

During the 1980s, competition within the fast-food industry increased dramatically. McDonald's attempted to carve a new market niche by producing healthy foods such as ready-to-eat salads and the McLean Deluxe. Despite expert claims that the fast-food industry was saturated, McDonald's continued to expand. McDonald's has employed extensive marketing campaigns and unique promotions such as "When the U.S. Wins, You Win" Olympic tie-ins. An annual advertising budget of more than $1.4 billion keeps product awareness high, while movie tie-ins and video offerings add merchandising to the mix.

Recently, McDonald's profits in the United States have climbed slowly. To boost sales, McDonald's has been exploring new markets and formats. The company has stepped up expansion overseas where there is less competition, lighter market saturation, and better name recognition.

McDonald's is in the mature phase of its life cycle. It has not only provided a service the American consumer needs, it has contributed to a lifestyle on which the public relies. By establishing the fast-food industry, McDonald's forever altered Americans' eating habits. With maturity has come new challenges. Operating worldwide, McDonald's faces issues such as globalization, politics, and environmental awareness.

Consistency is such an integral part of the McDonald's experience that many customers no longer just expect it but demand it. So far, McDonald's has met this daunting challenge. The central issue is how to maintain the integrity in all units no matter how far flung they are across the globe. According to restaurant analyst Allen Hickok,

> McDonald's is succeeding abroad because of the tight systems it has implemented over the years, and because of controlled growth. They are reaping the rewards of the infrastructure they began years ago. None of the others are anywhere close to the size, scale, scope and sophistication of McDonald's. McDonald's is in a world unto itself, and it is a world-class competitor.[1]

The Golden Arches have become an icon and a benchmark for other fast-food restaurants, especially since McDonald's changed its focus from local to global markets. Notes Brian Corcoran, staff director of global distribution/logistics for McDonald's International,

> In the 1970s, we were very focused on local sourcing. In the 1980s, we went to a more regional approach, or maximizing the supply system within a continent or a zone. Today we're moving toward a global approach to distribution, which involves being able to effectively purchase for a market from the best possible sources.[2]

To analyze the costs of product, shipping, and currency fluctuations, Corcoran is developing a database to analyze these factors. Corcoran also feels it is important to incorporate benchmarking for pricing to evaluate costing trends in the system. Because McDonald's is expanding its scope to include overseas suppliers to meet its needs, this database will aid with import/export issues. For example, McDonald's imports many Happy Meal toys from Asia.

The United States is still the biggest source of products and supplies for McDonald's restaurants. Approximately 70 percent of McDonald's U.S. exports go to Asia, 20 percent to Latin America, and 10 percent to Europe. Corcoran reports, "Asia and Europe are fairly equal in the number of stores." The Asian countries in which McDonald's operates—Japan, Korea, Hong Kong, Singapore, the Philippines, and Thailand—are not large food producers. Thus, they import many products from North America.

When contemplating entrance into a new market, McDonald's must evaluate a country's ability to provide food and supplies. Local governments can have a strong influence on the use of local products. In some cases, McDonald's has had to develop agricultural programs within a country before gaining approval to

[1] Wren, Jr., Worth, "McDonald's to Standardize Beef Supply," *Knight-Ridder/Tribune Business News*, April 7, 1998, p. 407B.
[2] Ibid.

import other needed products. According to Corcoran there are two dynamics:

We will probably increase exports to some smaller countries until they may in fact have sufficient size to produce their own. On the other hand, in some countries—for instance Singapore and Hong Kong— it's never likely that they're going to produce cattle. So they're going to continue to increase exports from the United States.[3]

The potential exists for one country to provide the entire stock of a certain product to all of the McDonald's markets. As it stands today, Mexico provides every sesame seed for all of the McDonald's buns in the world. James Cantalupo, CEO of McDonald's International, comments:

I feel these countries want McDonald's as a symbol of something—an economic maturity and that they are open to foreign investments. I don't think there is a country out there that we haven't gotten inquiries from. I have a parade of ambassadors and trade representatives in here regularly to tell us about their country and why McDonald's would be good for the country.[4]

To be a good corporate and global citizen, McDonald's has implemented a company-wide recycling program. In the late 1980s, corporate awareness of environmental issues was an important topic. Many companies felt threatened by the activists and tried to skirt the issue; McDonald's met the challenge head on. McDonald's collaborated with the Environmental Defense Fund (EDF) to explore ways to incorporate a responsible environmental policy into its existing operating system. EDF, recognizing McDonald's stature and influence, saw an opportunity to impact the entire fast-food industry.

It was a bold step for a private corporation to engage a public-interest organization to address environmental concerns. It was also a wise marketing decision. McDonald's was perceived as an environmental threat because its products were all served in disposable containers. The company, proving its flexibility, responded to changing consumer needs.

As it had done in the past, McDonald's looked for solutions that it could incorporate into its entire operating system. It felt that a separate department dedicated to environmental issues would only belittle the company's efforts, so all environmental initiatives were directed through operations development. It formed the Waste Reduction Task Force, which examined the full life cycle of all materials used by McDonald's. These included raw materials acquisition, manufacturing, distribution, food preparation, and packaging.

The task force found that, on average, each McDonald's generated 238 pounds of solid waste per day. This amount did not include the solid waste generated by take-out customers, which accounted for 40 to 60 percent of McDonald's' business. Contrary to public perception, the task force found that the bulk of solid waste generated came from food production, not from disposable packaging. To address this problem, McDonald's incorporated the help of its suppliers and franchisees. For instance, standard shipping pallets could only be used once or twice. This increased expenses in constant replacement and landfill fees. McDonald's introduced a more durable pallet that could be used 30 to 40 times. These pallets reduced waste, cut costs, and had minimal impaction on operations.

In addition to the behind-the-scenes changes, McDonald's reexamined their product packaging. McDonald's' announcement that it was going to switch from polystyrene (foam) clamshell containers to plastic ones ignited controversy. Initial response from the media was harsh. It accused McDonald's of "exploiting the clamshell's notoriety as an icon of the throwaway society, eschewing the less popular and more difficult solution." Bob Langert, a member of the task force, retorted, "Had we only been out to score with the public we would have returned to paperboard, which is actually worse for the environment but is perceived by the public as preferable to plastic." After a battery of tests, McDonald's finally decided on a three-layered wrap which consisted of an inside layer of tissue, a sheet of polythene, and an outer sheet of paper. By shifting to the quilted wraps, McDonald's reduced sandwich packaging waste by 90 percent and shipping packaging waste by 80 percent.

McDonald's also initiated a program called McRecycle USA. This program devoted $100 million annually to the promotion of recycled products in the construction and equipping of restaurants. Once again, McDonald's implemented the expertise of their suppliers to arrive at an equitable solution. Suppliers influenced the use of 100 percent recycled bags. Because they used unbleached material, the bags were brown instead of white. Initially, consumers did not like the new look. Once they realized the reasons for the color, they felt good using them. McDonald's capitalized on this, incorporating the recycled bag into its advertising campaign, making the look quite popular. More than 500 suppliers and manufacturers now par-

[3] Wren, "McDonald's to Standardize Beef Supply," p. 407B.
[4] Gibson, Richard and Moffett, Matt, "McDonald's Faces Hurdels in Quest for Global Expansion," *Wall Street Journal*, Europe, October 29, 1997, v. 15, p. 4(1).

ticipate in McRecycle USA. By implementing this program, McDonald's strengthened the market for recycled products.

In addition to recycling programs, McDonald's has researched energy efficiency projects. The company recently critically examined the design of its restaurants. In June 1996, McDonald's, in conjunction with Pacific Gas and Electric Company (PG&E), introduced a state-of-the-art energy-saving restaurant. Located near San Francisco, "The Energy-Efficient McDonald's" (TEEM) requires 25 percent less electricity than other McDonald's restaurants. Like the EDF project, the TEEM program was a joint effort between the public and private sectors. It involved input from the U.S. Department of Energy, the National Audubon Society, Commonwealth Edison, Sieben Energy Associates, and Tropic-Kool Engineering. The restaurant boasts the following features:

1. A computer-controlled heating, ventilation, and air-conditioning system, which reduces mechanical cooling at those times during the day and night when outdoor air temperatures fall within the desired range for indoor use.
2. Variable-speed exhaust fans on the fryer hood and above the griddle, which cycle down on cue, such as when the clamshell griddle or fryers are idle or doing light duty. The strategy not only cuts back on the use of power for the fans but also reduces the use of energy needed to "condition" outdoor air for use indoors by decreasing the amount of exhaust.
3. Triple-paned windows, which filter ultraviolet light and allow indoors just 2 percent of the heat from outdoors. Double-pane windows allow in as much as 70 percent of exterior heat.
4. A photosensor-controlled system of high-efficiency fluorescent lighting, which dims or brightens in response to the level of natural light in the restaurant.
5. Sensors, which turn the cooling system on or off based on the occupancy of the room, not a preset temperature. Occupancy is gauged by the level of carbon dioxide in the air, which is indicative of the amount of breathing taking place. Coolers with conventional controls can waste energy by cooling empty rooms.
6. "Light pipes," which capture sunlight striking the roof and redirect it into the interior areas of the restaurant not served by windows, such as the rest rooms and storerooms.
7. Occupancy sensors, which turn lights on and off in the walk-in cooler and freezer.
8. Infrared-sensor-controlled faucets and toilets in the rest rooms, which operate automatically when they detect a user.

Another feature being produced by the TEEM project is a sophisticated computer model of the restaurant. It tracks the performance of the TEEM site and compares it to a conventional site located nearby. The data obtained will be applied to future constructions in Atlanta, Chicago, and Phoenix.

Throughout the development of these various environmental initiatives, McDonald's has tried to remain focused on their main business objectives. "We're in the business of making hamburgers—of serving quality food at a low price. We're not in the packaging business." Even the hamburger is growing more competitive for McDonald's. Increasing domestic competition, explosive growth in the overseas markets, and the recent increase in social and political pressures have changed the atmosphere of the fast-food industry.

FINANCIAL AND PORTFOLIO ANALYSIS

Despite the recent flattening of domestic sales, McDonald's has again demonstrated the power of its worldwide operations with a growth in profits. In 1998, revenue was up 10 percent, to $12.4 billion. While net income was down in 1998, Return on equity improved to 19.5%.

System-wide sales increased by 7 percent, to $36 billion, for the year ending 12/31/98. System-wide sales consist of sales by company-operated, franchised, and affiliated restaurants. Total revenues, on the other hand, consist of sales by company-operated restaurants and fees from restaurants operated by franchisees and affiliates. These fees are based on a percentage of sales with specified minimum payments

Although McDonald's is showing strong financial results, this growth can be deceiving. Industry observers noted that domestic, same-store sales were down about 3 and 5 percent for the first and second quarters, respectively. McDonald's' recent growth should be credited to restaurant expansion rather than to the increased sales volume of existing stores. In 1998, for example, McDonald's added 92 new U.S. restaurants. This caused an increase in domestic sales, when, in actuality, comparable same-store U.S. sales were negative.

Sluggish sales are a new thing for many McDonald's franchisees. Most restaurant owners are quick to blame the fierce competition for the decline. John Weiss, a San Francisco securities analyst, describes the competitive situation between McDonald's, Wendy's, and Burger King as a "zero-sum game" where one improves and the other two decline. He continues:

They are adding about 8 percent to growth in stores, the demand is not growing more than 8 percent. If Burger King is showing improved same-store sales of

about 10 percent, as they are now, that doesn't leave much room for McDonald's to show improvement.

Former McDonald's CEO, Michael Quinlan, agrees that the competition has heated up. He said, "Our experience indicates that per-capita visits to McDonald's increase as we increase penetration. If we don't take advantage of these opportunities, the competition will." McDonald's has recently embraced this idea and changed its strategy to focus on increased market share rather than on individual store sales and profitability.

The corporation points to a recent test market as proof of this plan's success.

Year	Restaurant	Number of Stores	Market Share (percent)
1981	McDonald's	10	40
	Hardee's	5	20
1991	McDonald's	11	28
	Hardee's	18	40
1995	McDonald's	29	50
	Hardee's	17	35

In addition to the above percentage increases, the average volume per McDonald's restaurant increased by 50 percent; cash flow and profits per restaurant also improved. Jack Greenberg, the new McDonald's chairman, summed up this philosophy as not asking where to put the next new store, but rather where to put the next five new stores.

This plan has been met with reservation by some franchisees, who own 85 percent of the McDonald's restaurants. They worry that the saturation of new stores will cut into the business of already profitable stores or that there will be a long adjustment period before profits can be realized. Despite these reservations, McDonald's seems committed to a policy of rapid expansion.

McDonald's is now buying stores from its competitors, something it has never done before. In August 1996, McDonald's bought 184 Roy Rogers units from Hardee's. The restaurants are located in Roy Rogers' strongest territory, Baltimore and Washington, D.C. Expansion through purchase is primarily responsible for sales increases in McDonald's' overseas markets as well. McDonald's has bought 80 units of Burghy, a fast-food chain in Italy, and 17 units of Georgie Pie, a New Zealand chain.

Overseas markets are increasingly playing a larger role in McDonald's' profitability. Operating income from outside the United States contributed to 57 percent of total profits for year ended 1998. Michael Quinlan said:

We enjoy a significant lead over the competition outside of the United States. . . . Our objective is to *grow international sales at a compound annual rate in the mid- to high-teens and international operating income at a compound annual rate of 20 percent as measured over a five-year period.*[5]

The following comparison exemplifies the impact of foreign markets:

Year ending	U.S. Operations 1998	1997	Foreign Operations 1998	1997
Percent increase:				
Sales	6%	5%	8%	7%
Revenues	6%	0%	11%	12%
Operating Income	13%	0%	8%	8%
Sales/Revenue:				
Company operated	16.8	17.8	19.8	20.5
Franchised margins	81.7	82.7	81.7	82.1

With about 24,000 restaurants in 114 countries, McDonald's is by far the largest and most recognized global food-service retailer. Even as the market leader, McDonald's serves less than 1 percent of the world's population. Further global expansion is a tempting prospect. With the increased penetration into foreign markets, McDonald's is subject to certain financial risks. Fluctuations in exchange rates and the volatility of the foreign economy are major issues. To lessen short-term cash exposure, McDonald's purchases goods and services and finances in local currencies and hedges in foreign-denominated cash flows.

STOCK/INVESTMENT OUTLOOK

Although McDonald's met significant challenges in 1998, the general stock outlook is favorable. Some securities analysts feel that an industry "shakeout" is occurring, during which market share will change hands. Some analysts see McDonald's positioning itself to be the recipient of that change. People agreed, and McDonald's stock price rose 62% in 1998.

McDonald's' stock, which in 1998 was selling at 39 times the year's likely earnings, was not perceived as a bargain. While the earnings per share were estimated to grow by 13 percent per year over the next five years, same-store sales still had to improve. Generally, investors viewed McDonald's as a solid company and a good long-term buy.

RISK ANALYSIS

McDonald's has focused on the needs of families with children. This has been one of the main marketing strategies for McDonald's; it is one of the premises on which Ray Kroc founded the company.

---

[5] 1997 McDonald's Annual Report; Letter to Shareholders.

It is widely acknowledged in the fast-food industry that children heavily influence where the family will go to eat. For fast-food giants such as McDonald's, Taco Bell, and Burger King, families account for approximately one-third of the business. According to the National Restaurant Association, restaurants whose charge per person was under $8 reported that one-third of their business included children under the age of 13. Almost 50 percent of those restaurants used some sort of promotion targeted toward children.

To attract families, McDonald's has provided "child-friendly" atmospheres. These include child-sized portions sold at a reduced cost, tableside activities, McDonald's Playworld, special children's meals that include premium toys, such as the extremely popular "Happy Meal," and even "kids eat free" promotions. In recent years, movie tie-ins have also been very successful. In May 1996, McDonald's announced an unprecedented global marketing alliance with the Walt Disney Company. Beginning in January 1997, McDonald's became Disney's primary restaurant promotional partner. McDonald's will share exclusive marketing rights linking the restaurants to Disney movies, videos, and theme parks.

With the recent flattening of domestic sales, McDonald's has adopted an expanded marketing strategy. The company is focusing on the huge population of aging baby boomers who no longer have kids at home. McDonald's' research indicates that 72 percent of its customers think McDonald's is a good place for children; only 18 percent consider it ideal for adults. McDonald's views this adult market as largely untapped.

Attracting adults has proven to be a difficult task. Cheryl Russel, editor of *The Boomer Report*, notes that from 1989 to 1994, adults between the age of 45 and 54 reduced their dining out budgets by 19 percent and those between the ages of 35 and 44 reduced it by 24.5 percent. When these individuals do go out to eat, they are not going to restaurants that serve cheap, fattening foods. Said Russell, "As soon as their kids are old enough, they go elsewhere."

To lure these adults into the restaurants on a more consistent basis, McDonald's produced a new product line and "mature" marketing campaign. In the spring of 1996 McDonald's introduced the Arch Deluxe burger, followed by chicken and fish sandwiches in the summer. The company, hoping to produce another Big Mac, rolled out an incredible $200 million advertising campaign. The promotions featured the Arch Deluxe as "the burger with the grown-up taste." Ads featuring pouting kids making comments such as "Black-eyed peas. Spinach. Cauliflower. Now Arch Deluxe" were met with mixed reviews. Robert Shulman, coauthor of *The Marketing Revolution,* expressed doubts about the campaign. "It's a huge risk," he said. "It takes them away from their core audience—children—and potentially cannibalizes their original products."

Al Ries, chairman of Ries & Ries Market Research, offers the following advice; "McDonald's has to have the courage to realize that people do grow up and move on. You have to abandon some customers who outgrow their concept. That's the mark of a successful company. Coca-Cola said they could get into new-age beverages, but for the most part they've kept the focus on colas." But McDonald's, which is used to being the market leader, will not give up market share so easily. The company historically has not competed in the high-end sandwich arena, which is estimated to be a $5.1 billion product segment.

Unfortunately, the Arch Deluxe did not generate the expected profits the franchisees and the company desired. Its ability to lure adults back to McDonald's was painfully slow. The subsequent change in management structure was an indication of the company's frustration with the Arch Deluxe's performance. On October 8, 1996, CEO Michael Quinlan shuffled the company's top executives. The change signaled McDonald's determination for a more decisive business approach. "To some degree, they had to express their dissatisfaction with the trends," said Prudential analyst Janice Meyer. "This was just another effort to bring more leadership to the domestic business when it was clearly having a hard time."

INDUSTRY AND MARKET ANALYSIS

The McDonald's formula has been copied so often that there seems to be a fast-food restaurant on every street corner in America. Many critics say the fast-food industry has saturated the domestic market. Hungry Americans can now buy hamburgers at airports, train stations, sporting events, gas stations, supermarkets, college campuses, and discount stores. The industry is focusing on visibility, convenience, and one-stop shopping.

To satisfy consumer desires, the fast-food industry has set its sights on unusual places such as gas stations and convenience stores. Fast-food chains are focusing on developing their growth strategies on these companies for several reasons. First, gas stations occupy excellent locations. One industry expert commented "Let's face it, the petroleum companies own most of the best corners in America."

Another desirable aspect of gas stations and convenience stores is their ability to generate high consumer traffic throughout the day. It is rare for even the largest restaurant site to consistently generate that much traffic. Another attraction is the reduction in plant, property, and equipment costs. Sharing property and facility costs can be advantageous to both parties. In most cases, the site requires only modifications to an existing building, rather than building a brand new facility.

Although there are many advantages to co-branding, there are some risks. First, the market situation for co-branding is regional. The selection is on a market-by-market basis, especially when franchisees are involved. The store operator must be willing to upgrade the store image. Otherwise it can damage both companies. Dave Thomas, founder of Wendy's said,

> *You must maintain high standards to be successful in this business; be prepared to back up the national brand image with the best food quality, customer service, and affordable price. A national brand identity is very important. So be careful of who you work with. You must share the same philosophy.*[6]

The growth of the fast-food market is slowing in the United States. Many companies are looking to the less saturated overseas markets for expansion and growth. The introduction of alternative restaurant sites has boosted domestic sales. It is no surprise that McDonald's is at the forefront of this trend. When it comes to innovative marketing strategies, McDonald's has historically led the industry. These nontraditional sites are not restricted to gas stations and convenience stores.

In 1994, McDonald's opened its first trial restaurant in Wal-Mart; it now has more than 800 Wal-Mart locations nationwide. McDonald's now has operations in hospitals, airports, shopping malls, riverboats, military bases, ski lodges, theme parks, race tracks, casinos, and museums.

Alternative retail sites are not even a strategy limited to fast-food chains anymore. The trend has expanded to include retail stores such as The Body Shop, Sunglass Hut, Starbucks, Disney, and Au Bon Pain. Airports have seen the biggest growth in this market; they are expected to see even more. The number of airline passengers is projected to increase by 59 percent by the year 2007. Airports will be investing about $2 billion annually between 1997 and 2002 to improve retail space.

ROLE OF RESEARCH AND DEVELOPMENT:

What has set McDonald's apart from the average hamburger restaurant is its ability to recognize customers' needs and desires. It seems customers want fast, friendly service in a clean and orderly environment. McDonald's sees this as its main objective and addresses it as its primary business function. One of McDonald's most important critical success factors has been the ability to apply manufacturing functions to service activities. Mc-

Donald's has used this approval to bridge the dichotomy between service and manufacturing.

TECHNOLOGICAL STORY

The McDonald bothers identified simplicity as being important. Dick McDonald explained,

> *We said let's get rid of it all. Out went dishes, glasses and silverware. Out went service, the dishwashers and the long menu. We decided to serve just hamburgers, drinks, and french fries on paper plates. Everything prepared in advance, everything uniform. All geared to heavy volume in a short amount of time.*[7]

This idea is what attracted Ray Kroc, who felt this simple system was as ideal for franchising as it was ideal to duplicate. Kroc refined the brother's techniques into a strong operating system. The system consists of four distinct parts:

1. Develop supplier relationships.
2. Train and monitor franchises.
3. Improve products.
4. Improve equipment through technology.[8]

The ability to develop and adhere to this operating system proved to be a core competency for McDonald's.

One of Kroc's original managers wrote the first operations manual in 1957. It was later expanded to 750 pages to include every aspect of operating a McDonald's franchise. It outlines exact cooking times, proper temperature settings, and exact food portions. It is so detailed that it describes the quarter ounce of onions required for each hamburger, the number of slices per pound of cheese, and the precise thickness of a french fry that enhances the best taste ($\frac{9}{32}$ of an inch).

McDonald's attention to detail was revolutionary because it removed decision making from the employees. Nothing is left to chance. Raw hamburger patties are premeasured and prepackaged. In the kitchen, the ketchup and mustard are fitted with nozzles that dispense the correct amount with one squirt of the handle. To maintain a clean environment, numerous trashcans are carefully placed, not only within the restaurant, but also on the outside grounds.

The design of the restaurant itself controls the actions of the franchisees. The building is intended to handle only the predetermined product line. Work areas are arranged to prepare only the McDonald's limited menu. There is no room for discretion. The franchisee does not

---

[6] Thomas, R. David, "Dove's Way: A New Approach to Old Fashioned Success," 1992.

[7] Kroc, Ray, and Anderson, Robert, "Grinding it Out: The Making of McDonald's," 1990.
[8] Ibid.

have a choice on what food to sell nor how to prepare it. Thus, McDonald's controls its "agents in the field" by both contractual and facility limitations.

TECHNOLOGICAL INVESTMENT AND ANALYSIS

Typically, service and manufacturing are considered to be on opposite sides of the business spectrum. Service is perceived as being offered on an individual basis; one individual helping another individual. It is often performed "in the field," such as when a customer service agent goes out to a customer's home or business to maintain an item that was previously purchased. These customer service agents are working under variable conditions that are often difficult to control or supervise.

Providing good service requires maintaining a relationship with the customer. This means forging some type of emotional bond, such as trust, friendship, and familiarity. The company relies on these agents to establish these bonds, as customers become attached to these employees. In this vein, the idea of "service" is to individualize the product to please the customer. As a result, service industries are usually viewed as dealing with the human element and are, consequently, inefficient.

Manufacturing, on the other hand, focuses on speed and efficiency. The environment is highly centralized and organized. The work is performed by machines, producing vast quantities of uniform products. The products are made within the controlled environment of the factory and by individuals who are interchangeable. Personnel requirements are dictated by the needs of the machine, not by the customer. Relationships formed are strictly business-like, without human attachment.

McDonald's primary core competency is its ability to apply manufacturing principles to the service industry. By using "technocratic" thinking it is able to improve the quality and efficiency of service. McDonald's replaces high-cost and volatile "service" mentality with a low-cost and uniform "manufacturer's" system. The company carefully controls each restaurant's central functions, which are to:

1. Deliver a uniform product.
2. Meet certain quality standards.
3. Provide a clean environment.
4. Serve the customer in the shortest possible amount of time.

McDonald's operating system can be equated with an automobile assembly line. An assembly line is designed to guarantee that each product receives the same amount of time, attention, and detail. If any one worker is allowed discretion, the product becomes dif-

ferent and personalized. This highly structured and controlled environment produces high-quality products at low prices, especially when accomplished on a grand scale.

McDonald's has committed a considerable amount of research to site development. Once again, standardization has helped cut costs. Prefabricated building designs have reduced development costs in the United States from $1.6 to $1.1 million per restaurant. Reengineering kitchen equipment has also lowered costs from $80,000 to $50,000 per restaurant. In addition, a geographic information system is used to evaluate the demographics of potential site locations.

To ensure consistently high quality in all of its restaurants, McDonald's forged a strong relationship with its suppliers, demanding certain specifications for its products. Many large food suppliers such as Heinz, Kraft, and Swift, did not want to bend to such demands. For example, McDonald's analyzed meat in laboratories and developed requirements for their hamburgers. The meat must be 83 percent lean chuck (shoulder) from grass-fed cattle and 17 percent choice plates (lower rib cage) from grain-fed cattle.

Shunned by the large vendors, McDonald's collaborated with small suppliers who were willing to meet the stringent specifications. In return for their flexibility, McDonald's rewarded them with a high degree of loyalty. McDonald's guaranteed future orders, enabling suppliers to grow with the company. It turned out to be a very lucrative situation, given that a single McDonald's restaurant requires 1,800 pounds of hamburger meat and 3,000 pounds of potatoes per week. Jim Williams, of Golden State Foods, described how McDonald's changed the deal-making process:

> *Deals and kickbacks were a way of life. How long you let a guy stretch out his payments was more the determining factor of whether you got the business than the quality of the product you were selling. Kroc brought a supplier loyalty that the restaurant business had never seen. If you adhered to McDonald's specifications, and were basically competitive on price, you could depend on their order.*

The franchisees play a very important role at McDonald's. As of 1998, they generated 28 percent of the revenue for the corporation, including 42 percent of U.S. revenues. Therefore, McDonald's developed an operating system that focused on them. Franchisees are required to participate in a rigorous training program at one of the Hamburger University campuses located in Australia, England, Germany, Japan, and the United States.

Ray Kroc always referred to the franchisees as "partners" and insisted that corporate revenue depended on the success of the restaurants, not on the franchise fees. The success of the McDonald's operating system demanded that franchisees abide by the predetermined systems and regulations. These restrictions did not mean the franchisees were without input. The franchisees formed coalitions to introduce regional promotions and influence local suppliers. Franchisees were also influential in the development of new products, such as the Filet-O-Fish, the Egg McMuffin, and the McDLT.

Even though McDonald's encourages input from its franchisees, they are far from autonomous. McDonald's has always kept close tabs on the performance of the restaurants. In 1957, McDonald's sent a corporate employee "out in the field" to review the franchises. This field agent assigned a letter grade on the restaurant's quality, service, and cleanliness. This developed into a systematic method of evaluation known as the "QSC quotient" (later revised to QSCV—adding "V" for value). This successful program has grown with the company. McDonald's now has more than 300 field consultants, each visiting more than 20 restaurants a year. The QSCV quotient has also grown to include more than 500 specific performance points.

Even though suppliers and franchisees play a pivotal role in McDonald's operating system, the development of the food in conjunction with technology is by far the most important aspect of McDonald's unique system. The most impressive result of this focus is the success story of the McDonald's french fry. Nowhere else has one menu item made such an impact. In the early years of McDonald's, the company accounted for approximately 5 percent of the United States potato crop; 30 years later it was responsible for 25 percent of the market. McDonald's was responsible for making french fries a fast-food staple.

Last year, 80 percent of all McDonald's customers included fries with their meals. This translates into 4 million pounds sold every day in America alone. French fries are also a favorite of operators because they offer high profit margins and are a popular add-on sale. The only problem is that fries are the most difficult menu item to make. This is because french fries begin losing quality minutes after being cooked.

McDonald's has always used technology to produce superior food products. The company discovered that temperature settings on the fryers did not adequately control the temperature of the oil after cold potatoes were dropped in. By putting temperature sensors in the vat and on the potatoes, McDonald's found the best fries occurred when the oil temperature rose three degrees above the low-temperature setting. Armed with this information, McDonald's was able to design a fryer to duplicate this ideal cooking process.

McDonald's laboratories also discovered that potatoes cured for three weeks produced the best tasting fries. This is the time frame during which sugars convert into starches. To reduce browning, McDonald's requires potatoes with 21 percent starch content. To ensure that suppliers provide potatoes that meet these specifications, McDonald's provides field agents with hydrometers and directions to measure the starch content of potatoes floating in a bucket of water.

In 1965, McDonald's revolutionized the fry-making process. Recognizing distribution problems, Ray Kroc switched from fresh to frozen potatoes. This allowed a consistency not achievable before, further enhancing the fame of the McDonald's french fry. In the 1970s, McDonald's improved the freezing process by drying the french fries with air first to reduce moisture and prevent subsequent ice crystals from forming. Recent innovations include a new starch-based coating that retains moisture inside the potato to ensure crispness for longer periods of time.

McDonald's also implemented "technocratic" thinking to improve the preparation and service of the french fries. McDonald's wanted the appearance of generous portions, but excessive overfilling would prove costly to the company. In addition, filling containers with traditional tongs is very time consuming. The company hired an engineer to design an entire "french fry" system that filled the container directly.

Other advances include computer inventory systems and kitchen equipment with sensor technology to alert the user to faulty parts. McDonald's has rolled out a new cost-saving french fry machine called the "Automated Restaurant Crew Helper," otherwise known as ARCH. Edward Rensi, president and CEO of McDonald's USA, says the equipment is part of "significant initiatives to minimize labor shortages."

McDonald's influence has changed the way people eat. Through careful analysis of quality and procedures, McDonald's studied every component of its operation. This rigorous attention to detail provided the company with information to determine the best way to serve its customers and grow its business. McDonald's has used technology in an ingenious manner. By applying manufacturing principles to a typically labor-intensive situation, McDonald's has, in essence, turned a restaurant into a machine. Technology has harnessed unskilled labor to produce high-quality uniform food products on a mass scale.

TECHNOLOGICAL INNOVATIONS

NETWORKS

Networks are particularly important to McDonald's because they provide a mechanism to manage the franchises spread over large geographic areas. Networks reinforce the centralization of power by enabling headquarters to communicate with the franchises. This ensures standardization and quality control through the analysis of inventories and franchises. Networks achieve these functions at a comparatively low cost and without the time constraints of more mainframe-based communications.

SMART CARD TECHNOLOGY

Both McDonald's and Burger King are testing smart card technology in selected markets. The cash value of each card is stored on a computer chip or a magnetic strip on the back of each card.[9] Value can be added to the card through machines that accept cash or through ATM-like machines that add value by transferring funds out of a customer's bank account. Customers can use the cards, instead of cash, to make their food purchases. Corporate goals for smart card implementation include cost savings in relation to money handling, reduced shrinkage, and increased loyalty through incentives and premiums. Smart cards eliminate the need for merchants to communicate with banks for the authorization of purchases.

McDonald's is testing this technology at 870 restaurants across Germany.[10] Here, a payment system lets customers pay for goods using stored-value smart cards. Customers at McDonald's Deutschland, Inc., restaurants will be able to pay for goods by swiping smart cards through small, countertop terminals. They also will be able to add value to their smart cards by downloading money electronically from their bank accounts at touch-screen terminals in the restaurants. The terminals will lead users through the process of downloading new money to the cards.

McDonald's Deutschland continues to use smart card terminals in 55 stores. During the first 10 weeks of the trial, 30,000 transactions were conducted, using Hewlett-Packard Co.'s VeriFone unit, which provides the terminals.

Although smart cards are catching on in Germany, there has not been an easy way to add value to the cards. According to Rolf Kreiner, senior vice president of marketing at McDonald's Deutschland, by letting customers not only buy goods, but also add value to their cards, McDonald's is hoping to lead a trend toward the wide-scale acceptance of smart cards in Germany.[11] The German smart card payment infrastructure, known as GeldKarte-System, has about 40 million cards in circulation. McDonald's has committed to use VeriFone's SC552 smart card reader, which supports GeldKarte-System cards.[12]

The system that will let users add value to their cards will be separate from the smart card readers and will be called VeriFone's Transaction Automation Loading and Information System (TALIS). The system will let users add value to their cards separately from the smart card readers. While customers wait for TALIS terminals to connect to their banks, the screens flash advertising and marketing messages.

VeriFone's TALIS touch-screen terminals are equipped for two cards, permitting consumers to "transfer" monetary value from a debit or credit card to a smart card after first tapping in a personal identification number. Once the smart card has been filled with stored value, it can then be inserted into a smart card reader at the point of sale to make payment for goods or services.

Technologically, smart cards were designed to function in place of credit cards in the fast-food environment. Historically, credit card transactions were too slow. Their associated costs were too high in the face of small margins. Smart cards are an important step in resolving these issues. They enable restaurants to leverage sales and enhance the ease of credit card use. Authorization and settlement technology are rapidly improving.[13] The costs of network connectivity are decreasing.

INTERNET SITES

McDonald's first announced a web presence in 1994 with McDonald's interactive, an area in NBC Online on America Online. In 1995, the company developed and implemented a web site called McFamily (www.mcdonalds.com). It is aimed at families, perceived by McDonald's as its most important target market. The site features "seasonal ideas for fun family activities such as block parties, travel games, and household safety information." The Auditorium sponsors monthly guest speakers, including celebrities and parenting experts, and a Hey Kids area houses a gallery with McArt submitted by children with downloadable games and contests.[14] The goal of all of these web pages is to enhance the brand image that McDonald's is for families. McFamily includes a section on "helping others." This section features information on Ronald McDonald House and other related children's charities.[15] This section also features information on McDonald's efforts to preserve the environment.

[9] Essick, Kristi, "Smart Cards and Big Macs," *Information World*, August 24, 1998, v. 20, n. 34, p. 51(1).
[10] "Germans to Buy Big Macs with VerifFone's Smart Cards," *Newsbytes News Network*, August 17, 1998.
[11] Essick, Kristi, "Put a Big Mac on my Smart Card, Please," *Computerworld*, August 24, 1998, v. 32, n. 34, p. 45(1).
[12] Ibid.

[13] Keenan, Charles, "More Fast-Food Chains Taking Plastic Payment," *American Banker*, CLXIII(97):10, May 22, 1998.
[14] "McDonald's McCyberSpace," *Electronic Market Report*, September 5, 1995, v. 9, n. 17, p. 4(1).
[15] Rogers, Amy, "Plugged In: Ronald McDonald House Gets Internet Makeover," *Computer Reseller News*, January 4, 1999, p. 69(1).

The McDonald's web site cannot be used to sell food. However, it can capture revenue through the sales of merchandise related to McDonald's sponsorships. The "McStuff for You" section offers gear from McDonald's racing teams and the Olympic Games.[16] The web site is used to collect customer information and profiles through on-line surveys.[17]

DATABASES

Decision makers at McDonald's Corporation realize that customer preference is paramount. The chain is implementing a restaurant-level planning system, dubbed "Made For You." It enables each restaurant to eliminate its inventory of foods prepared in advance. Instead, workers make sandwiches based on actual demand without sacrificing any of the efficiency.

About 800 McDonald's restaurants use the system, which consists of PC-based cash registers running in-house software. Orders are routed to monitors at different food preparation tables to balance the workload among employees.

In McDonald's restaurants without the new system, workers must anticipate the demand for each type of sandwich in advance and place them in bins. When a customer wants a sandwich that is not ready-made or one with a different topping, the person at the register shouts out the order and workers move out of the assembly line for the special request. This slows the process and extends the customer's wait.

McDonald's introduced the new system in March at a meeting for its franchisees. The company is encouraging its 12,400 U.S. restaurants to incorporate the system, but the actual decision is left to each franchise. The technology eases the workload and could add up to a percentage point to the company's profit margin because it enables it to sell more food faster, according to Douglas Christopher, a financial analyst with Crowell Weedon & Co.[18]

Wal-Mart and McDonald's have joined together to share retail space. These two companies have been partners since 1993, with over 800 restaurants in Wal-Mart stores around the country. Now, McDonald's has taken this one step further. It actually uses Wal-Mart clerks and registers to sell McDonald's food.

In several test locations, when Wal-Mart shoppers pull their carts up to the checkout, there is a mat on the counter displaying the McDonald's products, much like what you would see at one of the restaurants. Each product, from hamburgers to Happy Meals, has a code number that the clerk scans into the Wal-Mart system while ringing up the customer's purchases. The orders are automatically relayed from the register to the kitchen using software jointly developed by McDonald's and Wal-Mart. The food is brought to the customers as they leave the store. Since the food appears on Wal-Mart's registers and receipts, customers can pay for it with a single credit card purchase. At the end of the day, the companies balance McDonald's portion of the proceeds.

This process only works in Wal-Marts with a McDonald's kitchen somewhere in the store, whether in a restaurant or a stand-alone counter. McDonald's hopes to continue implementing these systems as extensively as possible.

"It's an inevitable process," says Ross Telford, vice president of retail practice at NCR, the Dayton, Ohio-based company that has based its business on supplying point-of-sale (POS) systems and helping vendors and retailers such as Wal-Mart, JC Penney, and Qantas Airways capture, process, and analyze customer data. According to Telford, individuals are starting to use one another's environments and skills to reach as many potential customers as possible.

The Wal-Mart/McDonald's partnership is part of a much larger, industry-wide trend toward the cost-effective use of information at the cash register to increase profits. Known as "real-time cross-marketing," the concept enables the company to use information technology to get more than one sale out of every transaction. As the buyer produces his or her checkbook or wallet, the retailer offers another product that fits with the customer's original selection, or one that matches a profile of the customer's previous purchases stored in the database. Matching a customer's current or past purchases with new ones and completing the sale require both skill and tact. First, the information must be found; the product must then be presented in a way as to make the customer feel as if the company is not intruding. "Acquisition of detailed data is always a challenge. Even more challenging is how to use the data without being intrusive," says Steve Keller, director of general merchandising and industry marketing at NGR.[19]

To better manage its inventory, McDonald's has implemented supply-chain software that enables better management of inventory by sharing demand and supply information among its restaurants, suppliers, and distributors.[20]

[16] "McDonald's McCyberSpace," p. 4(1).
[17] Nash, Kim S., "McDonald's IT Plays Catch Up with Rivals," *Computerworld*, December 14, 1998, p. 111.
[18] Davey, Tom, "Personalized Service At Lower Cost—Hotels and Restaurants Turn to Transaction Processing and Real Time Communications to Get a Strategic Edge," *InformationWeek*, September 14, 1998, n. 700, p. 173(1).
[19] Frank, Diane, "The New ROI in Point of Sale," *Datamation*, November 1997, v. 43, n. 11, p. 73(4).
[20] "McDonald's Supply Chain," *InformationWeek*, April 13, 1998, n. 677, p. 30(1).

RECOMMENDATION FOR THE FUTURE

McDonald's appears to be at a crossroad. The company can continue on its traditional (and very successful) path of consistency and quality through standardization, or it can alter the basic strategies by allowing franchisee autonomy and continuing to provide a variety of offerings and service. It appears that CEO Jack Greenberg is rethinking many of the standards on which McDonald's is founded. At a company noted for standardization, emphasis on flexibility is quite a feat. This new outlook includes granting more freedom to franchisees to experiment with food and marketing, test new venues, such as satellite locations and co-branding, and develop new menu items.

These changes are innovative and risky. Current management is not considering minor adjustments. Experimenting with the much-copied operating system is a gamble. "If there was anything that was sacrosanct, it was the operating system," says former CEO Edward Rensi who was overseeing many of the changes. The system is a precisely organized machine; by introducing flexibility, the machine is in danger of becoming mired down with complexity. The danger lies in straying too far from what McDonald's has done in the past.

CASE QUESTIONS

Strategic Questions

1. What is the strategic/future direction of the corporation/organization?

2. Who or what forces are driving this direction?

3. Who has been the catalyst for change?

4. What are the critical success factors for this corporation/organization?

5. What are the core competencies for this corporation/organization?

6. What are the forces going against the success of McDonald's?

Technological Questions

7. What technologies has the corporation relied on?

8. What has caused a change in the use of technology in the corporation/organization?

9. How has this change been implemented?

10. Who has driven this change throughout the organization?

11. How successful has the technological change been?

12. How much will the smart card affect McDonald's' future sales and growths?

13. What criticisms has the stock market made of McDonald's?

Quantitative Questions

14. What has been the financial performance of the stock in the late 1990s?

15. What conclusions can be reached from an analysis of the financial information to support or contradict this financial ability?

16. What analysis can be made by examining the following ratio groups?

    Quick/Current:
    Debt:
    Revenue:
    Profit:
    Asset Utilization:
    Stock Price:

17. What conclusions can be reached by analyzing the financial trends?

18. Are long-term trends developing that seem to be problematic?

19. Is the industry stable?

20. Are there replacement products?

Internet Questions

21. What does the corporation's web page present about their business directives?

22. How does this compare to the conclusions reached by the writers of the articles mentioned in the case?

23. How does this compare to the conclusions reached by analyzing the financial information?

Industry Questions

24. What challenges and opportunities is the industry facing?

25. Is the industry oligopolistic or competitive?

26. Does the industry face a change in government regulation?

27. How will technology impact the industry?

Data Questions

28. What role do data play in the future of the corporation?

29. How important are data to the corporation's continued success?

30. How will the capture and maintenance of customer data impact the corporation's future?

RAINFOREST CAFE

Executive Summary

Case Name:	Rainforest Café
Case Industry:	Franchise (restaurant)
Major Technology Issue:	Using technology to enhance the dining experience.
Major Financial Issue:	How to keep its exponential financial growth going.
Major Strategic Issue:	The speed at which the restaurants should expand and (of course) the location, location, location of them.
Major Players/Leaders:	Steven Schussler (senior VP), Lyle Berman (CEO)
Main Web Page:	www.rainforestcafe.com
Case Conclusion/Recommendation:	The entertainment restaurant market seems to be saturated. Rainforest Café needs to find a way to encourage return customers and stranger loyalty.

CASE ANALYSIS

INTRODUCTORY STORY

Steven Schussler was an owner of a chain of nightclubs. He also loved exotic birds. For the benefit of his pet birds, he turned his house into a rain forest habitat. The project turned out so well that he decided to apply the rain forest idea he had developed to a rain forest-themed restaurant. Because the prototype was already in place he could use his home to convince potential investors to commit to the project. They did. The result is the hugely successful, multi-outlet, multimillion dollar enterprise known as Rainforest Café.

SHORT DESCRIPTION OF THE COMPANY

"One of the hottest concepts in themed retailing, Rainforest Café integrates food, entertainment, and retail into a carefully detailed, tropical-themed fantasyland."[1] Rainforest Café, Inc., owns, operates, and licenses rain forest-themed restaurants and retail stores. The first cafe opened in The Mall of America in October 1994. In April 1995, seven months after opening the first restaurant, the company went public.[2] In 1996, six restaurant/retail stores opened throughout the United States. In 1997, eight more opened. Rainforest Café has licensing agreements for restaurants in Mexico, Canada, and England.

The restaurant section of the cafe accounts for approximately 78 percent of store sales.[3] The menu is unique and always changing. Full-flavored cuisines from Mexico, Asia, the Caribbean, Italy, the American Southwest, Louisiana, and elsewhere greatly influence the dishes served.

The Rainforest Café's retail section accounts for approximately 22 percent of total sales.[4] Of this amount, general merchandise accounts for 45 percent of sales and private label items account for 50 percent of sales.[5] The private label items carry margins up to 50 percent. "The biggest potential for the Rainforest Café is the licensing of eight animal characters."[6] A move to push this licensing has not yet taken place.

The environmental awareness theme of the cafe is carried throughout the operation. The restaurant will not serve net-caught fish or beef raised on deforested land. Recycled products are used as much as possible and only organic cleaners are applied for cleaning. The cafe, along with many of its suppliers, donates a portion of its receipts to environmental groups or causes.[7]

SHORT HISTORY OF THE COMPANY

Rainforest Café's core competencies are in three separate areas of the business:

---

[1] "Rainforest Café: Welcome to the Jungle," *Chain Store Age Executive with Shopping Center Age,* March 1997, p. 94.

[2] "Rainforest Café Inc.," *Corporate Report–Minnesota,* October 1995, p. 47.

[3] Walkup, Carolyn, "Rainforest Café: It's a Jungle in There," *Nation's Restaurant News,* May 12, 1997, p. 129.

[4] Ibid, p. 130.

[5] "A Really Wild Place to Shop and Eat," *Discount Store News,* May 15, 1995, p. 78.

[6] Rubel, Chad, "New Menu for Restaurants: Talking Trees and Blackjack," *Marketing News,* July 29, 1996, p. 1.

[7] "A Really Wild Place," p. 79.

1. Rainforest Café demonstrates the ability to turn a great idea into a functional reality. The cafe provides customers an escape, if only for an hour, from the daily routine. The company has developed an eating experience that is not dining out, but an adventure.
2. Rainforest Café demonstrates fund-raising ability. Lyle Berman raised millions of dollars in capital with only one unit in operation. Many start-up companies have great ideas but fail because they are undercapitalized. Rainforest Café has not suffered this problem.
3. Rainforest Café has demonstrated the ability to develop a market niche in a very crowded industry sector. They have identified and appealed to a consumer segment wanting to be entertained and to act in ways perceived to being environmentally friendly.

FINANCIAL AND PORTFOLIO ANALYSIS

The Rainforest Café grew tremendously from 1994 through 1998. The large increase in sales can be attributed to the rapid expansion of the Rainforest Café throughout the world. Midway through 1994, the first Rainforest Café was opened in The Mall of America. By the end of 1998, there were 29 Rainforest Cafés in operation. Sales increased from $2,066,000 in 1994, to $13,451,000 in 1995, and to $213,900,000 in 1998 (Figure 1.2).[8]

---

[8] http://www.rainforestcafe.com; 1998 Annual Report.

The corresponding growth rate is 385.5 percent. Figure 1.2 illustrates Rainforest's Café's ability to exponentially increase sales through expansion. With seven or eight new units each year, sales doubled to around $100 million in 1997. Following a similar growth pattern, 16 new restaurants in 1998 doubled sales to over $200 million.

Accompanying the increase in sales has been a dramatic increase in net income (Figure 1.2). Rainforest Café started in 1994 with a net loss of $1,628,000. In 1995, net income would have been $1,169,000 without the extraordinary expense of extinguishing debt early. Net income for 1998 was $10,700,000.

The increase in the number of locations has contributed to the rise in net income. To increase net income, management must continue the efficient operation of each restaurant without losses. Efficient operation means cutting down on food waste and costs through strict controls, reducing labor costs through efficient employee utilization, and utilizing store space to maximize potential.

Rainforest Café's return on assets (ROA), in 1996 2.66 percent, falls well below that of the industry average, 8.12 percent. With start-up costs between $3 million and $5 million, and the relative newness of each restaurant, the return on these assets has yet to be realized.

Rainforest Café's return on equity (ROE), 2.9 percent, is very weak by all measures. Rainforest Café accumulated large amounts of equity to fund their expansion through 1999. Yet it still has few operating

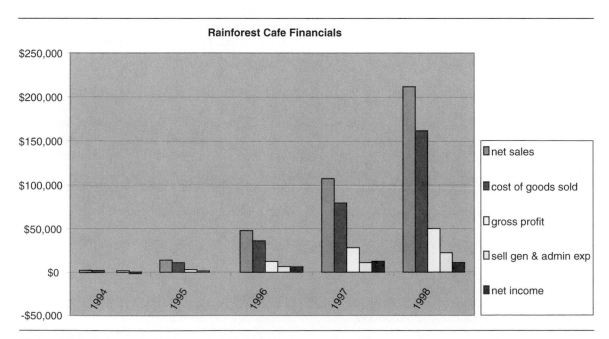

Figure 1.2 Rainforest Café financials, 1994–1998.

units.[9] Thus, a majority of the equity was placed in low interest-bearing investments until it is needed to construct Rainforest Cafés. The current ratio of 11.07 supports this analysis, indicating the high level of cash held by the company.

Rainforest Café's balance sheet must be examined to clearly illustrate the amount of cash and short-term investments held. At the end of 1996, more than half of the company's total assets, $119,828,000, were in cash or short-term investments. This level of cash holdings impacts the interpretation of financial ratios. The ratio of cash and short-term investments to total assets has fallen significantly since then.

Rainforest Café has very little long-term debt. In 1995, it took a $1.05 million charge to extinguish all the long-term debt,[10] converting it into common shares of stock. This practice is extraordinary in the restaurant industry, where most companies have a debt-to-equity ratio of 58 percent.[11] Rainforest Café did have $2.0 million in outstanding letters of credit in 1998. This small amount of long-term debt has very little impact on a corporation of this size. Rainforest Café's use of equity financing has generated enough capital to finance its rapid expansion.

STOCK/INVESTMENT OUTLOOK

Rainforest Café stock has been volatile. The stock closed at $25.125 on Thursday, July 3, 1997, but has remained below $10 a share since August of 1998.

The initial public offering was a success, raising $9 million with 1.5 million shares, or $6 per share. The initial offering floated 34 percent of the company's equity.[12] Two secondary issues generated another $170 million, which will be used for expansion through the year 1999.[13] Currently, approximately 17 million shares are outstanding with 790 shareholders.

The stock has traded from prices as low as $5 per share to prices above $50. In July 1996 the stock broke the $50 level and management declared a 3-for-2 stock split. Dividends are nonexistent and not expected.

Rainforest Café's price-to-earnings (P/E) ratio, 54.6, is very high, about twice that of other restaurants. By comparison, McDonald's PE ratio varies between 20 and 26.

This lofty PE ratio indicates one of two scenarios: Either the market has included the growth potential in the price for Rainforest or the stock is tremendously overvalued. If the company maintains its current growth rate and continues to produce the numbers it has already generated, the stock should hold value. Although this is a riskier endeavor than investing in McDonald's with its long track record, early indications seemed to predict substantial future growth. However, as theme restaurants fell out of favor in a saturated market, and as savings per share declined, the stock price stumbled and has yet to recover.

INDUSTRY AND MARKET ANALYSIS

The Rainforest Café has positioned itself in the themed restaurant niche. This niche has two distinct types of restaurants: passively themed restaurants and aggressively themed restaurants. Examples of passively themed restaurants include the Olive Garden, Red Lobster, and the Outback Steakhouse. Examples of aggressively themed restaurants include the Hard Rock Cafe, Planet Hollywood, and the Official All-Star Cafe. Consumers seem to enjoy the complete experience of themed restaurants. These experiences include good food, great entertainment, and a retail store all in the same location.

The restaurant industry has, in general, reached the mature stage of the business cycle. The theme restaurant industry is still in the growth cycle. The increased number of mergers and acquisitions are indicators of a mature industry. When there are fewer opportunities for physical expansion and increased competition within the industry, more consolidation is expected.[14] The Rainforest Café and other theme restaurants have avoided the major industry trend by concentrating on a niche that still has enormous potential for growth. The trend toward theme restaurants appears to be continuing as people expect more from their eating experience.

The year 1996 was difficult for the restaurant industry, primarily because there was poor weather, increased competition, price pressures, and people stayed home to watch the Olympics.[15] The restaurant industry's well-being is directly related to the economy's well-being. If the economy is doing well, consumer spending should be up and the restaurant industry should do well.[16] As the economy continues with low inflationary pressures, low interest rates, and high consumer confidence, the restaurant industry should continue to prosper. The market saturation, however, will continue to be a problem.

---

[9] "Rainforest Café, A Wild Place to Shop and Eat," *1996 Annual Report.*

[10] Hayes, Jack, "Rainforest Café Planting Seeds for Nationwide Growth," *Nation's Restaurant News,* August 21, 1995, p. 11.

[11] Sack, Kren J., "Industry Surveys, Restaurants," *Standard and Poor's Industry Surveys,* April 10, 1997, p. 21.

[12] Papiernik, Richard L., "Investors See No Clouds over Rainforest Stock Performance," *Nation's Restaurant News,* January 8, 1996, p. 12.

[13] *1996 Annual Report,* p. 3.

[14] Sack, "Industry Surveys," pp. 2–3.

[15] Schwartz, Matthew, "Which Way to the Web?" *Software Magazine,* September, 1998, v. 18, n. 12, p. 70(6).

[16] Ibid., p. 15.

The increase in the number of dual-income families and households earning more than $50,000 has resulted in people eating out more often. "According to the National Restaurant Association, Americans consumed an average of 4.1 commercially prepared meals per week in 1996."[17] The number has increased since then.

Rainforest Café has been outperforming the competition in the industry. Its table turnover ratio is seven times per day, twice that of the themed restaurant industry average.[18] Rainforest Café can potentially serve twice the number of people and meals than the competition, leading to substantially larger sales and profits on the investment. The increase in table turnover is due partly to the technology that Rainforest Café utilizes.

Rainforest Café is in a class with the two largest theme restaurant chains: Hard Rock Cafe and Planet Hollywood. Hard Rock Cafe has annual sales of $400 million with approximately 70 restaurants in 20 countries. Planet Hollywood reports annual sales of $373

million with 55 restaurants around the world.[19] With only six units open, Rainforest Café had over $48 million in sales (Figure 1.3).

Rainforest Café's future restaurant units range in size from 300 seats to more than 400.[20] Comparatively, Planet Hollywood has seating capacities ranging from 150 to 650 seats and Hard Rock Cafe's are slightly smaller.[21] The average check per person at Planet Hollywood is approximately $16 per person; at Hard Rock Cafe, it is $12 per person.[22] Comparatively, Rainforest Café's average check is $13.[23] Hard Rock Cafe has annual sales of $10.8 million (including food, drinks and merchandise), compared with Planet Hollywood's $14.3 million in annual sales.[24] Rainforest Café has annual sales of approximately $8 million.

---

[17] Ibid., pp. 1–4.
[18] Walkup, Carolyn, "Rainforest Café: It's a Jungle in There," *Nation's Restaurant News*, v. 31, n. 19, p. 128(2).

[19] Bernstein, Charles, "Hard Rock and Planet Hollywood: Head to Head," *Restaurants & Institutions*, April 1, 1997, p. 84.
[20] *1998 Annual Report*, p. 4.
[21] Bernstein, "Hard Rock and Planet Hollywood," p. 84.
[22] Ibid.
[23] *1998 Annual Report*.
[24] Bernstein, "Hard Rock and Planet Hollywood."

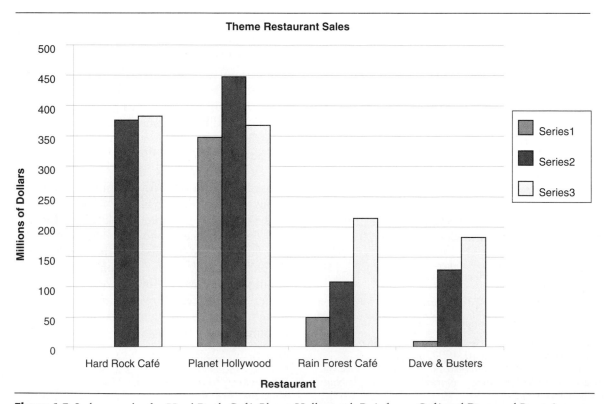

Figure 1.3 Industry sales for Hard Rock Café, Planet Hollywood, Rainforest Café and Dave and Buster's.

Rainforest Café's continued expansion into high traffic areas, such as large malls, Disneyland, and large tourist destinations, should provide continued growth in sales, profitability, and market share. Rainforest's aggressive growth should be beneficial throughout the company. If past performance is an indicator, sales should increase dramatically with each additional unit. With increased sales comes increased buying power. Rainforest should be able to negotiate lower prices with suppliers, thus increasing profit potential. The global and domestic expansion should slowly build Rainforest's market share.

The themed restaurant market appears to have substantial room for growth. Complete entertainment experiences have become more prevalent as the consumer demands more from every activity, including eating. With the increased number of players in the theme restaurant business, it is important to have first-mover advantage. The Rainforest Café has laid the groundwork to obtain and maintain this advantage. As long as Rainforest Café continues to stay one step ahead of the competition, success should continue. Like the Hard Rock Cafe, the Rainforest Café must develop a following of loyal customers to buffer the inevitable changes in consumer tastes and desires.

ROLE OF RESEARCH AND DEVELOPMENT

Technology is the driving force behind the entire Rainforest Café concept. Computer systems run the animatronics, the storms, the sounds, and the smells within the restaurant. The ambience makes the restaurant what it is; technology makes the environment possible.

TECHNOLOGICAL STORY

Technology has had a tremendous impact on the restaurant industry. In this industry, "the breadth of technology can shape the dining experience as well as the bottom line."[25] The smaller labor pool and the increased cost of labor have forced the industry to utilize computers and technology to increase worker productivity and efficiency. Rainforest Café is no exception.

Technology is used extensively throughout the company including point-of-sale (POS) workstations, computers that calculate a guest's waiting time for a table, and systems that control the animatronics and storms.

TECHNOLOGICAL INVESTMENT AND ANALYSIS

Rainforest Café uses eight Profit Series POS workstations with five preparation printers in each restaurant.

Rainforest executives chose the Profit Series manufactured by HSI for a number of reasons. The HSI Profit Series does not require proprietary hardware allowing system-wide integration in existing and new restaurants alike. Rainforest executives wanted to work with a mature company, like HSI, that could grow with them, and meet the company's future needs. The Profit Series system was user friendly. This made training easy, lowered costs, and increased flexibility.

The point-of-sale system simplifies the inventory tracking. The system indicates what sells the most, what needs to be ordered, when it needs to be ordered, and how much needs to be ordered. This lowers inventory costs. This saves time and eliminates ordering mistakes that could result in running out of needed items.[26]

Rainforest Café also uses a computer system to calculate waiting times for tables to within seven minutes.[27] With this knowledge, restaurant patrons can utilize their time more efficiently and shop or do whatever they desire before they reach their tables. The timing system also accounts for part of the increased table turnover.

RECOMMENDATION FOR THE FUTURE

Rainforest Café has had a successful start-up. Potential problems surround the rate of growth and the large cash holdings of the company.

Rainforest Café, Inc. has been methodically expanding. This market segment has become saturated. For this reason, Rainforest Café must quickly exploit these current conditions to maximize market share.

The available cash reserves for growth should be better utilized. A look at sales generated by Hard Rock Cafe and Planet Hollywood indicates that Rainforest Café has the potential to be the industry leader. By increasing the number of restaurants 10-fold, almost equal to the number of Hard Rock Cafes, Rainforest could potentially generate sales of $487 million. Compared to the Hard Rock Cafe's sales of $400 million and Planet Hollywood's sales of $373 million for this number of restaurants, this would make Rainforest Café the industry leader. Continued expansion is vital to the continued success of Rainforest Café.

Given the large start-up costs, the opening of each new unit is important to the success and health of the entire

---

[25] "News and Views from the IT Trenches," *Nation's Restaurant News*, May 19, 1997, p. 28.

[26] Rubenstein, Ed, "Rainforest Café Finds Cleaner, Greener Pastures with New Fryers," *Nation's Restaurant News*, March 15, 1998, v. 33, p. 20(1).

[27] Prewitt, Milford, "Eatertainment's Tinsel Tarnished," *Nation's Restaurant News*, December 14, 1998, v. 32, n. 50, p. 1(1).

company. The success of each unit lies in its location and the atmosphere of each restaurant. Thorough analysis must be conducted before a site is chosen. A poorly chosen site could lead to substantial losses if current and potential customer traffic does not meet expectations.

As the company grows, management must have the control systems in place to track operations. The current systems used by Rainforest work well; management must continually upgrade to remain on top of all operations. Staying on the cutting edge of technology will also help Rainforest Café increase the bottom line.

Linking the back office to the current POS system could reduce administrative costs and improve unit management. A total time system could track the hours of hourly wage employees. This system could then be tied to an automatic payroll system, cutting costs by reducing the time spent on payroll.[28]

The quality of the Rainforest Café must be maintained throughout all its stores. Rainforest Café sells an entire experience, not only food and merchandise. The experience must be uniform across all units.

Rainforest could facilitate its expansion through franchising. Planet Hollywood utilized this method of expansion with some success. In 1996, Planet Hollywood received more than $21 million in revenues from their franchisees. Rainforest could benefit from a similar plan of action. Quality control and training could be significant factors with franchising.

Uniformity and quality control are essential. Loosening control could cause difficulties for such a young company. Hard Rock Cafe has existed for 25 years and remains a privately held company. With almost 70 restaurants and a very strong position in the industry, Hard Rock illustrates that franchising is not the only alternative.

Currently, Rainforest Café is a leading contender in the themed restaurant sector of the restaurant industry. Expansion, continued growth, and innovation are all necessary for Rainforest Café to be the themed restaurant leader. Like Hard Rock Cafe and Planet Hollywood, Rainforest Café must focus on its strengths and use technology to continue its rapid growth.

---

[28] "News and Views from the IT Trenches," p. 24.

CASE QUESTIONS

Strategic Questions

1. What is the strategic outlook for the Rainforest Café?

2. What trends are driving this direction?

3. What are the critical success factors for this corporation/organization?

4. What are some of the core competencies of this company?

Technological Questions

5. What systems has the Rainforest Café been built on?

6. What has caused them to choose this technology?

7. How successful has the chosen technology been?

Quantitative Questions

8. What is the company's financial ability to commit to a continued high-technology infrastructure?

9. What conclusions can be reached from an analysis of the financial information to support or contradict this financial ability?

10. What conclusions can be reached by examining the following ratios?

Quick/Current
Debt
Revenue
Profit
Asset Utilization

11. What conclusions can be reached by analyzing the financial trends?

12. In its distribution methodology, what techniques does Rainforest Café use to apply technology to its ordering system?

Internet Questions

13. What does the corporation's web page present about their business directives? www.rainforestcafe.com

14. How does this compare to the conclusions reached by the writers of the articles?

15. How does this compare to the conclusions reached by analyzing the financial information?

Industry Questions

16. What challenges and opportunities is the industry facing?

17. Is the industry oligopolistic or competitive?

18. Does the industry face a change in government regulation?

19. How will technology impact the industry?

Data Questions

20. What role do data play in the future of the corporation?

21. How important are data to the corporation's continued success?

22. How will the capture and maintenance of customer data impact the corporation's future?

DAVE & BUSTER'S

Executive Summary

Case Name:	Dave & Buster's
Case Industry:	Restaurant industry
Major Technology Issue:	Making use of their technology in order to increase revenue in their amusement sales and to learn more about their customers
Major Financial Issue:	Maintaining a strong financial ground and continuing their profitability in order to fuel their growth in the upcoming years.
Major Strategic Issue:	Making themselves known as the first in their concept and establishing themselves as the premier provider of such a concept to an adult market.
Major Players/Leaders:	Dave Corriveau, president, Co-CEO, and cofounder Buster Corley , Co-CEO, and cofounder
Main Web Page:	www.daveandbusters.com
Case Conclusion/Recommendation:	Dave & Buster's is beginning to experience pressure from competitors that are using D&B's same basic concept and are therefore taking away from D&B's customer base. It will be up to D&B to take a more active role in attracting their targeted customers and putting in place the necessary technology to learn about their customers while maintaining their original concept.

CASE ANALYSIS

INTRODUCTORY STORY

Dave Corriveau met James Corley in Little Rock, Arkansas. Corriveau considers himself the "fun-and-games guy." He was still quite young when he opened up his own business in Little Rock. It was a game parlor and a saloon. In 1976, he opened a larger version named Slick Willy's World of Amusements. It has been rumored that Bill Clinton was among those who frequented the place. The 10,000-sq. ft. business generated sales in excess of $1.2 million while Corriveau was still in his early twenties.

During the same time, Corley was a general manager for T.G.I. Friday's in the same town. He also aspired to open up his own restaurant. He liked the location in which Slick Willy's was operating, a renovated train station. Corley approached Corriveau to request financial support to open his restaurant. Corriveau agreed and Corley opened right next door with a walkway connecting the businesses. Corley was also in his early twenties.

The walkway between these two businesses is probably the best thing that ever happened to the two entrepreneurs. The walkway enabled customers to migrate easily between the restaurant and the game parlor and saloon. Customers who initially came to one of the establishments would end up walking to the other. They came to eat something and then stayed to play a couple of games. Sometimes they came to play a couple of games and then stayed to eat. It was good business. The two owners soon realized the potential that existed for a complex that would combine both businesses under the same roof.

The Slick Willy Restaurant was sold to raise money. Corriveau and Corley then moved to Dallas. They were in Dallas a little over two years before they were able to open up their first restaurant. In 1982, inside a 40,000-sq. ft. building located next to an expressway, Dave & Buster's was born.

SHORT DESCRIPTION OF THE COMPANY

Dave & Buster's is a chain of 20 "eat-ertainment" complexes that combine food, fun, and games in major cities throughout the United States. Dave & Buster's restaurants are 30,000- to 70,000-sq. ft. complexes that have video games, virtual reality machines, murder mystery theaters, billiards, Las Vegas casino-style blackjack tables (just for fun, not money), and bars, all under the same roof. When the company says "There's no place quite like it"™ they really mean it. Dave and Buster's recently opened a new complex in the United Kingdom. They have plans to open seven more in the region. There are also plans to open complexes in the Middle East and along the Pacific Rim.[1]

SHORT HISTORY OF THE COMPANY

Dave and Buster's targets adults between the ages of 21 and 50 and discourages children and teenagers by requiring them to be accompanied by an adult. The concept has been successful so far. Their annual sales figures are shown in Figure 1.4.

Dave and Buster's is not merely a place to eat; it is also a place to have a drink and to be entertained among the video games, simulated casino tables, karaoke stations, simulated golf games, and even bowling lanes. The target age group of 21- to 50-year-olds seems to find the mix of entertainment and food attractive.

D&B's success is also attributable to the hosting of corporate private parties. To facilitate, banquet rooms are equipped with audiovisual equipment for presentations.[2] The locations are appealing to corporate organizers because after functions, entertainment is immediately available. Birthdays, high school reunions,

bachelor parties, and the like are also held in these rooms. Group business also adds volume to soft periods in the business cycle.

Dave and Buster's major competitor is Game Works, comprised of a collaboration between Universal Studios, Sega Enterprises, and film director Steven Spielberg's Dreamworks SKG. The agreement states that Game Works would become the exclusive distributor of Sega products in North America.[3] The team has aimed their efforts at 18- to 24-year-olds. The initial store openings have had major success. There are plans to open at least 100 more by the year 2000. Game Works has the necessary financial supporters to expand quickly.

The name Game Works has confused some customers into believing that it is just an upscale arcade. The company has initiated a marketing campaign to dispel such beliefs. Game Works also has a home page on the World Wide Web to assist them in marketing. This is something that Dave and Buster's was late to add.

FINANCIAL AND PORTFOLIO ANALYSIS

Revenues from group functions now represent 11 percent of sales, up from 8 percent two years ago.[4] Store

[1] "Dave & Buster's Accelerates International Expansion; Signs Two New Agreements to Develop D&B's in Pacific Rim and Europe," *Business Wire,* September 2, 1997.
[2] Brochure from Dave & Buster's restaurant.
[3] "Dave & Buster's Accelerates International Expansion; Signs Two New Agreements to Develop D&B's in Pacific Rim and Europe," *Business Wire,* September 2, 1997.
[4] "Highlights from DANB's Annual Meeting" and "Our Meeting with Management."

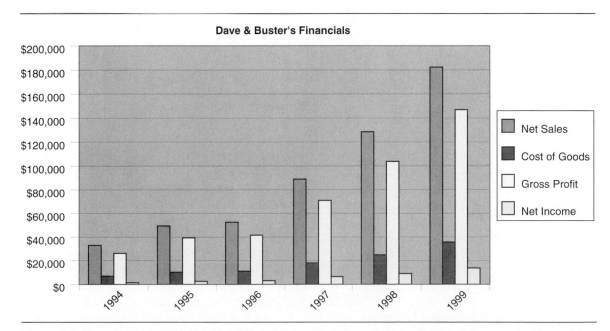

Figure 1.4 Dave & Buster's financials, 1994–1999. (Source: Dave & Buster's Annual Reports, 1994–1999.)

Table 1.1 D & B's Revenue Breakdown

Area of Revenue	Percentage
Amusement	44%
Food	33%
Beverage	21%
Merchandise	2%

managers are paid commissions on business they bring in and are required to build and maintain databases on corporate and group clients.[5]

The restaurant's financial success is attributable to revenue collected from the amusement segment of the business. As noted in Table 1.1, it constitutes the largest percentage of the revenue mix.[6] The revenue growth in this area has been fueled by the introduction of the PowerCard. The card has increased the buy-ins of video credits by 11 percent since its introduction late in 1997.[7]

There are several classifications for the number of restaurants in the industry. Such classifications are based on the concept they embody. The classifications range from the cafeteria/buffet concept (e.g., Morrison Restaurants) to the steakhouse concept (e.g., Outback Steakhouse). D&B falls under the celebrity/entertainment concept.[8] The difference in this segment is that it is capital intensive. In D&B's case, the opening of each restaurant costs around $11 million.[9] Such costs are justified by the average $10.5 million in annual sales[10] for these restaurants.

D&B maintained control of their expansion plans. Each store has opened on time while maintaining same store sales. Their three-year revenue growth of 41.83 percent put them above the industry average and certainly over the S&P 500.[11] As noted in Table 1.2, D&B has surpassed many of the industry averages. Net income growth of 80.88 percent is roughly 30 percent more than the industry average. The ROA of 6.38 percent is slightly above the industry's 4.95 percent.

D&B has made efforts to reduce costs in certain areas to increase profit margins. Comparing operations for the

Table 1.2 Peer Group Ratios

	Dave & Busters as of 08/22/97	S&P 500 as of 08/22/97	Industry as of 08/22/97
P/E	36.64	14.32	35.75
Div yield	0.00	2.09	1.10
Price/book	3.07	3.96	3.02
Price/cash flow	17.65	N.M.	30.77
Price/tang.book	3.49	10.21	0.20
3 yr rev growth	41.83	12.41	25.32
3 yr eps growth	N.M.	73.94	65.08
3 yr div growth	N.M.	10.06	22.49
Net income growth	80.88	154.39	53.51
Reinvestment rate	8.39	9.65	7.32
Net profit margin	7.14	7.39	6.64
Oper profit margin	12.08	13.18	13.39
ROE	8.41	17.97	14.76
ROA	6.38	5.59	4.95
Fixed charge coverage	282.13	16.31	6.69
Current ratio	1.15	1.78	1.22
Lg-term debt to equity	18.91	84.01	74.75
Total debt to equity	18.91	90.40	76.55

13 weeks ending August 3, 1997, with the 13 weeks ending August 4, 1996, cost of revenues, as a percentage of revenues, decreased to 19.4 percent from 20.4 percent. The decrease in cost of revenues was a result of lower costs associated with beverage revenues and a shift in the revenue mix toward more amusement income.

Operating payroll and benefits decreased to 28.4 percent from 29.7 percent in the prior comparable period. Operating payroll and benefits were lower due to cost reductions in variable and fixed labor and leverage from increased revenues. Other operating expenses increased to 25.6 percent compared to 22.4 percent in the prior comparable period. General and administrative expenses increased to 6.6 percent of revenues as compared to the 6.3 percent for the comparable period.[12]

STOCK INVESTMENT/OUTLOOK

Many investors have noted D&B's success. The stock price has increased. Since the initial public offering in

---

[5] Ibid.
[6] Rubel, Chad, "New Menu for Restaurants: Talking Trees and Blackjack," *Marketing News,* July 29, 1996, pp. 1, 16.
[7] Ibid.
[8] Restaurant Industry, Industry Report Source, Wheat, First Securities, Inc.; October 6, 1997.
[9] Mark, Dan, "New Restaurants Not Kidding Around," *Business Courier Serving Cincinnati–Northern Kentucky,* December 4, 1998, v. 15, n. 33, p. 1(2).
[10] Ibid.
[11] "Games Work," *Restaurant Business,* February 15, 1998, v. 87, n. 4, p. 60.

[12] Dave & Buster's Inc. (DANB) Quarterly Report, SEC Form 10-Q, September 16, 1997.

1995, the stock has gone up steadily and is seen as a good buy. Figure 1.5 shows the growth of the stock since the initial offering.

In December 1997, five out of six brokers recommended D&B's stock as a strong buy.[13] A consensus seemed to form on the future potential of D&B's stock. Sales at new restaurants remain high during the first two years and then stabilized. Another indication that D&B did not appear to be just another trend was the 6 percent increase in sales at the oldest location in Dallas, which had been open since 1982.

RISK ANALYSIS

Extreme business pressures face restaurant owners.[14] The relatively low cost of entry allows numerous start-ups to threaten existing restaurant businesses. Established businesses are continually improving their operations to cut costs, streamline production, and increase competitiveness.

In addition to market pressures, restaurateurs have many secondary risks:

- Identifying and reacting to changing consumer tastes and demands
- Hiring and retaining high quality employees
- Maintaining costs while providing high quality and impeccable service
- Partnering with suppliers and vendors
- Researching and analyzing geographic demographics
- Deploying and maintaining state-of-the-art technology infrastructures
- Investing in research and development.

---

[13] "YAHOO Finance," http://quote.yahoo.com/quotes?SYMBOLS=danb&detailed=r.
[14] "Serving the Supply Chains," Deloitte & Touche Consulting Group, http://www.dtcg.com/consumer_intensive_businesses/restaurants.htm.

Among the key points, the first one, identifying consumer tastes and demands, makes or breaks many restaurants. A research paper entitled *Dinner Decision Making—1996* found that 57 percent of on-premises diners were in pursuit of eating pleasure. The rising number of restaurants provides the consumer with extensive choice in the selective dining experience.

INDUSTRY AND MARKET ANALYSIS

The growth in restaurant industry sales is correlated with the positive changes in real income and the expanding economy.[15] As evidenced by the decline in industry sales that occurred during the 1974, 1980, and 1991 economic recessions, the industry is sensitive to the nation's business cycles and overall economic health.[16] Any outlook in the industry should examine in detail the forecasts made for the whole economy.

The long-range economic projections from the Bureau of Labor Statistics (BLS) up to the year 2005 are optimistic. BLS projects an average annual gain of 2.3 percent in real gross domestic product between 1994 and 2005. Real disposable income is expected to continue to grow at an average annual rate of 2.0 percent.[17] Also found in this report is a forecast for a 1.4 percent average annual increase in real spending for food and other nondurables. A separate study conducted by McKinsey & Company predicts that in the next decade 90 percent of incremental food expenditures will be for meals consumed away from home.[18]

---

[15] Riehle, Hudson, "Economics 2005," *Restaurants USA*, May 1997, pp. 39–46.
[16] Ibid.
[17] Ibid.
[18] Dolan, Kerry A., "Food Distributors: Restaurants Had a Checkered Year, But the Big Supermarkets Went to Town," *Forbes*, January 13, 1997, v. 159, n. 1, p. 158.

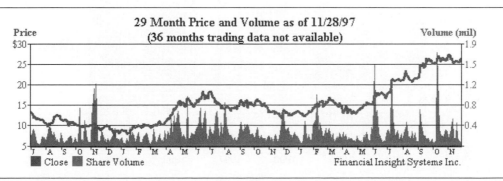

Figure 1.5 Growth of D&B's stock since 1995. (Graph taken from Market Guide web site <http://www.marketguide.com/ MGI/ PRODUCTS/chart.htm.>)

There are several indicators that the $320.4 billion restaurant industry will continue to grow.[19] Based on research conducted by the National Restaurant Association (NRA), the following statistics are positive signs for the industry:

- The typical person (eight years and older) consumed an average of 4.1 commercially prepared meals per week in 1996, up from 3.8 in 1991. Three out of four adults agreed that they have a larger selection of restaurants available to them in 1996 than they did in 1994.
- Forty-seven percent of adults agreed that they were cooking fewer meals at home in 1996 than they were in 1994.
- Almost two out of every five consumers (38 percent) considered meals prepared at a sitdown or fast-food restaurant to be essential to the way they lived.
- Two out of three adults felt that their favorite restaurant's food provided flavor and taste sensations that they could not easily duplicate in their home kitchens.
- Roughly three out ten adults indicated they were not eating on premises at eating places or purchasing takeout/delivery foods as often as they would like.

The NRA also noted that the restaurant industry experienced a growth rate of 5 percent from 1993 to 1996.[20] The baby boomers are credited with much of that growth since they account for at least 60 percent of the U.S. food-service spending.[21] Figure 1.6 illustrates the growth of the industry from 1970 to 1997.[22]

While the overall growth in the industry has been positive, the growth does not translate into stellar sale gains by individual restaurants. Three out four adults agree that they have a larger selection of restaurants from which to choose. Many large chains of restaurants have set out to expand the number of units at all costs. Applebee's International, for example, which had 660 restaurants by the end of 1995, opened 130 more by 1996.[23] Abe Gustin, chairman of Applebee's, said that despite the relatively flat growth in same-store sales, the company deliberately placed more units together when they found them operating at capacity in the same vicinity. Gustin conceded sales at the other Applebee's restaurants declined, but considered this "conscious cannibalization."[24]

While it may seem that larger chains are gaining in the restaurant industry, there is still growth in the

---

[19] "1997 Food Service Industry Forecasts," http://www.restaurant.org/RUSA/trends/ftmay97.htm.

[20] "Key Trends, Challenges Impact Operator's Growth Potential," *ID: The Voice of Food Service Distribution,* June 15, 1996, v. 32, n. 7, p. 13(5).
[21] Ibid.
[22] Ibid.
[23] Papiernik, Richard L., "Same-Store Sales Suffer as Chains Push Unit Growth," *Nation's Restaurant News,* March 25, 1996, v. 30, n. 12, p. 1(2).
[24] Ibid.

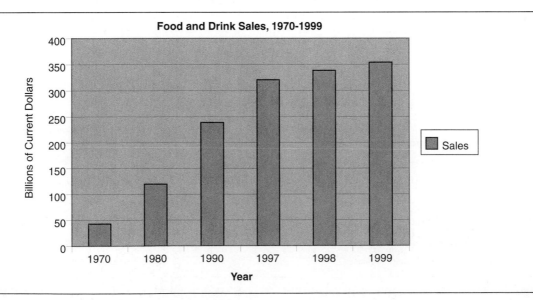

Figure 1.6 Growth of the food-service industry, 1970–1999.

number of individual restaurants. Research from the Census of Retail Trade used 1992 data (the latest available in this area) to report that 96 percent of all table service (not fast-food) restaurants were single-unit operations.[25] The data also show that 71 percent of those restaurants generated less than $500,000 in sales.

This data indicates that single-unit operations are still a major force in the industry. They have an ability that many larger chains cannot easily duplicate: to turn things around quickly when they are not working out. By virtue of their size, and sometimes bureaucracy, large chains take longer to react to customer's tastes and preferences.

Smaller restaurants are sometimes more in touch with customers and can easily meet their needs. This enables them to steal customers away from the larger chains that react more slowly to such demands. This flexibility will be a factor that many larger chains will need to address if they wish to increase their market share and/or maintain same store level sales.

As the total number of restaurants in the industry grows, competition will pressure restaurants to keep menu prices below inflation. An analyst from Wertheim Shroder & Co., a major investment bank, noted that "margin improvement and solid unit growth that produces adequate return on investment [is] where the battle is being fought."[26]

The restaurant industry not only provides a convenient place to eat and have an experience, it is also an integral part of the nation's economy. More than nine million people are employed in the restaurant industry. Employment is projected to be 11 million by 2005. The total annual wages and benefits of those employed in the restaurant industry equal $63 billion. Furthermore, more than one out of every four retail outlets is an eating or drinking establishment.[27] The industry sales projection for 1997 is $320 billion and is distributed among the three major industry sectors indicated in Table 1.3.

ROLE OF RESEARCH AND DEVELOPMENT

Apart from typical concerns of restaurants with kitchen, back office, and service efficiencies, Dave and Buster's must also deal with many other purchases that

Table 1.3 Industry Sales Projections for 1997

Industry Sector	1997 Sales Projections (billion $)
Commercial	$289
Institutional	$ 30
Military	$ 1
Total	$320

customers make in their restaurants. These purchases are the games. Any customer might make dozens of game purchases every visit. This is a service that Dave and Buster's is trying to address more efficiently.

TECHNOLOGY STORY

When the first D&B restaurant opened in Dallas in 1982, the games operated on tokens that could be retrieved from change machines located throughout the arcade area. Customers carried the coins in little velvet-like blue bags or, if they cashed over a certain amount, inside a golden tin bucket with a rainbow and a pot of gold. The coins could be used for video and ticket redemption games.

Gradually the stores began to integrate a system to replace the tokens with a rechargeable card that customers could easily carry inside their pockets. The Power Card works like a credit card. It enables players to place credits on the card by using the different charge stations around the establishment.

TECHNOLOGY INVESTMENT AND ANALYSIS

The Power Card provides convenience to the customer by taking away the burden of carrying around a bucket of coins and allows D&B to make gradual increases on the amount they can charge per game. Before prices could only be raised in whole increments (one token at a time). The card has done away with that by allowing incremental increases of 0.1 through 0.9 at a time. The customer simply swipes the card through a scanning mechanism located in front of each machine and the credit amount is automatically deducted from the card.

[25] DeLuca, Mike, "How Will Independent Restaurants Survive?" *Restaurant Hospitality*, August 1995, v. 79, n. 8, p. 18(1).
[26] Ibid.
[27] NRA 1997 Industry Pocket Fact book, http:/www.restaurant.org/research/pocket/index.htm.

The system has the capability to track what games have been played with each card and how much has been spent. Customers can verify the amount they have on their card by using analyzer/rechargers that are located throughout the arcade area. These analyzer/rechargers also allow customers to put more money on a card without standing in line. The tokens are still used for some of the ticket redemption games that involve skill activities.

A discount on the games is offered to those who have spent over a certain amount of credits on the same card. Members can sign up for the card by completing an application with particular information. They are then given a card with their name on it. The "gold" card gives the customer a 10 percent discount on the amount required to play the games.

The card offers bonuses to customers through a lottery-type system that matches the numbers on their card with a number drawn randomly by the computer. Credits are awarded accordingly to the card. The system used for the card does have certain limitations. The card can only be used at the issuing store, the credits are nontransferable, and no cash back is allowed on the remaining credit balance of the card. Furthermore, customers can only get bonuses from an attendant at one of the desks and not from the analyzer/rechargers.

RECOMMENDATION FOR THE FUTURE

Dave & Buster's must consider expanding at a faster rate in its market niche. There are many prime spots to place restaurants across the country. With Game Works well-financed and run by experienced operators, D&B's could find itself pushed out of the market niche they created. Besides hiring management to manage expansion, D&B's must consider finding new sources of capital to expand its locations and its games.

The corporate and group events customer segment must be more aggressively pursued. Sales personnel specifically targeting these customers should be hired. The divided attentions of the restaurant managers make them unsuitable for this function.

Other Power Card bonuses and use should be considered. Additional game buying power is certainly a fun incentive.

CASE QUESTIONS

Strategic Questions

1. What is the strategic direction of the corporation/organization?

2. Who or what forces are driving this direction?

3. What are the critical success factors for this company?

4. What are the core competencies for this company?

Technological Questions

5. What technologies has the corporation relied on?

6. What has caused a change in the use of technology in the corporation/organization?

7. How has this change been implemented?

8. Who has driven this change throughout the organization?

9. How successful has the technological change been?

Quantitative Questions

10. What analysis can be made by examining the following ratio groups?

Quick/Current:
Debt:
Revenue:
Profit
Asset Utilization

11. Is the industry stable? Are there replacement products?

Internet Questions

12. What does the corporation's web page present about their business?
13. How does this compare to the conclusions reached by the writers of the articles mentioned in the case?
14. How does this compare to the conclusions reached by analyzing the financial information?

Industry Questions

15. What challenges and opportunities is the industry facing?
16. Is the industry oligopolistic or competitive?

Data Questions

17. What role do data play in the future of the corporation?

18. How important are data to the corporation's continued success?

19. How will the capture and maintenance of customer data impact the corporation's future?

Database Questions

20. How could D&B use data collection to help manage their future?

21. What could D&B possibly do with such information and should they be interested in collecting the data themselves?

22. How could D&B collect these data?

23. What type of data should D&B be collecting from their customers?

Access Questions

24. Is there any trend in D&B's contracting of new customers?

25. Which location has the greatest restaurant occupancy capacity?

26. Is there a form that could be used to more efficiently enter new customers into the system?

27. How could the database limit the double booking of banquet rooms?

28. Are there any discrepancies in the booking of banquet room location capacity and their guest count?

STARBUCKS

Executive Summary

Case Name:	Starbucks Corporation
Case Industry:	Food/retail industry
Major Technology Issue:	Using "smart cards" for store purchases and using the Internet for retail extension are two technology issues facing the company.
Major Financial Issue:	Attracting and retaining high-quality employees depends on offering health and other benefits that are costly.
Major Strategic Issue:	To be a global brand by 2000, selling a coffee experience through novel distribution methods and new products.
Major Players/Leaders:	Chairman and CEO Howard Schultz is the driving force of the corporation.
Main Web Page:	www.starbucks.com
Case Conclusion/Recommendation:	Starbucks needs to master mass customization and one-to-one marketing at the same time.

CASE ANALYSIS

INTRODUCTORY STORY

Starbucks began as a sole gourmet coffee shop in Seattle's Pike Place Market in 1971. In the early 1980s, when the company consisted of just five stores, things began to change. A coffee buyer for Starbucks named Howard Schultz visited Milan, Italy. He was astounded at the crowds that gathered at the cafes. People who lived and worked in the city started and ended their days with a stop at their favorite cafe. Mr. Schultz thought this trend might be a success in the United States. He attempted to sell the idea to the owners of Starbucks.[1]

The owners of Starbucks rejected Schultz's idea. Opening a cafe meant getting into the restaurant business and that was not what the owners wanted to do. In light of this, Schultz resigned at Starbucks and raised sufficient funds to open his own cafe in April 1986. Less than a year later, Mr. Schultz opened two more cafes and bought out his former bosses for $4 million. Since then, Starbucks has grown to 1,145 company-owned or -licensed shops in North America with sales of $696 million.[2]

SHORT DESCRIPTION OF THE COMPANY

Starbucks is a limited restaurant that offers coffee products and light food items. The company purchases and roasts a wide variety of whole bean coffees. Many patrons buy coffees "to go" while others stay in the shop and enjoy the cafe atmosphere with friends and coworkers. Along with rich brewed coffees and espresso drinks, Starbucks also sells cookies, croissants, and other baked goods. Starbucks offers many derivatives of coffee such as Caffe Latte, Caffe Mocha, Caffe Americano, and Mocha Frappuccino.

SHORT HISTORY OF THE COMPANY

Starbucks, which on average opens a new store every business day, planned to open an additional 325 coffee shops in North America during 1997. Most of the existing coffee shops are located in malls or metropolitan areas. Starbucks has shops in airports, grocery stores, and bookstores. Starbucks continues to look to the future and is well on its way towards its goal to have 2,000 new shops by the year 2000.

In addition to its cafes in the United States and Canada, Starbucks has opened an outlet in Tokyo under a joint venture with a Japanese restaurant company, Sazabu, Inc. It also plans to open three shops in London in the near future. In two instances, existing stores have been so successful and the demand for the prod-

---

[1] Goldman, D. A., *et al.*, "Starbucks Corporation—Company Report," The Robinson-Humphrey Company, Inc., January 1, 1997.

[2] Ruggles, Ron, "Business Mix, Preserving Ambiance Shape Starbucks' In-Store Systems," *Nation's Restaurant News*, April 14, 1997, v. 31, n. 15, p. 52(1).

ucts has been so great that Starbucks opened competing shops across the street from the already existing outlets.[3]

The company empowers its employees to make business and customer service decisions on the spot. This empowerment, along with health insurance, professional training, and other benefits makes employees more eager to sell Starbucks products. Similar to the way the company takes pride in its coffee, it also takes pride in its professional work force.

Each new employee receives 24 hours of training taught by store managers who themselves have gone through facilitation workshops and are certified by the company as trainers. The training focuses on empowerment and what it means to the employee. Case scenarios are reviewed to illustrate common situations that arise. After these scenarios are reviewed, new employees are encouraged to give feedback and offer suggested actions. This feedback is important as a gauge for the trainers to decide when an employee feels empowered or hindered by management.[4]

Producing a quality product has allowed Starbucks to remain successful. This has always been the main strategy for Starbucks and is reflected in the company's mission statement: "To establish Starbucks as the premier purveyor of the finest coffee in the world while maintaining our uncompromising principles as we grow." Ingredients in making a good product are people like Dave Olsen, the company's coffee buyer. Olsen travels the world to inspect and purchase coffee beans. He will not purchase a bean just because it is from an historically good bean country. He knows countries can have both bad and good crops. Therefore, Olsen personally inspects all of the beans purchased by Starbucks.

The way in which beans are roasted also produces a quality product. Procter & Gamble, General Foods, and Nestlé all roast their beans through automation. Starbucks roasts its beans by hand in small quantities. Through years of experience, roasters at Starbucks are able to get peak flavor from each bean. This procedure is more time consuming and costly, yet it produces a richer more aromatic coffee.

Starbucks offers a multitude of coffee beans that can be ground at the store or sold whole. Customers can also enjoy cookies, croissants, scones, biscotti, and many other cafe delicacies. The main products at stores are coffee or espresso drinks. Black, decaf, latte, Americano, mocha, and Frappuccino are common orders heard in stores. Customers are allowed and encouraged to alter their orders by adding an extra shot of espresso or requesting steamed rather than foamed milk.[5]

Starbucks has become very good at building its stores. It takes only 6 weeks to open a new store, shortened from 13 weeks in 1997. Early deliveries by vendors of safes and refrigerators could mean that these objects needed to be constantly moved in order to install the floor tiles or other items. Instead of changing when deliveries were made, the management at Starbucks decided to revolutionize the process by which stores were constructed.[6]

The company opened two distribution facilities, one on each coast of the United States, to house the material and equipment needed to complete a store. The company was able to implement the concept of just-in-time (JIT) manufacturing to the construction of new stores. Using JIT, Starbucks is able to provide materials to construction sites on an as-needed basis.

FINANCIAL AND PORTFOLIO ANALYSIS

The products sold at Starbucks are not inexpensive. A small Coffee-of-the-Day costs $1.25 and an extra large, venti, Espresso Frappuccino costs $3.80. The muffins, scones, cookies, and other food items are also higher cost than comparable items offered at cafeterias or convenience stores. However, these prices are not out of line with the competitors in Starbucks' market niche. Gloria Jeans and Caribou are also priced in the same range. Starbucks is not fighting a price battle with its competitors, it is fighting a quality of product and service war. Patrons of cafes are not as concerned with price as they are with the enjoyment derived from the products purchased.[7]

Starbucks has grown tremendously since 1988. The annual growth rate for sales, net income, and earnings per share is 61.1, 75.3, and 56.5 percent, respectively. The company has achieved these numbers through their aggressive expansion effort and a near-zero total debt-to-equity ratio for the past three years. Instead of using debt to fund their expansion efforts, the company raised $20 million through an initial public offering of common stock in 1992. Additional capital was needed in 1994 to continue expansion and upgrade computer technology. At this time, Starbucks issued a second

[3] "Starbucks Corp.—Company Report," Moody's Investor Service, January 10, 1997.
[4] Stoeffel, J. P., et al., "Starbucks Corp.—Company Report," Smith Barney, March 4, 1997.
[5] "Ground Coffee," Mediamark Research, Inc., Spring 1995.
[6] Fysh, Graham, "Distribution Centers Help Starbucks Keep New Store Openings on Schedule," The News Tribune, Tacoma, WA, September 24, 1996.
[7] Simon, Howard, "Gourmet Coffee Firms Going Abroad," Journal of Commerce and Commercial, July, 1996, v. 409, n. 28761, p. 7B(1).

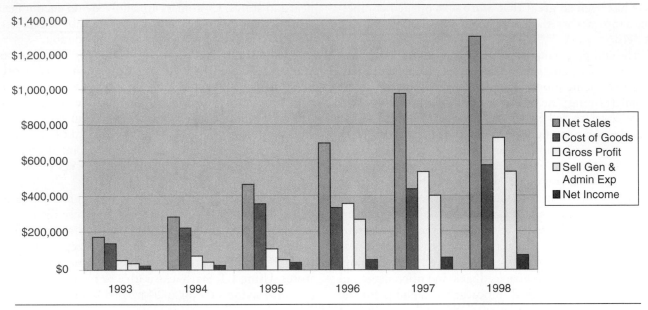

Figure 1.7 Starbucks' financials, 1993–1998. (Source: Starbucks' Annual Reports, 1993–1998.)

common stock offering at $28.50 per share and raised $156.8 million.[8]

Another reason Starbucks has not had to finance using debt is because it retains all earnings; dividends are not paid to the holders of common stock. The expectation is that as Starbucks shifts from being a growth company to a mature company, earnings will be distributed as the need for funding is reduced.

A reflection of a company's ability to make money in their core business is reflected in its earnings before interest, taxes, depreciation, and amortization (EBITDA). EBITDA does not take into account a company's investing activities, other income, or miscellaneous items. While net income has certainly increased, an average annual rate of 75.3 percent since 1992 indicate that EBITDA is growing even faster than net income. The slope of the EBITDA graph is increasing at a greater rate than the slope of the graph for net income. The provision for income taxes is the major factor that impacts income. Analysts often recommend an increase in depreciation and amortization to reduce taxes. Starbucks does not have a great deal of depreciable assets. Figure 1.7 shows Starbucks' net income for 1993 to 1998.

The ratios for Starbucks compare favorably to the restaurant industry. Starbucks' quick ratio has increased from 0.53 in 1994 to 1.02 in 1995 and to 2.44 in 1996. Compared to the Standard & Poor's industry index, Starbucks can cover short-term debt more easily than its competitors. The industry average quick ratios for 1994 and 1995 were 0.3 and 0.5, respectively. This can be attributed to Starbucks having very few current liabilities and the fact that these liabilities are growing slowly. Other factors aiding the quick ratio are growth in cash from $8.3 million in 1994 to $126 million in 1996 and growth in marketable securities to $103 million.

STOCK INVESTMENT/OUTLOOK

Standard & Poor's ranked Starbucks as the 795th largest company in the United States as of March 3, 1996. Smith Barney and The Robinson-Humphrey Company, Inc., continue to issue buy recommendations for the common stock.[9] Both research companies estimate 1997 earnings per share to be at $0.70, which makes the price-to-earnings (P/E) ratio 53. Robinson-Humphrey is looking for the common stock to reach $49.00 per share in 1997 but does not recommend purchases over $45.00 per share. Smith Barney estimates 1998 earnings per share at $0.95 while Robinson-Humphrey is more aggressive at $1.00. The forecasts translate into growth of 30 percent for 1997 and between 35 percent to 40 percent for 1998.[10]

---

[8] Prewitt, Milford, "Starbucks Nabs Over $155M in Secondary-Stock Offering," Lebnar-Friedman, Inc., 1994.

[9] Filipczak, Bob, "Push me, pull you," *Training*, January 1998, v. 34, n. 1, p. 92(2).
[10] "Starbucks Coffee," *The Weekly Home Furnishings Newspaper*, May 30, 1994, v. 68, n. 22, p. 57(1).

Stock Price For Week Ending: 07/30/99

Latest Trade Date:	07/31/99
Outstanding Shares (000s):	181,844
Volume:	2,953,300
High (or Asked):	25.25
Low (or Bid):	23.18
Close (or Average):	23.25
Market Value:	4,227,873

Earnings Information For 12 months Ending: 07/99

Earnings per Share:	0.50
Price/Earnings Ratio:	46.50

Figure 1.8 Starbucks' stock prices. (Source: Yahoo Finance)

The forecast for 1996–2001 is for Starbucks to grow at an annual rate of 35 to 40 percent. This is one of the fastest growth rates for companies followed by Robinson-Humphrey. This rate is far ahead of estimates for companies in this industry and the S&P 500. Analysts feel the growth momentum can be maintained through a combination of the introduction of new products, low cost expansion of stores into new geographic markets, new marketing efforts aimed at household consumption, and continued good management.[11]

RISK ANALYSIS

Demand in the coffee business is inherently inelastic. Although customers do cringe when they hear coffee futures are increasing in price, there is not much they do about the impending issue except discuss it over a cup of coffee. Reliance on coffee is addictive in nature. This enables Starbucks and other cafes to enjoy a loyal following, allowing more accurate prediction of cash flows and operating costs.

Starbucks is positioning itself to capture the coffee drinkers that brew coffee at home and the few people who are scared off by the high prices paid per cup at the store. On July 15, 1997, the business section of the *Chicago Tribune* ran an article titled "Starbucks' Latest Brew." It announced that Starbucks would use Chicago as a testing platform to introduce six new blends of coffee to the supermarket shelves.[12]

Three companies dominate the $3 billion wholesale supermarket coffee business. These companies,

Procter & Gamble, Kraft Foods Inc., and Nestlé, have large marketing departments and deep pockets to ward off possible invaders into the market. Jean-Michel Valette, an industry analyst at Hambrecht & Quist, predicts that any company entering this market will fail. However, Starbucks enjoys such brand recognition and a loyal following that it is making the attempt.

INDUSTRY AND MARKET ANALYSIS

Starbucks is classified as a member of the restaurant industry, which includes restaurants, bars, and other away-from-home dining facilities. Each of the almost 99 million households in the United States spent an average of $2,400 in the restaurant industry in 1996. The total spending amounts to $238 billion and does not include such other food locations as vending machines and employee cafeterias. Generally, this is not considered to be a high growth industry.[13]

Although $2,400 per household seems like a sizeable expenditure, the industry had anticipated a better year in 1996. January 1996 was very cold, which prompted many patrons to stay at home. The Olympics kept families glued to the television in the summer, and Thanksgiving and Christmas were situated in such a way that there were five fewer shopping days than in other years. These factors had a major impact on the industry, resulting in an increase in spending of only 2.1 percent over 1995. The National Restaurant Association (NRA) is estimating sales to grow 4.6 percent to $243.2 billion in 1997.

[11] Dwyer, Kevin, "Black Gold," *BC Business,* May 1994, v. 22, n. 5, p. 90(1).
[12] "Beverages Report," Mediamark Research, Inc., Spring 1995.
[13] Slywotzky, Adrian J., and Mundt, Kevin, "Hold the Sugar," *Across the Board,* September 1996, v. 33, n. 8, pp.39–43.

Table 1.4 Comparative Growth In Earnings per Share

	SBUX	IND	S&P 500	SBUX TO IND	SBUX TO S&P
FY97 vs FY96	46.80 percent	21.80 percent	12.50 percent	215 percent	376 percent
FY98 vs FY97	41.20 percent	17.90 percent	14.30 percent	231 percent	288 percent
FY 1998–2003	38.10 percent	15.80 percent	13.40 percent	241 percent	283 percent
FY 1993–1998	59.80 percent	18.00 percent	26.30 percent	331 percent	227 percent

The restaurant industry is relying on continued economic expansion, low unemployment, and low inflation to continue to boost its sales. High consumer confidence is the key ingredient to increased sales. In anticipation of an impending downturn in the economy, restaurants are streamlining their menus and offering less in the way of new products.[14]

A review of the industry's past ratios indicates that the industry is getting stronger, with the quick ratio keeping steady at 0.5 for the last six years. Debt ratios have shown tremendous improvement from 1990 to 1995, the times interest earned has grown from 3.8 to 6.7 and the debt-to-assets ratio has decreased from 42 to 26 percent. These debt ratios indicate that less debt is being used. This may occur as some food chains mature, which requires less debt. Or this may occur because capital needs are being met through the stock market or retained earnings, as is the case with Starbucks. Either way, less revenue is dedicated to servicing debt which will improve the bottom line figures. This is a highly competitive industry. This is evident in the fact that profit margins decreased to 24.04 percent in 1995 from 28.36 percent in 1994. It appears restaurants are either reducing their prices or not increasing them commensurate with their costs.[15]

Analysts predict Starbucks will remain a leader in earnings growth for its industry. This is a strong statement for an industry that, as a whole, is expected to outperform the S&P 500 in the next few years. Table 1.4 shows a comparative analysis of expected earnings for Starbucks, the restaurant industry, and the S&P 500.[16]

The restaurant industry is watched fairly closely by the government. The main concern of industry analysts is not the regulations but the increase in the minimum wage. The minimum wage was increased on October 1, 1996, and September 1, 1997. Although most restaurant employees are paid at wages higher than the minimum wage, this bottom-up pressure has a major impact upon employee costs.[17]

The typical Starbucks customer is one who thinks of himself or herself as more discriminating and willing to spend more money for a quality product. These customers do not consume large amounts of coffee and are therefore able to qualify why they are entitled to a good coffee product. To maintain this quality image Starbucks has entered into several joint ventures or strategic alliances with domestic and foreign companies to develop and market products ranging from coffee to coffee ice cream. So far, the company has yet to derive any profits from these joint ventures. Two investments do appear to be promising. The first is an alliance with PepsiCo for the development of a line of coffee-based bottled beverages sold through grocery stores. The second is with Dreyer's Ice Cream for coffee ice cream.

Figures 1.9 and 1.10 contain 1995 data compiled by Mediamark Research, Inc. The graph in Figure 1.10 illustrates the point of purchase of whole bean coffees by homemakers. This graph indicates why Starbucks wants to expand to the supermarkets. The second graph shows the dominance of the three main coffee brands in the ground coffee market. This is where the battle will occur. Starbucks is confident it will take market share away from the regional coffee brands. Starbucks' goal is to take market share from the big three coffee retailers.

In 1990, slightly more than 25 percent of table service operators used computers for scheduling employees' work hours. The figure jumped to more than 50 percent in 1996 according to the National Restaurant Association. The number of applicants for food-service jobs has decreased in recent years, reducing the quality of the applicants. To offset this, to become more effective, and to reduce error, point-of-sale computers are becoming more popular. Rather than writing orders on pads and handing them to the chef, waiters and waitresses submit customer orders to the kitchen electronically. This enables the waiter or waitress to

[14] Walkup, Carolyn, "Drive-Thru Java Craze Hits the Ground Running, Heads East, *Nation's Restaurant Review,* May 12, 1997, v. 31, n. 19, p. 6(1).

[15] "1996: A Difficult Year for the Industry," Standard & Poor's, Restaurants Industry Survey, April 10, 1997.

[16] "Starbucks Roasts the Competition," *Journal of Business Strategy,* November/December 1995, v. 16, n. 6, p. 56.

[17] Caminiti, Susan, "Coffee Chains Are Getting the Jitters," *Fortune,* November 27, 1995, v. 132, n. 11, pp. 42–44.

Whole Bean Point of Purchase

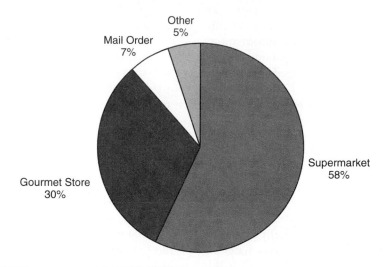

Figure 1.9 Whole bean coffee point-of-purchase percentages.

spend more time on the floor, in front of the customer, and to service more customers.[18]

The restaurant industry is fairly mature. New, untapped populations do not exist for the industry to exploit; competitors must steal business from each other. Rather than expanding by building more restaurants, existing restaurants are purchasing their competitors. This consolidation could profoundly impact the stocks of restaurants proposed for sale. On the other hand, the intent of the restaurants on the purchasing end is to reduce competition and increase market share.[19]

TECHNOLOGICAL STORY

Almost all transactions at Starbucks are completed on a cash basis. Many companies would be happy with this.

[18] http://www.sc-solutions.com/jax.html.

[19] Horsey, David, "Another Opinion," *Seattle Post-Intelligencer, Chicago Sun-Times,* July 15, 1997, p. op1.

Supermarket Sales – Ground Beans

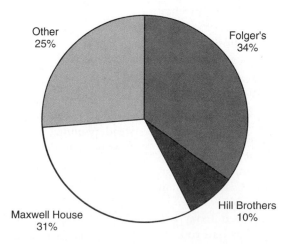

Figure 1.10 Supermarket sales of ground beans.

However, the management at Starbucks reviewed this process and envisioned a way of getting customers' money even before a transaction occurred. A customer smart card would enable Starbucks to accomplish this and enable the company to obtain valuable information.

Smart cards resemble credit cards and contain a microchip with encoded information. Smart cards do not require telephone linkages to a large central database when a purchase is made. Information is stored directly on the microchip in the card. All types of information can be contained on the smart card, making its use limitless. The card carrier's health information, picture ID, fingerprints, and other information can be encoded. An intelligent smart card has a central processing unit that allows information to be read and also stored while a memory smart card does not. The intelligent smart card can track the purchases made by the cardholder and actually give sales associates an idea of the shopper's tastes. Estee Lauder introduced the "At Your Service" system in Denmark in the summer of 1996. Magazine and Illum were the participating retailers and reported that the program worked well. When presented with the smart card, the sales associate merely put the card into the point-of-sale computer. A report was generated that contained the shopper's profile. Information such as skin type, hair color, beauty concerns, and product purchases was reported.[20]

TECHNOLOGICAL INVESTMENT AND ANALYSIS

As seen from the preceding section, the smart card is beneficial for both the purchaser and seller. No other businesses in the United States have embraced the concept. The card would certainly allow Starbucks to gain an edge on their competition by selling more coffee to existing clients. This would also reduce any mishandling of funds and reduce the reasons for robbery attempts. Implementation of the smart card would require a large investment in the production of cards and the changing of the point-of-sale terminals to accept both currency and smart cards.

While a Starbucks smart card would allow the company to receive cash at the time each card is loaded with funds, this will not be the case in the future. As smart cards become more commonplace, consumers will not want to carry more than one smart card. This means that the Starbucks smart card and other smart cards must be able to be used interchangeably. This will not allow Starbucks to receive the money as the card is loaded. In essence, Starbucks will be going from cash at time of purchase, to a cash prior to purchase, to cash at the end of the business day or other period.

As the number of stores has increased from 100 units to more than 1,145, technology has had to keep pace. Each store is outfitted with IBM 4695s as point-of-sale terminals with software designed by Progressive Software. These terminals are linked by way of a local-area network. The back office workstation acts as the network server as well as reconciling daily sales.[21]

Similar to Taco Bell and other fast-food restaurants, a touch-screen entry monitor would seem to be a perfect fit for this business. The basic sales process is for the customer to place an order with an employee, pay money, and receive the product that was ordered. The management at Starbucks reviewed the process at their stores and identified a public attraction. The customer liked the commotion. The customer enjoyed placing an order with the employee behind the register and having that employee bark out the order to the person creating the different beverages. At high time, the store seems to have the excitement of the trading pits at the Chicago Board of Trade. However, Starbucks does envision using the touch-screen monitor for use in drive-thru stores.[22]

TECHNOLOGICAL INNOVATIONS
Data

Starbucks finds fixes to its supply chain come slowly with the company's best-of-breed approach. This approach, in which companies hand-pick the best software product for each piece of the supply chain process, comes with its share of headaches. Among them are an extended vendor evaluation period, complex software integration hurdles, and version control problems.

Starbucks' expansive retail operation is just one piece of its supply chain. As part of its effort to establish itself as a major brand, Starbucks launched joint ventures with Dreyer's Grand Ice Cream Inc., Pepsi-Cola Co. and Redhook Ale Brewery to develop products based on its coffee. It also arranged with Capital Records to produce jazz compact disks, began selling its products through grocery stores, and distributed its coffee through Aramark Food & Services Inc., bookstore chain Barnes & Noble Inc., and United Airlines.

From 1988 to 1996, the only technology Starbucks used was a merchandise management system called JDA software, which ran on an AS/400. The rest of the supply chain processes were done manually. For a long time, production planning was not done at the SKU level. Instead, planning was based around the company's 30-odd flavors of coffee. In 1998, Starbucks managed about 3,000 SKUs with software from Manugistics.[23]

---

[20] http://www.best.com/percent7Erdcormia/search/smartcard.html.

[21] http://www.sc-solutions.com/estee.html.

[22] Sykes, Claire, "Starbucks Multi-Channel System Tackles Distribution Challenges," *Stores*, November 1997, v. 79, n. 11, p. 38(2).

[23] Treacy, Michael, "You Need a Value Discipline—But Which One?," *Fortune*, April 17, 1995, v. 131, n. 7, p. 195.

Forecasting was another area limited by the manual approach. Prior to the overhaul, it was essentially done through messages swapped between business unit managers and production managers on voice and e-mail. Now, business units use Retek Information Systems Inc.'s SkuPlan forecasting software to maintain a rolling monthly forecast for sales and a rolling 24-month forecast for SKUs. Those data are fed into Manugistics' software, which reports based upon an enterprise supply chain plan.

Starbucks had problems with the fundamental Bill of Materials (BOM). "There were as many BOMs in the company as the people who needed them." That meant higher costs because of redundancies and multiple and divergent forecasts. Today, BOMs are part of a comprehensive process run by several applications, including Numetrix Laboratories Ltd.'s Schedule X software. This software recommends the most efficient way to schedule the manufacturing resources.[24]

Initially, Starbucks presumed that an ERP package would be the best solution. With that in mind, the company's supply chain operations and IT groups defined the company's needs. Starbucks adapted Expert Buying Systems Choose Smart software to query more than 50 people inside and outside the company. The next step was to send out requests for information to top ERP vendors and consult with industry experts. Demonstrations and customer visits followed for five ERP vendors. Six months after the whole process began, Starbucks decided that none of these ERP packages could meet its needs. Instead, it opted for a best-of-breed approach. Starbucks purchased five of the applications outlined in its nine-piece plan. Software from Manugistics and Numetrix has been in place since 1996. Retek's SkuPlan went live in September 1997. Oracle Corporation's GEMMS (Global Enterprise Manufacturing Management System) was launched in October, 1997. IMI's order processing software was implemented in spring, 1998, while applications for transportation planning, purchasing, and warehousing/distribution were purchased and installed in mid-1999. The final implementation will be a data warehouse for sales and operations, a project that Starbucks will do by itself.

STARBUCKS ONLINE

After offering an Internet catalog on America Online for three years and maintaining a simple recruiting site, coffee retailer Starbucks launched its corporate Web site in 1998. "You see us in different places. Rarely do we get an opportunity to tell our story in our words," said John Williams, director of corporate marketing.

"This was a chance to share our brand story. It's an important move for us. It's a long-standing opportunity to extend all lines of business."

Williams said Starbucks.com, built by San Francisco web development agency Organic Online with the support of software giant Microsoft, was developed in response to feedback from its customers and employees after a test site during summer, 1997, brought a positive response.

"We think the [Internet] market is maturing and it's at a point now where it's becoming more and more a source of information and entertainment," Williams added. "The market is ready for us, and more importantly, we are also ready."[25]

The 250-page Starbucks web site contains four distinctive sections. Users can read about the company, its coffee, and other Starbucks products, such as coffee-flavored ice cream and packaged drinks. An electronic shopping component enables users to make coffee purchases online. A coffee taste-matching feature suggests coffee flavors based upon answers to a brief questionnaire.

Williams said Starbucks would promote its site through online advertising, as well as retail store promotions on its bags, cups, and napkins. Although he declined to discuss specific plans, Williams said he is considering a range of advertising opportunities, including banner ads, affiliate programs, and sponsorships. He said he expects advertising to accelerate as the holiday season approaches.[26]

RECOMMENDATION FOR THE FUTURE

Starbucks is continuing to focus its energy on its expansion efforts, the development of new markets, and joint ventures with other products. Targeting grocery stores continues to be a lucrative investment for Starbucks. Many individuals who are not willing to pay $2 for a cup of coffee **do** want gourmet coffee. In the grocery stores, the three large coffee companies sell their brands for around $5 per pound; Starbucks sells theirs for $10 to $12 per pound. While the Starbucks price is higher, it attracts many home brewers who want high quality coffee.

Starbucks has grown substantially since 1989. The company's sales have soared by an annual rate of 61.1. Net income has grown 75.3 percent annually. Starbucks boasts a talented management team and a terrific product. With continuing plans for expansion, new products, and upcoming technology, Starbucks has a good formula for growth. Market analysts agree that Starbucks will be a leader not only in its industry but among industries.

---

[24] Millman, Nancy, "Starbucks' Latest Brew," *Chicago Tribune*, July 15, 1997, Section 3, p. 1.

[25] http://www.lucent.com/press/0595/950531.cpa.html.
[26] Aragon, Lawrence, "Backup in the Espresso Lane," *Computer Select*, October 1998.

CASE QUESTIONS

Strategic Questions

1. What is Starbucks trying to market to the world?

2. Why is Starbucks more successful than other niche coffee retailers?

3. How important is Starbucks' workforce to their success?

Technological Questions

4. In what ways can technology help Starbucks grow and be successful?

5. What communications technologies are appropriate for Starbucks?

Quantitative Questions

6. What analysis can be made by examining the following ratio groups?

    Quick/Current
    Debt
    Revenue
    Profit
    Asset Utilization

7. Does Starbucks have the financial strength to continue its expansion?

8. How can distribution costs be reduced?

Internet Questions

9. How important has Starbucks Internet site been to its business development?

Industry Questions

10. What variables impact the coffee retailing industry?

11. To what degree is government regulation a factor in this industry?

Data Questions

12. How will the capture and maintenance of customer data impact Starbucks' future?

TECHNOLOGY TIPS

MICROSOFT WORD TIPS

USING A WIZARD AND A TEMPLATE

Do you need to write a resume, a memo to your boss, a cover letter for an important project? If you are not sure what are the formats or want to finish up your work quickly, Office 97 provides templates and wizards to assist you in completing such menial tasks. The following is an example for using a wizard and/or a template to develop your own resume.

Using a Resume Wizard

1. Start with a new document by clicking on FILE, then click on NEW.
2. A dialog box will appear with a number of tabs on the top. Click on the OTHER DOCUMENTS tab.
3. Double-click on the RESUME WIZARD icon.
4. A new dialog box will appear that will allow you to select how you would like your resume to look.
5. After making each selection click on the NEXT button on the bottom.
6. When you reach the ADD/SORT heading section make sure that the headings are in the order that you would like. If you wish to move them around simply click on the heading you would like to move and use the MOVE UP or MOVE DOWN buttons on the right to arrange the headings to your liking.
7. After you have made all of your selections you will reach the end of the wizard. At this point click on FINISH.

8. The wizard will process your information and will create a resume for you.
9. Type in your personal information in the blanks provided and modify the resume to reflect your experience.
10. Once you are done you can save the resume by simply clicking on the save button.

Using a Resume Template

1. Start with a new document by clicking on FILE, then click on NEW.
2. A dialog box will appear with number of tabs on the top. Click on the OTHER DOCUMENTS tab.
3. You can preview the template by clicking on it *once*. A sample will appear in the preview window on the right of the dialog box.
4. Double-click on the Resume template icon of your choice.
5. The template will appear on your screen and you may make modifications to it as you like. Simply substitute the information in the template with your personal data.
6. Additional headings can be added by placing the cursor where you want to add an additional header. Select a matching header from the NORMAL drop down box.
7. Once you are done you can save the resume by simply clicking on the save button.

ADDITIONAL NOTE

If you do not like your resume style after you have completed it, you can change the appearance in three clicks of the mouse. Do the following:

1. With the document open click on FORMAT.
2. Select STYLE GALLERY.
2. Your document will appear on the right in the preview window. Select the style of resume that you like and click OK when you are done. You can save several styles by saving the documents under different names using SAVE AS. . . .

MICROSOFT EXCEL BASICS

There are certain elements of the Excel worksheet window that this chapter will help familiarize you with in order to better understand the instructions being given in the following chapters. If you are familiar with the Excel worksheet window you may proceed to the next chapter. The window elements described here will help you to understand, and explain to others, basic tasks that are performed in Excel.

Menu bar—Standard toolbar—Formatting toolbar—Formula Bar

Sheet tabs: They allow you to work with several work sheets in a workbook. Each workbook starts out with three worksheets and can have a maximum of 255.

Worksheet window: This section of the Excel window contains a grid of columns and rows. The columns are labeled alphabetically and the rows are labeled numerically. The maximum number of columns is 256 and the maximum number of rows is 65,533. The point at which the rows and columns intersect is called a cell. The window shown above currently has the cell pointer at cell A1.

Status Bar: Located at the bottom of the screen, it provides a brief description of the task in progress or the active commands, The right side of the status bar shows the current condition of the scroll lock, number lock, caps lock key.

Standard and Formatting toolbar: The standard and formatting toolbar are similar to the toolbars used in Word, PowerPoint, and other Microsoft programs. Formula bar: It allows you to enter and edit data in the worksheet

Fill handle: When you point to the fill handle, the pointer changes to a black cross. To copy contents to adjacent cells or to fill in a series such as dates, drag the fill handle. To display a shortcut menu that contains fill options, hold down the right mouse button as you drag the fill handle.

MICROSOFT POWERPOINT TIPS

CREATING A PRESENTATION

While many may be familiar with Word, this may not be the case with PowerPoint. This will be a brief introduction on how to get started with PowerPoint. If you already have some experience with this program, you can skip ahead to the next chapter.

> Further assistance? Just click on the
>
>
>
> Office assistant button. Step by step instructions will be provided for each screen.

Using the AutoContent Wizard

This may be the easiest way to get started if you have little or no experience with PowerPoint.

1. Initiate the PowerPoint application.
2. A dialog box will appear that will prompt you and offer you four choices:
   - AutoContent wizard
   - Template
   - Blank presentation
   - Open an existing presentation
3. Click on the AutoContent wizard then click OK.
4. A new dialog box will appear that will aid you in starting the presentation. Click on NEXT button to advance to the next section; the BACK button to return to change a previous section.
5. Select from the different categories of presentation formats. These are just frameworks for your presentations. You can change their appearance later on.
6. Continue through the several steps and click on FINISH when you are done.
7. A text outline of each slide will appear with a slide miniature on the side. The changes you make in the outline will appear on the miniature slide.
8. If you wish to make changes directly to the PowerPoint slide click on VIEW from the toolbar. From the drop down menu click on the SLIDE button.
9. Go through and make the necessary changes on the individual slides. When you are done click on the SAVE button. Save the presentation in the location of your choice.

Using Presentation Layouts to Create a New Presentation

1. With the PowerPoint application open already.
2. Click on FILE from the tool bar menu, then click on NEW.
3. A dialog box will appear with four tabs on top. Click on the PRESENTATIONS tab.
4. A series of presentations already formatted into a standard presentation layout for the topic has already been developed (i.e. Business Plan, Company Meeting, etc.). You may preview the presentations by clicking once on the icon of your choice. Once you have found a presentation that you like you may select it by double clicking on it.
5. The first slide in the presentation will appear. If you wish to get an overall view of all the slides in the presentation click VIEW from the top toolbar and select Slide Sorter from the drop down menu. You may switch back to the Slide view by double clicking on the slide of your choice.
6. Modify slides as you like and save once you are done by clicking on the SAVE button.

Using a Blank Presentation

Blank presentations may come in handy when you do not wish to be distracted with the background designs selection. If you have a good idea of how you wish to format your presentation this method might be more useful.

1. With the PowerPoint application open already.
2. Click on FILE from the tool bar menu, then click on NEW.
3. A dialog box will appear with four tabs on top. Click on the GENERAL tab.
4. Double click on the Blank Presentation icon. A dialog box will appear on the screen asking you to select a slide layout. These may be changed later on so do not worry so much as to which layout you select at this point. Select one by double clicking on it.
5. Fill in the slide as you like. To create a new slide select INSERT from the toolbar and then the NEW SLIDE . . . You will be prompted to select a slide layout once again. Double click on your choice. Continue through these steps until you complete their presentation.
6. When you are done simply click on the SAVE [icon] button located on the toolbar.

MICROSOFT ACCESS TIPS
WHAT ARE DATABASES?

A database is a collection of related data. It is that simple. Creating a well-organized database on the other hand is not that simple. The following chapters will attempt to explain in a concise manner how to go about creating a simple database using Microsoft Access. The topics covered in these chapters will allow you to get started in Access and is not intended to be a definitive guide to databases. Once you have covered the topics in these chapters you will be able to move on to the more advanced features that Access has to offer. Remember that at any point help can be found using the Office Assistant or from the help files. Databases are covered in greater detail and advanced features are also covered. Click on the Office Assistant button [icon] or click on HELP located on the toolbar.

How Are Databases Organized?
The information in a database is organized in such a way that the data is related or connected in some way. This enables

searches for queries, creating reports, and locating specific records. Information in a database is organized in the following manner: fields, records, tables, and database. Fields are categories or topics such as book title or unit price. Groups of related fields are put together to form a record. An example of a record would be the mailing information of a customer, which would consist of fields such as city, state, and zip code. All of these records form part of a table. The database ends up being a collection of tables that can share information and is known as a relational database. The figure below illustrates how fields, records, and tables are linked together to form a database.

MICROSOFT FRONTPAGE TIPS
UNDERSTANDING THE WEB AND GETTING SOME TOOLS

The Internet
The Internet does not need much of an introduction most; people on the planet are familiar with the fact that it exists. A brief introduction, however, is probably appropriate to make sure that everyone has the same foundation of information. Put simply, it is a world-wide telecommunications network that is fully distributed and has no controlling nodes. Another way of looking at it is as an infrastructure that connects many different autonomous computers in a way that no individual computer plays a dominant role.

In the beginning stages, the Internet was a text-based system that allowed scientists, educators, and the government to communicate and interact using electronic mail and newsgroups.

The World Wide Web The fastest growing part of the Internet is the World Wide Web, which emerged in 1994. The Web uses a Graphical User Interface (GUI) to simplify and enhance operations on the Internet. Web Browsers are the front end product that allow users to access the Web. Browsers must be installed on any computer that intends to communicate on the Web. Although they may appear differ-

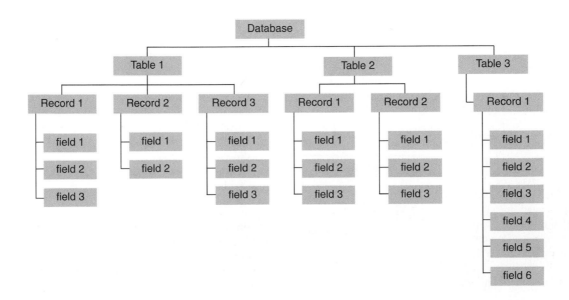

ent, web browsers from different manufacturers share the same protocols and communicate in the same manner. Since this book focuses on the Microsoft Suite, the Web Browser we will be using is Microsoft Internet Explorer (Version 4.01/5.0 at time of publication).

Once a computer is equipped with a web browser, the computer has the interface to communicate with the Internet. The computer must also have a physical connection to the Internet if communication is going to be successful. This connection is established with a modem that converts Web Browser instructions into Transmission Control Protocol/Internet Protocol (TCP/IP) instructions that can be transferred over the network or telephone lines and into the Internet. Different modems can transfer data at different speeds, which are measured in kilobytes per second (KPS). Most computers shipped today are equipped with a modem in their standard configuration. [Hint: an easy way to check for a modem is to check the back of your computer for a phone jack. This will either be a modem or a network card.]

Once a computer is equipped with a modem (or network modem) and browser, it can communicate on the World Wide Web. When you are "surfing the net," what you are doing is browsing different web servers. A web server is another computer that contains the applications, databases, or content that you are viewing. The browser on your computer is querying (asking questions of) the other machines and receiving responses in your computer's browser.

Exploring the Web To successfully explore the vast source of information the Web offers, you need to know where the information is located. Every web site on the Internet has a unique identifier called a Domain Name Server (DNS) that functions like a social security number. This domain name is a number that consists of a series of 4 numbers separated by periods. It would be very difficult and confusing for people to remember and explore the Web if they had to remember all these numbers. So, the process was simplified. HyperText Transfer Protocol (HTTP) is the language that simplifies and queries these DNS addresses to find a web site. Once a web

site is found, the content of the web site is often displayed in HyperText Markup Language (HTML). The result of this simplification process is that people can easily surf the net.

Necessary Tools

Which version of Explorer do I have and where is it located?

1. From the desktop, double click on **My Computer**.
2. Click once on the hard drive to highlight it.
3. Go up to **File** and right click once to get the menu of choices.
4. Pull the mouse down to **Find** and release the mouse button.
5. In the Named field type *Iexplore* and click on the **Find Now** button.
6. A number of files may appear in the box at the bottom of the window.

   We are looking for a file that is named *Iexplore* and is listed as an application in the type field. (If you cannot find this file then you will need to reload the Windows 95/98 system disk or notify your instructor.)

   The "in folder" field tells you where explorer is located. It will generally be in the Program Files Folder.
7. Left click on the *Iexplore* icon and pull down to Properties.
8. Click on the Version Tab. The file version should read 4.0 or higher.
9. If you do not have version 4.0 you will need to down load the file from Microsoft's web page (http://www.microsoft.com/windows/ie/download/all.htm?bShowPage).

Do I have Microsoft FrontPage Express so I can design my Web Page?

1. From the desktop, double click on **My Computer**.
2. Click once on the hard drive to highlight it.
3. Go up to **File** and right click once to get menu of choices.
4. Pull the mouse down to **Find** and release the mouse button.
5. In the Named field type *fpxpress* and click on the **Find Now** button.
6. A number of files may appear in the box at the bottom of the window.

   We are looking for a file that is named *fpxpress* and is listed as an application in the type field. (If you cannot find the file, download the component from Microsoft's web site. Make sure that you download from Microsoft's Internet Explorer web page (http://www.microsoft.com/windows/ie/download/all.htm?bShowPage).

I need to download a file. How do I do it?

1. Open the web browser (either Internet Explorer or Netscape Navigator).
2. In the address field, type in the *http* world wide web address. In this case it is http://www.microsoft.com/windows/ie/download/all.htm?bShowPage.
3. Select the file you need and follow the on-screen directions
4. If you are downloading Internet Explorer 5.0, you may have to customize the download by selecting FrontPage express as part of the download. Otherwise, FrontPage express will not be included in the standard download.

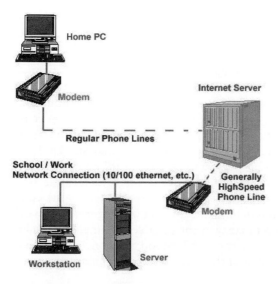

Home PC

Modem

Regular Phone Lines

Internet Server

School / Work
Network Connection (10/100 ethernet, etc.)

Generally
HighSpeed
Phone Line
Modem

Workstation   Server

CHAPTER 2

PERSONAL PRODUCTIVITY ENTREPRENEURIAL INDUSTRY

Personal Productivity

Technology can improve the way you conduct your personal affairs and help you do a better job at work. Many tools are available to improve your efficiency. This summary starts with the most obvious. It also includes representative tools that you may not have thought about to assist you in your work.

Microsoft Word The most widely used software today is word processing software. This software enables you to quickly enter information and continually edit and craft the words until they present exactly the information and ideas that the writer wants to convey. Only a few years ago, spelling and thesaurus packages were separate from word processing packages. Today they are neatly integrated as one.

Microsoft Excel The spreadsheet, in the form of VisiCalc, was what led to the rapid proliferation of the personal computer. For the first time, accountants and financial planners could make changes in their balance sheets and immediately see the results. Spreadsheets enable you to enter financial information and manipulate it in ways that result in a thorough analysis of the financial information. In addition, spreadsheets enable you to project financial information using "what if" analyses.

Microsoft PowerPoint Presentation tools, like Microsoft PowerPoint, enable you to graphically present your ideas using an overhead or written presentation. Integrating pictures and graphics, PowerPoint helps you present your ideas through words and symbols rather than strictly in a written paragraph format.

PowerPoint slides can be printed in a number of combinations for notes and handouts as well as presented directly from the computer.

Microsoft Access For many years, the size and complexity of databases required them to be maintained on a mainframe computer. The introduction of Access and its predecessors Paradox, dBase IV, and rBase enabled smaller databases to be moved to the personal computer. Access is based on the concept of tables, queries, forms, reports, macros, and modules. If the tables are set forth correctly, there are no repeating data cells, queries can be used efficiently to search for specific information, and reports can represent the information in specific tables. Rather than just entering data on a table, forms can be constructed to facilitate and leverage the data entry process. Reports can be written to summarize and present the results of the queries to management or customers. Macros and modules can speed the data entry and searching process.

Microsoft Project The military was the first entity to develop project management into a science and apply its concepts to actual decision making. Integrating decision trees, Gantt charts, and pert charts, project management tools enable the project manager to structure the project so that it can be examined and analyzed from different perspectives. "What if" analyses can then be run using different scenarios to determine which approach will yield the best results, given the constraints within which the project manager must work. The project management variables of time, cost, and risk can be more clearly understood and conveyed given the presentation of the variables in a graphic format.

Microsoft Internet Explorer or Netscape Navigator These powerful search engines enable the user to go to the World Wide Web and search for information. Information gained from the web can be saved and pulled into the Microsoft Suite. In this way, information can be obtained from the marketplace and used immediately to analyze a proposed project.

IBM Voice Type or Dragon Dictate These two products are among the first to bring voice transcription to the average user. Using a microphone and parsing technology, the words of the user are matched to the written words on the computer. After "training," the computer is able to represent the spoken word. The more the user uses the technology, the better the match between the spoken and written words.

Quick Books Quick Books can be used to organize and keep personal or business accounts. Based on a traditional accounting structure, they collect data and organize it in a format that can be easily applied to complete taxes or other accounting requirements.

Groupwise Electronic mail and calendar tools enable the user to receive and send electronic mail. These tools provide a standard interface to electronic mail. They also provide a way to store and retrieve information in this environment.

Objects, Components, or Modules Tools in the personal productivity environment are built on the concepts of objects, components, or modules. Each tool, while running separately, can also be combined. Excel can be used alone or its spreadsheets can be incorporated into a Word document or a PowerPoint presentation. Items from the World Wide Web can be easily copied, saved as GIF files, and incorporated into presentations or documents.

Today, much attention is paid to the particular Microsoft product or application in which you are working. The particular product becomes the gateway through which information is entered and ideas are formulated. As a result, significant time must be committed to learning the product and applying its rules to the final project.

In the future, the focus will be on the end product or the goal which is set to be accomplished. Integrating graphics, spreadsheets, or data into the base document will all be done as objects, components, or modules within the final product, rather than as separate programs, the results of which must then be integrated.

Word	W.1	Using Footnotes and Endnotes	Footnotes Endnotes
		Additional Note	
Excel	E.1	Entering, Copying, and Moving Data	Entering Data Copying Data Moving Data
		Additional Notes	
PowerPoint	P.1	Slide Views, New Slides, and Slide Show	Slide Views New Slides Slide Show
Access	A.1	Designing a Database	Determine the Purpose of Your Database
			Determine the Tables You Need
			Determine the Fields You Need
			Identify Fields with Unique Values
			Determine the Relatio-ships Between Tables
			Refine the Design
			Enter Data and Create Other Database Objects
FrontPage	I.1	Getting Started Planning Your Web Site	The Index Page Organizing Your Server Space

Equally important, standard tools will be purchased and used to develop the base document. Specialized inputs, used less frequently, will be purchased as plug-ins from the World Wide Web, rather than purchased and maintained through updates. Building on the theme of moving from fixed to variable costs, this will be a way to more efficiently purchase and implement the needed tools for the amount of time needed.

Entrepreneurial Industry

DESCRIPTION OF THE INDUSTRY

The entrepreneurship industry is thriving and vibrant. After years of being thought of as "oddballs," entrepreneurs are not only getting respect, they are admired and sought after. Entrepreneurs are people who go into business for themselves with a new way to do things or to market a new product. This differentiates the flower vendor on the corner (isn't he or she in business for himself or herself?) from the person and business we mean when we are talking about entrepreneurs.

Entrepreneurs used to be thought of as people who could not make it in corporate America; the word had a less than positive connotation. In the past 15 years, however, this has all changed. Nothing has brought about change in attitudes faster than when the countries in Asia seemed to pass the United States in productivity and ideas. Effective processes such as just-in-time manufacturing are becoming the norm in these countries. Suddenly, corporate America moved too slowly and the entrepreneurship style of thinking was needed. The entrepreneurial mind-set became desired for companies that wanted to succeed. How big is entrepreneurship these days? Venture capitalists, companies that look for ideas to invest in in return for a share of the profits, have poured millions of dollars into nothing much more than an idea and a prototype of the product. Only the volatility of the stock market threatens to dry up the liberal financing currently experienced by the entrepreneurial industry.

Entrepreneurship is so popular that a new type of entrepreneur is popping up: the well-to-do entrepreneur. This may be best explained by an example. Alex Mandl, the second in command at AT&T, quit his job in late 1997 to work at a start-up wireless communications company. The first week was spent hiring a secretary and trying to install a new phone system. Why did he do it? A team of venture capitalists had an idea; they hired Mandl to do everything else. They gave him a $20 million bonus plus a stake in the company. By definition, then, an entrepreneur is a person who risks his or her livelihood to start a business from scratch.

STOCK/INVESTMENT OUTLOOK

Investment in entrepreneurs is a risky proposition, to say the least. The great majority of new businesses fail within the first five years. Moreover, these types of businesses are usually very small and not publicly traded. Investing in them means contributing to the business directly in return for equity or partial ownership of the company. For that to happen, entrepreneur-driven businesses usually require tens of thousands of dollars.

With such a bleak outlook, who would invest and why? Venture capitalists, along with friends and family of the person starting the business, make these investments. Venture capitalists specialize in looking for good investment opportunities. Again, why invest in a start-up? If the concept seems reasonable, the person trying to get the funding is usually putting everything on the line, having already asked for money from everyone he or she knows. Investors know that if the business fails, it is probably not for a lack of effort. Venture capitalists, moreover, can provide general business guidance and advice so the new business will not fail for any obvious reasons. The payoff occurs when the business succeeds. The return can be substantial.

Following an entrepreneurship opportunity can be quite profitable. In a 1997 *Forbes* survey of the Forbes Four Hundred richest Americans, 72 percent of those were first-generation entrepreneurs such as Bill Gates, Steve Jobs, or Michael Dell. Today, a portion of this may accrue to the venture capitalist, making the returns quite attractive.

In short, investing in entrepreneur-type businesses is something generally best left to those willing to take risks and try new things. Personal investing in a small, entrepreneurial company should be done with the expectation that you might lose all the money.

POTENTIAL/PROSPECTIVE FOR GROWTH

The growth in the entrepreneurship industry is surprising. The lure of big profits and the ability to be your own boss entices many people. The potential for growth, however, remains phenomenal. Years of a healthy economy have loosened the purse strings of many venture capitalists, making it easier than ever to get money for new businesses. Luckily for entrepreneurs, the market volatility at the end of the 1990s only made venture capitalists cautious, not scared. Assuming the business gets off the ground, the potential for growth depends on a number of factors, including the need for the new product or service, the state of the economy, how the product or service is priced, marketed, and delivered, and the customer service that is provided.

With today's technology, it is easier than ever to compete with large companies offering similar services or products. There are even associations to help entrepreneurs get business advice, find mentors, and make business contacts. Combining the change in attitude toward entrepreneurs, the good economy, and willing venture capitalists, the chance for growth is better now than it has been in years. This also means that there may be more competition for investors' dollars.

COMPETITIVE STRUCTURE

The competitive structure of those in the entrepreneurship industry is constantly changing. Since entrepreneurs are not all selling the same product or service or even pursuing the same type of client, the competitive structure of the entrepreneur's business depends on the product or service they resemble most or the product or service they are trying to replace. If this is a completely new product or service, which few are, there are no competitors. In that case, however, customers need to be convinced that there is a new product or service they need or want. Store buyers must be convinced to give up some shelf space for the new product.

Getting a new offering off the ground is extremely difficult especially for entrepreneurs. They often lack the power and resources of multinational corporations, which also develop new products. Entrepreneurship is so well thought of, that many major manufacturing companies, from drug to toy makers, have encouraged entrepreneur-like behavior to develop new products and markets. Once these corporations have a new product, they have more clout in stores than a small company when asking for shelf space. If the new offer from the entrepreneur is a good idea and well-executed, the product or service will easily sell itself once the company starts growing. It usually takes time before the large corporations come in to compete with successful entrepreneurs. Reasons include believing that entering that market may not be worth it and being afraid of the longer time it takes for large companies to bring a product to the market.

THE ROLE OF RESEARCH AND DEVELOPMENT

Research and development is the reason entrepreneurs go into business for themselves. Entrepreneurs have vision of a product or service that is unique enough to warrant their full attention and financial support. The idea for a necessary product, for example, may come from simply saying "Wouldn't it be great if something existed that _____?" In this case, research needs to be conducted. Not only product research, but also market research. Would people be willing to pay for this? How much? How often would they buy it? As previously mentioned, some big companies make entrepreneur-like behavior a process. These companies realize that "thinking outside the box" does not just mean putting out today's fire in the most efficient way.

Merck and Company, the huge pharmaceutical company, has routinized the invention process. The scientists who develop drugs in Merck's laboratories are encouraged to commit time to looking for ideas outside the company and to develop and follow up on drug projects of their own liking. They can then make the case to a Merck board to finance the research or buy it from the outside. They are usually rewarded through stock options in their recommendations. Therefore, R&D is part of the entrepreneurship business. Someone simply opening a new store offering the same things as others in the same way at the same price could hardly be called an entrepreneur.

TECHNOLOGICAL INVESTMENT AND ANALYSIS

The amount of technological investment in an entrepreneurial company depends on the main product of that business. There is no doubt that technology and technological advancements have made being an entrepreneur easier and lowered the barriers to entry. Ironically, entrepreneurs have done best in the field of technology. Companies like Dell, Microsoft, and Netscape were all started as entrepreneurial businesses. In fact, Silicon Valley, the hotbed of computing-related innovations in the United States, is overrun with venture capitalists looking for the next Netscape. While a person selling a service or a simple product might not need to keep abreast of the latest technology to survive, eventually that business will need technology to grow.

It is not hard to see, then, that new technology is not only desirable for an entrepreneur, it can be critical to the success of the new entrepreneurial company. In fact, technology can deliver the competitive advantage that is driving the business. Consider, for example, the Internet's leading compact disc and video store, CDNow. CDNow sells millions of dollars worth of CDs each year. It went public in late 1997, making it less than five years old. It was started by two twin brothers in their twenties. To this day, CDNow remains a "virtual" store, with no warehouse or inventory. CDNow simply passes the order to the distributor, who ships it out. The people that work at CDNow work on customer service and web page design, and do not have the overhead and lease of a normal record store. The advent of new technology like the Internet allowed the business to exist successfully.

Technology can help a small entrepreneurial company compete against a large corporation on many levels. Using technology such as web sites on the Internet, combined with software packages to do everything from the payroll to professional-looking presentations and proposals, a single person with a computer can appear as professional as a much larger company. A technology setup of this kind, while not cheap, is certainly within reach of most small businesses. This has lowered barriers to entry in many industries.

Technology has lowered costs, reduced barriers to entry, and increased efficiency for entrepreneurs. It is the key element in many new entrepreneurial businesses.

RECOMMENDATION FOR THE FUTURE

Entrepreneurs need to be prepared for the worst, but work believing in the best. A good idea or product is not enough to make a successful business. Entrepreneurs need mentors. They need to visualize possible competitors (if it was so easy for me to start this business, what stops others from starting them if mine becomes successful?), and they must implement technology to give them an edge (or at the very least, make their lives easier). Technology also helps because the never-ending barrage of technological advances is constantly providing new entrepreneurial opportunities.

Entrepreneurs need to do R&D to make sure their concept is not only a viable one, but one for which there is a demand. One place to start looking is to use new technology to capitalize on current consumer trends. For example, the Internet has exploded because it makes data gathering so much faster when people seem to have less spare time. Now that the country has realized how important entrepreneurs are to keeping the country productive and innovative, it is important to implement their approach to benefit.

INDUSTRY WEB SITES

Entrepreneurial Industry

http://members.aol.com/vsgcoupon/index.html
http://www.natbrands.co.za/

Executive Summary

Case Name:	Amazon Co.
Case Industry:	Entrepreneurial industry
Major Technology Issue:	Staying at the forefront of web technology
Major Financial Issue:	Becoming profitable
Major Strategic Issue:	To be the leading online bookseller with the largest market share
Major Players/Leaders:	Jeff Bezos, founder and CEO
Main Web Page:	www.amazon.com
Case Conclusion/Recommendation:	Amazon must continue to be on the leading edge of web technology.

CASE ANALYSIS

INTRODUCTORY STORY

Despite its founding in Jeff Bezos's garage, Amazon.com does not fit the web start-up stereotype of twenty-somethings in ponytails. Bezos was a systems development executive at Bankers Trust in New York in the late 1980s—the bank's youngest Vice President ever. Yet, when the explosive growth of the World Wide Web caught his eye, he saw an even bigger opportunity: online commerce. Two years later Bezos, CEO of the Internet bookstore Amazon.com, was part of a group of young entrepreneurs using cyberspace technology to take market share from traditional businesses with strong consumer and industrial franchises.

This type of analytical thinking was not foreign to Bezos, given his Wall Street background. "I always wanted to start a business, but my wake-up call was when I found out the Internet was growing at a 2,300 percent rate," he said. "That's a market that nothing compares to. Then I sat down and made a list of twenty possible products to sell on the web. Books were the biggest commodity."

According to Bezos, the thing about books is that there are lots of them. At any given time, there are 1.5 million English-language books in print plus another 3 million worldwide. No other consumer commodity item comes close (music is a distant second, with about 200,000 titles available). Even the largest real-world bookstores maintain an inventory of only 170,000 books. Thus, the opportunity presented itself for an ideal electronic commerce business.

SHORT DESCRIPTION OF THE COMPANY

Amazon.com is an online Internet bookstore. It gets more than 80,000 visitors daily, totaling 29 million visits a year. Its stock value is $300 million. Customer service, a large selection, and the support of more than 8,000 affiliated sites, make it a market leader with a defensible market position.

SHORT HISTORY OF THE COMPANY

Since the July 1995 start-up, the Seattle-based company has consistently realized quarterly losses. The initial public offering (IPO) in May 1997 for Amazon.com was priced at $18 per share. The stock price rose to nearly $30 one day later before closing at $23.50, a 30 percent increase over its opening price.

Michael Murphy, editor of the *California Technology Stock Letter* in Half Moon Bay, said the number of Amazon.com shares to be sold increased from 2.5 million to 3 million in hope that the company would raise $42 million instead of the initial projection of $39 million.

According to the company's prospectus, the proceeds were to be used "for general corporate purposes, including working capital to fund anticipated operating losses and capital expenditures." Amazon.com also used the proceeds to "acquire or invest in complementary businesses and technologies."

Huge challenges loom. Even as Amazon.com seeks to raise its brand recognition to the level of retailing giants such as Barnes & Noble and Borders Books & Music, those competitors have launched their own web initiatives to compete with Amazon.com in cyberspace.

The easiest way to describe Amazon.com is to quote Bezos, "Ultimately, we're an information broker. On the left side we have lots of products, on the right side we have lots of customers. We're in the middle making the connections. The consequence is that we have two sets of customers: consumers looking for books and publishers looking for consumers. Readers find books or books find readers. Amazon.com handles online ordering, credit card charging, customer service, and fulfillment. It has book warehouses to use for its vast inventory of 2.5 million books."[1]

The most important components to sell successfully online are customer privacy, specialty services, timely customer response, and follow-up e-mail. Amazon.com can concentrate on these issues and be successful in electronic commerce because of its location in Seattle, Washington. Seattle has a large number of talented computer professionals and two huge book warehouses. Bezos claims that the key to Amazon.com's success is to hire and nurture talented employees. He still spends half of his time in recruiting activities.

Amazon.com generates all of its revenue from the Internet. Amazon.com's web site emphasizes information over graphics and includes a separate page for each book with capsule descriptions, customer reviews, and even author interviews. Amazon.com does not just sell books; it offers information about the books. It also markets music and auctions unique art and collectibles. Best of all, Amazon.com does not do the work itself. Amazon.com's software runs a questionnaire that the authors of the books may complete. It offers reviews from the media. Customers can add their own reviews of a book for other customers to read. The site also shows related books and books by the same author.

The customer reviews are valuable to Amazon.com because customer reviews provide the company with information about customers' tastes. The company can tie this information to its e-mail and postal addresses and use this tool to contact former customers during various times of the year. Publishers and competitors do not have access to this type of information. Even traditional bookstores cannot track this type of information about customers.

Previous customers, delighted by the choice of books, customer service, and the well-designed web page, started talking about Amazon.com in newsgroups and other online public forums. Instead of telling a few friends about their positive experience by word of mouth, they told many more by publishing the messages on the Internet. This type of free advertising remains priceless.

Amazon.com has increased its market share because it has always made customer service a central theme. It remains a niche player with skill in spotting trends and engaging customers.

Amazon.com has traditionally offered a 10 percent discount on hard- and soft-cover books. The company has established six groups of books that are offered at a 40 percent discount: Amazon.com's 500 best selling titles; the *New York Times* best sellers; and the top 50 titles in science fiction, mystery, literary and computer categories. Amazon.com will also offer the 40 percent discounts on books mentioned on National Public Radio and on Oprah's Book Club. The discount program pricing was put in place due to new competition in the online book selling industry.

To better position itself against its competitors, Amazon.com has recently increased its currently available inventory from 1.1 to 2.5 million books. Some critics of the company believe that there are not that many books in stock and that the company is falsely advertising. Bezos, for his part, seems unconcerned about the debate surrounding the number of books in inventory. "I'm actually quite pleased that our competitors think that what we do here is impossible," he said. "The longer they believe that, the better it will be for us."

Amazon.com can easily offer the first 400,000 books because they are directly ordered from the 12 wholesalers. The next 700,000 titles are ordered from 20,000 different publishers. The last million are out-of-print books that Amazon.com will try to locate. This increases the cost since Amazon.com's workforce must search for and locate requested books.

Once someone has shown the way, competitors have found it relatively easy to set up their own databases and agreements with distributors. A web site that used to be linked to Amazon.com may now link itself to Barnes & Noble or some upstart company if the commission is higher. The consumer may not have a loyalty to Amazon.com but to the initial web site they encounter. In this sense, Amazon.com relies on its great customer relationships and service to maintain its business relationships. Amazon.com's stiffest competition among the nonbookstore sites is the Internet Bookshop (http://www.bookshop.co.uk), a British company with 1.4 million titles, and Bookstacks (http://www.books.com), based in Cleveland, Ohio, with 4 million titles.

When Amazon.com first entered the online book selling business, it had little competition. Now it has competition from bookstores themselves, most notably Barnes & Noble and Borders Books. Barnes & Noble, based in New York, is the biggest bookseller in the world, with net income of $92,376,000 in fiscal year ending January 30, 1999, and $53,169,000 in fiscal year ending January 30, 1998 based upon sales of $3,005,608,000 and $2,796,852,000 respectively.

Traditional bookstores like Barnes & Noble and Borders have two distinct advantages. Their widely recognized names provide the opportunity to publicize

---

[1] http://www.amazon.com/exec/obidos/subst/misc/company-info.html, Bezos, Jeff (Interview). "Amazon is about value," *PC Week*, March 8, 1999, p. 16(1).

their web sites in their bookstores. Barnes & Noble's exclusive deal with America Online (AOL) gives it privileged access to much of this potential market. The mechanics of selling books online, however, are different than setting up a bookstore in a shopping mall. Barnes & Noble is offering immediate delivery of 600,000 books in its warehouses. Hardcover books will be discounted 30 to 40 percent and softcover books 20 percent.

Barnes and Noble offers online features similar to those of Amazon.com, including book reviews, author information, bestseller lists, editors' picks, and other editorial material. Amazon.com does not feel that Barnes and Noble will be able to challenge them. Paper-thin overhead and the laser-like web focus may make it difficult to match Amazon.com on price. Amazon.com can offer larger discounts because it does not have the cost of maintaining physical bookstores; the company boasts that it can beat the prices of competitors when shipping costs are included.

The biggest threat to Amazon.com may come from another kind of online bookseller, one that caters to a specialized audience. There are already specialized online booksellers, such as Pandora's Books, which sells out-of-print science fiction and mysteries. Such sites offer far more expertise in their subject area than a general bookseller like Amazon.com ever could. Even worse, from Amazon.com's point of view, science fiction buffs might be tempted to order other sorts of books from Ingram's (Amazon.com's largest supplier of recently published books) general list at the same time they pick up the latest science fiction book by Asimov.

Another challenge for the entire publishing industry is that some day soon people will be able to download and read books directly from the Internet.

The media hype that Amazon.com is receiving might be the one item that separates them from their competitors. Whether solicited or not, it has made Amazon.com the most talked about online bookseller in the world. The company's strenuous marketing campaign is fueling all of the publicity that Amazon.com is receiving lately. Funded by an undisclosed amount of venture capital, the campaign has enabled Bezos to purchase extensive ads in the *Wall Street Journal* and the *New York Times,* as well as parade his logo, in the form of banner ads, at the top of numerous book-related web sites.

This form of advertising has been very expensive for the company. Amazon.com spent $84.52 million for advertising in the first three quarters of 1998 (compared to $23.60 million over the same period in 1997). Amazon.com is spending roughly 23.7 percent of its incoming revenue on advertising, down from 28.9 percent in 1997. Even though the company has been able to bring about a decline in advertising costs, it has continued to experience a sharp increase in sales. Sales in the first three quarters of 1998 exceeded $357.103 mil-

lion (compared to $81.747). This is an increase in sales of over 435 percent for 1998.

Besides increasing advertising, decreasing prices, and expanding its inventory, Amazon.com has also redesigned and overhauled the graphics on its web site. The new interface is colorful, better organized, loads more quickly, and enables browsers to find selections more easily. The web pages now include book cover images and stylish typefaces.

FINANCIAL AND PORTFOLIO ANALYSIS

The company has grown rapidly since first opening its bookstore on the World Wide Web. Through the second quarter of 1999, Amazon.com had sales of more than $314,400,000 with an audience of 10.7 million visitors in November 1998. Compounded quarterly sales growth exceeded 100 percent from the first quarter of 1996 through the first quarter of 1997 and had surpassed 400 percent in 1998. This kind of sales growth has led to a high level of optimism about the company's future.

On the cost side, the company has incurred significant losses. As of March 31, 1999, Amazon.com had an accumulated deficit of $233.7 million. One of the major reasons for its losses is not the lack of customers. Amazon.com has defused this loss by arguing it must further develop its online market share. In terms of advertising, Amazon.com spent $3.4 million in FY1996, $19 million in FY1997, and over $60 million in 1998.[2] Amazon.com plans to continue to spend large dollar amounts on online advertising to establish its market position with the ultimate goal of becoming one of the top three booksellers.

Average daily visits to Amazon.com grew from 2,200 in December 1995 to approximately 50,000 in December 1996, to 80,000 in December 1997 and 8 million in November 1998. Forty percent of daily orders are from repeat customers. The main reason customers come back is the vast selection of 2.5 million books, competitive prices, and superior customer service. The importance in daily visits is reflected in Amazon.com's sales numbers of $0.5 million in 1995, $15.7 million in 1996, $147.76 million in 1997, and $610 million in 1998.[3] Comparing the third quarters of 1997 and 1998 is even more astounding. In 1997, third quarter sales were $37,887,000. In the third quarter, 1998, sales were $153,698,000.

Amazon.com keeps only 22 percent of sales after paying suppliers, salaries, and creditors. This low margin covers costs such as technology and overhead. This number is low compared to 36 percent for Barnes & Noble and 27 percent for Borders Group, Inc. These low margins on sales help to explain why the company

[2] http://www.sec.GOV/Amazon/; 10-K Annual Report, 1998.
[3] Ibid.

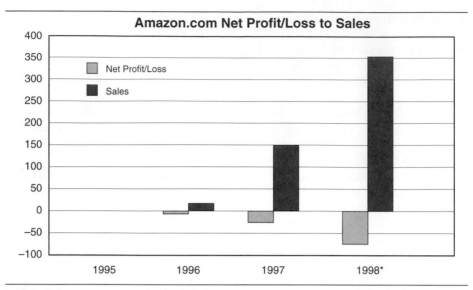

Figure 2.1 Amazon.com net profit/loss, 1996–1998. Values in thousands of U.S. dollars.
*(Note: 1998 includes only the first three quarters.)

had losses of $0.3 million in 1995, $5.8 million in 1996, $31 million in 1997, and $124 in 1998 (Figure 2.1).

Losses do not come as a surprise to the management of Amazon.com. From the beginning, Bezos predicted that the company would not turn a profit for five years. Through the third quarter of 1998, Amazon.com had $14.86 million in cash and cash equivalents. Combined with the proceeds from the IPO, Amazon.com believes it can meet anticipated cash needs for working capital and capital expenditures for many years to come.

Another problem with Amazon.com's current financial position is that Amazon.com relies on the Ingram Company for 59 percent of its inventory. Another notable risk is that Amazon.com does not have any long-term agreements with its vendors and relies upon them for the rapid fulfillment of its orders.

Amazom.com believes its success will depend in large part on its ability to extend its brand position and achieve sufficient sales volume to realize economies of scale. This is why the company continues to invest heavily in marketing and advertising. It must provide customers with outstanding value and a superior shopping experience as well.

Some observers speculate that Bezos is trying to dominate a particular part of the book selling industry to eventually sell Amazon.com to a competitor. Some indicators are that the company has yet to turn a profit and the main focus remains on market share. A high market share in a focused segment of a business is very attractive for a potential buyout since a competitor could immediately become a dominant player and would not have to invest additional money or expertise.

Bezos stated that he planned for Amazon.com to be a billion dollar company by the year 2000. This task is difficult if Amazon.com is only involved in selling books online. Barnes and Noble had revenues of $3.005 billion in 1998 and Borders had revenues $2.595 billion.[4] Since these two companies have both entered the online book selling business, Amazon.com's revenues of $357.103 million by the third quarter of 1998 are still rising (FY1997 sales in the third quarter were only $81.747 million). Amazon.com will have to convince more people to use the web to purchase more than books to reach this goal.

STOCK/INVESTMENT OUTLOOK

The company's stock price increased rapidly when it was first put on the market. The main reason is that many investors were eager to bet on a company based solely on Internet technology. The stock initially opened at $18 and rose to a high of $31 during the day before it dropped to $23.50 to close on the second day.

Because Amazon.com has suffered losses since incorporation, many analysts remain concerned about the ability of the company to turn a profit. The book value of the original investors' stock has been diluted due to the financial results thus far. In the IPO, 3 million shares were sold at $18 for a book value of $54 million. The adjusted tangible book value as of March 31, 1997, was only $51.2 million or approximately $15.85 per share. This should not be a surprise to an informed investor. By April 1999, the value of Amazon.com stock had skyrocketed to roughly $220 per share with a price-to-sales ratio of 52.57. Even with a company that has yet to turn a profit, its Internet presence made investors feel good

---

[4] http://www.hoovers.com/companyfinancials/Amazon/1998.

about Amazon.com, making the company worth over $15 billion in market capitalization. By August 1999, shares were around $100 per share due to the continued commitment by Amazon to gain market share at the expense of profitability.

RISK ANALYSIS

From the beginning, Bezos asserted that Amazon.com's strategy to gain market share quickly would result in steady losses. This was, however, mitigated by revenues that were higher than expected.

It is very important for Amazon.com to link itself to its consumers before the market changes and the Internet becomes crowded with competitors. Once Amazon.com has established itself as the dominant player in the online booksellers' environment, it is important to evaluate its advertising expenses (23.2 percent of sales in 1998 compared to 25 percent of sales in 1997).

INDUSTRY AND MARKET ANALYSIS

The worldwide book industry is large, growing, and relatively fragmented. According to Euromonitor, U.S. book sales were estimated to be approximately $26 billion in 1996 and are expected to grow to approximately $30 billion in 2000. Worldwide book sales were estimated at approximately $82 billion in 1996. Book sales are expected to reach $90 billion by 2000. The competitive environment on the web could mean better prices for book lovers everywhere.[5]

In the traditional bookstore business, publishers sell books both directly to retailers and to a network of distributors. Distributors serve as the primary vendors for many retailers and carry up to 350,000 of the best selling titles. The two largest U.S. retailers, which together are estimated to account for less than 25 percent of total United States book sales, have focused aggressively on superstore growth and have closed many of their smaller mall stores. Typical bookstores stock between 30,000 and 120,000 titles.[6]

Several characteristics of the traditional book industry have created inefficiencies for all participants. Physical store-based book retailers must make significant investments in inventory, real estate, and personnel for each retail location. This capital and real estate intensive business model, among other things, limits the amount of inventory that can be economically carried in any location. Another factor is that at any given time there are 1.5 million English-language books in print plus another 3 million worldwide.

In traditional book publishing, suppliers and retailers work at cross purposes. Publishers have to decide months in advance how many copies of a book to print. Yet they cannot accurately gauge demand until the book is presented to retailers. To encourage retailers to accept copies and display them prominently, publishers give stores the right to return unsold books for credit. Big chains like Barnes & Noble or Borders get the best deals. Retailers often over-order, since they want to be sure they have adequate stock on hand and since extra inventories pose little risk. As a result, returns in the book industry are high, leading to substantial additional costs.

Publishers and traditional book retailers cannot easily obtain demographic and behavioral data about customers, limiting opportunities for direct marketing and personalized services. The traditional book publishers cannot obtain this information because they do not collect and store the information like Amazon.com does.

Since Amazon.com sells books online without many of the traditional overhead items in a bookstore, Amazon.com can take advantage of an industry with an historically flawed process of conducting business.

The Internet is an increasingly significant global medium for communications, content, and online commerce. International Data Corporation (IDC) estimates that the number of web users grew to approximately 35 million by the end of 1996 and will reach over 163 million by the year 2000. The Internet economy will approach $200 billion in the year 2000, up from $15 billion in the late 1990s.

Growth in Internet use has been fueled by a number of factors, including the large and growing installed base of personal computers in the workplace and the home. Advances in the performance and speed of personal computers and modems, improvements in network infrastructure, and easier and cheaper access have increased the number of purchases made on the Internet.

The increasing functionality, accessibility, and overall usage of the Internet and online services have made them commercially attractive. The Internet and other online services are becoming unique sales and marketing channels, just as retail stores, mail-order catalogs, and television shopping have been in the past. Online retailers can interact directly with customers by frequently adjusting their featured selections, editorial insights, shopping interfaces, pricing, and visual presentations. The minimal cost to publish on the web, the ability to reach and serve a large and global group of customers electronically from a central location, and the potential for personalized low-cost customer interaction provide additional economic benefits for online retailers.

Unlike traditional retail channels, online retailers do not have the burdensome costs of managing and

---

[5] "Earnings Report: Amazon.com Inc.," *Computergram International*, July 22, 1999, n. 3208.
[6] Hogan, Mike, "Books," *PC/Computing*, July 1999, p. 156.

maintaining a significant retail store infrastructure or the continuous printing and mailing costs of catalog marketing. Because of these advantages over traditional retailers, online retailers have the potential to build large, global customer bases quickly and to achieve superior economic returns over the long term. An increasingly broad base of products is being sold successfully online, including computers, travel services, brokerage services, automobiles, and music.

The problem with the Internet is that the barriers to entry are minimal. Current and new competitors can launch new sites at a relatively low cost. In addition, the retail book industry is intensely competitive. Both Barnes & Noble and Borders have devoted substantial resources to online commerce. Barnes & Noble, specifically, has launched a web site to sell books online and has a relationship with AOL through which Barnes & Noble offers a broad selection of titles at discounted prices. Other traditional publishers, like Simon & Schuster, have also begun selling books through online sites.

The problems in the traditional book publishing industry and the minimal costs to enter the online industry have greatly reduced margins causing the extremely competitive price structure to become the norm. Barnes & Noble asserts that it will out-discount Amazon.com by offering hardcover books at a 30 to 40 percent discount and paperbacks at 20 percent discount.

ROLE OF RESEARCH AND DEVELOPMENT

Customers want a web site that is fast, easy, and fun. To maintain these qualities, Amazon.com must stay on the leading edge of technology. This is not always the easiest task and is usually quite expensive. Technology is the primary reason why Amazon.com spends so much time recruiting employees and one of the reasons it located in Seattle, Washington.

TECHNOLOGICAL STORY

To increase customer traffic and sell its vast inventory, Amazon.com uses an associates program. The associates program offers other web sites commissions of up to 15 percent on more than 400,000 titles and 5 percent on more than 1.1 million additional in-print titles. Amazon.com also pays 15 percent for sales of qualifying books that are linked to individual web sites and 5 percent on all other qualifying items, regardless of how many items are sold. Amazon.com knows that it will probably never be the very best site for rock-climbing information or quantum physics discussions. It has found, however, that sites specializing in such subjects can be great places to sell books. A link to Amazon.com is an easy—and potentially lucrative—way for such specialized sites to generate income through that one step. A click on the link takes a viewer to Amazon.com's relevant page.

The associates program is also a valuable tool for authors and web page publishers. They can link into Amazon.com to fulfill the order and collect the money. The author and publisher will not only get a royalty from the book sale, but also the 5 to 15 percent commission for linking the customer to Amazon.com's web page.

TECHNOLOGICAL INVESTMENT AND ANALYSIS

The company develops its web pages using its internal individuals. By having the technology in house, Amazon.com can control the programs more easily and keep its secrets from competitors. The disadvantage of keeping the technology development in house is that it limits itself to a small workforce for not only development, but also maintenance of the new product.

Amazon.com uses the Secure Netscape Commerce Server to transact book sales. Customers can enter their credit card number online by using a Netscape browser or any browser that supports the Secure Sockets Layer specification. If the customer does not have this technology, the order can be faxed in. Some people maintain that putting a credit card number on the Internet is no more dangerous than giving a credit card to a waiter in a restaurant. On the other hand, Kevin Mitnick, a computer hacker, stole 20,000 credit card numbers from just one site before being arrested. The security issue forces Amazon.com to continue research on the application of Internet security.

TECHNOLOGICAL INNOVATIONS

INTERNET SITES

According to Bill Burnham, an e-commerce analyst for CS First Boston, "To be successful as an Internet company, a company must be first, be dominant, and be the recognized leader."[7] Among cyber merchants that offer recommendation services, Amazon.com has an edge over competitors because its service, though complex, is accurate.[8]

Buying items on the web is part of the direct channel. It is growing at a rate comparable to that of the Internet itself. Interestingly, web sales have enhanced or added to sales at more traditional outlets. It has not replaced them. Amazon.com has not stopped people from visiting or making purchases in bookstores.

Web-based buying is particularly suited to products where instant access to updated pricing and configurations is advantageous. Sites can be expanded beyond this to provide a range of information, including special discounts, information on product availability, setup

---

[7] Wang, Nelson, "Wall Street Aims Its Love at Leaders," *Internet World,* September 14, 1998, v. 4, n. 29, p. IW9(1).
[8] Hof, Robert D., "Customizable Web Sites," *Business Week,* October 5, 1998, n. 3598, p. 176(2).

Table 2.1 Ten Best-Performing Stocks

Stock	Annualized Return (%)
1 Amazon.com	+496
2 Yahoo!	+214
3 MindSpring	+152
4 EarthLink	+143
5 @Home	+135
6 America Online	+109
7 CMG	+108
8 Onscale	+93
9 Broad Vision	+57
10 Mecklermedia	+52

(*Source:* Wang, Nelson, "Wall Street Aims Its Love at Leaders," *Internet World*, September 14, 1998, v. 4, n. 29, p. IW9(1).)

help, troubleshooting tips, driver updates, warranty information, and chat rooms.[9]

In competition with the Internet site of Amazon.com, Barnesandnoble.com is expanding its offerings in the business-to-business environment. Barnesandnoble.com continues to upgrade its intranet bookselling service. The Barnesandnoble.com service includes subscriptions to more than 42,000 newspapers and magazines, in addition to the books already offered. The publications are sold through a partnership with electronic commerce subscription vendor RoweCom in Cambridge, Massachusetts. RoweCom will also add direct account debiting and detailed financial reporting for corporate users, enabling Barnesandnoble.com to better track corporate expenditures on books and publications.

According to Michael Donahue, director of business solutions, Barnesandnoble.com enlisted 25 corporate customers in the service's first two months. Customers use specially developed tools to make links from their intranets to the Barnesandnoble.com business site. This enables them to list specific titles for their employees to see.[10]

Another alternative to buying books on a web site is the opportunity normally associated with bookstores; that is, the ability to browse and sample books. Silicon Valley-based BookBrowse has launched a new web site that publishes excerpts from popular U.S. bestsellers, as well as many top fiction and nonfiction titles. In addition to the excerpts, book summaries, author biographies, and reviews solidify the book buying process.

OVERALL DESIGN ASPECTS OF AMAZON.COM

Amazon.com's web site is divided into four main areas. Each of these areas can be accessed via the "tabs" at the top of the default screen. The simplified and low-bandwidth graphics allow customers to easily select the type of media they are interested in purchasing, including books, music, videos, or gift merchandise. This same simple design is used in each of the four main areas so users do not have to relearn navigation commands once they have become accustomed with their preferred media choice. The goal is to apply the same navigation structure to all the products that Amazon.com sells.

BOOKS

When a customer visits Amazon.com's web site (http://www.amazon.com), the default page is the book page. Linked to this page are immediately searchable fields that enable customers to go directly to the products for which they are searching. Navigation buttons have been conveniently placed at the top of each page to other book pages on the site, including Book Search, Browse Subjects, Bestsellers, Recommendation Center, Award Winners, Kids, Featured in the Media, and Computers & the Internet. These navigation buttons provide important assistance to those visitors who are simply browsing the aisles. Amazon.com also spotlights certain books on the default page in an effort to draw the customer's attention to the most recent books or books that Amazon.com wants the customer to know about. This product placement is reminiscent of point-of-purchase displays or end-of-aisle displays in a traditional retail store.

Book Search allows the customer to conduct a more detailed search of Amazon.com's database of products than the search field located at the top of every main area default page. Searches can be refined by Author, Title, Format (hard- or softcover), or Subject.

Browse Subjects categorizes book titles into 24 main topics, ranging from children's books to horror stories, from arts and music to mystery and thrillers. By choosing the subject of a book, the customer is taken to pages filled with subcategories, recommendations, and new book announcements (all within that subject field).

Bestsellers list the country's most popular books. They are categorized by soft/hardcover, fiction/nonfiction, and printed/not-yet-printed. These lists are compiled from the sales data Amazon.com receives. An interesting feature on these pages is the Amazon.com Hot 100, which updates the results from the bestsellers list every hour.

Recommendation Center provides customers with interactive sections to help them choose their purchase. These interactive sections ask questions about what type/style/author of books the customer likes and, based on these answers, makes suggestions for purchase.

---

[9] Blackford, John, "Toward Web-Savvy PC Buying," *Computer Shopper*, October 1998, v. 18, n. 10, p. 106(1).
[10] Machlis, Sharon, "Bookseller Bolsters Intranet Service," *Computerworld*, September 21, 1998, v. 32, n. 38, p. 101(1).

Award Winners collects books that have won various prizes, medals, accommodations, etc., and presents them to the customer.

Kids provides customers with the ability to further limit the type of book best suited for a certain range of children's ages. This provides assistance to parents or relatives who are interested in purchasing a book as a present for a child, but do not want to buy something too easy or too complex for the child's reading level.

Featured in the Media consolidates each month's selected reading lists from leading media sources, such as Oprah, the *New York Times, Time, Entertainment Weekly,* and the *Atlantic Monthly.* Customers familiar with these media sources can get to their anticipated lists, which are within easy reach for ordering.

Computers & the Internet presents computer and Internet-related books for quick reference. The pages also have links to other computer-based web sites that are related to the books Amazon.com has to offer.

MUSIC

Amazon.com also sells music on its web site. The music section of the site uses the same theme as the book area, simplicity. Just as the book area allows users to search for the book they want to purchase, so can a customer search for the CD they want to buy. Navigation buttons are located in the same location as in the book area. This allows customers to access Browse Styles, Chart Toppers, In the Media, and Recommendations.

Browse Styles offers genre-specific music in 14 main categories, complete with reviews, editors' picks, articles, interviews, bestsellers, and lists of recommended essential titles.

Chart Toppers includes the most popular and current music, all offered at a 30 percent discount. The area also features the Billboard Top 30 and CMJ college radio chart and national music charts from the United Kingdom, Germany, Japan, and Brazil.

In the Media lists CDs featured in 20 leading media outlets, including *Rolling Stone, Spin,* NPR, *Entertainment Weekly,* "The Tonight Show," and the "Late Show with David Letterman."

Recommendation Center offers a computerized recommendation service that is based on the user's preferences and favorite artists.

ACQUISITIONS

Amazon.com's sales for the first quarter ending March 31, 1999, jumped 236 percent to $293.6 million. Losses, however, rose to $61.7 million for the quarter, compared to a net loss of $10.4 million in 1998's first quarter. The 1999 loss includes a $25.3 million charge related to a number of acquisitions made by Amazon.com. Without the charges, the loss was $36.4 million.

CEO Bezos said that during the rest of 1999, Amazon plans to "invest more heavily than we have in the past." As a result, the losses are expected to increase even more. Areas targeted for investment include the Amazon.com distribution infrastructure. The company plans to open new distribution facilities in Coffeyville, Kansas, and Bad Hersfeld, Germany.

During first quarter, 1999, Amazon.com added 2.2 million customers, bringing the total number of accounts to more than 8.4 million. The company's Associates Program now has more than 260,000 members. The Amazon.com delivery service, which sends periodic e-mail updates about new book, music, and video titles, has more than one million participants.

One important new focus for Amazon.com is the online auction business. The increasing interest in this activity has prompted companies such as Amazon.com and America Online to develop their own sites where individuals can log on through the web and begin bidding. Amazon.com will concentrate on rare books, but they will also auction off everything from stereos to cruises.

With its auction launch, Amazon.com continues its move from bookseller to electronic commerce merchant. The auction area carries tens of thousands of items, including a signed copy of Ernest Hemingway's *A Farewell to Arms.* The company's goal is to build a place to find anything that customers might want to buy. The stock price jumped an additional 15 percent when the news of this addition was released.

In other expansion areas, Amazon.com acquired 46 percent of online pharmacy operator Drugstore.com. The new web site sells everything from aspirin to shampoo to prescription drugs. Detailed product information and on-line consultation with pharmacists is available. Amazon.com CEO Jeff Bezos estimates the market for drugs and health products to be about five times the market for books.

Drugstore.com faces stiff competition from PlanetRx, Rx.com, Rite Aid, Drug Emporium, and other chains that already have set up their own online stores or are in the process of doing so. Even Reader's Digest is in discussions with potential partners to begin direct marketing pharmaceuticals and vitamins in the year 2000. Walgreens will supply health and beauty aids and general merchandise items to Peapod's new home delivery distribution center in San Francisco.

RECOMMENDATION FOR THE FUTURE

Amazon.com added CDs in June, 1999. It also sells videotapes, audiotapes, digital video discs, and computer games. Continued initiatives are being made in video sales and rentals. Online software sales are projected to be the next probable acquisition.

Amazon.com has expanded in Europe by buying two online booksellers, Bookpages in Great Britain and Telebook in Germany. It bought Internet Movie Database in the United Kingdom as part of its plan to sell videos on-line.

In August, 1998, the company bought Junglee, a Sunnyvale, California, company whose "bot" technology allows consumers to search and compare products on the Internet, for $180 million. Amazon.com paid $90 million for PlanetAll, a Cambridge, Massachusetts, firm, that offers a web-based online address book, calendar, and reminder service.

Amazon.com is also stressing distribution. Most books are ordered directly from distributors or publishers. The company is increasing its warehouse space. Delivery is within two or three days, although obscure titles can take much longer. To improve product flow, Amazon.com hired Jimmy Wright, who was in charge of logistics for Wal-Mart, as vice president and chief logistics officer. The goal is to integrate this minimalist approach to distribution and warehousing into Amazon.com.

According to Internet analyst Genni Combes of the investment firm Hambrecht & Quist, these strategies will take Amazon.com in new directions from a long-term perspective. In the future, they will be not only a go-to site but a go-through site for other lines of products that they do not provide today. This direction is confirmed by the fact that in a June survey of Internet usage, Amazon.com appeared in the top 15 of a list compiled by the web ratings firm Media Metrix.

According to Michael Yang, co-founder and chief executive of MySimon Inc., a Sunnyvale based comparison-shopping service, "Amazon has two aspirations: One is to become the Wal-Mart of the Internet, the other is to become an e-commerce. This poses a challenge for the other portals in the industry."[11]

---

[11] Stephen Buel, "Amazon.com Bids to Be Online Superstore," Knight-Ridder/*Tribune Business News*, August 5, 1998, p. 2.

CASE QUESTIONS

Strategic Questions

1. What is the strategic direction of Amazon.com?

2. Who or what forces are driving this direction?

3. What has been the catalyst for change?

4. What are the critical success factors for this corporation?

5. What are the core competencies for this corporation?

Technological Questions

6. Upon which technologies has the corporation relied?

Quantitative Questions

7. What does the corporation advocate regarding its financial ability to embark on a major technological program of advancement?

8. What conclusions can be reached from an analysis of the financial information to support or contradict this financial ability?

9. Are there replacement services for Amazon.com?

Internet Questions

10. What does the corporation's web page present about their business?

11. Is the corporation's web page sufficiently sophisticated?

Industry Questions

12. What challenges and opportunities is the industry facing?

13. Is the industry oligopolistic or competitive?

14. Does the industry face a change in government regulation?

15. How will technology impact the industry?

Data Questions

16. What role do data play in the future of the corporation?

17. How important are data to the corporation's continued success?

18. How will the capture and maintenance of customer data impact the corporation's future?

PEAPOD

Executive Summary

Case Name:	Peapod
Case Industry:	Online shopping (or interactive grocery services)
Major Technology Issue:	Leveraging the value of the growing Peapod database.
Major Financial Issue:	Continued losses mean the high cost of order fulfillment must be addressed. Other means of increasing revenue also have to be explored.
Major Strategic Issue:	Dominating the market for interactive grocery services.
Major Players/Leaders:	Thomas and Andrew Parkinson, founders
Main Web Page:	www.peapod.com
Case Conclusion/Recommendation:	Peapod must further penetrate the market for its services, leverage its database, continue to work dynamically and learn from its partners, and leverage the Peapod name into line extensions and other online services.

CASE ANALYSIS

INTRODUCTORY STORY

Thomas and Andrew Parkinson founded Peapod in the Technical Center at Northwestern University in Evanston, Illinois, in 1989. It was developed on the premise that people are too busy to spend hours each week in the grocery store. Peapod has since become the number one online grocery shopping and delivery service in the world.

The founders, with backgrounds in sales and brand and product management, saw a growing market consisting primarily of women between the ages of 30 and 54 in upper-middle-class, dual-income families with median income exceeding $60,000 per year. Many have children and are too busy living their lives to spend time each week on the little favored task of grocery shopping.

The Parkinsons determined that this market segment would be willing to pay a premium for the time savings and convenience of having someone else do their grocery shopping for them, leaving them time for jobs, families, and other obligations. From this concept, Peapod became: "Smart Shopping for Busy People." This business idea has continued to thrive as confirmed by a 1995 survey by Andersen Consulting. The survey indicated that approximately 30 percent of consumers would pay a service fee for electronic ordering and grocery delivery services.

SHORT DESCRIPTION OF THE COMPANY

Peapod was founded in 1989. In 1990, the company introduced the first version of its online shopping software to a suburban Chicago test market using one fulfillment center and three employees. For the next two years, Peapod's main focus was to enhance its software and develop efficient operating systems.

In 1993, the company gradually expanded its operations in the Chicago area and set up operations in the San Francisco area. Peapod's goals for the future were to further enhance its software, improve operating processes, strengthen relations with local retailers, continue to expand service in Chicago and San Francisco, and raise additional capital from the sale of private equity.

SHORT HISTORY OF THE COMPANY

In 1995, Peapod released a new three-tiered software architecture, which included an updated version of the member shopping software. The new software allowed Peapod to execute its interactive marketing services to a number of national consumer goods companies including Ralston Purina Company, Ore-Ida Foods, Frito-Lay, Anheuser-Busch, Nestle U.S.A., M&M Mars, Kraft Foods, and others.

Peapod provides these companies with a forum for targeted interactive advertising, electronic couponing, and extensive product research by linking members from multiple markets into one network. It collects data regarding shopper motivation, purchasing behavior, and demographics. Peapod's database maintains extensive member profiles by collecting data from members' online shopping behaviors, purchase histories, attitudinal surveys, and demographic data. Through utilization of this data, Peapod can customize advertising and promotions to a demographic profile that has historically been difficult to reach through other direct response media channels.[1]

In 1995, together with its retail partner, Jewel/Osco, Peapod began its first media campaign in the Chicago area, utilizing radio and newspaper advertising. Prior to this time, the company relied primarily on word-of-mouth and point-of-purchase displays for member acquisition. That year membership grew by 4,600; 4,300 joined in the fourth quarter. Peapod has been advertising its own online services since this time to aid in its expansion into different markets.

Ironically, the company has found that traditional media have provided more successful advertising venues than high-tech media such as web banner advertising, even though Peapod still advertises in this manner on America Online. Radio spots have been the most successful medium used for attracting new customers to the Peapod web page. Direct mail, newspaper advertisements, and point-of-purchase displays in participating grocery stores have also been successful. The company is testing television advertising in its Chicago market.

Much of Peapod's advertising is conducted on a cooperative basis with its retail partners. Both partners contribute financial and management resources to member acquisition programs. Particularly in new markets, the advertising has focused on co-branding its service with the name recognition of the retail partner.

Aggressive expansion efforts began in September, 1996, with operations opening in Columbus, Ohio, and Boston, Massachusetts. Additional operations opened in Houston, Atlanta, Dallas, and Austin in 1997. As a result of these efforts, membership increased from 12,500 to 33,300 by the end of 1996 and more than tripled between January 1996 and March 1997. Now Peapod operates with more than 225 full-time and 1,075 part-time employees and serves over 5 million households.

In addition to time savings, Peapod boasts other benefits as well. Shoppers have the ability to save money. Peapod can assist customers in comparison shopping based on unit price, identify sale items, and accept manufacturer and electronic coupons. Customers will be more informed consumers by having the ability to shop for items by comparing nutritional content. Each Peapod order is guaranteed to be delivered fresh and on time with all items meeting acceptable levels of customer satisfaction. Other perks of the Peapod service include the use of Peapod e-mail and the availability of recipes in the Peapod Pantry.

Peapod is linked to the grocer's mainframe computer. Information on approximately 20,000 to 40,000 products is downloaded daily to reflect the most current prices, sale items, and selection. The proprietary database also incorporates the retailer's branded or regional products. These items can be viewed through "virtual aisles."

Each customer can sort products by category, name brand, which is useful for coupon holders, kosher products, nutritional value, and sale items. The customer can conduct word or category searches, and use personal lists for frequently purchased items. As an added convenience, Peapod presents a running total of the bill for reference as the member shops. While this service is also offered by phone or fax, an estimated 80 percent of the customers conduct their shopping online.

To use Peapod, customers must obtain a starter kit by downloading the software from the Peapod web site (www.peapod.com) or by calling the Peapod member care department at 1-800-5-PEAPOD. The software is free, takes little memory, and is available for both Windows and Macintosh users. Customers are able to shop the local affiliated grocery store aisles via computer and can place an order any time of day, seven days a week. Delivery is available Tuesday–Friday from 9:30 A.M. to 9:00 P.M. and Saturdays and Sundays from 9:30 A.M. to 2:00 P.M. Costs vary regionally, but usually include a monthly membership fee, delivery fee, and a charge of five percent of the total order cost. Additional surcharges are added for film processing, prescription pickup, and last minute orders or PinPoint delivery times (grocery delivery within a shorter delivery window).

Peapod carefully manages the number of deliveries in each period to avoid service problems that could result from over scheduling. Each order is centrally collected and electronically transmitted to the location where the order is filled. To streamline the packing process, orders are organized according to the layouts in each fulfillment center (shopping and packing facility). Shopping specialists fill the orders, which include fresh produce selected by specially trained produce shoppers, and meat, fish, and delicatessen items that are selected by the retailer's own experts. Packers organize and store the goods in temperature-controlled containers. A driver delivers the orders, ensures customer satisfaction, and collects nonelectronic payments and paper coupons.

---

[1] Muchuere, Michael W., "Virtual Supermarkets," *PC Magazine*, November 18, 1997, v. 16, n. 20, p. 41(1).

Peapod continues to focus on the customer service feature of its business. Given the delivery service and the premium price, the founders knew that the quality and customer orientation needed to be superior for customers to continue to use their service. For this reason, Peapod identified the vision of "fundamentally improving people's lives by bringing interactive shopping to a broad consumer market" and a passion of "amazing and delighting every one of its customers." To ensure that the dream and passion are realized, Peapod offers both toll-free telephone and electronic member support and technical assistance seven days per week. Peapod President Andrew Parkinson attributed the company's success to its development of easy-to-use software and delivery of the finest goods available.

The goal of customer satisfaction is stressed as early as the hiring process. Some of the qualities Peapod identifies as desirable for potential employees are people who persistently pursue goals and deliver on the company's promises, who show concern for customers and their families, who are team players, and who provide unsurpassed customer service. Once an employee is hired, each attends "Peapod University," the company's training program for all fulfillment personnel of the company and some of its retail partners. All shoppers, packers, drivers, and managers undergo hours of formal training, with additional training for produce shoppers, to ensure that service will be consistently excellent. The company rewards superior performance at all levels of the operation with structured incentive and recognition programs.[2]

Peapod has sought to partner with retail operations that have had similar goals and ideals when it comes to customer service. Among these partners are Jewel/Osco in the Chicago area, Safeway in the San Francisco/San Jose area, Kroger in the Columbus, Ohio, area, Stop & Shop in the Boston area, Tom Thumb in the Dallas area, Randall's in the Houston area, and Bruno's in the Atlanta area. Peapod has developed exclusive agreements with only one retailer in each of its markets. This includes the use of both its online delivery service and its marketing support. These agreements have terms of up to five years.

FINANCIAL AND PORTFOLIO ANALYSIS

Peapod primarily earns revenues through interactive marketing, member, and retail services. This includes subscription, service, and other fees paid by members and retail partners. While each of these revenue sources have been steadily increasing, they have not reflected the enormous growth since 1995.

In spite of its recent growth, Peapod has incurred losses since inception. By the end of 1997, membership had increased by more than seven times and member orders had increased by almost three times the first quarter 1995 amounts. However, while orders increased about 25 percent in 1998, membership remained flat compared to 1997 at around 100,000.[3] Cost increases have accompanied this growth, however.

It is difficult to project the impact of the company's expansion because the sales and order figures are subject to seasonal fluctuations. Historically, these numbers have been higher in the fourth and first quarters in the colder climate markets. Conversely, member orders decrease during the spring and summer months as a result of vacation schedules and better weather. The number of markets has increased, particularly noticeable between the second and third quarters of 1996. The number of members has increased only slightly, however. Member orders have decreased, as have grocery sales. At the same time, expenses increased due to the expansion, particularly in systems maintenance, general and administrative costs, and grocery operations.

While the number of orders continue to grow, so are the losses. The net loss for 1998 grew faster than the number of orders when compared to 1997 levels. These concerns bring into question the effectiveness of the company's expansion program and the success of continued growth in its current markets.

To operate profitably in the future, Peapod officers have identified several objectives: (1) increase grocery sales volume by adding new members, retaining existing members, and increasing member usage; (2) acquire market share in interactive marketing services; (3) develop and realize additional revenue sources, such as additional transactional, advertising, and informational services, and licensing; and (4) reduce costs of fulfillment.

On June 11, 1997, in an effort to raise $50 million to meet these objectives, Peapod executives announced an initial public offering of approximately 3.6 million shares of its common stock at $16 per share.

RISK ANALYSIS

Peapod has not experienced significant competition thus far from other electronic grocery and delivery services. Competition has only surfaced in Boston. There several less expensive, warehouse-based delivery services have recently emerged. Peapod's benefits over such services include its user-friendly and functional online shopping system, its substantially greater product selection, and,

---

[2] Bicknell, David, "Virtual Mall is Master of the Aisles," *Computer Weekly*, October 1, 1998, p. 300(1).

[3] http://www.sec.GOV/Archives/edgar/data/1036992/ 0001036992-99-000001.txt (SEC Edgar cite)
http://www.corporate-ir.net/ireye/ir_site.zhtml?ticker= ppod&script=2100&layout=7 (Peapod cite)

for the grocery retailer partner, the brand awareness generated through its cooperative marketing efforts.

Early on, Peapod successfully captured a segment of the online service industry that many larger competitors had yet to master. Online service carrier Prodigy began offering an electronic shopping service in 1988, but due to a weak response, withdrew it. America Online, for this reason, postponed their planned entrance into teleshopping.

Some of the retailers with which Peapod is paired tried to enter online shopping before developing a partnership. Kroger in Columbus, Ohio, is one such grocer. Kroger advertising manager Dale Hollandsworth knew that the market was ready for online shopping, but the stores were unable to accept the responsibility on their own. Other Columbus grocers also tried this tactic. Big Bear developed a delivery system in August 1995. After little success with online ordering, it decided to offer the service only through telephone or fax.

Some retailers have been more successful. Grand Rapids, Michigan-based Meijer offers a limited selection of 170 products online, including such goods as books, toys, household items, and holiday items. While this is not close to the 20,000 to 40,000 items Peapod makes available, the company has been trying to determine how much and which merchandise customers want to see online.

In some respects, competition exists from services similar to Peapod. Baltimore-based Shoppers Express is like Peapod in that it only partners with one grocer per market. Shoppers Express is currently available in 19 markets. Bethesda-based All Things Delivered also limits items. Many are purchased through warehouse clubs and only come in bulk sizes. While this helps to keep customer costs down, few families have the storage space or ability to consume these bulk-sized foods.

Peapod's primary competition in this segment exists in the Boston market from Westwood, Massachusetts-based Streamline. Streamline markets itself as a regular household replenishment service. It works with numerous retailers and provides such services as video rental, dry cleaning, and photo development, in addition to prepared meal delivery and grocery shopping.

Meijer doesn't charge for delivery, while both Peapod and Shoppers Express do. Peapod charges a monthly fee, delivery fee, and 5 percent of the total bill. Shoppers Express charges a flat $9.95 delivery fee and All Things Delivered charges a $7.00 fee for orders greater than $50.00. Streamline charges a $30.00 monthly fee for all services.[4]

---

[4] Muchuere, Michael W., "Virtual Supermarkets," *PC Magazine*, November 18, 1997, v. 16, n. 20, p. 41(1).

Future competitors may arise from large technology companies that, in conjunction with grocery retailers or independently, develop online grocery shopping systems. Because of the large capital investment required to develop and operate online grocery shopping and delivery systems, Peapod believes large, well-capitalized retailers or technology firms pose the most significant long-term competitive threat.

INDUSTRY AND MARKET ANALYSIS

Interactive grocery services is an emerging industry consisting of components of three major industries: online commerce, grocery retailing, and interactive marketing services.

ONLINE COMMERCE

The International Data Corporation (IDC) estimates that the number of households subscribing to Internet online services will grow from over 14 million in 1996 to over 42 million in the year 2000. IDC estimates that the total value of goods purchased over the web grew from $318 million in 1995 to an annualized rate of $5.4 billion in December 1996, and is expected to reach $95 billion by the year 2000 and $150 billion by 2004. Additionally, a September 1995 Supermarket Business survey estimated that supermarket home shopping sales will represent 5.5 percent of total grocery sales by the year 2000.

Although these figures for online growth look promising, it has been estimated that the rates at which subscribers cancel an online service are high. As a result, Peapod is not unlike other companies that compete to retain their members once they have registered for services. Peapod's average annual member retention rates (computed by averaging annual retention rates at the end of each month) were 62 percent in 1995 and 66 percent in 1996.

GROCERY RETAILING

The retail grocery business represented $311.7 billion in revenues in 1995, according to *Progressive Grocer's 1996 Marketing Guidebook*. Recent sales growth in the industry has only slightly exceeded inflation rates, while the competition has remained intense and the margins continue to narrow. Supermarkets continue to search for innovative ways to differentiate their stores through additional consumer services. Some grocery operators have begun to experiment with online shopping and home delivery and have found the service to be too complex and time and resource consuming to be successful. By establishing a partnership with Peapod for these services, the retailers gain access to Peapod's online sales channel at a lower cost than attempting the service themselves.

Peapod believes that the average online order size is five to six times the average in-store order. Members may not necessarily purchase more consumer goods for their households. For convenience, however, they move the purchase of other household goods from other retailers to the Peapod service. Through partnering with Peapod, retailers have the opportunity to generate revenue growth without the real estate investment usually associated with this expansion.

In addition to providing constant feedback on out-of-stock inventory and the quality of perishable items, Peapod's interactive marketing enables retailers to customize their stores online while experimenting with local merchandising, pricing, and promotional strategies. Peapod further provides retailers with transaction processing, electronic billing, and collection services. In return for these services, retailers pay Peapod both fixed and variable fees. The variable fees, paid monthly, are calculated as a percentage of the total monthly grocery sales. Retailers also pay a variety of management fees, based on geographic expansion and level of exclusivity.[5]

Peapod currently offers several flexible retail partnership programs. Under its full-service program, Peapod employees perform complete fulfillment services, including shopping, packing, and delivering of groceries. The retail partners provide access to the stores for use as fulfillment centers. In the Partners Fulfillment Program, the shopping, packing, and delivery services are performed by the retailer's employees who have been recruited, trained, and managed by the Peapod field management staff.

Future plans provide for nonexclusive licensing and system management programs through Peapod's Split Pea Software Division. Under this program, Peapod would provide software, hosting, and network management services, while the retailer would manage, under a private label, the marketing, fulfillment, transaction processing, and customer service components.

INTERACTIVE MARKETING SERVICES

According to NCH Promotional Services, companies spend approximately $6.5 billion on free-standing insert (FSI) coupon programs. While these programs are an effective way for consumer goods companies to generate additional demand for their products, this method of advertising is expensive to initiate, largely due to distribution and handling costs. The anonymous nature of the coupon programs makes it difficult to target their use and measure their effectiveness.

Consumer goods manufacturers have also gathered market information regarding consumer purchase behavior from in-store scanner data. Because scanner data capture only the product movement without associating it with particular consumers, it has limited utility as a tool for measuring consumer purchase intent or as a basis for targeted marketing.

The IDC estimates that interactive advertising spending grew from $280 million in 1996 to more than $2.3 billion by the year 2000. The Peapod system can capture product exposure, mouse clicks, coupon redemption, and product sales and can report the most complete information on the impact of a marketing program to the consumer goods companies. Peapod believes its personalized advertising and feedback on the impact of that advertising will provide a competitive advantage in the interactive marketplace.[6]

Peapod's user interface accommodates a variety of media displays, such as electronic coupons and information modules that support cost savings and "smart shopping." The database and membership profile enables the company's technology to deliver highly targeted, one-to-one advertising and promotion. Peapod's systems provide total accountability for every marketing event executed on the Peapod system so that exposures, mouse clicks, coupon redemptions, and sales are all captured for complete reporting of the impact of the marketing program. This accurate and comprehensive feedback is a valuable tool for consumer goods companies. This data enables them to pretest and refine marketing programs for execution in the more traditional media.

Companies operating in the electronic (computer, fax, or phone) grocery shopping and delivery business compete on several factors, including the ease of use, functionality, reliability of the shopping and ordering system, product selection, price, the reliability and professionalism of delivery operations and other customer services, and general brand awareness.

ROLE OF RESEARCH AND DEVELOPMENT

Research is extremely important to the success of Peapod. One area of success is its application features. They target various forms of redeemable content, such as advertisements, electronic coupons, online surveys, and product samples, to members based on a range of pre-defined criteria. Peapod has developed a Universal Event Processor. This is a flexible, high-performance database application that manages the targeting and redemption of these events.[7]

TECHNOLOGICAL STORY

The demand and market acceptance for online products and services is subject to a high level of uncer-

---

[5] "Peapod Launches Consumer Goods Research Service," *Newbytes PM*, April 6, 1999, v. 13, i7, p. NA.

[6] "Peapod's Customer Tracking System," *Computer World*, August 10, 1998, v. 32, n. 32, p. 1.
[7] Wang, Nelson, "Net Money," *Internet World*, April 13, 1998, v. 4, n. 14, p. 46(1).

tainty. The company's growth will depend, in part, on the number of consumers who own or have access to personal computers or other systems that can access online services on the Internet.

TECHNOLOGICAL INVESTMENT AND ANALYSIS

The Peapod consumer software is based on a three-tier architecture, which has positioned Peapod at the forefront of Internet computing. The first tier, the client layer, is located on the member's computer. This layer utilizes instructions from the application server to establish the user's interface, run the application, and return the input to the Peapod server. The two remaining tiers, the application and the database, are centrally maintained and manage all of the logic and data associated with the Peapod application.

Peapod believes that this "thin client" architecture has many advantages. The overall application performance is strong relative to other consumer network applications with comparable levels of interactivity. A major factor in the performance of a network application is the utilization of the narrow bandwidth connection between the consumer's computer and the server. Peapod makes efficient use of this bandwidth by processing on the member's computer and exchanging only application-relevant information between a member's computer and the Peapod server.

This architectural structure offers a high degree of scalability. Efficient interaction between the Peapod server and the member's computer and the processing of certain application activities on the client side reduces the processing requirements of the Peapod server. The separation of the application and the database enables Peapod to isolate and optimize the different processing requirements of those layers. As the membership base expands and the number of simultaneous users increases, Peapod can integrate additional application servers without impacting the rest of the application architecture.

Another advantage is the functionality and flexibility of the application. Because the application logic and data are maintained centrally, Peapod can change much of the content and appearance of the software without modifying or upgrading the software on the member's computer. Internet e-mail features were added to the application without any interruptions in client service or modifications to the customers' software. The centralized application logic also enables Peapod to present interactive marketing events and customize application appearances to individual members.[8]

The new version of Peapod software, version 5.0, will be based on Microsoft's ActiveX technology and

will be designed to offer an even greater level of integration with the web. Peapod will be able to incorporate web site content, such as HTML documents or Shockwave animated images, into its consumer interface. With this new version, Peapod will be able to adapt its consumer software to support new technologies.

Peapod software is easily accessible via the Internet or from a Peapod diskette. Once the software is downloaded to the member's computer, members can then access the Peapod servers via direct dial-up or the Internet. The Peapod client software currently supports both Windows and Macintosh user platforms.

Peapod has designed and integrated several business support systems with its shopping application to facilitate the administration of services. The fulfillment management application, installed at each of Peapod's fulfillment centers, enables Peapod field operations managers to access and print member orders according to store layout, manage delivery time availability, and update store-specific product offerings. The Peapod accounting system provides the billing, processing, and collection functions, which include the electronic link to process member credit card payments and funds transfer.

The next release of the fulfillment management applications will incorporate hand-held scanning technology to enhance and streamline the order picking and packing functions and electronically integrate member orders with the Peapod accounting systems.

Peapod's services are vulnerable to weaknesses in the communications medium (the Internet). This may compromise the security of confidential electronic information exchanged with members. Disruptions of service or security breaches could cause losses to Peapod, reduce member satisfaction, and deter new members from joining because of a lack of confidence in online commerce. Peapod has taken several steps to address these and other privacy concerns. It has restricted access to its database, limited the type of information made available to third parties, required each employee to sign a nondisclosure and confidentiality agreement, and implemented data security systems at the main data center.

TECHNOLOGICAL INNOVATIONS

TELECOMMUNICATIONS

Peapod remodeled its web site in 1998 to enable a variety of Internet-accessible devices, in addition to the standard PC/web browser combination, to access Peapod's virtual supermarket. The new site complements its SuRF proprietary shopping system. SuRF combines the multimedia capabilities of the World Wide Web with Peapod's WinSurfer application controls. This enables Peapod to offer shopping functionality and performance superior to those available from standard

---

[8] "Peapod Expanding," *Computerworld*, August 17, 1998. v. 32, n. 33, p. 33(1).

Internet technologies. This is particularly true considering the Internet's narrow bandwidths and conventional modem speeds.

DATA

Peapod developed a way to track not only if individuals respond to particular promotions, but how they respond. The software is called Universal Event Processor (UEP). It not only knows that you buy diapers, but it also records that you immediately used a two-for-one electronic coupon for raisin bagels even when you had never purchased bagels before, or that you ignore ads for cheese unless you are buying crackers. "It's routine to search databases for people who conform to a specific profile. We wanted to develop a system that automatically tracks the actual transactions that result," said Thomas Parkinson, Peapod's chief technology officer.[9]

"We found, for example, that we could sell five times as much Keri hand lotion by running a banner ad whenever a customer clicked on bananas," Parkinson said. This may seem illogical but it is invaluable marketing information.

Peapod believes it is too early to determine whether this has made individual consumers more loyal to Peapod. Nonetheless, it helps Peapod sell more products. The UEP has led data-hungry consumer goods manufacturers to Peapod's door.

Kraft Foods, Bristol-Myers Squibb Co., and Kellogg Co. use Peapod to test consumer tastes and behavior. They have seen on average a 10 to 15 percent increase in sales when they run a targeted banner advertisement. This is twice as much as with targeted electronic coupons, according to Tim Dorgan, who oversees market research for the consumer goods clients.

RECOMMENDATION FOR THE FUTURE

Peapod must build brand identity and awareness. This will be accomplished by using production and advertising to aggressively market its services to increase brand name recognition. Peapod will stress the functionality, quality, convenience, and value of its services to continue to build its brand identity.

Peapod must provide a superior member experience. Peapod is committed to providing its members with user-friendly, highly functional and cost-effective shopping tools, convenient delivery and pickup service, and exceptional product quality, each of which ensures member satisfaction and loyalty. Peapod must continue to gather consumer preference information to introduce more personalized services to its members. This will attract new members, retain existing members, increase member usage, and increase Peapod's share of members' household purchases.

Peapod must expand into new geographic markets and further penetrate existing markets. Peapod believes it can achieve competitive advantages in various markets by being the first to build a substantial online membership base. Peapod is currently in talks with grocery retailers in a dozen new markets. To take advantage of economies in fulfillment and advertising, Peapod plans to penetrate these markets quickly by opening multiple fulfillment centers in each new market.

The company considers numerous factors when choosing markets to expand into. Factors include size, population density, prevalence of personal computer users, demographic composition, market conditions, availability of a high-quality grocer, and other general economic factors.[10]

Peapod must build interactive marketing services and leverage its database. Peapod has pioneered, in partnership with consumer goods companies, innovative interactive marketing services consisting of advertising, promotion, and market research services. The company has a relationship with the M/A/R/C Group, a national marketing research organization, to develop and market custom and syndicated research applications that will bring the research benefits of Peapod to the marketplace.

Peapod plans to continue to use its database and online shopping channel to develop new services for its interactive marketing clients. As Peapod's membership increases, it is believed that consumer goods companies will find the interactive marketing services a more valuable and cost-effective research tool.

Peapod has been working closely with its retail partners to expand their roles in the fulfillment of member orders. This partnership has also been leveraged to improve product distribution and order fulfillment to reduce costs, improve quality, and enhance scalability. Technological support for these goals includes the recent development of a hand-held scanner which will be used to expedite the order picking and packing functions. Peapod has recently initiated efforts to license its technology to retailers on an international basis and in select United States markets.

Peapod has also developed new customer options to lower costs. In Houston, Peapod and its retail partner, Randall's, have implemented a drive-through pickup option. This option reduces the member's delivery fees and provides additional scheduling flexibility by enabling members to pick up their orders at their convenience. Peapod plans to incorporate this option in existing and future markets.

Peapod must leverage its membership and technology into other online services. Peapod recently entered into agreements with Geerlings & Wade, a

[9] "Peapod Spins Off Split Pea Software," *Computergram International*, January 15, 1999.

[10] Muchmore, Michael W., "Virtual Supermarkets," *PC Magazine*, November 18, 1997, v. 16, n. 20, p. 41(1).

national direct marketer of premium wines, to offer an online wine store, and Firefly Greetings, a provider of personal greeting cards and specialty products, to offer an online gift and specialty products center. Future plans include partnerships with nongrocery retailers to offer additional online services that would appeal to the company's membership base. Peapod also plans to make its services accessible on a national basis via the Internet. The companies with whom Peapod has partnered have agreed to pay Peapod development, management, and transactional fees so these services can be introduced in the next Peapod software version.[11]

---

[11] Peapod Launches Consumer Goods Research Service," *Newsbytes PM*, April 6, 1999, v. 13, i. 7, p. NA.

CASE QUESTIONS

Strategic Questions

1. What is the strategic direction of Peapod?
2. What forces are driving this direction?
3. What has been the catalyst for change?
4. What are the critical success factors for Peapod?
5. What are the core competencies for Peapod?

Technological Questions

6. What technologies has the corporation relied on?
7. What has caused a change in the use of technology in the corporation?
8. How successful has the technological change been?

Quantitative Questions

9. Has Peapod been profitable?
10. What conclusions can be reached from an analysis of the financial information?
11. Does Peapod have sufficient capital to sustain its rollout?

Internet Questions

12. Is the Internet important to Peapod?
13. What does the Peapod's web page emphasize?
14. How does this compare to other web sites?

Industry Questions

15. What challenges and opportunities is the industry facing?
16. Is the industry oligopolistic or competitive?
17. How will technology impact the industry?

Data Questions

18. What role do data play in the future of the corporation?
19. How important are data to Peapod's continued success?
20. How will the capture and maintenance of customer data impact Peapod's future?

TECHNOLOGY TIPS

MICROSOFT WORD TIPS

USING FOOTNOTES AND ENDNOTES

When writing long research papers it may be hard to keep track of what books, articles, research papers, and web sites you used. No matter how long or how short your paper is credit is due to those sources that you used. An easy way of keeping track of those sources is by using footnotes or endnotes. Footnotes will be located on the bottom of the page on which the reference appears. Endnotes will appear at the end of the document. Either one will save you time at the end from searching for the sources you used.

Footnotes

1. Place the cursor at the end of the sentence that you wish to insert a footnote.
2. Click on INSERT, then FOOTNOTE. . . .
3. A dialog box will appear that will ask you to select between a footnote or endnote. Click on FOOTNOTE.
4. Select either CUSTOM MARK or AUTONUMBER (Note: autonumber is suggested since it will change the footnote numbers automatically as you remove and insert footnotes.)
5. Once you have made your selections you can click on OK.
6. The bottom of the screen will open to the footnote section and will allow you to enter your source information.

7. You can keep the screen open if you like or close it by clicking on CLOSE.
8. You can add additional footnotes to your document by following steps 2 through 6.
9. If you wish to simply view your footnotes after closing the bottom screen you may do so by clicking on VIEW, then FOOTNOTES.

Endnotes

1. Place the cursor at the end of the sentence that you wish to insert a endnote.
2. Click on INSERT, then ENDNOTE. . . .
3. A dialog box will appear that will ask you to select between a footnote or endnote. Click on ENDNOTE.
4. Select either CUSTOM MARK or AUTONUMBER (Note: autonumber is suggested since it will change the endnote numbers automatically as you remove and insert endnotes.)
5. Once you have made your selections you can click on OK.
6. The bottom of the screen will open to the endnote section and will allow you to enter your source information.
7. You can keep the screen open if you like or close it by clicking on CLOSE.
8. You can add additional endnotes to your document by following steps 2 through 6.
9. If you wish to simply view your endnotes after closing the bottom screen you may do so by clicking on VIEW, then ENDNOTES.

ADDITIONAL NOTE

Instead of going back and forth between the footnote/endnote screen and your work screen you can view this information by placing your cursor on the footnote/endnote number. The information you entered for that particular footnote/endnote will appear in a small dialog box.

MICROSOFT EXCEL TIPS

ENTERING, COPYING, AND MOVING DATA

Entering Data

Entering data in the Excel worksheet is quite simple. Clicking on the cell in which you wish to enter the data, whether it is numbers or text, and then pressing enter, the tab key, or one of the arrow keys will make the entry into the cell. The order in which you enter data into your worksheet does not have to be in any particular order; however, to make the data entering easier the following order is suggested:

1. Type the text information to create a structure that will make it clear as to where to enter the numerical data.
2. Type the numerical data in the appropriate cells.
3. Add the necessary formulas to the worksheet.
4. Format the text, numbers, and formulas.

Copying Data

There are several methods to copy data from one cell to another. Any of the following methods will work.

Using Command Buttons

1. Click on the cell that will be copied
2. Click on the Copy button

3. Click on the cell that the data is to be copied into
4. Click on the Paste button

Dragging Data

1. Click on the cell that will be copied
2. Point to the border of the cell
3. While pressing the CONTROL key, drag the data to the new location in the worksheet
4. Release the mouse button when the cell that the data is to be copied in is highlighted

Fill Handle

1. Click on the cell that will be copied
2. Place the cursor on the fill handle and drag to fill adjacent cells
3. Release the mouse button when the last cell that is to be filled with the data has been reached

Moving Data

Moving data is different from copying since you will be removing the data from the cell and placing it in a different cell of the worksheet or workbook.

Using Command Buttons

1. Click on the cell that contains the data to be moved
2. Click on the Cut button
3. Click on the cell that the data is to be moved into
4. Click on the Paste button

Dragging Data

1. Click on the cell that contains the data to be moved
2. Place the mouse pointer at the edge of the cell
3. Drag to the new destination and "drop" the data in the cell of your choice.

ADDITIONAL NOTES

Another feature of using the right mouse button is to simply right click on the cell. This will provide a shortcut menu of command buttons that can be used with the cell selected.

The right mouse button can produce a number of shortcuts and minimize the movement of the mouse around the screen. When using the drag method to move and copy data use the right mouse button to drag instead of the left mouse button. This will make the shortcut menu on the right appear. You can then select from a number of choices what to do with the data.

MICROSOFT POWERPOINT TIPS

SLIDE VIEWS, NEW SLIDES, AND SLIDE SHOW

This section will allow you to select different views of your project, create a new slide once you have started your project, and perform a slide show in order to review your presentation.

Slide Views

There are several ways that you may view your presentations. Some views will be more useful during the creation of your presentation whereas others will be more useful once you have completed your presentation. There are at least four views to choose from, and they are as follows:

1. *Slide View:* This is the standard view of your slide and the one you will use most frequently. With the presentation *open* you will see five pushbuttons on the bottom left of the screen. The SLIDE VIEW will be the first 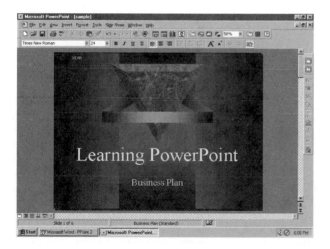 pushbutton.

2. *Outline View:* This view is probably the best view in which to organize ideas for your presentation. You can see how your main points flow from slide to slide. To switch to outline view, click the Outline View button. Use the buttons on the Outlining toolbar to move slides or text, show only slide titles, and change the indent level of titles and text.

3. *Slide Sorter View:* This view will allow you to see your entire presentation so you can easily add, delete, and move slides. To switch to slide sorter view, click the Slide Sorter View button.

4. *Notes Page View:* In notes page view, you can type speaker notes to use during your presentation. You also can print a copy of your notes for reference. To switch to notes page view, click the Notes Page View button. More will be discussed on this view in Chapter 10.

New Slides

Once you have your presentation open and you wish to add a new slide, do the following:
1. Switch to Slide Sorter view by clicking on the button.
2. Click on the slide that you would like to place the new slide *after.*
3. From the top toolbar click on INSERT and select NEW SLIDE.
4. A dialog box will appear asking you to select a slide layout. Select a layout and press OK.
5. To add more slides just repeat steps 1 through 4. (Note: it is not necessary to switch views. You may insert a new slide by selecting INSERT from the top toolbar and then NEW SLIDE.)

Slide Show

It may be useful to review your presentation by taking a look at the slide show. This will allow you to see how your presentation will appear to the audience. The presentation will start from the slide that you are currently on.

1. Simply click on the slide from which you want to start and click on the SLIDE SHOW button located on the bottom left of the screen next to the view buttons.
2. You may click on the left mouse button or the space bar to advance to the next slide.
3. To exit the slide show click on the right button of your mouse and select END SHOW from the pop-up menu. You may also advance through the whole presentation to the end. Once the show reaches the last slide the screen will revert back to the slide from which it started.

MICROSOFT ACCESS TIPS
DESIGNING A DATABASE

Before you use Access to actually build the tables, forms, and other objects that will make up your database, it is important to take time to design your database. A good database design is the keystone to creating a database that does what you want it to do effectively, accurately, and efficiently. Starting up Access and creating a series of tables is tempting, but chances are that later on you will be spending time trying to make sense of the database. The following steps will help you design your database and lessen the chances that you will have to troubleshoot the database later on.

1. Determine the purpose of your database.
2. Determine the tables you need in the database.
3. Determine the fields you need in the tables.
4. Identify fields with unique values.
5. Determine the relationships between tables.
6. Refine your design.
7. Add data and create other database objects.

Determine the Purpose of Your Database
The first step in designing a database is to determine the purpose of the database and how it will be used. You need to know what information you want from the database. From that, you can determine what subjects you need to store facts about (the tables) and what facts you need to store about each subject (the fields in the tables).

Talk to people who will use the database. Brainstorm about the questions you would like the database to answer. Sketch out the reports that could be produced by the database. Gather the forms you currently use to record your data. Examine well-designed databases similar to the one you are designing.

Determine the Tables You Need
Determining the tables can be the trickiest step in the database design process. That is because the results you want from your database, the reports you want to print, the forms you want to use, the questions you want answered, do not necessarily provide clues about the structure of the tables that produce them.

Paper and pencil are the tools that you should use first when designing your tables. As arcane as this may sound, they provide a good brainstorming session as to how the table should look and what information it should include. When you design your tables, divide up pieces of information by keeping these fundamental design principles in mind:

- A table should **not** contain duplicate information, and information should not be duplicated between tables.

When each piece of information is stored in only one table, you update it in one place. This is more efficient, and also eliminates the possibility of duplicate entries that contain different information. For example, you would want to store each customer address and phone number once, in one table.

- Each table should contain information about one subject.

When each table contains facts about only one subject, you can maintain information about each subject independently from other subjects. For example, you would store customer addresses in a different table from the customers' orders, so that you could delete one order and still maintain the customer information.

Determine the Fields You Need

Each table contains information about the same subject, and each field in a table contains individual facts about the tables subject. For example, a customer table may include company name, address, city, state, and phone number fields. When sketching out the fields for each table, keep these tips in mind:

- Relate each field directly to the subject of the table.
- Do not include derived or calculated data (data that is the result of an expression).
- Include all the information you need.
- Store information in its smallest logical parts (for example, First Name and Last Name, rather than Name).

Identify Fields with Unique Values

To enable Access to connect information stored in separate tables, each table in your database must include a field or set of fields that uniquely identifies each individual record in the table. Such a field or set of fields is called a primary key. An example of a primary key would be a customer number ID.

Determine the Relationships Between Tables

Now that you've divided your information into tables and identified primary key fields, you need a way to tell Access how to bring related information back together again in meaningful ways. To do this, you define relationships between tables.

Refine the Design

After you have designed the tables, fields, and relationships you need, it is time to study the design and detect any flaws that might remain. It is easier to change your database design now, rather than after you have filled the tables with data. Use Microsoft Access to create your tables, specify relationships between the tables, and enter a few records of data in each table. See if you can use the database to get the answers you want. Create rough drafts of your forms and re-ports and see if they show the data you expect. Look for unnecessary duplications of data and eliminate them.

Enter Data and Create Other Database Objects

When you are satisfied that the table structures meet the design goals described here, then it is time to go ahead and add all your existing data to the tables. You can then create any queries, forms, reports, macros, and modules that you may want.

MICROSOFT FRONTPAGE TIPS

GETTING STARTED

Now that you have a general idea of what the Internet is all about and you have the necessary tools, we can begin to create a web page. However, please understand that the following chapters merely scratch the surface on what is possible with web page development. At best, the following chapters should spark some interest and will have you searching the web for more information on what is possible with web pages. Information will be provided in the final chapter as to where you can go to further enhance your web page.

PLANNING YOUR WEB SITE

Before you start working on your web page look at other web sites and see how they work. Think about why you are creating a web site. What purpose will it serve? If possible, draw your web site. This will save you many headaches and will provide you with a sense of direction.

The Index Page

Understanding the index page is an important concept to grasp before creating your web page. The index page is the foundation of your web site. It is the page that people will view first and the page upon which all other pages are built.

An index page is like a default start page for a web site. When a browser searches a directory or folder, in the absence of a specific web page, it will return to the index page.

Example:

http://www.yourwebpage.edu/	Returns to your web page index page
http://www.yourwebpage.edu/photos.html	Returns your web page's photo page

You must have at least one index.html page for every web site. This is this page that will appear when people type in your web address.

Organizing Your Server Space

Depending on the size and complexity of your web site you may need to spend some time thinking about how you may want to organize the information on the server. Small sites containing one or two pages with only a few images may be fine with everything in the Public HTML folder. Larger sites may take more planning. You may have different folders or directories for different types of documents (Word Folder, PowerPoint Folder, Images Folder, etc.). The more planning and thought that goes into your site beforehand the fewer mistakes and less confusion you will have later on. Remember when adding folders that your links must include the names of the folder in their address.

Address	Will Open
http://www.yourname.edu/word/	index web page file in word folder
http://www.yourname.edu/word/paper.html	paper web page file in word folder
http://www.yourname.edu/ppt/	index web page file in ppt folder
http://www.yourname.edu/ppt/pres.html	pres web page file in ppt folder

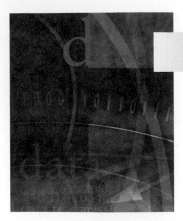

CHAPTER 3

SOLVING PROBLEMS
SPECIALTY RETAIL

Solving Problems

As the complexities of our society intensify, the problems of business are becoming increasingly complex and interrelated. Outsourcing, integrated supply chains, and electronic data interchange for the transfer of payments all expand the number of organizational entities and individuals with which the corporation must interact.

There are many approaches to solving problems. In the context of these technological complexities, the most important thing to remember is to break the problem into smaller, more understandable pieces. These individual pieces can then be examined in depth in relation to the problem and reassembled in ways that enable the identified problem to be addressed in a straightforward manner.

One approach to problem solving, in both business and technology, is the systems approach. A system is decomposed into the components of input, process, and output. *Input* includes all the variables that go into the organization or make up the problem. *Process* is the value added by the individual or organization. It is the manufacturing process, the communication skills, or the transfer that the organization does better than any other organization. *Output* process is the value provided to the buyers, given their bargaining power. This includes their need for new products, more cost-efficient products, or innovations in packaging, presentation, or additional features.

Allowed to run its own course, the input–process–output approach can become a system in itself. By their very nature, businesspeople focus on the refinement of internal processes, rather than on what the market needs. Often, an organization reaches a level of comfort with itself rather than maintaining focus on the needs of the current and potential marketplace. As a result, a cycle must be added to the process that requires the integration of customer information. Control and feedback become an important mechanism to ensure that the goal is reached.

Most business problems are too complex to address at once. An important step is to break the system into smaller components or a collection of subsystems. This enables the problem to be examined in sections. Each subpart can be separated from the others, enabling it to be examined independently.

Two approaches to productivity and problem solving include developing new ideas and putting them to effective use. This involves identifying innovations, bringing them into the workplace, and then making them work. Several methods exist to increase the ability to implement change in the organization. These include advocacy, rotation, leadership, and environmental uncertainty.

Advocacy The implementation of change in an organization is enhanced by one or more highly visible and respected persons in the organization who champions the diffusion of the innovation throughout the organization. This means that someone with visibility in the organization must advocate the change with passion.

Rotation Job rotation is an important way to implement new ideas and technologies in an organization. Moving staff among various functions broadens perspectives and clarifies the relationship between emerging new technologies and the business goals of the organization. It also spreads the newly learned expertise throughout the organization, accelerating the diffusion process.

Keeping employees in one place for an extended period of time causes groups to become insular and minimizes the identification with the organization as a whole. These individuals identify with the stability of the unchanging group and the resistance to change. Applications are localized and are further refined to meet the specific needs of the local group. This goes against identifying standards that can be implemented across the organization.

Leadership Senior management involvement is critical for the successful diffusion of innovations. Often, perception of leadership involvement is as important as the reality of the involvement. This leadership support for the innovation must be communicated through resource allocations and incentive and reward mechanisms.

Environmental Uncertainty Innovation and change are best accomplished in environments of high or low uncertainty. Departments that are fairly stable provide better environments to try new things. The resources and time commitments exist to try and implement innovations within the comfort level of stability. Likewise, departments ravaged by the threats of reorganization or dramatic resource cuts are more willing to innovate given the perception that preservation is not a viable option anyway. An environment in the middle, characterized by stability and predictability, is usually not uncomfortable enough to need change, nor comfortable enough to have the resources to commit to it.

Barriers/Obstacles to Productivity Improvement Barriers to adapting technology to address business problems could occur in four areas.

Motivation Commitment is required to distribute new technologies throughout an organization or department. Energy is required to learn a new tool, method, or technique and implement it into the daily work routine. A clear reward, either in money, position, or time allocation, is required to make this commitment in terms of energy and time. The advantages of innovations must be beneficial at both the individual and the organizational levels. If the individual does not see the advantage of the innovation to improve his or her own productivity, simplify work life, boost profit-sharing dividends, or win personnel respect or group recognition, there will be no reason to adopt the change.

Technological Intimidation Innovations in technology can compound the already difficult process of implementing technology. Not only can individuals develop an aversion to the new technology, they can also find its complexity intimidating and difficult. As a result, some are predisposed to failure before they start.

Resource Allocation The allocation of resources is important not just for the purchase of hardware and software, but also to pay for the implementation of the technology and its integration into the organization. Initial and continuing training on the new innovation is important to overcome the intimidation of a complicated new practice. Follow-up technical support is also important. Users of the technology must know whom to call when problems surface.

Senior Management Commitment Senior managers must be committed to the technology, not only with words, but also with their time and use. Technology that is used by senior management is far more likely to be adopted than technology that is only advocated by them. To achieve implementation success, opinion leaders must be convinced of the technology's importance. They must be trained to implement the change not only for themselves, but also for their organizations.

When faced, then, with problem situations related to productivity improvement, it is important to understand the role that technology may play in their resolution. Tremendous pressure is on workers and organizations to increase their productivity and decrease their costs in this environment. Time frames and cost constraints are increasingly being shortened and tightened.

To address these problems in the workplace, it is important to step back and take a macro view of the situation. Often these problems are not as formidable from a broader perspective. Second, one must break down the pieces to identify those elements that are most likely to cause problems. These smaller pieces can often be better addressed in a smaller, more focused manner. Third, it is important to evaluate carefully the productivity requirements in light of the organizational support for the problem resolutions being presented. In some cases, the problem might be the fact that the individual is pushing too hard, trying to achieve success with the implementation of an innovation for which there is not enough support. Finally, it is important to remember that technology, properly applied, might be the best means to address the problem.

Specialty Retail

DESCRIPTION OF THE INDUSTRY

Retail sales have been strong during the late 1990s, especially in light of the fact that the United States has a mature and saturated retail market. While sales have not been phenomenal, they have risen about 4 percent annually during most of the 1990s. Much of this increase can be attributed to the good economy of the decade. The 1990s have been marked by low interest

Word	W.1	Inserting Images in Your Word Document Additional Note	From Clip Art From a File Modifying the Image Web Images
Excel	E.1	Cell Ranges Selecting a Cell Range Naming a Range	Using the Mouse Using the Keyboard Using the Mouse and SHIFT Key Naming a Range
PowerPoint	P.1	Changing Slide Layouts Note	Changing an Existing Slide Layout
Access	A.1	Tables and Primary Keys Auto Number Primary Keys Single-Field Primary Keys Multiple-Field Primary Keys	
Front Page	I.1	Inserting Tables	Tables Inserting Rows and Columns Further Customizing the Table

rates, low inflation, and low unemployment, resulting in an increase in disposable income. Standard and Poor's predicts the economy will continue to grow, albeit at a slower pace. These factors, along with a strong consumer confidence index, all mean continued growth for the specialty retail industry, but at a moderate pace overall.

With favorable growth in so many areas including personal income, real earnings, disposable income, real consumer spending, and strong consumer confidence, and with low interest rates and low unemployment, why aren't retail sales growing more rapidly? The biggest culprit is the new shopping and spending trends of consumers. Recent studies indicate mall shopping is on the decline. In fact, the length of an average mall visit has dropped by more than a third. This may be partly because consumers are more pressed for time. As consumers have less time to shop, they are more likely to purchase only what they need and leave.

The Internet has also helped with precision shopping. In fact, Internet shopping has many advantages, which are not lost on the consumer. However, since home computers with Internet access are not universal in the United States, Internet shopping so far has made only a small dent in overall retail spending. As more consumers get Internet access and security becomes more standardized, Internet shopping will capture a bigger piece of the retail shopping market.

An important spending trend is the increased spending on leisure and entertainment, which reduces spending for retail shopping. This has not been lost on the sellers of entertainment and leisure services, as evidenced by the skyrocketing prices of big concert tours, plays, and unusual vacation packages. For example, concert tour ticket prices in the past few years for acts such as the Eagles, Rage, and Mettalica have ranged from $60 to over $100.

One last trend is affecting large specialty retailers planning to merge with each other: the federal government. The Federal Trade Commission blocked two retail mergers in 1998, one of which was the proposed merger of specialty retailers Office Depot and Staples. This type of intervention has helped keep specialty retailers from monopolizing the niche markets they serve.

STOCK/INVESTMENT OUTLOOK

The investment outlook looks best for those companies focused on specialty retail. The words *specialty retail* seem to imply a small store or chain. If we consider businesses such as Toys "R" Us and Bed Bath and Beyond specialty stores, the picture changes.

The future looks brightest for those companies poised to take advantage of the recent trends including superstores and "category killers." By attempting to stock every item in a certain line of merchandise, superstores/category killers gain the ability to charge low prices. OfficeMax is an example of a category killer in the office supply area. Other examples of category killers include the Toys "R" Us and Circuit City chains.

Those specialty retailers focused on becoming leaders in their category have the best investment outlook. As far as small specialty retailers go, the most successful seem to be serving a new trend or increasing need. Ikea furniture stores, for example, have found a hungry market for reasonably priced stylish furniture, even if the furniture is not built as solid as some might expect from the look of it. This has resulted in an expansion of their chain of retail stores.

POTENTIAL/PROSPECTIVE FOR GROWTH

One advantage specialty retailers will always have is that their fortunes do not necessarily move in step with that of the economy. By definition, a specialty retailer sells products only in specific categories serving niche markets. Therefore, a specialty retailer can make money as long as its niche market is profitable, regardless of the state of the economy as a whole. Likewise, a good economy is not enough to guarantee success for a specialty retailer.

Yet, while a healthy economy tends to help a smaller specialty retailer, the success of most specialty retailers depends heavily on the niche they are serving. Overall, specialty retailing is expanding, as people shop with more focused intent, and choose specialty retailers for their variety and/or value prices.

COMPETITIVE STRUCTURE

Specialty retail stores are normally thought of as the small stores competing for a small piece of the pie, the majority of which is owned by a few large players. While this is certainly true, this can change depending on the definition of what constitutes a specialty retailer. Certainly businesses such as Toys "R" Us, Staples, The Limited, and Radio Shack sell primarily one type of merchandise, yet they are large businesses. Therefore, specialty retailers can appear on both ends of the spectrum with regard to size.

Small specialty retailers can be either a national chain, regional, or local mom-and-pop stores. If a national chain, this is usually because there is a nationwide market for the particular niche products. This usually means there is one or a few large specialty retailers that have the lion's share of the market, which the small specialty retailer is competing against in an oligopolistic setting. An example is the smaller FAO Schwartz stores competing against Toys "R" Us. Smaller retailers generally compete, especially against category killers by focusing on something slightly different from the large category killer they are up against. They may, for exam-

ple, have only high-end or more expensive merchandise. FAO Schwartz, for example, focuses on more expensive and more profitable merchandise, while Sharper Image's toys are geared toward adults.

The large retailers have found that they can only remain on top by never resting on their laurels and carefully following overall retail trends like everyday value pricing, used by Home Depot. Some retailers seem happy to give up the leadership to retain their profitability. Borders Books and Music and Barnes and Noble are examples of bookstore chains that are competing through customer service rather than undercutting each other in prices.

The competitive structure depends on the particular niche market of interest. In general, a few large players capture a large share of the market. The rest of the retailers fight for the remainder, often less than half of the market.

ROLE OF RESEARCH AND DEVELOPMENT

Research and development has an important role in specialty retailing, although not in the traditional sense of R&D. Like all retailers, specialty retailers must research market conditions and keep tabs on the competitors. Unlike general retailers, specialty retailers must pay close attention to trends within their niche. For example, a retailer that only sold typewriters and carbon paper would be in a difficult situation if it did not change once personal computers became popular in the 1980's. General retailers can afford to be slightly behind the trends and still survive, since they do not make their entire living from one small section of the population. All of this is especially true of smaller specialty retailers.

New development is similar. Specialty retailers must develop new concepts and ideas for growth to keep from being passed by or stagnating. Development of faster and cheaper ways to do business is also important. Dell Computers has generated large profits from focusing on fast assembly and delivery methods in the time-sensitive market of home computers. The development in specialty retailing consists of refining the concept and shopping experience of their customers to keep pace with changing demands.

TECHNOLOGICAL INVESTMENT AND ANALYSIS

Specialty retailers are poised to take advantage of technological improvements in different ways. For innovations in areas all retailers face, such as inventory management, specialty retailers let larger, general retailers pay for research. They then apply the general solution to their particular niche markets. This enables specialty retailers, especially the smaller ones, to be quick adopters of technological advancements and improvements. They often apply new technology in innovative and unintended ways to gain competitive advantage over their rivals.

One small high-end men's apparel store in Washington, D.C., uses digital cameras to store pictures of suits that clients purchase. In that way, if an existing client needs to buy a replacement or needs a new shirt to match an already-purchased set of pants, a simple call may be all that is needed. The salesperson will pull up the picture in the computer of previous purchases and make suggestions and recommendations. General retail innovations such as EDI or Internet shopping have also been quickly adopted by specialty retailers.

The Internet seems to be an especially powerful tool for specialty retailers. A specialty retailer no longer needs a store or catalog to present itself professionally to customers. It can exist solely on the Internet. The Internet enables customers from all over the world to shop at the store. New information technology helps stores reduce and control costs and can provide key information about the business. The use of point-of-sale data can tell retailers quickly what is selling and what is not, enabling a faster response to market demands.

RECOMMENDATION FOR THE FUTURE

Specialty retailers must keep abreast of the latest trends in the general economy, in retailing, and, most importantly, in their niche. They must exploit improvements in technology to keep pace with their nimble competitors. Even large specialty retailers have small competitors that could turn operations around quickly. A more targeted and dedicated marketing approach seems to be the next trend in retail marketing. Standard and Poor's sees improvements in store design, customer service, merchandise quality, and technology as trends that will continue to influence this industry.

Some of these trends are already occurring, with suggestions for more merchandise coming from sales-clerks based on customers' previous purchases and demographics. With the Internet and the lack of time to shop, specialty retailers will have to work hard to keep customers. Location will become important again. Stores should be prepared to provide merchandise to customers or offer to deliver the merchandise if it is not available. Only increased service like this will maintain high margins and highly profitable customers.

INDUSTRY WEB SITES

Retail Sales Industry
   www.ey.com/home.asp
   www.ac.com/

BEN & JERRY'S

Executive Summary

Case Name:	Ben & Jerry's
Case Industry:	Frozen dessert/dairy products
Major Technology Issue:	Keep their operations as efficient as possible through the use of technology and maintaining a captivating web site
Major Financial Issue:	Keep their profits growing
Major Strategic Issue:	Maintain balance between good corporate citizenship and maximizing profits
Major Players/Leaders:	Robert Holland (CEO, 1998–1999), Perry Odak (CEO, 1999–), Ben Cohen, Jerry Greenfield
Main Web Page:	www.benjerry.com/
Case Conclusion/Recommendation:	B&J should concentrate on gaining market share and building brand awareness and loyalty. Regarding technology, B&J should concentrate on web site development and database marketing.

CASE ANALYSIS

INTRODUCTORY STORY

Ben & Jerry's beginnings can be traced back to a $5 correspondence course in ice cream making taken by friends Ben Cohen and Jerry Greenfield. Ben and Jerry grew up together in Merrick, New York. In 1978 Ben and Jerry gathered $12,000, $4,000 of which was borrowed, and opened an ice cream shop in a renovated gas station in Burlington, Vermont. The shop featured an antique rock-salt ice cream freezer and used a Volkswagen for deliveries. The shop soon became popular for its innovative flavors and ice cream using fresh Vermont milk and cream. Ben & Jerry's has grown into a $140 million powerhouse rivaled only by Haagen-Dazs in the super premium ice cream category.[1]

A sample of Ben & Jerry's innovation came with the "Yo! I'm Your CEO!" contest held in 1994 to find new leadership to take Ben & Jerry's out of its troubles of flat sales, lowered profits, and shrinking market price. The contest entailed writing a 100-word essay on "Why I Would Be a Great CEO for Ben & Jerry's." The winner would get to run the company, the runner-up would get a lifetime supply of Ben & Jerry's ice cream, and losers would get a rejection letter "suitable for framing." While the actual resulting CEO, Robert Hol-

land, did not participate in the contest until after he got the job, he did eventually write a 100-word poem.

SHORT DESCRIPTION OF THE COMPANY

Ben & Jerry's very distinct business philosophy stemmed from the shared ideals of its founders. From the beginning, Ben and Jerry believed that companies have a responsibility to do good for society, not just for the company. Formulated in 1988, the three-part mission statement personifies Ben & Jerry's dedication to a new corporate concept of linked prosperity.

Product Mission: To make, distribute, and sell the finest quality, all-natural ice cream and related products in a wide variety of innovative flavors made from Vermont dairy products.

Social Mission: To operate the company in a way that actively recognizes the central role that business plays in the structure of society by initiating innovative ways to improve the quality of life of a broad community—local, national, and international.

Economic Mission: To operate the company on a sound financial basis of profitable growth, increasing value for our shareholders, and creating career opportunities and financial rewards for our employees.[2]

---

[1] http://www.benjerry.com/co-index.html

[2] http://www.benjerry.com/mission.html

SHORT HISTORY OF THE COMPANY

Ben & Jerry's Homemade, Inc., is a publicly held corporation that was founded in 1978 by charismatic visionaries Ben Cohen and Jerry Greenfield. The corporation, headquartered in Burlington, Vermont, produces a plethora of frozen yogurt treats and ice cream novelties in traditional and unique flavors. The corporation currently competes in the dairy industry.

Ben & Jerry's markets its products through supermarkets, grocery stores, convenience stores, and food service operations. Ben & Jerry's has also established numerous "scoop shops" that are either licensed, franchised, or company owned. The corporation distributes over 50 products in all 50 states as well as international locations. Ben & Jerry's currently distributes and sells in Canada, Israel, and Europe.

Although a majority of Ben & Jerry's success can be attributed to their array of innovative flavors made with the freshest Vermont milk and cream, some individuals argue that the company's idealistic business philosophy has equally contributed to its success. Ben & Jerry's Homemade, Inc., operates in a socially conscious manner where the cofounders' values influence the corporate mission statement and strategy.

Among publicly held companies, Ben & Jerry's donates the highest percentage of its annual pretax earnings to community organizations and social causes. The company integrates social values into its daily operating activities, which makes it distinct from its competitors.

FINANCIAL AND PORTFOLIO ANALYSIS

Consumers purchased $2.9 billion worth of ice cream in supermarkets in 1997. Ben & Jerry's, focusing exclusively on the super premium ice cream market, continued to show a modest financial performance during the second quarter of 1997. Due to higher dairy costs, which forced the company to increase product prices and the rising demand for healthy, low-fat products, Ben & Jerry's experienced a 10.4 percent decrease in net income in the second quarter of 1997. Net income decreased to $1.7 million from $1.9 million in the second quarter of 1996.

Net sales during the quarter that ended June 28, 1997, increased 5.5 percent to $50.7 million compared to $48.0 million for the same period in 1996 (Table 3.1). The pint and 2.5-gallon container products experienced steady sales growth. The product line that had the highest volume of sales this quarter was the original Ben & Jerry's ice cream line rather than the frozen yogurt or sorbet lines. In previous quarters, low-fat product lines accounted for a higher percentage of volume sales. Total net sales include the sale of pints, 2.5 gallon bulk containers, novelty items, and retail store sales. Pint sales were 84 percent of total net sales, while 8 percent represented bulk container sales. An additional 7 percent of total sales came from the sale of novelty products, and the final remaining 1 percent of total net sales represented the company's retail stores.

Cost of sales in the second quarter of 1997 increased $18,000 or 0.2 percent over the same period in 1996, and overall gross profit was 37.8 percent in the second quarter of 1997 compared to 34.4 percent in the second quarter of 1996. Gross profit increased due to a price increase of 3 percent as well as improved operating efficiencies. During this quarter, the company faced increased dairy costs, which raised product prices. To offset the potential for additional income loss, Ben & Jerry's developed more efficient operating methods. If dairy costs continue to increase, the company will be negatively impacted and gross profit margins will reflect this as well.

Financial analysts recommended that Ben & Jerry's pursue numerous innovative measures to strengthen its financial performance for the third and fourth quarters of 1997. These areas of innovative development included additional promotional activities, creation of international joint ventures, further development of low-fat products, and more efficient manufacturing methods. If Ben & Jerry's properly implemented these strategies, analysts claimed the company would be able to offset increasing dairy costs and cater more to the health-conscious consumer while increasing profit margins at the same time.

Although Ben & Jerry's currently has 39 percent of the $261 million American market for super premium ice cream, sales growth has been slow in the past three years due to super premium ice cream entering the mature stage of the life cycle. To differentiate itself from fierce competition, Ben & Jerry's needs to increase its annual spending according to Kim Galle, an analyst at Adams, Harkeness & Hill. Marketing accounted for 27.2 percent of revenue in 1997. In 1996 it was only 23.5 percent of revenue. Galle proposed that marketing spending should rise to 30 percent in 1998. In the same year, the company ran its first widespread radio advertisements which continue to the present time. Television ads will follow in months to come. Thus, Ben & Jerry's is gradually funneling more revenue into marketing. This is likely to improve its financial performance.

According to Galle, the next step for increasing profitability is overseas expansion. Since market analysts classify ice cream as a mature product in the American market, Ben & Jerry's should anticipate little growth in

Table 3.1 Ben & Jerry's Financial Information

Fiscal Year Ending	12/26/98	12/27/97	12/28/96
Net sales ($000)	209,203	174,206	167,155
Net income ($000)	6,242	3,896	3,926

the United States and pursue international ventures. Competition still exists overseas from rival competitor Haagen-Dazs, which currently has international marketing and distribution advantages over Ben & Jerry's. Ben & Jerry's originally pursued international operations in 1986 in Israel. In 1992 the company set up a joint venture known as Iceverk in Russia. Unfortunately, this relationship ended in 1996. Although the company failed on this first joint venture attempt, Ben & Jerry's remains optimistic and realizes it must continue to enter new, emerging markets to increase the demand for super premium ice cream products.[3]

Due to changing consumption habits and lifestyle trends, Ben & Jerry's positioned itself as a leader in serving the health-conscious consumer in 1992 with the development of the low-fat frozen yogurt product. Analysts believe as the baby boomer population continues to age and become more health conscious, the industry should scramble to provide low-fat alternatives to satisfy their demands.

Because dairy costs have been increasing steadily, Ben & Jerry's has dealt with these costs by raising the prices of its products roughly 3 percent per year. According to analysts, the price increase has not had a dramatic impact on financial performance since the company chose to increase manufacturing efficiency by more than 50 percent during the same period. The company's St. Albans plant runs at 50 percent of capacity. This excess capacity situation provides Ben & Jerry's with the opportunity to co-pack other brands of ice cream with the remaining capacity. For example, Dreyer's ice cream recently stated that the company will have to arrange manufacturing facilities beyond their current plants. This presents an opportunity to companies with excess capacity, like Ben & Jerry's.

Numerous development alternatives are available for Ben & Jerry's to explore. The proposal most recommended by analysts to improve long-term financial performance is to focus on increasing market share and income growth in a mature industry. The ice cream industry has entered the mature stage of the product life cycle. This is evident from an examination of the net sales growth. Growth has been minimal within the industry since 1993, only fluctuating between one percentage point during the past three years. Since the product is mature, the only way for competitors to differentiate themselves is through continued promotional activities, which Galle claims will continue to be the trend.

Although the topic may be controversial in nature, several analysts believe Ben & Jerry's could reduce ad-

ditional administrative costs and increase net income by reducing the 7.5 percent of its annual pretax earnings which the company donates each year to charitable causes. Some analysts believe this donation is actually an expensive "cost" to the company and should be reduced if Ben & Jerry's wants to remain profitable in years to come. Additional funding from this reduced contribution could be spent on marketing to increase market share.

STOCK/INVESTMENT OUTLOOK

Ben & Jerry's went public in May 1984 by offering 73,500 shares of stock as an intrastate offering in Vermont at the rate of $10.50 per share. It was not until 1985 that the company issued 50,000 shares of stock as an initial public offering across the country for $13 per share. The company's stocks are traded on the NASDAQ exchange; the company's stock symbol is BJICA. Originally, individuals could only purchase Class A stocks through broker assistance.

In 1987, Ben & Jerry's began to sell Class B stock. The company purposely issued this stock to increase company strength, preventing any risks of takeovers. Ben & Jerry's has continued to operate with two classes of stock. The class A stocks are the only publicly traded ones since the Class B stocks are convertible, nontransferable stock.

The last significant stock activities took place in 1992 when Ben & Jerry's announced a 2-for-1 stock split. Within the same year, the company had another stock offering for 1,100,000 shares at $30.50 a share. At this time, there are over 11,000 shareholders; a majority of those shareholders are Vermont residents. Employees are able to purchase stock through a company plan.

By examining past stock performance of Ben & Jerry's combined with future financial expectations, analysts can make predictions as to the future price of a company's stock. For example, analyst Alex Taylor believes that the company reached a record high of $32 per share in August 1992 and will continue trading at a moderate level of $13 or less per share since Ben & Jerry's anticipates future losses due to the maturity of the product. During 1997, the company's stock ranged in price from $10.88 to $14.75. According to Zack's Investment Research, brokers continue to recommend the stock as either a moderate buy or moderate sell. Cash dividends have not been declared or paid to stockholders since the company's formation. The company reinvests earnings to ensure future growth.[4]

Ben & Jerry's was recently marked as a cautious buy by most investment managers. This is denoted in its 1.2

---

[3] Van Horten, Ben, "Harvest Time: As Chains Continue to Cultivate International Fields, They're Finding a Market," *Restaurant Business*, August 15, 1997, v. 96, n. 16, p. 71.

[4] "Ben & Jerry's Homemade, Inc. Announces 1999 Second Quarter Results," *PR Newswire*, July 19, 1999, p. 4529.

beta, which identifies it as a risky investment. At this time, investment managers are weary of the food processing industry as a whole. The industry has been above the S&P 500 index for quite some time. This trend, however, is not likely to continue in this heavily competitive industry.

RISK ANALYSIS

Future financial performance for Ben & Jerry's depends on a number of factors. The evaluation of the company's risk factors must include areas of business activity that could have the most adverse impact on long-term financial performance. According to *Moody's Investor Report* as well as top company officials, Ben & Jerry's must improve its efforts to eliminate risks in the areas of distribution, new product development, competition, raw materials, personnel, and charitable contributions.

Ben & Jerry's annual report has identified the company's primary risk to be the competition the company faces from independent ice cream distributors. The company continues to remain dependent on these distributors. These independent ice cream distributors act as primary distributors in assigned territories. Analysts believe that if relationships are poor, the company will be impacted financially since the loss of one or more distributor agreements could adversely impact Ben & Jerry's distribution strategy.

The next area of concern is product development. Ben & Jerry's must continue to rapidly introduce innovative product flavors on a regular basis to maintain its level of sales growth. In 1996, net sales were $167 million compared to $155 million in 1995. Thus, net sales increased 7.6 percent. Although sales in the super premium ice cream, frozen yogurt, and sorbet categories were stagnant, the company was still able to increase total net sales due to efficient production techniques and the ability to distribute new flavors. If Ben & Jerry's loses this strength, the company could experience a downturn in net sales.

By introducing innovative flavors and bringing them to the market quickly, Ben & Jerry's has gained a competitive advantage over other ice cream manufacturers. However, competition within the super premium frozen dessert market remains intense. Ben & Jerry's primary competitors such as Haagen-Dazs, Dreyer's, and Dannon are highly diversified and large in size. These companies have access to a greater pool of financial resources for marketing expenditures, distribution, and new product development.

Ben & Jerry's manufactures ice cream in three plants located in Vermont. The company's small size could have an adverse impact on performance since Ben & Jerry's must compete with larger companies for distribution and shelf space in retail food stores.

Although ongoing competition poses a financial threat to Ben & Jerry's, internal issues can also disrupt financial performance. The company relies on direction from top officials within the company. These include the chief executive officer, Perry Odak, chairperson of the Board and cofounder, Ben Cohen, and vice chairperson and cofounder, Jerry Greenfield.

Finally, Ben & Jerry's is considered an industry leader because of its ability to combine product innovation, profitability, and social consciousness into its company's mission statement. Ben & Jerry's was founded to serve the whole community through its socially conscious business philosophy. Although the company's charitable contributions have been generous during the past years, analysts fear that the company could soon run out of financial resources and energies to fund such causes. This could impact future profitability.

INDUSTRY AND MARKET ANALYSIS

Since Ben & Jerry's produces super premium ice cream, frozen yogurt, and sorbet, the company operates in the frozen dessert industry. Unfortunately, this industry experienced a 2.8 percent decline in unit sales in 1998, compared to 1997. Unit sales were $108 million. Private label ice cream was down 3.3 percent to 28.3 million units, while major public ice cream companies such as Ben & Jerry's and Dreyer's rose 30 percent in unit sales. Frozen yogurt experienced a 10 percent decline in sales.

Ben & Jerry's competes primarily against premium and super premium ice cream manufacturers in the frozen dessert industry. The company faces competition from both category sectors since there is little distinction between the super premium and premium brands of ice cream. The only distinctions are the richness of the ice cream and the price. Haagen-Dazs is still the principal competitor. Other major competitors include Dannon, Columbo, and Healthy Choice. Although there are numerous competitors including regional companies, Ben & Jerry's has targeted its marketing efforts on these companies. Increased competition and limited shelf space have introduced many barriers to entry for new entrants. The likelihood for success is minimal when entering this industry. Ben & Jerry's claims its competitive success factor has been its ability to develop new flavors and low-fat products on a regular basis to satisfy consumer demand.

In response to the demand for low-fat frozen dessert products, Ben & Jerry's developed its own line of low-fat frozen yogurt in 1992. Industry experts expect competition to remain strong in future years since proper distribution is difficult to obtain. In order for companies to maintain market share, they must increase promotional activities, especially in the premium and super premium categories. Since frozen dessert products are already in the maturity stage of the product life cycle, the potential for growth is minimal.

Although companies within the frozen dessert industry must remain aware of competitors' activities, they must also meet governmental regulations. Ben & Jerry's is subject to regulation by numerous governmental agencies, including the U.S. Food and Drug Administration and the Vermont Department of Agriculture. Companies also need to receive licenses from the states where the ice cream products are sold. New laws require additional labeling for low-fat products and other healthy foods. After the criteria were set, Ben & Jerry's had to make appropriate changes on its labels as well. Industry experts do not feel the FDA's stringent labeling requirements will have a significant negative financial impact on the frozen dessert industry.

Companies within this industry must also implement technological developments. Currently, companies including Ben & Jerry's are using advanced manufacturing systems for mixing and packing that require constant monitoring. Electronic communication systems are required. Ben & Jerry's has taken this idea one step further by implementing a "user-centered" manufacturing system that enables employees to remain up to date on all procedural steps that take place from start to finish. Major ice cream producers such as Haagen-Dazs and Dreyer's emphasize efficiency and improved productivity within their information systems. According to industry experts, companies must continue to implement systems to improve internal communication flow.

To remain competitive within this industry, ice cream manufacturers such as Ben & Jerry's must invest additional earnings in research and development of international ventures. Although the company has established outlets in Canada, Israel, and the United Kingdom, Ben & Jerry's formed a specific team to expedite the expansion process. Additional joint ventures overseas could provide growth for companies in this industry as well. Joint ventures provide low-cost methods to participate in international markets and require less capital investment. An ice cream manufacturer must also expand its distribution channels to differentiate itself among competitors.

Consumers' changing demands regarding food consumption also impact this industry. Standard & Poor's analysts claim that demographic changes such as an aging baby boomer population with increasingly healthy lifestyle preferences will force the industry to provide low-fat alternatives. As one analyst stated, the baby boomer generation's tastes have changed. However, Ben & Jerry's continues to target them with their premier, fattening product lines due to the products' expensive pricing strategy.

The super premium ice cream manufacturers will face additional competition from the premium sector as well. Competition did not exist among different categories in the past. Premium competitors such as Breyer's, which is owned by Unilever, and Dreyer's, which is partly owned by Nestle, are beginning to compete against super premium manufacturers, even though each category still uses different pricing strategies to market its products. Ben & Jerry's has a major disadvantage against these competitors since they are large, diversified multinational companies with numerous resources. Companies such as Dreyer's and Haagen-Dazs have greater market share in foreign countries than Ben & Jerry's. Although Ben & Jerry's claims that its primary competitive factor is the introduction of "innovative flavors on a periodic basis," the question remains whether this strategy will enable the company to maintain higher market share.

Given the outlook of the industry, Ben & Jerry's must set its course carefully to remain competitive in a maturing product marketplace.

ROLE OF RESEARCH AND DEVELOPMENT

According to Keynote's *Frozen Foods Market Report*, growth within the super premium ice cream category has always been driven by the introduction of new products. This is especially the case at Ben & Jerry's. Ben & Jerry's product menu includes over 50 different frozen items. Of these, 34 are packaged in pints and distributed through grocery stores.

The remainder of the products are distributed through the company's franchised "Scoop Shops" and restaurants. Since the company offers such a diverse product selection, Ben & Jerry's must invest heavily in the constant introduction of new flavors to satisfy customer demand and market trends.[5]

TECHNOLOGICAL STORY

Ben & Jerry's research and development process requires ample creativity and time, according to Peter Lind, the director of research and development at the company. Unfortunately, Lind claims the process does not take place overnight but rather requires the development of numerous prototypes before the proper flavor is developed. For example, 100 prototypes of the Cookie Dough flavor were developed and 500 prototypes of the Wavy Gravy flavor were tested before the appropriate flavor was selected. Lind's job is to "reinterpret classic dessert recipes" and reformulate them for ice cream. New "ice cream therapists" were recently added to Lind's department to facilitate the process. He admits that a majority of the department conducts "little research" yet engages mostly in new product development.

[5] Brown, Ed, "I Scream, You Scream—Saaay, Nice Carton!" *Fortune*, October 26, 1998, p. 60(1).

The ideas for ice cream flavor combinations often originate from conversations with customers, suppliers, management, and the marketplace. These unique combinations are profitable since Ben & Jerry's markets and distributes its products through the super premium sector. This category targets ice cream risk-takers who enjoy new tastes for adventure. The use of unusual flavor combinations is a critical success factor for Ben & Jerry's and enables the company to maintain its 28.7 percent market share against such competitors as Haagen-Dazs. The research and development process involved in getting these flavors to market requires more than just a simple recipe.

According to Lind, the company's Cookie Dough flavor was originally placed manually into vanilla ice cream before the company devised a way to automate the process for packing pints. It took the company four years to automate this process. Ben & Jerry's accomplished a quick return on the investment in this flavor since the company accomplished $23 million in sales with this product alone in its first year.

TECHNOLOGICAL INVESTMENT AND ANALYSIS

Ben & Jerry's currently utilizes technology in the following areas: customer database management, manufacturing, web site development, and multimedia. These areas drive the company's growth and require the most investment.

Customer database management has been a tool for satisfying customer needs and demands. The company currently uses its database to discover customer reaction to new product ideas and to involve customers in social concerns. According to cofounder Jerry Greenfield, "We use this database when we want to introduce new ideas and test new products."

Most of the database records are collected from the 100 franchised Scoop Shops that send in the names of people who want to be placed on Ben & Jerry's mailing list. This database is set up on a Macintosh system. By being placed on the mailing list, customers are sent catalogs and newsworthy updates on company happenings. Greenfield claims that the customer database builds relationships between the people and products.[6]

Within the area of manufacturing, Ben & Jerry's focused on a flexible, "user-centered" system which emphasizes efficiency and productivity. The system automates the production and storage process and connects or links the system with the business planning and control system. The benefits of this system include "product consistency, waste reduction, accurate reporting, quality improvement, and flexibility."

---

[6] Chheda, Tanvi, "Ice Cream Intelligence," *Information Week*, August 2, 1999, p. 14.

The new plant in St. Alban's, Vermont, was specifically designed for this type of manufacturing process. Factory workers control the flow process with a system that provides flexibility. Ben & Jerry's defines flexibility as the ability to change quickly to different product mixtures. As Jim Parshall, a systems engineer at Ben & Jerry's states, " We can actually run a vanilla-based ice cream mix followed by a chocolate one."

Although everyone is placed in operating teams, individual workers control the process by communicating with each other. Ben & Jerry's considers the operators within the plant to be the actual "users" of this system. This is why the company continues to claim it has a "user-centered manufacturing" system. Manufacturing is now broken down into "chunks" such as mix making, filling, and packaging. Each section operates independently, yet everyone communicates with one another and makes decisions through a process control architecture system based upon Allen Bradley PLC-5/20s, 5/40s, and Ethernet-compatible products.

TECHNOLOGICAL INNOVATIONS

NETWORKS

The Allen Bradley message protocol enables mix operators to immediately inform fill room operators regarding the type of mixes available. Another message can then be sent to the mix room to tell them how many gallons of the specific mix the operator decided to send. This message is confirmed and the action is executed.

The system architecture enables employees to exchange and analyze data. Company engineers and designers share product development information and constantly evaluate progress. The systems architecture also offers pattern recognition and process learning. If employees spot inefficient trends during the manufacturing process, proper adjustments can be made that are more effective for the company.

The company has integrated Macintosh computers with the PLC system since engineers believe Macintosh is also a user-centered company. Parshall claims, "Macintosh provides the best solution to our needs." Thus, the company will continue to use Macintosh for its supervisory system platform in the near future.

INTERNET

Although the manufacturing process is constantly being updated to improve efficiency, Ben & Jerry's also invests effort in web site development. The web site is an area of continuous technological growth and investment. The company's current web site, www.benjerry.com, features an interactive page with an animated tour guide helping visitors the site to answer their questions.

Unfortunately, according to Joe Wilkins, Ben & Jerry's World Wide Web director, the animation took minutes to download over typical telephone lines and thus discouraged visitors. To address this issue, Ben & Jerry's sought assistance from technological experts. Narrative Communications Corporation provided the company with an Enliven product suite. This suite package enabled users to quickly deliver large volumes of multimedia material over phone lines and modems.[7]

The Enliven suite has three main features: a client-side Netscape Communications plug-in viewer, a postproduction tool for importing material from multimedia development products, and the server software. The most important feature of the suite is, of course, the software package, which works with the web server to deliver the animation to the computers. The software requires Windows/NT and a web server. Wilkins believes Narrative has drastically improved the company's web site efforts. "Narrative has taken a process that was painfully slow and made it much more efficient."

Web site development is not the only area of technological advancement for Ben & Jerry's. The company is equally focused on the expanded use of multimedia applications in its day-to-day operations. Ben & Jerry's is specifically utilizing the videoconferencing element of multimedia. The company believes in close teamwork and practices Japanese-style management with employees. Since most employees are geographically scattered, videoconferencing provides a way for the company to build "tighter-than-ever" interaction.[8]

The videoconferences take place every other week to encourage the team communications concept and to help Ben & Jerry's socially conscious reputation by cutting down on automobile contaminants. Through videoconferencing technology, the company has linked its office/plant location in Waterbury, Vermont, to its plant in Springfield, Vermont. Within the next year, the company is considering using the videoconferencing system in all of its plants, three ice cream stores, a distribution center, and a few nationwide sales offices. Ben & Jerry's is currently using 728 kbit/second of a dedicated T1 line between sites for video since there are no switched data services in Vermont. The company invested $140,000 for the two end systems and spends $2,000 per month for T1 services.

RECOMMENDATION FOR THE FUTURE

Since Ben & Jerry's manufactures products in the mature stage of the product life cycle, the company should now focus on strengthened market share and building brand loyalty. Ben & Jerry's super premium ice cream product already has a committed customer base. The company will only gain new customers if consumers choose to switch super premium brands. In this stage of the product life cycle, emphasis must be placed upon building brand loyalty and customer satisfaction through the use of technology.

The company can build this loyalty through the effective use of web site development and database marketing. Although Ben & Jerry's recently updated its web site and increased the access speed, the company could further develop this site by including more online surveys that emphasize the importance of customer feedback. The question section should be prominently displayed in the table of contents, encouraging consumers to interact with the company. These questions also need to be answered promptly since consumers have complained of long delays for responses from Ben & Jerry's web page.[9]

Although graphic images add aesthetic quality to the web pages, a majority of these images are not needed and take too much time to download, slowing the process of retrieving the web pages. Although the company has attempted to improve the speed problem, the web site images still frustrate users.

Customer databases also need further emphasis and development. Ben & Jerry's is applying these databases to gather customer feedback and to introduce them to social concerns and volunteer organizations. Although these are major concerns for the company, customer feedback should be heard and recorded in other areas as well. Customers can be relied upon to recommend new flavors, additional channels of distribution, international opportunities, and new growth opportunities.

In addition to Scoop Shops, the company should obtain records from distribution channels, such as grocery stores and restaurants where customers purchase the products. Ben & Jerry's needs to develop a point-of-purchase display or sweepstakes where customers must send in additional information to obtain prizes or coupons. By collecting this information in customer databases, the company can distribute direct mail and newsletters more effectively.

Ben & Jerry's must continue to focus on the customer first, with a clear understanding of the importance of customer feedback and the use of technology to utilize it appropriately.

---

[7] Cole-Gomolski, Barb, "Ben & Jerry's: Serve Yourselves on Site," *Computerworld*, March 8, 1999, p. 20(1).
[8] Ibid.

[9] Ibid.

CASE QUESTIONS

Strategic Questions

1. What is the strategic direction of Ben & Jerry's?

2. Who or what forces are driving this direction?

3. What has been the catalyst for change?

4. What are the critical success factors for this corporation/organization?

5. What are the core competencies for this corporation/organization?

Technological Questions

6. What technologies has the corporation relied on?

7. What has caused a change in the use of technology in the corporation/organization?

8. How has this change been implemented?

9. Who has driven this change throughout the organization?

10. How successful has the technological change been?

Quantitative Questions

11. What does the corporation say about its financial ability to embark on a major technological program of advancement?

12. What conclusions can be reached from an analysis of the financial information to support or contradict this financial ability?

13. What analysis can be made by examining the following ratio groups?

    Quick/Current
    Debt
    Revenue
    Profit
    Asset Utilization

14. What conclusions can be reached by analyzing the financial trends? Are there long-term trends that seem to be problematic? Is the industry stable? Are there replacement products?

Internet Questions

15. What does the corporation's web page present about their business directives?

16. How does this compare to the description given in the case?

17. How does this compare to the conclusions reached by analyzing the financial information?

Industry Questions

18. What challenges and opportunities is the industry facing?

19. Is the industry oligopolistic or competitive?

20. Does the industry face a change in government regulation?

21. How will technology impact the industry?

Data Questions

22. What role do data play in the future of the corporation?

23. How important are data to the corporation's continued success?

24. How will the capture and maintenance of customer data impact the corporation's future?

THE GAP INC.

Executive Summary

Case Name:	The Gap, Inc.
Case Industry:	Specialty retail
Major Technology Issue:	Utilizing the new COBRA information system effectively
Major Financial Issue:	Increasing sales
Major Strategic Issue:	Differentiating The Gap from its competitors and furthering the Gap brand
Major Players/Leaders:	Donald Fisher, founder; Mickey Drexler, current president
Main Web Page:	www.gap.com
Case Conclusion/Recommendation:	The Gap must continue to experiment with its Internet presence. The Gap must explore the possibility of issuing its own credit cards to gather customer data.

CASE ANALYSIS

INTRODUCTORY STORY

Shopping can mean crowded malls, outrageous lines, and poorly stocked merchandise. Even when a salesperson attempts to locate the correct size or color at another store one can become discouraged and lose the impulse to buy. As competition remains high in the clothing industry, many retailers are turning to more innovative methods to attract customers. They need the technological ability to handle these increased customer demands.

SHORT DESCRIPTION OF THE COMPANY

All three of The Gap's main divisions—The Gap, Banana Republic, and Old Navy— have annual sales of more than $1 billion each. The Gap stores lead the way with $6 billion in annual sales. To keep this growth moving forward, The Gap built between 400 and 470 new stores in fiscal 1999, while remodeling and expanding at least 100. Half of the new stores were Gap brand stores in the United States, about 40 were new Banana Republics, and about 130 were Old Navy outlets. During 1999, The Gap also built 80 to 100 new Gap International stores. This occurred most notably in Japan, where the company doubled the number of stores from 30 to 60.

According to The Gap's 10-K, 1999's advertising budget was $550 million, more than half the company's $1 billion capital budget and up from $419 million in 1998. In 1997 The Gap spent just $175 million on advertising. Much of this advertising is the campy Old Navy and dancing Gap khaki campaigns.

Since 1995, Millard S. Drexler has been the hands-on CEO of The Gap, Inc. No detail from window displays to fabric blends escapes his attention. Every week, Drexler strolls anonymously into Gap stores from coast to coast to schmooze with customers and clerks in a constant drive to improve the company's products and services.

Drexler feels The Gap is limited only by its imagination. He has developed distinct identities for The Gap, Banana Republic, and Old Navy brands in a cluttered marketplace. Memorable TV ads include "jump and jive" dancers for The Gap and zany spots for Old Navy. This approach has enabled The Gap to soar, reversing the flat performance of the early 1990s when other retailers struggled. Due to strong showings in all of its divisions, The Gap earned $775 million, up 45 percent from 1997, on revenues of $8.8 billion in 1998.

Many experts say The Gap is one of the most popular shopping sites around. During the 1992 recession, annual gains in apparel spending dropped from about 6 percent pre-recession to less than 2 percent during the recession. The Gap, however, not only succeeded, it accelerated. Comparative sales, sales growth, and earnings all accelerated during this period.[1]

While the company will fill in existing markets, most growth will be in secondary and smaller market areas. Several hundred new store opportunities for both The

---

[1] Gallagher, Leigh, "Rebound," *Forbes*, May 3, 1999, p. 60(1).

Gap and Old Navy exist in small markets across the United States. These include cities like Lawrence, Kansas, Tupelo, Mississippi, Gainesville, Florida, Coraville, Iowa, College Station, Texas, and Billings, Montana. Innovative marketing concepts, including opening 20 flagship stores also occurred in 1999. For The Gap, the flagships are actually very profitable. According to the company, they are not loss-making marketing exercises, they are profit-making marketing exercises.[2]

The Gap controls only 3.5 percent of apparel market share in the United States and less than 0.2 percent of the apparel market share in the five international markets.

Short History of the Company

An example of rapid growth can be seen in The Gap, Inc. Donald Fisher, founder, began this jeans-only store in 1969. From the beginning it was clear he understood the market. The company's name is an allusion to the "generation gap." The idea to open a store came from a bad shopping experience, when Fisher tried to exchange a pair of blue jeans. The store's strategic focus was to be well-organized, well-stocked, and easy-to-shop.

By 1974, The Gap expanded so rapidly that it developed its own private-label clothing and accessories. Mickey Drexler became Gap president in 1983. He decided that to continue growth the company needed to broaden its target market. To meet the needs of different customer spending preferences, The Gap introduced Banana Republic and, later, Old Navy.[3] Banana Republic caters to a higher spending customer by offering more classically-styled, higher-quality clothing. Old Navy is a more trendy, value-priced version of The Gap.[4]

In 1986, to expand The Gap brand, Gap entered a then untapped market by opening Gap Kids. In 1990 The Gap extended the brand again with the introduction of Baby Gap. The Gap also expanded internationally, opening stores in the United Kingdom, Canada, France, Germany, and Japan. Private-label clothing sales increased so greatly that, in 1991, Gap announced that everything they sold would be under The Gap label.[5]

Taking cues from Nike, McDonald's, and Coca-Cola, Mickey Drexler implemented a strategy that changed The Gap from a jeans and T-shirt seller into a successful and influential retailer. Drexler decided to market The Gap as a brand rather than just a retail store. Eventually, The Gap's merchandise may be found at other retail stores.[6]

There are clear reasons why sales have soared from $480 million in 1983 to $5.3 billion in 1996. Sales have steadily increased from 1992 to 1996. This can be attributed to Drexler's ability to reach new market segments.

Most Gap products are designed, sourced, inspected, shipped, distributed, displayed, advertised, and sold under the supervision of Gap employees. In other words, The Gap has chosen a vertically integrated structure for its products to ensure quality, uniformity, and loyalty for each brand. This is a core competency for The Gap.[7]

A critical success factor for The Gap is the ability to produce innovative products and to market them well. The Gap must also address new markets with Gap products. It continues to expand by adding new stores domestically as well as internationally. New products such as Gap perfume or Gap sunglasses keep The Gap's product line growing.[8]

Due to its rapid growth, it has become increasingly important to build the best supporting technology. The Gap has restructured its information technology systems to handle this expansion. The emergence of the World Wide Web has provided The Gap with a new method for advertising and selling. The Gap's innovative web page provides the added convenience of online shopping.[9]

The recent introduction of online shopping has put The Gap's products at the fingertips of anyone with a PC and access to the Internet (www.gap.com). Customers are able to shop 24 hours a day, every day of the week. The Gap may encounter difficulties closing a sale because an actual "salesperson" is not there to "sell" the product. It is important to attract the impulse buyer. From a security standpoint, even though credit card numbers are encrypted during transmittal, it could be hard to convince a technologically leery customer of the safety of online shopping.[10]

The Old Navy stores are in the growth stage. They target families and value-oriented customers, but still provide style and quality in their products. In The

---

[2] Moltenbrey, Karen, "Setting up Shop," *Computer Graphics World*, May 1999, v. 22, i. 5, p. 56(1).

[3] Munk, Nina, "Gap Gets It," *Fortune*, August 3, 1998, v. 138, n. 3, p. 68(11).

[4] "The Forbes 400: The Richest People in America," *Forbes*, October 12, 1998, v. 162, n. 8, p. 280(50).

[5] Goldstein, Lauren, "Urban Wear Goes Suburban: As More and More White Kids Want to Dress Like Black Kids, 'urban' Fashion is Spreading from Watts to Wichita," Fortune, December 21, 1998, p. 169(1).

[6] Ibid.

[7] Moltenbrey, Karen, "Setting up Shop," *Computer Graphics World*, May 1999, v. 22, i. 5, p. 56(1).

[8] "How Levi's Trashed a Great American Brand," *Fortune*, April 12, 1999, v. 139, i. 7, p. 82(1).

[9] Amer, Suzie, Bianchi, Alessandra, Donahue, Sean, Ginsburg, Steven, Jeffers, Michelle, Patterson, Lee, and Pickering, Carol, "America's Best Technology Users," *Forbes*, August 24, 1998, v. 162, n. 4, p. S63(20).

[10] Hamel, Gary, and Sampler, Jeff, "The E-Corporation," *Fortune*, December 7, 1998, p. 80(1).

Gap's quarterly report from August 1997, they reported a strong performance from the men's segment of Old Navy, particularly cargo pants. Across all divisions, sweaters, knit tops, and men's basics (khaki and denim) have been big selling items.

Gap jeans have been viewed by customers to be dependable, high-quality products. The Gap's motto is to provide anyone with jeans that are the right size, style, and color. The jeans market may have reached a degree of maturity. A particular threat is the emergence of Levi's jeans that can be customized for an individual. Unless The Gap can compete with Levi's in pricing, Gap could lose its grip on this "cash cow."

FINANCIAL AND PORTFOLIO ANALYSIS

The cost and pricing structure of The Gap, Inc., varies among the three divisions of Banana Republic, The Gap, and Old Navy. All three offer different product lines, catering to different tastes and spending preferences. Banana Republic focuses on products that are higher in quality and price. The Gap is considered to have quality merchandise, but focuses on lower costs. It provides sales and discounts to move excess inventory. Old Navy targets the more cost-conscious buyer but provides quality comparable to the price paid. Old Navy also discounts its overstocked inventory.

As of August 15, 1997, The Gap Inc., experienced a 20 percent sales gain through intensified marketing efforts. This produced a 5.6 percent earnings gain in the second quarter. In the quarter ending August 2, 1997, earnings rose to $69.5 million, or 26 cents per share, from $65.8 million, or 23 cents per share in August, 1996. These results topped Wall Street's average estimate of 24 cents per share.

Sales grew to $1.34 billion in 1997 from $1.12 billion in 1996. From 1993–1997, sales increased by 15.5 percent, net income by 21 percent, and earnings per share by 21.6 percent. Mickey Drexler has effectively penetrated and explored new market segments, introduced new technology into the shopping experience, instituted online shopping, and changed the information systems at The Gap.[11]

Because The Gap is a retailer that uses sales or markdowns to sell slow-selling merchandise, gross margins during the fourth quarter of 1997 went down to 34.4 percent from 35.7 percent. Inventory turnover increased from 9.11 to 9.13 in 1997 compared to 1996. Selling, general, and administrative expenses were trimmed to 26.2 from 26.5 percent of sales.[12]

The company told analysts that higher advertising costs were offset by lower bonus accrual. Interest expense waned from $4 million third quarter 1997 down to $1.5 million fourth quarter 1997. Inventories increased 38 percent, during fourth quarter 1997, in an effort to maintain stock for the holiday season.

The company has long-term debt of $500 million. According to Hambrecht & Quist, this debt will be offered to the public, giving the company an opportunity to significantly increase its cash flow.

The future of The Gap is promising due to its innovations in information technology, especially the Internet. The Gap has also proven its ability to identify and develop new markets for its products. The primary areas of risk for The Gap are competition, market saturation, and competitive advantage in online shopping.

As The Gap continues to increase its product line, it is also increasing its advertising and marketing efforts, including national television ads for The Gap, Gap Kids, and Old Navy. According to Thomas Filandro, an analyst at Gerard Klauer Mattison, "The Gap avoided a major difficulty by being extremely disciplined with markdowns." The Gap is making a major push to gain market share, particularly in the men's clothing area. In an effort to avoid market saturation, it has introduced new stores and products frequently enough to maintain a good balance between successes and failures.[13]

Since Internet use is growing so rapidly, The Gap's decision to move toward online shopping was timely. As the success of The Gap's online shopping continues to grow and the financial results are being analyzed, more companies will compete in this area. Because of this, The Gap needs to continually improve its online services to stay at the forefront of its distribution channel.

STOCK / INVESTMENT OUTLOOK

According to Hambrecht & Quist, Gap stock is a recommended buy for investors. August 1997 in-store sales were up by 16 percent. This exceeded expectations of a 5 to 7 percent increase. Revenues during August 1997 also increased by 35 percent to $597 million. The results of The Gap's first back-to-school effort generated the company's first double-digit sales comparison since 1991.

Sales trends are strong in all regions, especially in Chicago, Texas, Boston, and San Francisco. These positive sales reports could lead to higher levels of interest in Gap shares, offering a good opportunity for long-term investment.

---

[11] Munk, Nina, "Gap Gets It," *Fortune*, August 3, 1998, v. 138, n. 3, p. 68(11).

[12] Ibid.

[13] Amer, Suzie, Bianchi, Alessandra, Donahue, Sean, Ginsburg, Steven, Jeffers, Michelle, Patterson, Lee, and Pickering, Carol, "America's Best Technology Users," *Forbes*, August 24, 1998, v. 162, n. 4, p. S63(20).

Three reasons to encourage investment in The Gap, Inc., stock are:

1. The company's new television advertising campaigns should continue to increase awareness of The Gap's brands.
2. The Gap's upcoming $500 million debt offering will give the company a significant cash infusion.
3. Gap's comparable store sales remain high; they increased 8 percent during 1997. According to a company report, reasons for long-term investment would be that The Gap is believed to represent "an excellent large capital growth holding for investors looking to a relatively safe haven in a volatile market environment." The Gap's stock "reflects investors' long-term interest in the company based on the strength of management and the company's strategic position."[14]

RISK ANALYSIS

Outside forces impacting The Gap, Inc.'s success are:

1. Threat of new entrants into the industry. Other retailers are constantly trying to compete with Old Navy, The Gap, and Banana Republic.
2. Bargaining power of buyers. While focusing on its current customers, The Gap must constantly find new ways to entice and develop new customers. From three different price points production costs must be tracked and compared for each level. The Gap must continue to search for what customers want by identifying and meeting their needs.
3. Threat of substitute products or services. In the retail industry, this is probably the biggest issue. Because competition is constant, The Gap must continually improve and develop products that are more desirable than others. The Gap's jean sales may be threatened by the recent popularity of Levi's campaign to make the perfect jeans through customization.
4. Bargaining power of suppliers. When a customer walks into a store to make a purchase, The Gap needs to have the item they want readily available or risk losing the sale. For this reason, price, quality, and delivery schedules are important.
5. Rivalry among existing competitors. Competitors such as Levi Strauss or The Limited may develop a more focused product line or a more effective advertising campaign. Internet presence will be an effective way to reduce competitors' threats and increase The Gap, Inc.'s competitive advantage.[15]

[14] http://www.gapinc.com/performance/annual reports/ annual reports.htm
[15] "Shopping Websites," *Fortune*, November 16, 1998, p. 244(1).

INDUSTRY AND MARKET ANALYSIS

Due to competition in the retail industry, one company's financial gain is often another's decline in income. Major competitors for The Gap, Inc., are The Limited, Inc., and Levi Strauss. Because Levi primarily competes against Gap jeans, it is more effective to compare and analyze The Gap with The Limited. These companies compete on many levels. When each company's five-year summaries are compared, The Gap's financial performance far exceeds The Limited's. For example, The Gap's sales were 8 percent higher, net income was 20 percent higher, and the earnings per share were 14 percent higher. As a result, Gap stock is favored in the industry.

The most glaring growth prospect is the emergence of online shopping. This will enable customers to shop 24 hours a day and provide better product availability. Online sales associates will help the customer coordinate and make the final purchase. This will enable The Gap to sell to customers that cannot or do not like visiting the malls or going to stores. This site can also assist with selecting the proper size and color combination. International sales also will provide The Gap with excellent growth opportunities.

ROLE OF RESEARCH AND DEVELOPMENT

Information technology is important to The Gap because it can provide more accurate and more efficient information for each of its stores. The sooner a manager or salesperson can get information about product availability, shipping information, or customer questions, the more efficiently things will run.

TECHNOLOGICAL STORY

On November 6, 1997, The Gap developed an online presence selling products identical to those in Gap stores. Gap Online is easy to navigate and uses much of the same interface as the corporate web site. Men and women's merchandise is organized by product categories. Virtual Style enables customers to see how different items look together in an outfit. Gap Online can be accessed any time and offers three ways to order: online, fax, or phone. Because credit card numbers are encrypted, safety is ensured. The Gap also offers a toll-free number for ordering if the customer so chooses.

Another feature offered at Gap Online is the Organizer, where customers can store their billing and shipping information as well as the names and addresses of friends and family to whom customers can send gifts. This Organizer provides a personalized gift reminder that will send an e-mail two weeks before a gift-giving date.

Several challenges exist. First, The Gap must develop ways to enhance impulse buys. Second, this feature must be constantly improved as more companies launch their own online sales campaigns. The Gap must be sure it can handle the volume of online shoppers, especially during holiday seasons.

One way The Gap hopes to increase traffic at its web site is by using Personify Inc.'s Real-Time Engine. This enables content and promotions to be dynamically generated and targeted toward specific users. The Gap also installed big screen video monitors and personal computer terminals in one of its San Francisco stores. This enables customers to become more familiar with the Gap Online site.

TECHNOLOGICAL INVESTMENT AND ANALYSIS

To achieve its annual growth rate of 20 percent, The Gap is moving toward an object-oriented architecture for sales force automation. Due to the rapid expansion, The Gap must provide access to the up-to-date information that is scattered across different technologies ranging from IBM legacy mainframes to Windows NT desktops.

The Gap has brought in web-enabling sales, inventory, and shipment information through its use of the Common Object Broker Request Architecture (COBRA). All users now have access to information from the mainframe through web browsers. Visigenic Soft-

ware's version of COBRA is the middleware link to the back-end databases.[16]

Phil Wilkerson, director of technical architecture at The Gap, said, "We knew we needed to get away from mainframes and a two-tier architecture and move toward the web and data warehousing." The information technology department's challenge is to keep its domestic and international chains up to speed with the most current information. The old system used IBM mainframes on the back end, Sun Microsystem Solaris servers in the middle tier, and OS/2 and Windows NT-based desktops.

To make the transition to web-enabled sales, inventory, and shipments, The Gap instituted COBRA, a platform-independent, object-oriented architecture. Java assisted with speed. Wilkerson added, "We have merchants and planners in offices around the world. They need access to purchase order information including styles and order quantity. Because we deal with a variety of suppliers in various locations, they need to be able to get this information wherever they are, whenever they need it. They will now be able to do this from The Gap's mainframe through their browser."

This type of structuring is relatively new in the retail industry. The Gap is applying object-oriented Java-

---

[16] Kroll, Luisa, "Digital Denim," *Forbes*, December 28, 1998, p. 102(1).

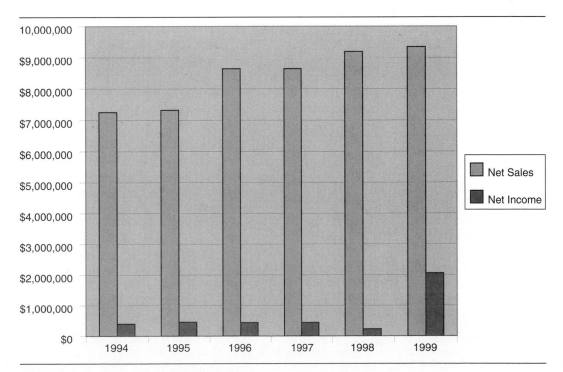

Figure 3.1 Gap, Inc., Financials, 1994–1999.

based applications to search its database more quickly, reducing costs. In using COBRA's object request broker (ORB), users can connect to browsers and access information in various databases. Because the ORB is cross-platform, it can provide information to and from databases, even if the information is on a UNIX machine, a mainframe, or an NT server. Wilkerson explained that without COBRA "users need specific hardware, software and exact protocols to access the kind of information they need. We're trying to sell pants. I've got to get them the information they need to sell pants. Right now, my support costs are up because I have to supply all these people with hardware, software, and networks."

When implementing any technological change, it is important to test the results and efficiencies. To test each of these new pieces, The Gap is using testing tools from Mercury Interactive Corporation to perform stress tests on the hardware, software, and networks. The goal is to make sure all of these pieces work well together.[17]

TECHNOLOGICAL INNOVATIONS

NETWORK

The Gap has reengineered its information systems to provide a stronger infrastructure for its 1,900 retail stores in a process it describes as "metamorphosis." It is not abandoning its Hitachi mainframe, which previously communicated directly with OS/2 workstations. It is isolating the "big iron" from end users and converting it to a DB/2 database server linked to UNIX Sun servers that communicate with Windows NT workstations.

Phil Wilkerson and his 300-person IS team recognized that they would need an effective reporting strategy. The company selected SQRIBE Technologies' SQR products for server-based enterprise reporting. They run the SQR server package on a Sun Solaris machine, where users can obtain web-based reports through the company intranet.

DATA

Wilkerson's team recognized collecting data is not enough. The data must also be available to the people who need it. The easier and more accessible data are, the better use the administrative people can make of the data.[18]

A key part of The Gap's information systems structure is data warehousing. A Hitachi mainframe (run-ning DB/2) handles the transaction processing, but reporting needs to be offloaded. Information Advantage is the key OLAP vendor. A detailed reporting architecture was developed independent of the data warehousing products. It is capable of providing the required reporting services. Part of these requirements include a web-based interface, which provides simplicity of operation and deployment. With over 4,000 workstations, the information systems group at The Gap wants to minimize the software that must be installed on each workstation.

Once the reporting architecture was defined, the search continued to fit products to the role. The same team that finalized the specification was also responsible for the implementation. As Wilkerson describes the concept, "I like to think we're a team of practicing theorists. In other words, yes, we have vision, but we're also practicing reality. A lot of architecture teams just draw pictures and never implement."

INTERNET

Analysts indicate one of the largest internet success stories is The Gap web page, which opened in 1997. The company debuted new sites for its Baby Gap and Gap Kids stores. It launched an ad campaign specifically targeting its online stores. Analysts applaud the way The Gap links its web page to its retail stores.[19] This is in contrast to Barnes and Noble, which delayed using its stores as promotional vehicles because of tax issues. Barnes and Noble did not utilize the core asset they have over Amazon. The Gap, by promoting its online store in its existing stores, is utilizing this linkage well.[20]

The Gap's success has been noted by others, particularly Levi Strauss & Co., which had an online store for jeans and its Dockers brand since November 1998.

RECOMMENDATION FOR THE FUTURE

Using COBRA and Java, The Gap could offer their own credit cards, much like The Limited does. This would enable them to measure what items are selling well and to whom. This will help The Gap track inventory problems and reduce overstocks.

The Gap should become innovative with Internet applications. A good start was the launch of the world's first online scent, Gap Blue. The online experience, Virtual Blue, takes one through sounds and images that capture the essence of the new fragrance, naturally, without using smell. Furthering this technique will bring additional "impulse" buyers to The Gap online.

[17] Orenstein, David, "Retailers Take Steps to Get Suppliers Y2K-Ready," *Computerworld*, October 26, 1998, p. 4(1).

[18] Gallagher, Leigh, "Where Are They Now? For Our Up & Comers, 1998 Was an Amazing Year," *Forbes*, January 11, 1999, p. 104(1).

[19] Kroll, Luisa, "Digital Denim," *Forbes*, December 28, 1998, p. 102(1).

[20] "E-Shopping Lies," *PC/Computing*, April 1999, v. 12, i. 4, p. 147(1).

CASE QUESTIONS

Strategic Questions

1. What is the strategic direction of The Gap?

2. Who or what forces are driving this direction?

3. What has been the catalyst for change?

4. What are the critical success factors for this corporation/organization?

5. What are the core competencies for this corporation/organization?

Technological Questions

6. What technologies has the corporation relied on?

7. What has caused a change in the use of technology in the corporation/organization?

8. How has this change been implemented?

9. Who has driven this change throughout the organization?

Quantitative Questions

10. What does the corporation say about its financial ability to embark on a major technological program of advancement?

11. What conclusions can be reached from an analysis of the financial information to support or contradict this financial ability?

12. What analysis can be made by examining the following ratio groups?

Gross margins
Inventory turnover
Interest expense
Long term debt

13. Is the industry stable?

Internet Questions

14. What does the corporation's web page present about its business?

15. What challenges does the corporation's home page face?

Industry Questions

16. What challenges and opportunities is the industry facing?

17. Is the industry oligopolistic or competitive?

18. Does the industry face a change in government regulation?

19. How will technology impact the industry?

Data Questions

20. What role do data play in the future of the corporation?

21. How important are data to the corporation's continued success?

22. How will the capture and maintenance of customer data impact the corporation's future?

THE LIMITED, INC.

Executive Summary

Case Name:	The Limited, Inc.
Case Industry:	Niche retail industry
Major Technology Issue:	Developing data warehousing and web-based commerce
Major Financial Issue:	Increasing net operating income
Major Strategic Issue:	Increasing market share through brand development
Major Players/Leaders:	Les Wexner, founder and CEO
Main Web Page:	www.limited.com
Case Conclusion/Recommendation:	The Limited must develop web-based commerce.

CASE ANALYSIS

INTRODUCTORY STORY

Les Wexner was among the first merchants to grasp the growing importance of niche retailing. By developing a vast network of suppliers in foreign countries that could manufacture private label goods inexpensively and quickly, The Limited could respond to "hot" fashion trends with amazing speed.

SHORT DESCRIPTION OF THE COMPANY

The Limited, Inc., is comprised of a unique family of brands. Included under the LTD ticker symbol are The Limited Stores, Express, Lerner New York, Lane Bryant, Henri Bendel, Structure, Limited Too, and Galyan's Trading Company. The Limited, Inc., also owns 83 percent of the shares of Intimate Brands, Inc. (IBI), which consists of Bath and Body Works, Cacique, Victoria's Secret stores, and Victoria's Secret catalog. The Limited also owns 84 percent of Abercrombie & Fitch, traded under the symbol ANF.

SHORT HISTORY OF THE COMPANY

On August 10, 1963, Leslie Wexner borrowed $5,000 from his aunt to finance the opening of a small women's clothing store in Columbus, Ohio. On his first day, Wexner sold $473 worth of merchandise. In the span of 34 years, Wexner's aunt's investment of $5,000 has become a $4.12 billion company with $8.64 billion in net sales. One man's vision, perseverance, and business savvy have made The Limited the leading specialty retailer in the United States. Currently the store employs over 120,000 people with a retail penetration of 5,690 stores in 13 retail businesses and several supporting industries.

Many of The Limited's holdings are household names. The major competitors are primarily The Gap Inc.'s holdings (Gap, Baby Gap, Gap Kids, and Banana Republic), the May Stores, and other direct retailers such as County Seat and Casual Corner.

The Limited has been able to separate itself from the competition by leveraging both existing and acquired brands. The Limited's early holdings (Limited and Express) were homegrown stores with concept and brand ideas generated by Wexner. The key to The Limited's success has been acquisitions of stores and brands that complement The Limited's lineup. The acquisition of Lane Bryant, Lerner, and Abercrombie & Fitch and the development of Structure are examples of these methods.[1]

Growing from one store in 1963 to a multistore, multibrand corporation in the 2000s has been the result of several strategic and operating efficiencies. The Limited built a distribution facility in Columbus, Ohio, next to the company headquarters. This enabled The Limited to ship inventory directly to the distribution center for prepackaging, price tagging, and order fulfillment. Additionally, the company acquired better control over inventory, storage, and shipping costs. They have since opened four additional distribution centers to accommodate the thousands of retail stores existing today.[2]

Another strategic initiative that contributes to overall brand perception and success is storefront saturation. Whenever possible, The Limited leases several contiguous spaces in new malls. It acts quickly to repo-

---

[1] Engler, Natalie, "Retail Wears IT—Gadzooks, Pacific Sunwear Expand Using Technology," *Information Week*, November 30, 1998, p. 136(1).
[2] Palmeri, Christopher, "Victoria's Little Secret," *Forbes*, August 24, 1998, v. 162, n. 4, p. 58(1).

sition their different stores in clusters in mall relocation and remodeling. This strategy enables the customer to virtually be surrounded with stores that are owned by The Limited. Otherwise, distractions like a cookie shop or a bookstore might flank a brand new Limited store. This retail space strategy leads to internal efficiencies as well. Contiguous stores can share break rooms, inventory rooms, management, and other resources. Interior passages between stores (for instance, connecting a Structure and Express) gives the customer the illusion of a much larger store. It also keeps customers inside The Limited stores and out of the mall.[3]

To manage this growth, The Limited has positioned several support subsidiaries to manage "back-office" activities and production for their retail presence, as discussed in the following paragraphs.[4]

Mast Industries Mast Industries, Inc., is one of the world's leading international contract manufacturers, importers, and distributors of apparel for men, women, and children. Product lines range from sportswear and ready-to-wear to lingerie. Mast delivers over 100 million garments a year to The Limited, retail and catalog divisions.

Limited Distribution Services Limited Distribution designs and implements operations that will provide the retail businesses with the most effective and efficient delivery operations available.

Limited Real Estate This subsidiary is responsible for locating and leasing all store sites for retail businesses of The Limited, Intimate Brands, and Abercrombie & Fitch.

Limited Store Planning The Limited Store Planning's mission is to develop the most innovative and successful stores in the retail business.

Gryphon Development Gryphon is one of the world's leading producers of cosmetics, fragrances, and personal care products.[5]

FINANCIAL AND PORTFOLIO ANALYSIS

At the end of fiscal year 1996, The Limited, Inc., operated 5,633 stores, occupied a total of 28,405,000 square feet, and employed 123,100 people. Just as sound store and corporate management contributed to the great success of the company, so did solid fiscal management.

At the close of 1998, net sales for the seventh consecutive year, increased. It should be noted that net in-

Table 3.2 Five-Year Summary

Date	Sales	Net Income	EPS
1999	9,346,911	2,053,646	9.060
1998	9,188,804	217,390	.797
1997	8,644,791	434,208	1.600
1996	8,644,791	434,208	1.54
1995	7,881,437	961,511	2.68

come remained relatively stable from 1992 through 1996, decreasing by one-half in 1997. Several factors contributed to this stable income in a time of increasing sales.

For the past 10 years, The Limited has shown strong net income growth and an impressive cost of goods sold/net sales performance. This ratio is critical to any retailing enterprise. The lower the percentage, the larger the net sales margin. This residual can be applied to other expenses used to operate the business and to leverage new and existing capital expenditures.[6]

From 1992 to 1996, at least 30 percent of the income from net sales has been available for operations. Since inventory costs are the largest component of any retailer's operating costs, The Limited fares well in the industry. It is important to note, however, that this ratio has not reduced and the operating margin has remained fairly static. If not for the large operating loss posted from a poor performance in the Express subsidiary, there would be an even smaller ratio for fiscal year 1996.[7]

Many forces beyond the company's control can impact gross income for a retailer. These include inflation, merchandising and sourcing costs, and indirect costs absorbed into the cost of goods sold. The milestone in any business is measured by its operating income performance.

Selling, General, and Administrative Expense has been on a steady increase in real dollars and as a percentage of income. (Table 3.3) In the 1996 annual report, the company explained the steady increase in these expenses.

General, administrative, and store operating expenses increased in the fourth quarter of 1996 compared on a pro-forma basis in the fourth quarter 1995. This increase was attributable to a 2.2% rate increase in the Intimate Brands Business (Victoria's Secret, Bath and Body Works, Cacique) and the inability to leverage expenses due to disappointing sales in the women's businesses, particularly Express.[8]

[3] Faircloth, Anne, "Brooks Brothers Dresses Down," *Fortune*, September 7, 1998, v. 138, n. 5, p. 44(2).
[4] Robillard, Pierre N., "The Role of Knowledge in Software Development," *Communications of the ACM*, January 1999, v. 42, i. 1, p. 87(1).
[5] http://www.limited.com/financial/index.asp.

[6] Ibid.
[7] DiPirro, Steven, "Managing System Availability," *Digital Systems Report*, Winter 1998, v. 20, i. 4, p. 7.
[8] http://www.limited.com/financial/index.asp.

Table 3.3 The Limited Balance Sheet 1995–1999

Fiscal Year Ending	01/30/99	01/31/98	02/01/97	02/03/96	01/28/95
Net Sales	9,346,911	9,188,804	8,644,791	8,644,791	7,320,792
Cost of Goods	6,348,945	6,370,827	6,148,212	6,148,212	5,206,429
Gross Profit	2,997,966	2,817,977	2,496,579	2,496,579	2,114,363
Selling/General/Administrative Expense	2,300,523	2,124,663	1,848,512	1,860,512	1,315,374
Net Income	2,053,646	217,390	434,208	434,208	448,343
Outstanding Shares	226,572	272,800	271,071	355,366	357,604

Building strong brands has been one of Wexner's greatest strengths. A loss of focus by the Express chain in 1996 cost The Limited substantial sales. Inventories had to be discounted so heavily that the margin on the sale items could not leverage their cost. As a result, the company's margin suffered on a consolidated business. In his Chairman's Letter in 1996, Wexner stated, "Let me make this plain: fixing Express, and fixing it quickly, is our top short-term priority. I am determined that it will again become the significant contributor it must be."

At fiscal year-end January 30, 1999, the total assets of The Limited were $4,549,708,000. This reflected the steady five percent growth in assets each year over the previous ten years, except for 1995. The approximately $1.14 drop in Total Assets and the corresponding drop in Total Equity was explained by a $1.615 billion treasury stock purchase. Without this purchase, the assets of the company would be approximately $5,735,002,000 (net of all other transactions), yielding a growth rate of 8.89 percent from 1995 results.

Table 3.4 indicates a plunge between 1995 and 1996 in Current Assets and Liabilities. Industry baselines for current ratios (liquidity) were at least 1.5. The previous years' performance indicates there was no cause for concern from investors.[9]

The current ratio, a measure of working capital, is well within industry and business standards (Table 3.5).

Looking at FY1996, the lowest number in the trend, presents a ratio of 1.7. Compared to 1995 results of 3.91, this looks somewhat dangerous. When the impact of the treasury stock purchase is considered, results again appear within the trend. Even with a current ratio of 1.70, the company had resources available to meet short term responsibilities and debt payments. This ratio is acceptable to financial institutions. If necessary, The Limited could borrow money to leverage capital projects. These include the deployment of an Internet commerce retailing system.

Turnover ratios are indicators of internal cash and inventory performance. Receivables turnover appears somewhat high for industry standards. A well-managed company should be able to collect outstanding debt in 60 to 90 days. The Limited is a multisubsidiary company. Not only are its subsidiaries involved in retailing merchandise, but others manufacture, source, distribute, market, and warehouse the very items they sell. On a nonconsolidated accounting basis, subsidiaries owe other subsidiaries money for intercompany services. These cannot be easily eliminated without distorting the company's actual outside receivables.

Inventory turnover, the measure of how quickly a company buys and sells inventoried goods, is also quite impressive for a retailer. From 1995 to 1997, the average number of turnover days was just over eight. Since the retail stores are not storing their own inventory, the time the goods remain on the shelves is more limited than for other retailers.

[9] Ibid.

Table 3.4

FY Ended	01/30/99	01/31/98	02/1/97	02/3/96	01/28/95	01/29/94
(thousands)						
Total Current Assets	2,318,184	2,031,151	1,545,097	2,800,032	2,547,666	2,220,625
Total Current Liabilities	1,247,935	1,093,412	906,893	716,575	797,555	707,444
Net Cash/Equivalents Available	1,070,249	937,739	638,204	2,083,457	1,750,111	1,513,181
Current Ratio	1.86	1.09	1.70	3.91	3.19	3.14

Table 3.5

Fiscal Year Ending	01/30/99	01/31/98	02/01/97
Current Ratio	1.86	1.86	1.70
SG & A/Sales	0.25	0.23	0.21
Receivables Turnover	120.27	110.22	124.68
Receivables Days Sales	2.99	3.27	2.89
Inventories Turnover	8.35	9.16	8.58
Inventories Days Sales	43.12	39.28	41.95
Net Sales/Total Assets	2.05	2.14	2.10
Net Sales/Employees	73,714	70,144	NA
Times Interest Earned	35.49	6.83	9.96
Current Debt/Equity	0.04	NA	NA
Long Term Debt/Equity	0.21	0.27	0.34
Total Debt/Equity	0.25	0.27	0.34
Net Income/Net Sales	0.22	0.02	0.05
Net Income/Common Equity	0.83	0.09	0.23

Table 3.6 Earnings per Share Growth Predictions

	Limited	Industry	S&P 500
FY98 VS FY97	7.90%	19.30%	10.90%
FY99 VS FY98	15.00%	17.50%	14.80%
Next 5 years	12.90%	16.20%	13.80%
Last 5 years	−4.40%	14.60%	26.60%

The warehousing arm of the company carries a small amount of inventory time. Once goods are shipped to the stores, they are considered "sold." This diminishes the inventory turnover ratio. Summarily, net of intercompany transactions, The Limited appears to have the ability to sell merchandise quickly. The speed of these internal operations provides a stable cash flow to operating expenses and leveraging capital expenditures.[10]

The results for 1996 net sales to working capital are again distorted by the treasury stock purchase. This period indicates a result of 13.55 versus 3.78 in 1995. Since available cash is a component of working capital, working capital is inflated. Averaging four times the amount of working capital, net company sales are shown to be far greater than the amount of working capital stated. This large sales margin funds the company's operating expenses and provides residual income to be used for capital projects.

Debt-to-equity ratios are not problematic either. The three-year average for 1995 to 1998 is 26 percent. This amount is within industry standards. Considering that there are companies, even start-ups, with debt-to-equity ratios of 60 percent to 70 percent that are still considered solvent on a cash flow basis, The Limited is capitalized well enough to meet its debts in a cash-crunch situation. Since income streams have been historically plentiful enough to cover operating costs, including debt repayment, the equity balances should not have to be used. Either with surplus operating revenue, or debt, The Limited can find its capital expenditures in information technology.

STOCK/INVESTMENT OUTLOOK

Many respected investment companies, such as American Express and FMR Corporation, own several million of The Limited's outstanding shares. This indicates a widely held perception of value in The Limited franchise.

One indicator of the quality and yield potential of stock investments is earnings per share (EPS). Comparing The Limited to the retailing industry and the Standard and Poor's 500 index provides the information given in Table 3.6. At first glance, one could assume that the growth prediction for the company's stock is somewhat disadvantaged when compared to the industry and the S&P 500. The table indicates that The Limited's EPS growth potential is not trailing behind the industry and S&P 500.

The stock price from 1997 through 1999 has remained stable, as shown in Table 3.7. There appears to be a cyclical pattern to stock prices. Historically, they are lowest in the late and early calendar months of the year; the stock price is highest in the middle of the year. This could be explained by the company timing of new merchandise releases and the seasonal nature of the selling season.[11]

RISK ANALYSIS

Working capital (current assets less current liabilities) from 1998 totaled $1,070,249,000. This figure should provide sufficient funds to continue research and development in technology to enable the purchase and distribution of items over the internet. Equally important, funds should be available to continue to collect and analyze user information from instore as well as online purchases.

INDUSTRY AND MARKET ANALYSIS

Retailers must constantly look for new ways to streamline branding, retain market focus, stay above acceptable profit margins, and mine data for information about customers.

In the early 1990s, it seemed that a new mall or shopping center was being built on every corner. Consumer

---

[10] Keener, Ronald E., "Problems for Everyone in IT Staffing Needs," *Health Management Technology*, May 1, 1999, v. 20, i. 4, p. 10(1).

[11] http://www.limited.com/financial/index.asp.

Table 3.7 Month End Market Prices (as of 9/30/97)

Month	1997	1996	1995	1994	1993
Jan	17.12	16.75	16.87	17.75	27.50
Feb	18.75	17.50	17.50	19.50	25.25
Mar	18.37	19.00	23.00	20.87	24.50
Apr	18.12	20.75	21.37	19.25	22.12
May	20.12	20.75	22.25	17.62	24.00
Jun	20.25	21.50	22.00	17.25	21.37
Jul	22.31	19.00	20.37	19.75	20.37
Aug	22.75	18.50	18.50	19.87	23.37
Sep	24.44	19.12	19.12	19.62	22.50
Oct	NA	18.37	18.50	18.50	21.37
Nov	NA	18.00	17.75	19.37	22.62
Dec	NA	18.37	17.12	18.12	17.00

demand was at an all-time high for new products and services. Despite the economic suppression of retail sales in the late 1980s, consumers returned to the stores in large numbers.

In the net income performance column, The Limited leads. Return on assets is highest for The Limited, followed by The Gap. In operating profit margin, The Gap is the leader, despite lower income performance. Both companies remain strong financial performers in the retailing industry.

Investment in retailing industries appears to be rising. According to the Standard and Poor's industry reports (June 1997), consumer consumption will continue to increase by 3.8 percent. Personal income should rise 6.0 percent. Trending models anticipate that price performance for the industry will increase from levels approximating 100 to 150 points.

Retailing is a fiercely competitive business. Corporate retail management competes by developing brand identities to which customers remain loyal. In the early 1990s, retailers tried to win markets through physical saturation. Not only was this ultimately expensive, it served to inundate and overwhelm the consumer. In response to these activities, Les Wexner made a salient point:

> Years ago, in our annual reports, I used to comment about never having closed a store. I'm over it. The world changes. No more so than in fashion. And we have to recognize what works. . . . Brands are not built through price promotions. Brands are built, money is made, wealth is created, on the sell side, not on the buy side.

Inside of this push to develop brands is the need to know individual customers and what they are willing to purchase, when, and where.

ROLE OF RESEARCH AND DEVELOPMENT

Much of the disposable income in U.S. households is spent on apparel and accessories. The challenge for retailers is to capture customers' loyalty. No other industry faces such rapid change, nor does any other industry have to work so hard to keep customers. Companies must position themselves to know their customers and respond quickly to market changes. Technology will play a vital part in this challenge. The focus will be marketing to individuals.

TECHNOLOGICAL STORY

Large amounts of money and energy are spent to identify customers in almost every type of business. In the area of finance and banking, where so much intimate and personal information is known about customers, data warehouses and market modeling tools are used to custom-fit products, services, and pricing to individuals.

Ernst and Young annually releases the results of their retail information technology survey *(http://www.ey.com/consumer/retailit/overview.htm)*. According to Stephanie Shern, of Ernst and Young:

> Retailers traditionally used Information Technology (IT) to deliver information to control markdowns and monitor costs. Leaders are now beginning to build the infrastructure to use data to support both top and bottom-line growth. The rise of the data warehouse, the increasing use of assortment management and the ongoing push to integrate business processes underscore this major trend.

All segments of the retail industry spend, on the average, 0.5 percent of their operating expenses as a percentage of sales on information technology. In apparel and accessories 1.35 percent of the operating expenses, the highest in the group, is spent on information technology. Shern states: "The trick will be to focus IT investments to best leverage spending to develop an enduring strategic advantage. That decision will be unique for each retailer."

Ernst and Young projections include:

1. Apparel and accessories retailers project average increases of 11 percent compared to an average personnel increase of 15 percent.
2. Eighty-two percent plan to add personnel for systems development; 45 percent will add staff for integration.
3. Apparel and accessories retailers have the highest number of information technology employees per $100 million: 10.5 employees per $100 million; these retailers increased annual capital spending for information technology by 23 percent.

TECHNOLOGICAL INVESTMENT AND ANALYSIS

The Limited employs over 120,000 people, has almost 20 self-managing subsidiaries, and has managed to accumulate over $4.1 billion in assets. Technology has helped The Limited manage inventory, manage product lines, control day-to-day activities at their retail stores, and provide information to management that enables them to grow the business.

DATA

While marketing is focused on developing markets of one, it is difficult. How can a retailer know each customer? Winners in the consumer information market will be expert managers of this data. Building on the successes of data warehousing in other business fields, retailers will have to find all the data they can about customers, analyze it, and proactively use that knowledge to increase profitability and retain market share.

Retailers are still in their infancy with data warehousing. According to Ernst and Young, "Two-thirds of respondents are using data warehouses that are less than 100 gigabytes in size. Nearly half say the data warehouse gets occasional use while 46% say that is has become vital to job tasks."

INTERNET

Also changing is retailers' use of the Internet to market goods, distribute corporate information, and attract customers. Specialty retailers like booksellers, T-shirt shops, and travel services have capitalized on doing business on the Internet. Why so little participation from large retailers? Again, Ernst and Young states:

Traditional retailers are fully aware of the opportunity/threat [from small Internet-based retailers]. 88% *operate or plan to launch Internet sites in the next 12 months [from October 1996], compared with 75% who planned to do so in 1995. Yet many may be ill-equipped to meet the challenges. Only 45%, for example, plan to outfit their sites to sell products and services. Internet applications account for only 2% of the average retailer's IT operating expenses.*

Technology will continue to play a vital role in determining the future of any retailing enterprise. The Limited is no exception. Being large and a market leader has led The Limited to take a somewhat conservative approach to technology.[12]

Data, hardware, and software are the building blocks of information technology. The integration of these objects enables a company to work, predict results, and make money. Most sales and customer data are collected at the point of purchase. Hardware enables stores to scan inventory items into an IBM terminal-based cash register programmed with custom sales tracking routines and inventory modules.[13] The sale is computed, payment is made, and the customer leaves. Nightly, store management closes the day's transactions and enters cash and payment balancing information to reconcile the day's activity. Leased-line connections from the store to central data repositories in Columbus, Ohio, make the transfer of sales data easy to accomplish. Inventory levels are adjusted, shipping orders are formulated, and data are stored for management review. A warehousing strategy is used to store data. In turn, the data can be mined to provide reports on store sales, product line productivity, and patterns of consumer behavior.[14]

The same principles are in operation in data warehousing. Intelligent handling systems track incoming goods, fill orders for stores, and monitor inventory levels. This hardware must be available to all levels of employees. Systems are also in place to automatically alert management of late shipments and deteriorating inventory levels. To make sure that the information stays current, custom software solutions track the flow of goods. Intranet-based database applications ensure smooth delivery to all warehouse personnel.[15]

[12] Hansell, Saul, "Got a Dime? Citibank and Chase End Test of Electronic Cash," *The New York Times*, November 4, 1998, v. 148, p. C1(L).

[13] Barnes, Darryl, "Java Card Application Development," *Dr. Dobb's Journal*, February 1999, v. 24, i. 2, p. 72(1).

[14] Keener, Ronald E., "Problems for Everyone in IT Staffing Needs," *Health Management Technology*, May 1, 1999, v. 20, i. 4, p. 10(1).

[15] Fiorito, Tony, "System Management 101: Managing Legacy Systems," *Digital Systems Report*, Spring 1999, v. 21, i. 1, p. 8.

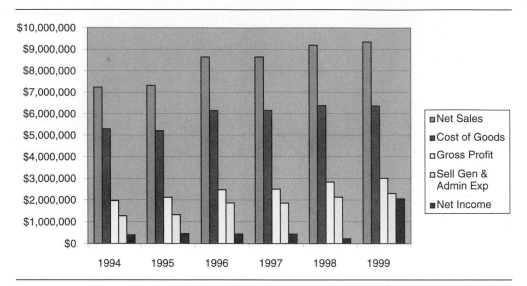

Figure 3.2 The Limited Financials, 1994–1999.

PC-based utilities are employed to manage employees, to share information between store and corporate management, and to facilitate client/server automation. These systems answer questions regarding future shipments and price and product availability. Home office users share information through local- and wide-area networks.

The Internet is playing a very important role in the future of The Limited's information technology focus. The Limited started a web site (www.Limited.com) in 1997. It is used primarily to distribute marketing and financial information. Newly developed commerce solutions could be plugged into the existing distribution channels with little infrastructural change.[16]

Knowing customers and their tastes is crucial to the development of brands that customers will buy. Web-enabled questionnaires and marketing forms could gather this critical information. PCs are being bought and used in the home and office internationally every year. Persons at home, work, or at an interactive kiosk in a store could volunteer information that could be used to feed decision support systems. Management would have the ability to use the technology to analyze the quantitative data. Customers' feelings toward products could be captured and analyzed.

A virtual store on the Internet requires a fraction of the overhead required by a physical store. Once established, transaction processes using a Common Gateway Interface or Java-enabled applications would record the

sale, produce entries in the data warehouse, and, by default, collect marketing data. This same interactive information could be modified into back-end management applications to monitor and predict sales results. This would leverage the IT expenditure to gain sales insight.[17]

From 1995 to 1997, developments in collaborative groupware and software have made sharing information across the enterprise less costly, more effective, and a valuable part of the information chain.

Support systems have been integrated to manage and share information. Since an intranet-based information solution can be integrated into the supply chain, the same technology could be used to integrate the front (marketing) and back (financial/operational) ends of the data. Employees would be able to share data, comment on contributions and new data, import and export raw data into other software application suites, such as Microsoft Office, and generate the reports required for financial and marketing needs.[18]

Data models could be built to answer questions regarding the profitability of the Internet commerce project or any other business decision. External sources could supply the static inputs and industry paradigms. Internal data could be applied to the model logic and the outflows would answer management hypotheses. Modeling enables companies to examine data through the use of constructed scenarios without actually exe-

---

[16] Carr, David F., "Application Server Products Take Aim at E-Commerce," *Internet World*, February 15, 1999, v. 5, i. 6, p. 15(1).

[17] Workman, Ronald, "Turning Java Into a Lean Virtual Machine," *Electronic Engineering Times*, March 1, 1999, p. 74(1).
[18] Fiorito, Tony, "System Management 101: Managing Legacy Systems," *Digital Systems Report*, Spring 1999, v. 21, i. 1, p. 8.

cuting the components of the model. In this way, the company can query data in countless formats not previously possible.

Technology will enable The Limited to answer questions regarding the profitability and effectiveness of the Internet. First, a descriptive model must be constructed to evaluate the impact of Internet commerce on supply and distribution chains, pricing, market segmentation, and information management. Inputs from all aspects of this marketing channel can be integrated. The model will evaluate the inputs and produce a set of descriptive outputs for management review. This data will complement a decision support system designed to evaluate the effectiveness of the distribution methodology.

RECOMMENDATION FOR THE FUTURE

The specialty retailing industry entered the technology arena late. As a result, they continue to make investments in technology to catch up. The Limited has the financial and management resources to test and deploy an Internet commerce system and should continue to do so. Their main competition, The Gap, has already made such a bold move.

The Limited must continue to refine its presence on the Internet by capturing and maintaining this influential market segment. The younger, contemporary market is easily impressed with trends and marketing savvy.

CASE QUESTIONS

Strategic Questions

1. What is the strategic direction of The Limited?

2. Who or what forces are driving this direction?

3. What are the critical success factors for this corporation/organization?

4. What are the core competencies for this corporation/organization?

Technological Questions

5. What technologies has the corporation relied on?

6. What has caused a change in the use of technology in the corporation?

7. How are customer data collected?

8. How successful has the technological change been?

Quantitative Questions

9. What does the corporation say about its financial ability to embark on a major technological program of advancement?

10. What conclusions can be reached from an analysis of the financial information to support or contradict this financial ability?

11. What analysis can be made by examining the following ratio groups?

    Current
    Inventory turnover

    Revenue
    Profit

12. Is the industry stable?

Internet Questions

13. What does the corporation's web page present about their business?

14. How sophisticated is the corporation's web page?

Industry Questions

15. What challenges and opportunities is the industry facing?

16. Is the industry oligopolistic or competitive?

17. Does the industry face a change in government regulation?

18. How will technology impact the industry?

Data Questions

19. What role do data play in the future of the corporation?

20. How important are data to the corporation's continued success?

21. How will the capture and maintenance of customer data impact the corporation's future?

TECHNOLOGY TIPS

MICROSOFT WORD TIPS

INSERTING IMAGES IN YOUR WORD DOCUMENT

Documents come to life and are more attractive when you place the right images in them. There are many sources for images. Office 97 has a clip art gallery, or you can retrieve photos from the web. The following will enable you to insert an image from the clip art gallery into your document.

From Clip Art

1. Place the cursor at the insertion point in your word document.
2. Click on INSERT, then click on PICTURE.
3. A side menu will appear. Click on CLIP ART. . . .
4. A clip art menu will appear with several choices. Double-click on your choice of clip art and the clip art will be inserted in your document.

From a File

1. Place the cursor at the insertion point in your word document.
2. Click on INSERT, then click on PICTURE.
3. Click on the FROM FILE . . . button.
4. Select from the dialog box the location of the picture you wish to insert in the document. A preview of the picture will appear in the preview box on the right.
5. Double-click on the file that contains the image you want and it will be inserted in your document.

Modifying the Image

1. You can adjust the size of the image by clicking on the image once.
2. Small boxes will appear at the corners of the picture. Click on one of these boxes with your mouse and while *holding down* the button resize the picture to your liking.
3. The picture can be moved around by clicking on it and dragging it to where you would like it in the document.

4. When you are finished modifying the picture click outside of the image to continue working with your document.

ADDITIONAL NOTE

Web Images

If you are surfing the web and see a graphic or picture that you like chances are that you may be able to use it in your document. Simply click on the image with your *right* button and from the pop-up menu click on SAVE IMAGE AS. . . . A dialog box will appear. Select where you would like to save the image (i.e., A: drive) and click on SAVE. Follow the directions listed above for inserting an image from a file to insert in your document.

MICROSOFT EXCEL TIPS

CELL RANGES

A cell range is a number of cells that are adjacent to each other and form a rectangle in a worksheet. Cell ranges can be copied, moved, and deleted.

SELECTING A CELL RANGE

Using the Mouse:

1. Click in the center of the cell that you want your range to start.
2. Click and hold down the left mouse button in the center of the cell and drag the mouse cursor to highlight the cells that are to be included in the range.
3. Release the mouse button once all the cells that are to in the range are highlighted.

Using the Keyboard:

1. Move the cell pointer to the cell that the range is to start
2. While holding down the SHIFT key, use the arrow keys to highlight the range of cells.
3. Release the SHIFT key.

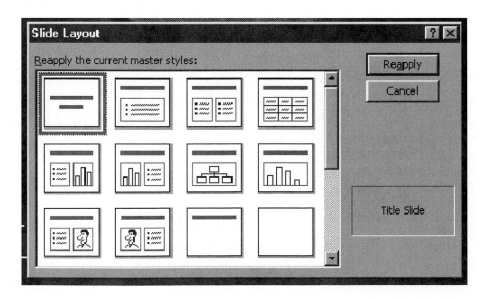

Using the Mouse and SHIFT key:

1. Select one corner of the range by clicking in the center of the cell.
2. While holding down the SHIFT key click on the cell that is to be the opposite corner in the range.
3. Release the SHIFT key.

NAMING A RANGE

Ranges can also be named. This aids in locating data that you know you will be working with frequently in formulas and/or need to locate. The name you give the range must not have spaces or symbols (i.e., *, %, $, #, etc.) and should be something meaningful and easy to remember.

Naming a Range:

1. Using one of the methods explained above, select a range.
2. Once the range has been selected click inside the Name box located next to the formula bar.
3. Type in the name for the range and press ENTER.
4. When you need to move to the range click on the list arrow on the name box to show the names of ranges and click on the name of the range you want.
5. The Excel worksheet window will change to show the range that you have selected.

MICROSOFT POWERPOINT TIPS

CHANGING SLIDE LAYOUTS

PowerPoint provides several layouts for slides that you may find useful in creating presentations. They save time by allowing you to select from preformatted layouts that serve as templates that you simply fill in with your presentation information. Also, this may be useful when you want to change a particular slide to a different layout without having to create a new slide.

Changing an Existing Slide Layout

1. While on the slide that you wish to change click on the right button (make sure the cursor is not over any of the slide's text or graphics). From the pop-up menu select SLIDE LAYOUT.
2. The dialog box on the right will appear. Select one of the slide styles by clicking on it. To apply the change to your slide click on the REAPPLY button.
3. There are 24 choices to choose from:

- *Title Slide*
- *Bulleted List*
- *2 Column Text*
- *Table*
- *Text & Chart*
- *Chart & Text*
- *Organization Chart*
- *Chart*
- *Text & Clip art*
- *Clip art & Text*
- *Title Only*
- *Blank*
- *Text & Object*
- *Object & Text*
- *Large Object*
- *Object*
- *Text & Media clip*
- *Media clip & Text*
- *Object over text*
- *Text over object*
- *Text & Two objects*
- *Two objects & Text*
- *Two objects over text*
- *Four objects*

4. When the slide appears you can simply fill in the blanks or double click on the clip art, organization chart, table, or chart icon to create it.

ADDITIONAL NOTE

If for any reason you are not pleased with the layout of the slide you can reverse your changes by selecting EDIT from the top tool bar, and UNDO from the drop down menu.

MICROSOFT ACCESS TIPS

TABLES AND PRIMARY KEYS

As explained in Chapter 1, tables are used in databases to organize data. When looking at Access tables remember that each row is a record and each column represents a field. The figure below shows how two tables are connected through the use of a primary key. The primary key is a field entry that is unique to a record. Your social security number or driver's license number is an example of a primary key. The tables below are connected through the Supplier ID field. There are three kinds of primary keys that can be defined in Access databases: AutoNumber, single-field, and multiple-field.

AUTONUMBER PRIMARY KEYS

An AutoNumber field can be set to automatically enter a sequential number as each record is added to the table. Designating such a field as the primary key for a table is the simplest way to create a primary key. If you do not set a primary key before saving a newly created table, Access will ask if you want it to create a primary key for you. If you answer Yes, AutoNumber primary key will be created.

SINGLE-FIELD PRIMARY KEYS

If you have a field that contains unique values such as ID numbers of part numbers, you can designate that field as the primary key. If the field you select as primary key does have duplicate or Null values, Microsoft Access will not set the primary key. You can run a Find Duplicates query to determine which records contain duplicate data. If you cannot readily eliminate duplicate entries by editing your data, you can either add an AutoNumber field and set it as the primary key or define a multiple-field primary key.

MULTIPLE-FIELD PRIMARY KEYS

In situations where you cannot guarantee the uniqueness of any single field, you may be able to designate two or more fields as the primary key. The most common situation where this arises is in the table used to relate two other tables in a many-to-many relationship. An example is when you have designated the primary key to be ProductID and it is used in the Order: Table and the Suppliers: Table. Many-to-many relationships are further explained in Chapter 6 along with an example.

MICROSOFT FRONT PAGE TIPS

INSERTING TABLES

Tables are easy to create with FrontPage Express. They make it easy for you to present information in an organized manner.

Whether it be pictures or a list of your favorite web sites, tables will make the information presentable and manageable.

Tables

1. Place the cursor in the area of the web page where you would like to insert the table.
2. Click on TABLE from the menu bar.
3. Select INSERT TABLE from the drop down menu.
4. The INSERT TABLE dialog box on the right will appear. Make the necessary entries in the fields (number of columns and rows, layout, etc.).
5. Click on OK.
6. The table will appear on the web page.

Inserting Rows and Columns

1. To insert a row or cell click inside the table where you would like to insert the row or column.
2. From the menu bar, click on TABLE and select INSERT ROWS AND COLUMNS from the drop down menu.
3. Click on ROWS or COLUMNS and the amount you would like to insert. Then click on OK.

4. The rows or columns will automatically be inserted in the table.

Further Customizing the Table

You can add a background, adjust the space between cells, add a caption to the table, and do a number of other modifications to the table in order to make it stand out. Explore the different options available to you to modify the appearance of your table.

1. Click inside the table then click on TABLE from the menu bar.
2. Select TABLE PROPERTIES from the drop down menu. (Notice that there are a several other choices to select from the drop down menu. Remember to come back and explore the other options.)
3. A dialog box will appear providing you with a number of options to modify your table.
4. Play around with the different options. Be creative. You might be amazed at what you can do.

CHAPTER 4

OPERATIONS AND TRANSACTIONS
RETAIL SALES

Operations and Transactions

All business revolves around transactions. A transaction is the exchange between individuals, areas, or companies. Technology's first step has always been to capture, store, and manipulate the basic data that surround a transaction or event. While some transactions occur within the organization, most transactions occur between the company and people outside the company. Transactions within the organization include production records, time sheets, employee evaluations, and interdepartmental transfers. Transactions outside the organization include those with customers (sales), suppliers (costs), and competitors (market share). Transactions occurring with outside parties are stored and maintained. This process is called *transaction processing*.

The basic element of a transaction is data. Data is the identifier that is used to separate the most finite elements of a business transaction. Data elements are combined or collected to produce information. Data is particularly valuable because it can be organized to summarize the current status of the organization. It can be manipulated to project sales, costs, and other figures into the future. Finally, it can be organized to support future recommendations.

Because data is so integral to the organization, it is important to preserve its quality. Sometimes this task is difficult because the transaction that is represented is complex. Quantity of data must also be considered. Storing and manipulating every piece of data surrounding a transaction would be inefficient. Companies must try to keep only relevant data; this data is summarized in reports whenever possible.

Data Integrity This is the process of keeping data accurate and correct as it is gathered and stored in the computer system. Each item must be correctly entered and the complete information recorded. Bar code numbers with a check digit as the last digit, for example, help maintain data integrity.

Multitasking Multitasking enables more than one task to be performed at a time. Whether on a single computer or within a series of networked computers, multitasking increases the ability of a computer system to run more than one operation at once.

Concurrency This is a problem that arises when applications attempt to modify the same piece of data at the same time. The application must know that several people might try to access the same piece of data at the same time. The software locks out all users except the current one. When this process is finished, other users can then access the application.

Data Volume The amount of data stored can be a problem when the business volume or the amount of information that must be kept increases substantially. Visa International expects the number of transactions processed daily to double in the span of a few years to over 40 million a day.

Three major types of business decisions exist: strategic, tactical, and operational. Strategic decisions have a long-term outlook and address issues such as competitive advantage and how to become a market leader. Tactical decisions fall between a long- and a short-term outlook, dealing with issues such as improving operations without restructuring the company. Operational decisions have to do with day-to-day actions to keep the company functioning.

Process Control This type of software is designed to coordinate operating decisions within manufacturing environments. It not only helps smooth the production process; it can also provide valuable data for future decision-making. Process control computers can monitor quality in the manufacturing process. This not only provides data to management; it also notifies operators if a problematic trend is occurring.

Point of Sale (POS) This term refers to the capture of transaction data at the location and time the transaction occurs. This maintains the accuracy of the data and enables transaction information to be used almost immediately. Several devices have been developed to capture this POS information. The most popular are bar code scanners that scan a product's universal product codes (UPCs). This provides the retailer with precise information about the item sold. It can be connected with Electronic Data Interchange (EDI) to make reordering easier.

Electronic Data Interchange (EDI) EDI is a method of automating data input. It also provides for the electronic transfer of documents between firms. Examples include the automatic electronic reordering of stock and the transmission of invoices and payments. Advantages include significantly decreased cost and increased accuracy in processing tasks such as placing orders. Disadvantages include security, compatibility, and privacy issues.

Accounting helps categorize and consolidate data to prepare management reports and meet government requirements. The increase in computing power over the years has led to a multitude of reports and other data to be generated for and from the accounting system. An important decision in accounting is the level of detail to maintain on the company's general ledger.

Human Resources This is an important area that lends itself to being automated by information systems. The need for accurate data and complicated applications in a timely and confidential manner has been addressed by human resource systems such as PeopleSoft. This application has enabled large efficiency gains to be attained by companies. Numerous laws and regulations govern employment. These change for each country. The power of computing has been used to improve compliance with local, state, and national governments.

Costs versus Benefits Costs must always be measured. Transaction processing and operations are no excep-

Word	W.1	Inserting a Table Additional Note	
Excel	E.1	Inserting Cells, Rows, and Columns	Inserting a Cell Inserting a Row Inserting a Column Inserting Several Rows and Columns Inserting in Nonadjacent Rows, Columns, and Cells
PowerPoint	P.1	Slide Transitions and Timing	Slide Transitions Timing Note
Access	A.1	Creating a Table Starting Access	Creating a Table
Front Page	I.1	Saving and Inserting Pictures from the Web	Saving a Picture/Graph from the Web Inserting Pictures in Your Web Page Modifying the Picture

tion. In transaction processing, for example, the cost of obtaining, maintaining, and storing additional data or developing additional reports must always be compared to the benefit gained by those activities. Deciding what processes are worthwhile to obtain data can be a difficult decision. For example, while the time of day sales happen is very important to restaurants, it is of varying importance to other businesses. An Internet store should be less than concerned about the time of a sale.

Retail Sales Industry

DESCRIPTION OF THE INDUSTRY

The retail sales industry encompasses all sales to end-product users—the consumers of the world. This industry is large and getting even larger as new and innovative means of reaching customers continue to be developed. Today a great deal of attention is focused on the Internet as a new medium for retail sales. The question is the extent to which people will buy over the Internet. Retail sales take place in department stores, warehouse stores, specialty stores, through mail order, and in many other venues.

FINANCIAL ANALYSIS OF RETAIL INDUSTRY

Retail sales have been robust for the past few years. Low inflation, rising income, falling unemployment rates, and an increase in consumer spending have led the drive in the retail sales industry bull market. In 1996, according to Reuters News Service, retail sales rose 5.3 percent, compared with 4.9, 7.5, and 5.6 percent for the prior years. Using the 1996 returns of the S&P's 500 as a measure of performance, the general retail industry produced return rates 21 percent higher on average the the S&P 500. Historically, normal valuation is only at 0.5 percent higher than the companies in this group.

Retail sales are generally cyclical in nature. Holiday sales are a significant measure of consumer sentiment. The National Retail Federation reports that December 1996 holiday market sales posted a 0.6 percent increase. This was above industry expectations for a 0.4 percent increase. The 0.6 rise was a 2.5 percent increase relative to December 1995 sales.

STOCK/INVESTMENT OUTLOOK

Retailers are expected to face problems, despite high levels of consumer confidence, because of the high levels of consumer debt and personal bankruptcy. According to NatWest Securities group—and by all historical standards—the growth in retail sales should begin to pull back. Consumer demand for luxury items may be at a peak. A slowdown in the economy may change consumers' willingness to purchase many luxury items. To economists, the numbers tell an old story: too many stores, too few consumer dollars.

POTENTIAL/PROSPECTIVE FOR GROWTH

The retail industry encompasses an extremely competitive and broad marketplace. The advancement in new retail avenues is ongoing. Sales over the Internet grew by an estimated 50 percent in 1995. This rate was much faster than the growth of retail in general. Over $2.2 trillion was spent in retail in 1997, with over $50 million of that amount in online retail shopping. The National Retail Federation believes that by the year 2005, 25 percent of basic merchandise could be bought over the Internet. While the use of online shopping will continue to increase, most retailers and consumers agree that online shopping will never be a complete replacement for the physical experience of browsing.

In addition to online Internet access, there is competition among stores to develop the shopping environment for the future. An example of this research is an idea presently being collaborated between J. C. Penney and Nordstrom. It proposes interactive home shopping through a consumer's television. This service would enable consumers to view merchandise on screen and make purchases through their television remote controls. Interactive home shopping networks are already in place; few allow the purchase of consumer goods through remote control.

Retailers who do not make information technology research and development a top prioritiy will be squeezed in the scramble to catch up. Retail industries must constantly address the changing demands, character, and demographics of their customers.

COMPETITIVE STRUCTURE

The retail sales industry is highly competitive in all areas. There are single store, franchise, and large retail outlets. Sandra Shaber of the WEFA group calls it either a "price business" or a "We've-got-a-gimmick business." Barriers to entry are not always high. There are always many trials of new concepts in progress. Retailers must react quickly to consumer preferences in the industry.

ROLE OF RESEARCH AND DEVELOPMENT

Extensive research and testing of Internet web sites is under way. It is not clear which concepts will work and how consumers will respond. Utilizing data warehousing technologies to obtain, gather, and analyze customer data/purchasing habits is being developed to the fullest by K-mart Corporation. In developing their idea of "Retail 2000," K-mart is researching cart scanning. This process enables a whole cart to be scanned at once to determine prices for checkout. Kiosks will enable customers to order products directly from a manufacturer. Marketing research and development is always under way in this industry.

TECHNOLOGICAL INVESTMENT AND ANALYSIS

Retailers have invested in many of the newest technologies. Technological improvements have allowed many retailers to thrive in this competitive industry. Tracking customer information with smart cards and computer programs designed for efficient stocking and warehousing have enabled retailers to cut costs and increase marketing capabilities. Web sites with online shopping capabilities extend the store hours to 24 hours a day. Information technology enables retailers to transact business deals around the clock and from any location on the globe.

RECOMMENDATIONS FOR THE FUTURE

Retailers must continue to take advantage of and innovate with the most up-to-date information technologies. They must seek ways to cut costs in a very competitive industry where much of the competition is based on overhead, inventory, and shipping costs.

WEB SITES

Retail Sales Industry

www.retailresources.com
smallbusiness.yahoo.com
www.fastcompany.com/home.html

Executive Summary

Case Name:	Home Depot
Case Industry:	Home improvement retail industry
Major Technology Issue:	The management of just-in-time type inventory control
Major Financial Issue:	Increasing same store sales
Major Strategic Issue:	Developing just-in-time inventory management techniques called "cross-docking," marketing to new customer groups (Hispanics), and maintaining ability to help and guide the do-it-yourself customers
Major Players/Leaders:	Founders Bernie Marcus and Arthur Blank
Main Web Page:	http://www.HomeDepot.com
Case Conclusion/Recommendation:	Home Depot must continue to train and prepare staff to help the do-it-yourself customers. This is a marketplace perception that differentiates them from their competitors.

CASE ANALYSIS

INTRODUCTORY STORY

Bryan Kahlow stepped back for a second to survey his work. He and his father-in-law had constructed a new deck. After receiving estimates in the $3,000 to $4,000 range, Bryan decided to investigate the possibility of completing the job himself. Of course, not being much of a handyman, he knew that he needed a lot of help.

One Saturday morning, the two men attended a short class at the neighborhood Home Depot store. There they learned all of the steps necessary to complete a deck. They were even given the name and phone number of their instructor who they could call in case they ran into trouble along the way. After two days of diligent work, they constructed a new deck. This was made possible by the friendly and courteous staff at Bryan Kahlow's local Home Depot.

A high level of customer service is what has helped Home Depot revolutionize the home improvement industry. Skilled contractors formerly dominated the industry. Now the industry includes many do-it-yourselfers eager to save time and money and achieve a sense of accomplishment.[1]

SHORT DESCRIPTION OF THE COMPANY

Home Depot is a chain of home improvement stores that stock approximately 40,000 to 50,000 different kinds of building materials, home improvement supplies, and lawn and garden products. The stores cater to both the do-it-yourselfer as well as home improvement, construction, and building maintenance professional. Home Depot operates five Home Depot Expo Design Centers, which focus on upscale interior design products. These include kitchen and bath products, light fixtures, and floor and wall coverings. Today, Home Depot dominates the $140 billion do-it-yourself retail business.

SHORT HISTORY OF THE COMPANY

When Bernard Marcus and Arthur Blank met 23 years ago, they were both managers for Handy Dan Improvement Centers, a regional hardware store chain based in Los Angeles. After a personality clash with their boss, they were both abruptly fired and found themselves searching for work in an industry they felt they understood.

The two executives analyzed their predicament and decided to open a new business. They chose to excel in areas in which Handy Dan could not compete. They came up with the format for a warehouse store that offered a wide variety of products and excellent customer service. In 1979, they chose Atlanta for their first location since the southeastern United States was growing so rapidly.[2]

The first year was a struggle. The shelves of the first stores were often empty because Home Depot could not

---

[1] Karpinski, Richard, "Home Depot Picks Its Spots," *InternetWeek*, September 28, 1998, n. 734, p. 13(1).

[2] "Home Depot Renovates," *Fortune*, November 23, 1998, p. 200(1).

afford to purchase inventory. Lack of adequate marketing and an extremely broad product line also confused many customers. The stores contained products from windshield wipers and automotive oil to unfinished wood furniture and soft drinks. Shoppers could not determine if Home Depot was a craft store or a warehouse department store. The result was a first year loss of nearly $1 million.

The following year, 1980, brought a more focused product line and better management. Sales doubled and the company recorded its first profit. In 1981 the company went public and expanded into Florida. Throughout most of the 1980s, Home Depot continued to grow at a phenomenal rate. They increased sales from $22.3 million in 1980 to nearly $3 billion in 1989. The company's stock split 10 times in the first decade and the expansion continues throughout the United States and Canada.[3]

Today, Home Depot is an innovator in the home improvement retail industry. It uniquely combines the economies of scale inherent in a warehouse format with a level of customer service never before achieved by warehouse-style retailers. Currently there are 540 stores in 40 U.S. states and 28 stores in three Canadian provinces. Home Depot expects to double the number of stores in the Americas to over 1,000 by the year 2000. The company announced plans for a joint venture with Falabella Retailing in Chile to open its first international store in Santiago, Chile, in 1998.[4]

In 1997, Home Depot attempted to increase brand recognition by aggressively marketing a new line of technology and media tools to assist customers with home improvement issues. In addition to a book entitled *Home Improvement 1-2-3*, Home Depot released CD-ROM software under the same name that contains over 2,000 detailed instructions for home repair jobs. The series had 50 narrated how-to videos, as well as a tool guide and skill scale. In September 1997, Home Depot introduced a daily do-it-yourself show, "House Smart," on the Discovery Channel. One of the goals of this media blitz is to increase brand recognition and establish a customer base in the 21 states where there are no Home Depot stores. The software and media efforts will also be tied to other promotions.

FINANCIAL AND PORTFOLIO ANALYSIS

The principal players in the home improvement industry, Wick's Lumber, Payless Cashways, and Hechingers,

have seen sales decrease, while Home Depot has continued to expand at 20 to 25 percent per year. In fact, Home Depot recently reported net earnings for the year ending February 2, 1997 at $937.7 million. That's up from $731.5 million the year before. Net sales were up 26.3 percent; comparable store sales were up 7 percent. Conversely, the three other players mentioned saw net sales plunge in 1996 and are struggling to stay competitive. Home Depot's recent $245 million acquisition of Maintenance Warehouse in an all-stock deal provides access to the business and institutional building and maintenance industry.

The one player who is fighting back is Sears. Arthur Martinez, CEO at Sears, plans to return the company to its previous position on top of the retail hardware industry. Moving away from the large department store concept, Martinez hopes to open several smaller retail outlets far from shopping malls and closer to the consumer. Additionally, he plans to invest $10 million in the expanding service operation. Bernie Marcus, CEO of Home Depot, once viewed Sears as a dying company but now views Sears as Home Depot's fiercest competitor.

Lowe's, another competitor, has essentially scrapped the 65 or so small retail hardware stores on which it built its company in favor of expanding the number of huge warehouse-like home repair stores. Lowe's has seen sales increase annually about 16 percent for the past five years and earnings per share rise at 25.7 percent. This is consistent with the growth rates of Home Depot. Lowe's hopes to reach 600 U.S. stores by the year 2000, while Home Depot plans to reach 1,100 stores in the same time frame. Lowe's is a formidable competitor, willing to change in a fluid industry.

During Home Depot's "great eighties" rapidly soaring stock prices as well as steadily increasing revenues made debt management quite simple. From 1993 to 1996 long-term debt was constant and even decreased in 1996. However, for fiscal year 1996, which ended February 2, 1997, debt increased drastically from $720 million to $1.2 billion. This increase can be attributed to the acquisition of Maintenance Warehouse and the continued expansion into untapped markets. Overall, however, the increase in debt is consistent with increases in other categories in the financials.

Home Depot reported gross sales of 19.5 billion in 1996, up from $15.5 billion in 1995. After seeing increases in current assets of 10 percent annually, fiscal year 1996 brought an increase of 33 percent (1996, $26.7 million; 1997, $37 million). Additionally, property, plant, and equipment increased from $49.6 million to $61.5 million in that year.

Most important to day-to-day operations, selling, general, and administrative expenses continued to remain at a consistent percentage of sales. This is most

---

[3] Sweat, Jeff, and Stein, Tom, "Killer Supply Chains—Six Companies Are Using Supply Chains to Transform the Way They Do Business," *InformationWeek*, November 9, 1998, p. 36(1).
[4] "Home Depot Renovates," *Fortune*, November 23, 1998, p. 200(1).

beneficial for Home Depot because it demonstrates that they can raise assets, debt, and equity without increasing operational costs significantly. Underlying this assessment are the changes in technological proficiency that have helped Home Depot operate more efficiently with fewer resources. This is why there has not been a significant decrease in cash flow.[5]

Management has been very cautious about expanding its specialty Home Depot Expo stores, which target the interior decorator customer. These stores have very few of the items found in the home improvement stores. The caution is due to mediocre profits from the five existing stores that are in large markets. These markets were chosen based on the number of stores in the region and the brand recognition already established. With expansion of its stores into new markets, including foreign markets, careful placement of Home Depot Expo stores will ensure that they limit exposure and losses.

To entice customers, Home Depot offers instruction classes inside stores. These classes teach an average customer some home improvement basics. For these classes, Home Depot hires sales associates who can help individual customers with projects. Home Depot keeps its stores stocked with virtually everything needed to complete any repair or home improvement task.

Ultimately, the success of the Home Depot stores depends upon the establishment of their brand and reputation. Competitors have duplicated Home Depot's strategies and built similar stores that offer the same features as Home Depot. In the Midwest, Menard's has expanded to many markets where Home Depot stores are not yet prevalent. In the South, Lowe's has aggressively and successfully become the principal competitor to Home Depot.

STOCK/INVESTMENT OUTLOOK

Home Depot saw rapid growth in all financial areas during the eighties and early nineties. As revenues soared and business expansion steadily continued, stock prices responded accordingly. Financial analysts have recommended the company for years. However, after the 10 stock splits in the first decade, Home Depot stock was stagnant at nearly $50 per share in the mid-1990s.

In the 10 years through December 1995, the stock price appreciated nearly 25 percent annually (Table 4.1). From 1996–1997 that number has dipped sharply to 3.8 percent and 5 percent, respectively. Earnings have slowed from the 25 percent pace. Growth is still expected in the 25 percent range.[6]

RISK ANALYSIS

Making the company-owned Home Depot Expo stores profitable ventures will present challenges and risks. The stores were opened in well-established Home Depot markets with the hope of using the brand recognition to attract customers to a home decorating store with the same customer service as the Home Depot home improvement stores. Sluggish profits have caused reassessment of the concept and management of the Expo stores. Management is moving cautiously to minimize the risk.

Expansion into the Hispanic communities has become a major focus of marketing efforts. Classes, advertisements, and software are now distributed in Spanish. Stores opened in the Hispanic community are staffed with Spanish-speaking sales associates.

Home Depot has revolutionized the home improvement industry and helped to spark a do-it-yourself movement. By continuing to offer quality brands, expert advice, and expanded product lines, Home Depot ensures their position as the leading retailer of home improvement products. The acquisition of Manufacturer's Warehouse gives Home Depot a foothold in the market for professional contractor products. Home Depot stores may soon begin selling appliances. This will further encroach upon a market traditionally dominated by Sears and Montgomery Ward.

---

[5] Sweat, Jeff, and Stein, Tom, "Killer Supply Chains—Six Companies Are Using Supply Chains to Transform the Way They Do Business," *Information Week*, November 9, 1998, p. 36(1).

[6] http://www.HomeDepot.com/.

Table 4.1

Ticker	Company	EPS 1996	EPS 1997E	P/E 1997E	Recent Price
EAGL	Eagle Hardware & Garden	$0.84	$0.93	22	$20.75
HECHA	Hechinger	−0.59	−0.26	NM	1.81
HD	Home Depot	1.94	2.38	23	55.75
LOW	Lowe's	1.71	2.04	19	38.25
PCS	Payless Cashways	−0.63	−0.20	NM	1.88
WKS	Wick's Lumber	0.07	NA	NA	5.75

INDUSTRY AND MARKET ANALYSIS

It is difficult to quantify the impact of Home Depot on the home improvement industry. Not only are they the industry leader, they are now principal players in several other industries as well. Home Depot is now the industry leader in the floor covering industry. It wants to make carpet and tile stores obsolete.

Home repair is a new industry. Baby boomers grew up going to local hardware stores like Ace or True Value. These stores provided basic hardware and home repair needs in a limited capacity. Typically, there was very little customer–staff interaction beyond the sale. If a customer wanted larger selection and the confidence of quality brands, he or she went to Sears, which has long been recognized for quality tools and hardware parts.

Home Depot developed the home repair industry by listening to customers and answering their questions. The industry was built on huge, low-frills warehouse-like stores containing 40,000 to 50,000 products, low prices, hassle-free shopping, and a great deal of do-it-yourself information. As a result, customers lacking the confidence to tackle complicated home repairs were empowered to try repairs in their home. With knowledgeable employees to advise customers in the store, an extensive list of low-cost contractors and independent handymen, and frequent free classes on home repair methods, Home Depot provided alternatives to the home repair customer.

As the industry expands, the competition will certainly grow with it. Rapid growth of the industry has meant that the secret to Home Depot's success is being copied. Competitors must either adapt to Home Depot's business model or they will fail to gain market share. Surprisingly, there are still very few major national players with many United States markets to enter. Additionally, the opportunity to expand into Canada, Mexico, and South America should keep the industry growing for the next 10 to 20 years.[7]

The biggest challenge to any competition will be the management of assets and inventories. For the major competitors, Lowe's and Home Depot, making the correct management decisions in terms of choosing new markets or increasing vertical integration will be challenging. Correctly analyzing the potential for future growth will determine the margin between first and second place in the home improvement industry.[8]

Home Depot stores boasted an industry-leading 14 percent of the $135 billion home improvement market in 1997. This is an increase from a 12% share in 1996. The next competitor in market share is Lowe's, which has a 6 percent share of the industry. Lowe's previously operated in small rural markets, and focused on supplying contractors. Lowe's opened 125 to 130 new stores between 1996 and 1997. They hope that these new stores, which average 110,000 square feet of floor space each, will enable them to gain a greater hold on the home improvement market. Their goal is to have 600 stores by the year 2000.[9]

To maintain market share, Home Depot has added several improvements to its operating strategy and vision. They have refocused on customer service and satisfaction through employee training. They also hope to differentiate themselves from imitators by promoting brands exclusive to its stores (Husky tools, Vigoro fertilizers, Scots riding mowers, etc.) Home Depot also wants to grow outside of the retail sector. In January 1997, they acquired Maintenance Warehouse America Corporation, a leading direct-mail marketer of maintenance, repair, and operations products to the building and facilities management market. This acquisition provided Home Depot with 100,000 names on a mail-order client list. This opened a new client base that includes apartment buildings and lodging facilities.

Another way Home Depot seeks to prosper is by cutting costs.[10] By introducing "cross-docking," or truck-to-store shelf inventory control, a form of just-in-time inventory management, they hope to reduce inventory costs and improve efficiency. Inventory management is an area that Home Depot wants to make a competitive advantage. Frequent surveys of customers and employees gives positive feedback regarding the products that customers would like to see on the shelves. This helps determine shelf space allocation as well as ordering cycles to minimize the time required to get needed products from suppliers to store shelves.[11]

TECHNOLOGICAL STORY

With business thriving and profits continuing to rise, the challenge to Home Depot is to continue to invest in their business for growth while minimizing risk. Minimizing risk is often a function of the level of preparation that goes into implementing a large change. In the area of technological progress and software implementation, the risks are particularly great because of the

[7] "Installations," *The Seybold Report on Publishing Systems*, March 2, 1999, v. 28, i. 11, p. NA(1).
[8] "A Tale of Two Economies," *Fortune*, April 26, 1999, v. 139, i. 8, p. 198(1).
[9] Ibid.
[10] Vaas, Lisa, "Companies Are Using Help Desk Technology for More Than Just IT Support," *PC Week*, February 22, 1999, p. 94(1).
[11] Berry, John, "Time To Justify IT Expenses," *InternetWeek*, April 12, 1999, p. 30(1).

rapid pace of change and the amount of capital required to implement a major technological upgrade.[12]

TECHNOLOGICAL INVESTMENT AND ANALYSIS

Future growth for Home Depot will be contingent on its ability to expand into new markets. The principles that built the company are the traits that will ensure its future success. Increased customer loyalty, expanded services within the store, and improved product lines will enable the company to operate more efficiently.

One of the ways Home Depot seeks to improve operating efficiency is through the implementation of a computer-assisted ordering system. This system reduces the time spent by associates ordering inventory and increases inventory availability. Sales increase since the required items are in stock and on the shelves when the customers want them. Inventory turnover is more efficient since inventory items that are not required are not stored in a warehouse.[13]

To provide better means of communications between individual stores and the home office in Atlanta, the company decided to move ahead quickly in the areas of communications and networking. Since they were interested in implementing an open system, they installed HP9000 UNIX processors from Hewlett-Packard in the stores. They connected them to headquarters using a (TCP/IP) Transmission Control Protocol/Internet Protocol connection. This is now the standard in open communications interconnections.[14]

The transition from in-store processors to a central TCP/IP hub was not difficult. However, Beach Clark, manager of network architecture at Home Depot, ran into problems finding an off-the-shelf package that would meet Home Depot's needs. To be effective, the package had to be able to handle data transport to and from the stores since the file transfer application for the Data General proprietary environment was not suitable for the TCP/IP network. Additionally, the package had to run in real time instead of processing in batch mode.

Corporate Microsystems (CMI) received the contract for its Mlink Advanced Communications Manager Software, which runs on a UNIX platform and delivers TCP/IP support. Mlink software offered capable data collection and downloading, connections for all the stores to the headquarters data, and coordination of e-mail between stores. By continuously polling stores for updates in areas such as price and inventory, the system was continuously updated instead of waiting until batch updates were performed each evening. Best of all, the system could run unattended and unobserved, reducing costs by minimizing operator interaction. The system improved all levels of communication and information processing between the stores and headquarters and also improved inventory management.[15]

Home Depot hopes to increase its customer base and improve customer service in its present markets. Implementing technological improvements in inventory management and improving its computer network will help control inventory and reduce costs.[16] Additionally, customer spending habits, rush orders, and general company information can be communicated instantly between individual stores and the home office.[17]

TECHNOLOGICAL INNOVATIONS

NETWORKS

Home Depot's computer operations do not spawn garden-variety headaches. The home improvement chain does face the normal service problems of too little time, too little money, and too many projects. It also adds some complexities of its own.

Location. Home Depot has nearly 700 retail stores, spread from Canada to Chile, with most scattered across the United States. Six hundred additional locations are planned.

Employment. There are 160,000 "associates," to be joined by another 100,000 new hires by the end of the year 2000. Why so many? To run the 600 new stores that are planned.

Finances. There is no budget for training the 100 new hires joining the company every day. These employees will be using computers and customer service applications to look up products and take returns.

The real task facing Mike Anderson, vice president of information technology, is to make computing in Home Depot's stores so easy that any employee can do it—without training. It's no small order, given that most workers have construction and trade backgrounds. Many associates panic when faced with a keyboard.

---

[12] Melymuka, Kathleen, "Walking With the Users: IT Pros Can Learn Valuable Lessons by Working the Other Side of the Fence," *Computerworld*, December 7, 1998, p. 60(1); Soat, John, "IT Confidential," *InformationWeek*, December 14, 1998, p. 158(1).

[13] Alter, Allan, "IT Needs a New Midlife Crisis," *Computerworld*, May 31, 1999, p. 32(1).

[14] Orenstein, David, "Home Depot Testing Linux for Mushrooming PC Volume," *Computerworld*, June 21, 1999, p. 4(1).

[15] Dalton, Gregory, "Home Depot Automates with Optika—Retailer Uses Workflow Application to Archive Documents Electronically," *InformationWeek*, June 7, 1999, p. 24.

[16] Vaas, Lisa, "Companies Are Using Help Desk Technology for More Than Just IT Support," *PC Week*, February 22, 1999, p. 94(1).

[17] Deckmyn, Dominique, "Home Depot Adds Imaging, Plans to Go 90%+ Paperless; Plans to Reach 90% Paperless State," *Computerworld*, June 7, 1999, p. 11(1).

As a result, Anderson decided to use Java and an object-oriented programming methodology for a new series of customer service applications. Planning started October 1996, products were acquired in December 1996, and software testing began in early summer 1997. About 40 locations use the software today.

"We didn't know how to write object-oriented applications or [much] about Java," Anderson says bluntly. Among the biggest obstacles were the objects themselves. If there was a bug in a software component, it might involve tracing the problem through 30 modules, each comprising many objects, to find the cause. Even when everything worked right, the applications were usually "far too slow."[18]

Why was Java chosen then? "We needed a graphical interface for the applications," says Danny Branch, director of information services, admitting that could be done in Visual Basic or C++ or a variety of other languages. Because the best Home Depot associates are experienced carpenters, electricians, painters, plumbers, and other trade professionals, the applications needed to be designed visually.

"We have several large Informix applications," Branch says. "But it's intimidating for many associates to go up to a keyboard and terminal. Visual applications are much less intimidating, especially with touch screens showing buttons saying 'Touch here to go forward' to help the associate.

"We also wanted an organized development framework and application architecture. We found a company, Novera Software Inc., that gave us a jump start in that area," Branch adds. In addition, Anderson insisted on pursuing the main promise of Java. A program should be written only once and then be able to run on any kind of server or workstation.[19]

The target server in nearly all Home Depot stores is a Hewlett-Packard Co. HP9000. This acts as an in-store processor. It runs all computerized retail operations. The only PCs found in a Home Depot store are special-purpose systems for projects such as kitchen design.

Home Depot avoided the graphical PC world on purpose, Branch says. "Keeping just six PCs operating in every store is difficult. We stayed away from PCs because of the cost of ownership."

However, Home Depot actually did not stay away from PCs. The company rejected network computers such as Java work stations because it believed they were immature; it chose IBM PCs and set them up so they could run only the new Java-based customer service applications.

Kathy Tadlock, information services project manager, helped define the three-part framework for the software: the interface, stored on the users' computers; the business logic; and the transaction data, stored on the in-store processor. Upgrading the software on user computers and servers promised to be fairly easy, separate tasks.

Because the goal was to make it unnecessary to train store personnel in computing, Home Depot chose to train programmers in store operations. "I have over eighty hours training on the tools the new client service program supports," Tadlock says. That's eighty hours on the tools—from drills to table saws—not on the application itself.[20]

SOFTWARE DECISIONS

The new software uses "storyboards" that lead users through a task, step by step, Tadlock says. The visual screen design makes the application easy to use even for people who have never seen it before. The product returns department was the first to receive this highly visual application. Many associates wind up at the returns desk during the day. They need to serve customers, not the computer.

"We wanted experienced plumbers working in our stores, not experienced computer operators. It's painful to see an associate frozen over a keyboard with a customer fuming behind them," Branch says.

Anderson wanted software that could share customer data across the company. He also wanted programs that did not care which operating system was in use for computers that ran such long-standing applications as credit verification and customer look-up.[21]

The team decided that putting the applications on users' computers would make it difficult to control the dissemination of software. Tools to install and maintain Java software on servers are also more effective. Anderson chose Java because he wanted to replace the HP in-store processors with newer, more powerful boxes. HP servers run on the UNIX operating system, while new machines under consideration from Compaq, IBM, and Sun run both Windows NT and UNIX.[22]

The use of Java saves programmer time and training. "We wanted a new application development framework for the future," Branch says, "not just a new program in Java."

As a result, Home Depot turned to Novera and its jBusiness product line, including the Novera Application Server and Novera Beans. The products take Java

[18] Dalton, Gregory, "Home Depot Automates with Optika— Retailer Uses Workflow Application to Archive Documents Electronically," *InformationWeek*, June 7, 1999, p. 24.
[19] Schreir Hohman, Robin, "Marimba Solves Home Depot Dilemma," *Network World*, February 1, 1999, p. 29(1).

[20] Stedman, Craig, "Retailers Adopt Different Strategies for Installing SAP R/3," *Computerworld*, January 25, 1999, p. 9(1).
[21] Stein, Tom, "Making ERP Add Up," *InformationWeek*, May 24, 1999, p. 59.
[22] Gonsalves, Antone, "EJB Technology Is Not Yet Fully Grown," *PC Week*, June 14, 1999, v. 16, i. 24, p. 23.

applications from programmers and add the code for object-oriented communication across the network.

Home Depot retrained programmers, who grew up writing for mainframes, to use Java. Novera's system took the complexity out of managing objects across dispersed networks and let "the programmers focus on pure Java," said Novera cofounder Michael Frey. "Novera took care of the networking portion, allowing Home Depot to write their business logic and define the user interface, then call our database wizards when they need access to remote data."

Customer information, for instance, is stored in an Informix database and is linked to other databases such as telephone look-up and credit verification. Databases are replicated back to a store support center in Atlanta.

"We save over three minutes filling in name and address information by using the telephone look-up," Tadlock says, describing the areas such as returns, special orders, and sales where customer data are needed. Phone record requests go from a countertop computer to the in-store processor to the main database in Atlanta and then back in less than a second. Receipts, if necessary for the particular service situation, are sent through a Java application.[23]

What has Home Depot learned in this process? Anderson wishes Java were more mature. "We had to write our own drivers for many devices, including the debit card readers, scan guns, and even the touch screens."

More than anything, Java's constant change over the past year required fast footwork. "HP's Virtual Java Machine was the slowest we tested, at the start," Branch said. Since the Virtual Machine is slow, it was necessary to switch to servers that were faster because the software to translate Java instructions was faster. That, in turn, meant vendors must stay current, ensuring that all their hardware and software incorporate improvements to Java or Java Virtual Machine technology. The reason is simple—Home Depot programmers have only one real objective. "If it doesn't help the stores sell more hammers faster, the managers don't want it," Branch said. "Every program has to show solid business benefits before it gets funded."[24]

INTERNET

Besides utilizing Java for in-store application development, Home Depot has also decided to implement other Internet technologies into the networking structure. Every evening, the Home Depot corporate headquarters in Atlanta must send an update to over 765 store databases to keep them in sync with the corporate

information system. This is a large amount of data, with each store's database being over 320MB in size. By transmitting all of this data to each store, the WAN (wide-area network) was over extended.[25]

By using Internet push technology developed by Marimba, called Castanet, Home Depot is able to transmit only the different data to each database. The Castanet Tuner integrates the new data with the store database. This technology changes the amount of data from 320MB to 1.2MB, enabling the update transmission to take approximately 30 seconds.[26] An additional benefit is that the technology enables the store server to accept the new data packet and hold it until the database can update, rather than canceling the transmission and requiring the Atlanta server to send it again.[27]

HOME DEPOT WEB SITE

The Home Depot web site carries the same color themes as their retail stores, complete with the now ubiquitous orange Home Depot logo. The site is designed around a frameset style, with the left-hand side of the site remaining stationary with the various site subdirectories, and the right-hand frame changing to reflect the visitor's selection.[28] The visitor can select from seven main sections: What's New, Project How-To's, Financial Information, Press Releases, Community Information, Depot Services, and Store Locator.[29]

What's New This section of the Home Depot web site gives the visitor a good assessment of where the company is heading, in terms of sponsorships, new store openings, new partnerships, and any other important corporate information.

Project How-To's The Project How-To's section carries a wealth of information that keeps customers coming back to Home Depot. Just as the retail stores have classes teaching people how to do home repair and home upgrades, the Home Depot web site offers the same type of expertise. This section is broken into three subcategories: Home, Yard, and Garden. Each of these three sections gives detailed explanations on how to prepare, start, and finish various projects. Examples of

---

[23] Ubois, Jeff, "Companies Turn to Outsourcers to Save Time and Money—Off-Site Web Sites," *InformationWeek*, October 12, 1998, n. 704, p. 55(1).

[24] Gaskin, James E., "Home Depot: Do-It-Yourself Java Programs," *Inter@ctive Week*, September 21, 1998, p. 9.

[25] Sliwa, Carol, and Orenstein, David, "Java Users in No Rush to Upgrade: Many See No Urgency to Implement Newest Runtime Environment," *Computerworld*, June 21, 1999, p. 12(1).

[26] Wilder, Clinton, "Taking Stock Online—Stockclick Lets Users Invest in Companies Online," *InformationWeek*, October 26, 1998, p. 69(1).

[27] Cox, John, "Java Heats Up Across Enterprise Networks: Big Shops Talk Up Their Java Applications at Annual Java-One Conference," *Network World*, June 14, 1999, p. 1.

[28] Colvin, Geoffrey, "A Century of Business," *Fortune*, April 26, 1999, v. 139, i. 8, p. 499(1).

[29] Wilder, Clinton, "E-Commerce: New Sense of Urgency," *InformationWeek*, May 24, 1999, p. 18.

such projects include "Repair Cracked Concrete" and "Replace Standard Wall Switch." By maintaining the same do-it-yourself attitude, Home Depot has successfully applied the approach used in their retail stores to their Internet presence.

Financial Info Home Depot discloses their financial information to the public, as well as the current stock price to visitors to this section.

Press Releases Any public press releases that the company has published are listed on this section of the web site. Home Depot includes all information that may be relevant to their customers, including new partnerships with manufacturers and distributors, and corporate earnings figures.

Community Information Home Depot uses this section to demonstrate its commitment to protection information.

Depot Services In-store demonstrations, classes, credit information, and professional advice are available free in this section.

Store Locator By utilizing Java script, Home Depot enables visitors to find the store located nearest to them. Rather than using a combination of zip code and state information, Home Depot has a dropdown list that contains the names of all states where a retail store is located. When users select their state, and press the GO button, the data is submitted to the Home Depot web server and a new page loads, containing thumbnail-sized images of store location maps and stores' address and telephone information. By clicking on one of the small maps, a large map will load, giving street coordinates of the store.

NETWORK

Home Depot has made a $50 million investment in thin-client workstations to lower their total cost of ownership. They use network computers, which are trimmed down computers that manipulate data in RAM and store information on a server rather than a local storage medium. The company saves on the cost of distributing new applications and information and minimizes inaccurate or out-of-date data files. This has been the primary driver for the decision to use thin-client workstations. By combining the more accessible Java application with the low-cost thin-client, Home Depot has been able to cut costs and increase their profitability.[30]

Both Albers and Vice President of IS Mike Anderson believe that the volume discount for 95,000 NCs should bring the cost per system to less than $500. "That's the purchase price we were really hoping for," Anderson said, noting that the company is as driven as others by the need to lower PC support costs. "Those costs eat away at the bottom line. We realize we must implement systems that will enable us to easily add new applications in the future."

The network computer model is a new technological direction, often considered by industry insiders to be too immature to be applied in large enterprise settings. Home Depot is cautious, citing concerns of future adaptability to new standards and Java developments.[31]

"That makes it difficult for us because we may want to develop applications using different methods," Albers says. "We've got to be sure the system we choose can adequately support multiple types of Java development methods." While it is time consuming to do the kind of real-world testing Home Depot does, Albers says that the 70 systems in each store require the company to benchmark these numbers.[32, 33]

RECOMMENDATION FOR THE FUTURE

In response to customer complaints about stores having inadequate staffing to answer questions, Home Depot has opened phone centers within selected stores to provide information on products, take orders, and give advice to customers. They are also investigating the possibility of opening 24-hour stores. All of these efforts attempt to establish a relationship with customers. When faced with many competitors in the industry, Home Depot wants customers to choose them. With the home improvement market so competitive, Home Depot recognizes the need to use creative marketing tools to make stores run more efficiently.

To provide more products to customers, Home Depot stores must devote more floor space to the products customers want most. These products include flooring products, lawn and garden supplies, and paints. Getting these products to the stores in larger quantities, providing sales associates with the requisite knowledge to assist customers, and providing assistance with delivery of merchandise are the ways in which Home Depot is trying to reestablish itself as the store of choice for home repair products.

---

[30] Sliwa, Carol, "Easing the 'Middle-Tier' Traffic Jam: Securities Firm Leads with Agent Technology," *Computerworld*, December 21, 1998, p. 14(1).

[31] Wilder, Clinton, "Taking Stock Online—Stockclick Lets Users Invest in Companies Online," *InformationWeek*, October 26, 1998, p. 69(1).

[32] Hohman, Robin Schreir, "Marimba Solves Home Depot Dilemma," *Network World*, February 1, 1999, p. 29(1).

[33] DePompa, Barbara, "A Thin Foothold—Thin Clients May Not Be Right for Every Business, But They're Finding a Market," *InformationWeek*, October 12, 1998, p. 146(1).

CASE QUESTIONS

Strategic Questions

1. What is the strategic direction of the corporation/organization?

2. What forces are driving this direction?

3. What has been the catalyst for change?

4. What are the critical success factors for this corporation/organization?

5. What are the core competencies for this corporation/organization?

Technological Questions

6. What technologies has the corporation relied on?

7. What has caused a change in the use of technology in the corporation/organization?

Quantitative Questions

8. What does the corporation say about its financial ability to embark on a major technological program of advancement?

9. What conclusions can be reached from an analysis of the financial information to support or contradict this financial ability?

10. What analysis can be made by examining the following ratio groups?
    Quick
    Current

Debt
Revenue
Profit

11. Are there long-term trends that seem to be problematic?

12. Is the industry stable?

13. Are there replacement products?

Internet Questions

14. What does Home Depot's web page present about their business direction?

15. Is the Internet a profit center for the company?

Industry Questions

16. What challenges and opportunities is the industry facing?

17. Is the industry oligopolistic or competitive?

18. Does the industry face a change in government regulation?

19. How will technology impact the industry?

Data Questions

20. What role do data play in the future of the corporation?

21. How important are data to the corporation's continued success?

TOYS "R" US, INC.

Executive Summary

Case Name:	Toys "R" Us, Inc.
Case Industry:	Retail toys
Major Technology Issue:	Developing a global data warehouse
Major Financial Issue:	Structuring the corporation in the most advantageous way
Major Strategic Issue:	Dominating their market segment
Major Players/Leaders:	Charles Lazarus, founder and CEO
Main Web Page:	www.toysrus.com
Case Conclusion/Recommendation:	The company must continue its progress to develop a global data warehouse that can also be used for regional decision making. The company must continue to expand internationally.

CASE ANALYSIS

INTRODUCTORY STORY

In 1957, Charles Lazarus saw the baby boom generation in the making. He observed that this was going to lead to a huge demand for baby products. In his mind this was mainly furniture.

The idea of selling just furniture did not last long. The furniture sold well, but Charles Lazarus got a lot of customers asking the same question: "Don't you stock any toys for my baby?" This led to the first "toy supermarket," which also opened in 1957. In the mid-1970s, Toys "R" Us became a public company. Since that time it has targeted other markets. These stores include Kids "R" Us, which concentrates mainly on children's clothes, Babies "R" Us, which markets products for younger aged toddlers, and Books "R" Us, which sells books for children.

SHORT DESCRIPTION OF THE COMPANY

Toys "R" Us has concentrated its present efforts in three core businesses, Toys "R" Us, Babies "R" Us, and Kids "R" Us. Toys "R" Us is in business "to offer a wide selection of toys, family recreational and educational products, including bicycles, video games/software, computer software, school supplies, sporting equipment, backyard swimming pools, playgrounds and swing sets, and children's books."

The company also offers products such as diapers, cribs, and strollers for infant and preschool-age children. Babies "R" Us focuses primarily on infants' needs. These stores, usually around 40,000 square feet in size, sell strollers, high chairs, cribs, chests, and baby furniture. Kids "R" Us is close to becoming the largest children's clothing store chain. These stores sell name brand children's clothes.

SHORT HISTORY OF THE COMPANY

Toys "R" Us uses sales and market domination as its measures of success. In describing the market domination that the store currently holds, Toys "R" Us speaks confidently. "We have not only created a niche, we totally dominate it," says one marketing representative. Toys "R" Us feels that they are not only in business to sell toys; it is very important that they make people happy.

Toys "R" Us participates in a number of programs benefiting child health and safety. These include such things as matching employee contributions to children's health care and educational institutions, awarding grants, providing books to homeless children, preventing the sale of unsafe toys and look-a-like toy guns, and researching toys to address the needs of children with disabilities.

The Toys "R" Us merchandising philosophy is "to provide the best selection of name-brand merchandise, stocked in depth, at everyday low prices, plus to ensure first class customer service."[1] Toys "R" Us plans to continue growing by "redesigning and updating the look of our stores and emphasizing customer service, pricing and selection." These plans are not only in place for the United States, but are especially strong for the global environment which they want to dominate.

---

[1] www.toysrus.com

FINANCIAL AND PORTFOLIO ANALYSIS

Toys "R" Us is a profitable company. However, it has had its ups and downs due to a series of restructurings and other changes. The major change, as far as restructuring, did not take place until the first quarter of 1996. On January 1, 1996, Toys "R" Us adopted a holding company form of organizational structure.

The new holding company provides Toys "R" Us with a framework to encourage future growth. This growth will come from internal operations, acquisitions, and joint ventures. It broadens the alternatives available for future financing and generally provides for greater administrative and operational flexibility. Toys "R" Us also closed 25 stores that were not meeting sales targets, mostly in Europe, and consolidated some distribution and administrative facilities to make the remaining stores more profitable. The name and the corporation changed to Toys "R" Us–Delaware, Inc.

The new holding company was predicted to increase 1996 earnings by $50 million. Another reason behind the change, besides increasing profitability and earnings, was to "improve the company's growth trends over the longer term," said Toys "R" Us CEO, Michael Goldstein. This restructuring would cause Toys "R" Us to take a one-time hit of $270 million, after taxes, in the fourth quarter of 1996. Along with the restructuring would come price cutting, increased advertising and promotions, and additional computer software.[2]

These actions were caused by several issues during the first quarter of 1996. The store's stock price had dropped to the lowest point in five years, $21.50 per share. This was due to the increased competition from stores such as K-mart, Wal-Mart, and, more recently, Target. These stores were cutting into the Toys "R" Us market share by offering toys and furniture similar to Toys "R" Us.

Toys "R" Us sales had been increasing by around 10 percent annually from 1992 through 1995. The company celebrated the opening of 113 new stores in the United States, 171 new international stores, a few clothing stores, and a more streamlined product mix. Advertising expenses increased due to extensive promotional activity especially in 1995. Net income also increased until the restructuring charge hit in 1995. This brought net income from $5.32 million in 1995 to $1.48 million in 1996.

The sales/cash ratio doubled from 1994 to 1995 and again from 1995 to 1996. Cash did not change while sales increased by 10 percent a year. Net sales as a percentage of working capital, plant and equipment, current assets, and total assets all increased. One important ratio that increased dramatically was inventory turnover. Based on the restructuring that took place, Toys "R" Us combined distribution activities to become more efficient in this area.[3]

STOCK/INVESTMENT OUTLOOK

Toys "R" Us has an obvious advantage over its competitors in name recognition, not to mention reputation. As long as the store continues to be on the cutting edge of technology, and carries the latest in video games and toys for children, it is likely to continue to have the highest market share, at least in the traditional toy sector.

INDUSTRY AND MARKET ANALYSIS

Toys "R" Us holds the highest market share in traditional toys, which include games, preschool and infant items, and electronic toys. It has approximately 21 percent of the market. The largest market shares are held by 10 stores including Wal-Mart, K-mart, Target, Kay-Bee, Service Merchandise, Hills, J.C. Penney, Ames, and Meijer. Wal-Mart has the second largest market share with approximately 15 percent.

In 1995, the industry posted retail sales of $20 billion, two-thirds of which occurs in the fourth quarter because of the holidays. The toy industry has one of the lowest markups among all consumer hard goods, with toys sometimes selling below the retailer's cost.

Several demographic trends impact toy companies. More families today have dual incomes and more disposable income. Since people are living longer, more grandparents and great-grandparents are involved in the family group. They tend to be purchasers of gifts and other items.

According to the 1996 Standard and Poor's Industry Surveys, Toys "R" Us is classified as a specialty store, while its two closest competitors, K-mart and Wal-Mart, are considered discount department stores. As such, Toys "R" Us's $532 million in net income fell behind Wal-Mart's $2.7 billion in net income and ahead of K-mart's $260 million.[4]

Environmental and product safety issues are important in the toy industry. One piece of environmental legislation impacting the industry is the Model Toxic Reduction Act of 1989. This law limits the presence of certain heavy metals in packaging and includes provision for further reductions.

Product safety is always a concern with toys. Toy Manufacturers of America, Inc., works closely with the government and other organizations on all product safety matters. These groups may include teachers, par-

[2] "Transforming Toys R Us," *Computer Retail Week*, September 21, 1998, v. 8, n. 219, p. 3(1).

[3] "Toys' FY Loss, Q4 Gain," *Computer Retail Week*, March 22, 1999, p. 7(1).
[4] "Toys R Us Profit Plummets," *Computer Retail Week*, August 24, 1998, v. 8, n. 216, p. 3(1).

ents, psychologists, or other specialists. New products or product prototypes are given to these groups for feedback and, after discussion, may be given to focus groups of children. A detailed evaluation is made at the end of the study period. Environmental and safety issues are taken very seriously. While competing in many ways, toy companies also have a joint commitment to public safety.

ROLE OF RESEARCH AND DEVELOPMENT

Toys "R" Us has two technology departments: information systems and information technology. The information systems department, "develops and maintains business applications for all Toys, USA divisions," while the information technology department "supports the company's hardware, operating systems, networking, and infrastructure needs."[5]

TECHNOLOGICAL STORY

One problem that toy stores have had is finding the right amount of computer software and hardware to add to their product mix. In the fall of 1995, Toys "R" Us began a test phase in which it decided to sell a few different computer systems and printers in selected stores. These stores, which numbered fewer than 20, carried Pentium Packard Bell systems and Lexmark color inkjet printers. This introduction came a year after the store's introduction of computer software into its product mix.

The computer hardware test was never successful. This may be due partly to laxness of Toys "R" Us management. Computer products have been more successful at smaller, newer stores such as Zany Brainy and Noodle Kidoodle. These stores are grabbing high margin market share. They have changed their marketing to center around the computer toy market. They each offer around 500 software titles and have many workstations in the store where kids can interact with the systems.[6]

TECHNOLOGICAL INVESTMENT AND ANALYSIS

The company's primary technology includes Unisys mainframes, IBM processors, and thousands of personal computers. Operating systems include DOS, Windows, and Windows NT all running under one protocol with IBM AS/400 midrange systems. Toys

"R" Us uses a wide-area network based on satellites, some local-area networks, and third-party networks.

It is important for the company to remain in constant contact with all locations. At the same time Toys "R" Us tries to maintain a decentralized focus, giving individual stores the autonomy they need to respond to local markets around the world.[7]

Joseph Giamelli, vice president of information systems, international division, decided to upgrade to Windows NT running on IBM AS/400 servers. The transition brought clients and distributed servers together under one standard open platform for Toys "R" Us stores around the world. With over 400,000 AS/400s in place, Toys "R" Us is the largest operator of data warehouses. As far as training goes, Giamelli states, "By going in with the AS/400, I had to train people on the application, eliminating the technical knowledge required and focusing on the business model."[8]

Also involved in the upgraded system was a global data warehouse that acknowledges 12 different languages and currencies. The length of time to remap data to the data warehouses in 12 languages and currencies was just six months. This upgrade enabled all software from around the world to run on the same platform and still allow all activities to be analyzed by the head office. As a result, Toys "R" Us analysts have been able to run better reports on a global basis by item, vendor, and category.

TECHNOLOGICAL INNOVATIONS

Toys "R" Us hopes to expand its customer base with its web site, www.toysrus.com. It offers services that are not available in stores, such as the ability to search for gifts by age and price range. Purchases can be gift wrapped and shipped with a personalized note. The original web site had been up since 1996 and served as a static corporate brochure. By 1997, the Toys "R" Us information systems department began the seed work for the web shopping site. The new unit took shape in February 1998.[9]

Toys "R" Us is facing competition from web startups eToys and Toys.com. By focusing on wrapping and other services, the company is hoping to attract upscale consumers. Toys "R" Us is playing catch-up to feisty

[5] Ricadela, Aaron, "Toy Retailer Slices Inventories, While Encouraging Consumers to See: The Software Side of Toys R Us," *Computer Retail Week*, July 27, 1998, v. 8, n. 220, p. 8(1).

[6] "Toys R Us Forms Web Unit," *Computer Retail Week*, May 10, 1999, p. 3(1).

[7] Wilder, Clinton, and Dalton, Gregory, "Kmart, Toys 'R' Us Turn to Internet for Sales Boost," *Information Week*, July 20, 1998, n. 692, p. 30(1).

[8] "Transforming Toys R Us," *Computer Retail Week*, September 21, 1998, v. 8, n. 219, p. 3(1).

[9] LaMonica, Martin, "At Toys R Us, Help Desk Application Is No Plaything," *InfoWorld*, October 5, 1998, v. 20, n. 40, p. 60(1).

competitor eToys Inc. (www.etoys.com), whose site has garnered rave reviews since its launch in October, 1997.[10] The site features more than 1,000 different toys, including those from well-known vendors BRIO, Mattel, and Fisher-Price.

Throughout the Internet development process, Kimball (CIO) wanted to make sure the team did not stray from the site's goals. "We had to constantly look at it from a customer perspective rather than getting wrapped up in technology." The first pass was not to have plug-ins, full-motion videos, or links to other manufacturers' pages. "Our challenge was to focus on simplicity," Kimball explains. "We could have added lots of graphics to be extremely appealing, but we didn't want the user to wait six minutes to download the thing," she said. "It comes up in about five to seven seconds."[11]

Users can track their packages' whereabouts via a link to the UPS online tracking service. The interface to the Toys "R" Us inventory system insures every item listed is in stock.[12]

---

[10] Wilder, Clinton, and Dalton, Gregory, "E-Commerce Dividends," *Information Week*, May 3, 1999, p. 18(1).

[11] Collett, Stacy, "Toys R Us Online Plan May Undermine Storefront Sales," *Computerworld*, May 3, 1999, p. 6(1).

[12] Leong, Kathy Chin, "Toys "R" Us Restructures for E-Comm," *InternetWeek*, June 8, 1998, n. 718, p. 47(2).

To stay on the right track, the company hired outside consultants, including New York-based InterWorld, to customize e-commerce software and Siegel and Gale for interface design. The Toys "R" Us web site is linked to the company's back-end inventory and fulfillment systems by commerce server software from InterWorld.[13]

"This was a fairly challenging project," according to Lisa Marchese, interactive strategist for Siegel and Gale. "Every detail had to be worked out. Other companies already had a catalog to start from, but Toys "R" Us had to start from scratch."[14]

RECOMMENDATION FOR THE FUTURE

Integrating the company's databases and putting decision-making power in the local store managers' hands gives Toys "R" Us a competitive edge. While operating locally, stores have the benefit of knowledge about the entire Toys "R" Us system. The company must expand into more countries, creating and expanding market share. In addition, it must integrate the Internet and store focus, getting cross-marketing benefits from both.

---

[13] Orenstein, David, "Retailers Struggle to Keep Techs," *Computerworld*, November 2, 1998, p. 39(1).

[14] Leong, Kathy Chin, "Toys "R" Us Restructures for E-Comm.," *InternetWeek*, June 8, 1998, n. 718, p. 47(2).

CASE QUESTIONS

Strategic Questions

1. What is the strategic direction of the corporation/organization?

2. Who or what forces are driving this direction?

3. What has been the catalyst for change?

4. What are the critical success factors for this corporation/organization?

5. What are the core competencies for this corporation/organization?

Technological Questions

6. What technologies has the corporation relied on?

7. What has caused a change in the use of technology in the corporation/organization?

8. How has this change been implemented?

9. Who has driven this change throughout the organization?

Quantitative Questions

10. What does the corporation say about its financial ability to embark on a major technological program of advancement?

11. What conclusions can be reached from an analysis of the financial information to support or contradict this financial ability?

12. What analysis can be made by examining the following ratio groups?

    Quick
    Current
    Long Term Debt/Equity
    Inventory Turnover
    Net Income/Net Sales

Internet Questions

13. What does Toys "R" Us's web page present about their business?

Industry Questions

14. What challenges and opportunities is the industry facing?

15. Is the industry oligopolistic or competitive?

16. Does the industry face a change in government regulation?

17. How will technology impact the industry?

Data Questions

18. What role do data play in the future of the corporation?

19. How important are data to the corporation's continued success?

20. How will the capture and maintenance of customer data impact the corporation's future?

SEARS, ROEBUCK AND CO.

Executive Summary

Case Name:	Sears, Roebuck and Co.
Case Industry:	Retail sales
Major Technology Issue:	How to handle the Prodigy online service
Major Financial Issue:	How to keep its stores profitable
Major Strategic Issue:	Is it smart to concentrate on the core business?
Major Players/Leaders:	Arthur Martinez, CEO, Sears; Ed Bennet, CEO, Prodigy
Main Web Page:	www.sears.com
Case Conclusion/Recommendation:	Sears has sold its share of the Prodigy online service, which did not offer customers what they wanted when subscriptions to online services exploded. With regard to their stores, Sears is spinning off its hardware sales into separate stores.

CASE ANALYSIS

INTRODUCTORY STORY

In February 1996, Sears' chairman and CEO Arthur Martinez told a meeting of analysts in New York that the company was looking for a way to sell its half of the Prodigy online service. Sears' spokesperson Jan Drummond said, "Prodigy did not fit into the company's long-term model for growth in terms of its core retail business."

"Sears' decision to seek a buyer resolves a long-standing issue," said Barry Kluger, Prodigy's senior vice president of corporate communications. "For Prodigy, it presents a wide array of new exciting options, all designed to continue to grow and enhance the asset."[1]

SHORT DESCRIPTION OF THE COMPANY

Sears is a multiline retailer which provides a wide array of merchandise and services through two segments: domestic operations and international operations.

The domestic operations segment includes the company's retail stores (comprised of full-line, home, and auto stores), home services and direct response marketing in the United States and Puerto Rico and the credit card portfolio. The credit card portfolio primarily relates to the Sears card, the largest proprietary credit card in the United States. The international operations segment consists of similar merchandising and service operations conducted through majority-owned subsidiaries in Canada and Mexico.[2]

The domestic retail merchandise business is highly competitive. "Convenience of shopping facilities, quality of merchandise, competitive prices, brand names and availability of services such as credit, product delivery, repair, and installation, are the principal factors which differentiate competitors."[3]

SHORT HISTORY OF THE COMPANY

In the late 1880s America had only 38 states. The country's population was 58 million of which 65 percent lived in rural areas. Only a few cities had 200,000 or more residents. The yearly national income was about $10 billion.

Richard W. Sears was an agent of a railway station in North Redwood, Minnesota. Sears' job as station agent left him plenty of spare time, so he sold lumber and coal to local residents to make extra money. Later, when he received a shipment of watches, unwanted by a neighboring Redwood Falls jeweler, Sears purchased them himself and sold the watches to other station agents up and down the line. He then ordered more for resale. In 1886 Sears began the R.W. Sears Watch Company in Minneapolis.

The following year, Sears moved his business to Chicago and placed an advertisement for a watchmaker. Alvah C. Roebuck answered the ad and Sears

---

[1] Ziegler, Bart, "Sears, Roebuck & Co. and IBM Sell Prodigy to International Wireless," *The Wall Street Journal*, May 13, 1996, p. B2.

[2] Sears, Roebuck & Co. Annual Report for the Fiscal Year Ended December 28, 1996.

[3] Standard & Poor's Industry Reports, April 1996, p. 74.

hired him. In 1893 the name of the firm became Sears, Roebuck and Co. The company was incorporated under the laws of New York in 1906 when common and preferred stocks were offered in the open market. The company has been publicly traded ever since.[4]

Sears maintains its corporate headquarters in Sears Tower, Chicago; the company's merchandise group is located in Hoffman Estates, Illinois.

In 1992, Sears outlined its five strategic priorities:

1. Focus on our core businesses.
2. Become a more compelling place to shop.
3. Achieve local market focus in products and services.
4. Accelerate cost and productivity improvements.
5. Create a winning culture and set of values.

The goal, supported by these strategies, is to make Sears a compelling place to shop, work, and invest.

In 1993 Sears started a $4 billion store revitalization program. It includes the mall-based store remodeling program and expansion of off-the-mall stores and home services.[5] The strategy is to revitalize the mall-based stores to strengthen apparel offerings and to provide the best value in malls. Off-the-mall furniture, hardware, and automotive stores position the company to benefit from changing demographics, which will expand the home and automotive aftermarket businesses.[6]

FINANCIAL AND PORTFOLIO ANALYSIS

Since 1992, Sears has established several financial goals: to attain an operating margin of 5 percent from the core retail operations and to give shareholders a total return in the top quartile of the S&P 500 over a five-year period. On average, the company's ratio of operating costs to revenues is not as low as benchmark targets in the industry but is improving due to efforts to increase revenues and cut costs.

Revenue growth, sales per square foot, operating margin, inventory turnover, and return on assets are important measures used internally to determine the company's progress in achieving its goals. Approximately $18 billion of funding at year-end 1994 was used primarily to support credit receivables. Retail store operations are essentially debt free, providing a solid foundation for growth.

From 1993 to 1997, Sears invested more than $4 billion in capital programs, funded largely by free cash

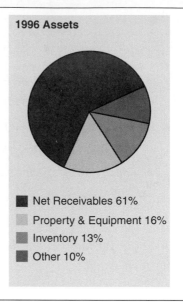

1996 Assets

- Net Receivables 61%
- Property & Equipment 16%
- Inventory 13%
- Other 10%

Figure 4.1 Sears' assets, 1996.

flow[7] (Figure 4.1). The spending revitalized the mall-based stores, grew off-the-mall formats, and improved costs and productivity. Spending increasingly will be directed to an accelerated off-the-mall store roll-out program. The capital program will expand total square footage by approximately 5 to 7 percent each year.[8]

The revitalization plan begun in 1993 has achieved the following goals:

- Increased productivity as measured by sales-per-selling-square-foot expanding from $289 at year-end 1992 to $346 at year-end 1994. Stores were remodeled, space allocated to apparel was increased, and merchandise offerings were revitalized.
- Expanded retail core operating margins by 160 basis points as revenues expanded by 21.5 percent from 1992 through 1994 and selling, general, and administrative expenses expanded by only 13.8 percent.
- Improved inventory turnover from 3.4 to 3.7 times from 1992 through 1994, through better inventory management, improved systems, and better vendor partnerships.
- Increased return on average assets from 2.1 to 3.1 percent through inventory management and improved sales per square foot.

The strategic sourcing initiative established in 1993 has identified more than $250 million in cost savings by fo-

[4] Sears, Roebuck & Co. Web Page, Sears History: http://www.sears.com, 1997; Gunn, Eileen P., "The Sultans of Sprawl: They Hit the Big Time by Helping to Pave the Planet," *Fortune*, June 21, 1999, v. 139, i. 12, p. 128(1).

[5] Gunn, Eileen P., "The Sultans of Sprawl: They Hit the Big Time by Helping to Pave the Planet," *Fortune*, June 21, 1999, v. 139, i. 12, p. 128(1).

[6] Sears, Roebuck & Co. Annual Report for the Fiscal Year Ended December 31, 1994.

[7] Tweney, Dylan, "Sears Joins the Revolution," *InfoWorld*, March 22, 1999, v. 21, i. 12, p. NA(1).

[8] Sears, Roebuck & Co. Annual Report for the Fiscal Year Ended December 28, 1996.

cusing on cost of goods sold, operating expenses, and capital expenditures. Specific categories reviewed include batteries, repair parts, paint, electronics, and paper and printing costs. Savings were used in three ways: to lower expenses, improve product quality, and provide better value to customers.

Logistics costs have been reduced significantly by consolidating distribution centers, increasing warehouse automation, and reducing transportation costs. The distribution cycle has also been shortened and logistic service levels (time and completeness of orders) have improved. Merchandise returns have been centralized to increase the potential for vendor credits.

Since 1994, Sears has reengineered its long-term incentive compensation toward making Sears a compelling place to shop, work, and invest. Arthur Martinez, chairman and CEO, believes that the leading indicators of the financial performance of the company are customers with a compelling place to shop and a workforce energized about its role in the process.

In 1996, Sears reported better-than-expected second-quarter earnings of $274 million, or $0.67 per share (Tables 4.2 and 4.3). This compares with $218 million, or $0.54 per share in 1997.[9]

[9] Ibid.

Table 4.2 Earnings per Share Statistics 1994–1996

	12/31/96	12/31/95	12/31/94
ROE - 12M	28.61	25.04	13.46
P/E 12 Mon	14.60	10.71	14.74
Beta	1.52	1.39	1.08
P/E 12 Mon	14.60	10.71	14.74
Trend EPS Growth	1.01	−2.89	1.86
EPS LT Growth %	14.63	13.21	12.50
EPS LTG % Std Dev	1.80	2.92	3.77
Actual EPS - 12M	3.15	3.64	2.13

(*Source:* Zacks Investment Research.)

According to management, merchandise margins increased in hardlines, apparel, automotive, and home, primarily due to fewer promotional markdowns and improved sourcing.[10] In addition, margins improved from a strong 9.4 percent increase in comp-store sales, leveraging buying and occupancy expense. The selling and store operating expense ratio declined 50 basis points to 21.3 from 21.8 percent leveraging payroll, benefits, and marketing expenses.[11]

[10] Andrews, Whit, "MP3's Clearly a Big Deal, But Is It a Revolution," *Internet World*, May 24, 1999, v. 5, i. 20, p. 14.
[11] Stein, Tom, "Making ERP Add Up," *Information Week*, May 24, 1999, p. 59.

Table 4.3 Sears, Roebuck & Co.—Stock's Outlook

Estimates (Dec)	1996A	1997E	1998E
EPS:	$3.12	$3.60	$4.15
P/E:	15.6x	13.5x	11.7x
EPS Change (Y-o-Y):	23.3%	15.4%	15.3%
Consensus EPS:		$3.59	$4.16
(First Call: 11-Apr-97)			
Q1 EPS (Mar):	$0.36		$0.41
Cash Flow/Share:	$4.93	$5.70	$6.50
P/CF:	9.8x	8.6x	7.5x
Dividend Rate:	$1.16	$0.92	$1.14
Dividend Yield:	2.4%	1.9%	2.3%
Opinion & Financial Data			
Investment Opinion:	B-2-1-7		
Mkt. Value/Shares Outstanding (mn):	$18,354 / 399		
Book Value/Share (Dec-96):	$12.39		
Price/Book Ratio:	3.9x		
ROE 1996 Average:	27.2%		
LT Liability % of Capital:	63.7%		
Est. 5 Year EPS Growth:	15.0%		
Stock Data (April 1997)			
52-Week Range:	$56¾–$39⅞		
Symbol / Exchange:	S / NYSE		
Options:	Chicago		
Institutional Ownership-Spectrum:	63.7%		
Brokers Covering (First Call):	26		

(*Source:* Merrill Lynch Capital Markets: Sears, Roebuck & Co.—Company Report.)

STOCK/INVESTMENT OUTLOOK

Growth in provisions for uncollectable accounts has hurt Sears' stock. The stock was down 21 percent from its 52-week high due to weakness in the retail group and concerns about growth in the provision for uncollectible accounts, which were up 73% in the second quarter, in the credit business about 50% of Sears' earnings (Table 4.3). At a price of $40 per share or below, the stock adequately discounted the potential problems in the credit business (Table 4.2).[12]

RISK ANALYSIS

While the provision for uncollectible accounts was rising, the net interest margin benefited from a uniform price increase in the second quarter of 1995, a standard $10 late fee and tighter grace standards implemented in the fourth quarter of 1995, and lower funding costs.[13] The APR rate was raised to 21 percent in 21 states on new balances in 1995.

INDUSTRY AND MARKET ANALYSIS

A number of factors will impact retailing and consumers over the next 10 years. There is a dominance of large, well-financed retailers benefiting from industry consolidation. Customers are increasingly demanding more value, defined as price, quality, merchandise assortment, and shopping convenience. Buying patterns are also changing as an aging population spends more on services.

In the first quarter of 1996, the near-term investment outlook for general merchandise retailers was neutral. There was an anticipation of continued weak consumer spending and pricing pressures. Excess retail square footage plagued the industry. Value pricing was the order of the day. Eventually the downward pressure in pricing abated. In 1995, the general merchandise index rose only 10.5 percent versus the S&P 500's gain of 34.1 percent. Year to date through March 29, 1996 the S&P 500 gained 4.8 percent, against a gain of 9.8 percent in the general merchandise index (Table 4.4).

The long-term investment outlook for general merchandise was neutral also (Figure 4.2a). Because of the highly competitive nature of general merchandising, retailers were forced to make cost cutting a top priority (Table 4.4). Major chains eliminated redundancies and closed underperforming stores (Figure 4.4).

Modest sales growth expectations forced retailers to trim inventories and invest in cost-cutting technology to boost productivity (Figure 4.3). Technology investments provided chains with better information about

---

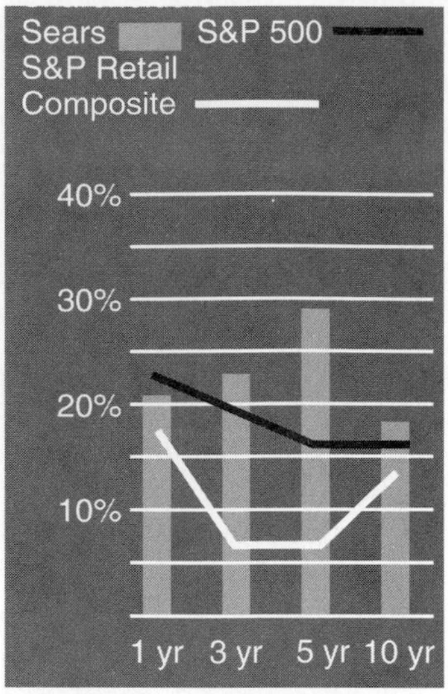

Figure 4.2a Total return to shareholders. (*Source:* Sears' 1996 annual report.)

sales trends. This enabled them to keep less merchandise in stock. Costs were brought in line through sales growth (Table 4.5). Over time the reduction in retail square footage made a better balance between supply and demand (Figure 4.2b).[14]

Sears was included in the computer software and services markets which were some of the fastest growing segments of the computer industry. In the first quarter of 1996, computer service stocks continued to outperform the market. These companies had strong

---

[14] Caldwell, Bruce, and Violino, Bob, "Supply-Chain Tests Begin," *Information Week*, February 8, 1999, p. 31(1).

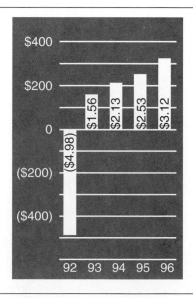

Figure 4.2b Income (loss) from continuing operations per common share. (*Source:* Sears' 1996 annual report.)

---

[12] Hood, W., *Investment Highlights Second Quarter Earnings, Outlook And Rating*, Prudential Securities Inc., The Investext Group, 1996.

[13] Sears, Roebuck & Co. Annual Report for the Fiscal Year Ended December 28, 1996.

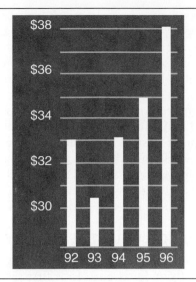

Figure 4.3 Revenues 1992–1996 (in billions).

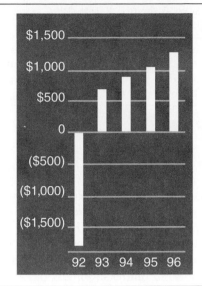

Figure 4.4 Income (loss) from continuing operations 1992–1996 (in millions).

growth characteristics, including a high level of repeat business, long contract life cycles, recurring revenues, earnings stability, and predictability (Figure 4.5).[15]

The availability of new, less costly, and more powerful computer workstations and communications technologies led to increasing demand for "client/server" computing systems, based on networks of desktop computers.[16] Client/server networks are cheaper, more reliable, and more versatile than traditional mainframe-based systems. The growing popularity of client/server computing led to *transformational outsourcing*. This was the practice where a computer services firm assisted customers to

change from a traditional mainframe computing environment to client/server systems.[17]

ROLE OF RESEARCH AND DEVELOPMENT

In 1995, 14 percent of Americans had access to the online world. The potential audience for online marketers and advertisers continues to grow. Subscriptions to consumer online services increased 37.3 percent to 8,498,376 in the second quarter of 1995.[18]

---

[15] Barry, D. D., et al, *Merrill Lynch Capital Markets: Sears, Roebuck & Co.–Company Report*, April 17, 1997, Merrill Lynch, Pierce, Fenner & Smith Incorporated, p. 19.
[16] Dalton, Gregory, "Focus On: Merging Physical, Virtual Sales Channels—Retailers Launch Cyber Kiosks," *Computer Reseller News*, May 24, 1999, p. 53.

[17] Dalton, Gregory, Colkin, Justin, and Hibbard, W. Eileen, "Virtual Shopping Gets Real—Sears, Borders to Install In-Store Intranet Kiosks To Make Entire Inventory Available," *Information Week*, May 17, 1999, p. 30(1).
[18] "Online Subscribers Grew 37.3% in 2Q (2nd Qtr. 1995)," SIMBA Information Inc., *Electronic Marketplace Report*, September 5, 1995, v. 9, n. 17, p. 5(1).

Table 4.4 Retail General Merchandise Index Ratios*

Valuation Ratios	As of 3/29/96	1995	1994	1988-95 Avg.
Price to Earnings Ratio	24.89	16.70	16.50	27.87
P/E Relative to S&P 500	1.31	0.96	0.98	1.33
Dividend Yield (%)	2.13	2.64	2.92	2.11
Dividend Payout Ratio	52.95	44.13	48.20	52.62
Price to Book Value	2.52	2.41	2.79	3.04
Price to Cash Flow	13.47	13.44	15.80	12.03
Structure & Profitability Ratios				
Debt to Equity Ratios	113.55	108.84	101.37	101.94
Return on Equity (%)	13.49	16.39	12.75	11.47
Return on Sales (%)	1.92	2.27	2.02	1.82

(*Source:* Standard & Poor's Industry Reports, April 1996.) *Per-share data adjusted to stock price level index. Average of stock prices indexes, 1970=10.

Table 4.5 Sears' Valuation Ratios, 1996 Sears: Structure & Profitability Ratios

Price to Earnings Ratio	16.6	Debt to Capital	73
Dividend Yield (%)	1.7	Return on Equity (%)	27.7
Price to Book Value	4.16	Return on Assets	16.4
Price to Cash Flow	9.84		

(*Source:* Zacks Investment Research.)

The key to Internet success, of course, is the ability to find the right information.[19] Sears attempted to compete in this area.[20] Prodigy Service Company, the first consumer online service in the United States, was a partnership formed between IBM and Sears in 1984. The online service was launched in the United States in 1988, and was available nationally in September 1990. Prodigy pioneered online shopping, banking, advertising, and stock trading.[21]

TECHNOLOGICAL STORY

In early 1995, online providers America Online, CompuServe, and Prodigy Services argued that Microsoft should take Microsoft Network out of Windows 95. These rivals were collectively denouncing Microsoft's plans to bundle Microsoft Network with Windows 95. After writing letters to Bill Gates and four influential congressmen, including then Senate Majority Leader

---

[19] "Sears, Roebuck and Co.," *Internet World*, May 17, 1999, v. 5, i. 19, p. 4(1).
[20] "Sears Selling Major Appliances Online 05/13/99," *Newsbytes*, May 13, 1999, p. NA.
[21] Varney, Sarah, "IBM, Sears Mulling Prodigy's Fate," January 15, 1996, Datamation, January 15, 1996, v. 42, n. 2, p. 40(8).

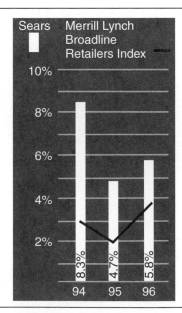

Figure 4.5 Comparable store sales growth.

Bob Dole, executives from America's largest three online services held a press conference in Washington to convince the public the integration of Microsoft's Network with Windows 95 would constitute an unfair competitive advantage. No plans to litigate over the issue were announced.

Microsoft's response was to charge the so-called Big Three with colluding to avert competition. The U.S. Department of Justice continued to investigate Microsoft Network, but withdrew a subpoena challenged by Microsoft. Microsoft shipped Windows 95 on August 24, 1995. Its first offering of Network included a WWW browser, previously scheduled for a later release.[22]

TECHNOLOGICAL INVESTMENT AND ANALYSIS

Prodigy was an industry leader when it began in 1990. It grew rapidly and was one of the first services to target consumers. It benefited from the marketing, funding, and distribution capabilities of IBM and Sears. Along the way, Prodigy consumed over $1 billion of its parents' funds without posting a profit in its 11 years of operation. It had a $3.8 million loss in 1994. In the fast-paced online marketplace, other services rose from start-up to profitability in far less time.

Prodigy has been called an underachiever. In January 1995, Prodigy became the first major online service to deliver a web browser to its members. Prodigy's Internet access focused on the World Wide Web, Usenet newsgroups, and Internet e-mail, with Gopher and FTP offered through the web browser. Nationwide access was limited to 14.4 Kbps until late 1995; America Online, on the other hand, was already offering 28.8-Kbps access.[23]

A former Prodigy Vice President, Scott Kurnit, launched prodigy's Internet strategy. He left Prodigy abruptly in April 1995 to head MCI's Internet business. Some observers say Kurnit left because he was not given enough free rein to pursue his vision. In May 1995, just one month after Kurnit's departure, Prodigy president Ross Glatzer announced his retirement from the online services business. The announcement included the appointment of former Viacom executive Ed Bennett as President. Bennett had free rein pushing Prodigy forward with a "we can't beat the net, so let's join it" plan. Bennett was the third company president in five years.

Industry analysts expected an IBM executive to take control of Prodigy. Glatzer, a former Sears marketing executive, had often endured criticism over the handling of the company's affairs. Press reports quoted

---

[22] Betts, Mitch, and Booker, Ellis, "Top 3 On-Line Providers Plead for Microsoft Mercy; Take Microsoft Network Out of Win95, They Ask," *Computerworld*, July 24, 1995, v. 29, n. 30, p. 4(1).
[23] Eng, Paul M., "Prodigy: A 5-Year-Old Underachiever," *Business Week*, October 30, 1995, n. 3448, p. 150(1).

IBM sources who suggested that they wanted to exert more control over the partnership. Bennett, an entertainment production veteran with experience marketing to niche segments hungry for innovative content, was viewed as a good compromise for Prodigy's "oddly paired owners."

Ed Bennett faced a large number of obstacles as Prodigy attempted to reposition and reinvent itself. "They're on the right track, but they need to move quickly," said Adam Schoenfeld, an analyst at Jupiter Communications Inc., an online services market research firm in New York. "Their corporate parents may have grown weary of throwing money down the sinkhole."[24]

For many years Prodigy used its proprietary NAPLPS programming language, which dated back to Prodigy's DOS and character-based origins in 1988. It was widely criticized for being both unwieldy and unsightly. In December 1994 Prodigy announced its second corporate downsizing in two years, laying off nearly 100 of its 700 employees. These were NAPLPS programmers as Prodigy converted its content from NAPLPS to the web standard HTML. NAPLPS skills were no longer needed for Prodigy's "net-centric" strategy.[25]

Glatzer and Kurnit presided over the "quiet dismantling" of the billion dollar lemon, replacing much of Prodigy's mainframe with lean microcomputers. These UNIX-based machines initially functioned as auxiliary components to the original back-end infrastructure. Over time, these computers handled an increasing percentage of Prodigy's back-end processing, including features such as chat and web browsing which became the most used parts of Prodigy.

In addition to layoffs, Prodigy was going through an extensive overhaul. In place of its own content, the company used outside suppliers, such as newspapers and magazines, to develop its online presence. Bennett suggested moving Prodigy's headquarters to SoHo in New York City.

Bennett compared the web to a "huge, bustling city" and Prodigy to "an easy-to-use Baedeker." "The Web is becoming so crowded, it's almost as if Hong Kong were built in a year," Bennett said. "If you were to visit that city and wanted to go to a tailor, how would you know which tailor? Prodigy will be the service that will help guide you."[26]

Prodigy was the first to develop special-interest areas that link to web sites. Still, Prodigy spent $10 mil-

lion on advertising to overcome its image problem. The company's new marketing tagline, Whatever You're Into,[27] was a part of a TV ad campaign launched in September 1995.

Bennett's initiative to move Prodigy's headquarters from suburban White Plains, New York, to SoHo, was rejected by Prodigy employees and IBM headquarters alike. The move was viewed "as too disruptive and jarring." So Prodigy maintained both offices, with Bennett splitting time between them. Most of the newly hired content developers worked from New York City.[28]

A well-defined Internet strategy was not enough for Prodigy. Stephen Eskenazi, an analyst for the online services industry for Alex Brown & Sons, identified two other major goals for Prodigy to achieve to survive: Build its subscriber base and make a profit.[29] "If they can't do that," Eskenazi said, "they could be a potential candidate for the consolidation this industry is bound to go through."

Bennett insisted that Sears would not back out, but Arthur Martinez, the new CEO at Sears, said publicly that the Chicago retail giant was going to "review" its role as co-owner. At a time when Sears divested all of its noncore businesses, including catalog sales, Allstate Insurance, Dean Witter investments, and Coldwell Banker, it seemed reasonable to evaluate the Prodigy investment.

"The problem was that IBM and Sears had so much money in Prodigy that any new expense caused eyebrows to go up at both companies," said Emily Green, an analyst at Forrester Research in Cambridge, Massachusetts. While Prodigy hesitated, competitors poured resources into the fastgrowing market. According to Bennet, "We need to make decisions faster. Under the IBM–Sears joint ownership, there was clearly a problem with that."[30]

America Online (AOL) captured the lion's share of new consumers coming online and quickly moved beyond Prodigy to become the market leader. Market rivals CompuServe and AOL gained market share while Prodigy lost subscribers.

With about 850,000 subscribers by February 1996, Prodigy ranked fourth among online services. The company that pioneered simple consumer online services was behind even the newly launched Microsoft Network, not to mention CompuServe and AOL.

---

[24] Mooradian, Mark, "Prodigy Ownership At Crossroads," *Interactive Content*, January 1996, v. 2, n. 21, p. 2(1).
[25] Hicks, Matt, "Sold on the Simplicity of Web Sites," *PC Week*, June 7, 1999, v. 16, i. 23, p. 77.
[26] Higgins, Steve, "Outsmarted By Its Rivals, A Humbled Prodigy Acts By," *Investors Business Daily*, Computers & Technology, May 25, 1995.

[27] Eng, Paul M., "War of the Web," *Business Week*, March 4, 1996, n. 3465, p. 71(2).
[28] Higgins, Steve, "Outsmarted By Its Rivals, A Humbled Prodigy Acts By," *Investors Business Daily*, Computers & Technology, May 25, 1995.
[29] King, Julia, and Hoffman, Thomas, "Sears Launches Do-It-Yourself Site," *Computerworld*, April 19, 1999, p. 4(1).
[30] Higgins, Steve, "How Prodigy Fell Behind—and Plans to Catch Up" *Investor's Business Daily*–Computers & Technology, May 14, 1996.

Sears lost faith in Prodigy's ability to persevere in the online service provider industry and decided to focus on growing its retail base instead of getting tangled in the World Wide Web.[31] After a decade of work and a $1 billion investment, IBM and Sears washed their hands of Prodigy. Once the market leader, in 1996 Prodigy needed about $100 million per year for a successful reorganization, according to industry analysts.[32]

In early 1996, Sears' Chairman Arthur Martinez announced that the company would divest its stake in Prodigy and would direct proceeds from the sale into building market share through acquisitions and new store openings. Sears backed out of the Prodigy investment citing that Prodigy "no longer fits into Sears strategy." Sears repeatedly hinted that it wanted to sell the service. The retail giant believed this was the optimal time to exit from its investment. A Reuters report put the value of Prodigy at $2 billion, with Sears' share at $1.2 billion.

Sears sold its 50 percent interest in Prodigy in June 1996 to International Wireless and 40 Prodigy managers. Prodigy executives started a privately held company that invested in cellular phone and Internet properties in Asia, Africa, and Mexico as well as Mexico's Grupo Carso. The sales price was just 25 percent of the estimated $1 billion that IBM and Sears invested in the service.[33]

TECHNOLOGICAL INNOVATIONS

NETWORK

Sears Vice President of Information Systems, Dennis Honan, led the project to equip his 14,000-person service unit with handheld PCs. The overall aim was to in-crease the efficiency of Sears' service technicians. They were all given handheld PCs linked by wireless WANs to the company's databases. This allowed users to access price estimates, place orders, check the availability of appliance parts, receive software upgrades, and get job schedule updates while on location. This enabled technicians to respond to and complete a higher number of calls every day.[34]

TELECOMMUNICATIONS

Sears deployed speech-recognition systems in 700 stores nationwide, enabling callers to tell a computer, rather than live operators, what department they want.

Sears expects the systems, which can handle four calls at a time, to transfer about 120,000 calls a day. "We see this as a tremendous customer service value," said Terry McGinnis, national manager of store office policy and procedure. "Instead of the phone ringing thirty or forty times, it will get answered and routed on the first ring."

The systems will tell customers to "speak the name of a department" and then verify with such responses as "Did you say shoes?" If a customer says "no" or the system doesn't recognize a command, the customer will be immediately routed to a live operator in Golden, Colorado, or Fort Wayne, Indiana. The operator will then route the call to the customer's local store department.[35]

RECOMMENDATIONS FOR THE FUTURE

In 1996, Sears marked its first full year of operations focused exclusively on retailing since 1931. Retail operations is the core competency for Sears. It is an important use of the company's financial and intellectual capital. Future efforts in Internet technology must revolve around this focus.

---

[31] Scott, Greg, "The Downside of IT Information," *ENT*, February 17, 1999, v. 4, i. 4, p. 54(1).
[32] "Sears to Sell Prodigy to Focus on Retailing" *Investor's Business Daily*–Business Brief, February 22, 1996.
[33] Wilder, Clinton, "Is There Still Time for Prodigy?" *Information Week*, December 4, 1995, n. 556, p. 47(3).

[34] Sears, Roebuck & Co., Annual Report for the Fiscal Year Ended December 28, 1996.
[35] Berry, Michael J. A., "Mining the Wallet," *Intelligent Enterprise*, June 22, 1999, v. 2, i. 9, p. 20.

CASE QUESTIONS

Strategic Questions

1. What is the strategic direction of the corporation/organization?

2. Who or what forces are driving this direction?

3. What has been the catalyst for change?

4. What are the critical success factors for this corporation/organization?

5. What are the core competencies for this corporation/organization?

Technological Questions

6. What technologies has the corporation relied on?

7. What has caused a change in the use of technology in the corporation/organization?

8. Who has driven this change throughout the organization?

9. How successful has the technological change been?

Quantitative Questions

10. What does the corporation say about its financial ability to embark on a major technological program of advancement?

11. What conclusions can be reached from an analysis of the financial information to support or contradict this financial ability?

12. What analysis can be made by examining the following ratio groups?
    Quick/Current
    Debt
    Revenue
    Profit
    Asset Utilization

13. What conclusions can be reached by analyzing the financial trends?

Internet Questions

14. What does the corporation's web page present about their business directives?

15. How does this compare to the conclusions reached by the writers of the articles?

16. How does this compare to the conclusions reached by analyzing the financial information?

Industry Questions

17. What challenges and opportunities is the industry facing?

18. Is the industry oligopolistic or competitive?

19. Does the industry face a change in government regulation?

20. How will technology impact the industry?

Data Questions

21. What role do data play in the future of the corporation?

22. How important are data to the corporation's continued success?

23. How will the capture and maintenance of customer data impact the corporation's future?

Executive Summary for Case

Case Name:	Walgreens
Case Industry:	Drugstore chains
Major Technology Issue:	Installation of Intercom Plus system for customer/doctor access to ordering prescriptions via telephone/online; operating the point of sale and inventory tracking equipment in all stores (Intercom Plus is an extension of the satellite linkage of all Walgreens' stores, called Intercom.)
Major Financial Issue:	Financing expansion without resorting to debt. Keeping costs low.
Major Strategic Issue:	Expanding market share; aggressively using technology to promote efficiency
Major Players/Leaders:	Charles Walgreen III, Chairman; Daniel Jorndt, President
Main Web Page:	www.walgreens.com
Case Conclusion/Recommendation:	Competitive advantage in the future, as in the past, will come from flexible, determined utilization of technology, especially networking of stores and databases.

CASE ANALYSIS

INTRODUCTORY STORY

Walgreens is the largest and most visited drugstore chain in the United States. It provides most types of prescription and nonprescription drugs. Walgreens also has a large variety of items used on a day-to-day basis such as milk, film, soda, batteries, school supplies, bread, chips, bandages, toothpaste, deodorant, chocolates, etc. Walgreens' success can be attributed to convenience but also to its successful logistics, distribution, and inventory systems.

SHORT DESCRIPTION OF THE COMPANY

Walgreens is the largest and fastest growing retail pharmacy chain in the United States. Its goal is to be the most convenient health care provider. Walgreens now ranks as one of the nations most successful and admired corporations. In September 1996, the company announced its 22nd consecutive year of record sales and earnings. Walgreens was listed among *Fortune's* "Most Admired Corporations in America" from 1992 through 1996 and is one of only 35 companies listed in all four editions of *The Best Stocks to Own in America.*

SHORT HISTORY OF THE COMPANY

Walgreens was founded by Charles Rudolph Walgreen Sr. In 1893 at the age of 20, Walgreen borrowed $20

from his sister, Clementine, and moved from the small town of Dixon, Illinois, to Chicago. While studying pharmacy, he worked at various drugstores.

When the United States went to war with Spain in 1898, Walgreen enlisted as a private in the Illinois National Guard. He was sent to Cuba. Malaria, yellow fever, and typhoid were rampant at the time. Walgreen fell victim to disease. The doctor, at one point, took Walgreens pulse and told the orderly, "this soldier is as good as dead." His name was entered in the casualty list and newspapers soon carried the report of his death.

Walgreen persevered and recovered. He moved back to Chicago, where he started working at a small drugstore, owned by Isaac W. Blood. In 1901, Walgreen purchased the drugstore for $6,000.

Walgreen was young, enthusiastic, vibrant, and focused on providing good customer service. One of his favorite customer service techniques consisted of answering the telephone himself and repeating the customer's order so the delivery boy would hear and begin work. While Walgreen conversed with the customer, the boy would leave with the order, sometimes arriving before the customer had finished talking with Walgreen.

In 1909, Walgreen purchased one of the busiest and most important drugstores on Chicago's South Side. This was a big opportunity, and he made the most of it. One of his first moves was to install eye-catching displays—a direct departure from the drab, lifeless drugstores of his day. He also manufactured his own line of drug products. By making certain drug items himself, Walgreen was able to ensure high quality and lower prices.

Aware that a successful ice cream fountain was an excellent traffic builder, he rented a vacant building next door, cut an arch through the wall and installed an ice cream fountain. He sold ice cream during the summer. To keep the room open during the winter, he converted the ice cream fountain into a sandwich and soup shop. The food was made by his wife, Myrtle. This was the forerunner of Walgreens' famous soda fountains of the 1920s through 1950s.

During the 1920s to 1950s, the soda fountain became a main attraction. Walgreens invented the milkshake in the early 1920s. The "double-rich chocolate malted milk" was famous. During this time Walgreens expanded rapidly, from 65 stores in 1925 to 397 stores by 1929. In 1933, Walgreens celebrated Chicago's spectacular Century of Progress by opening four stores on the fairgrounds. These stores experimented with advanced fixture design, new lighting techniques, and colors—ideas that helped modernize drugstore layout and design.

In the 1950s, Walgreens transitioned from total clerk service to self-service. Stores had to be remodeled to be twice the size to make room for aisles. Four hundred stores were remodeled and thousands of employees had to be retrained.

During the 1960s Walgreens filled its 100 millionth prescription, far more than any other drug chain at that time. In 1968, Walgreens became the first major drug chain to put its prescriptions into child-resistant containers, long before a federal mandate to do so. In the late 1970s, Walgreens began to upgrade its distribution network, investing in new facilities and sophisticated computer systems. Today, Walgreens is the leader in speedy, cost-efficient distribution with eight high-tech, full-service distribution centers.

In 1981, the first Intercom computers were installed in five Walgreens pharmacies in Des Moines, Iowa. Today, Walgreens has installed the Intercom Plus pharmacy system nationwide. In November 1991, the chain completed installation of point-of-sale scanning to speed checkouts. After opening its 1,000th store in 1984, Walgreens opened its 2,000th store in 1994. The company continues to open well over 200 new locations a year, with a goal of having 3,000 stores by the year 2000. During the 1990s, Walgreens pioneered the use of drive-through pharmacy windows and free-standing buildings for its stores, offering customers even greater convenience.[1]

---

[1] Barboza, David, "Keeping Walgreens on Main Street," *The New York Times*, December 6, 1998, p. BU2(L), c. 4.

FINANCIAL AND PORTFOLIO ANALYSIS

The Walgreen Company is America's largest drugstore retailer. During the fiscal year ended August 31, 1996, it had net sales of $11,778,408,000. The company served customers in 34 states and Puerto Rico through 2,191 retail drugstores and two mail-order facilities

Fiscal year 1996 was the 22nd consecutive year for record sales and earnings. Net earnings were $372 million or $1.50 per share, an increase of 15.9 percent from 1995 earnings of $321 million or $1.30 per share. Higher sales resulted in earnings increases and improved expense ratios.

Total net sales increased by 13.3 percent to $11.8 billion in fiscal year 1996 compared to increases of 12.6 percent in 1995 and 11.3 percent in 1994. Increases in drugstore sales resulted from sales gains in existing stores and added sales from new stores. In comparable drugstores, those open at least one year, sales were up 8.5 percent in 1996, 7.2 percent in 1995, and 5.5 percent in 1994.

New store openings accounted for 7.6 percent of the sales gains in 1996 and 1995 and 7.4 percent in 1994. The company operated 2,193 drugstores as of August 31, 1996, compared to 2,085 a year earlier. Sales are still growing every year. For a comparison of sales for 1996 and 1997 see Table 4.6 and Figure 4.6.

Gross margins as a percent of sales decreased to 27.7 percent of sales from 28.0 percent last year and 28.4 percent in fiscal year 1994. Prescription margins continued to decrease as third-party and mail-order service sales become larger portions of prescription sales. The company is responding to gross margin pressures by emphasizing minimum third-party profitability standards.

Selling, occupancy, and administrative expenses were 22.6 percent of sales in fiscal year 1996, 23.0 percent of sales in fiscal year 1995, and 23.4 percent of sales in fiscal year 1994. The fiscal year 1996 decrease, as a percent of sales, was caused by lower advertising expenses, reduced insurance costs, and improved accounts receivable collection. The fiscal year 1995 decrease, as a percent to sales, was caused by reduced store salary, insurance, and advertising expenditures.

Interest income was relatively constant over the three years. Average net investment levels were approximately $76 million in 1996, $59 million in 1995,

Table 4.6: Sales Increase Percentages for 1997 from 1996

Month	1996	1997	% Change
January	$953,905,000	$1,095,000,000	14.8
February	$964,118,000	$1,075,800,000	11.6
March	$996,240,000	$1,177,900,000	18.2
April	$982,699,000	$1,083,900,000	10.3
May	$1,009,899,000	$1,144,900,000	13.4

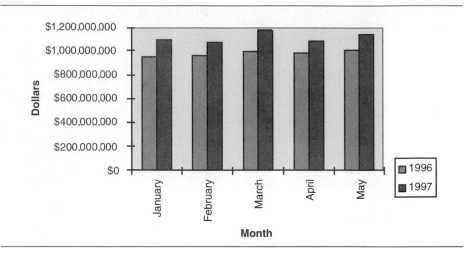

Figure 4.6 1996 versus 1997 sales.

and $105 million in 1994. The lower investment levels in fiscal year 1996 and 1995 were offset by higher interest rates.

Net cash provided by operating activities increased $66 million from 1995 to 1996, the result, primarily, of higher earnings. The company's ongoing profitability is expected to continue as the principal source for expansion and remodeling programs, dividends to shareholders, and funding for various technological improvements.

Walgreens goal is to attract the high-frequency shopper. Even though an average Walgreens store attracts fewer people through its doors than its competitors, Walgreens customers visit the store twice as often as other chains' customers visit their stores. This has helped set the company apart from competition and generate sustained, profitable growth matched by few stores in the retailing industry.

The ability to attract and retain high-frequency shoppers requires knowledge about who they are and what they want. Walgreens scanning technology has made information gathering easier and more accurate.

Scanners provide the following benefits:

1. Monitor customer purchases continually and adjust product mix accordingly.
2. Analyze outlet sales.
3. Monitor the impact of new sales strategies.
4. Control inventory replenishment.[2]

STOCK/INVESTMENT OUTLOOK

Financial returns for Walgreens continue to be impressive. Prescription sales increased 18.0 percent in 1996, 19.8 percent in 1995, and 18.9 percent in 1994.

Comparable drugstores were up 13.0, 13.8, and 12.1 percent in 1996, 1995, and 1994, respectively. Prescription sales were 45.2 percent of total sales for fiscal year 1996 compared to 43.4 percent in 1995 and 40.8 percent in 1994. In the overall industry, prescription drug sales climbed 16.7 percent on top of 1995's 17.7 percent rise.

Pharmacy sales trends are expected to continue primarily because of expansion into new markets, increased penetration in existing markets, and demographic changes such as an aging population. The market is thrilled with Walgreens success and has priced the stock at a high P/E ratio.

RISK ANALYSIS

Walgreens commands a healthy lead in the pharmacy industry. Goldman Sachs analyst John Heinbockel forecasts, "Without question, the drugstore sector will continue to produce perhaps the strongest unit growth—at about 5% to 6%—of any retailing sector."

Demographics and cost containment underlie Goldman's prediction. President Bill Clinton's 50th birthday party symbolized the coming of age, prescription age, that is, for the 78-million-member baby boom generation. This includes people born between 1946 and 1964. This group will be the fastest growing population segment over the next two decades. And as they age, they will flock to pharmacies. People 55 and older consume double the prescriptions used by the population as a whole.

The number of prescriptions taken annually per person is also increasing, from 13 in 1993 to 17 in 1995 for those over 70 years of age. This reflects new drug developments and health care cost consciousness, which leads to increased use of pharmaceutical therapy versus hospitalization and surgery. An aging popula-

---

[2] Ibid.

tion also increases sales through close-to-home, easy-access retail outlets.

Walgreens' strong market share, geographic dispersion, and full line of services offered through their pharmacy benefits manager, WHP Health Initiatives, increased third-party prescription sales 25 percent in 1996. Approximately 75 percent of their pharmacy business is now third party.

Overall, Walgreens fills more than 8 percent of all retail prescriptions in the United States. Other Walgreen services include long-term care prescriptions, durable medical equipment, home infusion services, and the Patient Care Center (PCC). Through the PCC, Walgreens monitors overall pharmaceutical care, working first to improve quality for the patient, and then to lower costs through managed care. Walgreens believes patient education presents the best opportunity to significantly impact both quality and cost. If patients are better educated in the use of their prescriptions, this will lower the cost of health care.

INDUSTRY AND MARKET ANALYSIS

In spite of broader and more spirited competition from discounters and supermarkets, chain drugstores continue to produce strong sales gains. The 7.1 percent increase in same-store sales in 1995 looks especially good in light of the poor performance in the rest of retailing.

Managed care pharmacy sales now account for more than two-thirds of all U.S. retail prescription sales. The pricing squeeze placed on pharmacy departments has fueled the rapid consolidation in drugstore retailing. Not surprisingly, independent drugstores and small chains have been hurt the most. In 1987, there were 33,788 independent drugstores; by 1995 that number declined by 16 percent to 28,222.

Chains have consolidated as larger chains expand and purchase the smaller ones. In 1987, there were 519 drug chains with four stores or more; by 1995, the number of chains had decreased to 463. According to *Drug Store News*, the top seven chains, with Walgreens at the top, recorded sales of $39.8 billion in 1995 and accounted for more than half of chain drugstore sales volume. In 1995, Walgreens recorded revenues of $10,400,000,000 (see Figure 4.7). In second, third, fourth, and fifth place were Rite Aid, Eckerd Corp., Revco D.S., and Longs Drug Stores Corp.

Consolidation has had numerous benefits. Chains can reduce prices at the cash register. This aids their competitive position in regard to supermarkets, discounters, and mail-order pharmacies. In an industry where market share is a barometer of strength, drug chains can use large-scale marketing strategies to their advantage. Chains can spread operating expenses over a larger store base. Walgreens, for example, has grown by adding new stores rather than acquiring them. In the past decade Walgreens lowered selling, occupancy, and administrative expenses by 2 percent while growing its base by more than 1,000 stores.

Walgreens leads the industry in net income and return on assets (see Figures 4.8 and 4.9). In other areas such as inventory turnover, yield, and price-to-earnings ratio, Walgreens does not occupy first place but is ranked among the top ten in the industry. From 1994 to 1996, Walgreens inventory turnover ratio has remained consistently in the range of 7.31 to 7.22 (see Figure 4.10).

ROLE OF RESEARCH AND DEVELOPMENT

Walgreens is applying technology to improve the accuracy and efficiency of the distribution and inventory system. This will improve the availability of

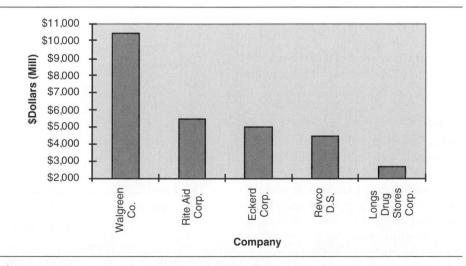

Figure 4.7 Drugstore industry revenues, 1995. (*Source: Moody's Industry Review*, v. 14, July 12, 1996.)

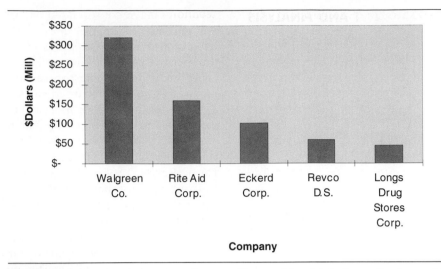

Figure 4.8 Drug store industry net income. (*Source: Moody's Industry Review*, v. 14, July 12, 1996.)

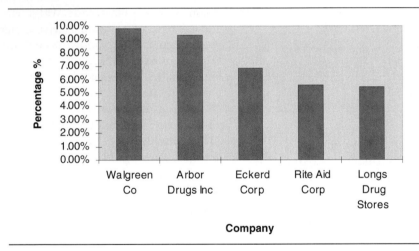

Figure 4.9 Drug store industry return on assets. (*Source: Moody's Industry Review*, v. 14, July 1996.)

information, reduce data entry errors, reduce shipment errors, and improve relationships with suppliers and customers.

TECHNOLOGICAL STORY

As the company grows, so will the amount of information the company handles. Walgreens is currently the technology leader in the drugstore industry. It was the first chain to link its computers via satellite. It was the first drugstore to install chain wide point-of-sale (POS) scanning systems to speed checkouts. The POS is combined with the distribution/inventory system to enable buyers to track item movement from the time merchandise arrives at the distribution centers to when the product is sold at the checkout.

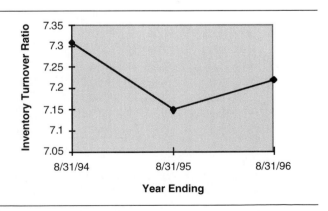

Figure 4.10 Walgreens inventory turnover ratio. (*Source: Walgreens' Financial Ratios, 1996.*)

TECHNOLOGICAL INVESTMENT AND ANALYSIS

Electronic data interchange (EDI) is used for the distribution/inventory system at Walgreens. The distribution/inventory system is the most automated in the industry, making extensive use of bar coding and radio-frequency technology to track and transmit distribution/inventory information.

Logistics, inventory, and distribution have always been important parts of the retail business. One of the newest retailing techniques is continuous replenishment. Predictability and trust is increased between buyer, seller, and third-party support agencies by eliminating duplicate inventory in the distribution channel. Continuous replenishment hinges on moving from push to pull strategies. This technique applies the use of new information technology and new methods of materials handling to speed information and cut cycle times up and down the pipeline. This technique has been adopted not only by Walgreens, but also by many of its competitors such as Wal-Mart and Target.[3]

Continuous replenishment begins at the planning and forecasting stage, which is established in conjunction with key vendors. The process requires the ongoing sharing of POS information. It concentrates on optimizing logistics planning to bring shipping and receiving in sync with sales floor trends. The system targets reduction of time and inventory throughout the supply chain to realize cost savings and productivity gains for both the retailer and the supplier.

Managing distribution to get the right merchandise to the right stores at the right time in the right amount, makes a big difference. Cost and productivity benefits are realized by distributing reduced up-front quantities to the stores. Replenishment is exact and frequent based on SKU level sales.

Cross-docking is currently being used by Walgreens for the distribution of their products. In the cross-docking system, the product is not consigned to storage but rather continuously flows across the dock until it is re-sorted and moves to a store. In this system, the distribution center becomes a sorting rather than a holding area. In some cross-docking systems, the merchandise is held at the dock less than 12 hours before it is moved to a store. The tighter the window on cross-docking, the more the inventory savings, and the more careful the coordination between buyer, seller, and third party needs to be.

The process saves everyone money. Workers in the warehouses only touch the product once when they audit and move it from truck to truck. Communications

technologies such as EDI are critical to this type of system.[4]

Good asset management requires knowledge of what the company owns and where these assets are located. Data inventory and tracking prevent property loss and theft. Asset management is made easier by technologies such as bar codes, radio-frequency tagging, laser coding, and newly developed desired state software management. These technologies assign identification tags to company assets that need to be tracked. Relevant data is applied to a central information system.

Laser technology is also used in the retailing industry for inventory control. This tool is similar to bar coding. The laser produces a permanent code without the use of inks or solvents. This code can be placed anywhere on the product. It is a low-maintenance, ink-less operation, with minimum downtime, maximum flexibility, and accurate, consistently reliable coding at high speeds.

These systems provide a constant interactive flow for up-to-date inventory information. Any mistake is identified immediately. Previously, everything was reactive. Now, armed with up-to-the-minute information, product coding enables Walgreens to make timely and accurate decisions, and become a more responsive partner to the customer.

Bar codes are used to identify inventory distribution costs. They provide the following:

1. Improve inventory accuracy from receiving to shipping.
2. Provide immediate availability of inventory information.
3. Reduce the percentage of data entry errors.
4. Make a permanent audit trail.
5. Reduce inventory levels previously inflated to compensate for errors.
6. Increase inventory turns.
7. Reduce shipment errors.
8. Improve relationships with customers and suppliers.
9. Reduce internal costs due to the elimination of errors, reduction of inventory levels, and accurate shipments.
10. Lower costs at all stages of the industrial/commercial channel.[5]

The inventory day sales ratio can be analyzed to confirm that inventory is being kept under control. Walgreens has been able to maintain inventory levels at a volume low enough to remain competitive (see Figure 4.11). The increase in the net sales per employee ratio (Figure 4.12) also demonstrates that the company is

---

[3] Collett, Stacy, "CVS Takes Shortcut to Web Commerce," *Computerworld*, May 24, 1999, p. 4(1).

[4] Salomon, Robert S., Jr., "Reinventing Retail," *Forbes*, October 19, 1998, v. 162, p. 171(1).
[5] Ibid.

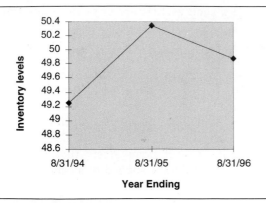

Figure 4.11 Inventory day sales ratio. (*Source:* Walgreens' Financial Ratios, 1996.)

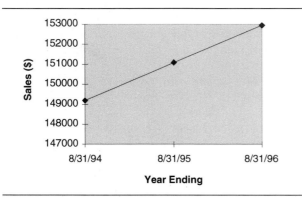

Figure 4.12 Walgreens' net sales per employee. (*Source:* Walgreens' Financial Ratios, 1996.)

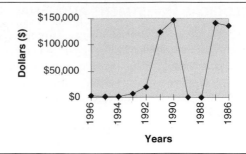

Figure 4.13 Walgreens' long-term debt. (*Source:* Walgreens' Income Statement, 1996.)

monitoring this number since it has been constantly increasing.

As can be seen in Figure 4.13, from right to left, the company's effort to reduce the amount of long-term debt has been successful. As the amount of long-term debt is reduced, additional revenues are available to invest in the firm.

TECHNOLOGICAL INNOVATIONS

NETWORKS

AT&T provides the connections to enable Walgreens to communicate instantaneously with their stores and pharmacists. In 1998, AT&T experienced a major T1 shortage. AT&T's standard frame relay backup options were rendered useless by the fact that the switches, rather than the physical routes, were out of service.

AT&T officials have worked to discover the root cause of the failure. AT&T Chairman and CEO C. Michael Armstrong briefed reporters that the company would not charge customers for frame relay service until the network was restored and the root cause was identified and fixed.

Some users thought AT&T had an obligation to go even further. In January, AT&T announced service-

level agreements (SLA) which included 99.99 percent availability for the frame relay network. At the same time, AT&T Data Services Vice President Steve Hindman promised a four-hour mean-time-to-repair guarantee. If this failed, customers would receive free ports and permanent virtual circuits (PVC) for a month. During this downtime, nearly every user reported that they did not have enough backup lines to keep their networks running. Many resorted to unusual measures. One giant pharmaceutical company called in a fleet of six jets to keep its networks of papers, services, and products working. Some of the pharmaceutical company's 80 sites had ISDN backup; others had only 9.6K modems. Only half of the company's orders were able to be submitted through dial-up. The company leased planes to fly paper orders to distribution centers. The company did not get its frame relay fully restored until Wednesday morning of the week of outage.

Walgreens does have financial protection because it contracted for a SLA from AT&T. Ray Sheedy, Walgreens director of corporate telecommunications, said 278 of the company's stores connected through AT&T lines were down for 24 hours. Walgreens' mail-order locations in Tempe, Arizona, and Orlando, Florida, which are ordinarily on the AT&T network, had backup frame relay capacity with MCI. Sheedy said Walgreens cannot afford dual networks in stores. He indicated that ISDN is too expensive to run to individual stores and is not available everywhere.[6]

Most analysts stressed the importance of discovering the root cause to prevent similar problems from occurring. Steve Sazegari, president of Tele.Mac, a Foster City, California, consulting firm, noted that data traffic typically spikes on Monday, the day the outage occurred. This is also the day order entry systems accept weekend mail orders and transactions.[7]

---

[6] Gittlen, Sandra, and Rohde, David, "AT&T Frame Relay Service Goes Down for the Count," *Network World,* April 20, 1998, v. 15, n. 16, p. 7(1).
[7] Ibid.

"These switches were never put under this kind of test in a public network before," Sazegari said. "Unlike a fiber cut which could be avoided through rerouting, eliminating an impact on the rest of the network, this switching interruption had an impact on the whole networking structure."[8]

INTERNET SITES

The Extensible Markup Language (XML) is a World Wide Web Consortium standard for tagging web content. The standard lets users make fields that name data. Search engines use these fields to make more accurate return lists. This technology enables companies to attach keywords to URLs so that typing in a simple word, not the whole name string, produces a document. Instead of typing in "www.walgreens.com," a user could simply program his search tool to look for "wal". Because the page was tagged with that name, the search tool would link directly to it.

Pete Van Valin, team leader for web systems at Walgreens, hopes to have XML up and running within 12 months on the company's web site. Currently, employees must place meta tags in their HTML documents. The goal is to automate the process with XML. Van Valin is still evaluating tools. Tagging is essential to examine all the information generated from the intranet's 10,000 users. His team has developed a list of standards and best practices for intranet documents but has not completed formal training on tagging, which is dependent upon precision. When that precision happens, the tagging process is greatly improved.[9]

Another approach is to use Bayesian logic to track word patterns in documents. This is based on the relationship between multiple variables and includes the extent to which one variable impacts the other. Rather than searching for individual words, search engines can be employed to examine patterns of words within documents and mark their occurrence. For example, if a user wants to search for information on Microsoft's Wolfpack, he/she is not interested in information about wolves in the wild. Because of the user's marked pattern, Autonomy's Agentware system, which was adopted for this purpose, recognizes this request is dealing with software and Microsoft.

SemioMap uses visualization to help users understand their search options. It offers a search tool that indexes text, makes clusters of content, and then generates visual maps of the location of those clusters. If a user searches on "NT," SemioMap will display the returns that directly pertain to that result, and then map related concepts such as Windows, Microsoft, and operating systems. This gives users a sense of the hierarchy of their searches.

To be successul at companies like Walgreens, searching mechanisms must incorporate the following:

1. They must be user-friendly and simplify searches, extending beyond Boolean search mechanisms.
2. They must gather and process external information and internal data.
3. Embedded agents must analyze search patterns and determine other ways to find information. They must study data-gathering behavior, store that information, and be able to build suggested query lists based on that information.
4. They must incorporate standards such as XML.[10]

RECOMMENDATION FOR THE FUTURE

Drugstores are becoming more adept at merchandising. Many drugstores have increased profitability by adding higher margin convenience items, such as greeting cards, body care products, toiletries, candy, and chocolates. Low-margin items like ice and milk help boost traffic. This results in a more profitable unit. The location of the stores has also become more important, with emphasis upon convenience, accessibility, ample parking, and 24-hour access.

Walgreens has continued to invest in new technologies to maintain its leadership status. The continuous improvement in sales, minimization of long-term debt, reduction in levels of inventory, and increase in research and development will keep Walgreens on the cutting edge of the pharmaceutical field.[11]

---

[8] Ibid.
[9] Gittlen, Sandra, "Leave it to the Hound," *Network World*, August 31, 1998, v. 15, n. 35, p. S13(1).

[10] Ibid.
[11] "Quest Awarded $9 Million Contract from Walgreens for Data and Voice Communications Services," *Cambridge Telecom Report*, May 10, 1999, p. NA.

CASE QUESTIONS

Strategic Questions

1. What is the strategic direction of the corporation/organization?

2. Who or what forces are driving this direction?

3. What has been the catalyst for change?

4. What are the critical success factors for this corporation/organization?

5. What are the core competencies for Walgreens?

Technological Questions

6. What technologies has the corporation relied on?

7. What has caused a change in the use of technology in the corporation/organization?

8. Who has driven this change throughout the organization?

9. How successful has the technological change been?

Quantitative Questions

10. What does the corporation say about its financial ability to embark on a major technological program of advancement?

11. What conclusions can be reached from an analysis of the financial information to support or contradict this financial ability?

12. What analysis can be made by examining the following ratio groups?
    Same-store sales
    Debt
    Revenue
    Profit

13. What conclusions can be reached by analyzing the financial trends?

Internet Questions

14. What is the purpose of Walgreens' home page?

Industry Questions

15. What challenges and opportunities is the industry facing?

16. Does the industry face a change in government regulation?

17. How will technology impact the industry?

Data Questions

18. What role do data play in the future of the corporation?

19. What are some of the other services Intercom Plus's data can allow Walgreens to perform?

20. How will the capture and maintenance of customer data impact the corporation's future?

TECHNOLOGY TIPS

MICROSOFT WORD TIP

INSERTING A TABLE

Inserting a table into a word document can help you display figures in an easier format for the reader to understand. If you do not have an Excel worksheet to copy and paste from, this is a quick and easy way to create a table in your word document.

1. From the toolbar, click on the Tables and Border button.

2. A tool bar will appear and your mouse pointer will appear as a pencil. You will now be able to draw a table to your preference.

3. While the pointer still appears as a pencil, click on the section of your document that you would like to insert a table.

4. While holding down on the left mouse button, click and drag the pointer to create a table to your preferred size.

5. Divide the table into cells and rows by dragging the pointer across the table, and dividing it up into as many cells and rows as you like.

6. You can enter data into the cells by clicking on the DRAW TABLE button. This will change the pointer back to its original form.

7. Data can be entered into the different cells by placing the cursor inside a cell and then typing the information. You can move the cursor around the table with the arrow key or the mouse.

8. The table can be adjusted by placing the pointer on the borders and dividers. The pointer will change in appearance to a double bar. While the pointer is still on the bar, click and drag the edges to the desired heights and widths. This will allow you to modify the shape and size of the table.

A *brief description is provided for the following Table toolbar buttons.*

	Autoformat Table: Changes appearance of table.
	Distributes rows evenly.
	Distributes columns evenly.
	Changes the pointer to an eraser.
	Changes the pointer to a "pencil" that allows you to draw tables.
	Changes the direction of text in cells or columns you have selected.
	Aligns text inside cells at the bottom.
	Aligns text inside cells in the center.
	Aligns text inside the cells at the top of the cell.
	Sorts data in cells in ascending order.
	Sorts data in cells in descending order.
	Placing the cursor at the bottom cell and then clicking this button will automatically add up the column of numbers.

ADDITIONAL NOTE:

The appearance of your table can be changed if you desire a less drab appearance. First, click inside the table and then click on the Autoformat Table button. A dialog box will appear with a preview box of the different formats available. Select the format that you like and then click OK. The table in your document will change to your selected style.

MICROSOFT EXCEL TIPS

INSERTING CELLS, ROWS, AND COLUMNS

Inserting cells, rows, and columns will be a task often performed when working with worksheets in Excel. The way of inserting these is similar and once you have inserted one of them (cell, row, and/or column) you will be familiar with how to insert the others.

Inserting a Cell
1. Click on the cell within the worksheet where the new cell is to be inserted.
2. Click on the right mouse button. The shortcut menu on the right will appear.
3. Select how you would like the cells to shift when you insert the new cell.
4. Click on OK.

Inserting a Row
1. Click on the cell within the worksheet where the new row is to be inserted.
2. Click on the right mouse button. The shortcut menu will appear.
3. Click on ENTIRE ROW and then click on OK.
4. The entire row beneath the cell selected will shift down to accommodate the new row.

Inserting a Column
1. Click on the cell within the worksheet where the new column is to be inserted.
2. Click on the right mouse button. The shortcut menu will appear.
3. Click on ENTIRE COLUMN and then click on OK.
4. The column will be inserted to the right of the cell selected. All columns will shift to the *right* of the cell selected in order to accommodate the new column.

Inserting Several Rows and Columns
1. Click in the *center* of the column/row heading where the new columns/rows are to be inserted.
2. Drag across the column/row headings and highlight the number of columns/rows you would like to insert (i.e. four highlighted columns/rows would prompt Excel to insert four columns/rows).
3. The number of rows highlighted will shift down, while the number of columns highlighted will shift to the right.

Inserting in Nonadjacent Rows, Columns, and Cells
1. Click in the center of the column/row heading or cell that is to be selected.
2. To select nonadjacent columns/rows, hold down the CONTROL key while you click in the center of the other column/rows heading or cell.

3. Click on the right mouse button to make the shortcut menu appear. Click on insert.
4. In the case of cells, the shortcut menu above will appear. How the cells will be shifted (right or down) can be selected. When selecting rows, the new rows will shift down the rows below it. In the case of columns they will be shifted to the right as shown at the right.

MICROSOFT POWERPOINT TIPS

SLIDE TRANSITIONS AND TIMING

As you are conducting your presentation, the transition from your slides can be adjusted to your liking. This includes the effect that the slide will have when going from one slide to another and/or the timing.

Slide Transitions
1. Select the slide you want to add a transition to. From the top toolbar, click on SLIDE SHOW. From the drop down menu, click on SLIDE TRANSITION.
2. The slide transition box on the right will appear. Select your transition from the drop down menu and the speed at which you want the transition effect to operate (slow, medium, or fast). An example of the transition will be shown each time you select an effect from the drop down menu.
3. When you are done with your selections, select APPLY (for the slides selected) or APPLY TO ALL.

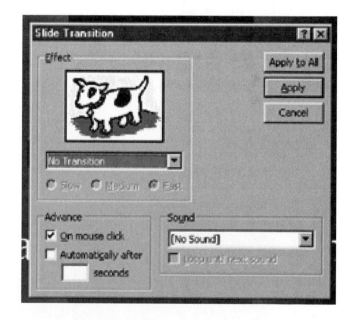

Timing
If you have rehearsed your presentation and have a good feeling of how much time you will spend on each slide, you can have PowerPoint advance to the next slide for you.

1. With your presentation already open, select the SLIDE SORTER view. Click on the slide that you wish to have PowerPoint advance for you.
2. Click on the slide with your right mouse button. Select SLIDE TRANSITION from the pop-up menu.

3. In the ADVANCE section of the slide transition box enter the number of seconds that you have the slide appear during the presentation.
4. Click on APPLY when you are done.
5. The time that you entered will appear underneath the slide. It will be in the following format hours/minutes/seconds.

Note:

About slide transitions: If you wish to add transitions to several slides at one time, switch to SLIDE SORTER view by clicking on the button on the bottom left-hand side of the PowerPoint screen. When the slide sorter view appears, *hold down* the shift key while clicking on the slides you want to add transitions to. The slides that are selected will appear highlighted on the screen.

About slide timing: During the course of the presentation, the slides that you have assigned time to will advance once the time you have entered has run out *or* on a mouse click.

MICROSOFT ACCESS TIP

CREATING A TABLE

We will be using Table Wizard to create a table. This is the easiest way to set primary keys and label the different fields in the table. There are a number of sample tables and fields in table wizard that will help you in creating a table. These are also good examples of how you should name your fields and how tables are broken down.

STARTING ACCESS

Microsoft Access

1. Click on START.
2. From the pop-up menu click on PROGRAMS.
3. Click on Microsoft Access to start the program.

Creating a Table

1. When Access starts, the dialog box in Figure 1 will appear prompting you to open an existing database or create a new one. Click on BLANK DATABASE. If you already had Access open, click on FILE from the toolbar and then NEW DATABASE from the drop down menu.

Figure 1

2. Click on the GENERAL tab of the NEW dialog box that appears in Figure 2. Click on BLANK DATABASE and then on the OK button.

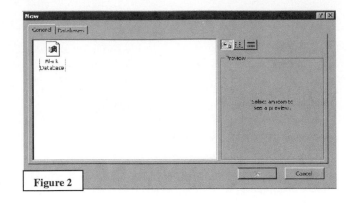

Figure 2

3. A new dialog box will appear which will allow you to select where the database will be saved and its filename. Click on CREATE once you have filled these fields.
4. From the new database window, click on the TABLES tab, then click on NEW.
5. Click on TABLE WIZARD in the next window that will appear and then click OK.
6. The Table Wizard dialog box in Figure 3 will appear. Different lists of tables will appear under the BUSINESS and PERSONAL options.

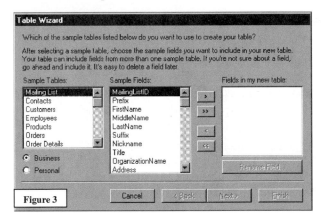

Figure 3

7. Click on a table from the table list. Notice how the sample fields will change to match the type of table selected.
8. Once a table has been selected, click on the fields that you would like to include in the table. To select fields for your table, click on the field and then click on the right arrow button. To select ALL of the fields click on the double arrow button.
9. When you are finished selecting fields for your tables, click on the NEXT button.
10. In the next dialog box you are required to name the table. Click on YES, SET A PRIMARY . . . to allow Access to set a primary key for you. Otherwise, you will be prompted in the next window to determine which field is to be the primary key. Click on the NEXT button when you are ready to move on.
11. In the last dialog box, you have three options to choose from. Click on an option and then click on the FINISH button to generate the table. In the next chapter, we will be modifying a table so choose the MODIFY THE

TABLE DESIGN if you want to continue on to the next chapter at this time.

MICROSOFT FRONTPAGE

SAVING AND INSERTING PICTURES FROM THE WEB

You have probably seen a number of pictures out in the web that you would like to use on your site. A lot of these pictures are up for grabs, but make sure that you notify the person that manages the web site and give credit to those who deserve it. Some pictures are protected by copyright laws so you do not want to get yourself in trouble just to spice up your web site.

Saving a Picture/Graphic from the Web

1. Once you have found the graphic or picture that you like on the web, use the RIGHT mouse button to click on it (this is for Internet Explorer)
2. A pop-up menu will appear with a list of choices. If the image you clicked on can be saved, the SAVE PICTURES AS. . . will appear as one of the choices. Click on it.
3. The SAVE PICTURE AS dialog box will come up on the screen. Select the file where you would like to save the picture. Also, rename the file with a name that will be easy for you to remember. Normally the pictures have very odd names that will mean nothing to you.
4. Click on SAVE. That is it. The picture is ready for you to use in your web page.

Inserting Pictures in Your Web Page

1. With your web page open in the edit mode, click on the part of the web page that you would like to insert the picture.
2. Click on INSERT from the menu bar. Select IMAGE from the drop down menu.
3. Click on the BROWSE button to locate the picture you want to use. Once you find it, click on it and then click on OPEN.
4. The image will then appear on your web page.

Modifying the Picture

1. Right click on the picture and select IMAGE PROPERTIES from the pop-up menu.
2. The IMAGE PROPERTIES dialog box will appear. Click on the different tabs and discover how you can change the picture (formatting, alignment, size, etc.)

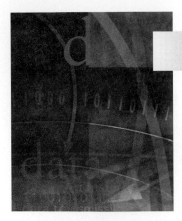

CHAPTER 5

DATABASE MANAGEMENT
AIRLINE INDUSTRY

Database Management

Information is important to everyone. Rarely is anyone interested in looking at all of it. Managing collections of data have been made easier with computers. Relational database management is a popular technique. This allows multiple-read access to the data while documenting who has write access to the database. An important, but usually unappreciated job, is to maintain databases to ensure their integrity.

The databases should be set up correctly. Each table should refer to one concept; the data should be divided keeping that in mind. Once these tables have been defined, users can develop input screens, reports, and views. It is important to know which tool is needed. Whether a database or a spreadsheet is needed depends on the requirements of the users and the type of information available. Increasing amounts of information are kept on commercial databases which users pay to access, rather than maintaining their own database.

Database Management System (DBMS) This software provides control over the data to ensure its accuracy and integrity. DBMSs are designed to deal with multiple users at the same time.

Relational Databases These are databases in which the data are stored in tables. They consist of columns with rows of data. Each table has a name and represents objects or relationships to the data. Reports can be developed easily based upon the relationships the table contains. Different tables can be linked using common fields such as customer or product number.

Data Independence This approach separates the data from the programs. It allows the data to be changed without impacting the programs that access the data and vice versa. A DBMS uses this approach.

Data Integrity This is the method of insuring that the data in a database are up-to-date and accurate. This is crucial to maintain, since an unreliable database can cause more harm than no database at all.

Query This is a way to retrieve data from a database. Two common methods are query by example (QBE) and SQL. Query by example works by making your selections on the screen. SQL, while more difficult to learn, is supported by more database systems with easier to read results. Both types of query methods can also perform simple calculations. Multiple tables of data can be joined by common fields, making queries more powerful.

Designing a Database The tables must be defined, as well as what data go into each field. Data input screens must be designed to ease input into the database. First, data must be defined. A primary key, which uniquely identifies each row, must be chosen. Menus can be helpful to guide you through a database. Menus can also help when inputting data into the database, in the form of input forms. Reports coming fom the database must follow pre-defined formats.

Database Administrator A person who knows, manages, and makes decisions regarding an organization's databases is a database administrator. The administrator is responsible for all operations involving the database. Standards, documentation, testing, backup, and recovery techniques and procedures are important to facilitate what a database administrator uses.

Commercial Databases These databases are focused on business issues. This provides information to individuals and firms for whom gathering the data themselves might be impossible or too expensive. These databases offer a large array of information, from entertainment to legal case information. Examples are America Online, CompuServe, Lexis-Nexis, and Compact Disclosure. Some of this information is available on CD-ROM to subscribers. Issues involving the use of commercial databases include the cost of using the data, data integrity, and privacy.

Airline Industry

DESCRIPTION OF THE INDUSTRY

The airline industry is an important component of today's global economy. Over 1.25 billion passengers per year rely on the world's airlines for business and vacation travel. Approximately a quarter of the world's manufactured exports by value are transported by air. Since the first jet airliner flew in 1949, use of commercial aviation has expanded more than 65 times.

The industry is mature but is still changing and growing. The passenger segment of the airline industry is the largest. In 1995 it accounted for over $69 billion in revenues or 73.7 percent of the industry's total revenues. Other major segments include freight and express (9 percent), charter (3.5 percent), and mail (1.3 percent). Economically, the airline industry is an imperfect oligopoly, in which a few carriers dominate in long-haul passenger traffic. Several dozen small carriers compete for short-haul flights. The Department of Transportation classifies air carriers by the size of their revenue base. In the United States, 34 carriers have a fleet of 25 or more aircraft.

Major airlines: Annual revenues exceed $1 billion; American, United, Delta, Northwest, Southwest, and US Airlines. Each has fleets of 300 or more aircraft.

National airlines: Annual revenues are between $100 million and $1 billion; more regional in focus with smaller seating capacities.

Regional airlines: Annual revenues are less than $100 million; commuter lines and start-up carriers.

Airline industry demand is cyclical. Travel generally follows economic activity. Economic models for forecasting airline traffic are commonly based on projections for gross domestic product (GDP), disposable personal income, and consumer confidence levels. While air traffic volume reflects economic factors, the cost and convenience of alternative modes of transportation also impact air traffic. Demand for discretionary travel, such

Word	W.1	Writing Around Images	Using Text Wrapping on an Image
		Additional Note	Using Text Wrapping on a Text Box
Excel	E.1	Filtering Data	Column Labels
			Row and Column Contents
			How to Filter the Data
PowerPoint	P.1	Changing Background Colors, Color Schemes, and Design Templates	Changing Design Templates
			Changing Color Schemes
			Changing Background Colors
Access	A.1	Modifying a Table	
Front Page	I.1	Creating Links	Creating a Link in FrontPage Express
			To Edit a Link in FrontPage Express
			To Remove a Link in FrontPage Express

as vacations, tends to be more price sensitive. In recent years, corporate travel budgets have also become price sensitive. High fares stifle air traffic demand, while low fares spur greater demand.

The federal government has not regulated airlines since deregulation in 1978. Since deregulation, the industry has grown significantly more concentrated. Since 1985, mergers played a significant role in this concentration. Between 1986 and 1987, Texas Air merged with Eastern and People's Express, Northwest Airlines with Republic Airlines, and Delta with Western. Industry consolidation has resulted from slowing traffic growth and the exhaustion of conventional cost-cutting measures. Mergers offer savings opportunities through the consolidation of administrative, distribution, and maintenance operations. Bankruptcies in the 1990s, most notably Pan American and Eastern, have also led to the consolidation of the industry.

All major airlines with the exception of Southwest operate through hub-and-spoke networks. In a hub system, passengers are gathered from surrounding "spoke" cities to a central hub airport where they must transfer to the second leg of their flight. This enables densities to be built for the longer portion of the flight, better matching equipment to demand. Competitive challenges are rare once an airline is established in a hub. This has led to the stabilization of airfares and profit margins.

Despite deregulation, the Federal Aviation Administration (FAA) still imposes safety standards on carriers. It certifies aircraft and airlines and establishes age and medical requirements for pilots. A series of tragic airplane crashes in 1996 pushed air safety to the forefront. The crash of a ValuJet airplane in the Florida Everglades in May was followed in July by the mysterious explosion and crash of TWA's Flight 800 over the Atlantic Ocean. The ValuJet crash prodded regulators to tighten their scrutiny of start-up airlines and the practices of maintenance contractors. Certification of a new airline now takes twice as long as before. The number of aircraft that a new airline can operate is also limited based on the carrier's financial and managerial resources.

The Department of Transportation (DOT) levies civil penalties against airlines that engage in fraudulent marketing practices and violate code-sharing rules. It also decides airline ownership and control issues. Internationally, the DOT plays an important role by negotiating bilateral aviation treaties with foreign nations.

FINANCIAL ANALYSIS

From 1994 to 1996, the growth rate in the airline industry averaged 6.7 percent each year. In 1997, the growth rate averaged 7.1 percent per year, with an average load factor of just over 70.6 percent. Compared to other transportation industries, this rate is high, due to the fact that regional and international airlines continue to increase their service to underserved destinations.

The airline industry includes high barriers to entry. It requires a huge capital investment, not only for purchasing aircraft but also for labor, gate fees, advertising, fuel, etc. Nonetheless, the airline industry is easier to enter now than it was before 1978 when deregulation was passed. Flight equipment accounts for more than 62 percent of total airline assets.

A newer trend for start-ups, as well as major carriers, is to lease rather than buy planes. If aircraft are purchased, tax implications occur such as charges for depreciation and financing costs such as interest or preferred dividend payments. Among major airlines, depreciation averages 4.7 percent. For Southwest Airlines, depreciation increased 4.9 percent compared to an increase in the percentage of owned aircraft.

An important measure is yield, or the revenue generated per passenger mile (RPM). Comparing the absolute yield level for different carriers is only useful if the carriers have a similar mix of flights. Another consideration is revenues from nonfare sources. Since these can account for as much as 10 percent of an airline's total revenues, this contribution can make the difference between an operating profit and loss.

Industry revenues are strongly linked to corporate earnings and disposable income. The second and third quarters, along with holidays, have commonly been the times when demand was highest and operating conditions most favorable. From 1990 to mid-1994, the industry suffered $12 billion in losses. In the third quarter of 1995, the airline industry reported record profits of nearly $2.4 billion. Total operating revenues increased by 3.6 percent while total operating expenses increased by 3.3 percent. At the same time, passenger revenues increased by 6.2 percent along with freight and express revenues, which increased by 16.4 percent. The rate of return on investment rose by 6.8 percent. As a result of these factors, the operating profit margin increased by 3.1 percent along with the net profit margin, which increased by 2.9 percent.

The outlook is even more promising for the worldwide airline industry as a whole (Table 5.1). The profits for 1995 reached a net figure of $5.2 billion dollars, based on international service revenues of $129.6 billion. Net profit of 4 percent of revenue set an all-time record for the industry. International revenues for 1996 reached $140 billion, resulting in a $6.0 billion net profit or 4.3 percent of revenue. With the airline industry's new profitability, and provided that the airlines continue to focus their efforts on the balance sheets, this industry will become a very attractive investment in the next century.

Table 5.1 1995 Balance Sheet ($000) for U.S. Scheduled Airlines

	1994	1995
Assets		
Current Assets	18,157,623	19,947,250
Investments and Special Funds	7,140,591	8,097,537
Flight Equipment Owned	52,017,495	55,973,650
Ground Equipment and Property	15,853,279	16,801,863
Reserve for Depreciation (owned)	(26,484,944)	(29,052,534)
Leased Equipment and Property Capitalized	6,797,817	7,130,706
Reserve for Depreciation (Leased)	(2,538,537)	(2,574,200)
Other Property	11,169,633	11,314,747
Deferred Charges	2,420,056	2,142,008
Total Assets	84,533,013	89,781,027
Liabilities		
Current Liabilities	25,787,765	27,288,358
Long-Term Debt	17,622,152	16,473,060
Other Non Current	19,129,373	19,031,438
Deferred Credit	8,820,904	9,783,529
Stockholders' Equity—Net Treasury Stock	13,172,819	17,204,642
Preferred Stock	10,414	12,599
Common Stock	761,962	618,713
Other Paid In Capital	10,529,115	11,752,511
Retained Earnings	2,167,969	4,974,966
Less: Treasury Stock	296,895	317,648
Total Liabilities and Stockholders' Equity	84,533,013	89,781,027

(*Source:* Air Transportation Association of America, *1996 Handbook.*)

STOCK/INVESTMENT OUTLOOK

The airline industry is expected to continue to grow with the U.S. economy. As the outlook for corporate profits and personal income growth improves, continued profits also appear likely. Forecasters warn, however, that this industry is highly cyclical, and is prone to overcapacity resulting in high levels of competition.

Airline stocks are the most cyclical on Wall Street. Investors tend to bid up shares of airlines when they look weakest and substantial losses are incurred. Once profits are returned, investors move on, dumping stocks with depressed price-to-earnings ratios. Investors tend to favor growth airlines with wide profit margins rather than those with a strong service performance and a young fleet. The biggest rally gains in equity airlines go to the "worst" airlines because investors anticipate a larger gain from a depressed base in that carrier's bottom line.

POTENTIAL/PROSPECTIVE FOR GROWTH

The airline industry remains one of the fastest growing sectors of the world economy. Passenger and freight traffic is expected to increase at an average annual rate of 5 to 6 percent between 1997 and 2010. This is significantly greater than the expected growth of global GDP. By 2005, the number of people traveling by air is projected to exceed 2.5 billion a year. Growth in air travel will be led by the Asia market. Demand for this region is anticipated to grow by an average of 8.6 percent annually between now and 2010.

Experts attribute the rapid rate of growth to the increasing disposable incomes of consumers and the decreasing fares being charged. Airfares today are 70 percent less after adjustment for inflation than they were in 1970. As world economic growth continues to accelerate, so should growth in the airline industry. A significant change in the structure of the industry is "open skies." This term refers to the process of *internationally* deregulating air transportation services, an area with many regulations and restrictions.

For instance, the United States and Canada signed a new bilateral air services agreement in February 1995. The agreement provides for unlimited nonstop air services between two-thirds of the 100 largest U.S. cities and any major Canadian cities that previously did not have air services. This agreement should continue to greatly expand air traffic between the two countries, with projections for annual growth to 20 million passengers annually. The United States has also been negotiating "open skies" agreements with several European nations. Discussions are focused on initiating new transatlantic routes, increasing flight frequency on existing routes, and lifting pricing restrictions.

Another area for substantial growth is the regional airline market. Largely overlooked during deregulation, this market has become a bottom line profit booster for the national airlines, feeding passengers into their hubs. During the 1970s, the regional airline industry was made up of local commuter airlines serving local cities and connecting outlying communities to metropolitan areas.

After deregulation, national and major airlines ended service to smaller communities, concentrating on higher yield routes. The smaller commuter airlines began to acquire larger turboprop aircraft and replace the major airlines on these low yield routes. In the 1980s, commuter airlines grew through industry consolidation and code sharing with larger airlines. In the 1990s, they grew into large regional carriers serving numerous cities and operating turbojet aircraft. This has enabled them to service new routes previously not possible without the longer range regional jet aircraft. The three leading regional airports in 1995 were:

Dallas/Fort Worth (DFW): 370 departures per day
Los Angeles (LAX):   342 departures per day
Cincinnati (CVG):   255 departures per day

Technological advancements have enabled *code sharing*, which is a key to growth in the regional airlines. This enables airlines to use a single ticket source by using the ticket codes of the larger national airlines. This facilitates the coordination of schedules through a smooth transfer of passengers from one airline (regional) to another code sharing partner (national). Code sharing has contributed to the consolidation of smaller commuter carriers into larger regional carriers. The number of regional carriers decreased 51 percent to 124 carriers in 1995. The average trip length doubled from 121 miles in 1978 to 223 miles in 1995. The number of passengers grew from 11.3 million in 1978 to 57.2 million in 1995.

In 1995, the two largest regional airlines were Simmons Airlines, Inc., an American Eagle carrier, and ComAir, Inc., a Delta Airlines carrier. Simmons flies a fleet of 92 turboprops out of Dallas/Fort Worth and Chicago O'Hare, serving over 50 cities with 586 flights per day and carrying 4.98 million passengers. ComAir flies out of Cincinnati and Orlando, serving 79 cities with 680 flights per day.

COMPETITIVE STRUCTURE

Ten major airlines (airlines with annual revenues over $1 billion) currently account for over 75 percent of all operating revenue and 90 percent of passenger revenue (Figure 5.1). The other 10 percent are made up of over 100 airlines. The market share of other airlines has been increasing at the expense of the major airlines.

The competitiveness in the airline industry was enhanced by deregulation in 1978. Deregulation allowed airlines to fly wherever they wished. It also allowed new small airlines to compete with the existing major airlines. Some small airlines, like Southwest, have done well with point-to-point, short-haul, and high-frequency operations.

Airlines do not sell a tangible product but are simply suppliers of transportation. Aside from certain frills, the service airlines provide is basically undifferentiated. Some of these frills are more leg room, better food, newer movies, telephone service, and most recently hookups for fax and online communication. Frequent flyer programs and rewards are also used to distinguish airlines from their peers. Passenger pricing has become more and more transparent, particularly due to consumer access to fares on the Internet. In sum, the airline industry is highly competitive.

Besides competing with each other on service and price, airlines compete with a variety of transportation modes, including automobiles, railroads, and buses. For business travelers, the frequency of flights during a particular time of day is critical. Schedule reliability also influences airline selection. Smaller airlines unable to obtain gate space during peak travel times are unable to attract business travelers.

Airlines use frequent flyer programs to build brand loyalty and distinguish themselves from the competi-

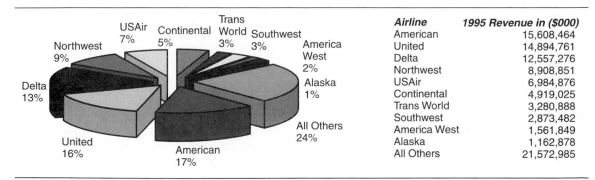

Airline	1995 Revenue in ($000)
American	15,608,464
United	14,894,761
Delta	12,557,276
Northwest	8,908,851
USAir	6,984,876
Continental	4,919,025
Trans World	3,280,888
Southwest	2,873,482
America West	1,561,849
Alaska	1,162,878
All Others	21,572,985

Figure 5.1 Operating revenues of U.S. scheduled airlines.

tion. Frequent flyer programs have been developed in an attempt to gain customer loyalty and promote repeat business. Frequent flyers represent only 8 percent of the total number of passengers. The miles they fly equal 45 percent of all miles flown. Satisfying these passengers can be key to an airline's success.

ROLE OF RESEARCH AND DEVELOPMENT

The airline industry is always seeking to improve safety. To do so, airlines have used technology to address the weakest link in air safety, the factor of human judgment. In developing new, more reliable systems for aircraft and more advanced simulators for pilot training, the airlines can help pilots identify and avoid problems before they become irreversible.

Airport capacity is another crucial issue facing the industry. It is usually cheaper to expand existing airports than to build new ones; thus it is crucial to squeeze more capacity out of existing airports. The FAA is responsible for making decisions regarding flight paths and determines when an airport is overcrowded. With the development of the global positioning system (GPS), a new system called *free flight* may reduce congestion and save time, energy, and the need for new airports.

TECHNOLOGICAL INVESTMENT AND ANALYSIS

Technology presents a tremendous potential to cut costs and simplify the process of air travel. The airline industry has improved its operating efficiency by applying new information and communication technologies. Staffing levels can be cut because computers, modems, and ATM-like machines enable fast and efficient communication and ticket distribution.

In 1995, airlines established home pages on the World Wide Web. These sites display information about schedules and fleets, contain financial and promotional material, give listings of in-flight movie offerings, and let travelers check the status of their frequent flyer accounts. Since 1996, ticketless travel enabled ticket purchases to be made on the web. Once the reservation is paid for, passengers can board the airline by showing a valid driver's license. This eliminates the security surrounding ticket stock as well as the accounting procedures required to track the used tickets.

In 1997, 2 percent of air travel reservations were made through Internet bookings. As travelers use the Internet to obtain frequently sought information, airlines are cutting customer service operators. The Internet makes airfares publicly available and comparable on the World Wide Web. This enables consumers to compare and shop for the lowest prices.

Airlines are using technology to reduce operating costs. Early in 1995, the airline industry realized the partial elimination of the traditional paper ticket. The "electronic ticket" was its replacement. It brings signif-

icant savings to airlines in the cost of ticket distribution. Whether passengers welcome the change is not entirely clear.

The airline smart card is another new product. It provides frequent travelers with the ability to quickly identify themselves, board a flight, obtain a ticket, and pay for other products and services. It also saves airline ticket distribution costs, allows more passengers use of self-service facilities, and provides a better means of identification.

Most airline smart cards are co-branded. This means that they are issued by banks or credit card companies and contain airline industry applications. The cards have the capability to provide information regarding airline and seating preferences. Space also exists for visa and immigration data for some governments.

All major airlines, with the exception of Southwest Airlines, are part of an intricate computer system that enables travel agents to book flights for customers. The nation's 30,000 travel agents sell 85 percent of the tickets. Major airlines are able to offer a high concentration and variety of flights with availability. This makes it easier for agents to schedule. In addition, major airlines are able to offer more incentives to travel agents who sell the airlines seats. Early in 1995, most major airlines imposed a $50 cap on all seats over $500 sold by agents.

RECOMMENDATION FOR THE FUTURE

For airlines to survive in this highly competitive industry, they need to strive to become as cost efficient as possible. Only with low costs can airlines compete with low fares. Technology can cut costs and provide convenience as shown with the electronic tickets and smart cards.

To gain a competitive advantage in the industry, airlines should seek to gain access to emerging markets in Asia. As China and other countries become more involved in the global marketplace, their rate of economic growth will rise. This will lead to a greater demand for air travel. If an airline is able to capture this market, the returns will be considerable.

One method that could be utilized to capture this market would be the smart card. If an airline introduces the card for its passengers, other airline's procedures would seem tedious in comparison. Consumers would not want to switch from the smart card due to costs and inconvenience. This would enable the new market to be captured, at least for a limited time.

INDUSTRY WEB SITES

Airline Industry

www.atag.org
www.air_transport.org
www.iata.org
www.raa.org

AMERICAN AIRLINES

Executive Summary

Case Name:	American Airlines and British Airways "The Skies Just Got Friendlier"
Case Industry:	Airline industry
Major Technology Issue:	SABRE: groundbreaking computer reservation system; method to track frequent flyer miles (AAdvantage Program); supersaver fares (discounted fares for public not flying); code sharing
Major Financial Issue:	Reallocation of resources to make core airline business stronger; better focus airline in high-margin markets
Major Strategic Issue:	Alliance between American Airlines and British Airways; antitrust consideration; American: capture and profit from British's control of Heathrow; British: untapped U.S. market; obtain state of the art technology
Major Players/Leaders:	Robert Crandall, President and CEO
Main Web Page:	www.aa.com
Case Conclusion/Recommendation:	Boost revenues and market share. American gained market entry to Britain and Heathrow airport. Use technology to distance airlines from competition.

CASE ANALYSIS

INTRODUCTORY STORY

In early 1977, hearings were held in Washington regarding airline deregulation. The hearings proceeded without incident for much of the day. Phil Bakes, the legal counsel for Senator Ted Kennedy, remembers sitting in the hushed hearing room as a panel of airline witnesses finished testifying. As he glanced up from his seat, he noticed an unfamiliar, tough looking man coming right at him.

> *"You academic pinhead!" the man shouted, "you don't know anything. You can't deregulate this industry, you're going to wreck it. You don't know a thing!"*[1]

And so it was that this distinguished legal mind and other spectators got their first public introduction to Robert Crandall, Vice President and future President and CEO of American Airlines.

While Crandall lost this initial fight over airline deregulation, from that day on the rest of the airline industry knew he was a force to be reckoned with. Almost 20 years later, Crandall once again thrust him-

self into the spotlight, but this time with a plan to change the airline industry forever.

In the spring of 1996 Crandall announced that American Airlines and British Airways were pursuing an alliance. It would be classified as an operational merger, in that they would cooperate on pricing, sales, and marketing, and share revenues; yet they would retain separate entities. The rest of the industry immediately protested in fury, claiming this would cause monopoly-like conditions and shut almost everyone out of the United States–European gateways. Yet, Crandall, with his slicked back hair and tireless spirit, decided he would take on government, his competitors, industry naysayers and all others, to push through the merger.

SHORT DESCRIPTION OF THE COMPANY

American Airlines (or AMR Corporation) is composed of the Air Transportation Group, SABRE Group, and Management Services Group. The Air Transportation Group has historically been made up of American Airlines and American Eagle. Together, they have now grown to the point that they serve over 300 destinations around the world. Their strong name recognition is probably their greatest strength. Although they experienced a fatal crash in Columbia at the end of 1995, consumer confidence remains high.

---

[1] Peterson, Barbara, and Glab, James, *Rapid Descent*, Simon & Schuster, New York, 1994, p. 49.

The SABRE Group is a continuation of a trend-setting reservations system developed by American in 1946. They provided the industry's first electrical/mechanical device for controlling seat inventory. The network system continued to grow from coast to coast until it reached its current level. Today, 300,000 devices are connected to SABRE. Personal computers can be used to access SABRE and make air, hotel, or car rental reservations.

The Management Services Group is AMR's attempt to break ground in new areas, while testing to see if there is opportunity for major growth. Many of the subgroups in this line of business have adopted a consulting role to the clients in one aspect of transportation or another.

SHORT HISTORY OF THE COMPANY

American Airlines has a history of being an airline maverick. Charles Lindbergh was the chief pilot for one of the scores of small companies that was consolidated into American in the late 1920s and early 1930s.[2] Although dependent on mail service in its earliest days, the company quickly realized that the future of air transportation resided in the development of passenger services. American inaugurated commercial flights with the Douglas DC-3 between Chicago and New York on June 25, 1936.[3]

Robert Crandall fit no one's mold as the prototypical president. He liked it that way. For what he lacked in polish, he more then compensated for in grit. The man that some people regarded as the "most feared and powerful man in the global airlines industry,"[4] had a burning desire not only to succeed, but an almost bloodthirsty drive to bury the competition in the process. Although not a fan of anything other than business, he revered the hard-nosed reputations of men like legendary Green Bay Packers coach Vince Lombardi. At a company-wide dinner, he climbed on the stage and cried out, "We'll crunch our competitors so hard even Lombardi will hear it, and nobody will need a hearing aid to know we knocked them off their feet!"[5] His heightened level of intensity was matched with his unyielding knack for innovation.

Crandall was originally attracted to American because of its groundbreaking computer reservation system, SABRE. He had been on the cutting edge of data processing and information systems in his time at Kodak

and Hallmark. Those businesses were not fast paced and exciting enough for him. In addition to leading the charge to update the SABRE system, he helped to propel American to the zenith of the airline industry with groundbreaking programs and incentives. He is probably best known for the two ideas that revolutionized the relationship between the airline and the passenger.

The AAdvantage Program This program was one of the earliest frequent flyer programs. It was based on the concept that frequent travelers with American Airlines should be rewarded with free tickets and gifts. When the program was conceived it was estimated that 50,000 members would join in its initial campaign. Instead, it met with phenomenal public response, and had more than a million participants before the end of the first year, 1981.

The Supersaver Fares The question to be addressed was how to offer highly discounted fares for the public that would not otherwise fly, while holding as many full-priced seats as possible for the people who traveled no matter what. The answer was to give the discounts to people who made reservations well in advance and intended to stay a minimum number of days. This would effectively eliminate many businesspeople from obtaining these fares. Marketed under the name "super-savers," they were a huge success. An individual could now fly coast-to-coast on a regularly scheduled American flight for $227 instead of $412.[6]

For all of Crandall's success in making American Airlines a world class power, the airline fell on hard times, along with the rest of the industry, in the late 1980s and early 1990s. American fell prey to the myth in the airline industry that bigger is better. It tried to win market share in too many different cities, spreading itself too thin.

In addition, American continued to buy aircraft at a dizzying rate with no consideration for the impact or the balance sheet. As recently as 1989, American placed a $7 billion order for aircraft. By the end of 1992–93, management reached the decision that for the company to succeed a new strategy was needed. As a result, they rolled out the "transition plan."[7] The plan had a three-pronged mission:

1. To reallocate resources to make their core airline business stronger where it was economically justified.
2. To shrink and reduce the airline in markets that they deemed they could no longer compete profitably.
3. To encourage and support the growth of the information and management services division.

[2] "The Fly Boys: They Shrank the Globe and—Even Harder—Made Money in the Process," *Fortune*, May 24, 1999, v. 139, i. 10, p. 238(1).
[3] *A Brief History*, American Airlines, 1995, p. 62.
[4] Petzinger, Thomas, *Hard Landing*, Random House, New York, 1995, p. 49.
[5] Ibid., p. 50.
[6] Ibid., p. 50.
[7] American Airlines Annual Report, 1995, p. 17.

From this plan grew a "leaner, meaner" company. As American's financial fortunes began to improve, Crandall continued to search for a new way to give the company an edge in the industry. His management team came to the conclusion that it was time for American to expand on an idea that was beginning to catch hold in the industry, the alliance. Crandall resisted at first, having long been an opponent of airline alliances. The more he looked at the issues, the more he became convinced this was the direction to follow. Yet, Robert Crandall would not be happy to just form any alliance; he now focused on formulating the biggest and most dominant alliance that the airline industry had ever seen.

FINANCIAL AND PORTFOLIO ANALYSIS

While both American Airlines and British Airways took pride in the fact that they were among the elite of the industry, it became clear that they would need each other to claim their spot as the largest airline in the world. While each offered specific advantages to the partner, the sheer magnitude of the financial, mechanical, and industrial expertise between the two was enough to leave industry observers gaping. The main area of concentration between this new alliance was the single most profitable route in the world, the transatlantic United States to Great Britain route.

The alliance would be the largest United States–European airline alliance ever, nearly twice the size of the United–Lufthansa alliance and over five times the size of Delta's alliance with Sabena, SwissAir, and Austrian Airlines. It would fly more seats than all of its competitors combined from 8 of 10 United States gateways. It would be the only service provider in 4 of these ten markets.[8]

Heathrow Airport is a major player in North Atlantic air travel. It handles more international passengers than any other airport in the world. The number of people that pass through grows more staggering each year, with the figures for 1995 reaching over 54 million passengers.[9] With so many airlines flying through Heathrow, it was difficult to associate all of them. As a result, British Airways, the government-owned airline, had a virtual monopoly on space at Heathrow for years.

In 1977, the United States hammered out the terms of the United States–United Kingdom Air Transport Agreement (known as "Bermuda 2"). This agreement guaranteed a limited number of gates to Pan Am and TWA (at that time the most dominant American international air-

lines) at Heathrow, with the agreement that there would never be more than those two airlines from the United States. Over the years, American Airlines executives have asserted that this was one of the most poorly negotiated deals in the history of the industry. The United States government defended itself with the argument that limited access was better than no access at all.

As both Pan Am and TWA fell upon increasingly difficult financial fortunes in the late 1980s, they attempted to sell their routes to American and United, respectively, for approximately $750 million. The problem was that the Bermuda 2 agreement specifically spelled out that Pan Am and TWA were the only United States airlines allowed to serve Heathrow, with all the others relegated to the poorly situated Gatwick Airport. By 1991, a deal was negotiated that enabled another United States carrier to operate out of Heathrow. In exchange, British airlines received a number of new operating rights, including the right to code share in most United States–United Kingdom city pairs.[10]

While American and United Airlines initially praised the deal, they continued to grow discontented with their limited space and the inability to grow along with the increased traffic through Heathrow. Some airlines gave up on Heathrow and looked elsewhere. United, while still using all of its owned routes to Heathrow, is rapidly expanding its operation in Frankfurt, as a result of its merger with Lufthansa. In the same vein, Delta has continued to push for a loosening of regulation at Heathrow. This has led to development of other European hubs in the home nations of their alliance partners. With the advent of the BA/American alliance, American will leap to the top of the transatlantic airlines. With their newly unlimited access to Heathrow, they will not have to go through the same trouble as the other airlines in trying to develop a hub. The new alliance will command almost 70 percent of the availability for United States–United Kingdom traffic spots.

Many years ago, British Airways realized that to fully maximize their potential, they would need to gain a strong foothold in the United States. After years of posturing and studying the possibilities, CEO Sir Colin Marshall decided the best way to proceed was to get a piece of the action himself. He went out and purchased nearly 25 percent of USAir Group Inc., in reality making them part of the British Airways world network. The merger did not work. USAir had control of inconvenient airports and USAir was in worse financial shape than was initially realized.

American appeared to be an attractive alternative. With a substantial market share in almost every major American city, there would be no problems with incon-

[8] "Branson Blasts the Proposed Alliance," *PR Newswire*, October 9, 1996.

[9] Bryant, Adam, "Rivals of American and British Air Quickly Assail New Alliance as Anticompetitive," *New York Times*, June 12, 1996, p. D4.

[10] Mathias, Dick, "What Makes a Code-Share Fly?," *Journal of Commerce*, December 7, 1993, p. 18A.

venient gateways. Financially, American had rebounded strongly from financial difficulties in the late 1980s and early 1990s, to the point that they posted positive results by 1995. The deciding factor was American's command of information systems and technology.

RISK ANALYSIS

The airline industry as a whole was faced with a major problem but did not appear to have an answer. The combination of deregulation, greater competition, and the ability to transport larger numbers of people at one time was reducing margins.

Boeing, the world's largest aircraft manufacturer, released a study that indicated that noted yields, the revenue received for each mile a passenger is carried, were in a long-term decline. Boeing further noted that yields had been falling by about 2 percent a year in real terms since 1960. It expected the decline to continue at a rate of 1.1 percent a year between 1995 and 2014.[11] Even as raw passenger numbers increased, this did not relieve the pressure on companies to eliminate superfluous costs.

INDUSTRY AND MARKET ANALYSIS

While corporations focus on market growth and year-end profits, governments are responsible for the impact on the economics of an entire nation. Since deregulation in the 1970s, agencies such as the DOT and FAA have worked to assess the impact of mergers, deregulation, the economy, and the financial viability at the airline industry.

From the outset of deregulation, the United States government went to great lengths to ease the restrictions that foreign governments placed on international travel. The government was confident that if deregulation was implemented in other countries, the concentration on customer service and technological expertise would be superior to the national airlines that dominated their home markets. Other governments were concerned about the same outcome and sought to protect their interests from airlines from Britain and the United States. As a result, they closely restricted the number of flights that foreign airlines could fly into and out of their airports.

For much of the '80s, the antitrust laws of the United States did not apply to the airline industry. The Reagan administration's laissez-faire stance enabled a surging tide of mergers to change the face of the airlines, resulting in only 10 airline holding companies operating nationally. Together, they controlled about 95 percent of the airline market in the United States.[12] As a new administration was ushered in with the 1992 elections, so

was a new activist spirit. In 1992, when Northwest indicated their interest in an alliance with the Dutch airline KLM, the government sent a strong message to the Netherlands that without a formal open skies agreement between the two counties, there would be no chance for antitrust immunity. As a result, the final agreement included an open skies agreement.

The United States government studied the impact of this early alliance and further tightened its policy as it moved forward. In the case of United/Lufthansa and Delta/Sabena/Austrian/SwissAir, the government not only required an open skies agreement from all of its airlines home nations, which it received, but it further restricted some routes to remain nonalliance.[13] For example, Delta and SwissAir are the only two airlines that offer service between Cincinnati and Zurich; they must remain competitive on that route and not collude on prices.

Given the large number of restricted routes, and the demand that Britain sign an open skies agreement, the United States government may be a major factor in preventing this alliance from happening. Britain has always been extremely firm at the negotiating table; there is little reason to think this time will be different. British Airways may persuade the British government to open its skies, and to complete the deal with American.

While United States policy is influenced by everyone from travel agents to airports to consumer advocates, transportation policy in the European Union is decided by a relatively tight-knit circle. As a result, British civil aviation policy has grown into a complex network of bilateral aviation treaties. Most of them are severely outdated; some are decades old. They continue past their useful life because of the lack of direction in transportation.[14]

Not long after BA and American made their June announcement, the European Commission gathered in Brussels to prepare the launch of its bid to negotiate full traffic rights with the United States on behalf of the European nations. They immediately realized they needed to gain control of the fastest growing threat to outside intervention: the alliances. While other alliances provided little concern compared to the BA/AA monolith, the commission announced that it would simultaneously investigate all of the current transatlantic alliances.[15]

The source of power that Brussels claimed was the little known, and even less frequently used, Article 89 of the Treaty of Rome. This article allows member

[11] Skapinker, Michael, "Airlines Rush to Adapt to Big Changes in the Skies," *Financial Times*, November 16, 1995, p. 27.
[12] Petzinger, Thomas, *Hard Landing*, Random House, New York, 1995, p. 53.

[13] Feldman, Joan, "Some Call It Oligopoly," *Air Transport World*, May 1996, pp. 45–47.
[14] "Flying in Formation," *Economist*, June 15, 1996, p. 15.
[15] "Antitrust Is the Key in Open Skies Talks," *Airline Business*, August, 1996, p. 18.

nations to investigate dominant positions in Europe. While the member states are legally bound to cooperate with the commission, in practice this does not mean they will follow its recommendations. The negotiating stance of the commission seems to be weakened by the apparent inability of the nations of Europe to work as one. The EU claimed a small victory in June, 1996, by securing a mandate from all the member states to negotiate an air agreement with Washington. However, nine nations had already made bilateral deals with the United States.[16]

For all of its potential roadblocks, it is possible that it took this "mother of all alliances" to get the rest of Europe to work together in the transportation arena. If there is consensus throughout the European Community against the structure of the alliance, the British government may be forced to rethink their own policy.

Delta Airlines released a statement that described the potential alliance as "frightening," and promised that it would fight the plan, unless meaningful access to Heathrow was given in exchange.[17] Executives of airlines throughout the United States made it a top agenda item to paint a vision of a monopoly if the deal went through. When presented with a public survey that said that 50 percent of the people asked believed the alliance would be fairly to extremely helpful, Richard Hirst, senior vice president at Northwest Airlines, remarked, "If that's true, I'd eat American's annual report—in public. No condiments, just raw."[18]

Robert Crandall has been called a lot of things throughout his career, but one label that few could argue against is visionary. He seems to be an individual who can sense change, and has the courage to pursue it. Yet, understanding his strategy at this juncture might be a little more difficult. It was obvious he wanted to increase the influence of American Airlines by seizing control of Heathrow.

ROLE OF RESEARCH AND DEVELOPMENT

Robert Crandall came from a systems background, and was determined to maintain American's technological leadership. His goal is to use technology to make every aspect of the airline as efficient and well run as possible. One brainchild was the American Airlines Decision Technologies Group (AADT), which originated as a developer of decision support tools.

The goal of this venture was to have a computer analyze all the different possibilities in complex decisions and produce recommendations based on its analysis of the financials and other factors. As the group developed these cutting edge tools, they soon found that the information base needed to apply these tools did not exist.[19] They had to develop it.

TECHNOLOGICAL STORY

In the area of information technology, British Airways had grown comfortable. Since going public in 1987, it had an unbroken record of profits through fiscal year 1995.[20] It dominated its home market to the point of near monopoly, while signing key alliances internationally to continue to expand. It had good management and a nearly untarnished reputation.

The belief that the status quo would remain good enough soon began to haunt the company. They found themselves at a point where they had no reliable vehicle to study and analyze their internal work practices and flows. They were trying to find ways to slash costs through automation of their systems, rather than resorting to desperation and replacing full-time employees with either less skilled or part-time workers.

As BA looked within and realized that their greatest internal liability lay in the area of information technologies and systems, American appeared as not only a perfect fit, but also nearly a necessity. American had long been recognized as a leader in technology in the industry. This dated to the invention of SABRE and the development of the American Airlines Decision Technologies Group.

TECHNOLOGICAL INVESTMENT AND ANALYSIS

The first move American Airlines Decision Technologies Group (AADTG) made was to closely align itself with the SABRE Technologies Group, to apply the expertise of the people already on that staff. As this newly defined group began to take shape, they realized their first hurdle would be to develop the appropriate core modules in relational databases, and make sure the stand-alone systems could interact with the core.[21] They settled on four core modules, which they felt would cover a larger percentage of the areas addressed by the decision support tools.

Aircraft records: As John Simmons, a director of the group explained, "it keeps track of hours,

[16] Barnard, Bruce, "EU Launches Probe of Airline Alliance," *Journal of Commerce*, 10/3/96, p. 4B; Branson, Richard, "You're Building a Monopoly," *Wall Street Journal*, January 1, 1997, p. A.16.

[17] Bryant, Adam, "Rivals of American and British Air Quickly Assail New Alliance as Anticompetitive," *New York Times*, June 12, 1996, p. D4.

[18] Kayal, Michael, "American Airlines poll: Public favors BA Alliance," *Journal of Commerce*, September 6, 1996, p. 3B.

[19] Henderson, Danna, "Seeking the IT Holy Grail," *Air Transport World*, March 1996, p. 77.

[20] Feldman, Joan, "Trying to raise the crossbar," *Air Transport World*, June 1996, p. 23.

[21] Henderson, Danna, "Seeking the IT Holy Grail," *Air Transport World*, March 1996, p. 78.

cycles, components, the airframe, the engines, and tells you exactly where you stand, whether a part is attached to an aircraft, or in a shop or a warehouse."[22]

Materials: This encompasses inventory, purchasing, warehousing, warranty tracking, and related activities.

Training module: This tracks mechanic and inspector licenses, as well as recurrent training requirements. The module provides a clear history of all personnel records.

Production control: This develops the package for a specific aircraft's base visit and then transfers the package electronically to mechanics anywhere in the world.

These modules were put in place in 1992 for American's own fleet. SABRE technologies built an interface that tied the module into mainframe applications such as inventory control, flight scheduling, and financial analysis. Johnson explained the power of the tools when they are programmed to work as one:

A mechanic can look up a part number at a terminal on the floor of the hangar and order the part; the front end interfaces with the mainframe to order the part, get it delivered to him, document the cost, assign the cost to the specific airplane he's working on, and change the inventory. The inventory system then automatically reorders, to maintain current inventory levels.[23]

Equally impressive are the labor reports, which allow a mechanic to log onto and off a work card and indicate that a piece of work is in process. This provides a real-time status of hours, materials, and labor for any ongoing project. The history database enables a mechanic to examine 20 to 30 airplanes and predict with a very large degree of certainty the exact parts that are going to be needed. This means that airlines do not have to stock everything needed for an airplane, which has a major impact on the levels of inventory that need to be maintained.

These technological strides keep American ahead of all the other competitors. BA could not help but notice that the technologies that American was developing were those that directly addressed the main problems BA was facing. Areas like efficiency, usage, and maintenance were presenting serious problems for BA, while American was transforming itself into a technologically driven organization. If BA wanted to buy the technologies, not only would it have to make a major outlay of cash, but it would actually be supporting one of its competitors. This

was because BA needed to continually pay American personnel as consultants to keep the systems running.

American began to develop technologies that would further implement the AA/BA concept of seamless travel through the alliance. Perhaps the program that provides the most obvious and appreciated results is American's newly developed AAccess electronic ticketing. Most of the major airlines went to the option of electronic ticketing in 1996. Consumers do not need a hardcopy or paper ticket, they just have to check in at the gate with a picture ID to claim their boarding pass. American believes the AAccess program will take this concept to a new level, enabling a traveler to go from home computer to airplane seat without any intervening stops inside the terminal.

The system combines online reservation and electronic ticketing with IER gate readers that allow e-ticketed passengers not checking bags to board their aircraft at 21 United States airports merely by inserting any credit card to identify themselves.[24] This distinguishes the system as the only one that does not require the traveler to stop at a ticket or gate counter. American has begun testing airport kiosks that will be called AAccess self-service devices. At the selected test airports, passengers will be able to change their seats, check their AAdvantage mileage, or accomplish their own upgrades. These innovations make American even more attractive as a partner with British Airways.

TECHNOLOGICAL INNOVATIONS
TELECOMMUNICATIONS

American Airlines has leveraged web technologies to reduce call-center volume, sell vacant seats, and expand its affinity marketing programs. At the same time, the company is deploying intranet tools to knit together its distributed enterprise, which at any given time can have personnel spread across 115 different cities worldwide.

"What we've done is put the primary burden for developing the Internet strategy on the department heads," says Scott Nason, American's vice president of information technology. "If you are running the operations department, it is your and your manager's job to figure out how to run your department better."

By pushing business managers to take responsibility, American has developed solutions to difficult problems. An ever-increasing appetite for call-center ticketing support has been satisfied through Internet electronic commerce. Unused inventory is being reduced through discount sales at its NetSavers site.

"The number of people buying online is still small, but there will be ongoing cost implications and broader

22 Ibid.
23 Henderson, Danna, "Seeking the IT Holy Grail," *Air Transport World*, March 1996, p. 81.
24 Henderson, Danna, "On the Bar-Code Road," *Air Transport World*, September 1996, p. 87.

marketing programs for the distribution of product from here on," said John Samuel, American's managing director of interactive marketing.

DATA

American Airline's Revenue Accounting Data Access Resource (RADAR) started as a departmental data mart for use by 40 accountants in March 1997. It is now accessed by more than 100 users in diverse departments such as marketing and security. The data mart took about nine months to build.[25]

RADAR consists of a Sybase IQ 11.5 running on a Sun Enterprise 5000 12-way server, which pulls data from a mainframe ticketing system that each year issues more than 125 million pieces of travel-related documents. The front end is IQ/Objects from IQ Software, which translates GUI-driven commands into valid SQL for custom, ad hoc queries. RADAR development required several months of combing through data, looking for a corrupted index. The finished data mart has 20 tables and completes the average query in seven minutes, with about 40 percent of the queries being done in less than four minutes.

The return on investment has exceeded expectation. During its first week, RADAR saved $60,000 by spotting improper ticketing procedures. American Airlines says that the $400,000 project has paid for itself many times over in cost savings.

RECOMMENDATION FOR THE FUTURE

It was not only American's technology in the behind-the-scenes working of an airline that made it attractive, but also its ability to stay on the cutting edge of what the consumer wanted. BA's own surveys indicated that travelers perceived its service to be "impersonal." This slippage was evident during the winter storms of 1995

in the United States. While American Airlines was calling passengers with rebookings, BA was telling even business fliers to come out to the airport and standby.[26] These events led to the public perception that BA was out of touch with the consumer, only putting effort into initiatives that would have a direct impact on its bottom line.

Public perception of American is at the other end of that spectrum. Dating back to the supersaver fares and frequent flyer plans of Crandall's early days, AA has consistently found ways to distinguish itself in the area of customer service. In recent years, it has seized the lead in the area it sees as most important as far as the convenience of the consumer, the Internet.[27]

In the fourth quarter of 1995, American placed sixth among all companies in World Wide Web advertising.[28] The important thing is not just that American is reaching people on the web, but that it is providing a service the consumer wants. One example of this is easy-SABRE, American's consumer-oriented version of the system that had previously been available only to travel agents. Consumers can now access this service online. In 1995 alone, American sold 1.6 million tickets through this medium. In addition, there are millions who have signed up for NetSAAvers on the American Airlines web site. Through this service, consumers are alerted to specials once a week through e-mail, helping to fill seats that would have otherwise remained empty.[29]

American must push ahead with its technological energy. The alliance with British Airways will be beneficial and should be pursued.

---

[25] Amer, Suzie, Bianchi, Alessandra, Donahue, Sean, Ginsburg, Steven, Jeffers, Michelle, Patterson, Lee, and Pickering, Carol, "America's Best Technology Users," *Forbes*, August 24, 1998, v. 162, n. 4, p. S63(20).

[26] Feldman, Joan, "Alliances: Are We Making Money Yet?," *Air Transport World*, October 1995, p. 25.
[27] "The Best of Online Travel," *Computerworld*, October 26, 1998, p. 92(1).
[28] *Marketing Computers*, "Big Spenders Online," January 1996, p. 12.
[29] Gunther, Marc, "Travel Planning in Cyberspace," *Fortune*, September 9, 1996, p. 187.

CASE QUESTIONS

Strategic Questions

1. What is the strategic/future direction of the corporation/organization?

2. Who or what forces are driving this direction?

3. What has been the catalyst for change?

4. What are the critical success factors for this corporation/organization?

5. What are the core competencies for this corporation/organization?

6. What are the forces going against the Alliance?

Technological Questions

7. What technologies has the corporation relied on?

8. What has caused a change in the use of technology in the corporation/organization?

9. How has this change been implemented?

10. Who has driven this change throughout the organization?

11. How successful has the technological change been?

12. What are the criticisms of the proposed alliance?

Quantitative Questions

13. What does the corporation say about its financial ability to embark on a major technological program of advancement?

14. What conclusions can be reached from an analysis of the financial information to support or contradict this financial ability?

15. What analysis can be made by examining the following ratio groups?
    Quick/Current
    Debt
    Revenue
    Profit
    Asset Utilization

16. What conclusions can be reached by analyzing the financial trends?

17. Are there long-term trends that seem to be problematic?

18. Is the industry stable?

19. Are there replacement products?

Internet Questions

20. What does the corporation's web page present about its business directives?

21. How does this compare to the conclusions reached by the case?

22. How does this compare to the conclusions reached by analyzing the financial information?

Industry Questions

23. What challenges and opportunities is the industry facing?

24. Is the industry oligopolistic or competitive?

25. Does the industry face a change in government regulation?

26. How will technology impact the industry?

Data Questions

27. What role do data play in the future of the corporation?

28. How important are data to the corporation's continued success?

29. How will the capture and maintenance of customer data impact the corporation's future?

SOUTHWEST AIRLINES

Executive Summary

Case Name:	Southwest Airlines
Case Industry:	Airline industry
Major Technology Issue:	Choosing the correct technologies that will help them lower costs ahead of their competitors
Major Financial Issue:	Keeping their unbroken string of profitable years
Major Strategic Issue:	How to deal with the new competition
Major Players/Leaders:	Herb Kelleher, CEO
Main Web Page:	www.americanair.com
Case Conclusion/Recommendation:	Southwest Airlines has succeeded in a very competitive industry by holding down costs and passing that savings on to the consumer. They will need to continuously invest in the right technologies to remain ahead of competitors.

CASE ANALYSIS

INTRODUCTORY STORY

Look! Up in the sky! It's a bird. It's a plane. It's . . . Shamu? Sound crazy? If you have ever flown on Southwest Airlines, nothing seems more natural than munching peanuts inside a black-and-white painted killer whale. There is more. Imagine sitting in an aisle seat. Just as you lay your head back, a bunny-suited flight attendant pops out of the overhead bin and yells "Surprise!" Or at the end of a trip, your flight attendant requests: "Please pass all the plastic cups to the center aisle so we can wash them and use them for the next group of passengers."

These are examples of the unconventionality that characterizes Southwest Airlines.

SHORT DESCRIPTION OF THE COMPANY

Southwest Airlines is the fifth largest United States airline. Unique among airlines, the company has enjoyed more than 20 years of steady growth by specializing in frequent nonstop flights that are less than two hours in duration. The company views its principal competition as the automobile rather than other airlines. Southwest's operating philosophy combines rock-bottom fares with no-frills flights.

Southwest neither serves meals on board nor checks bags through to connecting flights. There is no reserved seating. Boarding passes are reused. The company flies only Boeing 737s to simplify maintenance. With its unique operating philosophy, South-

west is a maverick in the highly competitive airline industry.[1]

SHORT HISTORY OF THE COMPANY

Southwest Air was founded in 1966 when a group of Texas investors, including Texas businessman Rollin King and lawyer Herbert D. Kelleher. They pooled $560,000 to form the Air Southwest Company. Incorporated in 1967, the company was a commuter airline serving three cities in Texas: Dallas, Houston, and San Antonio. Three competing airlines filed suit, questioning whether the region needed another airline. Kelleher took the case all the way to the U.S. Supreme Court, which ruled in favor of Air Southwest in 1970.

The airline soon changed its name to Southwest Air, sold stock, and began operations. In 1971, it offered 6 daily round-trip flights between Dallas and San Antonio and 12 daily round-trip flights between Dallas and Houston. One-way tickets cost $20.[2]

The company stressed no-frills convenience. In reference to Love Field in Dallas, its home base, it made "love" its promotional theme. Its early ad campaigns featured stewardesses wearing hot pants and serving love potions (drinks) and love bites (peanuts) to the company's clientele of mostly business fliers.

---

[1] Branch, Shelly, "The 100 Best Companies To Work For In America," *Fortune*, January 11, 1999, v. 139, i. 1, p. 118(1).
[2] "Why CEOs Fail: It's Rarely for Lack of Smarts or Vision. Most Unsuccessful CEOs Stumble Because of One Simple, Fatal Shortcoming," *Fortune*, June 21, 1999, v. 139, i. 12, p. 68(1).

When the other airlines moved to the Dallas-Fort Worth airport in 1974, Southwest stayed at Love Field, gaining a virtual monopoly at the airfield. This was a cheaper, more convenient airport that, along with Houston's Hobby Airport, provided the basis for broader operations.

Expansion began in 1975, when the airline inaugurated service to the Rio Grande Valley, with four round-trip flights each day to South Padre Island. By the end of that year, the company had acquired a fifth plane. Soon, it got clearance to offer service from Corpus Christi, Lubbock, El Paso, Austin, and Midland/Odessa. In the following years, more cities were added to the company's list of destinations.

In 1979, Southwest introduced self-ticketing machines in many of its airports to speed up and simplify passenger ticketing. In 1981, Herb Kelleher became the president and CEO of Southwest Airlines.[3] He brought his flamboyant personal style to the job of running the company. With Kelleher at the helm, the airline's pace of expansion picked up markedly, despite the nationwide recession.[4]

In 1982 Southwest departed from its previous strategy of sticking to short-haul flights and inaugurated routes from San Antonio and El Paso to Los Angeles. This entry into long-haul markets curtailed profits during this period.

By 1986, Southwest had scheduled flights from 25 cities. The airline introduced a number of fare-cutting measures to maintain its market share in the heavily competitive postderegulation airline industry. "Incredible Pair Fares," "Fly Now, Pay Less," programs, $25 tickets for senior citizens and, finally "Fun Fares" became part of the strategy to lure more flyers to the skies. In this same year, the company made "fun" its new corporate byword and implemented a "fun" uniform of T-shirts, surfer shorts, and tennis shoes, along with inflight games and giveaways.[5]

Faced with the demands of business flyers, Southwest introduced its first frequent flyer program. Unlike the programs of other airlines, which presented awards based on accrued mileage, Southwest's program was designed to reward the short-haul flyer, allotting awards on the basis of the number of trips taken.[6]

As a result of its steady growth, Southwest entered the 1990s as a major airline with a fleet of 94 planes serving 27 cities. Relying on conservative financial management, the company was able to avoid the pitfalls of debt that crippled many other carriers in the early 1990s. Southwest returned an overall profit during those years.

In 1995 Southwest launched a "ticketless" travel system to trim travel agent commissions. The company also inaugurated a new computer reservation system for an automated booking of passengers. In 1996, Southwest won its fifth annual Triple Crown—for best on-time record, best baggage handling, and fewest customer complaints.[7]

Within 25 years, the airline company became the fifth largest major airline in America. Today, it owns over 240 of the newest jets in the nation and flies over 44 million passengers a year to 50 cities. Given its record of solid growth and its development of a unique niche in the American transportation industry, it appears likely that Southwest airlines will continue to thrive.[8]

FINANCIAL AND PORTFOLIO ANALYSIS

A carrier's load factor is derived by dividing its revenue per mile by its total available seat miles (ASMs). This forms a key measure of capacity utilization. Given the airlines' high fixed cost structure, the more passengers that can be boarded before each scheduled departure, the more profitable the flight will be. The average load factor for United States domestic flights was estimated at nearly 70 percent last year. Short-haul commuter airlines, such as Southwest, often have load factors well below the major airline since they trade higher aircraft turnaround for lower load factors. In fact, Southwest can operate profitably at load factors of 50 percent or less. The airline's operating costs are among the lowest in the industry because of its high productivity of assets and labor, the offering of "no frills" and point-to-point service.

Salaries, wages, and benefits per ASM have increased. This is due to an increase in the number of reservations sales agents, as well as in average headcount, in line with capacity. Southwest also offers generous profit sharing, with 15 percent of net profits returned to workers. It matches up to 100 percent of employee contributions to 401(k) plans, depending on union contract provisions. Fuel and oil expenses have also increased in the last couple of years, primarily due to the rise in the average jet fuel cost per gallon from 1995. Maintenance, materials, and repairs per ASM

[3] Labich, Kenneth, "Is Herb Kelleher America's Best CEO?," *Fortune*, May 2, 1997, p. 44.

[4] "The Jack and Herb Show," *Fortune*, January 11, 1999, v. 139, i. 1, p. 163(1).

[5] Nirenberg, John, "Review Nuts! Southwest Airlines Crazy Recipe for Business and Personal Success," *International Journal Of Organizational Analysis*, p. 212.

[6] Sunoo, Brenda Paik, "How Fun Flies At Southwest Airlines," *Personnel Journal*, June 1995, p. 62.

[7] "Southwest Goes Live," *Travel Weekly*, April 3, 1995, p. 55.

[8] Branch, Shelly, "The 100 Best Companies to Work for in America," *Fortune*, January 11, 1999, v. 139, i. 1, p. 122(1).

have increased in the last year due to the increased scheduled frame inspections. Agency commissions per ASM have decreased, even more than the year before. This is partially due to the increased number of bookings by customers directly over the Internet. Depreciation expense per ASM increased 4.7 percent in 1996 compared to 1995 due to an increase in the percentage of owned aircraft. Aircraft rentals per ASM increased in the last few years. This rise resulted primarily from sale/leaseback transactions involving ten new 737-300 aircraft and a higher percentage of the fleet consisting of leased aircraft.[9] Other operating expenses have also gone up due to increased advertising costs resulting from expansion into new markets, tax on commercial aviation jet fuel purchased for use in domestic operations, and increased airport security costs.[10]

Fierce cost control is one of the secrets to Southwest's profitability. Kelleher personally approves every expenditure over $1,000 and constantly monitors the key industry standard, cost per available seat mile, to make sure he stays a penny or two behind the rest of the industry.[11]

Southwest has the strongest balance sheet in the industry. Cash at the end of 1996 was $582 million, almost twice the level of cash held in 1995. Long-term debt of $650 million at the end of 1996 comprised 22 percent of capitalization. Long-term debt decreased by $11 million from 1995 to 1996.[12]

Debt to total capital (long-term debt divided by total invested capital) is currently 30 percent, well below the industry average. Shareholder equity is on a continuous rise and equals $1.7 billion. Total current assets almost doubled from $473 million in 1995 to $750 million in 1996. The company's consolidated net income for 1996 was $207.3 million ($1.37 per share), compared to the corresponding 1995 amount of $182.6 million ($1.23 per share), an increase of 13.5 percent. Operating revenues (net sales and other operating revenues) have been increasing by at least 30 percent every year since 1993.[13] Operating expenses, although lowest in the industry, have also increased, but only by 10 percent on average. Fuel and oil expenses have gone up because the price of fuel went up considerably in 1996; maintenance, materials and repairs, agency commissions, aircraft rentals, landing fees, and depreciation expenses have also gone up, but only in line with the expansion of capacity. Cash flow provided by operating activity has increased 25 percent since 1995. The cash flow provided by investing activity and by financing activity has gone down. The current ratio (current assets divided by current liabilities) is at 98 percent. This percentage is an indicator of the company's liquidity. Obviously, Southwest does not have an issue in this area. Debt as percent of net working capital (long-term debt divided by the difference of current assets and current liabilities) is also a measure of a company's liquidity and is above the industry average.

In contrast with the industry as a whole, which has lost billions of dollars, Southwest has accumulated 25 consecutive years of profits—a record unmatched in the U.S. airline industry. With its unique approach to travel, Southwest is far different from industry's international megacarriers. Different is even putting it mildly. Southwest has been described as having succeeded in differentiating itself through its focus on service, operations, cost control, marketing, its people, and its corporate culture. Southwest has grown to become one of the largest and best loved commercial airlines in history. No other airline has contributed more to the advancement of the commercial airline industry. The airline's annual employee turnover rate is 7 percent, the lowest in the industry.[14]

Unlike models of lean and modular production, Southwest places little emphasis on its formal organizational structure. Employee participation is largely informal. Southwest is known for its unique culture and its committed workforce. This culture values individual styles, humor, and fun at work. The company is also known for its cooperative labor/management relations, which have promoted a work environment free of rigid rules. The high-commitment culture is supported by the fact that Southwest has never had a layoff. An employee profit-sharing plan, one of the first in the airline industry, provides employees with a stake in Southwest's performance.

A key component of Southwest's success is its emphasis on extensive training and continuous learning for its workforce. Every major work area—mechanics, in-flight activities, customer service, operations, provisioning, and reservations—has its own training department, which provides training in technical skills. Employees also receive specialized courses on customer service, team building, decision making, employee relations, performance appraisal, communications, stress management, and career development.[15]

9 Beeker, H., "Southwest Airlines—Company Report," *Smith Barney*, May 22, 1997, p. 1.
10 "Southwest Airlines Co.—Company Report," *Institutional Shareholder Services*, March 20, 1997, p. 1.
11 Melymuka, Kathleen, "Sky King," *Computerworld*, September 28, 1998, v. 32, n. 39, p. 68(1).
12 Browning, C., et. al., "Southwest Airlines Co.—Company Report," *Merrill Lynch Capital Investments*, July 24, 1997, p. 1.
13 Buttrick, S., et al., "Southwest Airlines—Company Report," *PaineWebber Inc.*, January 23, 1997, p. 1.

14 Caldwell, Bruce, "Airlines Outsource," *Information Week*, January 4, 1999, p. 104(1).
15 Branch, Shelly, "The 100 Best Companies to Work for in America," *Fortune*, January 11, 1999, v. 139, i. 1, p. 124(1).

Through a set of innovative work and human resource practices including training, information sharing, innovative compensation plans, and employee involvement, the committed workforce at Southwest has shaped the company around the vision of quality, flexibility, and customer service. As a result, Southwest has achieved the vision of high performance, sustained over time.

STOCK/INVESTMENT OUTLOOK

At the end of July 1997, Southwest had 150,448,000 shares outstanding. Officers, directors, and employees of the company hold 13 percent of those shares. The market value of company's outstanding shares was $4,362,992,000.

There has been a 300 percent increase in the value of Southwest's stock since 1990. The stock for Southwest is priced fairly, with current growth of 10 percent per year. It is usually rated outperform, which means that it is expected to outperform the market by 5 to 15 percentage points. The EPS are expected to rise in the future—some say even by as much as 25 percent per year despite the lower projected percentage in capacity increase.[16]

With the company stepping up its growth, the stock remains attractive. Southwest's prospects are also very favorable because it is the leading player in the low-fare sector of the airline industry. Southwest should show at least a 10 to 12 percent compounded annual earnings growth for the foreseeable future.

RISK ANALYSIS

Over the past several years, Southwest has faced increased competition in its established markets (e.g., United Airlines Inc.'s Shuttle on the West Coast) and in new markets (e.g., Northeast to Florida, where it competes against Delta Air Lines Inc.'s low-cost, low-fare operation and Delta Express). While the competition has, in some cases, reduced pricing, Southwest has fared extremely well in most of these markets.

INDUSTRY AND MARKET ANALYSIS

In the airline industry today, low costs are and will remain the determining factor between winners and losers. Southwest has focused on the maintenance of the industry's highest level of aircraft utilization. This is possible because the point-to-point, non–hub-and-spokes route system enables Southwest to achieve 23-minute aircraft turnaround times. This is the time between when the aircraft arrives at the gate and when it pushes back from it.

Southwest benefits greatly from a highly motivated and productive workforce that embraces the SW spirit of fun and family. Although 85 percent of Southwest's employees are unionized, there is a much greater spirit of cooperation and "we're in this together" attitude than at the vast majority of airlines.

The cost of ticket sales for Southwest are low. This is largely because only 40 percent of Southwest tickets are sold through travel agents compared with 80 to 85 percent for the airline industry. This enables Southwest to circumvent travel agent commissions, which are around 10 percent of the ticket price. Some 45 percent of Southwest customers use ticketless travel. Since Southwest focuses on point-to-point service with 23-minute aircraft turnarounds, only about 20 percent of its passengers are connecting. This minimizes opportunities for lost baggage and flight delays due to the late arrival of connecting flights. Southwest's primary market is people who are concerned about the cost of airfare. Usually, those people travel for leisure. However, with some technological investments, Southwest was able to attract businesspeople as well.[17]

Air travelers can also book flights and secure flight information through the Internet. Airlines enable flights to be booked through their home pages on the World Wide Web. Another option for passengers is to book flights through the Internet via intermediaries that integrate all airline schedules into a synthetic variant of a CRS.

ROLE OF RESEARCH AND DEVELOPMENT

Southwest Airlines understands the importance of technology in today's business world. Being in a highly competitive airline industry, it has no other alternative. This industry relies on technology, and companies have used it successfully in the past to differentiate themselves. Others had to keep up in order to stay competitive.

Southwest Airlines, however, does not like to simply keep up with technological trends—it prefers being a few steps ahead. All of their technological investments have thus far proven to be immensely successful and have helped Southwest Airlines.

TECHNOLOGICAL STORY

While most airlines rely on independent travel agents to sell the majority of their tickets, Southwest has refused to connect with the computer reservation system that the agents use. Agents who wish to book a Southwest flight have to pick up the phone like anyone else or go to the Southwest home page. Many try to persuade customers to pick another carrier or to make the call themselves. The result is that nearly half of all Southwest

[16] "Southwest Airlines Declares a 3-for-2 Stock Split and Increases Dividend," *PR Newswire*, September 26, 1997, p. 926.

[17] McCartney, Scott, "Southwest Puts New York on Map," *The Wall Street Journal*, November 4, 1998, p. B1(E), c. 3.

tickets are sold directly to passengers, with an annual savings to the airline of about $30 million. The percentage of Southwest tickets sold by agents is in the "mid-40s," which is far below the industry average.

Southwest Airlines, which participates only in the SABRE CRS, offers electronic booking options to agencies with more features than the Web site. Southwest's Direct Access software product, which enables non-SABRE agents to dial into the airline's computer system, gives an agent more information and allows cancellations.

In 1996, Southwest Airlines became one of the first airlines on the Internet to offer "26 different types of information" from its own site, the Southwest Airlines Home Gate. The ultimate goal has been to add booking capability so passengers can make ticketless reservations from their personal computers. Southwest's strong customer orientation led them to invest in this customer-focused technology. Once it added the option of bookings through the web site, the company expected it to build gradually. The company advertised for the service, both online and in other media. So far it has proven to be very successful. As with other web booking systems, Southwest's site accepts only bookings from a browser that can encrypt data, which means the latest versions of Netscape Navigator and Internet Explorer.[18]

TECHNOLOGICAL INVESTMENT AND ANALYSIS

In a move to significantly improve the productivity of business travelers, Southwest Airlines and McCaw Cellular's Claircom Communications unveiled the world's first broadly available air-to-ground commercial fax and data service through the AirOne Communications Network in 1994. Prior to this, the wealth of data services accessible by computer on the ground were not available to the air traveler. Through the same AirOne system that delivers telephone calls from a plane, passengers can attach to electronic networks to get the latest news, weather, sports, and travel information or even play video games.

The AirOne system, installed throughout the Southwest fleet, provides high-quality, digital air-to-ground service using AT&T's long-distance service. Passengers on all Southwest's planes can access electronic mail networks and information networks such as CompuServe, Prodigy, and Dow Jones. The AirOne System offers the most comprehensive fax and data services in the market. It can send and retrieve faxes, data, and electronic mail through conventional laptop computers, portable fax machines, and personal data assistants.

In the preceding example, Southwest Airlines demonstrated that they recognized ahead of time the significant demand for this type of service because of the increased productivity and accessibility it provides to the business traveler. Southwest was the first airline in the world to make this type of communication technology broadly available to its customers.

Southwest used Object Design, Inc.'s ObjectStore software, an object database management system, to help build a ticketless reservation system into its Home Gate corporate web site. The company was looking for a system that would make the online booking process easy to use, responsive, and quick to build. Object-oriented programming was chosen and ObjectStore was selected after an exhaustive search, mainly because of the product's Virtual Memory Mapping technology and the company's reputation. Southwest Airlines' 10-GB database stores passenger, fare, confirmation, and schedule data.[19] The ObjectStore database is designed specifically for building Internet and intranet applications. In the expanding web environment, the product supports rapid development of applications, including those that call for extended data types such as image, free text, video, audio, HTML, and Java software objects.[20]

The Home Gate web page is easy to use.[21] Customers simply click on the departing location, their destination, travel date, and approximate departure time. Home Gate looks up the fare and schedule information and returns relevant information. The customer can then make a reservation, type in his or her credit card number, and purchase the ticket. The system replies with a confirmation number, which the customer takes directly to a Southwest Airlines gate to obtain a boarding pass. The purchasing process is secured through encryption technology.

Southwest's newest investment is shifting from SABRE Group's SAAS hosted TPF reservation system to an in-house reservation system developed in partnership with Hewlett-Packard. The new system is a "hybrid" of mainframe and client/server technology and combines a central inventory database with local schedule and fare databases through a proprietary operating system.

TECHNOLOGICAL INNOVATIONS

Southwest migrated from a legacy multiprotocol network to a routed TCP/IP network in 1998. While the

[18] Walker, Jay, "Internet Alters Business DNA," *Information Week*, February 15, 1999, p. 202(1).
[19] Hayes, Frank, "Some Sites Soar, While Others Fuel Reservations About E-Commerce," *Computer World*, February 24, 1997, p. 72.
[20] "Internet Access: MCI WorldCom Creates Alliance with CompuServe to Launch Consumer Internet Service," *EDGE*, on & About AT&T, February 8, 1999, p. NA; "Top Management Toolbox for Managing Corporate IT," *Communications of the ACM*, April 1999, v. 42, i. 4, p. 93.
[21] Stahl, Ed., "Southwest Goes Online," *Travel Weekly*, May 13, 1996, p. 85.

frame relay WAN is currently in its infancy phase and handles operational traffic, it will eventually handle passenger reservations and updates. The WAN currently transports traffic from operational applications such as e-mail, accounting, and procurement and links the check-in terminals at 51 airports, nine reservations hubs, headquarters, and 20 additional locations.[22]

[22] "New Servers: HP Redefines Internet-Age Computing With New N-Class Midrange Server," *EDGE: Work-Group Computing Report*, April 19, 1999, p. NA.

RECOMMENDATION FOR THE FUTURE

With 25 consecutive profitable years, including 5 successive years of record profits, there is little reason to alter Southwest's successful formula of providing inexpensive, no-frills transportation. Southwest thrives by focusing on individuals who pay their own travel expenses both for business and pleasure. No other carrier in the airline industry has demonstrated the operating skills and cultural cohesiveness required to approach Southwest's standards of service and reliability on a broad scale. No other carrier has obtained as clear a reputation in the world of technology investments.

CASE QUESTIONS

Strategic Questions

1. What is the strategic direction of the corporation/organization?
2. Who or what forces are driving this direction?
3. What has been the catalyst for change?
4. What are the critical success factors for this corporation/organization?
5. What are the core competencies for this corporation/organization?

Technological Questions

6. What technologies has the corporation relied on?
7. What has caused a change in the use of technology in the corporation/organization?
8. How has this change been implemented?
9. Who has driven this change throughout the organization?
10. How successful has the technological change been?

Quantitative Questions

11. What does the corporation say about its financial ability to embark on a major technological program of advancement?
12. What conclusions can be reached from an analysis of the financial information to support or contradict this financial ability?
13. What analysis can be made by examining the following ratio groups?
Quick/Current
Debt

Revenue
Profit

14. What conclusions can be reached by analyzing the financial trends? Are there long-term trends that seem to be problematic? Is the industry stable? Are there replacement products?

Internet Questions

15. What does the corporation's web page present about their business directives?
16. How does this compare to the conclusions reached by the writers of the articles?
17. How does this compare to the conclusions reached by analyzing the financial information?

Industry Questions

18. What challenges and opportunities is the industry facing?
19. Is the industry oligopolistic or competitive?
20. Does the industry face a change in government regulation?
21. How will technology impact the industry?

Data Questions

22. What role do data play in the future of the corporation?
23. How important are data to the corporation's continued success?
24. How will the capture and maintenance of customer data impact the corporation's future?

TECHNOLOGY TIPS

MICROSOFT WORD TIPS

WRITING AROUND IMAGES

The images you use in your document can help you illustrate what you want to say. However, they may also get in the way of what you are writing. You can overcome this by seamlessly integrating the image into the document text. The following will allow you to write around images.

Using Text Wrapping on an Image

1. Once you have inserted the image, click on the image with the right mouse button.
2. The picture tool bar will appear along with a pop-up menu. If the tool bar does not appear simply click on SHOW PICTURE TOOLBAR.
3. From the tool bar click on the TEXT WRAPPING button.
4. A drop-down menu will appear that has six selections:
   - Square
   - Tight
   - Through
   - None
   - Top and Bottom
   - Edit Wrap Points
5. Select a text wrapping that works best for your document. The text wrapping style used with the image to the right is the TIGHT style.

Using Text Wrapping on a Text Box

If you have inserted a text box in your document the Text Wrapping feature is still available, but accessing this feature takes different steps.

1. Click inside the text box. A border will appear around the text box.
2. Click on the border of the text box with your *right* mouse button. A pop-up menu will appear. Click on FORMAT TEXT BOX. . . .
3. A dialog box will appear that will have several tabs on top. Click on WRAPPING tab.
4. The dialog box will change to the wrapping choices available for text boxes. Click on your choice of wrapping and click on OK when you are done.

ADDITIONAL NOTE

There will be times when you would like the text to be closer to the picture or further from it. It is possible to adjust the wrap points of most images that you insert into a word by using the "edit wrap points" feature from the picture tool bar. This can be very useful when you are trying to make text take shape around an image. This feature is not available with tables and text boxes.

1. Simply click on the image with your right button.
2. If the picture tool bar does not appear automatically, click on SHOW PICTURE TOOL BAR from the pop-up menu.
3. From the picture tool bar click on the Text Wrapping button.
4. From the drop-down menu click on the edit wrap points button.

5. A series of red dotted lines will appear around your image. Click and drag the lines out to give the image the shape you want. The text around the image will adjust itself according to the way you edit the wrap points.
6. When you are done editing the wrap points click outside of the image.

MICROSOFT EXCEL TIPS

FILTERING DATA

Worksheets can sometimes contain so much data that it becomes difficult to draw any type of conclusions from the data entered. Filtering provides a way of sorting your data for trends or helping you find values that you designate. In order to make full use of this feature create your worksheet using the following guidelines.

Column Labels

- Create column labels in the first row of the list. Excel uses the labels to create reports and to find and organize data.
- Use a font, alignment, format, pattern, border, or capitalization style for column labels that is different from the format you assign to the data in the list.
- When you want to separate labels from data, use cell borders, not blank rows or dashed lines, to insert lines below the labels.

Row and Column Contents

- Design the list so that all rows have similar items in the same column.
- Do not insert extra spaces at the beginning of a cell; extra spaces affect sorting and searching.
- Do not use a blank row to separate column labels from the first row of data.

How to Filter the Data

1. To filter a column, click any cell in the column. Click on DATA from toolbar and then on FILTER from the side menu. Finally, click on AUTOFILTER.
2. Excel will display arrows to the right of the column labels.
3. To filter the data for the value you want, click the arrow and then click on the value from the drop-down list.
4. Once you select a value, a filtered list will appear displaying the value selected.
5. To display all of the data again, click on the arrow from the column that you filtered and select ALL from the drop down list.

AUTOFILTER Option	What does it do?
ALL	Displays all of the data
TOP 10	Displays all rows that fall within the upper or lower limits you specify, either by item or percentage
CUSTOM	Applies two criteria values within the current column, or use comparison operators other than AND (the default operator)
BLANKS*	Displays only rows that contain a blank cell in the column
NONBLANKS*	Displays only rows that contain a value in the column

MICROSOFT POWERPOINT TIPS

CHANGING BACKGROUND COLORS, COLOR SCHEMES, AND DESIGN TEMPLATES

There are several design templates to choose from when preparing your presentation. You can always change the design template in order to suit your audience or yourself. The design template's background and colors can be modified for each single slide or for all slides. It is suggested that you explore the different combinations of backgrounds and color schemes that will make your presentation stand out from the rest.

Changing Design Templates

1. With the presentation open click on APPLY DESIGN button from the top toolbar.
2. The Apply Design dialog box will appear with a list of the design templates available. Previews of the designs can be seen in the right half of the dialog box by clicking on the different titles.
3. Once a particular design has been selected click on APPLY. All your slides will be changed to the design selected.

Changing Color Schemes

1. With the presentation open click on FORMAT from the top tool bar and then click on SLIDE COLOR SCHEME.
2. The slide color scheme dialog box will appear. There will be some preset color schemes available to choose from. However, the color scheme of the slide can be changed in its entirety by clicking on the custom tab. From this section the parts of the slide that you want to change can be selected individually.
3. Preview changes by clicking on the PREVIEW button to see what the slide will look like.
4. Once the colors have been selected click on APPLY TO ALL if all slides are to get the new changes. Click on APPLY if only the selected slide is to receive the color changes.

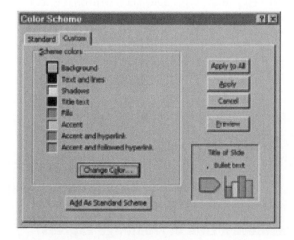

Changing Background Colors

The background color can be changed while changing the slide color schemes, but more can be done from the background dialog box. You can have a picture in the background, adjust the gradient, include textures, and alter the patterns.

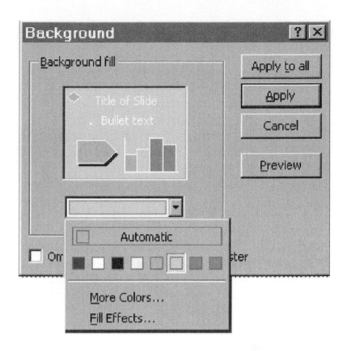

1. Click on the right mouse button on an empty spot of the slide that will be changed. From the pop-up menu click on BACKGROUND.
2. The dialog box (on the right) will appear. Colors for the background can be selected by clicking on the drop-down arrow. A second menu will appear (as shown on the right) that will provide several options.
3. Click on the FILL EFFECTS to get a greater variety of backgrounds. The combinations are endless, but take caution with how they will appear in a presentation.
4. Preview the slide by clicking on PREVIEW to see what types of changes have been made to the slide.
5. If the changes are satisfactory click on APPLY to make changes to one slide or APPLY TO ALL if you wish to make changes to all slides.

MICROSOFT ACCESS TIPS

MODIFYING A TABLE

Tables need to be modified from time to time to add field labels, delete field labels, or organize the structure of the table. For whatever reason you may have to modify the table, the following steps will guide you through the process.

1. If you are continuing from the previous chapter you should now be in the design view window. If you are not continuing from the previous chapter, open a table from the database window by selecting a table and clicking on the DESIGN button. If the table is already open, the design view can also be accessed by clicking on the design view button located on the toolbar.
2. In the design view you can change the field name, data type, and make a number of other changes to the table. To change the data type click on the data type cell of the field you want to change, and click on the drop-down menu to select the data type that you want to apply. Descriptions of the different types of data can be found in the table on page 164.

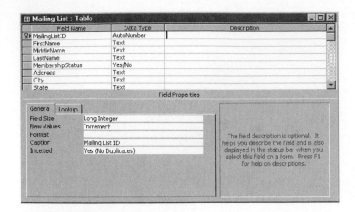

3. Notice that as you select different data types the FIELD PROPERTIES located at the bottom of the window will change. Explore the different options available with each data type including the input mask. Click inside the different FIELD PROPERTIES options. The list button will appear next to it to allow for further choices.

4. When you are done making changes to the table click on the SAVE button.   Note: Before changing views you will always be prompted to save the table.

Available Data Types

Type	Description
Text	Text or combinations of text and numbers, such as addresses. Also numbers that do not require calculations, such as phone numbers, part numbers, or postal codes.
Memo	Lengthy text and numbers, such as notes or descriptions.
Number	Numeric data to be used for mathematical calculations, except calculations involving money (use Currency type). Set the Field-Size property to define the specific Number type.
Date\Time	Dates and times.
Currency	Currency values. Use the Currency data type to prevent rounding off during calculations. Accurate to 15 digits to the left of the decimal point and 4 digits to the right.
AutoNumber	Unique sequential (incrementing by 1) or random numbers automatically inserted when a record is added.
Yes/No	Fields that will contain only one of two values, such as Yes/No, True/False, On/Off.
OLE Object	Objects (such as Microsoft Word documents, Microsoft Excel spreadsheets, pictures, sounds, or other binary data), created in other programs using the OLE protocol, that can be linked to or embedded in a Microsoft Access table. You must

Type	Description
	use a bound object frame in a form or report to display the OLE object.
Hyperlink	Field that will store hyperlinks. A hyperlink can be a UNC path or a URL.
Lookup Wizard	Creates a field that allows you to choose a value from another table or from a list of values using a combo box. Choosing this option in the data type list starts a wizard to define this for you.

MICROSOFT FRONTPAGE TIPS

CREATING LINKS

Hyperlinks are a very important aspect of the Web. They add to web site usability and flexibility while enhancing user involvement and participation in a site. Links can take on a number of forms. They can be words or phrases or they can be images or pictures on a web page. Links are designed as objects that allow the user to be redirected to areas of interest or more information.

Links function very much in the same way as a map. They help you navigate to new areas of interest by providing a way of determining alternative routes to different information destinations. As a designer of web pages, your use of links is important because it allows you to explain to visitors what information is available and where and how to find it.

Once you have created a number of different web pages that contain information about you or a topic that you are interested in, you can connect these web pages using links.

Creating a Link in FrontPage Express

1. Highlight the word, text phrase, or image that you wish to use as a link.
2. From the Insert pull down menu, select hyperlink (also use the Globe with Link Icon).
3. The Hyperlink type field should probably read, *http:* (This is the most common type. You may also use *mailto:*).
4. In the URL field, you need to type the address of the web page where you want the link to redirect to. Ensure that the URL you enter is correct. Otherwise, the link will not work.

To Edit a Link in FrontPage Express

1. Highlight the word, text phrase, or image that you wish to use as a link.
2. From the Edit pull down menu, select hyperlink (also use the Globe with Link Icon).
3. In the URL field, you need to change the address of the web page where you want the link to redirect to.

To Remove a Link in FrontPage Express

1. Highlight the word or text phrase that you wish to use as a link.
2. From the Insert pull down menu, select hyperlink (also use the Globe with Link Icon).
3. Hit the clear button.

CHAPTER 6

NETWORKS AND TELECOMMUNICATIONS
WHOLESALE INDUSTRY

Networks and Telecommunications

The exchange of information between people and groups is a basic necessity in the workplace. Computers can greatly assist in the transfer and execution of data and ideas. To ease communication between users, computer networks have been developed and implemented. The planning, designing, and maintenance of a computer network is a complex process. Software and hardware must be designed and shared, access to the workstations and network must be monitored, and the compatibility between many different types of workstations and programs must be examined.

Local-area networks (LANs) are an efficient way to share data between users by keeping vast amounts of transaction data on large central computers, while connecting individual personal computers to them. This facilitates data sharing, including electronic messages and provides access to the data people need. LANs are well-suited solutions for the current trend of proliferating personal computers to run smaller applications, along with central or mainframe computers that maintain large amounts of data and run large applications.

Change is inevitable; the change in the telecommunications industry is impacted by the way computers are connected when they are geographically far apart. With high-speed data lines such as ISDN and T1 becoming more available and cheaper, quick communication between computers across entire nations or regions be-

comes more commonplace. Due to many differences in infrastructure, standards, and politics, communications and connections between countries are even more complicated than within a country.

Sharing Data Sharing data is one of the main uses of networks. Networks can be used to share data with respect to transactions, decisions and searches, messages, bulletin boards, calendars and scheduling, teamwork and authorship, and backup. With transactions, connecting a company's computers enables a central database to maintain the current inventory and sales data. Decisions and searches can be made from the most recent data if the data are stored in one central location with all appropriate parties having access to the data. Messages sent through electronic mail (e-mail) through the network are quickly becoming the norm in sharing information with coworkers.

Electronic bulletin boards are computer networks that allow geographically dispersed individuals to access information on the bulletin board. To improve scheduling, computer networks can be linked to workers' calendars to make sure everyone is available for a meeting and even determine the meeting time. Groupware applies computer networks to sharing data for teamwork and authorship. Backup is made easier through computer networks by connecting a computer with the backed up data to the source computer at all times.

Sharing Hardware Hardware, such as printers, storage devices, and special processors, is also usually shared through a computer network. Sharing printers in this way gives each person access to whatever type of printer is needed for a specific job. Storage devices such as large mainframe computers can also be shared through networks. Large amounts of data can be kept. Computers with expensive specialized processors can also be shared through a network, making them available to all who need them without having to buy more specialized computers than necessary.

Sharing Software Networks have become extremely popular for sharing software. A software program can be stored in the main computer, normally called a file server. All users connected to that file server use the same software. This has many advantages. First, upgrades are easier because there is only one computer in which the upgrade needs to be performed. Companies are also able to purchase a smaller number of software licenses than the number of workstations connected to that file server. For example, 25 computers may be connected to the file server. If no more than 10 people need a program at a given time, the company can purchase only 10 copies or licenses of the software for concurrent use through the network.

Voice and Video Communication Telephones have long been valuable tools for business. More recently, video communication, or teleconferencing, has become more prevalent. This is due to better technology, the increased use of networks across entire companies, and the cost difference between meeting in person and teleconferencing. Even though the hardware may be expensive, teleconferencing is almost always cheaper and faster in terms of time commitment than traveling to meet face to face.

Components of a Network Computer networks have four basic components: computers, transmission media, connection devices, and software. To complicate matters, there are different manufacturers, brands, and varieties for each computer.

Almost any computer can be connected to a network. An attached computer becomes either a client or a server. Servers are more powerful and distinguished by the fact that they store data used by other computers in the network. Clients are used by individuals and access the server whenever they need data. Networks where computers perform both as a client and as a server are called peer-to-peer networks.

Transmission media must be chosen carefully to balance the pros and cons of each medium. The choice dictates the speed of the network. Changing an installed network medium is usually very costly. The most popular transmission media are electric cables, fiber optics, and radio, micro, and infrared waves.

Other issues to consider are the transmission capacity of each medium and the combination of different

media. The two primary types of electric cable are twisted-pair wire, the oldest form of electrical wiring, and coaxial cable. Twisted-pair wire cannot carry a large amount of information and is subject to interference. Coaxial cable is much better in terms of capacity and reduced interference and is not much more expensive. Fiber optic uses light waves instead of electricity. While fiber optic cable is much quicker and smaller, the cable itself is much more expensive. The connection devices are also more expensive; the connecting network is more limited in size.

The use of radio, micro, and infrared waves as transmission media does not require cables since signals are transmitted over the air.

Transmission capacity, the amount of data a medium can carry at one time, varies widely between the mediums, as does the price of the materials and the labor necessary to install them. Media are sometimes combined, placing the fastest media between distant locations, and slower, but cheaper, media within a building.

Connection devices include network interface cards (NICs) or LAN cards that translate signals and transmissions between computers and the network. Other commonly used devices connect different networks, especially if the networks use different transmission media. It is important to use an operating system that allows multiple users, such as Windows/NT, Office 2000, Novell, or UNIX.

Internet The Internet is a worldwide network of computer networks. It began as a means of exchanging data between universities and the U.S. military. Since the early 1990s, the number of computers connected to the Internet has grown exponentially. To enable this growth the Internet is defined by a set of standards that set the protocol computers must use to exchange data. No single group is in charge of the Internet. Anyone with a computer connected to the Internet has the ability to give other users access to the data stored on that computer, if they so choose.

Three ways exist to grant outside access: telnet, FTP, or database access through the World Wide Web. Telnet allows users of one computer to log onto a different computer. Once logged on, the individual is treated like any other user on the system. The person logging on must have an account on the other computer to control access. File Transfer Protocol (FTP) is a standard method of transferring files between computers. The person or organization that controls the computer can determine the specific files that are available to other users. The advantage is that each user does not have to have an account to access the "public" files on the other computer. Files can be transferred in either direction between the two computers, if the "owner" of each computer gives that permission.

The World Wide Web (WWW) is most easily accessed through a browser like Netscape's Navigator or Microsoft's Internet Explorer. The browsers read and interpret a computer file written in markup language, such as HTML (HyperText Markup Language). This organizes the computer files into a series of interrelated associative links.

The Internet possesses an incredible amount of useful data. Finding your way through this data can prove interesting and time consuming. Search engines such as Yahoo!, Hotbot, Lycos, Goto.com, Excite, and AltaVista supply input systems and advanced data search capability to match the information to the request.

The Internet offers great opportunities to conduct business transactions within the constraints of security concerns. As security is increased through techniques such as encryption, and as customers feel more comfortable with the security of the transfer of funds, Internet transactions will continue to grow. Since the Internet is a network of networks, a credit card number travels through a series of different computers before it reaches the vendor. Encryption scrambles this number and protects it throughout the transmission process.

Wholesale Industry

DESCRIPTION OF THE INDUSTRY

The wholesale industry is a diverse and fragmented industry with multiple channels of distribution and over $250 billion in annual sales. Wholesalers market to a number of distribution channels including retail outlets, small distributorships, national, regional, and local distributors, direct mail suppliers, large warehouses, and manufacturers' direct sales forces. The industry is focused primarily on the food, health, and industrial maintenance and repair sectors.

INDUSTRY AND MARKET ANALYSIS

The wholesale industry's customers have reduced overall costs by limiting the number of suppliers and maintaining relationships with those that can offer a broad product selection, automated order processing, and advanced services such as inventory management and nationwide support. To remain competitive, distributors must provide customers with wider product selection, lower costs, and value-added service.

Word	W.1	Inserting an Excel Spreadsheet Additional Note	What is a Linked Object?
Excel	E.1	Sorting Data Note	How to Sort Data Direction of Highlighting Matters What is the Sorting Order?
PowerPoint	P.1	Inserting Slides from Other Presentations	Inserting Slides Using INSERT Copying/Pasting Slides into the Presentation
Access	A.1	Making the Database Work: Relationships How Do Relationships Work? A One-to-Many Relationship A Many-to-Many Relationship Defining Relationships	
Front Page	I.1	Backgrounds	

The principal means by which wholesalers compete with manufacturers and other distributors is by providing value-added services in the areas of local stocks, efficient service, account managers, competitive prices, catalogs, extensive technical and application data, and procurement process services. These tools permit retailers to lower their total costs.

The wholesalers' advantage lies in the ability to supply product faster and allow smaller inventories to be held by the customer. Wholesalers allow customers to have access to one-stop shopping. This reduces the number of suppliers and transactions required to procure the supplies needed.

FINANCIAL ANALYSIS

Since 1990, producer prices have been falling, limiting the wholesale industry's ability to increase prices. In the absence of price inflation, industry consolidation will likely continue as it has over the past decade. Bottom line gains are coming from increased productivity, not from increased prices.

STOCK/INVESTMENT OUTLOOK

The investment outlook for the wholesale sector is neutral. The lack of inflation has a negative impact on profits given the companies' traditionally low profit margins. Only productivity gains and premiums paid for outright purchases are likely to influence the stock prices of wholesale companies.

POTENTIAL/PROSPECTIVE FOR GROWTH

Growth in the wholesale industry is not expected to be strong. The industry is threatened by advances in communications and freight systems. Growth in individual companies will be primarily through acquisitions. Some overseas growth is possible since American companies are often at the forefront of utilizing new technologies to increase productivity.

COMPETITIVE STRUCTURE

The competitive structure of the industry has been changing. The wholesale industry now competes with more companies than ever before since manufacturers are able to reach more customers directly. Internally,

competition has not allowed prices to rise and has focused on productivity gains and industry consolidation. One of the most consolidated areas is drug wholesalers where three companies now account for over 50 percent of the industry's sales.

ROLE OF RESEARCH AND DEVELOPMENT

The ability of wholesalers to succeed depends on their ability to increase productivity. Research and development to increase productivity depends on creative and thoughtful use of the many off-the-shelf products available. These technologies include bar code scanners, wireless communications, data warehousing, and Internet communications.

TECHNOLOGY INVESTMENT AND ANALYSIS

Wholesalers are using technology to provide many types of value-added services to product distribution. Some of the services include sophisticated, continuous replenishment programs for customers, warehouse and inventory management, customized labeling, bar coding, and special packaging. All of these services are communications intensive, requiring powerful computer systems and data warehousing and management.

RECOMMENDATION FOR THE FUTURE

The wholesale industry is under threat from the globalization of the world economy. Advances in communications, transportation, and data warehousing technology are decreasing the time and space that separate retailers and consumers from manufacturers. The speed with which these technological advances have been adopted varies from industry to industry. A definite trend toward the elimination of the middleperson is in place. It is only by offering unique, value-added services in addition to the physical movement of goods that the wholesale industry will have opportunities for future success.

INDUSTRY WEB SITES

Wholesale Industry
www.awba.com/
www.genbus.com/
www.indexfresh.com/

FISHER SCIENTIFIC

Executive Summary

Case Name:	Fisher Scientific International
Case Industry:	Manufacturer and distributor of laboratory supplies
Major Technology Issue:	The continuing need for distribution innovations from the Fisher Technology Group
Major Financial Issue:	Increasing debt and the threat of takeover attempts
Major Strategic Issue:	Expanding fast enough to be the largest global player
Major Players/Leaders:	Chester G. Fisher, founder
Main Web Page:	www.fisher1.com
Case Conclusion/Recommendation:	Expand internationally, especially in Europe. Develop Internet commerce business-to-business services. Focus on large contract business.

CASE ANALYSIS

INTRODUCTORY STORY

In 1902, Chester G. Fisher, 22, of the Western University of Pennsylvania opened his own business. He saw a need for someone to supply scientific laboratories so he purchased a local storeroom to begin a scientific supply business.

At that time laboratory work was based on simple experiments involving solid, liquid, and gaseous materials. Fisher's earliest products included microscopes, burettes, pipettes, litmus paper, balances, and calorimeters.[1]

SHORT DESCRIPTION OF THE COMPANY

Fisher Scientific International is a world leading distributor and manufacturer of laboratory supplies, equipment, and chemicals. The company services the research, educational, governmental, and technical communities. Almost every area of equipment supply including instrumentation, chemicals, consumables, and safety and training aids is covered in their tremendous selection of products.

Thousands of companies across the United States and worldwide have preferred supplier agreements with Fisher or are visited by a Fisher representative. These efforts have enabled Fisher's total sales to top over $2 billion dollars, making Fisher the largest laboratory supplier in the world.

SHORT HISTORY OF THE COMPANY

In 1904, Fisher published the *Scientific Materials Company Catalog of Apparatus & Supplies*, one of the first scientific catalogs of its time. Fisher Scientific continues to produce a 2,000 plus page catalog for its customers. It distributes more than 180,000 products and services for the biotechnology, biomedical, pharmaceutical, clinical, educational, quality control, chemical, environmental, safety, food technology, and other research markets.

At the beginning of World War I, Fisher started its own research, development, and manufacturing efforts. The Fisher Bunsen burner was introduced in 1921 and retailed at $3.00. It was hailed as "the best improvement in burners since the original Bunsen." Other advancements of Fisher's facilities enabled Fisher to be a technical leader in the research, education, and technical community in the United States. In 1940, Fisher acquired Eimer & Amend's laboratory supply business.

In 1965 Fisher Scientific went public. After decades of scientific advancements and minor acquisitions, the Fisher family decided to sell its remaining shares to Allied Signal Corporation in 1981. Fisher was lost in the Allied portfolio of 30 marginal businesses for a number of years. This lasted until 1991, when Fisher became independent and elected Paul Montrone as CEO.[2] After this period, which included a shift in focus away from the medical supply industry, Fisher saw tremendous stock growth and completed several mergers and acquisitions.

---

[1] http://www.frco.com/fisher/fisher.html.

[2] Ibid.

Fisher's sales tripled during the course of the 1990s. This was the result of a series of strategic mergers and targeted marketing. Fisher employs a direct sales force. Sales for the year ended December 31, 1996, increased 49 percent to $2,144.4 million from $1,435.8 million for 1995. The sales increase primarily reflects sales from the acquisition of CMS and FSE in October 1995, as well as growth in North American operations. Excluding sales from acquisitions, Fisher experienced a slowdown in the rate of North American sales growth in 1997.[3]

FINANCIAL AND PORTFOLIO ANALYSIS

Despite large expenditures for various mergers and acquisitions, Fisher Scientific International has remained profitable, vigorously increasing sales in recent years. It has remained the largest supplier of laboratory consumables and supplies (chemicals, test supplies, glasswares, and others), and laboratory instruments and equipment (balances, centrifuges, microscopes, etc.). Net sales increased 49 percent in fiscal year 1997, and averaged 27.4 percent from 1992 to 1997.[4] This is due to Fisher's focus on establishing a wide product line and dominating market share through acquisitions.

Net income steadily rose from $6 million in 1988 to over $35 million in 1996. During the 1980s a series of owners bought and sold the company. This caused earnings to remain stagnant.[5] The new rise in profitability can be attributed to an intense effort to focus on sales volume. This strengthened relationships with customers despite discounting. Fisher has also diversified into different areas. This includes the Fisher Technology Group, which consults with outside companies on the best way to improve their technological systems.

Total assets steadily increased in 1996 due to various acquisitions such as CMS, Fisons, Hamilton, and a software developer. Total assets stabilized in 1995 and 1996 and are expected to drop after Fisher fully consolidates the facilities and operations of CMS and Fisons.

Long-term debt experienced a sharp increase from $12 to $45 million in 1995 largely due to the $304 million acquisition of Fisons and CMS in 1995. Fisher laid off about 10 percent of the combined workforce of CMS and Fisher to help with this acquisition.

Recently, the Trinity 1 Investment Group headed by the Bass brothers submitted an unsolicited bid to purchase Fisher at $48 per share. This placed a value of $1 billion on Fisher Scientific International. In response, Fisher adopted a "poison pill" in the form of a dilutive-shareholder rights plan to thwart the possible takeover. CEO Paul Montrone said, "The rights will not prevent a takeover, but should encourage anyone seeking to acquire the company to negotiate with the board prior to attempting a takeover."[6] Fisher will need to seek ways to increase debt to make it less attractive while still maintaining its high investment grade rating.

Fisher's SG&A expenses have gradually increased since 1988. This increase is the result of lower margins and increased competition in the health care field. Fisher's international presence continues to rise, further increasing SG&A expense rather than domestic operations. The 1995 acquisition of Fisons provided Fisher the opportunity to centralize its European operations. New distribution centers in South Korea, Germany, and Mexico contribute to this rising figure. These expenses should decline as international operations become established.[7]

Examining Fisher's net sales per employee data indicates that while sales per employee dropped dramatically in 1995 due to the acquisition of CMS and Fisons, it rebounded in 1996. This shows that management cut the necessary expenses to integrate the operations of the acquired companies and move sales per employee from $240,000 in 1994 to $325,000 in 1996.

STOCK/INVESTMENT OUTLOOK

According to the S&P Stock Reports, Fisher has been classified as bearish since May 1997. This is due to a decrease in earnings estimates. Speculation about a takeover has caused Fisher to regain most of this loss.

From 1991 through 1996, the five years since Fisher returned to being a separate public company, sales increased 183 percent, at a compound annual rate of 23 percent. This is higher than any other period in Fisher's history. Net income rose sharply in 1991 and 1992 and is again increasing significantly after recent restructuring and related charges.

Long-term holders of Fisher Scientific stock have seen the share price increase 222 percent, equal to a compound annual return of 25 percent from Fisher's last IPO in 1991 to March 14, 1997. This compares with a 134 percent increase, equal to a total annual return of 18 percent for the S&P 500.[8]

RISK ANALYSIS

Fisher downgraded its estimated earnings for 1997 claiming that cost cutting in the health care industry is slowing demand for some of its product line.[9] As a result, Fisher will need to continue its aggressive expansion and diversification efforts.

---

[3] Ibid.
[4] Fisher Scientific International Annual Report, 1998.
[5] Ibid.
[6] Ibid.
[7] Ibid.
[8] Ibid.
[9] "DCR Fisher Scientific Remains on Rating Watch—Down," *PR Newswire*, August 8, 1997, p. 3.

INDUSTRY AND MARKET ANALYSIS

Classifying Fisher Scientific International in an exact industry is somewhat difficult. Their operations cover many SIC codes, primarily 5049, Professional Equipment. A large area is also found under 5047, Medical and Hospital Equipment and 3826, Analytical Instruments and various chemically related SIC codes.

Fisher crosses many competitive paths with different distributors and manufactures such as Baxter and Owens & Minor for medical supplies; VWR, Beckman Instruments, and Cole-Parmer Instrument Company for analytical instruments; and Aldrich, VWR, Sigma, and others in the chemical industry.

A more telling descriptor of Fisher's industry is laboratory consumables, supplies, equipment, and instruments. In a survey of chemists, Fisher is mentioned 50 percent more times than any other company as the primary source for both laboratory supplies and chemicals. Fisher remains the leader in this industry. Given Fisher's sales as a leader and the number of competitors mentioned, the lab market Fisher targets is probably between $5 and $10 billion. In 1992, Paul Montrone diverted Fisher's focus from the medical area to avoid direct competition with Baxter.

The market share that Fisher enjoys as a result of its acquisition of CMS and Fisons in the instrumentation market is staggering. These acquisitions were mainly responsible for the 49 percent jump in sales in 1996. Competitors such as VWR and Beckman have seen growth rates averaging 10 to 20 percent. While sales estimates for these companies remain in the 8 to 12 percent range through 2000, long-term buy recommendations are scare because of the competitive nature of the industry and the shrinking availability of domestic market share.[10]

The medical equipment and supply industry experienced moderate growth from 1994 to 1998. The predictions for the next few years are relatively stagnant with even a 5 percent drop in overall sales.[11] Forecasts for major players such as Baxter predict 15 to 20 percent sales gains over the next year.[12] Capturing domestic and international market share will be crucial to expanding sales during this time.

The chemical industry has enjoyed consistent growth over the last five years and is expected to see 8 percent growth on average over the next five years. Fisher's main focus is on supplying chemicals to laboratories. This is only a small part of the chemical industry overall.

Fisher has a separate educational division that supplies teaching aids for science education, and a safety division that offers health and safety supplies. Fisher distributes over 245,000 products worldwide from over 6,000 different suppliers.

Fisher has positioned itself to be the only company that can significantly attract large worldwide contracts from major pharmaceutical companies.[13] Its aggressive efforts to expand into international markets not dominated by any major player should help Fisher gain worldwide market share. Investments in plants and distribution centers in South Korea, Germany, and a recently purchased controlling interest in Monterey-based Casa Rocas, S.A. de C.V in Mexico, reflect Fisher's desire to capture the international market share that already totals 15 percent of 1996's $2.14 billion.[14] Fisher hopes this figure, excluding 10 percent in sales from Canada, reaches 25 percent in the next two years.

ROLE OF RESEARCH AND DEVELOPMENT

The Fisher of today looks much different than the Fisher of 20 years ago. In recent years, Fisher has diversified many of it resources and focuses on technology areas. On the instrument side, Fisher was the first to develop new generations of technologically advanced products throughout the middle of the 20th century.

Fisher's commitment to using technology to streamline internal procedure started in 1962 when the company installed an IBM system that would record and track inventory for all of their products. By 1967, this system became Fisher's "Fastback" computer system, which was linked to all Fisher branches by 1970. This provided Fisher with inventory control and management capabilities many of its competitors lacked at the time. This capability was developed before banks or airlines began to use them.

TECHNOLOGICAL STORY

In 1978, Fisher installed computer terminals at its major customers' sites. This enabled them to place orders directly and receive immediate order verification. Customers were able to look up information on past purchases and other financial information. A year later, Fisher expanded this system to increase the speed and accessibility of the customer's terminals.[15]

In 1994, Fisher became the first catalog distributor in the industry to have the majority of its product offering

[10] "AccuMed International Establishes Strategic Marketing Partnership with Curtin Matheson Scientific, a Division of Fisher Scientific," *PR Newswire*, September 16, 1996.

[11] http://www.frco.com/fisher/fisher.html.

[12] Karon, Paul, "Technologically Savvy Team Shares Wealth with Customers," *Infoworld*, May 13, 1996, v. 18, n. 20, p. 76(1).

[13] http://www.frco.com/fisher/fisher.html.

[14] "Fisher Scientific Purchases Majority Interest in Mexican Distributor Casa Rocas," *Business Wire*, December 4, 1996.

[15] Frock, John Evan, "E-Commerce Receives Real-Time Price Boosting," *Internet Week*, August 3, 1998, n. 726, p. 8(1).

available to its customers on CD-ROM and for purchase on its web site. Fisher's spending on computer technology has increased its efficiency and enabled it to win large preferred supplier agreements such as the Department of Defense to handle smaller instrumentation and operational products.[16]

The years 1995 and 1996 saw the beginning of several information technology developments. The strategic objective was to maximize return on assets by increasing sales volume through all global trade channels. The Fisher Technology Group, dedicated to the development and support of advanced technology for businesses over computer networks, introduced developments to expand Internet services and provide other electronic solutions to increase business productivity.

TECHNOLOGICAL INVESTMENT AND ANALYSIS

The Fisher Technology Group is a unit of Fisher Scientific International. Fisher Technology specializes in electronic commerce and is best known for its ProcureNet electronic mall. Formed in 1995, Fisher Technology Group is dedicated to the development and support of advanced technology for business-to-business electronic commerce over public and private computer networks. Fisher Technology Group (FTG) develops, licenses, and supports software systems and related services for electronic marketing and procurement. These solutions are Internet-, intranet-, and client/server-based.

SupplyLink manages the entire product procurement process and centralizes all supplier information, making internal referencing of vendor's products more efficient. Integrated SupplyNet is a customer-specific electronic catalog that enables customers to maintain existing contracts with suppliers, including net prices.

Another leading-edge technology development of Fisher's Technology Group is ProcureNet, an online mall of over 50 scientific suppliers run by Fisher. Even Fisher's competitors are lining up to participate. ProcureNet (www.procurenet.com) was the first public, business-to-business electronic mall that enables actual transactions to occur. ProcureNet provides vendors with an electronic storefront to maximize exposure for their company and actually sell over the Internet. This site was developed by The Fisher Technology Group. Its main software product "CornerStone," which ProcureNet is based on, is available for sale to companies that need this technology function. CornerStone operates much like its own catalog division. It includes online product descriptions and ordering and availability information.[17]

The quality of this Internet commerce product has been so well received that IBM and Oracle plan to resell Fisher's software as part of their own Internet commerce products. This new business area will help Fisher offset downtrends in the laboratory markets and give Fisher a new area for future growth.

Given the high margins and after sale consulting revenue that is involved with software licensing for Internet commerce products, this area could prove to be extremely profitable for Fisher. The incentive for the Fisher Technology Group is that for every dollar of licensing products shipped, approximately $10 of consulting and service revenue will follow. Given the alignment with IBM, Fisher has a high-profile distribution mechanism to launch its future marketing efforts. Fisher Technology Group's acquisition of UniKix will add to their expertise and capabilities in the electronic commerce area.

Fisher Technology is now part of ProcureNet Inc. whose flagship product is OneSource. With over 15 years of experience in the procurement industry, ProcureNet was formed in early 1999 as the result of merging four established organizations with collective experience in procurement applications, electronic catalogs, data rationalization tools, and procurement services.[18]

TECHNOLOGICAL INNOVATIONS

TELECOMMUNICATIONS

Fisher Scientific launched a new Internet commerce site based on IBM's Net.Commerce server. It performs real-time contract pricing, payment processing, and manages EDI transactions, according to Mark Munson, general manager of ProcureNet.

The Trilogy and IBM servers calculate pricing and other variables in real time to accommodate the nuances of business relationships. Variables include volume discounts, delivery logistics, multiple-supplier outsourcing, automated replenishment, sales forecasting, and reporting.

INTERNET

The latest release of Fisher's flagship software product, CornerStone, recently advanced the company's goal of providing users with a better capability to build their own Internet commerce web sites.

While not yet available for the AS/400, CornerStone 3.5 currently runs on the RS/6000. "Fisher is currently working with IBM to migrate CornerStone to the AS/400," says Amelia Mills, VP of product management at Fisher Technology. "The new AS/400e series should facilitate such migration." CornerStone 3.5 features several enhancements to existing versions, including customer registration features, personalized ordering capabilities, multiple supply source functions, contract pricing and

---

[16] Ibid.
[17] "Web Trading Hub Moves a Step Closer to Reality," *PC Week*, March 29, 1999, v. 16, i. 13, p. N13(1).

[18] Dalton, Gregory, Colkin, Eileen, and Wilder, Clinton, "Simpler E-Business," *Information Week*, February 15, 1999, p. 26(1).

availability data, request for quote (RFQ) support, and transaction services. Customer registration consists of user registration, profiles, and log-on. CornerStone stores information such as company name, shipping and billing addresses, account numbers, and orders in progress for registered users.

Personalized ordering capabilities include the ability to modify and enter header and line-item information, an unlimited number of comments and customer-specific data, the option to bypass the catalog search and selection process by entering part numbers directly on the order, and the ability to select a supplier at the line-item level.[19]

With regard to multiple supply source functions, CornerStone can divide supplier lists and generate separate RFQs or purchase orders for each supplier. Users are also able to check for their specific contract price and product availability before placing an order. In addition, CornerStone 3.5 supports full EDI for the management of quoting and purchasing activities between customers and suppliers.

CornerStone 3.5 works as a stand-alone application or can interface with a business's legacy purchase systems. This depends on how the business is structured and whether it requires a data warehouse for all orders, according to Mills. Another strength, she says, is the product's ability to help companies develop full-featured, content-rich online catalogs, as opposed to an Oracle-like database or table type of catalog. "The goal is to help with anything an enterprise might order, and manage information about the product they ordered."[20]

Fisher Technology licenses the CornerStone architecture for both private buying solutions and marketplace selling solutions. One example is Fisher Technology's part in creating and maintaining the web site of its parent company, Fisher Scientific. "In the business-to-business market, credit card capability requirements are different from consumer-to-business markets in that they do not need to have instantaneous response from a clearing house," Mills says.

One Fisher Technology client, Zeneca Pharmaceuticals (Wilmington, Del.), has about 75 end users working with CornerStone 3.5. Zeneca procures lab supplies and miscellaneous requirements from the system through an intranet. "Our users can actually look right into the Fisher catalog," says Steve Trader, purchasing supervisor in logistics and safety at Zeneca.

Trader says Zeneca also plans to add access to third-party catalogs on its corporate intranet, in conjunction with Fisher Scientific's offerings. For now, the phased implementation has worked well, according to Trader. "Initial feedback has been good," he says. "Most of our customers are people comfortable using this technology."[21]

Costs for CornerStone vary according to the services Fisher provides. Web site design and implementation is $18,000, while the license fee for hosting CornerStone behind a client's firewall is $150,000. The fee for electronic catalog and content authoring varies as well.[22]

DATABASES

Fisher Scientific in Europe uses Pindar's Active Catalog to search the catalog on the Internet. Pindar replaced its "WebCat" HTML interface option with a more comprehensive web catalog product, Active Catalog. An important characteristic of Active Catalog is its support for features that are tailored to the individual user, based on log-in. The features can include user-specific language support, pricing, promotional offers, and even some aspects of the look and feel. User-specific bookmarks are maintained by the system, as is the user's purchase history. The user can retrieve a previous order, perhaps change a few items or quantities, and re-submit the order very easily.[23]

Fisher has upgraded CornerStone to include application programming interfaces to SAP and Oracle ERP systems. A company is able to place product orders in CornerStone and simultaneously update tables in SAP or Oracle. This is important for integrated database maintenance.

RECOMMENDATION FOR THE FUTURE

The Fisher Technology Group has laid the groundwork for a promising start in the Internet commerce business. This should be further developed to help Fisher diversify its revenues across different industries and further focus on its competencies. Fisher has taken the lead versus other business-to-business sites on the web. It should continue to seize the opportunity to be the first to market with a top-quality product. This focus will keep Fisher close to its customers by making the procurement process the most convenient and efficient in the industry.

ProcureNet, originally a service of Fisher Technology Group, has over 100 tenants. It won the "marketplace" award at the Internet Commerce Expo for being the top business-to-business electronic mall. The relatively new ProcureNet Inc. should be aggressive in its expansion and try to become the leading provider for business procurement services.

[19] Engler, Natalie, "The New Business Technologists," *Computerworld*, November 16, 1998, p. 106(1).
[20] Hennings, Tom, "E-Commerce Offers Advantages, Challenges to Traditional Retailers," *Computer Retail Week*, September 7, 1998, v. 8, n. 217, p. 19(1).

[21] Berney, Jesse, "Managing Customer Relationships," *Intelligent Enterprise*, November 1998, p. 6(1).
[22] Greenemeier, Larry, "Fisher Casting Into AS/400e Waters," *Midrange Systems*, September 26, 1997, p. 62.
[23] They Seybold Report on Publishing Systems, Updated Catalog Offerings from Pindar, April 13, 1998, p. 209.

CASE QUESTIONS

Strategic Questions

1. What is the strategic direction of the corporation/organization?

2. What are the critical success factors for this corporation/organization?

3. What are the core competencies for this corporation/organization?

Technological Questions

4. What technologies has the corporation relied on?

5. What has caused a change in the use of technology?

6. How successful have the technological changes been?

Quantitative Questions

7. What does the corporation say about its financial ability to embark on a major program of advancement?

8. What conclusions can be reached from an analysis of the financial information to support or contradict this financial ability?

9. What analysis can be made by examining the following ratio groups?

   Quick/Current
   Debt

   Revenue
   Net sales/employee

10. What conclusions can be reached by analyzing the financial trends?

Internet Questions

11. What does the corporation's web page present about their business direction?

12. Does the web site provide a service to customers?

Industry Questions

13. What challenges and opportunities is the industry facing?

14. Does the industry face a change in government regulation?

15. How will technology impact the industry?

Data Questions

16. What role do data play in the future of the corporation?

17. How important are data to the corporation's continued success?

18. How will the capture and maintenance of customer data impact the corporation's future?

W. W. GRAINGER

Executive Summary

Case Name:	W. W. Grainger
Case Industry:	Wholesale distributor of maintenance, repair, and operations supplies
Major Technology Issue:	Determining the best way to use technology to reach customers and to cut costs
Major Financial Issue:	Cutting the cost of operations
Major Strategic Issue:	Developing a method to reach and service customers directly
Major Players/Leaders:	William Grainger, founder; David Grainger, grandson; Richard Keyser, new CEO in 1995
Main Web Page:	www.grainger.com
Case Conclusion/Recommendation:	Grainger must continue to anticipate and read customers needs.

CASE ANALYSIS

INTRODUCTORY STORY

When driving along the Edens Expressway (Interstate 94) just north of Chicago, a large sign spelling the name W. W. Grainger is visible. In fact, this name is visible no matter what state you live in. W. W. Grainger provides the products that keep the electricity flowing to all areas of America's buildings—hand and power tools, the lights that illuminate offices and classrooms, and cleaning, safety, and sanitary supplies.

SHORT DESCRIPTION OF THE COMPANY

W. W. Grainger is the nation's largest wholesale distributor of maintenance, repair, and operations (MRO) supplies. Although they do sell some products under private labels, Grainger no longer manufactures its own products. Grainger realized that its core competencies were in inventory control and distribution, not product development and manufacturing. By divesting itself of manufacturing, Grainger was able to concentrate its energies on the logistics of getting the product to the customer in the fastest and most cost-efficient manner possible.

SHORT HISTORY OF THE COMPANY

William W. Grainger and his wife Margaret founded W. W. Grainger in 1927. Their goal was to provide alternating current (ac) motors to an industry that was primarily supplied with direct current (dc) products. There were no national competitors and no national freight systems to put a meaningful limit on the future growth of Grainger. Coupled with electricity growth at 7 to 8 percent annually, with two-thirds of all electricity thought to be powering electric motors,[1] this industry was perfect for investment.

Grainger's vision was based on service, speed, and convenience. Their goal was to provide the product when the customer needed it. The key was getting their catalog into as many hands as possible and increasing the product offering. Starting with a catalog of 8 pages, Grainger's catalog now has over 4,000 pages with over 78,000 catalog items to choose from. In 1995 the catalog was distributed to 2 million customers. Grainger has grown from a small distribution center in Chicago to over 350 branches nationwide.

The motto "The Right Products, Right Here, Right Now" continues to be the focal point. In fact, 70 percent of U.S. companies are within 20 minutes of a Grainger branch.[2] Grainger occupies branches in all 50 states and Puerto Rico and is continuing to expand in North America. This market saturation has allowed Grainger to maintain and increase market share, especially in the metropolitan areas.

Until the mid-1990s, Grainger's management focused on utilizing resellers and local distributors to access new markets. The management under David Grainger, grandson of William W. Grainger, continued with the belief that the utilization of these distribution channels would increase market share in current and untapped markets. For the periods of Grainger's most

---

[1] Internet, http://sbweb3.med.iacnet.com/infotrac/ses...xrn_16&bkm_66#Investment Thesis Positives / July 11, 1997.
[2] Internet, www.grainger.com / June 18, 1997.

rapid growth, resellers accounted for 60 percent of total sales.[3]

From 1979–1983, Grainger's growth declined. During this period, Grainger's sales growth was weaker than the overall growth in the wholesale electrical merchandising market.[4] Grainger responded by cutting back on branch openings, product introduction, and additions to their sales force.

From 1980 until 1982, only seven new salesmen and four branches were added to the company. These cutbacks only complicated matters, since the addition of branches, products, and sales force in the past had helped drive sales. Instead of leveraging net income and rebounding from single-digit growth, management cost reduction initiatives contributed to a decrease in customer service. Management decided the best way to increase growth was for the Grainger division to penetrate metropolitan areas more aggressively, diversify into other market segments, and ultimately divest itself of its manufacturing division.

In 1995, Richard Keyser was selected to replace David Grainger as president and chief executive officer of W. W. Grainger. He became the first nonfamily member to lead the company.[5] Keyser set Grainger's strategic direction "to focus on groups of customers that have like needs, and that tend to be small, medium, and large. On the very high end, Grainger would focus on integrated supply."[6]

In 1995, management realized that the Grainger Metropolitan Branch Program positioned Grainger against the resellers on which they relied. The realization was that the resellers were beginning to limit growth. Instead of valued customers, they were becoming a network of competitors. This was opposed to Grainger's intention to get closer to its customers[7] by focusing directly on them. While the company still services resellers and local distributors, the ultimate goal is to service customers directly.

By actively pursuing metropolitan areas, which for so long had been the domain of the resellers, Grainger was sending a clear message to the industry. They expanded stores in the metropolitan areas and directly contacted customers that had been serviced by the resellers. An even stronger message was the fact that Grainger would no longer ship directly to the customer or remove prices on invoices for the resellers.

In 1987 Grainger had 231 stores nationwide. They realized they had not tapped all available markets. A strategic study showed that market share was high within 20 minutes of a branch, but then dropped. The answer to increased market share was clearly more branches, in particular, more metropolitan branches. This initiated the Metropolitan Branch Program. What followed was the immediate addition of 55 stores in 1988 and 25 in 1989, bringing the total to the count of 327 branches.

Grainger was stepping in between established relationships, taking market share and margins away from resellers, and possibly forcing the resellers to become allies of their competition. This was an effort to get closer to the end user and expand in more profitable market segments.

Grainger had become so proficient in servicing the resellers that they essentially transferred these skill sets to the end user customers. Customers found that by dealing directly with Grainger, they were eliminating a step in the procurement process, with potential savings in both time and money.

Grainger's success stems from their reputation for service and the breadth and depth of inventory. In order for Grainger to capitalize on market share, they had to enter market arenas in which they had not previously participated, continually expand the number of their stores, and make sure that the catalog was everywhere. In the late 1980s, in keeping with the company vision of building leadership positions in selected distribution markets, Grainger management saw an opportunity to develop other Grainger-like businesses in different specialty distribution markets.

The company chose spare parts (Grainger Parts Operation), safety products (Allied Safety), sanitary and janitorial supplies (Jani-Serv), general distribution (Bossert), and several smaller businesses (with total sales of $245 million) and aligned them under the Specialty Distribution Group (a division of W. W. Grainger). Although the Grainger Parts Operation was built internally, all other divisions were established mainly through acquisition.[8]

Over the years, the Grainger Division integrated its Specialty Division groups, realizing that once they had acquired the products and brands they felt were crucial to the markets they wished to serve, they would need to market them under the Grainger umbrella. W. W. Grainger is now comprised of three business units: the Grainger Division, Lab Safety Supply, and Grainger Parts Operation.

Grainger seeks to provide expertise in finding appropriate products for customers and then having them available. This is accomplished through a large local inventory and same-day shipping. Another key is

[3] Internet, http://sbweb3.med.iacnet.com/infotrac/ses...xrn_16&bkm_66#Investment Thesis Positives / July 11, 1997.
[4] Ibid.
[5] *Industrial Distribution*, June 1996, v. 85, n. 6, p. 48(2).
[6] Ibid.
[7] Internet, http://sbweb3.med.iacnet.com/infotrac/ses...xrn_16&bkm_66#Investment Thesis Positives / July 11, 1997.

[8] Internet, http://www.sec.gov/Archives/edgar/data/277135/0000277135-96-000004.txt / June 18, 1997.

Grainger Parts Operation (GPO). Grainger has over 350 branches nationwide, one national distribution center (NDC), two regional distribution centers (RDCs), and six zone distribution centers (ZDCs), all of which when combined supply 24-hour replenishment to the branch network.

Although the services may vary, Grainger enjoys a unique ability to offer the same selection of goods to various customers with varying needs. Grainger's customer base is typically contractors, manufacturers, industrial and commercial accounts, and institutional accounts, such as schools, health care facilities, and government agencies. Part of their customer base, small business, is primarily concerned with speed and convenience in getting their products. The other section, large business, which constitutes over two-thirds of the revenues, is focused on reducing total cost and supplier base and on product standardization. Regardless of the customer, Grainger's technology and services enable them to effectively serve a diverse customer base while maintaining a competitive advantage.

FINANCIAL AND PORTFOLIO ANALYSIS

In the decades from its founding in 1927 through the 1970s, Grainger grew at annual rates in excess of 20 percent. This was the result of strong entrepreneurial management and a vision to take a unique company concept nationwide.[9]

Sales have grown dramatically over the last 11 years, from $1,159,595,000 in 1986 to $3,537,207,000 in 1996. The number of employees has also grown from 5,578 in 1986 to the present count of 14,601. The year 1996 marked record sales and earnings for Grainger,

---

[9] Internet, http://sbweb3.med.iacnet.com/infotrac/ses...xrn_16&bkm_66#Investment Thesis Positives / July 11, 1997.

Table 6.1 Cumulative Sales Growth Rates to Date

Period	Grainger (%)	Nominal GNP (%)	Grainger vs. GNP
1976–1980	99.80	53.30	1.9
1981–1985	32.70	31.50	1.0
1986–1990	66.90	29.40	2.3

recording sales of $3,537,207,000, up 7.9 percent over prior year and net earnings of $208,526,000, an increase of 11.7 percent from 1995 (Figure 6.1).

The primary driver for sales has been the increase in the number of offerings in the general catalog and increased sales force. Although net sales increased by 7.9 percent, sales per employee were down from $276,462 in 1995 to $242,259 in 1996. This occurred even though 2,700 new employees were added to the payroll.

Grainger's compound growth rate is accelerating at twice the rate of others in their respective industry (Table 6.1). This growth can be attributed to the expansion of branches, increase in sales force, distribution of general catalogs, and the expansion of the catalog into electronic mediums like PC-based software and the Internet service.

Current assets increased every year except for 2 from 1984 until 1995. Total assets increased every year. This is seen in the continual expansion of stores, inventory, and capital expenditures. Capital expenditures for 1996 were focused on four primary areas: construction, relocation, and expansion of stores; additions and upgrades to data processing systems; expansion of the distribution logistics network; and the initial phase of the new corporate headquarters in unincorporated Mettawa, Illinois.

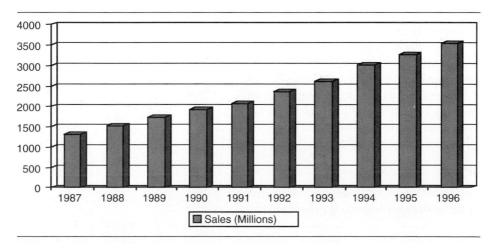

Figure 6.1 Grainger sales growth 1987–1996.

Earnings as a percentage of net sales decreased from 1987 until 1995. Long-term debt as a percent of total capitalization continually decreased from 1984 until 1995, with the exception of 1 year. Grainger continues to maintain a low debt-to-equity ratio and a strong liquidity position. The current assets to current liabilities ratio is 2:1. Grainger's long- and short-term success can be attributed to their expansion of stores as well as their inventory management.

In 1996, Grainger launched a campaign to centralize shipping from their zone distribution centers and stock the most commonly purchased items in each branch. The purpose of this national stocking model was to remove obsolete or slow-moving inventory from the branches, reallocate it to the NDC, and have the critical items on hand in local branches. Shipping from centralized points consolidated orders for customers, saving on freight charges for both parties. This model has resulted in higher service levels. It has reduced inventory and freight costs.

In 1996, Grainger implemented a system to automatically seek stores with excess inventory levels of a certain item to complete a customer order. This system, called *Smart-LINQ,* provides rapid recovery for a stocked-out store, while reducing overstocks in surrounding stores and shrinking redundant inventories. This system enabled Grainger to reduce inventory in 1996 by over $38 million. These changes should help improve an already impressive average inventory turnover rate of 3.5.

STOCK/INVESTMENT OUTLOOK

Grainger is continuing a comprehensive modernization of its management information systems and a reengineering of its nationwide distribution network. As a result, it has decreased its cost structure, increased its value to its customers, and strengthened its competitive position.[10]

Grainger stock is sold on the NYSE and the CSE under the symbol GWW and is currently selling around $90 per share. Grainger's more than $3 billion in annual sales reflects its emphasis on meeting and surpassing customers' expectations through their service, technology, and sharpening focus.

In 1995, capital expenditures were $62 million. In 1997 they were $85 million as Grainger continued to optimize the company's branch and logistics network, enhance information systems capabilities, and continue construction at their Lake Forest facility.

RISK ANALYSIS

Grainger's rate of growth is heavily dependent on the overall health of the general economy. If growth in the economy were to falter due to higher interest rates or other factors, the company's performance could be impacted.[11]

Grainger is also affected by weather conditions. Extreme measures of any particular season can bolster sales. Extreme heat, cold, or rain can have a very positive impact on sales since Grainger's products can help alleviate the effects of these conditions. Just as adverse weather has a positive impact on sales, calm or mild weather seems to flatten sales.

In December 1996, in an effort to increase market penetration and respond to the entry of competition such as Home Depot and Wal-Mart in North America, Grainger completed the acquisition of Canada's largest industrial distributor, Ackland's. This overnight expansion moved Grainger's Canadian presence from one sales office to 180 branches.[12] This $251 million acquisition was financed with $135 million in cash and the remainder in shares of Grainger stock.[13]

In addition to Grainger's expansion northward, 1997 marked the first time the company opened a non-U.S.-based facility. The company opened a branch in Monterey, Mexico. Grainger clearly decided that expansion in greater North America was advantageous. They have also begun to study the Pacific Rim region for potential expansion.

INDUSTRY AND MARKET ANALYSIS

MRO supplies is a broad and fragmented industry with multiple channels of distribution and approximately $250 billion in annual sales (Table 6.2). The market for MRO supplies is served through a number of distribution channels including retail outlets, small distributorships, national, regional, and local distributors, direct mail suppliers, large warehouses and manufacturers' direct sales forces.[14]

Table 6.2 Sales and Market Share (Billions)

Period	Grainger	Electric Wholesale Market	Grainger Market Share (%)
1976–1980	2.8	184.9	1.50
1981–1985	4.6	349.6	1.30
1986–1990	7.0	514.2	1.40

[10] Internet, http://www.sec.gov/Archives/edgar/data/277135/0000277135-96-000004.txt / June 18, 1997.

[11] Internet, http://sbweb3.med.iacnet.com/infotrac/ses... 4272828/66!xrn_18&bkm_66# Industry Overview / June 18, 1997.

[12] *Industrial Distribution*, February 1997, v. 86, n. 2, p. S3(2).

[13] Ibid.

[14] Internet, http://sbweb3.med.iacnet.com/infotrac/ses... 4272828/66!xrn_18&bkm_66# Industry Overview / June 18, 1997.

It is estimated that the top 50 industrial distributors account for less than 10 percent of the total market and that over 100,000 small retailers, distributors, and dealerships, each averaging less than $10 million in annual sales, supply over 65 percent of this market.[15] Grainger continues to aggressively increase its branch count, believing that a more intensive approach can raise penetration in what it considers a minimal market share.

Customers within the industry have increasingly focused on reducing overall costs by dealing with fewer suppliers and maintaining relationships with those that can offer a broad product selection, automated order processing, and advanced services such as inventory management and nationwide support. To remain competitive, it has become increasingly important for distributors to provide customers with wider product selection, lower costs, and value-added service.[16]

In the past there was no effective competition; developments in freight systems and communications have made competition easier.[17] Companies are now able to service the marketplace with far fewer facilities than a company like Grainger. Grainger also faces competition from manufacturers, including some of the company's own suppliers, that sell directly to certain segments of the market and from wholesale distributors, catalog houses, and certain retail enterprises.

The procedure that Grainger employs to compete with manufacturers and other distributors is to provide local stock, efficient service, account managers, competitive prices, several catalogs, extensive technical and application data, procurement process consulting services, and other efforts to assist customers in lowering their total MRO costs.[18]

Grainger's competition ranges from small hardware stores to companies such as General Electric, MSC Industrial Direct, Wesco, Graybar, McMaster Carr, and the growing Home Depot stores. Interestingly enough, a company like McMaster Carr operates out of only four branches nationwide, markets exclusively by telephone, and delivers overnight via United Parcel Service. Advances in freight systems and communications have given a boost to competitors eager to capture a portion of Grainger's market.[19]

Grainger's advantage lies in its ability to supply products faster, supporting smaller inventories for the customer. Grainger enables customers to access one-stop shopping, reducing the number of suppliers and transactions required to procure the supplies needed. A report from the Value Line Investment Survey states "Electrical equipment companies expect to increase earnings growth in this industry with new product development, increased market penetration, divestments and acquisitions.[20] This parallels Grainger's strategic direction.

ROLE OF RESEARCH AND DEVELOPMENT

Grainger's electronic services have transformed the way Grainger and its customers conduct business. Their services cut cycle times to improve business processes, both for customers and suppliers, as well as within the company.[21] Moreover, these services have provided seamless integration with Grainger stores and the sales force. These services must be continuously refined and updated to reduce costs and to meet customer needs.

TECHNOLOGICAL STORY

Grainger has not always been on the cutting edge of technology. Twenty years ago, the only way workers at Grainger could check stock on a particular item was to run into the warehouse and physically look for the item or call another store and have them do the same. The way to ensure that customers had their products when they needed them was for Grainger to saturate each branch with inventory. Today Grainger has implemented technologies that not only enable their employees to check stock and availability nationwide but also to enable Grainger to manage their inventories more efficiently. Grainger realized that developments in freight systems and communications, increased competition, and customers' growing needs required them to find ways to get to the customer faster and make it easier for the customer to do business. This did not always mean having a branch at the front doorstep of every business. The first step was to understand how technology could improve efficiencies. The second step was to match available technology to strategic goals and customer needs in a way that would not only execute flawlessly but also support the business.

TECHNOLOGICAL INVESTMENT AND ANALYSIS

In 1981, Grainger redefined their method of retrieving and replenishing inventory when they installed their automated storage and retrieval system (AS/RS) at the Niles, Illinois-based regional data center. This massive 10-aisle system was designed to supply over 60 percent

[15] Ibid.
[16] Ibid.
[17] Internet, http://www.sec.gov/Archives/edgar/data/277135/0000277135-96-000004.txt / June 18, 1997.
[18] Internet, http://sbweb3.med.iacnet.com/infotrac/ses.../432/399/4272828/66!xrn_18&bkm_66#outlook/July 11, 1997.
[19] Gillooly, "Brian, "Online Marketplaces—Death of a Salesman," *Information Week*, May 10, 1999, p. 8(1).

[20] *The Value Line Investment Survey*, Part 3–Ratings & Reports, January 26, 1996, v. 51, n. 20, p. 1001(19).
[21] *Manufacturing & Distribution Issues*, Grant Thornton Newsletter for Industrial Companies, 1996, v. 7, n. 3, p. 10.

of the replenishment stock to forward picking locations at a rate of 210 pallet loads an hour.[22]

This AS/RS has greatly increased efficiencies in getting product to the customer as well as to the branches. Although the AS/RS expedited inventory, it was only one component in improving customer service and efficiencies. The other component was speeding information.

Information transmission has been enhanced through the use of satellite communications. Grainger utilizes a satellite communications network, which substantially reduces its reliance on phone lines by linking stores and other facilities through a network control center. This was enhanced in 1995–1996 when Grainger completed the installation of IBM minicomputers at each branch, office, and distribution center. This Grainger network enables all portions of the business to be linked by satellite network to provide the convenience of instant product availability information and real-time inventory management for more than $1 billion worth of inventory.

This network has decreased Grainger's response time through the almost instantaneous transmission of information. This expedites the completion of sales transactions and the initiation of stock replenishment.[23] This in turn increases levels of customer satisfaction. It has also enabled Grainger to distribute software across the network with greater efficiency.

Grainger offers their general catalog on CD-ROM, free to Grainger customers. In 1996, the company introduced a web site. With the introduction of their web site, Grainger became one of the first business-to-business web sites to accept orders over the Internet. Grainger's state-of-the-art technology helps Grainger customers look up products instantaneously. When doing so, they utilize a guided interactive search engine that can search by description, brand name, specification, manufacturer's model number, and Grainger stock number to check the company-specific pricing.

Grainger has integrated the CD-ROM catalog version with Datastream products. Datastream is a leading manufacturer of computer software programs such as MRP2 and Maintain It, a purchasing and preventive maintenance software program. Now users of these Datastream products can click on an icon and immediately be transferred to the Grainger CD-ROM catalog (ECAT—electronic catalog).[24]

Utilizing Grainger's Web Site, http://www.grainger.com, customers can order online 24 hours a day, 7 days a week, to find over 200,000 products quickly and easily. This provides the customer with fast and cost-effective paperless services. In addition, customers can utilize the web site for inquiries and feedback. Grainger's Internet site has dramatically increased the number of companies using Grainger's distribution system.[25]

Barbara M. Chilson, Grainger's vice president and general manager for electronic commerce, stated "Grainger's Internet commerce convenience was created in response to feedback received from our customers."[26] Grainger's online catalog (Web Cat) allows multiple users per account to order online. This provides a significant advantage to larger companies, which often give more than one employee purchasing responsibility.[27]

Items such as the CD-ROM catalog and Web Cat give customers greater access to products in the general catalog. The CD-ROM version enables customers to access more than 500,000 product cross-references. The Internet provides over 1 million cross-references. Other electronic services include electronic data interchange (EDI), electronic funds transfer (EFT), and computerized maintenance management programs with built-in interface to the Grainger CD-ROM catalog.[28]

According to James T. Ryan, Grainger's vice president of information services, "The company is continually upgrading its information systems to better serve its customers." In 1995, Grainger started moving major applications from the mainframe into a more distributed client/server network. Every branch now uses minicomputers and "intelligent" workstations. As a result, Grainger is now positioned to respond much faster to customer needs with more computing power resident at the branch level.[29]

Technology has enabled Grainger to offer more products and services and open more locations. Grainger's direct sales focus is shifting from servicing resellers, other distributors, and small customers, to medium to large customers, integrated supply chains, and national accounts. Grainger has been careful not to make the critical mistake of ignoring its smaller customers, who until the mid-1980s had been the largest source of Grainger's profit. To ensure smaller customers were not neglected, Dick Keyser piloted a telesales project in 1996. It was designed to better address the accounts for whom direct mail alone was not sufficient.

[22] *Modern Materials Handling*, May 1996, v. 51, n. 6, p. 32(4).

[23] Internet, http://sbweb3.med.iacnet.com/infotrac/ses...267661/4!xrn_1&bkm_4#Business Description / July 11, 1997.

[24] Wilder, Clinton, "Online Supplies Purchases via R/3—W.W. Grainger Teams with SAP on Electronic–Commerce," *Information Week*, September 14, 1998, n. 700, p. 32(1).

[25] Machlis, Sharon, "Supplier Seeks Sales via Web Searches," *Computerworld*, September 14, 1998, v. 32, n. 37, p. 20(1).

[26] Internet, http://mro-explorer.com/news/mtrmatch.htm/ June 18, 1997.

[27] *PR Newswire*, June 9, 1997, p. 609DEM037.

[28] Kirby, Peter S., "Plug And Play: The Future of eCommerce," *Electronic News*—1991, December 7, 1998, p. 8(1).

[29] *Manufacturing & Distribution Issues*, a Grant Thornton Newsletter for Industrial Companies, 1996, v. 7, n. 3.

Realizing that integrated supply was more than a fad, Grainger formalized a new division—Grainger Integrated Supply Operation (GISO). With GISO, a customer uses Grainger to supply some or all of its maintenance, repair, and operating supplies. According to Donald E. Bielinski, senior vice president of marketing and sales, "Most GISO customers are large corporations because GISO customers typically order about $1 million of product per location per year from Grainger. Currently, annual orders of less than $1 million are not cost effective for Grainger to fulfill within the GISO program."[30]

As technology improves, Bielinski estimates it will become cost effective for the company to accept smaller orders. Bielinski estimates the national market for integrated supply to be around $2 to $3 billion. GISO is paying off. Grainger recently signed American Airlines at its Dallas-Fort Worth airport operation and Fel-Pro, out of Skokie, Illinois, as GISO customers. GISO currently has about 40 customers. Looking to the future, Bielinski adds that "Grainger will continue to work on the three major areas that any distributor must constantly strengthen. This includes continuing to improve the physical movement of products, the flow of information, and the efficiency of transactions." In keeping with Bielinski's iteration of the critical factors for future growth, it seems that technology has found a home with Grainger. The use of technology will allow Grainger to meet its customers' and internal goals.

The Grainger web site and CD-ROM catalog has improved customer service and cut the costs of producing catalogs. The web site affords customers access to Grainger 24 hours a day from around the world. In addition, the web site and CD-ROM has reduced the costs of catalog distribution. In 1995, more than two million copies of the general catalog were distributed to businesses nationwide. Given the freight charge to ship a catalog approximately 5 inches thick, the savings are substantial when a CD-ROM is shipped.

Not only do freight costs decrease when more users go online or utilize the CD-ROM catalog, but costs are also saved on catalog production (paper version versus CD-ROM). Since 1995, Grainger has produced the general catalog once a year instead of twice (spring and fall). This has greatly reduced the production costs, directing the money back into the company.

TECHNOLOGICAL INNOVATIONS

TELECOMMUNICATIONS

W. W. Grainger is teaming with SAP to let customers use the R/3 application to buy products from Grainger

through the web. Grainger views the web as a growth vehicle for business-to-business sales. The web site accounts for less than 1 percent of Grainger's total sales but is growing as much as 100 percent a quarter.

Grainger will use electronic catalog technology from Requisite Technology Inc. in Boulder, Colorado, to provide the online content for all its web initiatives. Requisite will also provide catalog technology to support Grainger's web site and intranet. Sales representatives use these sites to get information to fulfill orders and answer customers' questions.[31]

TECHNOLOGICAL INNOVATIONS

INTERNET

Grainger has launched a pilot of a unified E-commerce site for procuring products and services from six business-to-business suppliers. It is the first stage of a larger procurement system that covers products and services needed by businesses.

The OrderZone.com web site was developed in conjunction with Perot Systems. Using Perot's Digital Marketplace technology, it offers a single point of entry to online procurement sites from Cintas, Corporate Express, Grainger Industrial Supply, Lab Safety Supply, Marshall Industries, and VWR Scientific Products.[32]

The web-based system pools suppliers' business processes so customers can securely access each vendor's site through OrderZone.com, place orders using a single form, and receive one invoice, payable electronically. Daniel Hamburger, president of Grainger Internet Commerce, says OrderZone.com is catering to businesses that "want procurement of all indirect supplies to be easier."[33] Other sites on OrderZone.com provide business products such as office supplies, uniforms, and security equipment.

An important aspect of the Grainger web site is the development of an accurate, user-friendly web site for its catalog operations. Inaccurate, unhelpful search engines have long been a complaint of customers using catalog sites. Grainger is focusing on web-search technology because helping corporate customers pinpoint the parts they need is a critical success factor for its $4 billion-per-year parts ordering business.

According to Don Bielinski, group president, "There's nothing 'special' about our products. You can get them anywhere." The value add we provide is in the

---

[30] Ibid.

[31] Karpinski, Richard, "E-Commerce Tools, Standards Alleviate," *InternetWeek*, May 17, 1999, p. 9(1).

[32] Wilder, Clinton, and Dalton, Gregory, "E-Commerce Dividends," *InformationWeek*, May 3, 1999 p. 18(1).

[33] Dalton, Gregory, Colkin, Eileen, and Wilder, Clinton, "Simpler E-Business—Grainger Debut Web Sites," *InformationWeek*, February 15, 1999, p. 26(1).

business process."[34] The web site enables Grainger to carry a broad array of products, from lighting to motors to security products. The advantage is one-stop shopping and the ability to order products quickly and easily.[35]

Traditionally, if a Grainger customer needed a replacement motor for an air compressor, he/she would leaf through the company's thick red paper catalog of 70,000 products and search for the appropriate motor. The buyer usually called a sales assistant to request help before ordering.

On Grainger's old web site, www.Grainger.com, the customer would enter "motor" and then have to go through dozens of listings. The new site, Order-Zone.com, responds to the inquiry with a series of questions based on the user's desired product type. For motors, that might mean queries about brand name, enclosure, horsepower, and revolutions per minute.

To accomplish this transition, Grainger has entered into a "multiyear, multimillion-dollar" deal with Requisite to electronically catalog Grainger's products and develop relevant search questions.

According to Don Bielinski, web sales account for less than 1 percent of Grainger's business, but are "the fastest growing thing we have."[36]

SMART CARD

As Tom Condon, director of Information Systems, moves about the sprawling maze of workstations at Grainger's Custom Solutions Center, his identification badge emits infrared signals. The signals are picked up by receivers on the ceiling that report his whereabouts to the company's personnel directory on the intranet.

If a customer needs Condon in a hurry, the receptionist merely clicks on his name in the company's personnel directory to find his location, which is updated every five seconds. The directory sends him a targeted audio message from an overhead speaker.

Grainger adopted this technology because the price and quality of competing products are very close in the maintenance equipment industry. As a result, customer service is becoming the differentiator. Executives are eliminating phone tag, pagers, and public address systems in favor of employee-tracking through the intranet.[37]

Over 200 employees are connected to a browser-based suite of tools called ArialView from Arial Systems Corporation. Condon believes Grainger's $100,000 investment in the system will pay off because it helps the company respond to customer calls about five minutes faster. With the number of ArialView "searches" reaching 1,500 per day, Grainger is projected to realize $500,000 per year in productivity savings.

According to Condon, "The identification badge system is a tool to reduce time in solving problems and improving customer satisfaction."[38]

Condon is often asked whether employees feel comfortable being monitored. According to Jere Brown, marketing manager, no one at Grainger has publicly complained about wearing the badges. Given Grainger's team-oriented approach, there is almost peer pressure to wear it. According to Jim Alland, CEO of Arial Systems, ArialView does not monitor employees in the rest rooms. The system does track when employees enter and leave the building and who they are with.[39]

According to Esther Roditti, a New York attorney specializing in high-tech law, no federal laws prohibit employee monitoring of this nature. She recommends, however, that companies use common sense and notify employees of any monitoring activity and maintain "reasonable standards of privacy" at work. Roditti concluded by stating, "It personally disturbs me."[40]

RECOMMENDATION FOR THE FUTURE

Grainger must continue to focus on technology to improve efficiencies, increase customer service levels, effectively manage inventory, and facilitate access to existing markets. In short, they must implement technology that will improve distribution processes as well as give them the upper hand against current and future competition. Technology is being used to align customer needs with the company vision. Technology has taken Grainger from 347 branches to the virtual store that can be accessed any time from any place.

Although Grainger still focuses on market saturation, it can now be accomplished without huge capital expenditures in every branch location. Grainger's financial position over the last decade and a half has put the company in a position of embracing the technology and its ever-changing environment. The ability to finance from within the company and through cash and stocks positions it well for the technological investments it must face. Grainger should utilize technology to further decrease internal costs such as paperless picking and ship-

[34] Machlis, Sharon, "Supplier Seeks Sales via Web Searches," *Computerworld,* September 14, 1998, v. 32, n. 37, p. 20(1).
[35] Frook, John Evan, "Blue-Collar Business on the Web," *InternetWeek,* September 14, 1998, n. 732, p. 43(1).
[36] Machlis, Sharon, "Supplier Seeks Sales via Web Searches," *Computerworld,* September 14, 1998, v. 32, n. 37, p. 20(1).
[37] "Enhancing the Value Chain," *e-Business Advisor,* May 1999, v. 17, i. 5, p. 8(1).

[38] Collett, Stacy, "Infrared System Keeps its Eye on Employees," *Computerworld,* May 24, 1999, p. 40(1).
[39] Ibid.
[40] Ibid.

ping, and direct links to their suppliers for direct shipments to customers as well as those of the customers.

The acquisition of Acklands was instrumental in shaking up the industry and Grainger's current and future stock price. Grainger has always started new ventures or acquisitions to keep the company in the spotlight and drive up the market value. Grainger represents a solid investment with a new management group with global vision and the tools and capital to bring it to fruition.

Grainger believes the key to integrating technology and the customers' needs lies in the ability to align investments in technology with the company's business objectives. In doing so, Grainger's success will be determined by how well it anticipates the needs of their customers and how well they respond to those needs. A key factor for Grainger's future is the decision to follow other companies and customers across national boundaries into the international marketplace.

CASE QUESTIONS

Strategic Questions

1. What is the strategic direction of the corporation/organization?

2. Who or what forces are driving this direction?

3. What has been the catalyst for change in the company?

4. What are the critical success factors for this corporation/organization?

5. What are the core competencies for this corporation/organization?

Technological Questions

6. What technologies has the corporation relied on?

7. What has caused a change in the use of technology in the corporation/organization?

8. How has this change been implemented?

9. How successful has the technological change been?

Quantitative Questions

10. What does the corporation say about its financial ability to embark on a major program of advancement?

11. What conclusions can be reached from an analysis of the financial information to support or contradict this financial ability?

12. What analysis can be made by examining the following ratio groups?

   Quick/current
   Debt
   Revenue
   Sales per employee
   Profit

Internet Questions

13. What does the corporation's web page present about their business direction?

Industry Questions

14. What challenges and opportunities is the industry facing?

15. Is the industry oligopolistic or competitive?

16. How will technology impact the industry?

Data Questions

17. What role do data play in the future of the corporation?

18. How important are data to the corporation's continued success?

19. How will the capture and maintenance of customer data impact the corporation's future?

US ROBOTICS

Executive Summary

Case Name:	US Robotics, Inc.
Case Industry:	Wholesale manufacturing industry
Major Technology Issue:	Staying ahead of the competition by delivering the latest in modem and information transfer technology
Major Financial Issue:	There are no major financial issues.
Major Strategic Issue:	Placing themselves as the product of choice now and in the future
Major Players/Leaders:	Casey Coswell, CEO
Main Web Page:	www.3com.com
Case Conclusion/Recommendation:	US Robotics needs to take advantage of their merger with 3COM by maximizing the potential of creating a complete line of communication products that will address the future needs of consumers and the changes that the industry will undergo.

CASE ANALYSIS

SHORT DESCRIPTION OF THE COMPANY

US Robotics researches, designs, and builds modems and communications servers for retail customers and business applications. The company was incorporated in 1976 and is based in Skokie, Illinois. It was recently acquired by 3COM Corporation.

SHORT HISTORY OF THE COMPANY

US Robotics was started by Casey Cowell, a graduate of the University of Chicago. At age 23, he dropped out of a doctoral program and collaborated with former classmates to make plans to build a keyboard and acoustic coupler for communication over phone lines. The original name, US Robot, was inspired by Isaac Asimov's novel *Robot*. To avoid confusion, the name was changed to Robotics.

The first product was a perfection of their previous acoustic coupler and a keyboard, which they started to market to generate for cash. Their sales increased through word of mouth. Within a short time, a range of equipment made by Teletype, DEC, General Electric, and Applied Digital Data Televideo was added to the US Robotics product line.[1]

The company launched its second product, a modem, in 1979, after FCC regulations changed to allow non-AT&T equipment to be connected directly to the telephone network. Cowell placed an ad in *Byte* magazine; soon orders for the modems began rolling in.

In 1984, the company relocated to a large factory space in Skokie, and the modem became US Robotics' only product. Through research and development, modems were eight times faster than they were in 1976. There were three major competitors: Motorola with Codex and UDS divisions and Hayes Microcomputer products. US Robotics built its own computer chip data pump to control the modem's transmission features.[2]

US Robotics modems were built to their own specifications, not those of Rockwell and other chip manufacturers that supplied Hayes and Motorola. This enabled US Robotics to develop faster modems and get them to market more quickly than its competitors. By 1990 rates of 9,600 bits/second (bps) were becoming common. During this time US Robotics began the development of the 14,400 bps modem. After the introduction of its new product and while maintaining third place in the general modem market, it captured a 43 percent share of the market. Companies previously unfamiliar with US Robotics became customers and identified themselves as targets for future marketing efforts.

FINANCIAL AND PORTFOLIO ANALYSIS

Net sales for 1996 increased $1,977,512,000.[3] This increase was the result of higher unit sales in both the

---

[1] International Directory of Company Histories, v. 9, p. 514.

[2] Ibid.

[3] http://www.sec.gov/Archives/edgar/data/895642/0000950135-97-001575.txt.

PC-related product categories, including high-speed desktop and PC card modems,[4] and the systems product category, including modem pools, network hubs, remote access servers, and LAN switching products. The increase in the average selling price of the PC-related products contributed to the substantial increase in revenue during 1996.

The increases in unit sales were driven by strong market demand for devices that provided online access to information through computers and networks. This reflected the continued growth of online information and trends in organizational and personal computing patterns and capabilities. Gross profit increases constituted a 41.9 percent of net sales compared to 41.4 percent in 1995.

International sales represented 26 percent of total sales. Concentrated in Canada and Europe, these sales increased by 125 percent to $517.2 million in 1996 compared to 1995. International sales in 1996 represented approximately 26 percent of net sales. The increase resulted from higher unit sales, reflecting a worldwide trend toward information technology. Casey Cowell's dream was that one day international sales would constitute at least one-half of the company's sales. US Robotics is now building the organizational infrastructure needed to achieve the same dramatic growth in the Asia-Pacific region.

The cost of goods sold doubled, $1,149 million compared to $521 million, in 1995. Selling and marketing expenses accounted for 13.7 percent of net sales compared to 15.4 percent in 1995 and 17.2 percent in 1994. During 1995 and 1996 US Robotics substantially increased spending for promotional programs designed for the continued development of technical support programs and for recruiting and training new resellers.[5] Selling and marketing expenses decreased as a percentage of net sales due to the significant growth in sales and the semipermanent nature of these expenses.[6]

General and administrative expenses in 1996 were 4.7 percent of net sales, compared to 4.8 percent in 1995. The dollar increase in 1996, from $261 to $528 million, was attributed to expenses associated with additional administrative staff, computer systems, and outside professional and consulting services necessary to support US Robotics' expanded level of business activity.

Research and development costs increased in relative terms from 5.9 percent in 1995 to 5.6 percent in 1996. Net earnings for 1996 were $170.0 million, compared to $66.0 million and $36.1 million for 1995 and 1994,

respectively. Net sales doubled but net earnings almost tripled.

Long-term obligations of the company followed a downward direction from 1994. In that year US Robotics had $69 million in long-term debt. In 1995, this number dropped to $65 million and in 1996 to $54 million.

Cash and cash equivalents decreased from $136 million to only $16 million. Even though cash flows from operating activities, excluding changes in assets and liabilities, increased to $248.8 million in 1996 from $87.3 million in 1995, the acquisition of Scorpio Ltd. took a large portion of the cash reserves, almost $54 million.

The company expects to continue to make significant investments in the future to support its overall growth. Currently, ongoing operations will be financed from internally generated funds. Several factors could impact the company's ability to generate cash from operations in 1997. These include economic conditions, market competition, and market acceptance of new products.

To maintain its financial flexibility, US Robotics entered an agreement with a group of banks to provide initial credit of $300 million, expandable to $600 million under certain circumstances. The management of US Robotics believes that this anticipated cash flow from operations and access to debt and equity markets will permit the financing of its business requirements in an orderly manner for the foreseeable future.

Accounts receivable turnover increased from 5.28 to 10.64. Inventory turnover went from 8.63 to 43.47. This indicates improved merchandising. From a working capital point of view, a company with a high turnover requires a smaller investment in inventory than one producing the same sales with a low turnover.

STOCK / INVESTMENT OUTLOOK

US Robotics' year-end stock gains in 1997 were $1.79 per share, compared with $0.77 and $0.47 in 1996 and 1995, respectively. This was a 3.8 multiple in three years.

3COM, a leading U.S. network equipment manufacturer, agreed to merge with US Robotics, the leading modem manufacturer, in a deal estimated to be worth $6 billion. US Robotics shareholders received 1.75 shares of 3COM stock for each share of US Robotics stock they held.

RISK ANALYSIS

The data communications industry is intensely competitive and characterized by rapid technological advances and emerging industry standards. Failure to keep up with technological advances would adversely impact the company's competitive position and the results of operations. Primary competitors with respect to systems

---

[4] *Breaking the Barriers 1996 Annual Report*, p. 21.
[5] *International Directory of Company Histories*, v. 9, p. 514.
[6] "Rockwell:56-Kbit . . . Corner," *Electronic News*, February 10, 1997, v. 43, n. 2154, p. 20(1); http://www.sec.gov/Archives/edgar/data/895642/0000950135-97-001575.txt.

products domestically include Ascend Communications, Lucent, Motorola, Microcom, and Multitech.

The primary competitors with respect to desktop products domestically include Hayes Microcomputer, Best Data, Motorola, Boca Research, Zoom Telephonies, and Cardinal. Primary competitors with respect to mobile communications products include Motorola, TDK, and Hayes. Competitors, with respect to handheld electronic organizers are Sharp, Hewlett-Packard, and Casio.[7]

INDUSTRY AND MARKET ANALYSIS

Modems began as primarily tools of business, but they quickly entered homes during the last decade, with increased application during the last four years, due to the Internet.

At the end of 1995, US Robotics constituted 21.9 percent of the entire market (Figure 6.2). Maxtech had 18.4 percent, Hayes 8.6 percent, Boca and Compaq 5.8 and 5.1 percent, respectively. US Robotics sales were $889 million in 1995 with net income of $65.9 million (Figure 6.3). Boca Research sales accounted for $143 million during the same year with net income of $9.5 million. Hayes had sales of $631 million and net income of $6.8 million in 1995. Since 1995 US Robotics sales have skyrocketed. The increase from 1995 to 1996 was 88 percent.

Hayes Microcomputer is trying to reestablish its leadership in the computer modem business. Hayes was forced to file Chapter 11 bankruptcy in 1994 due to the intense competition. Its market share dropped from 35 percent of the market to 8.4 percent with $45 million of debt. By introducing the 56K upgrade program and cutting prices on other modems, they hoped to move ahead of US Robotics and be the first to introduce new products.[8]

Hayes witnessed a drop in market share after 1994. With the expectation of new products, its stock is expected to go up. Boca Research witnessed an increase

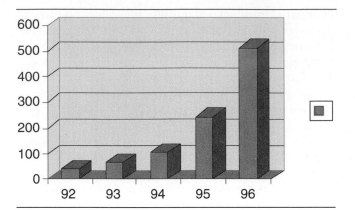

Figure 6.3 US Robotics international revenues in millions of dollars.

in share earnings of $0.72 compared to a $1.07 increase in 1996. US Robotics witnessed a $1.79 per share increase in 1996 compared to a $0.77 per share increase in 1995.

The FCC has a rule limiting the data transmission power over a telephone line. On January 22, 1997, the FCC held hearings to explore ways to provide telecommunication companies with incentives to develop high-speed telephone connections to reduce network congestion.[9] Lucent Technologies, Rockwell International, and US Robotics have been developing technology for the 56K modems, which will offer a cheaper alternative to technologies such as digital telephone lines, cable modems, and high-speed satellite links.[10] The US Robotics X2 is highly spoken of by Internet users. The Hayes 56K, or the Rockwell modem, has received limited publicity and interest.

ROLE OF RESEARCH AND DEVELOPMENT

US Robotics concentrates on extensive research and development. Their strategies are based on access, speed, and solutions. Their goal is to develop comprehensive solutions that add value for those who sell and use US Robotics products and technologies.[11] The company's objective is to maintain and enhance its leadership position in the information access market by leveraging its strengths in the areas of communications technologies, customer-driven product design, marketing and distribution channel partnerships, international presence, manufacturing, and human and financial resources.

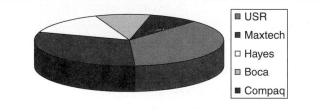

Figure 6.2 Market share before the introduction of the X2 modem.

---

[7] *Electronic News*, April 21, 1997, v. 43, n. 2164, p. 10(4); *Computerworld*, August 26, 1996, v. 30, n. 35, p. 10(1).
[8] http://hayes.com/.

[9] "FCC Rule Stands in Way of Faster Modems," *Los Angeles Times*, January 24, 1997, v. 116, p. D3, c. 2.
[10] "MCI, US West Test ADSL . . . , Modems," *InfoWorld*, April 8, 1996, v. 18, n. 15, p. 6(1).
[11] "Leading Modem Makers," *Market Share Reporter—1997*, p. 258.

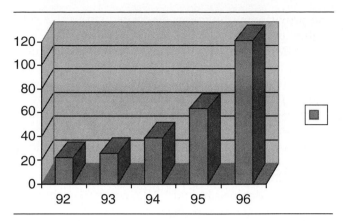

Figure 6.4 Research and development in millions of dollars.

Figure 6.4 shows that the amount of money allocated to R&D multiplied from $15 million in 1992 to $114 mil in 1996. By introducing the 33.6K and the X2 56K modems, US Robotics has achieved the highest quality in the marketplace, the most advanced products, and the best service.

US Robotics continues to emphasize research and development. To sustain their growth, they must be early to the market with the latest technologies. This will also help ensure that their products are the standard bearers for the industry, with a high level of industry dominance.

On February 26, 1997, 3COM and US Robotics agreed to enter into the largest merger in the history of the data networking industry. The merger was completed on June 12, 1997. According to 3COM, this move strengthened 3COM's capacity to compete with Cisco Systems, the world's leader in network equipment.[12] The combined company will be an undisputed industry leader in each of its network access businesses. The combination of the distinct, but complementary, strengths and products of the two companies will result in a leading market position in several markets. Both companies have a common vision for the fundamental trends that drive the network markets and a common strategy to capitalize on those trends. Together they have a unique ability to deliver end-to-end connectivity solutions across both LANs and WANs. With the combination, they became the industry and market leaders at the edge of local- and wide-area networks, having connected more users to networks than any other vendor in the industry.[13]

At the time of the merger, the market was consolidating around a few leaders within each segment. As a result, it was extremely important to quickly establish a clear market leadership. The merger further solidified the strengths of the 3COM and US Robotics brands among end users and resellers. This has provided them with a market position that has remained unparalleled in the industry. US Robotics has been dominant since 1990 in WAN information access, products, and systems that connect computers and other equipment over analog and switched cellular networks. Beginning in 1996, other companies merged or cooperated—like Hayes and Alcatel, MCI and U S West, GTE and Pacific Bell. These mergers have developed new digital connections for online communication. In 1997, US Robotics began to acquire LAN equipment companies, indicating a shift toward remote access servers. Yet, 3COM remained the industry leader in LAN systems. The boundaries between LANs and WANs are converging. Customers are now expecting higher levels of integration between their LAN and WAN access solutions, from both a user and a management perspective.[14] 3COM can leverage US Robotics' well-established retail channels of distribution as well as maximize US Robotics' significant presence in the carrier and Internet service provider markets. Together, 3COM and US Robotics have a unique ability to deliver end-to-end connectivity solutions across both LANs and WANs.[15]

TECHNOLOGICAL INNOVATIONS

NETWORKS

3COM Corporation has launched its bidirectional Cable Access System for the delivery of broadband communications. This high-speed, cable-return Internet access system includes 3COM's Total Control Cable Modem Termination System (CMTS) and network management software for the front end and the US Robotics Cable Modem CMX for consumers. The system components are all based on the Data Over Cable Service Interface Specification (DOCSIS).

3COM's end-to-end system enables offices and homes to access the Internet through cable connections and receive multimedia information and entertainment at speeds up to 100 times faster than conventional analog modems. In addition, the system will support future digital services such as Internet telephony and videoconferencing. The 3COM Cable Access system is scheduled for deployment by Tele-Communications, Inc. (TCI),

[12] "Ethos," http://194.70.69.3/ethos/news/lit1/5282htm.
[13] Medford, Cassimir, "New Services—3Com Takes Its VARs To the Edge," *VARbusiness*, June 21, 1999, p. 14.
[14] Benhamou, Eric, "3Com/US Robotics Combination," http://www.3com.com/0files/releases/1226eab.html#epaisley.
[15] Burgess, Mark S., "Security By Route," *e-Business Advisor*, August 1998, v. 16, n. 8, p. 34(7).

and is currently used by FiberTel-TC12 (Argentina), Northern Cable (Canada), ISP Channel and BlazeNet (USA), and other operators in the United States, Germany, Holland, Switzerland, Spain, and Taiwan.

"Our technology helps make cable networks the preferred on-ramp to the digital highway. We can now deliver more than static information," said Richard Edson, senior vice president for 3COM's New Business Initiatives Group. "The state-of-the-art high end system and cable modems enable new services and revenue opportunities for individuals, businesses, and cable operators around the world."[16]

"This is the result of significant and continued investment by 3COM in the emerging cable industry, DOCSIS standards, and the retail channel," said Levent Gun, vice president and general manager of 3COM's Cable Access Group. "Partners like TCI have helped us design the optimal platform for current high-speed Internet access services and the applications to be delivered in the next century."

3COM supports flexible loads and centralized management. 3COM's CMTS is built on the leading Total Control remote access platform, making it an easy and reliable choice for cable operators' delivery and management of high-speed digital services. The system consists of both hardware and software, providing a reliable, modular architecture with decoupled upstream and downstream access cards. It includes the capability to support cable-return (two-way) and telco-return (one-way) cable modems from a single Total Control chassis. This enables cable operators to build high-density scalable systems, generating one of the lowest costs per marginal subscriber in the field.

Unlike most routing-based approaches with limited scalability, the 3COM remote access platform preserves front-end investments by accommodating multiple "hot-swappable" cable access cards in each chassis. The system can easily expand to meet increased user demand by adding more cards in nearly any upstream/downstream ratio. Furthermore, 3COM's network management software is SNMP based, allowing centralized control of all network components. Operators can manage and run diagnostics remotely on the system's user-friendly interface.

The Total Control chassis allows cable operators to use voice-over-Internet protocol (VoIP) gateways available from 3COM. In addition to VoIP capabilities, other 3COM Total Control servers provide caching and provisioning functions associated with cable subscriber services.

3COM/US Robotics Cable Modem CMX is user friendly and retail-ready. The 3COM/US Robotics Cable Modem CMX is simple to install, easy to use, and supports raw throughput of up to 38 Mbps downstream and up to 10 Mbps upstream. The modem is based on the same size and stackable design as 3COM's popular OfficeConnect family of networking equipment for consumers and small- and medium-sized businesses. The new cable modem also supports Windows, Macintosh, and UNIX computers through a standard Ethernet interface.[17]

All 3COM modems ship with a Cable Connection CD-ROM that provides the latest broadband applications, installation software, and tools to maximize high-speed Internet access. With Comfax software, 3COM cable modem users can send and receive digital faxes over a global network of Internet fax servers, bypassing traditional dial-up telephone networks. Thus, 3COM cable modem users can substantially reduce fax charges and dedicated phone lines.[18]

The 3COM Cable Access system and modem family enables high-speed data communications over cable networks. It is compatible with all 3COM routers, switches, and NICs. The 3COM CMTS is currently supporting multiple Internet telephony demonstrations. The US Robotics cable modems are available in select markets and retail storefronts in North America.

RECOMMENDATION FOR THE FUTURE

The growth potential, especially outside the United States, is phenomenal for connectivity of all kinds including LANs, WANs, and modems. Competition forces all the companies to focus on product innovation and quick introduction to the marketplace.

The option of additional mergers or cooperation should be constantly considered. Cooperation between hardware firms and telephone service providers is the direction taken by Hayes and Alcatel. It may prove to be successful.

The new 3COM/US Robotics firm must act as one company, focus unrelentingly on growth, adopt a global perspective, and remain intensely competitive.

---

[16] Dalton, Gregory, "Bazaar Advantages," *Information Week*, May 10, 1999, p. 42(1).

[17] "3Com Intros US Robotics V.90 56Kbps Message Modem 03/24/99," *Newsbytes*, March 24, 1999, p. NA. COPYRIGHT 1999 Newsbytes Inc.

[18] "3Com Unveils Small Business Year 2000 Program 12/03/98," *Newsbytes*, December 3, 1998, p. NA. COPYRIGHT 1998 Newsbytes Inc.

CASE QUESTIONS

Strategic Questions

1. What is the strategic direction of the corporation/organization?

2. Who or what forces are driving this direction?

3. What has been the catalyst for change?

4. What are the critical success factors for this corporation/organization?

5. What are the core competencies for this corporation/organization?

Technological Questions

6. What technologies has the corporation relied upon?

7. What has fueled US Robotics' drive for making faster modems?

8. How has this change been implemented?

9. Who has driven this change throughout the organization?

10. How successful has the technological change been?

Quantitative Questions

11. What does the corporation say about its financial ability to embark on a major technological program of advancement?

12. What conclusions can be reached from an analysis of the financial information to support or contradict this financial ability?

13. What analysis can be made by examining the following ratio groups?

   Current ratio
   Debt
   Revenue

14. What conclusions can be reached by analyzing the financial trends?

Internet Questions

15. What does the corporation's web page present about their business directives?

16. What can be found at the web page?

17. How does this compare to the conclusions reached by analyzing the financial information?

Industry Questions

18. What challenges and opportunities is the industry facing?

19. Is the industry oligopolistic or competitive?

20. How will technology impact the industry?

Data Questions

21. What role do data play in the future of the corporation?

22. How important are data to the corporation's continued success?

23. How will the capture and maintenance of customer data impact the corporation's future?

TECHNOLOGY TIPS

MICROSOFT WORD TIPS

INSERTING AN EXCEL SPREADSHEET

Inserting an Excel spreadsheet into your document is easier than creating a table. This is true if you already have your spreadsheet done. The following steps will create a linked object and allow you to integrate a spreadsheet or parts of your spreadsheet into your word document.

1. Click on the part of your Word document where you would like to insert your spreadsheet.
2. Minimize your Word document and open the Microsoft Excel workbook that contains the data you want to create a linked object from.
3. Switch to Microsoft Excel, and then select the entire worksheet, a range of cells, or the chart you want.
4. Click on the Copy button.
5. Switch to the Word document, and then click on EDIT.
6. From the drop-down Edit menu, click PASTE SPECIAL.
7. From the dialog box click PASTE LINK.
8. In the AS box in the middle of the dialog box click on *Microsoft Excel Worksheet Object*.
9. Click OK. Your worksheet is now inside your Word document.
10. If you want to enable the Excel features just double click on the worksheet. You will be switched over to the Excel workbook. All changes made will automatically be made in the Word document.

ADDITIONAL NOTE

What Is a Linked Object?

A linked worksheet or chart is displayed in your document, but its information is stored in the original Microsoft Excel workbook. Whenever you edit the data in Microsoft Excel, Word can automatically update the worksheet or chart in your document. Linking is useful when you want to include information that is maintained independently, such as data collected by a different department, and when you need to keep that information in Word up to date. Because the linked data is stored in another location, linking can also help minimize the file size of your Word document. The files must be accessible to each other if you use this feature (i.e., both on the C: drive; A: drive, etc.). If you do not need to use this feature just click on PASTE in the dialog box in step 7.

MICROSOFT EXCEL TIPS

SORTING DATA

Excel is able to sort the data in a column in a descending or ascending order. This will help in organizing the data in alphabetical or numerical order for lists and printouts. There are some important things to note when using the sort feature. Unlike filtering, sorting is a permanent change to the Excel sheet. If you want to change the worksheet to its original state you must the change using the UNDO button or exit the worksheet WITHOUT saving. Also, the sorting feature works only on the columns highlighted and disregards the data in the other columns. If the data located in the rows must remain together you must highlight all columns that are relative to each other.

How to Sort Data

1. Highlight the cells that you want to sort.
2. Click on the ascending order button or the descending order button.
3. The cells highlighted will be organized according to the button you clicked.

Direction of Highlighting Matters

If you highlight from left to right the sorting order will start with the leftmost column. If you highlighted from right to left the sorting order will start with the rightmost column.

What Is the Sorting Order?

Excel uses sort orders to organize data according to the value, not the format, of the data. When you sort text, Excel sorts left to right, character by character. In an ascending sort, Excel uses the following order:

• Numbers are sorted from the smallest negative number to the largest positive number.
• Text and text that includes numbers are sorted in the following order:

0 1 2 3 4 5 6 7 8 9 ' - (space) ! " # $ % & ( ) * , . / :
; ? @ [\ ] ^ _ ` { | } ~ + = A B C D E F G H I J K L M
N O P Q R S T U V W X Y Z

In logical values, FALSE is sorted before TRUE.
• All error values are equal.
• Blanks are always sorted last.

NOTE

When using the descending sort, the sort order is reversed except for blank cells, which are always sorted last.

MICROSOFT POWERPOINT TIPS

INSERTING SLIDES FROM OTHER PRESENTATIONS

If you need to insert slides that were created in a different presentation you can do so with ease. This may be useful when you have members of a team working on different parts of a presentation and then need to integrate their work into one final presentation.

Inserting Slides Using INSERT

1. Open the presentation in which you want to insert the slides.
2. Click to the SLIDE SORTER VIEW.
3. The slide that you click on in SLIDE SORTER VIEW will have all the new slides inserted after it.
4. From the top toolbar click on INSERT. From the drop-down menu click on SLIDES FROM FILES. . .
5. The slide finder dialog box below will appear on the screen. Click on the BROWSE button and select the file that contains the presentation. Open the presentation by double clicking on the file.
6. Once you are back to the dialog box below, click on the DISPLAY button. This will show all the slides that are available for insertion into your presentation.
7. Click on the slides that you want to insert. The surrounding area of the slide will become bold when you have selected it. If you wish to insert all slides simply click on INSERT ALL.
8. Click the CLOSE button. The slides will appear in your presentation with the design template that was used with the rest of the presentation.

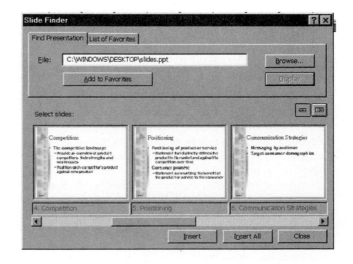

Copy/Pasting Slides into the Presentation

1. Open the presentation into which you want to insert slides. Also open the presentation from which you want to copy slides.
2. Switch to SLIDE SORTER VIEW in the presentation from which you will be copying slides.
3. Click on the slide you wish to copy (to copy several slides at a time hold down the SHIFT key while selecting on slides).
4. Click on the right mouse button. From the pop-up menu click on COPY.
5. Switch to the presentation into which you want to copy the slide. Your presentation should be in the SLIDE SORTER VIEW. Click on the slide that you want to insert the slide *after*.
6. Click on the right mouse button. Click on PASTE from the pop-up menu.
7. Your slide will be inserted into your presentation using the design template that is being used in the presentation.

MICROSOFT ACCESS TIPS

MAKING THE DATABASE WORK: RELATIONSHIPS

After you have set up different tables for each subject in your database, you need a way of telling Access how to bring that information back together again. The first step in this process is to define relationships between your tables. Once this is done, you can create queries, forms, and reports to display information from several tables at once. For example, this form includes information from five tables.

HOW DO RELATIONSHIPS WORK?

The form on the right brings together the fields of five different tables to display information about the same order. This coordination is accomplished with relationships between tables. A relationship works by matching data in key fields. In most cases, these matching fields are the primary key from one table, which provides a unique identifier for each record, and a foreign key in the other table. For example, employees can be associated with orders they are responsible for by creating a relationship between the Employees table and the Orders table using the EmployeeID fields.

A ONE-TO-MANY RELATIONSHIP

A one-to-many relationship is the most common type of relationship. In a one-to-many relationship, a record in Table A can have many matching records in Table B, but a record in Table B has only one matching record in Table A.

A MANY-TO-MANY RELATIONSHIP

In a many-to-many relationship, a record in Table A can have many matching records in Table B, and a record in Table B can have many matching records in Table A. This type of relationship is only possible by defining a third table (called a junction table) whose primary key consists of two fields: the foreign keys from both Tables A and B. A many-to-many relationship is really two one-to-many relationships with a third table. For example, the Orders table and the Products table

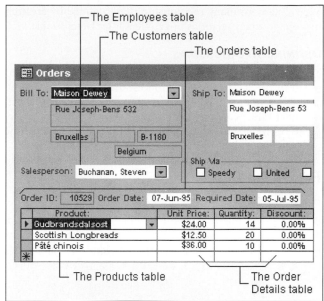

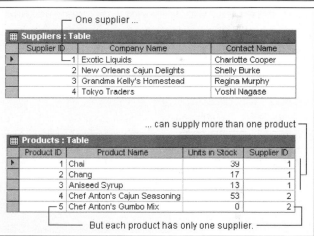

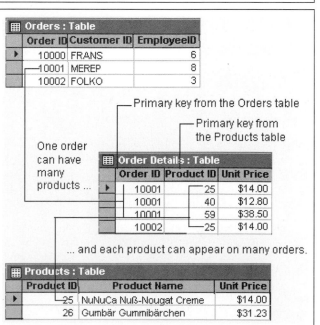

have a many-to-many relationship that's defined by creating two one-to-many relationships to the Order Details table.

DEFINING RELATIONSHIPS

You define a relationship by adding the tables you want to relate to the Relationships window, and then dragging the key field from one table and dropping it on the key field in the other table. Click on the RELATIONSHIPS button in order to open the window and begin creating links among your tables.

FRONTPAGE TIPS

BACKGROUNDS

As you surf through the web you will notice that many sites have different backgrounds. You can also make your background different by using an image or simply changing colors. Just make sure that visitors to your web site are still able to read the information on your web page, and it is not too distracting.

1. Click on FORMAT from the top menu bar.
2. Select BACKGROUND from the drop-down menu.
3. The PAGE PROPERTIES dialog box on the right will appear. Click on the BACKGROUND tab.
4. You can either select a picture as a background (check off on BACKGROUND IMAGE) or change the background color.

There are a number of web sites that are dedicated to creating backgrounds for web sites. Use a search engine (YAHOO!, Lycos, AOL NetFinder, etc.) to find the different sites dedicated to creating these. Once you find a background you like, save it in the same way you would a picture, as explained in Chapter 4.

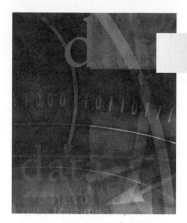

CHAPTER 7

INTEGRATION OF INFORMATION
AUTOMOBILE INDUSTRY

Integration of Information

Sharing data effectively is crucial for success in today's competitive environment. Managers must know how to use a variety of tools. There are many ways to integrate types of data, such as using a spreadsheet or a word processor as the foundation document. A newer method is to begin with a database report. Software is available to help integrate different types of information. Integration requires combining data from many different locations. Networks enable work done by different people to be linked. Workgroup software combines features to facilitate group work by supporting different tasks such as communication and integration of data types. GDSS software enables workers to contribute at the same time.

Integrated Data Integrated data takes information from different sources and puts it together in a meaningful and useful way. One of the difficulties of this is the diversity in hardware and software. Recent programs share data through links. An important distinction is between static and dynamic integration.

Static Integration Static integration uses a base document that contains static or "snapshot" copies of other objects. The disadvantage is that if the original or source documents change, the user must recopy the changed items to the integrated document. The advantage is that one can keep track of the changes in the source documents, since changing the original does not change the integrated object.

Dynamic Integration Dynamic integration uses a base document that always contains the current or most re-

cent version of the source documents it contains. One advantage of this approach is that you do not have to remember what other documents use your source documents, since the most recent version will always be applied. Other names for dynamic integration are hot links, dynamic data exchange (DDE), or object linking and embedding (OLE).

Integration over Networks Integration over networks reaps all the benefits of dynamic integration. This effort requires worker coordination, particularly in the use of compatible software packages. Security controls are needed to specify which workers access what.

Groupware Groupware refers to software tools designed for workgroup integration, such as Lotus Notes. Three components exist for groupware: communication, compound documents, and databases. Examples of groupware include e-mail and scheduling. Compound documents can be documents worked on by more than one person and containing different types of data, such as text, graphs, and images. Groupware applications can be used to automate teamwork, develop discrete business solutions, build enterprise-wide systems, and even extend the enterprise.

Legacy Systems Legacy systems are older systems that usually contain valuable data, but can have incompatible or outdated software.

Data Warehouse A data warehouse is a single consolidation point for an organization's data from diverse production systems. Data are usually stored in a central computer, sometimes even in a single large file. Data need and sources need to be identified. The data must be transformed and integrated so it can be searched and analyzed efficiently. One problem with a data warehouse is that it usually represents a static copy, not a dynamic link, of the total data in the company. As a result, some of the information may not be available.

Open Systems Open systems technology represents a method to organize information technology in an entity. In this case, the software and data are separate from the hardware. This would allow a simple transfer of the data and software whenever the organization or entity purchases new hardware. Windows NT was one of the first to offer a commercial solution to the challenge of running common software and data on different types of hardware. The problem with a proprietary operating platform such as Windows is that the maker, Microsoft, defines the interface and the standards. Developing open or nonproprietary standards involves extensive time and effort.

Group Decision Support System A GDSS is a groupware tool designed to help teams make decisions. Most versions of a GDSS use a special room in which each participant is seated in front of a networked terminal. A facilitator directs the meeting. All participants can have immediate input. Depending upon the arrangement, participants can remain anonymous, giving managers more honest feedback and ideas. Limitations of a GDSS include the loss of oral interaction, the requirement that participants type their input, and the expense of maintaining a separate, networked meeting room.

Software Available to Support Integration

Spreadsheets Spreadsheets were an early type of integration software. They also generate representative graphs. An important development is the ability to dynamically link the information in a spreadsheet to other files or even different software packages. This keeps the information constantly up-to-date.

Word Processors Since most reports are primarily text, this is a popular way to integrate data. Diagrams, charts, and spreadsheets can be imported into the document. Word processors allow dynamic integration of data from spreadsheets or graphic packages.

Database Reports These reports are similar to word processors. The major difference is that in a word processor all the information to be included must be explicitly presented in the report. With a database management system report writer, a person can develop a template for a single row of data that is to be shown in the report. That template can be applied to as much data in a database as needed. This is useful with problems that involve repetitive types of information.

Clipboard Clipboards provide a way to integrate data when the operating system uses "windows." The clipboard is an area where data can be imported to be held until it is exported elsewhere, even into a different software package. This can be a static copy of the information or a dynamic link. The information can be imported into the clipboard by selecting the data and copying, cutting, or extracting it into the clipboard. The destination document is then selected; data is pasted into it.

Automobile Industry

DESCRIPTION OF THE INDUSTRY

The automobile manufacturing industry is an increasingly competitive industry with respect to a number of factors. Automobile companies compete on quality, price, development, appearance, size, special options, safety, and financing terms.

Word	W.1	Creating Charts Additional Notes	Creating a Chart Quicker and Easier
Excel	E.1	Formatting Cells	Coloring Cells Formatting Data within Cells Text Alignment Cell Borders
PowerPoint	P.1	Inserting Clip Art and Web Images	Inserting Clip Art Web Images
Access	A.1	Creating Forms Using Form Wizard	Using Form Wizard
Front Page	I.1	Creating a Scrolling Marquee	Modifying the Marquee

Three types of automobile manufacturers dominate the industry:

1. Original equipment manufacturers: These companies supply inputs such as windshields, seats, and brake systems directly into a specific stage in the assembly process.
2. After-Market/Replacement Parts: Manufacture parts such as brake pads and batteries are supplied to assemblers and the replacement market.
3. Capital Goods: These organizations provide manufacturing and assembly line equipment to the assemblers.

FINANCIAL ANALYSIS

The automobile industry has benefited from several factors during the past few years. The first is the improved economic condition in the United States. The second is the result mostly of favorable exchange rates. This provides a cost advantage compared to vehicles manufactured in Japan or those vehicles with a significant portion of the parts manufactured in Japan.

Automakers and suppliers are also impacted by the season. Operating results vary primarily because of the variability in types and numbers of vehicles sold in different seasons. Results are impacted by new product launches, sales incentives, and costs of materials and production changes.

STOCK/INVESTMENT OUTLOOK

Automobile manufacturers in the United States continue to struggle to remain in a leadership position in terms of quality and market share. In 1994 and 1995, operating revenues increased while net income decreased. This lowered return on investment. Stock prices vary greatly in the automobile industry, depending upon economic growth, the stability of the economy, and interest rates.

POTENTIAL/PROSPECTIVE FOR GROWTH

Quality has become the focal point for improvement in the domestic auto industry. Even though important advances have been made, the perception persists that U.S. automobiles do not meet the same high standards as certain foreign manufacturers.

Several trends in automobile manufacturing are setting the stage for the future growth of smart automobiles. As the industry responds to demands for safer and more environmentally responsible vehicles, emerging innovations are flourishing. A Dataquest Report suggests three main sectors for growth:

1. Advanced driver information and communication systems, including keyless entry, navigation systems, and near obstacle recognition. These products enhance the driver's awareness of personal safety as well as the safety of road conditions through power steering, electronic brakes, and collision avoidance.
2. Powertrain electronics, including active suspension.
3. Body control electronics, or the application of "black boxes" for automobile and security systems.

The next generation of smart cars will enable its passengers to automatically keep pace with the vehicle in front and signal emergency services regarding the exact location of an accident without driver action.

A Harvard study predicts that world demand for automobiles will continue to increase. Production capacity is likely to continue to exceed demand. Europe has become the primary battleground for car manufacturers with unified Germany now being the biggest single market. Eastern Europe and South America offer limited growth as well as high risk with significant market opportunities in the years 2000 to 2010. China, India, and the Asian countries represent the greatest opportunities and challenges to Japanese, U.S., and European manufacturers.

COMPETITIVE STRUCTURE

Automobile manufacturing remains a highly competitive industry ranging from the Big Three automakers to a variety of suppliers. In addition, a number of foreign automobile companies are investing in North America.

Automakers are taking advantage of new management tools and techniques. One trend is the just-in-time (JIT) manufacturing system, which ultimately cuts down on the number of suppliers needed. American automakers traditionally utilized thousands of different suppliers in short-term contract relationships, based upon cost. Today, by implementing JIT, manufacturers reduce the number of suppliers by establishing long-term relationships with fewer suppliers.

Most European car manufacturers have significant positions only within Europe. U.S. companies tend to have major shares domestically and in Europe, while only two major Japanese companies claim to be truly global. Although the industry is becoming concentrated, no single company is close to dominating the market. In fact, seven companies have between 10 and 15 percent of the market. A variety of alliances and joint ventures have been utilized as a means of growth. Consolidation will continue to dramatically alter the profile of the entire industry. Ford is trying to move further up market with the acquisition of the Aston Martin and Jaguar brands. Facing tough Japanese competition in the U.S. market, Ford is set to challenge GM for second place in Europe with the purchase of 51 percent of Mazda.

Consolidation in supplier relationships will also dramatically alter the industry profile over the next 10 to 15 years. Ford had 2,300 direct suppliers in 1995 and reduced this figure to 1,150 in 2000. Chrysler reduced its direct suppliers from 2,000 to 1,500 over the same period. BMW recently announced its intention to reduce its line suppliers from the current figure of 1,400 to just 200.

ROLE OF RESEARCH AND DEVELOPMENT

Research and development in the domestic automobile manufacturing industry never ceases. Automakers and suppliers continuously strive to improve their product and its functions to remain ahead of competition in the United States and in foreign countries.

In the Ford 2000 program, Ford set the goal of global standardization of environmental systems and processes at all Ford facilities worldwide. Ford is standardizing their operational procedures while still striving for consistency and continuous improvement in their facilities.

Automobile pollution is a worldwide problem. Automobiles currently have 80 percent of the global personal transport market and 55 percent of goods transportation. Their impact on the environment is large. Noise and solid waste also contribute to environmental deterioration. According to a study done by Harvard University, more than 500 kg of every car produced ends up in landfill sites, accounting for 4 percent of the total rubbish weight.

Recycling is another way to deal with the pollution problems that cars pose. About 75 percent of current cars are steel and therefore easily recyclable. The remaining 25 percent consist of plastic, glass, and rubber. Legislation will force reductions of the latter to 15 percent by 2002 and to 5 percent in the longer term. Alternatives to plastics include resin-bonded flax, which can be used as agricultural fertilizer when the car is eventually recycled. Green networks are being built to collect batteries, catalytic converters, and bumpers and recycle them directly in the production of new vehicles.

Reducing fuel consumption is a major research area. Engines are being developed with reduced friction, more efficient combustion, and better ignition. Diesel cars are an alternative; work also continues on small electric cars. Engines capable of using renewable fuels such as soya oil have been in existence since the 1970s. These renewable fuels will not become cost effective unless there is a change in oil prices or in the presence of government incentives.

Weight reduction is another area of research. In the future, car bodies may be composed of lighter, high-strength steels, alloys, polymers, and composites.

TECHNOLOGICAL INVESTMENT AND ANALYSIS

Robot manufacturing companies like Motoman Inc., and Fanuc Robotics, have impacted the automobile manufacturers. Robots are capable of completing jobs humans have difficulty with or find tedious and boring. Once properly designed and calibrated, robots make fewer errors in production tasks. Today, they can be operated from familiar Windows-based PCs.

To speed up the design cycle, the Big Three U.S. automakers bring their electronics suppliers into the design cycle at much earlier junctures than in the past. According to Alex Popovic, automotive marketing manager at National Semiconductor Corporation, "The sooner we (suppliers) get involved, the more cost-effective and better-performing system the customer gets." Early supplier involvement has another advantage in the automotive market. Working from the design stage, the systems engineers can implement diagnostic techniques that will reduce the automaker's future warranty costs. Alex Popovic states, "We try to eliminate problems early by increasing the accuracy of the diagnosis of the problems."

Most of the 1.1 million employees working for Chrysler, Ford, and General Motors are expected to eventually use web applications. The Big Three automakers are proving that intranets and extranets can open communications in the supply chain, improve international communications, and save money on support. The automakers are also looking to networking as a way to lower costs and improve profit margins. The Big Three are already among the leaders in providing web access to their employees.

Members of the Automotive Industry Action Group trade association are working to help GM, Ford, and Chrysler overcome Year 2000 problems and issues at parts manufacturers that threaten to disrupt the supply chain. A Year 2000 problem at even a small company could cripple a giant automaker because most companies tightly manage their business partners and use just-in-time inventory. These efforts are important because most of the automobile industry is running on old legacy computer systems and applications.

RECOMMENDATION FOR THE FUTURE

Although the automotive industry has had its ups and downs in the recent past, automakers and suppliers must continuously improve their processes to survive in today's marketplace. This means taking advantage of the latest technology to cut costs.

Quality control must also be a major goal of U.S. automobile manufacturers. This increasingly means providing customer service long after the completion of the sale.

WEB SITES

Automobile Industry
www.mel.nist.gov/
www.nationalservice.com/

FORD MOTOR CO.

Executive Summary

Case Name:	Ford Motor Co.
Case Industry:	Auto industry
Major Technology Issue:	Implementing Global Studio communications
Major Financial Issue:	Cutting development costs
Major Strategic Issue:	Implementing the global mission of Ford 2000
Major Players/Leaders:	Alex Trotman, CEO; the Ford family
Main Web Page:	www.ford.com/us/
Case Conclusion/Recommendation:	Go forward with Ford 2000 program.

CASE ANALYSIS

INTRODUCTORY STORY

In 1996, Alex Trotman, president, CEO, and chairman of the board of Ford Motor Company, hosted a Ford family meeting. Trotman has hosted the Ford family every year since being appointed CEO in 1993. Approximately 20 Fords gathered to tour facilities, drive new models on the test track, lunch with the board of directors, and drill Trotman on everything from sales in Latin America, productive capacity, and environmental issues to, importantly for the Fords, dividends.

The Ford family received roughly $88 million in dividends in 1995. Trotman knows the value of staying on their good side. Although publicly held, the family exerts significant influence on the company. They are also protective of their investment. One outside director said of the Ford Company, "With all this cash, if it weren't for this family, I'd take over this company." After former chairman and CEO Donald Petersen rubbed the family the wrong way, he prematurely retired. Trotman hopes to retain the Ford family support. He needs it now more than ever as he attempts to "win the world over" all over again.

In late 1995, Elena Anne Ford, the great-great-granddaughter of Henry Ford, became the first member of the fifth generation to go to work for Ford. The event is a small reminder that the Ford family is a constant presence. The special Class B stock the Fords own gives them 40 percent of the shareholder votes.

The Fords also have a strong presence on the board of directors—with seats being held by Edsel B. Ford II, William Clay Ford, and William Clay Ford, Jr. Edsel and his cousin Bill, Jr., have also been mentioned as possible candidates to become CEO. However, Bill Jr. resigned from the company in 1995 to succeed his fa-

ther as chairman of the finance committee of the board, a position reserved for an outside director.[1]

SHORT DESCRIPTION OF THE COMPANY

In addition to manufacturing cars, Ford is the world's largest producer of trucks. Ford has operations in 30 countries and over 200 markets. For the fiscal year ended December 31, 1996, Ford's net income was $4.4 billion on sales and revenues of $147.0 billion.

Ford's operations are divided into two business units: Ford Automotive Operations (FAO) and Financial Services. FAO is responsible for the design, manufacture, assembly, sales, and marketing of cars, trucks, and related parts and accessories for Ford, Lincoln, Mercury, and Jaguar, a wholly owned subsidiary. FAO also has interests in Aston-Martin, Kia, and Mazda. Financial Services consists of financing, leasing, insurance, and rental operations through the Ford Motor Credit Company ("Ford Credit"), the Hertz Corporation, and American Road Insurance Company subsidiaries.

SHORT HISTORY OF THE COMPANY

In 1903, the first Ford production car, the Model A, was sold in the United States. Henry Ford started the company with a capital base of $28,000, a dozen or so employees, and a small production facility in Detroit. The Model T, introduced in 1908, was sold in two types and one color: black. The vehicle was tremendously popular, and Ford was forced to continue to develop and refine the mass-production concepts first introduced by Ransom Olds.

Henry Ford II succeeded his grandfather at the helm of Ford and began a 35-year tenure that ended with his

---

[1] Hayes, Mary, "The Search for Simplicity," *Information-Week*, March 8, 1999, p. 38(1).

retirement in 1980. It was during this time that Ford began to take the shape of the present-day Ford Motor Company. When Henry Ford II took over operations, he found a company in which the market share was eroding, the cash reserves were low, and the organizational structure was highly politicized.

Wanting to instill strong fiscal control, Henry Ford II fired hundreds of executives and hired a group of 10 former U.S. Air Force officers. Known as the "Whiz Kids," they quickly revamped Ford's operations and created a Finance Department. For example, Alex Trotman is the first person since 1945 to hold Ford's highest position who did *not* advance from the Finance Department.

Ford's success through the years was attributed to what it did *not* provide for automobile owners, specifically variety and high quality. Typically offering one-half the number of models that General Motors (GM) offered, Ford enjoyed tremendous economies of scale and avoided the expenses inherent in diverse product lines.

Success did not come without criticism, however. Ford has not been a creative leader in the industry since the 1920s. Ford seldom innovated with new concepts and in turn watched from the sidelines as a former Ford employee developed the revolutionary minivan for Chrysler. Chrysler developed the small sport utility vehicle (SUV) and GM led the way in large SUVs. Ford was known as a low-cost provider of value vehicles.[2]

Historically, Ford has been reluctant to admit financial difficulties, preferring to blame problems on market conditions. In a 1996 meeting called by Ford officials for the media and Wall Street analysts, Ford admitted that "our product development costs are too high, our investment in new products is excessive, [and] our profit margins are down because our costs are too high." The announcement was monumental considering the company's history.

Ford went to the 1996 meeting with a plan of action to regain the top spot among the Big Three. The following initiatives were outlined:

1. Huge reductions in product development costs
2. A commitment to reducing the cost of every car and truck each year from 1996 through 2000
3. An investment in a new vehicles cost reduction plan, calling for the reuse of existing facilities and platforms
4. A reduction in passenger car and truck platforms, enabling the use of more common components across all product lines. This was mandated by Ford 2000.

Some say Ford's troubles began when the company strove to emulate Toyota in product quality. No one knows how many buyers have spurned Ford's new passenger cars because of the increases in sticker prices, even with the increase in quality and comfort. Jim Harbour of *Automotive Industries* said Ford's current difficulties began in 1993–1994 when Chrysler, after a second brush with bankruptcy in 1991, emerged lean and revitalized.

Harbour said Chrysler was able to knock Ford off the pedestal it had been on since the late 1980s by introducing hot new products, utilizing an efficient product development process, and realizing gains in manufacturing productivity with little or no investment in existing facilities. As a result, Chrysler was able to earn $1,250 and $628 per vehicle in 1994 and 1995, respectively. This compared to Ford's $625 and $415. Either way, Ford was no longer blaming market conditions for its difficulties.[3]

When Ford redesigned its product lines, the company neglected to adequately target cost the development process. *Target costing* is the process of establishing variable cost and investment targets prior to program approval, then designing every part of the vehicle so that it meets the target. Chrysler perfected the process with the Viper. Even GM is target costing with results in both cost advantage and highly satisfied customers.

What Ford needs to concentrate on is what it does right—within a cost-conscious environment. Critical to the success of the company are trucks. Ford is the undisputed leader in the design, manufacture, and sale of trucks. In 1996, Ford, for the first time ever, spent more to develop trucks than it did passenger cars. Ford's success with the F-150, Ranger, Expedition, and the hugely popular Explorer is the envy of the industry.

Though Henry Ford once spurned the consumer credit business, the largest captive automotive finance company in the world is now Ford Credit. With net income in 1995 of $1.4 billion, Ford Credit is also the world's largest and most profitable auto financing company. Ford Credit is the leader in providing financial services to dealers and retail customers. The division operates in approximately 35 countries and provides financial services to over 11,000 dealers and 7.4 million retail customers, 3.5 million in 1995 alone.

In addition to financing, Ford Credit offers extended service contracts and credit and disability insurance to retail customers. Ford Credit also serves non-Ford customers and dealers through PRIMUS Automotive Financial Services. PRIMUS provides financing for Mazda, Jaguar, and other car companies in the United States, Canada, and Europe.[4]

---

[2] Hibbard, Justin, "Assembly Online," *InformationWeek,* April 12, 1999, p. 85(1).

[3] Moad, Jeff, "Ford Shifts Gears," *PC Week,* April 12, 1999, v. 16, i. 15, p. 91(1).
[4] Brown, Eryn, *Fortune,* May 24, 1999, v. 139, i. 10, p. 112(1).

Keys to Ford Credit's success are growth and customer service. As Ford sets its sights on new market opportunities throughout the world, Ford Credit has geared up to meet the demand for financing. Ford Credit is opening a location in Australia to serve as headquarters for the Asia-Pacific region and to oversee new joint ventures in Indonesia, South Korea, and South Africa. Ford Credit is also expanding its operations in Europe and South America. It recently assumed management responsibility for financing operations in Brazil and Argentina following the dissolution of a Ford–Volkswagen joint venture.

In Europe, Ford Credit now has activities in Poland, Greece, the Czech Republic, and Hungary. Even in the United States, the subsidiary is developing growth opportunities. The company recently launched a sub-prime financing business as a way to entice new customers into the Ford family of customers. This line of business provides financing to customers who would normally not qualify for conventional financing. Serving the customer is also a key to Ford Credit's success. It enjoys a high customer satisfaction rating, which benefits both Ford Credit and Ford. Research shows Ford Credit customers are "one-third more likely to replace a Ford car or truck with a new Ford vehicle."[5]

Ford used to operate regionally. This resulted in duplicate efforts in some areas and underserved markets in others. To avoid this overlap and better identify market opportunities, Ford integrated its North American Automotive Operations (NAO) and European Automotive Operations (EAO) into a new group called FAO (previously identified as Ford Automotive Operations). The inclusion of NAO and EAO into FAO will not impact Ford's operations in the Asia-Pacific Rim or Latin America. It will also not affect Ford's relations with Mazda, Volkswagen, or Nissan.[6]

In November 1993, Alex Trotman was named the CEO of Ford. Trotman's appointment was a first for the industry: he is the first non-American to hold the position of CEO of any major U.S. auto manufacturer ("Big Three"). In late 1994, Trotman introduced Ford 2000, a bold venture that will be the Company's largest reorganization effort ever. The initiative took effect on January 1, 1995.

The purpose of Ford 2000 is to transform Ford into a global company, to take advantage of global economies of scale, and to make Ford the best and most profitable automaker in the world. Ford 2000 will permeate every aspect of Ford's operations with far-reaching effects from information systems to new product development,

from the assembly line to suppliers, from Dearborn to New Delhi.

Ford 2000 is not Ford's first reorganization effort on either a domestic or global scale. Ford literally had to reinvent itself in the early 1980s after suffering over $3 billion in losses during the 1980–1982 time period. One executive vice president described the situation: "We *really* believed Ford could die . . . from top executives through middle management and down to the hourly employees." But by 1988, Ford was posting record profits and its vehicles were winning awards. For example, in 1986, the Taurus was named *Motor Trend's* "Car of the Year." In 1987, the Thunderbird Turbo Coupe was also named "Car of the Year."

Ford was able to accomplish this remarkable turnaround in a relatively short period of time by emphasizing product quality, production efficiencies, product and capital investments, process improvements, and more employee involvement.[7]

Ford made a commitment to quality, placing it at the center of its new mission statement. Ford was thus able to extract a 65 percent increase in quality from 1980 to 1988, 80 percent of which came from people—not automation. Ford also built a worldwide computer network for the design headquarters. The network allowed product development teams to work on vehicle designs concurrently rather than in the traditional manner of mail and/or facsimile.

Ford invested in its future by continuing to spend money on capital improvements. Ford spent five times more on capital expenditures than it generated from operations in 1980 and 1981. The company's debt-to-equity ratio increased 55 percent in three years. Although the company's bond ratings fell, the initiative signaled that Ford was determined to make changes. Capital expenditures in 1988 alone were $4.7 billion, funded by the issue of short-term debt.

Ford kept production capacity low, closed 15 plants worldwide, and cut workforces during the period from 1978 to 1986. Ford also decided against building new facilities because internal studies indicated the company could possibly save 30 to 50 percent of the cost to build a new facility by retooling existing plants. Ford took measures to reduce the number of suppliers as a means of exerting control over product quality and delivery times.

Ford solicited employee involvement at all levels on the best way to improve product quality. A top-down approach left a clear impression that change was not only possible to achieve, it was essential to the long-term survival of the company. As a result, employee satisfaction actually grew. The reorganization effort was smoothly implemented.

[5] "Ford Credit: Financing the World Over," Ford Credit Press Release, May 1, 1996, p. 2.
[6] Arnold, Bill and Greenberg, Barry, "Accelerating New Development," Electronic Buyers' News, March 1, 1999, p. E19(1).
[7] Moad, Jeff, "Ford Shifts Gears," *PC Week*, April 12, 1999, v. 16, i. 15, p. 91(1).

Ford also changed how it developed a vehicle. To take advantage of the expertise that existed throughout the world, "development of a specific car or component [was centralized] in whichever Ford technical center worldwide had the greatest expertise in that product. Designers in each market then styled exteriors and passenger compartments to appeal to local tastes."[8]

Previous efforts to become more global had failed. These attempts had focused on the "global car"—a vehicle that would be built with common parts assembled in different locations throughout the world and slightly tailored to appeal to regional tastes. The first global vehicle put into production was the European-designed Escort. Ultimately, the measure failed as each geographic region redesigned the car. In the United States, only six of the Escort's 5,000 parts remained common with their European counterparts.[9]

Ford's most recent attempt at a "global car" was the CDW27 line of cars under the Mondeo (non-U.S.), Ford Contour, and Mercury Mystique names. The time and cost expended to bring the trio into production was $6 billion over a seven-year period. The cars have not sold well in the United States. Critics have called the cars "duds [which] have dated styling, and are not appealing to middle-income families put off by the high price and lack of passenger space."[10] This unprofitable expenditure of time and money is believed to be a driving impetus for the implementation of Ford 2000.

Trotman was appointed CEO in 1993 when Ford's economic situation was excellent. Ford's net income had increased an incredible 110 percent over the previous year, sales growth was strong, the balance sheet was solid, Ford's pension fund was fully funded, and its 5 percent dividend yield was impressive for an automobile manufacturer. Nonetheless, Trotman had bigger ideas for the company. He wanted Ford to be the biggest and the best automobile manufacturer in the world. That meant exceeding General Motors, the world's number one producer of vehicles, and Toyota, the automotive industry's standard-setter in manufacturing efficiencies and car designs. To achieve this two-pronged goal, Ford needed a global mission to unite the company throughout the world. Ford 2000 was Trotman's global mission. Proponents at Ford say that Ford 2000 will achieve the global mission by breaking down regional barriers within the company and replacing it with a single, global management team.

The program, which cuts management levels from 14 to 7, involves eliminating expensive duplication, increasing efficiency, achieving economies of scale, streamlining processes, and pushing responsibility for decision making and accountability throughout the organization.

Ford anticipates annual savings of $2 to 3 billion to come from three major areas. Engineering efficiencies will eliminate duplication of effort. A more efficient utilization of parts and components facilities will lead to plant and equipment manufacturing savings. Finally, a reduction of the supplier base will result from the efficiencies achieved in other areas.

Ford is not only learning from its own mistakes, but is also making concerted efforts not to repeat the mistakes of others. Ford used GM's 1984 reorganization as a model of what to avoid. GM's chaotic reorganization paralyzed the Company for nearly two years, throwing its North American operations into a tailspin from which it is only now recovering.[11] Ford believes management plays a central role in transitioning the company to Ford 2000. Therefore, the company has assigned the top 60 executives with the responsibility of organizing and implementing Ford.

One aspect of Ford 2000 that Ford is stringently applying is the elimination of duplication from the design and manufacturing process. In 1993 alone, Ford needed five passenger cars and seven light- and heavy-duty truck platforms in North America to achieve sales of 4.1 million units. In Europe, it needed five and two, respectively, to achieve sales of 1.3 million units. These numbers do not include Kia, Mazda, Jaguar, or Aston-Martin. Under Ford 2000, Ford will spread the cost of producing units over 5 basic platforms instead of the 19 previously required. Additionally, the following duplication is noted in Ford's production system:

- Six different types of four-cylinder engines
- Five types of V6s
- Five types of V8s
- Twelve types of manual and automatic transmissions
- Forty-six different steering wheels
- Thirty-three different types of batteries in the United States and/or Europe alone.

Ford's efforts not only affect its operations, they also impact Ford's suppliers in important ways. A long-term relationship with Ford both excites and worries suppliers. As Ford consolidates the supplier base, volume for suppliers to bid on will increase. Common sizing will mean fewer redundancies—fewer components mean fewer programs on which to bid.

Ford wants key, full-service suppliers to provide materials that account for 60 percent of Ford's costs. To make being a full-service provider lucrative, Ford is integrating suppliers into the design and development

[8] Pelofsky, Mark, "Transformation at Ford," *Harvard Business School*, 9-390-083, November 15, 1991, p. 14.
[9] Ibid., p. 10.
[10] Walton, Mary, "When Your Partner Fails You," *Fortune*, May 1997, p. 134.
[11] McElroy, John, "Trotman Re-Engineers Ford," *Automotive Industries*, May 1994, p. 33.

processes earlier, with more of a long-term stake in product development.[12] For example, Johnson Controls began designing the seats for Ford's then secret Expedition SUV in 1992.

For suppliers, doing business with the new Ford means they will probably have to make some changes in their organizations. For suppliers who already have operations in North America and Europe, Ford 2000 means they no longer need two different strategies. "It does clarify the interfaces," says ITT automobile boss Tim Leuliotte. "Today, it does not take more than electronic mail for any quote that goes into Ford Europe to show up on a desk in Dearborn, and vice-versa."[13]

A significant problem for suppliers may be getting familiar with Ford's new organizational system. With fewer levels of management, suppliers face an ever-changing company. Another challenge was how to achieve the 5 percent annual savings reduction between 1996 and 1999 called for by Carlos Mazzorin, vice president of production and purchasing.[14]

The mandate has not gone over well with suppliers who believe Ford is merely pushing all the cost reduction efforts onto them. Mazzorin clarifies the issue by saying that these savings can come either from Ford's or the suppliers' efforts. "I'm not after the margins of the suppliers. I believe we're going to do it together."[15] The rewards are long-term, large-volume contracts with the company.

The gamble is huge. If successful, Ford "could be a big winner as the industry consolidates. If [it] fails, it will be one of the most expensive re-engineering lessons ever."[16] Ford has not disclosed how much the Ford 2000 program is costing the company in implementation and reorganization costs.

FINANCIAL AND PORTFOLIO ANALYSIS

Ford recorded net income in 1996 of $4.4 billion on sales and revenues of $147 million. Total unit sales were up 47,000 units to 6,653,000. Consistent with the Ford 2000 initiatives begun in 1995, capital expenditures were down $467 million from 1995. The Ford 2000 reorganization program seeks to reuse existing Ford facilities as part of Ford cost-cutting efforts.

Although sales of the Taurus and Contour/Mystique have not met company hopes and expectations, customer reception of the Expedition and Jaguar XK8, both of which were introduced in 1996, is strong. In fact, demand for the Expedition is so strong that Ford has dedicated a production facility to the Expedition that is currently running on a 24-hour basis. In the United States and Canada, Ford has also completed launches of its highest volume vehicles, the Escort and F-Series pickup truck.

Financial Services continues to perform well and is becoming a more important part of the overall success of Ford. This unit posted net income of $2.8 billion in 1996, an increase of 34 percent over the previous fiscal year. A one-time action, the sale of USL Capital's assets of $512 million, accounted for the majority of the increase. Ford Credit, which represents approximately 52 percent of Financial Services' consolidated net income, posted a lower net income in 1996 over 1995 due mainly to higher credit losses and higher loss reserve requirements. The losses were partially offset by higher earnings on assets and improved net interest margins.[17]

Ford's preferred method of marketing its vehicles is advertising through print and television media. In fact, automakers as a whole spend more on advertising to promote their vehicles than any other product. When Ford introduced the new generation Taurus in 1995, it spent $55 million on promotion through the mass media and media-sponsored events. Between 1995 and 1997, advertising expenditures for the Taurus increased by 18 percent.

RISK ANALYSIS

In addition to competitive pressure from other vehicle manufacturers, Ford faced extensive government regulation. Ford was the subject of three separate federal investigations concerning ignition switches. Ford disclosed it was studying the potential problems in the ignition switches, which were installed in approximately 23 million cars and trucks spanning the 1984 to 1993 model years. On April 25, 1996, Ford recalled approximately 8.7 million cars and trucks for faulty ignition switches that could cause the vehicles to catch fire even if the vehicles were not running. The vehicles included in the recall were the bulk of the 1988 to 1992 (and some 1993) model year vehicles. The recall was prompted by eight class action suits and media pressure. Although not part of a formal recall, Ford stated that pre-1988 vehicle owners might wish to replace the ignition switches at their own expense if concerned about the potential for fires.

[12] "Ford 2000 Calls for More Engineering by Suppliers," *Machine Design*, October 2, 1995, p. 26.
[13] McElroy, John, "Trotman Re-Engineers Ford," *Automotive Industries*, May 1994, p. 33.
[14] "E-Commerce Starts and Stops," *InternetWeek*, May 3, 1999, p. 7(1).
[15] Keenan, Tim, "Waste Warriors: Automaker Purchasing Chiefs Want Leaner Suppliers," *Ward's Auto World*, December 1995, p. 59.
[16] "Trotman's Global Gambit," *Chief Executive*, September 1996, p. 49.

[17] Cronin, Mary J., *Fortune*, May 24, 1999, v. 139, i. 10, p. 114(1).

All automobile manufacturers are under pressure from the federal government to make vehicles that are safer, more fuel efficient, and less harmful to the environment. The National Vehicle and Fuel Emissions Laboratory of the EPA has outlined the Clean Air Act of 1990 as having "provisions to further control ground-level ozone (urban smog), carbon monoxide, particle emissions from diesel engines, air toxins, and acid rain."

Automobile manufacturers are subject to government safety standards and regulations that require corporate average fuel economy (CAFÉ), damageability, and theft protection of new motor vehicles. Regulations govern manufacturing and assembly facilities relating to air emissions, water discharge (covered under the Federal Water Pollution Control Act), and hazardous waste disposal. The federal government is also urging automakers to develop alternative fuel source vehicles, specifically, electric cars. Ford has an electric vehicle in the design phase.[18]

Ford is also a defendant in several product liability suits and other litigation including suits for damages arising out of alleged defects in occupant restraint systems. Nine class action lawsuits are currently pending against Ford that allege that Ford Bronco II utility vehicles have a tendency to roll over. Other legal actions seek damages from contact with Ford parts and products that contain asbestos. Ford is also a defendant in four separate patent infringement actions and six class action lawsuits that allege defects in paint processes used by Ford on certain vehicles.

INDUSTRY AND MARKET ANALYSIS

Ford operates in a highly competitive industry due to broad competition and the cyclical nature of the industry. Demand for Ford cars and trucks is dependent on economic conditions, the cost of raw materials and labor, and the availability of financing.

In 1994, Ford had 5 of the top 10 selling vehicles in the United States with the following models: Escort, Taurus, F-150 pickup truck series, Ranger small pickup truck series, and the Explorer SUV. With a net income of $5.3 billion, 1994 was also Ford's best year on record. Despite Ford's recent success, Ford stumbled. Net income fell by 22 percent in 1995; the company fell behind GM in product quality, as measured by J.D. Power and Associates. Chrysler won in styling and Toyota led in factory logistics and efficiency.[19]

During the 1990s Ford patterned itself after Toyota, the industry leader in quality vehicles. Two of Ford's recent efforts, the Ford Taurus and the Contour/Mystique, made dramatic strides in quality but with a corresponding increase in price. Whether or not the traditional Ford customer is willing to spend more for this new generation of Ford products remains to be seen.

ROLE OF RESEARCH AND DEVELOPMENT

Ford is trying to expand the market for its vehicles. One interesting approach is a concept car for the elderly. Previously written off as having no economic clout, Ford now recognizes that the elderly are a burgeoning demographic group that is living and driving longer. Ford has developed a car for the over-60 population that allows drivers to continue to enjoy driving while the vehicle aids the senior driver suffering from poor vision, restricted movement, and slower reaction times. Some of the technology Ford is incorporating into these cars includes:

- Seats that swivel.
- Heads-up displays which project speed and mileage onto the windshield so the driver does not have to take his/her eyes off the road.
- Magnified rear-view mirrors.
- Radar-assisted parking.
- Button touch brakes.
- Larger instrument panels.

Ford spoke to scores of elderly motorists about the difficulties they experienced while driving and simulated the problems associated with aging to facilitate their research. Eventually, Ford plans to incorporate these ideas into all models and says that the changes in vehicle design will be welcomed by drivers of all ages.[20]

TECHNOLOGICAL STORY

Ford 2000 has had a profound impact on Ford's technology and information systems. Ford expanded the computer network begun in the late 1980s and is attempting to centralize the operations of the design and manufacturing teams. Because Ford is adamant about removing redundancy and Ford 2000 aims to integrate systems into a single, global environment, the computer network is critical to success.

In a recent *Fortune* article, Mary Walton, whose new book about Ford, *Car: A Drama of the American Workplace*, discusses the failure of the Taurus in the marketplace. One of the reasons for the failure of the redesigned vehicle and the automaker's present difficulties is the implementation of Ford 2000. Ms. Walton spent two years with the Taurus development team observing the trials and tribulations of updating the five-time "Best Selling Car in America."

Ms. Walton noted that the circumstances under which the Taurus was originally developed, a sense of

---

[18] Nauss, Donald W., "Ford Unveils Plan to Become World's Biggest Recycler," *Los Angeles Times,* April 27, 1999, p. C1 c. 2.

[19] Taylor, Alex III, "Ford's Really Big Leap at the Future: It's Risky, It's Worth It, and It May Not Work," *Fortune,* September 8, 1995, p. 134.

[20] Wilder, Clinton, "GM Goes Online for Buying," *InformationWeek,* March 22, 1999, p. 26(1).

market urgency and shared mission, were absent during the redesign phase. Instead, the focus of the Taurus development team and the company's corporate culture was on meeting tight production schedules and financial targets. The focus was an about-face for Ford. In trying to avoid the financial fiasco of the CDW27 vehicles, Ford placed so much emphasis on cost control that the development process became rigid. The obsession with controlling cost and keeping the vehicle on schedule also alienated suppliers.

TECHNOLOGICAL INVESTMENT AND ANALYSIS

The global computer network, Global Studio, enables team members throughout the world to work online with one another and impact design and manufacture changes instantaneously. Coupled with other technology being implemented, the global network system will also help avoid lengthy and expensive product simulations, enable designers to view products being developed in other parts of the world, replace sketches and clay models as design tools and stages, and facilitate global communication. The Global Studio will allow teams to share data on a variety of subjects, including ergonomic studies, air flow analyses, crash simulations, digital mockups, and general and group engineering review.

Ford has encountered difficulty in implementing the process. Information technology (IT) has over 5,000 people who labor to support 7,000 engineering workstations and 85,000 PCs. Migration to the new system has been difficult. Convincing the system users of the advantages of Global Studio has been a laborious task. IT director Bill Powers has even encountered resistance from information technology personnel.[21]

To facilitate the retraining process and ensure further integration of the worldwide systems, Powers has permanently moved the head engineers from each of Ford's systems to the Systems Integration Center in Dearborn, Michigan, where they work to establish the best infrastructure for the company. The integration issue is likely to become more difficult as employees are forced to work as a team and understand elements that were not previously part of their jobs. Smaller teams may be able to integrate faster, but as "larger units grapple with issues of time, costs, redundancy, and training, Powers is likely to discover many issues forming that could slow down the re-engineering effort."[22]

The implementation of the Global Studio is severely limited by technological parameters such as bandwidth. This limits the amount of information that can be sent at once. Local communications laws define what can

and cannot be done. The infrastructure and the capabilities of each country vary significantly.

In 1996, Ford launched a project called C3P, or CAD/CAM/CAE, and Product Information Management. The goal is to assist Ford to cut prototype costs by 50 percent, improve efficiencies by 20 to 30 percent, and eliminate one-half of the company's costly late development design changes. Before C3P, it used to take two to three months to build, assemble, and test a prototype of a car's chassis. "Using the C3P technologies, Ford can do all that in less than two weeks," says Richard Riff, a C3P project officer. The system should help Ford reduce its product development lead time even further.

While developing the Global Studio, Ford has also had to contend with issues of security. Ford uses the Total Control Security Server, a system that manages sign-on requests originating from a SecureID card, a separate device from Security Dynamics. The SecureID card is a changing "lock and key" device that generates one-time passwords for user authentication. The credit card-sized device, which is synchronized with the security server, generates a new six-digit number every 60 seconds on an LCD display creating a cryptographic key. When an employee types in the number displayed and her unique PIN to request remote access, the security server runs an algorithm using the time and the cryptographic key. It then matches the number to the card it comes from. If all the pieces fit together, the server accepts the sign-on.

TECHNOLOGICAL INNOVATIONS

NETWORK

Ford's intranet connects about 120,000 of Ford's computers around the world to web sites containing proprietary company information such as market research, rankings of suppliers' parts, and analyses of competitors' components. The chief benefit of this network is that Ford is able to bring new models into full production in 24 months compared with 36 months before.

The intranet is expected to save the company billions of dollars. Ford plans to use its intranet to achieve manufacturing on demand. This would be a process that involves coordination of delivery and assembly of thousands of components. The company plans to manufacture most of its vehicles on a demand basis by 1999. This will require linking its 15,000 dealers around the world to the intranet.[23]

TELECOMMUNICATIONS

Ford has a pilot test in which consumers in Houston and Boston can use the Internet to buy used Fords, Mercurys,

[21] Leong, Kathy Chin, "Intranet Drives Ford's Efforts," *InternetWeek*, October 26, 1998, p. 47(1).

[22] Callaway, Erin, "Global Gamble," *PC Week*, May 22, 1995, p. E1.

[23] Medford, Cassimir, "Inside Outsourcing," *VARbusiness*, June 14, 1999, p. 72.

and Lincolns (www. fordpreowned.com). In recent years, Ford has found it far more difficult to sell used cars than the new models. Many used cars come off multiyear leases and have up to 36,000 miles on the odometer.[24]

DATA

In 1996, Ford awarded an outsourcing contract to Ryder Integrated Logistics Inc. to design and manage an integrated just-in-time supply chain and transportation system for Ford's 20 North American manufacturing plants. This is in conjunction with a project to integrate its plants' individual supply chain systems.[25] It will connect them to suppliers for real-time information about component and part inventories, as well as real-time tracking of deliveries. The system will help Ford "squeeze out" the cost of transporting parts and components to its plants. The consolidated system would let Ford managers monitor when plants in the same area need deliveries of similar auto parts. Currently, each plant's shipments are delivered individually by separate trucks. Managers will be able to coordinate parts transportation to multiple plants in the same region using just one truck.[26]

RECOMMENDATION FOR THE FUTURE

Alex Trotman will be judged by the success or failure of his Ford 2000 initiative. If successful, the ghosts of Henry Ford II may be dispelled and the office of CEO will be known as Trotman's office as well. If unsuccessful, Ford may find itself in a situation similar to the late 1970s and early 1980s. Ford 2000 and Trotman are already being blamed for the dip in profits. The most vocal critique of the Ford 2000 performance to date seems to come from automotive analysts and Wall Street. Some critics contend that the Ford recovery may take 10 years to accomplish.[27]

---

[24] Wilder, Clinton, "Slow Revolution in E-Commerce," *InformationWeek,* February 8, 1999, p. ER18(1).
[25] Sweat, Jeff, and Stein, Tom, "Killer Supply Chains," *InformationWeek,* November 9, 1998, p. 36(1).

[26] Wallace, Bob, "Ford Suppliers Get Call to Design," *Computerworld,* March 8, 1999, p. 1(1).
[27] Moad, Jeff, "Ford Shifts Gears," *PC Week,* April 12, 1999, v. 16, i. 15, p. 90(1).

CASE QUESTIONS

Strategic Questions

1. What is the strategic direction of the corporation/organization?

2. Who or what forces are driving this direction?

3. What has been the catalyst for change?

4. What are the critical success factors for this corporation/organization?

5. What are the core competencies for this corporation/organization?

Technological Questions

6. What technologies has the corporation relied on?

7. What has caused a change in the use of technology in the corporation/organization?

8. How has this change been implemented?

9. Who has driven this change throughout the organization?

10. How successful has the technological change been?

Quantitative Questions

11. What does the corporation say about its financial ability to embark on a major technological program of advancement?

12. What conclusions can be reached from an analysis of the financial information to support or contradict this financial ability?

13. Are there long-term trends that seem to be problematic?

Industry Questions

14. What challenges and opportunities is the industry facing?

15. Is the industry oligopolistic or competitive?

16. Does the industry face a change in government regulation?

Data Questions

17. What role do data play in the future of the corporation?

18. How important are data to the corporation's continued success?

19. How will the capture and maintenance of customer data impact the corporation's future?

GENERAL MOTORS CO.

Executive Summary

Case Name:	General Motors Co.
Case Industry:	Automobile industry
Major Technology Issue:	Integrating all of the different GM computer systems into a common system
Major Financial Issue:	Reducing the costs of production and improving profitability per unit
Major Strategic Issue:	Regaining market share lost, growing the business, and competing on a global basis
Major Player:	John F. Smith, Jr., President and CEO
Main Web Page:	www.gm.com
Recommendations:	The implementation of improved strategic technology to better understand the customer, streamline development efforts, and reduce manufacturing costs.

CASE ANALYSIS

INTRODUCTORY STORY

"I ask you to think back to the 1980s for the moment. GM was even called a dinosaur. We have since restructured our company, lowered our costs, improved our quality, wholeheartedly embraced lean manufacturing and common processes, and produced an entire new line of exciting cars and trucks," said John F. Smith, Jr., president and CEO of General Motors, in a speech delivered to The Executives' Club of Chicago on April 17, 1997.

Information systems and computer services have had an important role in this process. The push toward a consistent information system (IS) infrastructure has been a great challenge for GM since 1984 when GM bought Electronic Data Systems (EDS) for $2.5 billion. After 12 controversial years, GM spun-off EDS and looked for a CIO to build an internal information strategy and management capability.

Effective June 28, 1996, GM named Ralf J. Szygenda, former CIO of Bell Atlantic, to the position of vice president and CIO. Szygenda had to face two major challenges. One was to impose order on a highly autonomous information systems groups within GM's operational units. The other was to ensure that outsourcing vendor EDS provided the best service at the best price as it sought to build its non-GM business after being spun-off from GM. Szygenda's main work was to develop and implement information technology strategy that would help CEO Smith fully implement his four top priority goals:

- getting common
- running lean
- competing on a global basis
- growing the business

SHORT DESCRIPTION OF THE COMPANY

General Motors Corporation (GM) is the largest producer of automobiles and one of the biggest manufacturers in the world. GM designs, manufactures, and markets cars, trucks, automotive systems, heavy-duty transmissions, and locomotives worldwide. The company employs 649,000 people and total revenues exceeded $164 million in 1996. GM owns 250 manufacturing, distribution, and service facilities in the United States. It also operates in more than 50 countries. General Motors Corporation consists of the following five major divisions:

GM-NAO/Delphi. General Motors North American Operations designs, manufactures, and markets vehicles for the following nameplates: Chevrolet, Pontiac, Oldsmobile, Buick, Cadillac, GMC, Saturn, and EV 1. Delphi Automotive Systems is the world's most diverse supplier of automotive systems and components. Operating in 36 countries, Delphi offers expertise in the areas of chassis, interior, lighting, electric energy and electric management, steering and thermal systems. In 1996, 32.7 percent of Delphi's sales were to non-GM-NAO customers.[1]

---

[1] *GM Annual Report 1996*, p. 25.

GM-IO. General Motors International Operations designs, manufactures, and markets automobiles outside North America. The nameplates include Opel in Germany, Vauxhall in the United Kingdom, Holden in Australia, Isuzu in Japan, and Saab in Sweden.

GMAC. General Motors Acceptance Corporation provides a broad range of financial services, including consumer vehicle financing, full-service leasing and truck extended service contracts, residential and mortgage services, and vehicle and homeowners insurance. GMAC's businesses span 33 markets around the world. In 1996, GMAC became the first automotive financial services company to offer an online credit application on the Internet.[2]

Hughes. Hughes Electronic Corporation designs, manufactures, and markets advanced technology electronic systems, products and services for the telecommunications, space, automotive electronics, and aerospace and defense industries on a global basis. Hughes also includes Delco Electronics, which manufactures electronics products and components primarily for the automotive industry.

Others. Other GM businesses include GM Locomotive Group and Allison Transmissions, which is the world's largest manufacturer of heavy-duty automatic transmissions for trucks and buses, off-highway equipment, and military equipment.

In 1996, the highest income was generated by GM-O, followed by GM-NAO. Although GM is a car company, its nonautomotive businesses generate sales sufficient to rank among the top 30 in the Fortune 500. International operations are strong, as is the financial company. GM-NAO, on the other hand, is fighting for market share and trying to increase profitability. The new information systems policy and its implementation is particularly significant to the improvement of GM-NAO.

SHORT HISTORY OF THE COMPANY

The beginning of General Motors can be traced to 1898 when R. E. Olds converted his father's naval and industry engine factory into the Olds Motor Vehicle Company.[3] The first model proved to be successful. Olds founded the first American factory dedicated exclusively to the production of automobiles. A few years later, David Buick started a factory as well.

Market forces made some manufacturers disappear and others form consortiums. William Durant, the son of a Michigan governor who served as a director of the Buick Motor Company at that time, brought Oldsmobile and Buick together to organize the General Motors Company in 1908. Chevrolet joined the company in 1918. By 1920, more than 30 companies were acquired.[4] The corporation suffered during the years of the Great Depression, but did produce a profit even during this difficult period.[5]

By 1941, General Motors accounted for 44 percent of the total U.S. automotive sales, compared with 12 percent in 1921. During World War II GM retooled its factories for the defense effort. From 1940 to 1945 GM manufactured products from small bearings to large tanks, naval ships, fighting planes, bombers, guns, cannons, and projectiles worth $12.3 billion.

Car manufacturing resumed after the war. Postwar expansion resulted in increased production. Record automotive sales and innovations in styling and engineering characterized the decade of the 1950s. General Motors improved aerodynamics and introduced automatic transmissions.

In the second half of the 1950s, GM underestimated demand for smaller European cars. The small models GM introduced in the late 1950s failed to attract customers' interest and its market share slipped. In 1956, a year of decreasing sales, Ford, Chrysler, and General Motors lost 15 percent in sales while imports virtually doubled their market penetration.

In the 1960s, GM prospered again by diversifying into home appliances, insurance, locomotives, electronics, banking, and finance. By the late 1960s after-tax profits for the industry reached a 13 percent return on investment. General Motors' return on investment increased from 16.5 percent to 25.8 percent.[6]

Like the rest of the industry, General Motors had largely ignored the importance of air pollution control. The oil crisis of the early 1970s caused additional troubles. General Motors' luxury, gas guzzling car sales dropped 35 percent in 1974. The company's compact and subcompact sales rose steadily to attain a 40 percent market share. Ford, Chrysler, and General Motors were unprepared for the shift in consumer demand. General Motors suffered the greatest losses. The company spent $2.25 billion in 1974 and 1975 to meet local and federal regulations on pollution control. By the end of 1977 that figure doubled.[7]

Management's strategy in the 1980s was to pursue strategic initiatives that reflected the kind of foresight that seemed to be missing in previous years. The com-

---

[2] Ibid., p. 26.
[3] *International Directory of Company History,* 1998 ed., v. I, p. 171.

[4] Ibid.
[5] *The World Book Multimedia Encyclopedia,* General Motors Corporation, p. 433.
[6] *International Directory,* p. 172
[7] Ibid.

Table 7.1 GM Hourly Employees at Year-End

	1996	1995	1994	1993
U.S. Hourly Employees*	236,600	247,300	248,700	262,200
Excluding Delphi & amp; Delco	161,000	169,600	169,900	172,600

*Excludes Electromotive, New Venture Gear, Allison Transmission, and other nonautomotive subsidiaries. Includes active, protective, temporary layoff, and indefinite layoff.
(*Source:* Company data and Morgan Stanley Research.)

pany made two major acquisitions. In 1994, GM bought Ross Perot's EDS, a highly successful computer services company. The purpose of this takeover was to introduce information systems that would speed all operations and eliminate unnecessary labor. Another acquisition, Hughes Aircraft, was to provide GM with the best technology in microelectronics and system engineering.

GM's auto market share slipped during the 1980s and in 1990 and 1991 it lost more than $6 billion. GM sought to regain profitability by consolidating operations and reducing excess manufacturing capacity. In 1991, the company announced that over 20 plants would close by 1995 and 74,000 workers would be laid off (Table 7.1).

New management led by Jack Smith was introduced in 1992.[8] Having exceeded its break-even goal in 1994, GM's management laid out a long-term goal to earn an average 5 percent return on sales over an economic cycle's full course. To achieve this, GM shifted gears from accelerated restructuring and workforce reduction to rebuilding its product lines and boosting productivity from its downsized plant network.[9]

In the second half of the 1990s, GM refocused on its core business. To begin, GM completed the spin-off of EDS in June 1996. In January 1997, General Motors announced a series of planned "Hughes Transactions." The transactions included the tax-free spin-off of the Hughes defense business, followed immediately by the tax-free merger of that business with Raytheon Company. At the same time, Delco Electronics, the automotive electronics subsidiary of Hughes, was transferred from Hughes to General Motors' Delphi Automotive Systems unit.

GM has unique handicaps rooted in its history and culture. GM-NAO grew up as a collection of six separate vehicle makers. Lacking unity and direction, the division became easy prey for powerful independent constituencies: suppliers, dealers, and labor unions. Thus, GM-NAO had nearly a half million employees and operated without centralized manufacturing, purchasing, data processing, advertising, or market research.[10]

With 82 models of cars and trucks, GM is a big believer in shelf space. Rather than building a single family sedan—like Toyota Camry or Honda Accord—GM sells four sedans aimed at different segments, ranging from conservative to sporty. GM executives think that people have been compromising their tastes to buy a Camry just to get the quality.

In 1996, GM implemented brand management in North America to determine a better way to separate individual models and still maintain the economies of scale that come from common engineering. GM adopted a process of defining and targeting discrete groups of customers through a research technique called *needs segmentation.* After completing a lengthy survey of tens of thousands of car buyers, it divided them into about 30 needs segments based on such characteristics as income, age, family size, and driving habits. Buyers of sport utility vehicles, for instance, were subdivided into six segments. A group of brand managers and their teams are focused on building strong brand equity and clearer, more specific roles for each vehicle brand.

The goal of the new direction is to supply a full product line of vehicles with distinctive personalities for every stage of a customer's life.[11] This is a very controversial approach to building cars. GM rigorously tests concepts with customers, then shows them scale models of the actual vehicle all the way through the design process. Customers even get a chance to feel how the car will drive by climbing into a $1 million programmable mockup. Like everything else at GM, product development suffered from multiple processes and personalities. The "large number of segments and various products" approach puts even more importance on implementing common and standardized production. To achieve acceptable margin it is crucial to coordinate research and development, supplier relations, and manufacturing process through an integrated information system.[12]

FINANCIAL AND PORTFOLIO ANALYSIS

After interest and taxes, General Motors' North American Operations had 1996 net income of $1.2 billion, compared with over $2 billion in 1995 and $677

---

[8] *GM Annual Report 1996,* p. 3.
[9] *Standard & Poor Industry Survey, Autos-Auto Parts,* January 1997, p. A86.
[10] Taylor III, Alex, "GM: Time to Get in Gear," *Fortune 500,* April 1997, p. 96.

[11] *GM Annual Report 1996,* p. 28.
[12] "Sell to Seniors," *Computerworld,* May 24, 1999, p. 37(1).

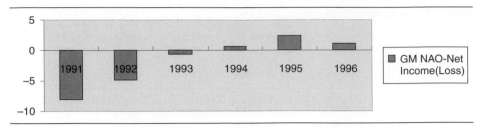

Figure 7.1 GM-NAO net income (loss) in billions of U.S. dollars. (*Source:* Company data.)

million in 1994. But the three previous years were disastrous, with GM suffering net losses of $600 million (1993), $4.8 billion (1992), and $8.1 billion (1991) (Figure 7.1).

The 1995 net income increase was due primarily to revenue growth, global sourcing savings, and previously reduced manufacturing costs. GM's 1996 performance was hurt by several strikes, higher sales incentives to sell older models, and numerous new product launches. In 1998, net income decreased to $2.9 billion from $6.7 billion in 1997.

Over the last few years, GM's profit per unit in North America has been the lowest of the Big Three by a wide margin. In 1996, GM-NAO posted a pretax profit per unit of $172—$672 behind Ford's $844 profit per unit in North America and sharply lower than Chrysler's $2,207. See Tables 7.2 and 7.3. The results were exceptionally poor because GM had launch costs and labor disruptions that reduced profitability in the most recent quarters.

Production of new generation vehicles is increasing. As a result, profits in North America from vehicle production should increase beyond that which might be attributable to volume increase alone.

Table 7.2 GM-NAO Pretax Profit Per Unit

	1993	1994	1995	1996
Ford	$381	$1,013	$634	$844
GM	($230)	$284	$592	$172
Chrysler WW	$1,644	$2,284	$1,214	$2,207

Note: GM results do not adjust for the strike. (*Source:* Morgan Stanley.)

Table 7.3 GM-NAO Pretax Profit Per Unit

	1993	1994	1995	1996
GM B/(W) than Ford	($611)	($730)	($41)	($672)
GM B/(W) than Chrysler	($1,874)	($2,001)	($622)	($2,035)

B/(W) = Better / (Worse) (*Source:* Morgan Stanley.)

Rebuilding product lines and boosting productivity from the downsized plant network has resulted in significant improvements in return on assets since 1993 (Figure 7.2). GM's ROA of 3.3 percent in 1995 was even better than Ford's 1.8 percent, but still far below Chrysler's 4.1 percent.

SG&A expense has been increasing as a result of the company's full-court press to reestablish/increase "brand equity." SGA expense as a percentage of sales was equal to 7.5 percent in the first quarter. That compares with 7.0 percent in 1996, 6.2 percent in 1995, and 6.5 percent in 1994. The brand equity strategy is to stabilize, as much as possible, pricing over the life cycle of models.[13] The intent is not to eliminate the need for incentives, but rather to mitigate and smooth their impact over the product's life cycle.

GM's cash flow is strong and the company has adequate liquidity to maintain spending through the next downturn, assuming that the company performs in a similar manner as in the last downturn. GM used $7.6 billion in cash during the last recession. In addition, because of its underfunded pension, GM contributed $6.3 billion worth of GM class E stock to its pension fund. However, GM's cash flow would have been even worse had the company not cut capital spending sharply. Capital spending at GM averaged $6.6 billion per year in the late 1980s, or 6 percent of sales. In the early 1990s, GM reduced its capital spending to $6.3 billion per year or 5 percent of sales. See Table 7.4 for details.

During 1995 and 1996, GM invested heavily again, on equipment such as new presses, dies, and tool sets. The company purchased roughly 2,400 new dies for an estimated $800 million. As a result, depreciation and amortization remained at relatively high levels. Given these modernization efforts in body fabrication, body-in-white engineering, and die engineering, the machinery and tool costs of manufacturing decreased. Had GM kept capital spending at a constant percentage of sales over the period, cash flow would have reached a negative $16.7 billion.

---

[13] *GM Company Report,* Prudential Securities, April 23, 1997, p. 11.

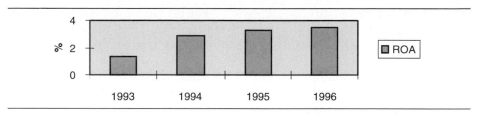

Figure 7.2 GM's return on assets. (*Source:* Standard & Poor, Morgan Stanley.)

Table 7.4 GM Automotive—Capital Spending

	Sales	**Depreciation**	**Capx**	**Depreciation-Capx**	**Depreciation-Capx/sh**	**Capx/Sales**
1991	$ 94,828.00*	$4,671.10	$5,783.60	($1,112.50)	($1.81)	6.10%
1992	$103,004.90	$5,209.10	$5,349.10	($140.00)	($0.21)	5.20%
1993	$108,027.20	$5,281.90	$5,164.80	$117.10	$0.17	4.80%
1994[†]	$123,670.30	$5,873.00	$5,545.40	$327.60	$0.28	4.50%
1995[†]	$132,261.80	$6,299.00	$8,215.00	($1,916.00)	($2.56)	6.20%
1996[†]	$133,725.70	$6,585.00	$8,953.70	($2,368.70)	($3.13)	6.70%

*Dollars in thousands, except for share data.
[†]Excluding EDS. (*Source:* Morgan Stanley.)

With GM now having $10.6 billion in net cash on its books, it appears that it still needs roughly $6 billion to weather another downturn of similar magnitude to the last recession and to maintain capital spending. This should be more than offset by the value of GMH stock expected to be left after the sale of defense operations is complete.[14]

STOCK/INVESTMENT OUTLOOK

Like the rest of the automobile industry, GM's stock performance is cyclical in relation to the market, business growth, and the interest rate.

RISK ANALYSIS

To compete successfully with its United States and, even more importantly, Japanese competitors, GM has simplified and standardized its manufacturing processes. Even stamping, a simple process, is unbelievably complicated at GM. Pieces stamped by Pontiac for a particular model do not fit on a nearly identical car made by Buick. GM is spending $850 million to standardize the die production at 13 plants and reduce the number of press line setups from 57 to 6. GM will spend about $2,700 per ton for stamping, compared to $2,300 at Toyota.

GM's assembly plants are as complicated as the stamping process. The Pontiac Grand Prix, introduced in 1988, was built in its own dedicated plant in Fairfax, near Kansas City. But when Grand Prix sales fell off, production was cut from two shifts to one, and the factory lost money for years. Now the Fairfax plant has been reengineered with flexible machinery; it can build both the Grand Prix and a new Oldsmobile called the Intrigue. The plant now runs on two shifts. With the expensive equipment fully utilized, the Grand Prix has changed from a money loser to a moneymaker. GM takes 29 hours to put together the Pontiac at the Fairfax plant. GM hoped to improve this number to 22 hours by the end of 1999. Yet, Toyota already assembles Camrys in 20 hours.[15]

GM is pursuing other avenues to improve productivity. Its primary goal is to redesign vehicles to require fewer parts and less manufacturing time. GM's newest vehicle designs incorporate 20 to 30 percent fewer individual parts and require 25 percent fewer assembly labor hours than their predecessors. Some of the previous vehicles were designed as long ago as 1981. The reduction in part counts and labor requirements will lead to substantially lower manufacturing costs when the plants producing these vehicles reach full capacity. As GM expands these advances to the rest of its product line, we can anticipate large increases in its production

[14] *GM Company Report*, Morgan Stanley, March 12, 1997, p. 12.

[15] Taylor, "GM: Time to Get in Gear," p. 100.

efficiency, improvement in vehicle quality measurements, and wider profit margins.[16]

Even if GM significantly improves its quality and productivity, the company has to make sure it makes cars customers want. GM was accused of no longer listening to the customer in 1978, when internal politics and misinterpreted customer research defeated a GM minivan prototype. Six years later Chrysler introduced the hot-selling Dodge Caravan. This decision cost GM billions in sales.[17]

INDUSTRY AND MARKET ANALYSIS

Car manufacturing is one of the largest industries in the United States, accounting directly and indirectly for one out of seven U.S. jobs. The period between 1950 and 1956 was particularly prosperous in the United States, with a rise in demand for a second car in the family. However, Americans were beginning to show real interest in smaller European cars. By 1956, a year of decreasing sales, Ford, Chrysler, and General Motors had lost some 15 percent in sales while imports were virtually doubling their market penetration. In 1957 the United States imported more cars than it exported. Despite a recession, imports accounted for more than 8 percent of U.S. car sales.[18] There was a strong revival in the 1980s. Total vehicle sales reached an all time high in 1986 with 16.3 million vehicles sold.[19] During this period, the Japanese automakers strengthened their position and gained significant market share in the United States.

The slow growth in disposable personal income since 1990 caused a gradual upturn in vehicle sales beginning in 1993 and 1994.

In the first half of the 1990s, a persistent rise in the value of the Japanese yen compared with the dollar severely eroded the cost competitiveness of Japanese vehicles in the United States market and dramatically improved the Big Three's competitive position. These gains would erode if the yen continued to weaken compared with the dollar.

The Big Three automakers were benefiting not only from the exchange rate shift, but also from a decade of restructuring, reengineering, and rebuilding their business base. Favorable economic conditions combined with increased efficiency, productivity gains, and improvements in quality and design resulted in record-high earnings for the Big Three in 1994 and strong aggregate profits in 1995.

For the OEMs, growth opportunities arise from several sources. First, there is the rush to add high-tech features to vehicles to distinguish them and to comply with safety and emission regulations. In addition, opportunities are improving to gain business from Japanese automakers in the United States and in Japan following the 1995 United States–Japan trade accord. Global expansion is also helping those parts producers that are structuring their businesses to support U.S. automakers' efforts to consolidate designs across their international operations and expand their international businesses.

Automakers are asking parts makers to extend their capabilities so they can deliver assemblies instead of just parts. This has sparked a new round of consolidation in the auto parts industry among suppliers with complementary parts to support geographic expansion. The Big Three require substantial cost reductions from their outside parts suppliers. Suppliers, in turn, are responding with aggressive programs to enhance productivity and improve efficiency. They are learning to function in an era of price freezes and reductions.

To stimulate further manufacturing cost improvements, automakers are resorting to new product development strategies that give parts manufacturers greater input and allows them to share the benefits of cost savings and productivity enhancements. Parts manufacturers are rewarded for bearing some of the risk entailed in developing new vehicle systems. This gain-sharing approach has worked best for Ford and Chrysler. General Motors has been slow to implement such a strategy, partly because of more vertical integration. General Motors produces 70 percent of its vehicle content, compared with 50 percent at Ford and less than 30 percent at Chrysler.

Currency fluctuations have encouraged the trend toward increased productions of foreign models in North America and a reduced flow of actual imports. In particular, the long-term appreciation of the Japanese yen versus the dollar has now reversed. This has caused many Japanese automakers to increase their North American manufacturing capacity to maintain competitive prices on their core products.

As the 21st century nears, the auto industry is under pressure from the federal government and environmentalists to develop and market automobiles that run on fuels other than gasoline. California, which has the nation's most serious air quality problems and the most stringent emissions standards, has adopted vehicle-related clean air rules that are even stricter than the federal legislation.

With the exception of a few years that registered small increases, the number of franchised auto dealerships in the United States has steadily declined since the end of World War II. In contrast to 1949, when some 49,000

---

[16] *Standard & Poor Industry Survey,* p. 15.
[17] Maglitta, Joseph, "MindMeld," *Computerworld,* Internet edition, October 30, 1995, p. 65.
[18] *International Directory,* p. 172.
[19] *Standard & Poor Industry Survey,* p. 1.

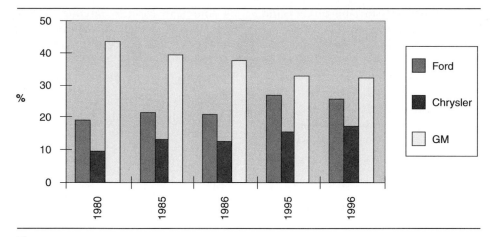

Figure 7.3 GM's market share in North America, cars and light trucks. (*Source:* Company Data.)

dealers were operating in the United States, there were about 22,300 dealers in business as of January 1, 1996.

In the next few years, both General Motors and Chrysler will consolidate their dealer bases and eliminate unprofitable or marginal dealers or those that cannibalize sales from nearby outlets. Most of the 1,700 units that GM has targeted for consolidation, for example, are located in urban areas.

General Motors has led the U.S. automobile market since 1930. However, GM's total 1995 market share of 33.9 percent represents a steep decline from the company's 1978 peak of 47.7 percent. Since then, GM's share has declined steadily, with a particularly severe drop in 1986 (Figure 7.3). For the most part, GM's market share decline resulted from two significant problems that plagued the company in the mid-1980s: quality and style. Potential buyers felt that certain models were of poor quality and were too similar in appearance. These criticisms were specifically aimed at GM's first generation of front-wheel drive cars and certain compact and subcompact models. These cars had been hastily brought to market to comply with government fuel-efficiency requirements and to respond to the sudden shift in consumer demand for smaller cars that resulted from higher fuel prices.

GM has lost the home-field advantage and makes almost no money in North America, where it has higher costs than its competitors and some of the weakest brands. Labor relations, never healthy, hit a postwar low as UAW strikes in 1996 kept GM from building 300,000 vehicles, at a cost of $1.2 billion after tax. Overall, GM-NAO returned 1.2 percent on sales. Excluding the Delphi parts, as GM began doing in March 1996, GM-NAO's return shrank to 0.8 percent. That's well below GM's target of 5 percent.[20]

Table 7.5 GM's New Models for 1997

New Product	Model Being Replaced	Segment
Saturn Coupe	Old Saturn Coupe	Small
Grand Prix	Old Grand Prix	Middle
Malibu/Cutlass	Corsica/Beretta, Ciera	Middle
Century/Regal	Old Century/Regal	Middle
Intrigue	Cutlass Supreme	Middle
Corvette	Old Corvette	Luxury
Park Avenue	Old Park Avenue	Luxury
Minivans	Old Minivans	Minivan
Full-sized Van	Old full-sized van	Full-sized Van
Catera	None	Luxury

(*Source:* Morgan Stanley.)

Despite improved vehicle quality and product identity in recent years, further challenges remain. In particular, the company faces continuous pressure to reduce costs sharply and to boost the performance of its now profitable North American operations. GM launched a record number of new products in 1997 (Table 7.5). For GM, getting production of a new car up to full assembly-line speed requires 3.5 months—*if* things go smoothly. Honda changes models over a weekend by doing more preproduction planning. While GM dealers wait for the new cars, they have to keep selling old ones that must be heavily discounted.

The success of these new products is critical for several reasons. First, the new products should carry significantly lower costs than those they replace. Thus, if mix and price remain favorable, profitability should improve. Second, the new products should give a much-needed lift to GM's sagging market share, helping to reduce average fixed costs.[21]

---

[20] Taylor, "GM: Time to Get in Gear," p. 96.

[21] *GM Company Report,* Morgan Stanley, March 12, 1997, p. 11.

Early indications of the 1997 start-up quality and market reaction were quite encouraging. The Chevrolet Malibu was selected the 1997 Motor Trend "Car of the Year" and the new EV1 electric vehicle received numerous awards for leading-edge technology. Apparently, the new models are better designed, better built, and cheaper to produce than the ones they replaced. They were launched into a healthy economy, even though the competitive environment is fierce. GM will have to battle Ford and Chrysler for truck sales, and Toyota, Nissan, and Honda for car sales.[22]

ROLE OF RESEARCH AND DEVELOPMENT

GM has introduced new inventions and focused on R&D since it was founded. GM used the electric self-starter, an engineering breakthrough designed by Charles F. Kettering, in its 1912 Cadillac to eliminate the dangerous and unpredictable hand crank. Kettering's company merged with GM. The inventor became the scientific director of the corporation.[23]

The public interest in automatic gears after World War II convinced GM to concentrate their research in this field. General Motors was one of the leaders in the invention and development of power-assisted steering and brakes. They led in the implementation of safety features such as front seat safety belts and air bags.

Following the environmental needs and tightening of government air pollution regulations, GM engineers developed the EV1. EV1 is the only purpose-built electric vehicle on the road today. It has gained several awards for leading-edge technology.

TECHNOLOGICAL STORY

In recent years, GM's research has been focused on bringing new information technologies to enhance safety and differentiate its products from competition. The OnStar, an interactive mobile information and communications system, is an example of how GM is incorporating information technology into its products to gain competitive advantage in the luxury car market.

OnStar provides advanced features. Emergency medical services are automatically notified when the vehicle's air bag inflates. The system features a voice-activated cellular telephone from Hughes Electronics that links the car and driver to GM's OnStar call center in Farmington, Michigan. The communications links are made by American Mobile Satellite. The vehicle is located through a Rockwell global positioning satellite.[24] Experts say OnStar puts GM ahead of its smart-car rivals.

TECHNOLOGICAL INVESTMENT AND ANALYSIS

In the early 1980s when GM owned 40 percent of the U.S. auto market with revenues over $100 billion, the company did not have a unified information system that would satisfy its needs. GM used electronic data interchange (EDI) to order parts automatically from suppliers since the concept was proposed in the early 1970s. Yet different divisions and sections within divisions used different computers and software.

Thus, GM was forced to handle many tasks manually, whereas a unified computer system would eliminate the need for much of that work. If two sets of engineers were not using the same computers to communicate with each other, they would often have to reenter data and change their formats.[25]

Roger Smith, CEO from 1981 to 1991, envisioned a system where everyone at GM was connected to one network. Design, engineering, administration, telephones, payroll, health insurance, financing, and the factories would all be integrated into one system. Smith felt that data processing was at the heart of General Motors and should be handled only by an internal group.

Since GM did not have strong IS capabilities he went outside the company and hired Salomon Brothers to assist him with acquisition of a computer services company. Out of several potential candidates, Smith chose Electronic Data Systems. First, it was a highly successful, if not small, by GM standards, data processing firm. Second, it had a corporate culture which minimized the red tape and bureaucracy that Smith hated so much.[26] EDS merged with General Motors in 1984 and immediately assumed control of GM system and inventory. Overnight, thousands of GM workers became EDS workers.

The integration of EDS into General Motors turned out to be a very painful and long-term process. Aside from the clash of cultures and resentment of EDS's intrusion into GM turf, there were professional complaints with GM's new subsidiary. When GM acquired EDS, the computer company had no automotive experience and little background in distributed systems. Also, EDS lacked experience with management control systems, robotics, computer-aided design, and manufacturing, of which were a large part of GM's computer systems. GM people complained that EDS mishandled

---

[22] Taylor, "GM: Time to Get in Gear," p. 96; Flint, Jerry, "Backseat Driver: The Assault on Fortress GM," *Forbes*, March 8, 1999, p. 88(1).

[23] *International Directory*, p. 171.

[24] "Not Your Father's Cadillac," *Computerworld*, Internet edition, April 8, 1996.

[25] "Ross Perot and General Motors," *Harvard Business Review*, p. 1.

[26] Ibid., p. 6.

parts supplying, often buying far too many or too few, resulting either in overstock or factory delays.[27]

However, EDS scored successes in consolidating purchases, improving payroll databases, and standardizing PC systems at GM. Ever since the merger, EDS tried to implement commercial packages. Automakers have been notorious for developing homegrown software. GM led its competitors in this regard.[28]

EDS coordinated a project for GM North American Operations called consistent office environment (COE). COE was a three-year plan focused on replacing a hodgepodge of desktop models, network operating systems, and application development tools with a shorter and more manageable list of vendors and technology platforms. COE represented the fastest and largest IS infrastructure upgrade in GM's history. This laid the foundation for the implementation of a common business communication strategy across General Motors. The goal was to change the way GM handled information on the desktop, in the workgroup, and across the enterprise.[29] In 1993, GM had 27 e-mail systems, 10 word processing programs, five spreadsheet applications, and seven business graphics packages.

All the contracts for COE were, by design, signed within 90 days of one another in mid-1993. The contracts were structured on a per-user/per-month basis. This allowed GM to ramp up the new system without incurring capital spikes.

Obviously, COE was a landmark for the few lucky vendors tapped by GM/EDS to supply hardware and software components. Lotus Development Corporation, which supplied its Notes groupware platform, was said to have made its largest single Notes sale to EDS for the project. Similarly, Compaq Computer Corporation, which supplied the desktop and laptop system, was believed to be looking at one of its largest nongovernment sales ever.[30]

In June 1996, GM filled its top information systems job with Ralph Szygenda, former chief information officer at Bell Atlantic Corp. Before joining Bell Atlantic, Szygenda was CIO at Texas Instruments.[31] In his job, Szygenda chairs GM's Corporate Information Council, which includes the IS heads from GM's business sectors. Szygenda reports to GM Vice Chairman Harry Pearce. Szygenda's job is to develop and manage GM's global information technology strategy as well as its relationship with outsourcers, most notably Electronic Data Systems (EDS).

Szygenda relied on EDS for much of his IS needs at a time when the newly liberated systems integrator was focused elsewhere. Getting a lower price from an outsourcer is good news for a CIO. It was more complicated for GM's CIO because lower earnings for EDS could reduce the value of EDS stock held by GM pension funds. That, in turn, could require GM to make special payments to those funds in compensation. The CIO was not responsible for the pension fund, but GM's contracts were important to the vitality of EDS. Therefore, GM had to phase in the shift of its business to EDS's competitors.

"Despite this semi-captive relationship, EDS is responding well to the cost-reduction effort. We need to align all of our investments in information systems with our business priorities [while] running information systems and services like a business," Szygenda said in late December 1996.[32]

Szygenda was pleasantly surprised to find 2,200 IS employees "hidden" within GM and not shipped off to EDS. Among the handful of corporate IS staff, he picked Raymond Kahn to head Year 2000 compliance efforts for the company's 2 billion lines of code. This project was estimated to cost hundreds of millions of dollars. Most of the new IS executives were to come from outside to assist Szygenda in accomplishing his mission.

Although GM management had been imposing tighter controls on IS for several years, Szygenda wanted to cut hundreds of millions of dollars more from GM's current information technology budget of more than $4 billion. To achieve this goal, he focused his hiring on individuals who would help him accomplish his goals by finding common software, processes, and expertise that could be reused across the company.

Integration and common global product development is critical to GM's prosperity. Because of EDS, GM's IS infrastructure was in relatively good shape. Applications, however, were developed piecemeal by GM's units, leading to about 7,000 separate systems. Szygenda wanted to see at least half of GM's $4 billion IS budget go to developing applications. He wanted to finish GM's struggle to standardize and to collaborate globally.

GM took a step toward common systems in December 1996 when it announced it would standardize on EDS's Unigraphics CAD/CAM solid modeling software. Shortly after that, GM began automatic transmission of solid model data to its suppliers, which use

---

[27] Madden, John, "EDS Slims Down to Refocus on Growth Markets," *PC Week*, March 15, 1999, v. 16, i. 11, p. 1(1).
[28] Booker, Ellis, "GM Seeks Consistency," *Computerworld*, Internet edition, March 14, 1994.
[29] Ibid.
[30] Ibid
[31] Scheier, Robert, "GM Taps Bell Atlantic CIO for Top IS Job," *Computerworld*, Internet edition, June 20, 1996.

[32] Scheier, Robert L., "GM's First IT Chief Seeks 300 CIOs," *Computerworld*, Internet edition, December 23, 1996.

a variety of CAD/CAM systems, to cut costs and product development time.[33]

Another major step toward a unified IS was a comprehensive business software system. General Motors implemented R/3 from the German company SAP. R/3 ties together and automates the basic processes of accounting. These include order taking, credit checking, payment verification, and account balancing. SAP's R/3 is becoming the new standard equipment for global corporations.

INTERNET

An intranet is helping GM develop products more efficiently. GM engineers need to share knowledge. If they do not, dozens of people write the same bug fix or work with out-of-date versions of objects, simply because nobody knows what coworkers have already done. Without a process to track changes and revisions, all large projects can get out of control.

GM's Powertrain Control Center uses its intranet to coordinate the work of more than 300 engineers all over the world. Prior to the intranet web servers, GM engineers filed paper documents and distributed them through the internal mail system. In 1994, they installed a UNIX-based shared file server. It lacked data organization, control, and file naming standards. By using the continuus/web intranet solutions, instead of completing dozens of disjointed efforts, everyone works with consistent standards, procedures, documentation, and code. Colleagues, whether in Michigan or Munich, can access this document through their Netscape browsers. An e-mail notification system automatically notifies users every time a relevant document changes.[34]

A second intranet deploys executable files, the code that runs the "black boxes." Customers, including manufacturing companies, the GM service organization, auto dealers, and assembly plants use the software to program the Powertrain and transmission controllers.

The intranet does not solve all the problems, however. GM engineers still wrestle with incompatibility issues, such as reconciling the difference between UNIX and Windows file formats and tools. The intranet does not help them balance the need for security with the need for usability. The continuous intranet solution still has much to achieve to reach its ultimate objective of moving its "entire" software development process to a single database and communicating all that information through a web server. It has accomplished the important interim goal of consistency.[35]

Another area of GM's business that needed standardization and efficiency improvements was communication with the dealership network. GM did not have a common communications system in place for its dealerships.[36] The old Dealer Communication System, which dated from 1975, required the dealers to take piecemeal technical downloads that took hours and then cut and paste the messages into a cohesive format. To improve communications and information exchange between GM headquarters and its dealer network, the company asked EDS to introduce a new dealership automation program. The system was named GM Access. EDS chose Microsoft's Windows NT as the server to link dealerships nationwide.[37] The main objective of GM Access was to distribute data about the availability of new cars to GM's car dealerships through a satellite network. The satellite network replaced the outdated X.25 network, which required hours to download information.[38]

General Motors installed Lotus Notes at its 8,500 U.S. dealerships as the platform for GM Access in the first half of 1996. Dealers use Lotus Notes to check inventories, locate specific vehicles matching customer requirements, and find information on pricing, incentives, and service. Lotus Notes is estimated to reduce by 30 percent the time it takes to disseminate sales and service information to GM dealers.[39]

GM Access allows dealers to access inventory data that is no more than 24 hours old, read service manuals and technical bulletins, and get recall notices and parts availability information. GM Access also enables dealers to use an online search engine to find individual models or configurations. This information will be downloaded within 14 seconds to the dealerships to increase efficiency and get consumers the most up-to-date information. GM Access also allows GM and its dealerships to standardize the entire system. Previously, Pontiac, Buick, and GMAC all submitted their paperwork differently, which was an administrative nightmare.[40]

To further cut the time it takes to get information to its dealerships, General Motors decided to implement an emerging technology called IP multicasting. IP multicasting broadcasts data from one main site to multiple receiving stations. It was more efficient than developing an individual link from the central site to every remote location.[41] "We went from trans-

---

[33] Caldwell, Bruce, "IS Hiring Drive Is on at GM," *Informationweek,* December 23, 1996, n. 611.

[34] Wilder, Clinton, "GM Goes Online for Buying," *Information Week,* March 22, 1999, p. 26(1).

[35] Engler, Natalie, "Code Conspirators," *Computerworld,* Internet edition, May 26, 1997.

[36] "GM Rolls Out Notes at Dealerships," *Computerworld,* Internet edition, June 6, 1996.

[37] DiDio, Laura, "GM Access Revs Up," *Computerworld,* Internet edition, July 8, 1996.

[38] "Gateways for GM Dealers," *Information Week,* April 5, 1999, p. 97(1).

[39] "GM Rolls Out."

[40] DiDio, Laura, "GM Access."

[41] Wallace, Bob, "GM Revs Up Data Delivery to Dealers," *Computerworld,* Internet edition, December 23, 1996.

mitting a 1M-byte file to a very limited number of dealers in roughly 30 minutes to sending the same file to 500 dealers in three minutes," said Wayne Stein, a project manager at EDS.[42] IP multicasting lets GM provide dealerships with timely software updates, sales incentive data, service bulletins, and car availability information. In the past, this was done by numerous point-to-point transfers or by mailing diskettes to dealerships. All 8,500 GM dealerships nationwide were scheduled to be online by September 1997.

GM is using the Internet extensively in its advertising effort which is focused on increasing brand equity. GM was a true pioneer in the automotive industry when it began to broadcast its messages through the web.[43] GM first used "push" technology at the end of 1996 to send an animated advisory to subscribers of the GM Channel. It announced the launch of the 1997 Buick Regal. A click on that notice sent users to the Regal's own web site, which included video clips and chat areas. "We envision a group of different experiments to see how this aids the branding efforts for GM," said Larry Lozon, senior vice president and director of the GM's new-media strategy arm.[44]

While the Internet advertising succeeds in attracting new customers, GM is also using the net to make it easier for its customers to get financing. GM's financial division, General Motors Acceptance Corporation, became the first automotive financial services company to offer an online credit application on the Internet in 1996.

In addition to promotion and customer services activities, the Internet is expected to be used extensively in areas such as market research and employee training. In the near future, by clicking on a picture of a red Corvette, a market analyst at General Motors might be able to obtain a profile of red Corvette buyers. If he wants to break that up by region, he might circle and click on a map. All in the same motion, he might view a GM sales-training film to see whether the sales pitch is appropriate, given the most recent market trends.[45]

TECHNOLOGICAL INNOVATIONS

NETWORK

GM began a two-year global rollout of an ambitious information technology architecture that will provide up to 175,000 GM users with web access. Called GM OnLine, the rollout includes new applications as well as Compaq Computer PCs. "GM OnLine is a new integrated intranet infrastructure that gives our users access to the Internet," said GM CIO Ralph Szygenda. "It will be our platform for knowledge-sharing and collaboration and the nucleus for a number of future applications." Besides the Compaq Windows NT-based desktops, GM OnLine includes Lotus Domino, Microsoft Office, and Tivoli Systems' TME 10 enterprise management system.

TELECOMMUNICATIONS

GM has launched its response to web sites such as Auto-by-Tel and Microsoft CarPoint, which let consumers shop for cars online. GM enables customers to configure and price GM cars and trucks on its corporate web site (www.gm.com) and divisional sites such as www.buick.com and www.pontiac.com.

Dealers will still be utilized. Web users will be directed to the nearest GM dealer stocking the model in the desired color and with the desired options. The customer will be able to directly receive the manufacturer's suggested retail price and financing terms from General Motors Acceptance Corporation, GM's credit unit.

Price negotiation, ordering, and payment will still be handled by the dealer using traditional means. GM does have long-term plans to link from the web into dealer inventory systems to enable online ordering, according to Craig Norwood, interactive retail systems manager in Warren, Michigan.[46]

The configuration application will run on the web-enabled version of Signature Plus interactive selling software from CWC Inc. in Mankato, Minnesota. GM dealers in North America already use a customized client/server application from CWC. Named Prospec it can configure, locate, and order cars from GM. The GM web site application is the first customer deployment of the web version of Signature Plus.

DATA

GM is evaluating several data mining products for projects for the GMAC loan division and its credit card area.

GM has experimented with data mining on a few scientific projects. Only recently has the automaker tried to use data mining in production work to solve problems. Some of these problems are database marketing. They use customer data and warranty information. If GM can use warranty data to identify very specific problems, GM can fix those processes or parts and save on future warranty expenses.

[42] Ibid.
[43] "Car-buying Site Could Help Out GM on the Road Again," *Computerworld,* March 8, 1999, p. 43(1).
[44] Bank, David, "Instead of Clicking Pages, Users View Channels on the Desktop," The *Wall Street Journal,* interactive edition, December 13, 1996.
[45] Halper, Mark, "Welcome to 21st-Century Data," *Forbes,* April 8, 1996, p. S48.
[46] Karpinski, Richard, "GM Expands E-Biz Scope," *InternetWeek,* March 15, 1999, p. 1(1).

RECOMMENDATION FOR THE FUTURE

Although GM is still the largest manufacturer of automobiles in the world, its global position and competitiveness has been worsening over the last 20 years. The following are some areas of weakness:

- GM's market share in North America has decreased from 47.7 percent in 1978 to 31.9 percent in 1997.
- GM had by far the lowest profit margin of the Big Three automakers in 1996.
- GM has the lowest pretax profit per unit of the Big Three automakers.
- GM still does not have a common global system to run its business processes, R&D, manufacturing, sales, and marketing activities worldwide.

Several approaches would help GM be more successful:

1. Focus on core businesses and discontinue others. A series of spin-offs could improve cash flow and enable investments where needed.
2. Restructure and reduce workforce. Initiatives in these areas slowed during the second half of the decade.
3. Implement common design processes, worldwide purchasing, body fabrication, body-in-white engineering, and die engineering.
4. Undertake thorough market research and implement brand management.

Since GM's cash flow is strong, financial resources are available to pursue investment in information technology. Successful implementation of the COE project demonstrated that consolidation of the IS environment does not have to bring additional costs.

CASE QUESTIONS

Strategic Questions

1. Where does the company see itself heading?

2. Who or what forces are driving this direction?

3. What will GM need to succeed with their new strategy?

4. What are the core competencies for this corporation/organization?

Technological Questions

5. What technologies has the corporation relied on?

6. What has caused a change in the use of technology in the corporation/organization?

7. How has this change been implemented?

8. Who has driven this change throughout the organization?

9. How successful has the technological change been?

Quantitative Questions

10. What does the corporation say about its financial ability to embark on a major technological program of advancement?

11. What conclusions can be reached from an analysis of the financial information to support or contradict this financial ability?

12. What conclusions can be reached by analyzing the financial trends? Are there long term trends that seem to be problematic?

13. Is the industry stable?

14. Are there replacement products?

Internet Questions

15. What does the corporation's web page present about its business directives?

16. Does the company make use of its Web page in order to collect data from its visitors?

Industry Questions

17. What challenges and opportunities is the industry facing?

18. Is the industry oligopolistic or competitive?

19. Does the industry face a change in government regulation?

Data Questions

20. How will GM be using data to implement its strategy?

21. How important is data to GM's strategy?

22. How will the quality of the customer data impact the corporation's future?

TECHNOLOGY TIPS

MICROSOFT WORD TIPS

CREATING CHARTS

Charts can make numbers easier to understand. If you would like to graphically present some numerical data, with a graph it can be done quite easily. The following instructions teach you how to create a basic bar chart from the data included in the table. You can use your data instead if you like.

Creating a Chart

1. Place the cursor on your document where you would like to insert your chart.
2. Click on INSERT. From the drop-down menu click on PICTURE.
3. A side menu will appear. Click on the CHART button.

4. A graph will appear along with an example table. Replace the numbers on the table with the numbers shown or use your own numbers. Notice that your tool bar will change to show the Graph tool bar on top.
5. Notice that as you input numbers in the different cells on the table the graph will change when you move on to the next cell.
6. After you finish entering the data into the cells click outside the graph on the document itself. This will close out the toolbar and show the completed graph.
7. To make any changes to the graph double-click on the graph, and the graph tool bar along with the data sheet will appear. You can move the graph around by clicking and dragging on it.

Division	1996 Sales	1997 Sales	1998 Sales
Extron	$256879	$287342	$334231
Filoak	$356045	$378908	$381908

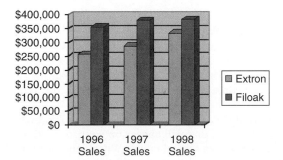

ADDITIONAL NOTES

Quicker and Easier

You can skip entering data into the data sheet if you already have a table created. Word will automatically fill in the blanks for you with the cells that you highlight from the table created in the document.

1. Highlight the cells in your table including text that you would like to appear on the graph.

2. Click on INSERT and from the drop-down menu click on PICTURE. Now click on CHART.
3. Automatically the chart will appear using the numbers that were highlighted in the table.
4. Adjust the cells to show any additional information you want.
5. Click outside the graph when you are done.
6. To modify the chart later on just double-click on the graph and the data sheet and graph tool bar will appear.

MICROSOFT EXCEL TIPS

FORMATTING CELLS

The appearance of the worksheet can be modified in more ways than can be demonstrated here. This chapter will cover the formatting of individual cells to highlight certain data, to improve the appearance, or to make the data easier to read.

Coloring Cells

1. Click on a cell or highlight the cells that will have color added by dragging across the cells.
2. Click on the right button while in the highlighted cell or range of cells. Select FORMAT CELLS from the shortcut menu.
3. The Format cells dialog box will appear. Click on the PATTERNS tab inside the dialog box. The dialog box will change to show the menu choices on the right.
4. Select a color and/or pattern to apply to the cells selected.
5. Click on OK to make the changes.

Formatting Data within Cells

1. Click on a cell or highlight the cells that will be formatted by dragging across the cells.
2. Click on the right button while in the highlighted cell or range of cells. Select FORMAT CELLS from the shortcut menu.
3. The Format cells dialog box will appear. Click on the NUMBER tab inside the dialog box. The dialog box will change to show the menu choices on the right.
4. Click on the type of format that is suitable to the cells that have been selected. Brief explanations of the formats and examples are shown in the dialog box when the category is clicked.
5. Click on OK to apply the changes to the cells.

Text Alignment

1. Click on a cell or highlight the cells that will be formatted by dragging across the cells.
2. Click on the right button while in the highlighted cell or range of cells. Select FORMAT CELLS from the shortcut menu.
3. The Format cells dialog box will appear. Click on the ALIGNMENT tab inside the dialog box. The dialog box will change to show the menu choices on the right.
4. Click and drag on the text orientation indicator, align the data inside the cell, or click on the Vertical Text Alignment window that has TEXT written in it.
5. Click on OK to apply the changes to the cells.

Cell Borders

1. Click on a cell or highlight the cells that will be formatted by dragging across the cells.
2. Click on the right button while in the highlighted cell or range of cells. Select FORMAT CELLS from the shortcut menu.
3. The Format cells dialog box will appear. Click on the NUMBER tab inside the dialog box. The dialog box will change to show the menu choices on the right.
4. Select the color, style, and borders that you want to format the cells with. Click on OK to apply the changes to the cells.

MICROSOFT POWERPOINT TIPS

INSERTING CLIP ART AND WEB IMAGES

The use of images in presentations can sometimes help you explain a point that words alone cannot. A resource that comes with the PowerPoint presentation package is Clip Art. Although it is somewhat limited on the number of images it offers, it can still help bring some life to the presentation. If you have access to the World Wide Web your selection of images will grow exponentially.

Inserting Clip Art

1. You must be in SLIDE VIEW in order to insert Clip Art.
2. Click on the slide into which you want to insert the Clip Art.
3. Click on INSERT from the top toolbar. Click on PICTURE from the drop-down menu and then click on Clip Art from the side menu.
4. The Clip Art box on the right will appear. The Clip Art library may vary depending on what has been loaded into your computer.
5. Select the image you wish to use by clicking on it and then clicking on INSERT. You can also double-click on the image in order to insert it.
6. The presentation slide will appear once again with the Clip Art. The image can be resized by clicking on the image and then dragging the corners. The image can be moved around by clicking on it once and dragging it to any place within the slide.

Web Images

You can download Clip Art and images from the WWW at anytime and insert them in your presentation. Follow steps 1 through 4 above and click on the web button to gain access to the web (you must have Internet access to use this feature). The web browser will open up at Microsoft's Clip Gallery Live. You can follow the instructions here to download images to your computer and use them in future presentations. If you wish to insert other images from other web sites do the following:

1. Go to the web page that you wish to copy the image from.
2. Place the cursor over the image that you wish to insert into the presentation and click on the right mouse button.
3. Select SAVE PICTURE AS. . . from the pop-up menu.
4. The SAVE PICTURE dialog box will appear. Save it in a location that will be easy for you to remember later (i.e., a floppy or the desktop).
5. Once the picture has been saved you can access it from PowerPoint. Open the presentation and go to the slide in which the picture will be placed. The slide should be open in the SLIDE VIEW.
6. From the top toolbar click on INSERT, then click on PICTURE, and finally, click on FROM FILE.
7. From the INSERT PICTURE dialog box look for the picture that was saved from the web. Click on the file and a preview will be shown. Click on INSERT to have the picture inserted in the presentation or double-click on the file name.
8. The picture will appear in your presentation. You can adjust the size and placement of the picture as explained in step 6 above.

MICROSOFT ACCESS TIPS

CREATING FORMS USING FORM WIZARD

Forms make it easier for you to present your data to others and, as you will see in later chapters, they can help you in entering your data. Although forms can be created from scratch, you may want to use the Form Wizard to get ideas for layouts.

Using Form Wizard

1. From the database window click on the FORMS tab.
2. Click on the NEW button and click on FORM WIZARD from the pop-up menu. Click on the drop-down arrow to list the tables and queries that you can use to create your form.
3. Click on OK. A dialog box will appear asking you to select the fields that will appear on your form. You can select fields from several tables. When you have completed your selections click on the NEXT button.
4. In the next dialog box select the layout of your form. Click on the NEXT button when you are done.
5. The following dialog box will allow you to select a style for your form. Browse through the different styles and click on the NEXT button when you are done.
6. In the last dialog box you name the form and select whether you would like to view your form and enter data, or open it in the design view to modify it. Make your selections and click on the FINISH button.

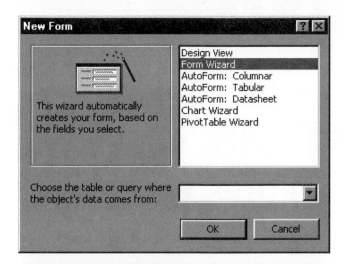

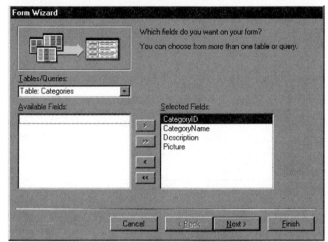

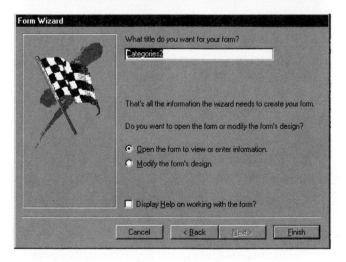

The name you give the form in the last dialog box will appear in the database window under the FORMS tab. To open it just double-click on it. The next chapter will show you how to make modifications to the form and customize it to suit your needs.

MICROSOFT FRONT PAGE TIPS

CREATING A SCROLLING MARQUEE

If you want some text to scroll across the page while someone is looking at your web page you can do this with the Marquee feature. This might be useful if you are trying to catch the visitor's attention.

1. Click on the part of the web page where you would like the marquee to appear
2. From the top menu bar, click on INSERT. Select MARQUEE from the drop-down menu
3. The MARQUEE dialog box will appear. Type the text that you would like to appear inside the TEXT field
4. Experiment with the other features to see how the marquee can change
5. When you have finished click on the OK button

Modifying the Marquee

Whenever you want to modify the marquee simply double-click on it and the dialog box will appear.

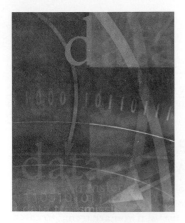

CHAPTER 8

MODELS AND DECISION SUPPORT
COMPUTER HARDWARE INDUSTRY

Models and Decision Support

Models are important to analyze problems and make decisions. Models can be simple or complex. Their output can be exact or subject to interpretation. Businesses use models of the past (to improve processes) to help with the present (to evaluate choices) and to guide the future (to forecasting alternatives). Management information systems can help manage and collect the data models used. Word processors and graphic software are used to turn the output into a meaningful final report. As a user, you will be responsible for understanding basic business models and choosing the right combination to apply to your work situation. Enterprise information systems are models of the entire business. They are designed to help managers monitor corporate performance, identify problems, and retrieve data.

Model A model is a simplified, abstract representation of a real system. It can be a mathematical expression, graph, or even subjective description.

Operations versus Tactical Decisions Tactical problems tend to be well defined and impact business for a short period of time. Operations decisions involve less evident problems that require a more complex model.

Decision Bias The four primary types of decision bias are (1) acquisition (input), (2) processing, (3) output, and (4) feedback. Acquisition bias occurs when people put too much emphasis on events that were just observed or on prior beliefs or assumptions. Processing

mistakes occur when people have difficulty making consistent decisions and incorporating new data. Output bias happens when the format of the output, such as the scale of a graph, distorts the interpretation of the final report. Feedback bias occurs when feedback received is misinterpreted. Biases point out the need for models to incorporate, use, and interpret data consistently. Information systems can help with the data acquisition, execution, and interpretation of the model.

Types of Models

Physical. Physical models, such as a miniature building an architect might build, are the most common. They are meant to replicate the original as much as possible in a cost-effective manner. Physical models can be expensive to build. New tools such as computer-aided design (CAD) make it easier to visualize physical models.

Process. Process models are symbolic or descriptive, such as diagrams or graphs. They often use models and pictures to simulate objects, and mathematical relationships to represent processes.

Business Modeling. Business models help describe businesses and business decisions. Dividing a company into functional departments is a business model. Reengineering is a business modeling technique that has gained momentum as corporations have tried to become more efficient.

Application of Models

Optimization. These models use mathematics or other analytical tools that evaluate different alternatives while choosing the best decision.

Prediction. This model is based on an historical approach and develops a projection of what the system should look like.

Simulation. This modeling technique applies a model to the effects of changes and situations on the item being studied. These types of modeling techniques tend to be mathematical and project the extent of change taking place.

Decision Support Systems (DSS) DSS provides support through data collection, analysis of models, and the presentation of output. DSSs consist primarily of a database or data warehouse, modeling tools, and presentation software.

Building Models

Assumptions. Since models are built to simplify a real-life siutation, assumptions must be built into the model that are reasonable, accurate, and well-communicated.

Input/Output Variables. Choosing the correct input and output variable is very important. The selected input variables must be correlated to the output variables identified for analysis.

Processes/Equations. It is important to identify and understand the processes that are represented in the equation and calculations at the process model.

Software. DSS software can be either generic or pre-programmed and specific. Generic modeling tools can be applied to any situation. Examples include tools that are graphic based, such as SAS, GPSS, SIMSCRIPT, and MODSIM III. Developing the right model is the hardest part of choosing this option. Preprogrammed (specific) models can be easier to use, but can be limiting if the user is resricted to the variables defined in the underlying model. Providing the user with too much control can introduce so many variables that the user is confused because he/she is not familiar with the process being studied.

Model Limitations

Cost. Models can be expensive to build, both in terms of time and dollars. This cost must be factored into the evaluation process. Time restrictions must also be taken into account when considering the complexity of the model.

Word	W.1	Modifying a Chart
		Additional Note
			Changing Chart Type
			Changing the Data
			Adding Labels, Chart
			  Titles, and Moving the
			  Legend Around
			Other Modifications

Excel	E.1	Formating Worksheets Using AutoFormat Additional Note	Using AutoFormat

PowerPoint	P.1	Creating
		  Organizational Charts
			Getting Started
			Adding Boxes
			Deleting Boxes
			Changing the Organizational Chart Style
			Modifying Boxes,
			  Borders, Lines, Colors
			  and Text
			Saving the Chart and
			  Making Further
			  Changes

Access	A.1	Modifying Forms	Form in the Design View Modifying the Picture Re-sizing the Picture
Front Page	I.1	WebBots: Time Stamp	Time Stamp Changing the Time Stamp Options

Errors. Since models are simulations of real life, there are more opportunities for errors in the assumptions built into the model. The three main type of errors in models are (1) mistakes in the input data, (2) errors in the equations used in the model, and (3) flaws in the display or interpretation of the results.

Enterprise Information System (EIS) An EIS is based on a model for the entire firm. These systems use existing transaction data to summarize and display information for top executives. Normally, the information is displayed on a screen and the executive can change the parameters of the data he or she wants to display. The user can also "drill down" to see the detail behind the numbers and get more information. The EIS should be connected to data sources such as a data warehouse, which will provide data such as people, wages, materials, and sales. These inputs will be turned into more meaningful numbers by the EIS. These include profits, regional and total sales, and trends. Advantages of an EIS include easy and current access to data by executives. Disadvantages include possible incompatibility if the system that provides the data is significantly different from the traditional source.

Computer Hardware Industry

DESCRIPTION OF INDUSTRY

The computer hardware industry is a maturing industry in rapid and constant change. In 1997, Intel had sales of about $25 billion. Yet, more than 90 percent of Intel's revenue came from products that did not even exist the previous year. This represents product life cycles at their shortest.

Growth in computer hardware spending has been driven largely by business purchases. The computer hardware industry can be divided into three segments: (1) systems and servers (including mainframes and supercomputers), (2) personal computers (PCs), and (3) workstations. Of the $600 billion spent on information technology in 1996, 40 percent was spent on hardware.

FINANCIAL ANALYSIS

The growth of the computer hardware industry has dramatically increased revenues to companies in the industry. Profit margins are much slimmer in the United States due to fierce competition and the price wars waged for the sake of market share. Nonetheless, computer hardware companies are expanding internationally where profit margins are significantly higher.

Due to the very fast market cycle, inventory turnover must be extremely high. Any company with lower inventory turnover than its competitors will quickly begin experiencing balance sheet problems.

STOCK/INVESTMENT OUTLOOK

The outlook for the computer hardware industry is positive. The continued build-out of LANs, WANs, and client/server computing generates the need for PCs. The increasing consumer interest in web access is also positive for the industry. In 1996, web users increased by 115 percent. Only 40 percent of U.S. households have a PC and far fewer do worldwide. Thus, the PC market is not saturated.

Stock in computer hardware companies remains volatile. Since the technologies involved are changing quickly, hopes and fears are also rising and falling in step. Expectations of future earnings and success will be difficult to gauge. Will Microsoft and Intel dominate the markets further? Will there be successful challenges to their leadership? Will technological breakthroughs in other areas like communications or physics change the industry? Will the Internet change the hardware and software requirements?

COMPETITIVE STRUCTURE

The top 10 PC suppliers control 65 percent of the market. Competition is fierce. In fact, the PC market in some ways resembles a commodity market; top vendors target market share over margins. New entrants to the industry have slowed and the product offerings of existing vendors have widened.

"Wintel" is an acronym for the Intel–Microsoft leadership that dominates the PC market. Worldwide, 83 percent of PCs use the Windows operating system and 85 percent of all PCs use an Intel microprocessor. This is a concern of many, including the U.S. Department of Justice. One feature of this market domination, unlike in other monopoly situations, is constant innovation.

Intel and Microsoft spend 13 percent of their combined sales on R&D. This is far ahead of other computer hardware vendors, which only invest 3 to 5 percent of sales on R&D. This constant innovation and improvement generates ever shorter product life cycles. In fact, the need or perceived need to upgrade PC systems has benefited the entire industry.

POTENTIAL/PROSPECTIVE FOR GROWTH

The tremendous increases in the power and flexibilty of PCs and the ability to amplify PC strengths by networking in local-area networks (LANs) and wide-area networks (WANs) has made the PC segment the largest. This segment is biggest in both units and dollars. Between 1991 and 1995, PC shipments increased by 20 percent annually. Shipment growth of 15 percent annually is projected to continue.

Large systems and services account for about 35 percent of the spending on computer hardware. Mainframe sales have dropped. Sales of servers have increased. Servers enable the development of LANs and WANs.

Workstations constitute only 5 percent of spending on computer hardware. They combine powerful processors, networking, and graphical user interfaces. They are available in packages aimed at transaction intensive professions like engineering, 3-D animation, and scientific applications. The increasing powers of PCs have infringed on the market segment dominated by UNIX vendors to this point.

TECHNOLOGY INVESTMENT AND ANALYSIS

The investment in technology is particularly pronounced in the manufacturing aspect of computer hardware. Due to the fierce competition in the industry, cost control is very important. The price differentials between direct PC and retail PC sellers have narrowed greatly due to the control of costs. The increased competition means there is less room for error by those in the industry.

The technical and scientific feats of further innovation in processor speeds and storage capabilities demand ever more complicated manufacturing constraints. Constant advantage must be integrated from the latest technologizes in manufacturing and research.

RECOMMENDATION FOR THE FUTURE

In the future, the computer hardware industry must broaden itself to satisfy market needs. Presently, PCs fit the description "One type fits all." There is really only one type of PC with a few interchangeable parts of varying degrees of newness. Does one have a 133-MHz microprocessor or a 200-MHz microprocessor? In many ways, it does not really matter.

The market could fragment in many ways useful to both consumers and businesses. E-mail stations, word processing units, stand-alone web browsing units, and web-TV are all segments that could meet the particular needs of individuals. Some will always want the newest and fastest components. Yet, many needs can be met by existing technology.

Upgrading can be a costly expense. Will simpler, task-specific machines be web based? Which companies will ensure that old software can talk to new software by making translators for the technology?

INDUSTRY WEB SITES

Computer Hardware Industry
shopping.yahoo.com/computers/
www.compaq.com
www.dell.com

Executive Summary

Case Name:	Dell Computer Corporation
Case Industry:	Computer manufacturer
Major Technology Issue:	The best way to incorporate the latest technology into its systems
Major Financial Issue:	How should their explosive revenue growth be handled?
Major Strategic Issue:	Should Dell continue with its direct sales strategy or go into retail? How should Dell continue to segment the workstation market?
Major Players/Leaders:	Michael Dell, founder and CEO
Main Web Page:	www.dell.com
Case Conclusion/Recommendation:	While Dell seems to be able to sustain a high growth rate, it must be careful in every major decision. A closer look at the company reveals how past mistakes have severely impacted margins. Overall, the company is healthy financially with a good prognosis for the future.

CASE ANALYSIS

INTRODUCTORY STORY

Many people get their first job during high school, but few are as successful in high school as was Michael Dell. Dell made $18,000 selling newspapers in one year. One of his techniques was to identify the newspaper purchased most by newlyweds and new families in the area. He then targeted those individuals for newspaper sales. Dell tracked this market segment through the city marriage license bureau, lists of new home purchases, and other sources. Later that year, he bought a BMW with $18,000 cash. The ingenuity and persistence he demonstrated at an early age confirmed his strong entrepreneurial spirit. The formation of Dell Computer Corporation occurred only two years later.[1]

SHORT DESCRIPTION OF THE COMPANY

Dell Computer Corporation sells personal computers directly to the consumer, mostly through mail order. Approximately 90 percent of the company's annual revenues of $12.3 billion are from corporations, governments, and educational institutions. Over 80 percent of the Fortune 500 companies are Dell customers.[2]

Dell Computer introduced the concept of selling personal computer systems to customers on a built-to-order basis, providing direct toll-free support and next day on-site service.[3] The corporate philosophy is to "Cut out the middleperson and sell directly to customers." Since its incorporation in 1984, Dell Computer has become one of the largest manufacturers of computer systems in the world.[4]

SHORT HISTORY OF THE COMPANY

In 1983, Michael Dell entered the University of Texas at Austin as a college freshman. Rather than enjoy the freedom that comes with living away from home in a college dormitory, Michael was concerned primarily with how to make his dorm room into a warehouse. Soon it was filled with unsold PC stock purchased from local dealers.

With the room full of inventory, Dell added components and assembled them into clones of IBM computers. To compete with the retail segment, Dell offered the IBM clones to customers through mail order. Within months, Dell averaged $50,000 to $80,000 in revenues per month. Dell dropped out of college in 1984 to work full time on the concept of Dell Comput-

[1] Dennis Sylvia, "Dell Founder Paints Optomistic Picture of PC Industry," *Computing Canada,* July 9, 1999, v. 25, i. 27, p. 4.
[2] Fraone, Gina, and Brown, Stanley H., "The Top of the Heap," *Electronic Business,* July 1999, v. 25, i. 7, p. 99.

[3] Dell, Michael, "Selling Secrets of a PC Tycoon," *Computer Weekly,* February 11, 1999, p. 1(1).
[4] Wang, Stan, and Dille, Steven, "Turn Business Information Into Strategic Assets," *Business Advisor,* June 1999, v. 17, i. 6, p. 26.

ers. His explanation for dropping out was "I prefer to compete with IBM."

Dell determined that the best way to succeed in selling PCs was to build to suit and to ship directly to the customer. The PC market was changing so rapidly that fast turnaround of each order was paramount. The company would use low-cost direct marketing in computer magazines. This would undersell the better known computers being sold through retail dealers who typically had higher overhead. A Dell customer placed orders by dialing a toll-free number or faxing a purchase request. In its first full year in business, Dell Computer achieved sales of $6 million. This was a stunning justification of Dell's savvy read of the market. Dell has since become the top brand name in the direct mail market.[5]

Annual revenues in the second year were $40 million. By 1987, Dell had moved to become the dominant company in the mail-order market. To continue its rapid growth, Dell expanded internationally, starting in London. The London office sold $4 million in computers the following month. During this time, Dell also formed a Canadian subsidiary.[6] The company has since opened offices in 28 countries. With sales reaching just over $159 million in 1987, the firm went public at $8.50 a share.[7]

The increased competition from the foreign markets moved Dell to produce PCs using Intel Corporation's 80386 microprocessor (the most powerful PC chip at that time) and file servers using the sophisticated UNIX operating system. In 1990, Dell Computer set up subsidiaries in Italy and France. This had a direct impact on the company, vaulting them from twenty-second to the sixth largest PC maker in the United States. Due to the manufacturing of too many memory chips, the company abandoned the project (PCs with the Intel chip) to produce a line of workstations. Although Dell managed to double their sales in 1990, profits fell 65 percent primarily from the abandonment of the project.

In the early 1990s, consumers looked toward the benefits of notebook sized computers. As a result, Dell devoted resources to producing a notebook model, which it released in 1991.[8] However, the company's product line experienced technological difficulties. By the latter part of 1992, earnings deflated by $20 mil-

lion as a result of the cancellation of a series of notebook computers.[9]

The technical errors and increased competition prompted the company to cut prices by as much as $1,400 on their entire product line. The goal was to maintain their market share. Due to counterattacks from the competition, Dell introduced its "Dimensions" by Dell, a line of low-cost PCs.[10]

With price wars continuing and consolidation taking place, Dell experienced its first loss ever with a quarterly loss of $75 million in 1993. Dell saw opportunity in price wars and consolidations. The company sought market share from companies going out of business. Dell succeeded. By the end of 1996, Dell ranked number five in the worldwide PC market.[11]

FINANCIAL AND PORTFOLIO ANALYSIS

Despite the recession of the early 1990s and litigation that was eventually lost to Compaq, Dell has managed to recover. Net profits went from $5 million in 1990 to just over $944 million for 1998.[12] Unit volumes increased from 48 to 55 percent for fiscal year 1997. This change resulted from continued, rapid growth of the company's entire product line. Desktops and workstations make up 78 percent of the company's revenues while the other 22 percent consists of notebooks and servers.

The company has also experienced rapid growth in the international market. Growth in North and South America has been three times faster than the United States market. In Europe, where economic conditions have worsened, Dell has continued to advance on the strength of 36 percent sales growth. Dell has offices in 14 countries and just over 2,000 employees. This moved Dell to the number two position in the overseas market with sales of more than $2 billion in 1997.[13]

The Asia/Pacific/Japan region has become one of Dell's major emphases for growth. With direct operations in 11 countries and distribution alliances serving another 37, Asian sales grew 38 percent in 1997 over fiscal year 1996. With margins and growth higher outside the United States, Dell finished construction in Malaysia of a 238,000 square foot manufacturing and customer-support facility. This facility allows Dell to deliver its products more quickly and less expensively in Asia, not to mention customizing products to regional

[5] Wagner, Mitch, "The InternetWeek Interview—Michael Dell, Chairman and CEO, Dell Computer," *InternetWeek,* November 9, 1998, p. 10(1).
[6] "Dell Computer Corp.," *International Directory of Company Histories,* St. James Press, 1994.
[7] Kleinbard, David, "Big Tech Vendors Build Up Huge Cash Reserves," *Information Week,* May 31, 1999, p. 115.
[8] "Dell Computer Corp.," *International Directory of Company Histories,* St. James Press, 1994.

[9] Ibid.
[10] "Low-Cost PCs Boost the Market," *Computergram International,* July 27, 1999, p. NA.
[11] "Amazon.com Standardizes on Dell Desktops," *EDGE: Work-Group Computing Report,* August 16, 1999, p. NA.
[12] *Annual Report 1997,* June 18, 1997, www.dell.com.
[13] "Dell's Direct Approach," *Management Today,* February 1997, p. 62(3).

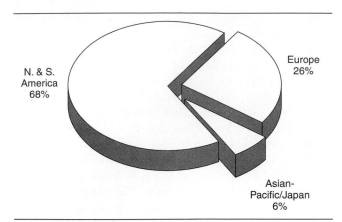

N. & S. America 68%

Europe 26%

Asian-Pacific/Japan 6%

Figure 8.1 Revenue by geographic region.

and national tastes. Dell's management projects that the "mix of our business over time should be geographically a lot different from what it is today."[14] Figure 8.1 summarizes the company's areas of operation.

Gross margins as a percentage of consolidated net sales have increased. This is due in large part to declining component costs and shifting of the product mix to notebooks, servers, and higher end desktops.

Although Dell continues to grow and demonstrate strong financial results, the company is in a precarious position. Upon entering the PC market in 1984, Michael Dell sold by direct sales only. The company's ultimate success factor has been and continues to be its direct-sell and build-to-order philosophy. Direct selling occurs through ads in computer magazines and telephone calls directly to the company. Build-to-order means that the PC is built only when an order is placed.

Through Dell's direct-sell and build-to-order philosophy, the company maintains a strong competitive advantage. The Dell philosophy is to have no inventory and no middleperson and avoid the related price markups. PC components drop in cost an average of 32 percent a year. Retailers like Compaq carry inventory 70 days longer than does Dell. As a result, parts cost Dell 6.1 percent less. Then dealers add a 7 percent markup on PCs. Direct marketing and sales expenses add an additional 1.1 percent to the cost of a PC. Overall, no inventory and no middleperson gives Dell a 12 percent (6.1 percent + 5.9 percent) cost advantage over resellers.[15]

In 1993, Dell added computer retailers to their distribution channel. At the time, the retail sector ap-

peared to have a large growth potential. Dell hired retail veteran David Turnbull from Acer America to run the division. Over a year's time, Dell only managed to obtain 2 to 10 percent of its revenue from the retail dealers. Compaq was better known with individual consumers and Packard Bell PCs were cheaper. Thus, against the advice of financial analysts, Dell abandoned the retail market in 1994.

During the early 1990s, the United States experienced a recession, causing sales to weaken. As a result, PC makers engaged in extensive price wars, resulting in a decline in profits. In actuality, Dell benefited from the recession. Consumers had less money but still required computers. With this in mind, consumers purchased Dell's inexpensive, yet technologically innovative, IBM clones in large numbers. This resulted in annual sales of $1 billion.

Dell has stressed the vital aspect of knowing their customers and the individualized treatment each requires. Moving into the 21st century, customer service-oriented companies must differentiate themselves from the competition. Direct relationship marketing has been a goal of Dell from the outset. Salespeople take direct responsibility for complete satisfaction of each customer.[16]

Sales personnel are trained for approximately six weeks before taking a seat at the "phonebank." They are trained to promote products while customizing orders. Specifications are then sent to a nearby plant where orders are filled within five days.[17] Staff technicians solve over 91 percent of customer problems. Problems that cannot be solved quickly are discussed in weekly staff meetings. If all else fails, customers can choose next-day, on-site service.

The company's net sales for the three fiscal years 1994 through 1996 were attributable to the increased units sold. The increased unit volume was offset by a 6 percent decline in average revenue per unit compared to fiscal 1996. The company has experienced growth in net sales in all geographic regions (see Figure 8.2 for a sales analysis).

Gross margins were affected as a result of several factors such as declines in component costs (offset by price reductions) and a product mix shift to higher margin products such as notebooks and servers of 18 percent and 4 percent, respectively. The company maintained a direct business model that involves low levels of inventory. A decrease in components inventory had a direct impact on overall product costs. The low level of inventory lessened the risk associated with price pro-

[14] "Runaway Horse: Michael Dell Wants to Rein in Growth; Shareholders Want the Whip," *Financial World,* October 24, 1995, v. 164, n. 22, p. 36.
[15] "Houston, We Have Some Problems," *Fortune,* June 23, 1997, p. 102(3).

[16] Donnelly, Brian, "Enterprise Application Integration," *Enterprise Systems Journal,* May 1999, v. 14, i. 5, p. 80(1).
[17] "PC Slump? What PC Slump?," *Business Week,* July 1, 1991, p. 66(7).

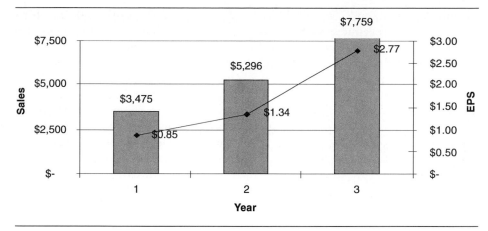

Figure 8.2 Net sales and earnings per share (EPS), in millions except per share data (1) 1/29/1995, (2) 1/28/1996, (3) 2/2/1997.

tection and returns. One last factor that maximized margins was the large discounts that Dell receives from Microsoft for copies of Microsoft Office.[18]

Despite Dell's fallout with notebook computing in 1993, sales have grown astronomically. The company's net income increased 90 percent to $518 million from 1996 to 1997 and 82 percent to $944 million from 1997 to 1998. Property, plant, and equipment have shown continued growth to meet the growing demand for products with percentage increases for these years of 31 and 40 percent, respectively.[19]

The cost of goods sold, research and development, and selling, general, and administrative expenses will continue to increase to meet demand as Dell further penetrates the Internet and the server market.

To further evaluate the stability of Dell Computer, financial ratios need to be analyzed carefully. Looking at net sales to the number of employees, the net sales have increased greatly while the number of people working for Dell has also steadily increased. The ratio of inventory to day's sales has decreased dramatically from fiscal year 1996 to 1997 and decreased 50 percent in 1998. Since fiscal year 1995, the inventory to day's sales ratio has gone from roughly 30 to 6 days. This indicates a combination of a decrease in the amount of inventory at the plants and sales growth to where inventory only lasts 6 days on the shelves, minimizing the level of inventory. Additionally, the net income to net sales ratio has grown moderately, indicating that operating expenses have decreased and net sales have grown.[20]

However, even the industry innovator in build-to-order solutions can face stiff competition. In the fourth quarter of 1998, Apple Computer, a recent adopter of the build-to-order philosophy, developed an inventory system that was 25 percent lower than Dell's inventory level. With competition chipping away at Dell's most prized cost-cutting measures, the company may still have to face cost-cutting issues.[21]

The total debt to equity ratio has steadily decreased, indicating that the company's debt has decreased while the company's equity has grown. This consistent, steady growth has enabled Dell to absorb market fluctuations and achieve an average operating profit of 6 percent over the previous year for 1990-1998.

STOCK/INVESTMENT OUTLOOK

From 1990–1998, Dell shares have appreciated more than 2,800 percent (adjusted for stock splits). Dell had the highest share price growth for the first nine months of 1996 of any U.S. company in the Dow Jones World Stock Index. Investor's love Dell Computer. The company's stock ranked second behind Western Digital as the highest total return to investors with 206 percent for 1996. The company approved a two-for-one stock split for stockholders of record as of November 25, 1996. Following the quarterly earnings announcement in early February 1997, Dell once again announced a two-for-one stock split to shareholders of record on July 18, 1997. This was their fourth stock split in five years.

As of June 2, 1997, Standard & Poor's revised Dell's outlook from stable to positive and affirmed their rating at triple B minus.[22] As the company expands into the

[18] Wilder, Clinton, "Rethinking ROI E-Business Strategic Investment," *Information Week*, May 24, 1999, p. 47.

[19] DiCarlo, Lisa, "Changes Afoot in PC Industry," *PC Week*, April 26, 1999, v. 16, i. 17, p. 1(1).

[20] "IBM and Dell Computer Corporation," *Midrange Systems*, April 26, 1999, v. 12, i. 6, p. 4(1).

[21] Dell, Michael S., "Computing According to Dell," *Computer Shopper*, December 1, 1998, p. 180(1).

[22] "Dell Computer Corp.'s Outlook to Positive by S&P; Affirms Rating," *PR Newswire*, June 2, 1997.

PC server and workstation market, and keeps its industry fundamentals intact, strong revenue growth is expected. The stock splits and outlook status work toward Dell's goal of providing consistent financial results and superior value to their shareholders.

RISK ANALYSIS

As we move toward the 21st century, the Internet is the new mass medium for advertising. Dell's home page remains the model web page for technology companies. Ads on the Web cost roughly $9 per user compared to $116 for radio, $340 for broadcast TV, and $586 for newspaper. Increased web advertising fits into Dell's strategy of being the low-cost direct seller of PCs.

Compaq is currently reevaluating their distribution channel. They are considering a merger with Micron Computer or Gateway 2000 to enter the direct-sell market. The biggest danger to Dell is that Compaq will overhaul its sales strategy to be more like Dell. Fortunately for Dell, adding a direct distribution channel to their current operations would cause numerous problems for Compaq. For instance, if a customer has the choice of purchasing a PC from a retailer or a direct seller over the Internet, the customer will probably go to the cheaper outlet. Compaq could cannibalize their own retail sales.

INDUSTRY AND MARKET ANALYSIS

Growth in the PC sector was up 20 percent in 1996. Internet users in 1996 were 25 million compared to the 150 million users expected by 2000. U.S sales are 40 percent of the total PC market, up 17 percent compared to the prior year. Large numbers of international areas have not been penetrated. The Western European market has 24 percent of the market, up 13 percent. Asia/Pacific has 13 percent of the market, up 23 percent, while Japan has 12 percent of the market, up 44 percent. Portable computers and servers are growing over 30 percent per year. If sales for network computers rise, sales for servers will skyrocket.[23]

Balancing resellers and direct sales is very difficult. If Compaq were to add the direct model to their distribution channel, a domino effect may occur because every effort to go direct is greeted with a number of resellers threatening to jump ship. Although Compaq is still growing rapidly (14 percent for first quarter 1997), direct-seller Dell is growing even faster (57 percent for first quarter 1997). See Figure 8.3 for comparisons.[24]

IBM's response to Dell's growth has been a massive marketing and sales effort for their new SystemCare hardware and service. SystemCare aims at corporations that budget $250,000 to $5 million annually on PC hardware and services. The goal is to reduce the total costs of ownership for the corporations.

SystemCare was developed to enable IBM to offer technology life cycle leasing, LAN management, asset management, maintenance, and other services as SKUs that resellers can market to their customers.[25] This system, however, does not have any details at this point. Resellers do not know how much money they can make and training needs to be done. With that in mind, SystemCare was not fully implemented until 1998.

Demand for servers remains strong, with Compaq positioned as the market share leader for servers that run smaller LANs. Servers are the fastest growing segment in the computer hardware industry. The main reason is that corporate America is reducing its use of large, expensive mainframes in favor of more flexible hardware. IBM feels the effects of this firsthand. Although IBM saw a 50 percent growth in mainframe

---

[23] Davey, Tom, "Dell Turns to Servers," *Information Week,* April 27, 1998, n. 679, p. 156(1).
[24] Smith, Tom, "Dell Ties E-Storefront to Buyer Processes," *Internet Week,* May 17, 1999, p. 6(1).
[25] "IBM Readying its SystemCare Effort," *Computer Reseller News,* June 2, 1997, p. 40.

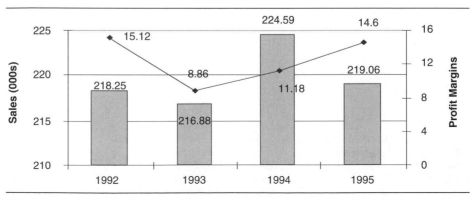

Figure 8.3 PC sales and profit margins (industry).

MIPS (million instructions per second), they were forced to reduce prices dramatically to remain competitive with less expensive servers.

ROLE OF RESEARCH AND DEVELOPMENT

Dell's main emphasis in research and development is refining their direct sales approach. This has worked well but must constantly be adapted to new technologies and opportunities.[26]

TECHNOLOGICAL STORY

In 1991, Dell produced its first notebook model. In 1992, it introduced a full-color notebook with Intel's 486 chip. Quality and internal issues stemming from Dell's growth forced the company to cancel a series of notebook computers before they were even introduced. As a result, Dell changed management's strategic outlook. Michael Dell hired industry veterans, particularly from companies like Apple, Hewlett-Packard, IBM, and Motorola. One of them was Mort Topfer, who headed Motorola's land mobile products division. Another was John Medica, the former leader of Apple Computer's Powerbook team. Today, they run Dell's notebook computer unit.[27]

TECHNOLOGICAL INVESTMENT AND ANALYSIS

With competitors attempting to copy Dell's sales model, Dell focused on another direct route, the Internet.[28] Compaq, Packard Bell, and other companies that sell through retailers allow "surfers" to browse through a product line catalog on the Internet.[29] But as consumers look through Compaq's product line, others are purchasing PCs through Dell's home page. Dell has revenues in excess of $1 million a day in Internet sales.[30]

Dell recently incorporated an electronic link with its larger corporate customers.[31] Purchases of Dell products can be made directly through corporate accounting systems of a suitably outfitted corporation or institution.[32]

Dell Computer also focuses on the server market.[33] Servers account for 6 percent of the company's system revenue. Dell currently ranks number four behind IBM in server sales. Dell Computer has made stronger efforts to move up in ranking by cutting server prices by 16 percent on its midrange and high-end Pentium® Pro processor-based PowerEdge® network servers. The price cuts make Dell's PowerEdge servers as much as 30 to 35 percent lower than comparable systems offered by Dell's major competitors.[34]

Dell Computer entered the workstation market with the delivery of Windows NT-based workstations in 1998. The company targets financial services, software development, and mechanical CAD/CAM/CAE/graphics markets. Workstations, when compared to a standard IBM clone PC, integrate hardware and software into a solution for specialized tasks such as financial analysis, computer-aided design, or software development.

Dell has also gone direct internationally. Last year, the company moved into 9 markets in Asia, enabling customers to purchase a computer online in Australia, Hong Kong, New Zealand, Thailand, Korea, Malaysia, Singapore, Taiwan, and Japan. Dell has various web pages for different countries, each developed in local languages and local currencies. To cut delivery costs, computers are manufactured in foreign plants rather than in the United States.[35]

TECHNOLOGICAL INNOVATIONS

NETWORK

Dell has not adopted the same strategy as Compaq for networks. Some components of networking are tied to the server, including the components in the box and the network adapters. Network accessories and products that connect to the server could be easily sold by Dell. In contrast, Compaq must convince the reseller to sell the Compaq server and the Compaq router or the Compaq switch, rather than the Cisco or 3Com product.[36] That is not easy. Larger network users have bought into architectures. For someone to influence a

[26] Whiting, Rick, "Warehouse ROI: Data Warehouses Are Getting the Same Scrutiny As Other Projects," *Information Week*, May 24, 1999, p. 99.

[27] Pendery, David, Briody, Dan, and Schwartz, Ephraim, "What Dell Does Best," *Info World*, April 6, 1998, v. 20, n. 14, p. 1(2).

[28] Cheek, Michael, "Online Buying is Good for Feds, Vendors," *Government Computer News*, March 23, 1998, v. 17, n. 7, p. 24(1).

[29] Lundquist, Eric, "Dell's Web Tie-in Could Unravel Compaq," *PC Week*, May 17, 1999, v. 16, i. 20, p. 122.

[30] Karpinski, Richard, "Web Transforms Businesses: E-Commerce Pioneers Say Online Participation is Critical to Success," *Internet Week*, April 5, 1999, p. 12(1).

[31] Steermann, Hank, "Measuring Data Warehouse Success: Eight Signs You're on the Right Track," *Intelligent Enterprise*, March 30, 1999, v. 2, i. 5, p. 12(1).

[32] "The Direct Route," *InfoWorld*, June 2, 1997, pp. 1, 19.

[33] Burger, Dale, "Dell Hits Fork in Road over Network Computer," *Computing Canada*, February 3, 1997, v. 23, n. 3, p. 17(1).

[34] "Dell Strengthens Server Leadership with Price Cuts of Up to 16 Percent," *Wall Street Journal*, May 15, 1997, p. B1.

[35] Frerichs, Robert N., "Supply Chain Management," *Electronic Business*, August 1999, v. 25, i. 8, p. 8.

[36] Schwartz, Ephraim, "Dell Set to Launch Internet Service Provider Business," *Info World*, August 2, 1999, v. 21, i. 31, p. 42.

company to switch from their current architecture, a compelling argument must be presented. As such, Dell is committed to pursuing the server market only.[37]

CEO Michael Dell believes his company's strategy is appropriate and will be sufficient to make it the number one server supplier. Dell's own efforts have been enhanced by the move toward product standardization with the introduction of Microsoft's Windows NT. The company will continue to push for industry standards and does not see itself as a technology innovator.[38]

TELECOMMUNICATIONS

Dell's telecommunication plans are broad. They include customized web sites for business customers, which let a company's employees buy computers directly over the Internet based on automated policies. Dell is also focusing on automated service and support based on the latest configuration information of a company. Currently under design is a workflow capability that will automate the purchase-approval process within businesses.

---

[37] "Dell Adds Giganet for NT Cluster Stategy," *Computergram International*, May 19, 1999, p. NA.
[38] Hoog, Robert, "Use Your Intranet for Effective Knowledge Management," *e-Business Advisor*, April 1999, v. 17, i. 4, p. 27(1).

RECOMMENDATION FOR THE FUTURE

Dell plans to increase its presence in the technology sector through the perfection of the direct distribution channel. The company has grown to the point that they are currently ranked as number four in worldwide PC sales. Although passing Packard Bell, IBM, and Compaq may take some time, they must look toward the notebook and server market to complement the PC market.[39]

Without the benefit of the retail market, they can only continue their growth rate by maintaining and revolutionizing the direct market. As a result of Dell's growth, Compaq, IBM, and other computer companies have reexamined their distribution channels. The decreasing margins will cause an increase of mergers and acquisitions among PC manufacturers. Most importantly, Dell must continue to focus on the founding philosophy. Dell must constantly keep its direct-sell and build-to-order philosophy along with customer service vital for the company's continued success.

Dell must make its presence felt internationally by expanding current facilities and building new distribution channels as international demand grows. The facility built in Malaysia in 1996 has strategically minimized shipping costs.[40]

---

[39] "Low-Cost PCs Boost the Market," *Computergram International*, July 27, 1999, p. NA.
[40] Serwer, Andrew E., "Michael Dell Turns the PC World Inside Out," *Fortune*, September 8, 1997, v. 136, n. 5, p. 76(7).

CASE QUESTIONS

Strategic Questions

1. What is the strategic direction of the corporation/organization?

2. Who or what forces are driving this direction?

3. What has been the catalyst for change?

4. What are the critical success factors for this corporation/organization?

5. What are the core competencies for this corporation/organization?

Technological Questions

6. What technologies has the corporation relied on?

7. What has caused a change in the use of technology in the corporation/organization?

8. How has this change been implemented?

9. Who has driven this change throughout the organization?

10. How successful has the technology been?

Quantitative Questions

11. What does the corporation say about its financial ability to embark on a major technological program of advancement?

12. What conclusions can be reached from an analysis of the financial information to support or contradict this financial ability?

13. What analysis can be made by examining the following ratio groups?
    Quick/Current
    Debt

Revenue
Profit
Asset Utilization

14. What conclusions can be reached by analyzing the financial trends? Are there long-term trends that seem to be problematic? Is the industry stable? Are there replacement products?

Internet Questions

15. What does the corporation's web page present about their business directives?

16. How does this compare to the conclusions reached from the case?

17. How does this compare to the conclusions reached by analyzing the financial information?

Industry Questions

18. What challenges and opportunities is the industry facing?

19. Is the industry oligopolistic or competitive?

20. Does the industry face a change in government regulation?

21. How will technology impact the industry?

Data Questions

22. What role do data play in the future of the corporation?

23. How important are data to the corporation's continued success?

24. How will the capture and maintenance of customer data impact the corporation's future?

GATEWAY 2000

Executive Summary

Case Name:	Gateway 2000
Case Industry:	Computer hardware manufacturer
Major Technology Issue:	How to include the latest technology in its computers
Major Financial Issue:	How to maintain its fast growth in revenue and profits
Major Strategic Issue:	How to keep prices down while customizing computers
Major Players/Leaders:	Ted Waitt, CEO
Main Web Page:	www.gw2k.com
Case Conclusion/Recommendation:	Gateway 2000 has been able to grow faster than the market by selling customized computers directly and at very competitive prices. Gateway needs to accurately predict customers' wants and needs to continue its high growth strategy.

CASE ANALYSIS

INTRODUCTORY STORY

Ted Waitt founded TIPC (Texas Instruments PCs) Network in August 1985 after dropping out of college. He brought in his friend Mike Hammond to work the technical side of the business. Contrary to popular belief, the pair started their business in an empty office on the Waitt cattle farm and not in a barn. The company sold upgrades and accessories to owners of Texas Instruments (TI) PCs. Waitt's grandmother guaranteed the $10,000 loan that founded TIPC. Norm Waitt, Ted's older brother, joined the company in early 1986 to take care of the company's finances.

In 1987, Texas Instruments offered its customers a chance to upgrade their old computers to IBM-compatible PCs for $3,500. Waitt and Hammond saw this as a great opportunity, since they knew they could do the same for a lot less. The first Gateway computer had two floppy drives, a deluxe color monitor, and more memory than most PCs at the time. The $2,000 asking price was comparable to other models, but the Gateway PC offered far greater performance.

SHORT DESCRIPTION OF THE COMPANY

Gateway 2000 is a direct marketer of personal computers. Gateway 2000 develops, manufactures, and supports a broad line of desktop and portable PCs. Domestic sales account for 84 percent of total sales; the remainder are international sales.

Individuals, small businesses, and home offices account for 65 percent of Gateway's customers. Large cor-

porations, government agencies, and educational institutions account for 35 percent (Figure 8.4). Desktop computers represent 90 percent of the revenues. Gateway 2000's strategy is to offer quality, high-performance products using the latest technology at competitive prices with outstanding service and support.

SHORT HISTORY OF THE COMPANY

Gateway's significant advantage over its competitors has been its ability to provide quick response to its customers. Once a customer calls and places an order with the desired features, the system is designed, packaged, and shipped in about five days. Gateway maintains a large financial advantage by building computers when orders are placed. The company holds virtually no inventory.

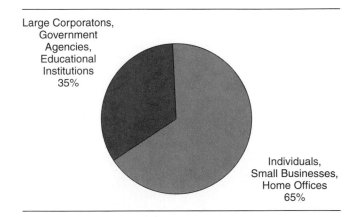

Figure 8.4 Gateway 2000 customers.

Gateway often changes configuration designs every three days and is able to change prices every day. With this processing format, Gateway is able to avoid the financial risk caused by excess inventory. Gateway is also able to pass along the savings to customers almost immediately.

The company grew from $1.5 million in sales in 1987 to $12 million in sales in 1988. Gateway annual sales were nearly double the industry average for 1993–1996 (Figure 8.5). Gateway has experienced annual sales growth of 40 to 50 percent, surpassing the $5 billion plateau in 1996. Sales surpassed $6.5 billion in 1997 and $8.5 billion in 1998.

Gateway assembles computers with components developed by other manufacturers, avoiding high research and development costs. In 1990, the company was renamed Gateway 2000 and built a new headquarters in South Dakota. At the time, Gateway 2000 employed 185 people and shipped 225 PCs a day. Today Gateway employs 9,700 people.

Gateway 2000 distributed advertisements with self-mocking headlines such as "Computers from Iowa?" The company headquarters and all shipping boxes are designed with black and white spots to resemble the hide of a Holstein cow. The company markets itself strictly through advertising. On an annual basis, advertising costs are approximately $90 million. Gateway's sales passed the billion-dollar plateau in 1992 and rose to $3.7 billion in 1995. The company went international in 1993 when it opened a marketing and manufacturing plant in Ireland. The company also completed its IPO in 1993.

Waitt's instincts have led him to pioneer the mail order computer industry. In 1988, Gateway was the first to make EGA monitors standard on all of its systems. In 1990, it was the first to make Windows the standard operating system on all of its systems. In 1994, Gateway made the Pentium chip and CD-ROM drives standard before its competitors. In 1996, Gateway become the first computer maker to enable its customers to custom order and pay for new computers over the World Wide Web.

Gateway has developed an extensive customer support base. Gateway customers can call the toll-free technical support line and receive professional assistance for any difficulty they may be experiencing.[1] Gateway is considered to be the industry leader in customer service and support.[2]

Gateway's vision and research has led to its remarkable growth pattern for the past 10 years. That same foresight is expected to help Gateway remain a step ahead of the competition in offering the best priced, most powerful computers available to consumers. Gateway has been slowly gaining market share as more individuals feel comfortable buying their second computers through a direct manufacturer such as Gateway.[3]

Gateway seeks to continue its pioneering efforts by offering new and innovative products. As PCs become a more important part of the every day household, Gateway hopes to continue to develop new products. Ted Waitt believes that by the year 2002, Gateway could be a $90 billion company. He hopes to build a global computer manufacturing power from what started as a two-man shop just over 10 years ago.[4]

FINANCIAL AND PORTFOLIO ANALYSIS

The growth of the computer industry has continued to move forward at an aggressive pace. As competition

[1] Myron, David, "Face-to-Face Support," *VARbusiness*, June 21, 1999, p. 15.
[2] "Gateway Sees Greener Pastures in Urban Stores," *Computer Shopper*, August 1999, p. 151.
[3] Speir, Michelle, "Six Sensational Systems," *Federal Computer Week*, November 16, 1998, v. 12.
[4] Swisher, Kara, and Ramstad, Evan, "Gateway Is in Talks to Acquire EarthLink," *The Wall Street Journal*, June 23, 1999, p. B6(W), p. B6(E), 1.

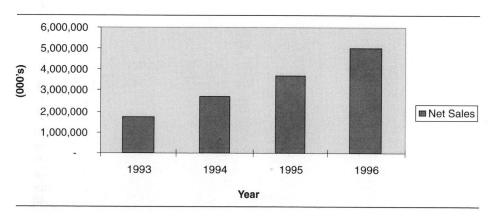

Figure 8.5 Gateway 2000 net sales, 1993–1996.

has lowered prices, industry profit margins have decreased. Gateway has continued to grow rapidly. All signs indicate continued growth.

Gateway 2000 has experienced a more difficult time selling computers on the international market. It expects sales to improve in Europe with the exception of Germany. International revenue as a percentage of total sales, currently 16 percent, is not expected to increase.

The company is able to immediately change the price structure of its PCs. This flexibility helps the company maintain strong earnings by continually passing along savings to the consumer without a break in sales or lost inventory. Earnings per share have soared (Figure 8.6).

The company has been decreasing long-term debt, thereby decreasing the debt to equity ratios. Overhead expenses as a percentage of sales decreased in the fourth quarter of 1996 to 11.3 from 11.9 percent. The improvement was primarily due to a strong seasonal increase in sales, leading to a change in operating margins. The company's growth has been funded through increased profits and improved cost measures, not through increased debt.

While the net sales to plant and equipment ratio and the net sales to total assets ratio have decreased, the decrease has been due to significant increases in property, plant, and equipment to support the accelerated growth pattern Gateway has experienced. The decrease in net sales to current assets seems to be largely due to cash difficulties in December 31, 1996, as compared to the prior year-end cash positions. The total debt to equity ratio has steadily declined to 0.03 for fiscal year 1996 from 0.04 for fiscal year 1995 and 0.08 for fiscal year 1994. Figure 8.7 depicts the decline in long-term debt.

The net sales to employee ratio improved to $519,096 in 1996 from $395,304 in 1995. Operating margins improved to 8.2 percent, compared to 7.3 percent for the previous quarter. Gateway reported an unusually high gross margin of 19.3 percent in the fourth quarter of 1996. The company has continued to improve the gross profits as depicted in Figure 8.8.

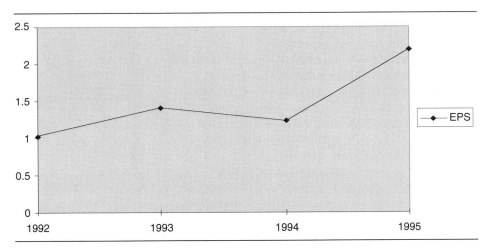

Figure 8.6 Gateway 2000 earnings per share, 1992–1995.

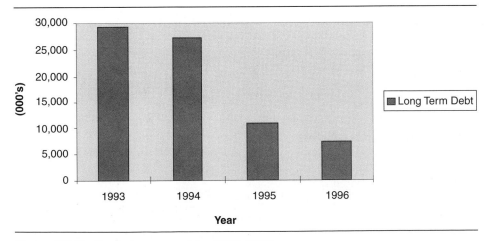

Figure 8.7 Decline in long-term debt, 1993–1996.

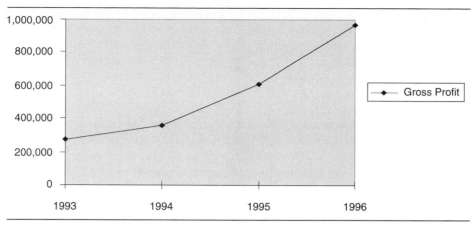

Figure 8.8 Gross profit, 1993–1996.

The introduction of the new MMX microprocessors strengthened sales during the first quarter of 1997.

STOCK/INVESTMENT OUTLOOK

While the computer manufacturing industry is competitive, Gateway 2000's outlook remains positive. The company has a good mix between personal and business customers. This will enable the company to survive and adjust to changes in buying trends. New technology, such as the faster MMX processor, will maintain consumer demand. Corporate demand should remain constant in the near future, as more corporations continue to shift to Windows NT. Gateway 2000's direct marketing should enable the company to continue a strong growth pattern despite increased competition, as it takes market share from other indirect manufacturers.

Experts generally agree that the near-term growth pattern for Gateway should continue to progress at a steady pace. Gross margins remained above 19 percent through 1997. Operating expenses remained at 12 percent. Earnings per share improved 34 percent for fiscal year 1997. While sales continued to increase in 1997, gross margins and operating expenses remained in line with fiscal year 1996. This continued to fuel positive expectations for the company and the industry.

RISK ANALYSIS

Gateway 2000 operates in a highly price competitive industry. Gateway must continue to price its systems to remain in the market with other PC manufacturers. Market price wars and the resulting decline in margins directly impact stock value. A change in the buying habits of consumers could impact the success of the company. While the market has been very strong in recent years, a change in buying patterns by either corporations or consumers could have a negative impact on demand. Gateway 2000 stock is currently trading at a premium value relative to its price history. If the valuation returns to normal, the stock could experience downward pressure.[5]

Another major threat to Gateway may come from the industry heavyweight, Compaq. Compaq has been discussing the idea of more direct distribution plans. If Compaq were to build this direct network, the impact would most likely be felt more in the corporate rather than the consumer market. Gateway may be able to deflect some of this risk, as the majority of computer hardware sales are with the consumer market.

One major obstacle for Compaq remains: the fact that Compaq has significantly higher pricing for products when compared to Gateway. Compaq may be able to compete with Gateway for the corporate customers in the near future, but individual customers will remain difficult for Compaq to capture. While Gateway has been developing international sales, their exposure is still much lower than other major PC manufacturers.[6]

INDUSTRY AND MARKET ANALYSIS

The worldwide information technology (IT) market reached $570 billion in 1996. This market includes computer hardware, software, and services. Computer hardware is the largest of these segments and comprised approximately 40 percent of the total IT market in 1996. Further, computer hardware consists of personal computers, large/multiuser systems, and workstations. PCs comprise nearly 60 percent of all computer hardware sales.

[5] Blackford, John, "The Return of the Corner Store," *Computer Shopper,* July 1999, v. 19, i. 7, p. 88.
[6] Caldwell, Bruce, "Gateway Outsources IT to Lockheed Martin, Keane," *Information Week,* May 31, 1999, p. 36.

The number one computer manufacturer in terms of market share for 1996 was Compaq Computer (Figure 8.9). Compaq holds a 9.7 percent share of the worldwide PC market, which is slightly less than the 10 percent market share it held at the end of 1995. Although Compaq's annual sales growth was below the industry average at 14 percent, the company is still highly regarded as the model of success in the very competitive PC marketplace.

Compaq offers the most comprehensive product line. The company also has a very large and comprehensive global manufacturing and distribution infrastructure. It remains the most profitable vendor in the PC industry with operating margins well above the competition. These margins have helped Compaq maintain pressure on the competition with aggressive advertising and marketing programs. Compaq has recently updated their product line. This should help them retain their worldwide market share.

IBM holds the second largest share in the PC industry with 8.8 percent of the PC market. IBM increased its share from 8 percent in 1995 largely as a result of a strong 30 percent increase in sales for 1996. Compaq displaced IBM as the world leader in 1994, but IBM has been making gains to recapture the top spot. IBM has accomplished this by drastically cutting the number of brand offerings, restructuring its manufacturing and forecasting units, and adapting to the ever-changing PC environment more quickly than its competition.

Apple Computer holds the third spot worldwide with a 5.3 percent market share. Apple Computer's share has dropped from the 7.8 percent share it held at the end of 1995 but seems to have stabilized. NEC, a Japanese vendor, is fourth with a 5.1 percent market share, and Hewlett-Packard is fifth with a 4.3 percent worldwide market share.

The personal computer business has benefited largely from increased spending by businesses and consumers in recent years. The PC industry has experienced five con-secutive years of double-digit growth. However, signs are beginning to indicate that a slight decrease in growth may be forthcoming. The industry has experienced growth of 20 to 30 percent annually. Experts believe a more sustainable growth rate is 10 to 15 percent annually.

The two primary direct-mail companies, Dell Computer Corporation and Gateway 2000, have experienced growth patterns that have been approximately double the industry average, ranging from 40 to 50 percent. These companies offer a very attractive product to second-time purchasers with aggressive pricing and custom-built configurations.[7]

New technology and products will keep demand strong in the future. Improved technology has reduced component costs, enabling vendors to offer PC systems with many features at very affordable prices. Research and development costs are major investments for the industry leaders. While profit margins for existing technology products continue to shrink, the industry leaders will benefit from the larger margins that result from new technology. For example, the cost of dynamic random access memory (DRAM) chips has recently experienced a dramatic decrease, which in turn has resulted in lower cost PCs.

New technology will continue to drive the success of the computer industry. LAN servers are gaining a larger piece of the revenue pie as customers are implementing server-based LANs rather than centralized mainframe systems. LAN servers are available in many different sizes. Smaller servers are used for productivity applications such as e-mail. Larger servers, which use several microprocessors, are assuming the tasks of the more traditional large and midrange computers.[8]

---

[7] Pereira, Pedro, "Not Out to Pasture Yet: Gateway Gets Serious About the Channel," *Computer Reseller News,* June 7, 1999, p. 59.

[8] Conlin, Michael, "For Whom the Dell Tolls," *Forbes,* August 10, 1998, v. 162, n. 3, p. 46(1).

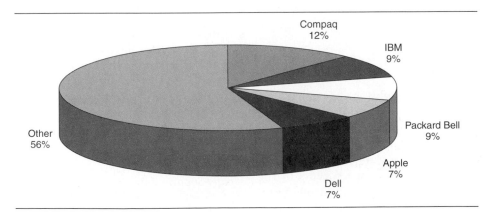

Figure 8.9 United States PC market share.

The increased popularity of the World Wide Web, now estimated at over 100 million users, has helped both PC and server vendors. Consumers and businesses alike are quickly replacing old computer hardware with faster modems and more powerful PCs.

The use of the PC for entertainment and television is pushing forward a new and exciting frontier. The merging of these technologies should enhance graphics and multimedia demand. The convergence is expected to develop increased popularity for the web as consumers bring this technology into their living rooms.

New processors, such as the Pentium Pro and the MMX, help improve the speed and abilities of multimedia applications. They will continue to keep PC demand strong in the future. Technological advances will enable the industry to maintain a comfortable growth pattern.

All computer hardware vendors will experience difficulty maintaining profit margins as the average selling prices of products decline sharply. Competition within the industry has been strong. PC demand is expected to slow sharply as the market matures and a larger percentage of households purchase PCs.

PC vendors have bundled more and more of their products with CD-ROM drives and high-speed modems. The added features have pushed the average price for consumers to $1,200 for an entry-level computer. Industry studies show that average U.S. households with an income over $50,000 have already purchased a computer. With the relatively high prices, PCs are not an affordable option for many consumers. Figure 8.10 depicts the continued expected decline in the price of personal computers.

Purchasers have come to expect prices to decline and expect more features in each new generation of computers. As processors continue to improve performance, Intel has aggressively reduced the price of its microprocessors.

ROLE OF RESEARCH AND DEVELOPMENT

As a direct manufacturer, Gateway is able to avoid extensive research and development costs. However, the company must constantly research the computer industry to be able to continue to constantly provide leading-edge technology to its customers. Gateway has purchased other companies to obtain an advantage over competitors. For instance, they acquired Advanced Logic Research (ALR), an industry leader in the design and manufacturing of high-performance computer systems. The knowledge gained from this investment has helped Gateway provide the latest technological advances to consumers ahead of the competition.

As Gateway continues to grow in the ever-changing computer industry, they must also continue to invest in the development of their employees. By continually investing to update the knowledge level of support staff, Gateway will ensure they maintain an edge over the competition not only with new products, but also with superior customer support.[9]

Technological advances have caused setbacks for many companies in the computer industry. The industry is one of the fastest innovating industries in history. As new technology becomes available, current inventories become outdated. One of the challenges facing industry leaders continues to be the proper management of inventory.[10]

---

[9] Waitt, Ted, "Gateway Looks Ahead," *Computer Shopper*, December 1, 1998, p. 180(1).

[10] Hagendorf, Jennifer, "Ted Waitt: Gateway—A Direct Marketer Attempts to Bridge Multiple Channels While Sticking to His Roots," *Computer Reseller News*, November 9, 1998, p. 131(1).

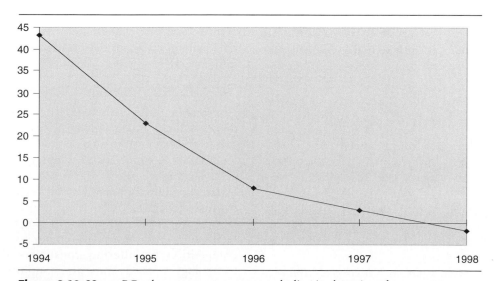

Figure 8.10 Home PC sales, year-to-year percent decline in the price of a computer.

TECHNOLOGICAL STORY

The MMX processor was introduced in January 1997. Through diligent research, Gateway was able to capitalize on the new technology. Gateway was able to offer PCs with the new processor to consumers prior to many its competitors. Consumer demand decreased in the fourth quarter of FY1996 in anticipation of the MMX introduction.

Gateway capitalized on the introduction of the MMX processor by immediately offering the new processor as soon as consumers demanded it. Gateway experienced larger than expected demand in the first quarter of FY1997 for PCs with this new technology.

TECHNOLOGICAL INVESTMENT AND ANALYSIS

DATABASES

Some industry analysts believe recordable CD drives will soon take the place of Zip and even floppy drives. Gateway must agree, having outfitted the G6-450 with a Philips CD-RW drive. Its sticker price includes a 14.4GB IBM Deskstar hard drive, a Riva TNT-equipped graphics card, a way-cool keyboard, and loads of software. The keyboard features audio-CD controls for use with the other optical drive, a Toshiba DVD-ROM; modem controls for accessing the speakerphone and voice mail; and a sleep button for putting the machine into standby mode. Inside there are four PCI slots and a lone PCI/ISA slot, which is occupied by a TelePath modem made for Gateway by 3Com Corporation.

Gateway provides a wealth of software with the computer, including Microsoft Home Essentials and a choice of three additional Microsoft collections (one for business users, one for children, and one for game players). Purchasers also receive easy-to-use CD recording and duplication utilities for use with the Philips drive and two blank CD-R and CD-RW discs.

Gateway's warranty is exemplary: three years on parts and labor, including one year of on-site service. Two extra years of on-site service costs just $99. The company also provides an unmatched variety of support options, including forums on America Online and CompuServe.

NETWORKS

Gateway 2000's E-1000N is a network PC-compliant system designed for high-volume network environments. The E-1000N, which shipped in the third quarter of 1998, is compatible with the Network PC System Design Guidelines.[11]

The E-1000N is based on Gateway's E-1000 platform with additional modifications to deliver the advanced management capabilities and hardware features

specifically called for in the network PC guidelines. Both systems include high levels of manageability, integrated networking, a space saving form factor, and exceptional price/performance. The E-1000N and the balance of Gateway's E-series line aim to reduce PC ownership costs by incorporating technologies that provide remote configuration and maintenance and remote software download from a central point. Hardware features also have been added to increase the control that IS managers have over PC implementations. At the same time, the E-1000N maintains critical features of the traditional PC, such as compatibility with existing Windows business software.

"Providing the E-1000N as Gateway's Net PC configuration will help our customers better identify the systems that best meet their specific needs," said Bill Shea, vice president of Gateway 2000 Major Accounts. "This continues our tradition of delivering high-value products with the flexibility needed by organizations in today's marketplace."

"One of the strengths of the Net PC System Design Guidelines is its comprehensive approach to manageability," said Mike Aymar, Intel vice president and general manager of the Desktop Products Group. "Gateway's E-1000N, by taking advantage of those guidelines, provides customers with a system designed specifically for centralized administration while still delivering the performance and flexibility they expect from Gateway PCs."

"Gateway 2000 customers benefit from the increased manageability and lower costs of the E-1000N," said Rich Tong, vice president of marketing, personal and business systems group at Microsoft Corp. The E-1000N joins the E-series line from Gateway 2000. The E-series family includes the E-1000, the E-3000 mainstream desktops, and E-5000 Pentium II workstations. The dual-mode approach of the E-1000 platform allows customers to deploy the E-1000N as a network PC alongside fully featured E-1000 PCs according to their user needs. At the same time, customers benefit from maintaining common architecture, interchanging common components, and the flexibility to adopt their computing infrastructure to future needs.

RECOMMENDATION FOR THE FUTURE

Competition within the computer manufacturing industry will continue to lower prices for their products. Gateway must continue to expand on the core competencies that have made the company a worldwide success. The ability to offer a powerful product at prices below the industry norm will be key to the company's continued success.

Gateway must continue monitoring the ever-changing technology environment to remain a step ahead of the competition by offering consumers the latest new technology. Gateway must also continue to invest in the extensive training of their support staff to maintain

---

[11] Ricadela, Aaron, "Gateway Gets Networked," *Information Week,* June 23, 1999, p. 43.

their competitive advantage in customer support. A lapse of foresight could result in a serious setback for the company.[12]

_____

[12] Hagendorf, Jennifer, "Ted Waitt: Gateway—A Direct Marketer Attempts to Bridge Multiple Channels While Sticking to His Roots," *Computer Reseller News*, November 9, 1998, p. 131(1).

Gateway 2000 has displayed the ability to aggressively develop new PCs with the latest technology and pass along the savings from that improved technology directly to the consumer. This management style should enable Gateway 2000 to continue the growth the company has experienced.

CASE QUESTIONS

Strategic Questions

1. What is the strategic direction of the corporation/organization?

2. Who or what forces are driving this direction?

3. What has been the catalyst for change?

4. What are the critical success factors for this corporation/organization?

5. What are the core competencies for this corporation/organization?

Technological Questions

6. What technologies has the corporation relied on?

7. What has caused a change in the use of technology in the corporation/organization?

8. What change has been implemented?

9. How successful is the technological change expected to be?

Quantitative Questions

10. What does the corporation say about its financial ability to embark on a major technological program of advancement?

11. What conclusions can be reached from an analysis of the financial information to support or contradict this financial ability?

12. What analysis can be made by examining the following ratio groups?
Quick/Current
Debt
Revenue

Profit
Asset Utilization

13. What conclusions can be reached by analyzing the financial trends? Are there long-term trends that seem to be problematic? Is the industry stable? Are there replacement products?

Internet Questions

14. What does the corporation's web page present about their business directives?

15. How does this compare to the conclusions reached from the case?

16. How does this compare to the conclusions reached by analyzing the financial information?

Industry Questions

17. What challenges and opportunities is the industry facing?

18. Is the industry oligopolistic or competitive?

19. Does the industry face a change in government regulation?

20. How will technology impact the industry?

Data Questions

21. What role do data play in the future of the corporation?

22. How important are data to the corporation's continued success?

23. How will the capture and maintenance of customer data impact the corporation's future?

TECHNOLOGY TIPS

MICROSOFT WORD TIPS

MODIFYING A CHART

Modifying the appearance or data of your graph can be done without having to "draw" a new one. If you have followed the directions in the previous chapter or created a graph using Word's graph wizard, then the following will help you modify your graph in several ways.

Changing Chart Type

If you want to change the chart to a pie chart, columns, radar, surface, or any of the other type of chart styles, do the following:

1. After creating your chart, double-click on the chart itself. Borders will appear around the chart area.
2. Click on the graph with the right mouse button. From the pop-up menu, select CHART TYPE.
3. A dialog box will appear providing examples of the different types of charts available.
4. To preview a chart, click on the style you want and hold on the PRESS AND HOLD TO VIEW SAMPLE button. A sample of the chart will appear (depending on your data, some charts will not be available for display).
5. Once you have selected a chart type click on OK.

Changing the Data

If your data has changed after creating the chart, you can correct the chart to reflect the changes by doing the following:

1. Double-click inside the chart area. Borders will appear around the chart area box and the chart toolbar will appear.
2. If the data sheet does not appear, click on the data sheet button from the chart tool bar.
3. A data sheet will appear with the information you entered. Edit the data in the cells that you want to change. As you move from cell to cell, you will notice that your chart will change to reflect your changes.
4. Once you have made the necessary changes click on OK.

Adding Labels, Chart Titles, and Moving the Legend Around

If you want to add a title to your chart, attach labels to designated graph areas, or move the legend around the chart area, this can be done from the chart options dialog box. Do the following:

1. Double-click on the chart itself. After the borders have appeared around the chart area, click in the chart area (but *not* on the graph itself) with the right mouse button.
2. Click on CHART OPTIONS from the pop-up menu. A dialog box will appear with several options.
3. Click on the tab that has what you would like to change (TITLES, LEGEND, or DATA LABELS).

4. An example of what the chart looks like with your changes will appear in the preview box.
5. When you are done with the changes click on OK.

ADDITIONAL NOTE

Other Modifications

There are thousands of modifications that can be applied to each chart. Not all modifications can be covered here, but feel free to explore all of the possibilities. Many of these can be uncovered by double-clicking on certain areas of the chart. There are many easy-to-follow dialog boxes that will assist you with the modifications when you click with your right mouse button on these same areas. Remember that any changes you make can be undone by clicking on the UNDO button. So be creative and feel free to explore.

MICROSOFT EXCEL TIPS

FORMATTING WORKSHEETS USING AUTOFORMAT

The previous chapter demonstrated how a cell, or range of cells, could be formatted. If such detail is not required, the entire worksheet can be formatted at once using the AutoFormat feature in Excel. This feature makes use of 16 preset formats that can be applied to individual worksheets in a workbook. Although it is recommended that this feature be used once all the data has been entered in the worksheet, it is not necessary to do so.

Using AutoFormat

1. Highlight the range of cells that is to be formatted or click on a cell. All cells that contain data that are adjacent to the cell highlighted will be formatted.
2. From the Menu bar, click on FORMAT, then click on AUTOFORMAT from the drop-down menu.
3. The AutoFormat dialog box will appear.
4. From the list that appears under Table format, a sample of the format highlighted will appear in the sample box.
5. Once a format is selected, click on OK. Excel will format the range of cells according to the format selected.

ADDITIONAL NOTE

The formatting is not permanent and can be modified just like any other worksheet. If you do not like the formatting changes made, you can use the UNDO button to revert to the original worksheet format.

If you have made several changes and wish to undo all formatting, do the following:

1. Highlight the range of cells that is to be changed.
2. From the Menu bar, click on FORMAT, then click on AUTOFORMAT from the drop-down menu.
3. The AutoFormat dialog box will appear.
4. Scroll down on the Table Format box and select NONE.
5. Click on OK.

This will remove all formatting from the cells that were highlighted and revert back to the standard Excel format.

MICROSOFT POWERPOINT TIPS

CREATING ORGANIZATION CHARTS

The organization chart can help you visualize both the placement of officers in an organization and the relationship between ideas. These types of charts can be created in Power-Point slides with tools that are already included in the program.

Getting Started

1. Start with new slide. Click on the NEW SLIDE button from the top toolbar.

2. The NEW SLIDE dialog box will appear. Look for the organization chart slide and double click on it.

3. A new slide will appear on the screen. Double click on the organization chart icon to open the program. The initial chart will appear with boxes containing labels.

4. Double-click on the box that you want to enter information to. The box will now display the fields it contains. Press ENTER or TAB to move to the next field. It is not necessary to fill all the fields.

5. Click outside the box to deselect it and make your entries final.

Adding Boxes

The oranization chart program has its own menu and toolbar to make changes to the chart. Use the buttons on the toolbar to complete the following:

1. Click on the type of box that you would like to add (Subordinate, Co-Worker, etc.).

2. In the chart, click on the box that you would like to attach the new box to.

3. To add several boxes at once, click on the box button for the number of boxes you would like to add (i.e. three clicks for three boxes).

4. Click on the box that you want to attach the new boxes to.

Deleting Boxes

1. Click on the box that you want to delete.
2. Press DELETE.

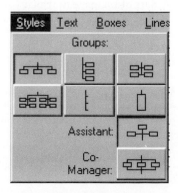

Changing the Organization Chart Style

1. Select the boxes that you want to change. Several boxes can be selected at once by holding down the SHIFT key as other boxes are clicked on.

2. Click on STYLES from the tool bar and select a style.

Modifying Boxes, Borders, Lines, Colors, and Text

1. Click the right mouse button over the box that you want to modify. . . .

2. *COLOR:* From the pop-up menu, select COLOR to change the box color.

3. *BORDERS:* Select Border Style, Shadow, or Line Style from the pop-up menu to modify the outside border of the box selected.

4. *LINES:* Click the right mouse button over the *line.* From the pop-up menu you can change the Thickness, Style, and Color of the line selected. NOTE: all lines attached to the line selected will be subject to the changes made.

5. *TEXT:* Click on the box in which you want to modify the text. From the top toolbar, select TEXT. The Color, Font, and Alignment of text can be modified from this menu.

Saving the Chart and Making Further Changes

1. To save the chart to your presentation, click on FILE and then UPDATE from the drop-down menu. You can also click on CLOSE AND RETURN to exit out of the program and incorporate the chart.

2. To make changes to the chart once it has been added to the presentation, simply double click on the organization chart to launch the program.

MICROSOFT ACCESS TIPS

MODIFYING FORMS

Forms can be modified once they have been created. Modifications may include inserting a company logo, adding a new field label, changing the tab order, or any number of other changes. In this chapter we will show how to open your form in the design view in order to make modifications. We will also insert a logo in the form.

Form in the Design View

1. Open your database and click on the FORMS tab located on the database window.

2. Click on the form that will be modified and click on the DESIGN button on database window. If you already have the form open, click on the DESIGN view button located on the toolbar.

3. Your form will appear in the design view. It should look similar to the view on the right.

4. Click on INSERT from the standard toolbar and select PICTURE.

5. The INSERT PICTURE dialog box will appear. Look for the file that contains the picture you want to insert. If you want to see a preview of the picture before selecting it, click on the PREVIEW button.

6. Click on file that contains your picture and click on the OK button.

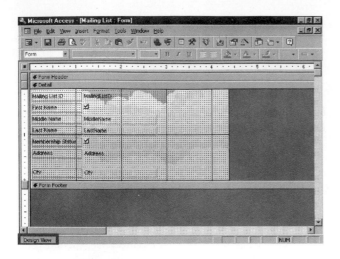

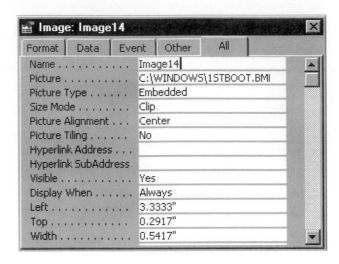

7. Once the picture appears on your form you can click on it and move it around the form.

8. To see what the form will look like with the inserted picture, click on the FORM view button.

Modifying the Picture

1. To modify the picture, right click on the picture.
2. From the pop-up menu, select PROPERTIES.
3. A dialog box will appear with four tabs to select from.

From this dialog box you can make the picture trigger a series of commands (EVENT tab), change the alignment (FORMAT tab), or make a number of other modifications. However, unlike the other Office97 Suite applications, Access does not have a DRAWING toolbar. If there are any special modifications that you wish to make to the picture, do them before inserting the picture.

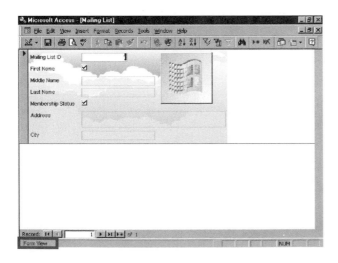

Re-sizing the Picture

You may find that adjusting the size of the picture is not as easy as dragging the corners of the picture. A slight change will have to be made in the image properties dialog box.

1. Double click on the picture to open the properties dialog box.
2. Click on the FORMAT or ALL tab.

3. Click inside the SIZE MODE field.
4. A drop down arrow will appear inside the field. Click on it and select STRETCH from the list.
5. Close the dialog box.

Now you will be able to resize the picture by simply dragging the corners of the image. The picture will adjust to the size of the box.

MICROSOFT FRONTPAGE TIPS

WEBBOTS: TIME STAMP

WebBot components are features that you can add to your webpage without the need of writing complex code. A Web-Bot is a "dynamic object" on a web page that runs when you save the web page on the web server or, in some cases, when you use the page. There are three WebBots included with FrontPage Express: Time Stamp, Include, and Search. The time stamp will be discussed in this chapter.

Time Stamp

This WebBot places a date (and the time, if you like) on your web page that shows when your web page was last updated. Every time you begin to edit your web page, the date and time will be updated to reflect the date and time that your computer has. It might be a good idea to include this in your web page so you can keep track of when you updated your web page and inform visitors of how recent the information is. To include this WebBot do the following:

1. Click on the part of the page in which you would like to include this WebBot
2. From the toolbar, click on the WebBot button.
3. A window will appear asking you to select from the different WebBot components. Select Time Stamp and click on OK.
4. The time stamp window below will appear allowing you to make some selections. These can be changed later so do not worry too much about which you select. Make your selections and click on OK.
5. The time stamp format that you selected will appear on the page. Every time you update the page using Front-Page Express, the time stamp will be updated.

Changing the Time Stamp Options

If you want to change some of the options you had selected for the Time Stamp WebBot, do the following:

1. Open the page in the FrontPage Express editor.
2. Double click on the time stamp on the page.

3. The time stamp properties window (the same as above) will appear, allowing you to make any changes you want. Once you are done changing the properties of the time stamp click on OK.

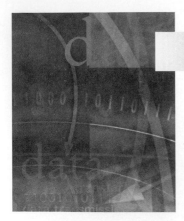

CHAPTER 9

DECISIONS IN BUSINESS AREAS
PACKAGE DELIVERY INDUSTRY

Decisions in Business Areas

Models can be applied to help make decisions in business. There are similarities among business models and how MIS supports these models. The first line of help MIS provides is in retrieving the data needed, while advances like graphics capabilities in PCs have aided greatly in interpreting the results of these data searches. This has resulted in a constant flow of software to help design, run, and evaluate business models. While some of these programs are very specific in what they are trying to solve, generic ones (such as spreadsheets) enable individuals to build their own models.

Accounting Accounting is dependent upon recording transactions and producing standardized reports. Tracking financial data provides a model, which helps support tactical management. The fundamental support MIS provides in this environment includes the use of databases to store the data, control shared access and authorized users, and produce the reports. MIS can also help evaluate basic accounting models. It can assist a firm in the application of its accounting data to make strategic decisions by integrating the data with mathematical decision models. One such model is activity-based costing (ABC). This allocates cost by attaching individual costs to the activity that makes the company incur the cost.

Finance There are two main categories of models: investment and financial management. Most of the in-vestment models deal with managing portfolios of financial instruments such as securities. Managing securities can easily yield thousands of data entries. To help manage the data in a timely fashion, computers have worked on financial mathematical models to evaluate investments and strategies. At the most basic level, MIS support in corporate financial management uses computerized databases to monitor financial transactions. Other uses of MIS to support financial management include providing access to external data such as that from the government, forecasting and simulation, and financial modeling tools.

MIS and Marketing Marketing models are used to evaluate consumer preferences, forecast sales, and analyze promotional campaigns. Models can also help users choose between various marketing strategies. Recommendations are made based upon the enormous amount of data available to a company, both internal and external. Target marketing's goal is to clearly define a target market and address it accordingly.

Human Resource Management (HRM) In today's more litigious environment, MIS has helped HRM grow from merely keeping payroll records to expanding employee records in databases. This results in more accurate tracking of items such as career paths, payroll taxes, training, performance reviews, and vacation.

Production and Design Advanced computer capabilities have enabled robots and machines to perform more complex duties or lower costs for the same task. Other uses of computers in manufacturing include process control, inventory management, and production design.

Process control is the use of computers to monitor and control the production machines, such as robots. This can lead to improved quality, reduced down time, and fewer mistakes.

Inventory control is a classic business problem that computers have helped alleviate. The ideal situation is to have in stock only those raw materials and end products needed for each day or manufacturing cycle to save on inventory warehousing. Computers have helped this goal become a more affordable solution. In a manufacturing system of material requirements planning (MRP), the production line drives the information system. At each stage of production, the use of raw materials and new inventory levels needed are calculated. Manufacturing resource planning (MRP II) is an integrated approach. A "demand" system is based on projected sales, which drive the raw materials planning and scheduling. Just-in-time (JIT) scheduling is a manufacturing technique popularized by the Japanese in which the raw materials arrive at the manufacturing line just as they are needed. This requires more frequent deliveries of product, better forecasting in the amount of materials needed, and smaller shipments.

Computers are now used heavily in the design process. Computer-aided design (CAD) programs draw engineering prints that can be quickly and easily changed. These programs can also keep track of raw materials needs and costs.

Geographic Information Systems (GIS) GIS have been designed to identify and show relationships between physical locations and business data. This helps with many operational decisions, especially in a manufacturing company. Usually, a map is used as the base. The maps can be developed and stored using either pictures or digitized map data. The digital map data gives the most flexibility since the maps can be overlaid with the business data of interest. Data can come from external sources, such as the population density from the last government census. The latest and most advanced map system is the Global Positioning System (GPS), which is a set of satellites maintained by the U.S. government. GPS allows a portable receiver to identify its location within 50 feet. The United States government has announced plans to make the technology for the next phase with more exact pinpointing (much less than within 50 feet) available for consumer use in the near future.

Package Delivery Industry

DESCRIPTION OF THE INDUSTRY

The secret to being a successful package delivery company is timeliness, efficiency, and affordability. In the

Word	W.1	Bullets, Numbers, and Outlines	Bullets and Numbers
		Additional Note	Creating an Outline
			Changing the Outline Format
			Customizing Bullets, Numbers, and Outlines
Excel	E.1	Graphs	Using Chart Wizard
			Making Changes to the Chart
			Data Changed?
PowerPoint	P.1	Printing Presentations	Printing Handouts
			Printing Speaker's Notes
			Printing Slides
			Printing an Outline
Access	A.1	Using Forms to Enter Data	
		Printing Out Records Using Forms	
		Printing Out All Records Using Forms	
Front Page	I.1	WebBots: Include Important Note	Modifying the Content

last 20 years, guaranteed two-day and overnight delivery service have resulted in drastic changes in businesses' perceptions of "timely." The Pony Express delivered messages for only a few months until the telegraph rendered it obsolete. Many think that fax machines and e-mail may do the same thing to the overnight market. So far this has not been the case. The industry has continued to change nonetheless, hastened by the march of technology.

As manufacturers and sellers have focused on driving costs down in a more competitive marketplace, inventory management has become an increasingly important issue. The package delivery industry has responded with products and services that make better inventory management possible. The industry offers many price structures, timing options, and tracking information alternatives for a variety of different needs.

FINANCIAL ANALYSIS

While moderate to high market growth continues in the industry, prices have declined due to fierce competition. Technological advances and efficiencies have enabled the industry to continuously cut costs. UPS and FedEx, the two most technologically advanced companies, have reported profit increases greater than yearly sales increases (Table 9.1).

STOCK/INVESTMENT OUTLOOK

The stock projection for the package delivery industry remains positive. Most of the large delivery companies are rated a buy or outperform for the next three to four years. Those companies that are competing on price, such as Airborne Express, may face a bleaker future than those that have prepared to offer technologically differentiated services, such as UPS or Federal Express. Other carriers, such as Emery and DHL, have identified niches by specializing in delivery of heavier packages or in international delivery.

POTENTIAL/PROSPECTIVE FOR GROWTH

The package delivery market continues to grow 3 to 5 percent each year. Competition remains fierce among the established players. Alternative messaging services,

including the Internet, faxes, and e-mail, may decrease document delivery growth in the future. Alternatively, Internet usage may increase package delivery growth as more individuals purchase from the Internet and as business conditions continue to get more efficient and less dependent on location.

Alliances between manufacturing and delivery companies are becoming increasingly prevalent and important. Recently, the United Parcel Service joined the online computer services CompuServe and Prodigy. The software for FedEx is pre-installed on Apple and IBM personal computers.

With the decrease in air transportation costs, increasing amounts of lower value and heavier manufacturing products are being shipped by airfreight. Increasingly, carriers market their service not as airfreight, but as "time-definite" transportation. Pricing is based on the speed with which the shipment is delivered and the distance it travels. This contrasts with trucking, where rates are set by weight and distance. This strategy has served to narrow the price difference between these two modes of delivery.

The other major area for growth is international, especially in Southeast Asia (Table 9.2). Those companies with the resources to build new facilities and new networks in this region will realize a huge advantage over those competitors without these resources or vision.

COMPETITIVE STRUCTURE

The U.S. market is made up of seven large companies, dozens of smaller entities, and the U.S. Postal Service. The biggest shake-up in the package delivery industry occurred when the UPS, the sleeping giant, awoke. For years, UPS was the industry cash cow. It owned the package delivery market and was a very staid company trying to do one thing well—mass-produced delivery. After the upstart FedEx began the new overnight market, UPS slowly transformed itself to expand into that and other markets (Figure 9.1). One of the ways UPS transformed itself was to increase its marketing department from 7 to 600 people, with the goal of attracting and retaining corporate customers.

Given the high cost of entry, the oligopoly in the marketplace will continue. Billions are needed to develop facilities in trucking, delivery, computer, and air networks. These costs keep new companies from entering or becoming a dominant force in the marketplace. As time goes on, more buyouts, mergers, and alliances may further restrict the number of players.

Mergers will continue to play an important role in the consolidation of the industry. FedEx acquired Flying Tiger in 1988. Airborne formed an alliance with Roadway to complement its strengths. Airborne brought planes to the alliance; Roadway had a well-established truck network.

Table 9.1 Percent Increases of Sales and Profits for UPS and FedEx, 1996–1999

| | UPS % Changes | | FedEx % Changes | |
	Sales	Profit	Sales	Profit
1996	+6	+259	+35	+22
1997	+0	+10	+12	+11
1998	+10	+10	+11	+15
1999			+5	+7

Table 9.2 Pacific Rim—U.S. Cargo Capacity Deployment (Eastbound; Annual Metric Tons, Belly and Freighter Capacity)

Carrier	1995 (Tons)	Forecast 1996 (Tons)	2000 (Tons)	Growth Rate 1993–1995 (%)	1995–2000 (%)
FedEx	142,768	151,741	191,531	8.3	6.1
UPS	70,343	98,498	158,807	27.1	17.7
Other	997,853	1,027,060	1,284,986	11.6	5.2
Total	1,210,964	1,277,300	1,635,326	11.9	6.2
FedEx/UPS Share	17.6%	19.8%	21.4%		

(*Source:* MergeGlobal, Inc., *Aviation Week & Space Technology,* August 26, 1996.)

The U.S. Postal Service has also increased its role and tenacity in the marketplace. The post office enjoys several advantages not enjoyed by private industry. They have an entire restricted market, daily mail delivery, and a well-established infrastructure, including trucks and airplanes.

ROLE OF RESEARCH AND DEVELOPMENT

The role of research and development in the package delivery industry is to develop new technologies that will cut the cost of shipping or provide better services to customers. Recent initiatives include new software installed at customer sites that enable customers to track packages themselves. Other software links package label printing with customer databases to better track shipped packages.

TECHNOLOGICAL INVESTMENT AND ANALYSIS

FedEx and UPS are leading the industry in technological spending. They are attempting to integrate all facets of the delivery process. They want their customers to use their software to print shipping labels, track packages, and receive bills. Eventually these delivery companies want to become the shipping departments for corporations. Once FedEx and UPS introduce their software into customers' routines, it is more difficult and troublesome for customers to switch to other delivery services. This is similar to the way some travel companies have set up sites as in-house corporate travel departments.

Assets that provide the means to physically move goods are undifferentiated and generically available to all players. Technology has emerged as the method with which to distinguish a company's products, improve service quality, and lower costs. As such, it has become increasingly important to manufacturers and retailers to be able to access real-time information about the status of parts, materials, and finished goods in a world of just-in-time inventory management. Technology is increasingly being used to manage complex physical networks, enhance asset utilization, and reinforce the reliability and predictability of package delivery. Technology is the leading component of the effort to add extra value for service and mitigate the downward spiral on prices. In spite of this focus on technology, the package delivery business is a labor- and capital-intensive business.

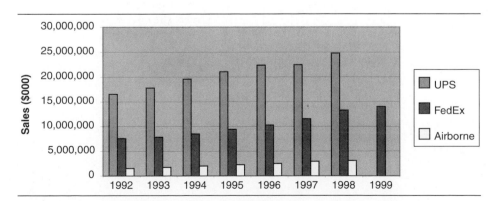

Figure 9.1 Package delivery sales comparison—"the big keep getting bigger."

RECOMMENDATION FOR THE FUTURE

The future appears bright for those companies with the resources to continue their expansion into Asia and onto the Internet. These are growth areas and should be exploited with the latest technology.

As more companies cut costs and reduce the number of employees through outsourcing, they may outsource their shipping department to the larger package delivery companies as well. This is a service area of the business that could be expanded by the larger companies.

Smaller package delivery companies, such as Emery, DHL, and Airborne, will have to find specific niches, like transportation for heavy, valuable, or dangerous items, to survive.

WEB SITES

Package Delivery Industry
  www.aircourier.org
  www.airborne.com

FEDERAL EXPRESS

Executive Summary

Case Name:	Federal Express Corporation
Case Industry:	Package delivery
Major Technology Issue:	Determine which technology platform to adopt
Major Financial Issue:	Decreasing profit margins due to increased competition
Major Strategic Issue:	Whether FedEx should expand into different businesses
Major Players/Leaders:	Fred Smith, founder, chairman, president, and CEO
Main Web Page:	www.fedex.com
Case Conclusion/Recommendation:	FedEx should continue using cutting-edge technology such as its web site and geopositioning to increase value to its customers, drive costs down, and offer new services. FedEx should also continue to grow its international expansion.

CASE ANALYSIS

INTRODUCTORY STORY

The Pony Express was a pony relay mail system between St. Joseph, Missouri, and Sacramento, California. It operated between April 1860 and October 1861. The system had 100 stations, 80 riders, and between 400 and 500 horses.

Two technological breakthroughs led to the end of the Pony Express: the connection of the East and West by the intercontinental railroad in 1861, and the completion of the intercontinental telegraph in 1861. These advances enabled Americans to send messages across the country in minutes and packages and freight in weeks as opposed to several months. The march of technology continues.

SHORT DESCRIPTION OF THE COMPANY

Federal Express is the world's largest express transportation company. It delivers more than 2.5 million items to over 200 countries each business day. It employs more than 120,000 people worldwide, operates 552 aircraft and more than 35,000 vehicles in its integrated system. The carrier's planes travel more than 430,000 miles within 24 hours, equivalent to about 15 trips around the equator. FedEx has regional hubs in Indianapolis, Newark, Oakland, and Fort Worth. Anchorage is a gateway port.

FedEx was the first company to offer overnight package delivery, to introduce the overnight letter, to offer 10:30 A.M. next-day service, and to offer Saturday delivery.

Technology has been integral to FedEx's growth and success. The company pioneered the first automated customer service center. It also launched bar code scanning for shipments, which provides real-time tracking for each shipment. Today, FedEx customers can interact with FedEx in many ways, including Powership Hardware Systems, FedEx Ship Software, and the FedEx Internet home page.

SHORT HISTORY OF THE COMPANY

In 1971, no company provided one-day delivery in the United States. Fred Smith, the founder of Federal Express Corporation (FedEx), then an undergraduate student at Yale University, conceived the idea of an express delivery system that revolved around a hub and provided next-day delivery. His idea was to provide overnight delivery of small, high-value items.[1] In May and June 1972 two New York market researchers, Art Bass and Roger Frock, separately studied the need for fast on-time air express. In 1972, they concluded that there was a high degree of dissatisfaction with existing airfreight services.

The industry was dominated by Emery Air Freight and Flying Tiger, both launched at the end of World War II. Each generated annual revenues of $100 million, but their deliveries were erratic and frequently late. Roger Frock and Art Bass's independent studies concluded that there was a large untapped market for fast, on-time air express. Moreover, it could be lucrative: the potential revenue for the airfreight industry

---

[1] Mason, Richard O., McKenney, James L., Carlson, Walter, and Copeland, Duncan, "Absolutely, Positively Operations Research: The Federal Express Story," *Interfaces*, March–April 1997, v. 27, p. 18.

was as much as $1 billion a year.[2] Fred Smith's vision was summed up in one quote:

> *This company is nothing short of being the logistics arm of a whole new society that is building up in our economy—a society that isn't built around automobile and steel production, but that is built up instead around service industries and high technology endeavors in electronics and optics and medical science. It is the movement of these support items that Federal Express is all about.*[3]

Fred Smith's plan called for 30 Falcons to pick up packages in as many or more cities around the United States and arrive around midnight at a hub at Little Rock's Adams Field. There an "army of night workers" would sort, assemble, and load the packages for departure around three in the morning to arrive at the appropriate destination cities by dawn. This was in answer to the observation that the majority of air express users wanted their parcels not only to travel overnight by air, but to be delivered promptly by ground courier. Customers indicated they were willing to pay a premium for door-to-door service.[4]

To continue its success, FedEx had to pick up, transport, and deliver packages to and from the most lucrative cities as efficiently as possible. This all had to be done from offices that closed at 9:00 P.M. with packages that had to be delivered by 10:30 A.M. the next morning. To meet these increased pressures, FedEx developed a three-model management planning system. It used these models to make both ongoing operational decisions and crucial strategic decisions[5]:

1. *Origin-destination flow model:* This model used an improved origin-destination flow approach to determine the what, when, and where of package volumes from and to actual and potential cities in the system.
2. *FLY model:* This model produced schedules and determined resource requirements for selected cities. Using actual past volumes to review performance, this model tested other options and recalibrated its coefficients.
3. *Financial planning model:* This model examined the overall economic and financial implications of alternative route structures and flying schedules.

For FedEx to have optimal margins it must have very high load factors. This is the percentage of an aircraft's total capacity that is utilized. Many common carriers operate at load factors between 60 and 69 percent. FedEx was able to maintain a load factor between 82 and 93 percent, with an average of 87 percent. This level was maintained while reconfiguring its route structure every month, implementing schedule changes within a few days, and keeping its financial performance in line.[6]

For customer service, FedEx considered developing a reservation system similar to the one used by Avis Car Rental. FedEx formed a team that modeled different types of systems and called the project "Sydney." The preliminary tests suggested that the solution was a central telephone answering system. They tested the system in its worst performing city, Newark, New Jersey, and at the company's main hub in Memphis. The prototype proved to be a great improvement over the old method and resulted in improved customer service. Eventually, FedEx handled all of its customer calls in centralized call centers. The call centers sent requests to dispatch centers in the cities served.[7]

Since the beginning, the most debated question was the use of a single hub as opposed to the use of a series or multi-hub system. FedEx had established two hubs that ran in parallel, in Memphis and Pittsburgh. These parallel hubs were independent. In a series multi-hub system, the hubs would be dependent on each other with all functions flowing through the system in a set order. Each function could not be started until the preceding functions were completed. FedEx's expansion, once again, raised the debate of a single-hub system over a multi-hub system. Several key executives were convinced that a series, multi-hub system was the way to go.[8]

With high-cost aircraft and facilities used intensively for compressed periods of time under conditions that demand near perfect performance, the single hub worked best. Memphis remained the single hub in the system. In July 1979, FedEx broke ground for the massive, highly automated SuperHub.[9] The SuperHub and the centralized call centers moved FedEx from a decentralized to a centralized structure with strict standards and few redundancies.

Soon after the SuperHub opened, the model required additional adjustments. As a competitive move, Smith wanted to change the committed delivery time from 12:00 noon to 10:30 A.M. The model showed that the FedEx system could deliver on that promise. A competitive analysis application of the model revealed that UPS, FedEx's major competitor, could not effectively

---

[2] Trimble, Vance H., *Overnight Success: Federal Express and Fredrick Smith, Its Renagade Creator,* Crown Publishers, New York, 1993, p. 126.
[3] Mason *et al.,* "Absolutely, Positively," p. 17.
[4] Trimble, *Overnight Success,* pp. 126–127.
[5] Ibid., pp. 21 and 22.

[6] Ibid., p. 22.
[7] Karpinski, Richard, "The Logistics of E-Business—Web Commerce Demands New Approach to Inventory, Shipping," *InternetWeek,* May 31, 1999, p. 1.
[8] Trimble, *Overnight Success,* p. 28.
[9] Ibid., pp. 28, 29.

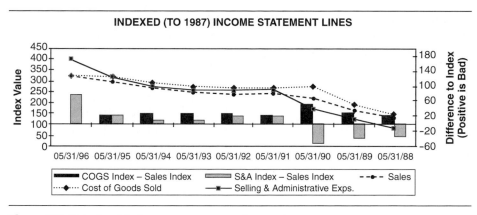

INDEXED (TO 1987) INCOME STATEMENT LINES

Figure 9.2 Relationship between revenue and operating expenses.

meet this deadline. In late 1982, FedEx's modeling capability gave FedEx this competitive advantage, confirming its position as the leader in the implementation of new methods and technology. FedEx's use of technology also enabled it to survive and lead in the low-margin business of package delivery.

Various models had predicted that the SuperHub concept would reach its capacity in 1987. FedEx concluded, through its modeling, that as the SuperHub reached its capacity it would be better to adapt an overlay hub methodology. In an overlay hub system each pickup station makes a decision to send a package for redistribution within the region by sending it to the regional hub or to send the package to the Memphis SuperHub. Today, FedEx operates an overlay hub system with regional hubs in Newark, Chicago, and Oakland as well as sorting centers in Memphis, Indianapolis, Fort Worth, and Anchorage.

Volume growth accelerated rapidly. In 1979 FedEx enhanced its Sydney system, which resulted in COSMOS (Customer, Operations, Service, Management Operating System). COSMOS is a mainframe-based order and dispatching system. It was designed to eventually keep track of every package through the entire FedEx system.

The bar code FedEx uses contains a three-letter symbol for the regional station and a two-letter symbol that represents the sorting facility. The bar code information is used to determine the route of the package. The pickup scan records specific package information, customer information, receiver information, and weight. The information is sent to a mainframe and is used for package routing, tracking, billing, forecasting, and planning. A scan takes place every time a package moves from one place to another. When a courier drops the packages at the pickup station, the packages are scanned and then sent to the predetermined overlay hub.[10]

[10] Radosevich, Lynda, "Going Global Overnight," *Infoworld*, April 19, 1999, v. 21, i. 16, p. 1(1).

FINANCIAL AND PORTFOLIO ANALYSIS

Revenue growth drives a company's overall success. Profitability is driven by the relationship between revenue and operating expenses. Figure 9.2 illustrates the relationship between revenue and operating expenditures and the growth of these components. The lines in the chart illustrate the growth of revenue, cost of goods sold, and selling and administrative expenses. The black bar illustrates the difference between cost of goods sold and revenues and the gray bar illustrates the difference between selling and administrative expenses and revenues. A positive value for the bars signals a negative implication. Federal Express is increasing revenues.

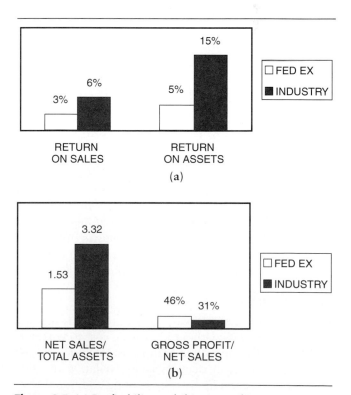

Figure 9.3 (a) Profitability and (b) asset utilization ratios.

Cost of goods sold and selling and administrative expenses have been increasing at a faster rate.

FedEx is not utilizing its assets as well as its competitors as illustrated in Figure 9.3b. However, top-line profitability is better than the industry as illustrated in the asset utilization chart, gross profit to net sales ratio. The two asset utilization ratios suggest that FedEx must decrease its selling and administrative expense and increase its sales. FedEx's profitability is much lower than the industry as shown in Figure 9.3a. Return on sales and return on assets are significantly lower than its industry averages. The profitability of the companies in the airfreight industry is driven by asset utilization and cost control. One of the company's goals must be to increase gross profit and control selling and administrative expenses.

FedEx has invested a significant amount of its revenues in technological enhancements. They have financed the investment with internally generated cash flow while decreasing debt, especially long-term debt. The company's strategy of becoming an even larger presence in the logistics business will enable FedEx to better utilize its investments in technology.

STOCK/INVESTMENT ANALYSIS

Smith Barney said of FedEx stock on July 14, 1997:

FedEx is one of the best positioned companies in the future growth of world trade. The airline has an international route structure that is unmatched by any other airline. The only concern we have is that the company will continue to invest more than $2 billion annually in the business. At current prices, the upside seems relatively limited in the short term, so we are maintaining our 3H (Neutral, High Risk) rating on these shares. Long term, as the market looks ahead, we believe these shares could become attractive.

Donaldson, Lufkin & Jenrette Securities said on July 1, 1997:

Going forward, the company has key marketing initiatives that take effect today, including the adoption of distance-based pricing, some shifts in the format of its pricing, and the introduction of new deferred services, including a three-day domestic option and its first deferred international option. We continue to rate the stock market performance excellent.

RISK ANALYSIS

In this cost-focused industry, all competing forces are trying to add value without increasing cost to win market share. Even the United States Postal Service, whose reputation for timely delivery is not stellar, is applying pressure on Federal Express by making additional cost-cutting measures to become more competitive. The United States Postal Service's classification reform will lower shipping rates by as much as 30 percent for companies that use bar coding in their mail preparation.[11] This change may affect volumes for all carriers.

INDUSTRY AND MARKET ANALYSIS

United Parcel Service, Federal Express, CNF Transportation, Airborne Freight, and Air Express International are the largest airfreight providers. However, Federal Express has a 50 percent share of the overnight delivery business. Since deregulation of the trucking industry in the late 1970s and the airline industry in the early 1980s, there has been a growing consolidation in the transportation industry.

The domestic airfreight market, as measured by ton-miles, grew at an 8 percent compound annual rate between 1991 and 1995, during which time air cargo rates reached levels that priced some shippers out of the air freight market. As a result, growth slowed dramatically to just 2.2 percent in 1996, as less-than-truckload motor carriers and ground express carriers captured market share. Air cargo rates have also come down, sliding 3.5 percent in 1996. As of 1997's first quarter, they were up just 1 percent, year to year.

On the international side, where most air carriers operate as forwarders, ton-miles in 1996 increased by 6.5 percent, experiencing better growth than domestic cargo. International and domestic traffic growth accelerated in 1997. Domestic air ton-miles, excluding mail, rose 6.0 percent in 1997's first quarter, while international volumes increased 16.9 percent. By holding the line on rates and absorbing much of the increase in fuel costs, airfreight carriers have been able to recover lost business.[12]

Airfreight carriers focus on the highest value and the most time-sensitive packages. The airfreight business has very thin margins. In this type of environment a company must utilize its fixed assets as much as possible and keep costs as low as possible. A major cost to airfreight providers is fuel cost. An unexpected increase in fuel costs could drive the least efficient operators into bankruptcy.

Airfreight accounted for $40 billion (9 percent) of the United States commercial freight transportation market in 1996. On the domestic side of the business, estimated at $25 billion in 1996, 85 percent of the revenues are generated by "integrators." These are companies which control both ground and air transportation. Federal Express was the largest integrated carrier, with

---

[11] *Insurance & Technology*, pp. 9–10.
[12] "Transportation: Commercial," *Standard & Poor's Industry Survey,* July 17, 1997, pp. 2 and 3.

revenues of $7.5 billion in 1996. In second place was the United Parcel Service, with $4.8 billion in revenues, followed by Airborne Express ($1.9 billion). Airfreight forwarders and passenger airlines accounted for the remaining 15 percent ($15 billion) of domestic airfreight revenues.[13]

Pricing was based primarily on the speed with which the shipment was delivered and secondarily on the distance the package traveled. With trucking, by contrast, rates are set primarily by weight and distance. Because airfreight rates have not risen as much in recent years as ground transportation rates, the price differential between the two modes has narrowed.[14] Half of Federal Express's volume is shipped entirely by ground transportation.

ROLE OF RESEARCH AND DEVELOPMENT

Federal Express is expanding its ability to become a logistics giant. The company is well-positioned to become an integrated logistics company offering warehousing, inventory management, and shipping. FedEx distribution centers enable customers to place an order directly with its system, ship the package, and manage the inventory of its customers.

Federal Express is positioning itself to take advantage of the corporate outsourcing of the warehousing and inventory management functions. Federal Express continues to treat information as a resource, investing about 10 percent of its revenues in customer-serving and productivity-enhancing technologies.

In 1996, total logistics spending was about $800 billion (11 percent of GDP). Logistics spending is broken down into three components: inventory carrying costs ($310 billion), transportation ($460 billion), and administration ($30 billion). Of the $460 billion spent on transportation, trucking accounted for 80 percent. Surveys indicate that 66 percent of United States corporations and nearly half of the corporations in Europe and some in Asia are seeking to re-engineer their supply chains.[15] To meet this need, FedEx now offers FedEx Express, a warehousing, inventory management, and distribution service.

In October 1997 Federal Express purchased Caliber System Incorporated. Caliber was composed of five components: (1) RPS was the nation's second largest ground and second-day-air small package deliverer, (2) Viking Freight was a regional trucking company that operated in the West, (3) Robert's Express was one of the world's largest nonstop trucking companies, (4) Caliber Logistics provided contracts to handle the shipping needs of companies worldwide, and (5) Caliber Technology was the information subsidiary of the Caliber System.

TECHNOLOGY STORY

In 1992, in an effort to remain ahead of his competition, Smith made plans to provide Zapmail, a proprietary fax service. He felt this new technology would make a superhighway that would divert traffic from the older routes, such as express or regular mail. Smith thought that by completely controlling this new superhighway he could earn revenues every time it was used. He based his decision on the fact that there was no standard in facsimile technology. He wanted his service to become that standard.

Correct in many of his predictions about the popularity of the fax machine, Smith was unable to foresee the quick development of a single fax technology standard and the nearly instant price decline that made fax machines ubiquitous. As machines became affordable to smaller companies and even individuals, the service as provided by Federal Express became unnecessary. Only after a significant investment in an extensive system of electronic data transfer lines and the hardware necessary to send and receive data across those lines was Federal Express able to recognize that this service would not be profitable.

TECHNOLOGICAL INVESTMENT AND ANALYSIS

Federal Express's extranet is a network integrating elements of both the intranet and Internet. It was established for secure communication and data exchange between internal and external users.[16] It differs from the Internet in that selected information from an organization's intranet is made available to its external users. In other words, the extranet is the integration of the intranet and the Internet. The Federal Express site lets customers key in their account and airbill numbers, then tap into the overnight courier's own operational system to track the progress of their shipments. High-volume corporate customers can handle their shipments automatically by integrating their order and warehousing data systems with FedEx's intake, billing, and package tracking software.[17]

In late 1996, FedEx decided to terminate its development of a version of its FedEx Ship software for Lotus Notes. Instead, the company focused its attention on the development of its web site. In contrast, FedEx Ship for Notes would have required users to have a Notes or a basic Windows client.

FedEx utilizes the Internet to provide information to its customers and enable its customers to place orders.

[13] Ibid., p. 8.
[14] Ibid., p. 17.
[15] Johnson, Gregory S., "Alliances Shape the Future of the Logistics Industry; Information Rivals Transportation Itself," *Journal of Commerce,* October 6, 1997, p. 11A.
[16] Basch, Reva, "What on Earth Is an Extranet?," *Link-Up,* February 17, 1997, n. 723, p. 248.
[17] Ibid.

Equally important, the Internet provides customers with the ability to track their packages by linking to the FedEx mainframe over the telephone lines through a modem or EDI. The Internet runs in conjunction with the customer call center, which provides the same services to FedEx customers. For its customers who currently use a PC to dial into FedEx, the Internet will eliminate the need for customers to have FedEx ordering and tracking software installed on their PC.

The FedEx web site opened in November 1994. Since then, approximately five million customers visit each month. Handling 900,000 online tracking requests each month is substantially cheaper than fielding them in the FedEx call center. Setup costs for the web site were minimal, because FedEx modified applications that were already in development for its proprietary InterNetShip network. The web site, which is protected by a firewall, runs on Netscape Commerce Server software hosted by dual Sun SPARC web servers. Secure socket layer (SSL) security protects information sent over the web.[18] The exponential growth in the use of FedEx's web site has forced FedEx's IS department to service its external customers. "Customers expect everything to work perfectly all the time or they get very frustrated. If they don't get what they want, they go elsewhere," said Susan Goeldner, manager of Internet technologies at Federal Express. Unlike internal users, who are hostages of IS, external customers can demand immediate attention.

The relationship between IS and marketing at FedEx has not always been smooth, according to Goeldner. The need to develop a viable presence online has driven them together.[19] Federal Express is trying to focus the IS department on the strategic need for Internet commerce. Given the growth of PCs in the business world, electronic commerce over the Internet is a viable way to capture customers and reduce costs.[20]

An experimental courier route planning system project is also under way. FedEx is using geo-coding and geo-positioning technology to plot a courier's pickups and deliveries on a map route based upon longitude and latitude. One use of the map is to show the courier the exact route she followed and to suggest possibilities for more efficient sequencing. Soon to follow are shortest time path estimates. These will help station managers plan the work of couriers under supervision. Preliminary estimates show that a 5 to 10 percent productivity improvement is possible, almost all of which goes to the bottom line.

Another application involves plotting an entire station's deliveries by route number on the station's service area map. This will reveal operating problems in the route structure. Since customer volumes are always changing, and new customers appear and old ones disappear, route balancing is a constant challenge. Couriers' routes are currently plotted by hand. When the geo-coding experiment is completed, the computer program will accomplish the task more efficiently.

TECHNOLOGICAL INNOVATIONS

NETWORK

Federal Express Corporation uses a set of package tracking and shipping Application Programming Interfaces (APIs) that link corporate networks, intranets, and World Wide Web sites directly to internal FedEx applications that hold shipping status information. Such tight links with customers' systems can make electronic commerce easier and faster, according to Michael W. Janes, FedEx's vice president of marketing for logistics and electronic commerce. To provide a higher level of customer support, the Memphis-based delivery giant is investing millions of dollars in the installation of distributed application and management software.

Federal Express has found that network computers have yet to prove to be the answer to the company's network problems. While the company has not ruled them out as part of its future computing environment, it is unclear whether the devices will be rolled out as the sole replacement for 75,000 dumb terminals.

Federal Express Corporation will continue to implement Java-based network computers as the company's thin client of choice. Dennis Jones, executive vice president and chief information officer, said the company would continue a five-year testing program of thin clients. "We believe that thin-client technology will play an important part in the future, including Java PCs,"[21] Jones said. With dipping PC prices and turmoil in the network computer market, FedEx sees PCs as the client of choice for now.

TELECOMMUNICATIONS

Federal Express's fedex.com began in the spring of 1995 but did not add the ability to track packages until April 1996. The site added servers and bandwidth as traffic increased, particularly during the UPS strike in August 1997. During this time, the number of hits to the site doubled from 140,000 to 280,000 per day. The company uses ten 200-MHz Sun Microsystems Ultra 2 web servers running Netscape Enterprise

[18] Walsh, Mark, "The Air Bill Joins the 8-Track," *Internet World,* August 1997, v. 8, n. 83, p. 43.
[19] Ibid.
[20] Stone, Martin, "FedEx Delivers Online Interactive Site," *Computing Canada,* January 15, 1999, v. 25, i. 2, p. 7(1).

[21] Pereira, Pedro, "FedEx Opens Doors to World," *Computer Reseller News,* October 21, 1996, v. 30, n. 43, p. 55.

Server 3.5.1: five run Solaris 2.6 and five run Netscape 2.5.1.[22]

Although FedEx does not break out details on how many packages are shipped or tracked through fedex.com alone, the company did confirm that 2 million of the current daily average of 3 million packages are shipped or tracked through the web site or through FedEx's Windows software over a proprietary data network.

Federal Express has implemented IntraNetShip. This is a workgroup-enabled extranet application that links to customer intranets and automates package tracking and authorization processes. IntraNetShip runs on customer servers and interfaces with fedex.com. The application centralizes policy management at user sites and standardizes authorization procedures. It represents an expansion of FedEx's Internet strategy, from web-based package tracking and other services to a model based on server applications at customer sites.

Federal Express is also beta testing software that enables corporate customers to take a virtual look inside packages in transit to reveal their contents and value. The application establishes a central administrator who can

---

[22] Methvin, David W., and Silverman, Paul, "In Brief—Track It Down," *Windows Magazine*, March 1, 1999, p. 162(1).

distribute inventory, packing, and shipping instructions to appropriate departments. Ultimately not only the path of the package but also the contents and value of the box will be tracked, according to Rohan Champion, vice president of strategic alliances at Federal Express.

RECOMMENDATION FOR THE FUTURE

FedEx should continue its focus on customer service through web site development. Better integration of data for internal and external customers will continue to result in increased cost savings.

With the purchase of the Caliber System, Federal Express will be able to utilize its technology to capture more revenues and profits. The airfreight business has very low margins and Federal Express has proven to be a leader in its industry. However, the inventory management and logistics businesses have wider margins. Expanding in this market will enable Federal Express to better utilize its fixed assets. The outsourcing of corporate warehousing, ordering, and shipping functions will provide a growing market for Federal Express to capture more revenues and improve profit margins.

Since the international market is growing at about twice the rate of the domestic market, Federal Express should continue to invest in its international operations.

CASE QUESTIONS

Strategic Questions

1. What is the strategic direction of the corporation/organization?

2. Who or what forces are driving this direction?

3. What has been the catalyst for change?

4. What are the critical success factors for this corporation/organization?

5. What are the core competencies for this corporation/organization?

Technological Questions

6. What technologies has the corporation relied on?

7. What has caused a change in the use of technology in the corporation/organization?

8. How has this change been implemented?

9. Who has driven this change throughout the organization?

10. How successful has the technological change been?

Quantitative Questions

11. What does the corporation say about its financial ability to embark on a major technological program of advancement?

12. What conclusions can be reached from an analysis of the financial information to support or contradict this financial ability?

13. What analysis can be made by examining the following ratio groups?

    Revenue
    Asset Utilization

14. What conclusions can be reached by analyzing the financial trends? Are there long-term trends that seem to be problematic? Is the industry stable? Are there replacement products?

Internet Questions

15. What does the corporation's web page present about their business directives?

16. How does this compare to the conclusions reached in the case?

17. How does this compare to the conclusions reached by analyzing the financial information?

Industry Questions

18. What challenges and opportunities is the industry facing?

19. Is the industry oligopolistic or competitive?

20. Does the industry face a change in government regulation?

21. How will technology impact the industry?

Data Questions

22. What role do data play in the future of the corporation?

23. How important are data to the corporation's continued success?

24. How will the capture and maintenance of customer data impact the corporation's future?

UNITED PARCEL SERVICE

Executive Summary

Case Name:	United Parcel Service, Inc. (UPS)
Case Industry:	Package delivery
Major Technology Issue:	Determine which technologies will help separate UPS from its competitors
Major Financial Issue:	How to keep profits growing while expanding into new markets
Major Strategic Issue:	Determining whether UPS should expand into Europe, where FedEx failed
Major Players/Leaders:	Kent Nelson, CEO; Ken Lacy, Chief Information Officer
Main Web Page:	www.ups.com
Case Conclusion/Recommendation:	UPS must continue to invest in new technologies that will enable it to not only compete with its rivals, but also set itself apart. To succeed, UPS must maintain its economies of scale, smart use of technology, and strategic alliances.

CASE ANALYSIS

INTRODUCTORY STORY

The new chief information officer for UPS, Ken Lacy, faced a daunting task. Simply put, he was charged with taking an enormous, geographically diverse company and updating its central nervous system. He had to do this in a hurry because the competition was ferocious. Federal Express, UPS's most feared competitor, had the potential to corner the parcel delivery market much like Kleenex or Xerox did in their markets. "Go fed-ex this for me, would you?" or "I just got a fed-ex from my uncle in Baltimore" are phrases that Lacy or, more importantly, Lacy's boss, chairman and CEO Kent Nelson, never wanted to hear.

Lacy had the chairman's support as well as the company's cash to spend. In a time of deregulation, more competition, and cost cutting, investments in technology were increasingly important to maintain competitive position.

SHORT DESCRIPTION OF THE COMPANY

UPS operates in over 200 countries worldwide and offers an array of products and services. General services include ground delivery, domestic air, international delivery, and other services customized to meet the demands of the consumer.

UPS's core business, however, is its ground transportation service. UPS offers the standard delivery service associated with the UPS name. UPS Hundredweight

Service is a contracted service to customers sending multiple package shipments with a combined weight of more than 200 pounds. UPS Groundsaver, another contracted service, provides business-to-business shipments to specified ZIP codes.

Ground transportation revenue increased 2 percent from 1994 to 1995 due to an increase in rates. Ground transportation is the core process of UPS. It has become somewhat of a commodity in the industry. Severe competition and market saturation have caused the margins to deteriorate.

SHORT HISTORY OF THE COMPANY

In the early 1900's, a teenage entrepreneur named Jim Casey and his brother George started a new company. With few telephones in households and no formal parcel delivery service, personal messages and small packages had to be delivered privately by hand. To meet this labor intensive demand, the American Messenger Company was founded in Seattle, Washington.

Since those early years, UPS has grown into one of the most successful private companies in America. UPS offers transportation of small and large packages by ground or air to over 200 countries and territories worldwide. In 1995, UPS delivered over 11.5 million packages, sales were over $21 billion, and total assets exceeded $12.6 billion.

UPS has developed a simple yet effective delivery system. They pick up a package and bring it to a hub, or central sorting facility. From there, UPS's large volume transport transfers the packages to another hub from which they are delivered to their final destination.

To deal with logistics, UPS has developed precise, standardized procedures and sophisticated technological systems. A UPS satellite, hundreds of thousands of miles of communication lines, 1,300 distribution centers, a fleet of Boeing airplanes, and specially developed tractor trailers and trucks are just some of the equipment UPS utilizes each day to complete package deliveries.

In an effort to keep its high standard in place, the company has spent $3.4 billion on technology improvements since 1995. This focus has made UPS a leader in the industry and has positioned the company to become a first-class, technologically superior service provider in the global marketplace.[1]

FINANCIAL AND PORTFOLIO ANALYSIS

A faster growth, greater profit margin service for UPS is in domestic air services. Segments within this area are differentiated by speed of delivery. For example, UPS's newest service, UPS SonicAir Service, offers same-day or "next flight out" delivery service to almost any location in the United States. Meanwhile, UPS 3-Day Select guarantees delivery in three business days for a lower rate. Tracking service is provided by TotalTrack, UPS's online cellular tracking system. Domestic air services, as a whole, have grown 14 percent in volume and 11 percent in revenue from 1994 to 1995. This accounts for approximately 86.7 percent of the total consolidated revenue for 1995.

This growth trend reflects consumer demand in the industry for this type of service. UPS has continued to invest heavily by acquiring additional aircraft, replacing older aircraft, improving existing air hub sites, and beginning construction on a sixth regional hub in Colombia, South Carolina. This area has been of importance for UPS not only because of its greater profit margins, but also because it most directly competes with the express delivery services of the U.S. Postal Service and Federal Express.

A third area of service UPS offers is the international delivery service. This is where Kent Nelson, the CEO, is investing for the future of UPS. These investments have reduced the positive nature of the financial statement. In the past, UPS has not done well outside the Americas. Overall, international deliveries contributed 13.3 percent of total consolidated revenues and led to a loss of more than $212 million in 1995. The positive news is that there is a worldwide increase in demand for parcel services. There is also a trend toward a reduction in border restrictions and a positive recogni-

tion of the UPS name in other countries. These trends, along with efficiencies from the implementation of UPS's technologies, have all contributed to a 35.2 percent reduction, or $115 million decrease, in losses from 1994 to 1995.

The last general area of UPS is the other services category. This consists of UPS GroundTrac, UPS TotalTrack, UPS MaxiTrac, UPS MaxiShip System, and other customized services. These services are for certain types of customers that use products such as consignee billing and delivery confirmation services. All of these UPS products use or support the core UPS services such as ground or air delivery.

Other lines of business include UPS Logistics Group, Inc.; UPS Worldwide Logistics, Inc., under which UPS Inventory Express service is offered; and UPS Truck Leasing, Inc. Except for UPS Truck Leasing, these other lines of businesses originated with UPS in 1994. These lines offer consultative services, technological assistance, and other logistical services. These new lines will be closely monitored because they have higher margins and the potential to open new frontiers for the entire industry.[2]

UPS has historically been an industry leader in both size and scope. It is the largest distribution company in the world with total assets of $417 billion as of December 31, 1998, and net income of $1.7 billion for the year ended 1998. Its cash flow provided by operations was $2.9 billion for 1998. This compares with $1.95 billion in 1995. Sales increased to $24.8 billion in 1998 (Figure 9.4). Operating expenses reached $21.7 billion. An EPS of $1.83 in 1995 was the highest EPS from 1990–95.

The first area of interest is the increase in sales and its impact on the other areas of the financial structure of the company. UPS has experienced a steady increase in sales from 1990 to 1998. Sales for 1998 reached $24.8 billion, a 10% increase over 1997. This increase is substantiated by ratios supporting such trends. The ratios also point out new issues that accompany this increase. Inventory turnover has increased from 38.5 in 1996 to 53.96 in 1997 to 65.23 in 1998 (Figure 9.5). This demonstrates the increased demand for United Parcel Service services. During this same period, the receivables turnover ratio has decreased from 9.55 to 9.34 to 9.14. This success should encourage UPS to continue to address its billing and collection procedures.

A steady increase in debt from 1991 to 1997 reinforces management's commitment to long-term development (Figure 9.6). Increased demand accompanied by more intense competition led to additional spending

---

[1] Kay, Russell, "Preview the Future of E-Commerce," *Computerworld,* June 21, 1999, p. 88(1).

[2] Ibid.

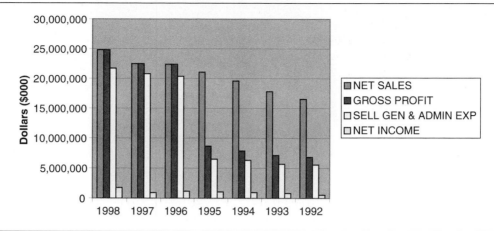

Figure 9.4 United Parcel Service financials, 1992–1998.

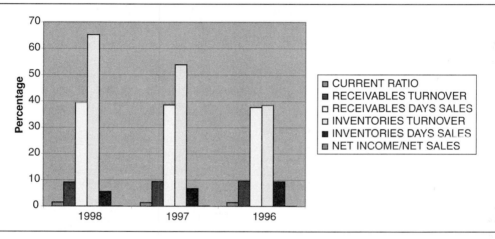

Figure 9.5 Key turnover ratios.

for expansion, technology, and upgrades. More specifically, long-term debt increased from $830,634 million in 1991 to a high of $2.583 billion in 1997. The long-term debt-to-equity ratio has increased from .01 in 1997 to .06 in 1998.

Cash increased from $460 million in 1997 to $1.24 billion in 1998. Major components of this increase can be traced to several issuances. A $200 million issuance of 5.5 percent Eurobond notes due in January 1999 and $166 million issuance of 3.25 percent Swiss franc notes due in October 1999 were two of the largest debt offerings UPS made.

UPS's leverage pattern reveals a great deal about its intentions to expand and grow. The increase in debt and the utilization of cash indicates that UPS has risked its business on the growth of their product within a growing industry. UPS is positioning itself for the future. The company has confidence in its ability to manage this growth and has invested in new equipment,

buildings, lines of business, markets, and, of course, technologies. UPS intended to spend $2.3 billion for land, buildings, equipment, and aircraft in 1996 alone. UPS believes there is a long-term sales potential in the European market and is borrowing heavily to finance this expansion.

UPS remains confident enough in their operations and ideas that they placed themselves in a risky position despite heavy losses in the European market from 1990–1995. Losses in the foreign markets were in excess of $200 million per year for 1993–1995. Nevertheless, UPS has taken on more debt to purchase assets in an effort to realize its long-term goals of expansion and increased market share.

Legal issues may also impact UPS in a financially detrimental manner. The majority of these issues surround allegations by the IRS that UPS owes back taxes because it incorrectly listed assets from 1983 through 1987. Because of rules set by the SEC in disclosing such

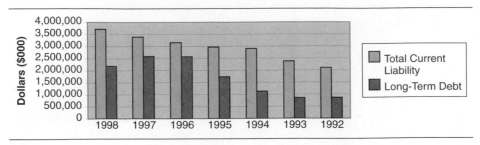

Figure 9.6 Debt and liability, 1992–1998.

litigation, all the suits are published in the annual reports and other publications. In sum, UPS may be liable for almost $399 million not including penalties, interest, and other expenses. Legal counsel for UPS recognizes the potential liability.

UPS has a unique opportunity to expand and further increase its profitability. Although not a publicly traded company, UPS has filings with the SEC that do provide some insight. Management's strategies can be categorized into three sections:

1. Increase business in the higher margin areas.
2. Expand in Europe and other continents to increase volume and market share.
3. Increase information technology to compete with Federal Express and smaller, niche competitors.

To maintain its edge with premium products, UPS has taken advantage of its economies of scale and restructured its prices, using distance-based pricing for its air express services. UPS can charge higher rates for customers needing services requiring longer distances and lower prices for those customers who have shorter distance needs.

Short-distance prices for UPS Next Day Air have dropped 40 percent while pricing for longer distance service has increased 28%. Overall, however, these newly structured services have increased prices 4.9 percent along with increased profitability. International rates have also increased with a 4.9 percent increase for UPS Worldwide Express, a 6.9 percent for UPS Worldwide Expedited, and a 3.9 percent for standard delivery to Canada. The focus on profitability has resulted in less emphasis on markets with lower margins like the residential delivery segment. This management strategy coincides with current market conditions of increased demand for higher priced air services. UPS still leads the domestic ground market by a wide margin over the Roadway Package System.

Another initiative at UPS is globalization. With investments in information technology, acquisitions, and strategic alliances, UPS has increased its presence in the global arena. Historically, FedEx and Airborne had significantly newer and more sophisticated systems to handle international shipments. UPS has upgraded its systems as well. UPS has invested a significant portion of their funds in the cargo versions of Boeing's new 777 plane, as well as acquiring a new $3 million operations center in Hong Kong.

UPS has strengthened ties and entered into negotiations for joint ventures in Indonesia, the Philippines, and India. UPS's presence in Asia has increased with growing businesses in China and Japan. In October 1996, UPS reached an agreement with Nippon Cargo under which the companies will ship freight on each other's aircraft and negotiate a code-sharing arrangement for Pacific crossing flights. These relatively new developments and interests in Asia have placed UPS in direct competition with FedEx, the leading shipper in the Asian market.

The final, and most significant, initiative management has introduced is the implementation of new technologies and upgrades of older, outdated technologies. This initiative is at the core of all of their expansions and is set at center stage in UPS's future plans. UPS has consistently spent approximately $500 million a year on technology from 1985 to 1995 and over $3.4 billion from 1996 through 2000. This is a dramatic change from the less than $50 million per year spent from 1980 to 1984.

RISK ANALYSIS

From an operational standpoint, UPS must consider the implications of the shift from less to more skilled employees. In 1994, UPS suffered volume decreases as a result of an International Brotherhood of Teamsters labor strike that lasted just one day. As labor intensive as UPS is with its over 320,000 mostly union employees, it cannot afford to have long strikes.

As UPS shifts toward a more skilled workforce as a result of increased technologies, the employees are going to be more difficult to replace. Stiffer competition has resulted in higher pay for competent workers. Even common truck drivers at UPS have to know how to link to satellites and download information through DVAs and other sophisticated devices.

UPS has taken steps to change the compensation program for their employees. Managers are now given stock options after two years. Others are able to advance within the company on a faster track. Yet employee turnover is still a concern in this service sector company.

INDUSTRY AND MARKET ANALYSIS

In the parcel delivery industry, the weight of goods shipped usually ranges from less than 1 pound to 600 pounds, and is characterized by two- to three-day ground delivery and next-day delivery services. Other services similar to the description and scope of UPS's include the United States Postal Service and other country's postal services, specifically identified companies such as Federal Express, DHL, and Roadway Services, and other more general companies that include motor carriers, express companies, freight forwarders, and air couriers. Primary rivals of UPS are the United States Postal Service and Federal Express.

Private, public, and government owned companies are included in this industry, with public companies being the largest and most predominant group. UPS, with its employee-owned private status, is an exception.

Parcel delivery and trucking as an industry is directly tied to economic and industrial growth. Although fluctuations arise from the business cycle, in general, there is a direct relationship between the economy and the parcel delivery service.

Industry deregulation has been occuring on several fronts, including:

The European Union single market: This eliminates confining trade restrictions in Europe and sets the stage for uniform codes and restrictions. This will enable the parcel industry to trade more efficiently in the European marketplace.
NAFTA: In 2000, this Act lifts all ownership restrictions and trade barriers between the North American countries. This places new demands on time-sensitive package shipping.
Intermodal Surface Transportation Efficiency Act of 1991: This Act reduces the paperwork associated with interstate trucking and transportation.

Since deregulation, many companies have entered the industry, filling the needs of niche markets. The trucking industry has gone from 18,000 licensed carriers in 1985 to over 55,000 licensed carriers in 1995. To cope with this increased competition, companies have reduced prices and cut expenses. Nevertheless, the industry as a whole has experienced steady growth.

The most significant trend in the industry is the move toward just-in-time inventory systems. This is in an attempt to reduce the expenses associated with inventory warehousing, loss, waste, and depreciation. This trend has led to shorter delivery routes, increased demand for express deliveries, and the request for more information regarding the packages delivered. These demands have become a crucial issue for the survival of the parcel industry's companies and have fostered extensive change. A significant increase in technology expenses has occurred in the short run. Technology will continue to reshape operations and customer service levels.

The most visible change in technology is a focus on the Internet as a medium of interaction between the parcel company and the customer. FedEx, UPS, DHL, and almost all other parcel delivery companies have web sites that offer information and tracking for customers' individual packages. Web sites offer individualized support without increased requirements. Most importantly, web sites have the ability to reach current and potential customers without the constraints of geography, time, or availability.

In UPS's case, a user can type in a parcel number on the UPS web site and initiate an automatic search. In just a few seconds, a user can receive an update on where a package is and get information estimating the time of delivery. The user can also request this information through e-mail. This trend of using web sites in the industry has led to increased customer satisfaction.

Another emphasis is increased spending on the newest and most advanced customer-focused technologies. Increased consumer spending on package delivery services and increased competition to fulfill these needs have led parcel companies to look for the highest level of performance. DHL and FedEx have developed Windows- and Macintosh-based software that lets their customers dial into their servers through toll-free numbers to gain access to their accounts and package status. DHL will even provide a customer that meets minimal standards with a 486 PC with Super VGA monitor, a 14.4-Kbps modem, printer, package scale, bar code reader, and software. This kind of dedication to spending on technology to meet the customers' needs has been a strong drive in the parcel industry.[3]

ROLE OF RESEARCH AND DEVELOPMENT

In light of industry trends and forces, UPS has taken the initiative to implement a series of projects to upgrade and revamp old systems and introduce new ones. UPS perceives themselves as leaders in their industry and does not want to lose to the faster, smaller companies such as FedEx and Roadway or even local competitors.

[3] Hamblen, Matt, "UPS to Upgrade Handhelds for Real-Time Parcel Tracking," *Computerworld,* June 21, 1999, p. 16(1).

TECHNOLOGICAL STORY

The UPS mainframes support finance, marketing, and operations departments. The customer service department is supported by UPS MaxiTrac applications. UPS MaxiTrac manages the data traffic so users can access the database quickly and easily. UPS is also taking advantage of the potential of the Internet as a platform for transactions. It has implemented Internet Electronic Data Interchange software provided by a California company called Premenos Inc.

Through alliances with technology and communications companies, UPS has demonstrated its long-term commitment to information systems while also concentrating on the core industry of parcel delivery.

TECHNOLOGICAL INVESTMENT AND ANALYSIS

Database facilities in Atlanta, Georgia and New Jersey house what UPS claims is the largest db2 database in the world. The database has more than 7,000 gigabytes of records, including tracking information for all UPS packages shipped in an 18-month period. This kind of computing power translates into information regarding senders, receivers, billing, bar codes, time sent, estimated destinations, and other information for more than 4 billion packages.

The new Atlanta, Georgia site is primarily backup for New Jersey operations in case of disasters or expansion needs. Input into these new centralized computing facilities is through DIADs, or delivery information acquisition devices, specially developed for UPS by Motorola. These devices are handheld by the delivery person and feature 1.5 MB of RAM, digital signature capability, and an optical coupler. The optical coupler transfers information and signatures into the DVA or DIAD vehicle adapter, where data are then transferred through a cellular phone or modem. UPSnet transfers the data to the data facilities in New Jersey and Atlanta. UPSnet accomplishes this through a network of 500,000 miles of dedicated cables, more than 200 switching nodes, and a UPS satellite.

Outsourcing of certain IS functions that need expert advice and partnerships is under way. To send all the information from the delivery trucks through the DVA using UPS TotalTrack, UPS has alliances with more than 90 local and regional cellular carriers including AT&T Wireless Communications, AirTouch Cellular, Southwestern Bell Mobile Systems, Pacific Telesis, GTE Mobilnet, and others. Northern Telecom switches provision UPSnet's dedicated cables, which are directly linked to the central computing facilities. Several types of products from several companies result in a 100 percent uptime for the network.

Users of UPS MaxiTrac dial through lines provided by AT&T and Sprint. For data warehousing, UPS has chosen EMC Corporation and a system developed by Hewlett-Packard Company and Oracle Corporation. UPS's existing mainframes were not meeting the speed and availability needs required to service the vast amounts of data. With the help of EMC, data warehousing will now be state of the art. These cooperative agreements have lessened UPS's technology-related responsibilities and have focused UPS's energies on more core issues.

The final implementation of UPS's technological initiative is the development and upgrade of software application products. One of the results of this initiative is UPS Online. This service is a Windows-based system that lets the customer manage finances related to packages, track the status of packages, and print shipping summaries. This system integrates UPS into the customers' daily operations while providing more valuable information. This enables the customer to react to situations in real time.

Another new product is the UPS web site. The customer can use the site to locate where a package is at a particular point in time. A browser can also find information about the company, what is new in the company, employment information, news releases, and a host of other information related to UPS. In this way, even casual, noncompany-related customers can access most of the information that users of UPS Online would have.

Another technological enhancement is the new and improved help desk that services internal and external users in an attempt to "empower our [employees and customers] to become as independent as possible in using technology." A more formalized operation was launched in 1995 as the volume and the sophistication of UPS and its software grew and the need for support for these new technologies increased. With the internal and external operations combined, the help desk received approximately 70,000 calls per month, a dramatic increase compared to approximately 14,000 calls per month in 1991. The external operation is run by 130 front-line experts. The internal group is directed by 65 first-line consultants in the Mahwah, New Jersey, campus.[4]

The intimidating task of coordinating all the software at UPS is directed by the Windows-based Expert Advisor from the Software Artistry company. Previously, the help desk function was supported by IBM's mainframe-based Infoman. Its limitations became evident with the move to PC-based operations from

---

[4] Karpinski, Richard, "New Tools Ship Data Into Enterprises," *InternetWeek*, April 19, 1999, p. 17(1).

mainframe operations. Expert Advisor allows UPS to store more data online to provide standardized assistance quickly and efficiently. The help desk technicians no longer have to flip through binders full of information to solve an issue. Rather, they type the problem into Expert Advisor. With its dynamic ability to constantly update and incorporate new diagnostic tools and solutions into the system, Expert Advisor has enhanced the help desk function at UPS.[5]

TECHNOLOGICAL INNOVATIONS

TELECOMMUNICATIONS

In 1998, UPS launched an Internet-based delivery service that the company advertises could make life easier for firms sending sensitive documents on tight deadlines. The service is called UPS Document Exchange. It is a suite of delivery and information management services that provides a choice from two Internet delivery services: UPS OnLine Courier and UPS OnLine Dossier.[6]

UPS OnLine Courier uses either the UPS web site or a separate software package and enables customers to send documents to anyone, regardless of the e-mail software package, operating system, or hardware on either side of the delivery process. The product is built in an open environment. "It has a Portable Document Format (PDF) and Adobe PDF built into it. If the recipient does not have the same software, it does not hinder their ability to read it. That's a benefit of the Courier," said Joan Schnorbus, a UPS spokesperson.

UPS OnLine Dossier takes UPS OnLine Courier one step further by using a double-encryption process and offering insurance. The document will self-destruct if tampered with. UPS OnLine Dossier authenticates identities using digital certificates. These are required by both the sender and receiver.[7]

Also available is the integration of UPS package-tracking capabilities with a customer's web site. This enables customers to track information for their orders from the company's site where they placed the order, rather than requiring them to jump to the UPS site.

RECOMMENDATION FOR THE FUTURE

UPS knows where they are strong and where they must focus their strengths. The company must continue to focus on the fact that UPS is a parcel delivery company. New technologies must be incorporated into this core business. The management focus is clear—they want higher returns from a global marketplace.

UPS has launched an intensive advertising program for its new package tracking service. It has entered large volume strategic alliances with companies. This segments the competition and gains market share. UPS's resources go a long way as it strives to gain a foothold in the European market. It seems clear that UPS is on the move to defend itself from others, trying to break away from the competition. Economies of scale, good management, and the public embrace of the new technologies are needed to continue to differentiate UPS in the marketplace.

---

[5] Ibid.
[6] Karpinski, Richard, "The Logistics of E-Business," *InternetWeek,* May 31, 1999, p. 1.

[7] Thyfault, Mary E., "UPS Upgrades Data-Delivery Devices," *InformationWeek,* June 21, 1999, p. 24.

CASE QUESTIONS

Strategic Questions

1. What is the strategic direction of the corporation/organization?

2. Who or what forces are driving this direction?

3. What has been the catalyst for change?

4. What are the critical success factors for this corporation/organization?

5. What are the core competencies for this corporation/organization?

Technological Questions

6. What technologies has the corporation relied on?

7. What has caused a change in the use of technology in the corporation/organization?

8. How has this change been implemented?

9. Who has driven this change throughout the organization?

10. How successful has the technological change been?

Quantitative Questions

11. What does the corporation say about its financial ability to embark on a major technological program of advancement?

12. What conclusions can be reached from an analysis of the financial information to support or contradict this financial ability?

13. What analysis can be made by examining the following ratio groups?

    Debt
    Revenue
    Profit
    Asset Utilization

14. What conclusions can be reached by analyzing the financial trends? Are there long-term trends that seem to be problematic? Is the industry stable? Are there replacement products?

Internet Questions

15. What does the corporation's web page present about their business directives?

16. How does this compare to the conclusions reached in the case?

17. How does this compare to the conclusions reached by analyzing the financial information?

Industry Questions

18. What challenges and opportunities is the industry facing?

19. Is the industry oligopolistic or competitive?

20. Does the industry face a change in government regulation?

21. How will technology impact the industry?

Data Questions

22. What role do data play in the future of the corporation?

23. How important are data to the corporation's continued success?

24. How will the capture and maintenance of customer data impact the corporation's future?

TECHNOLOGY TIPS

MICROSOFT WORD TIPS

BULLETS, NUMBERS, AND OUTLINES

There will always be times that you will want to list a number of points, bullet a list, or create an outline. The following will allow you to create these.

Bullets and Numbers

1. Place the cursor where you want to start the bulleted/number list.
2. Click on your right mouse button. From the pop-up menu, click on BULLETS AND NUMBERING.
3. From the dialog box, click on the BULLETED tab or NUMBERED tab. Select your preferences.
4. Click on OK when you are done.
5. A new bullet or number will appear when you hit ENTER at the end of the sentence.
6. Hitting the ENTER button twice will disable the numbering/bullet feature.

Creating an Outline

1. Place the cursor where you want to start the outline.
2. Click on your right mouse button. From the pop-up menu, click on BULLETS AND NUMBERING.
3. Click on the OUTLINE NUMBERED tab. Make your selection from the choices offered.
4. Click on OK when you are done.
5. The new outline numbered heading will appear.
6. Type in your information.
7. To begin the next section of the outline, hit ENTER.

Then click on the NUMBERING button from the toolbar. The next section of your outline will appear.

8. To change the numbered outline heading to the appropriate numbering level, click on the DECREASE INDENT button or INCREASE INDENT button. These buttons will allow you to move the headings through the different outline levels.

Changing the Outline Format

1. If you would like to change the format of the outline, place the cursor at the first entry in your outline.
2. Click on your right mouse button. Click on BULLETS AND NUMBERING from the pop-up menu.
3. Click on the OUTLINE NUMBERED tab. Select your outline style preference by double clicking on it.

ADDITIONAL NOTE

Customizing Bullets, Numbers, and Outlines

You can customize the bullets and outlines to your preferences. In the Bullets and Numbering dialog box, click on one of the tabs. Then click on one of the bullet or numbered styles. Now click on the CUSTOMIZE button. A new dialog box will appear that will allow you to make changes to the styles that are available. Make the necessary changes and then click on OK when you are done.

MICROSOFT EXCEL TIPS

GRAPHS

Using graphs to point out highlights of the data you are entering in the Excel spreadsheets can help users understand the data. Graphs are easily created in Excel and there are many options to choose from. At least ten chapters could easily be written on the creation of graphs in Excel, but this chapter will simply acquaint you with creating a simple graph. It is suggested that you explore the many options available to enhance your graph.

Using Chart Wizard

Chart Wizard is located on the standard tool bar. It can also be accessed by clicking on INSERT and CHART from the drop down menu. The Chart Wizard walks you through all the necessary steps to create a chart, including graph style, data to be used, chart labels, and how it should be saved (on a separate spreadsheet or as an object within the current spreadsheet). The following is an example of how to create a simple chart:

1. Highlight the data that you want to create a graph for. In this example, the labels are also highlighted since they will be integrated into the graph.
2. Click on the Chart Wizard button. The Chart Wizard dialog box will appear and will walk you through the steps necessary to create the chart.
3. Select the chart style, data range, chart options, and location where the chart will be placed. Click on the NEXT button after making your selections. Click on the BACK button to return to the previous step.
4. Once the selections have been made, click on the FINISH button and Excel will create the chart.

Making Changes to the Chart

Once the chart is created and changes need to be made, right click on the area of the chart that needs to be changed. A different pop-up menu will appear, depending on which area of the chart you click on. Experiment with the different options available to customize the charts.

Data Changed?

There is no need to create a new chart if the data in the worksheets used to create the charts changes. As the data is changed in the worksheet, the chart will be automatically updated.

MICROSOFT POWERPOINT TIPS

PRINTING PRESENTATIONS

There are many formats in which you can print a presentation, but the process for each is pretty much the same. Since each format has a purpose, it will benefit you to learn each one in order to help your audience follow you (handouts) and help you practice (speaker's notes).

Printing Handouts

1. Open your presentation in PowerPoint. Click on FILE, then click on PRINT.

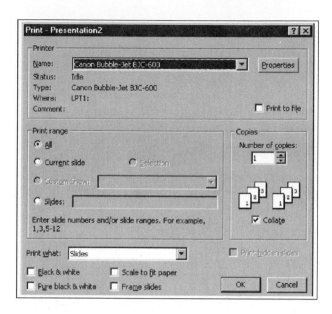

2. The print dialog box on the right will appear. Click on the drop-down arrow located in the PRINT WHAT section.
3. Select 2, 3, or 6 slides per page handouts.
4. Click on OK when you have completed your selections.

Printing Speaker's Notes

If you made use of the speaker's notes view and typed in information under each slide, or would like to have some space to write some notes under each page, do the following:

1. Open your presentation in PowerPoint. Click on FILE, then click on PRINT.
2. The print dialog box will appear. Click on the drop-down arrow located in the PRINT WHAT section.
3. Select Notes Pages.
4. Click on OK to print.

Printing Slides

1. Open your presentation in PowerPoint. Click on FILE, then click on PRINT.
2. The print dialog box will appear. If SLIDES does not appear in the PRINT WHAT section, click on the drop-down arrow and select it.
3. If you want to print all of the slides, simply click on OK. If you want to print certain slides, click on SLIDES and enter the slide number or range of slides that you want to print.
4. Click on OK to print.

Printing an Outline

An outline of your presentation is produced automatically as you prepare your presentation. If you wish to print it, do the following:

1. Open your presentation in PowerPoint. Click on FILE, then click on PRINT.
2. The print dialog box will appear. Click on the drop-down arrow located in the PRINT WHAT section.
3. Select OUTLINE from the drop-down menu.
4. Click on OK to print.

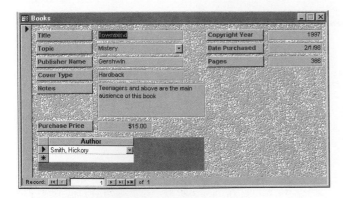

MICROSOFT ACCESS TIPS

USING FORMS TO ENTER DATA

You are not restricted to using the tables to enter data. Once you have created a form, it can be used to enter data into the tables. This may make it easier for someone who will be working with the database and is not familiar with the table format. Also, you can get a printout of a record using the form if you need to distribute it to co-workers or a customer.

1. From the database window, click on the FORMS tab, then double click on the form you want to use to enter data (if you have not created a form already, chapter 8 explains how to do so).
2. When the FORM appears on your screen, click on the NEW RECORD button ▶* located on the form.
3. Enter the appropriate data in the different fields by using the TAB key to advance through each field on the form.
4. When you are done filling out the different fields, press the ENTER key. Click on the NEW RECORD button to advance to the next new record. Notice that the record counter located at the bottom will show that a new record has been added.

PRINTING OUT RECORDS USING FORMS

To print out a single record:

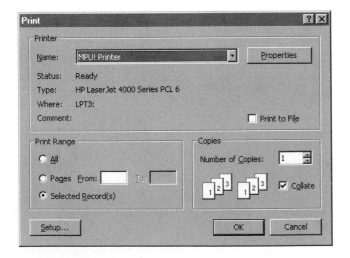

1. Make sure that the record you want to print is displayed in the form.
2. Click on FILE from the tool bar and PRINT from the drop-down menu.
3. Click on the SELECTED RECORD(S) radio button.
4. Click on the OK button.

The record that appeared in your form will print out using the form layout you created.

PRINTING OUT ALL RECORDS USING FORMS

A quick way to get a print out of all your records is to use the PRINT button. Once you have the form open, just click on the PRINT button and all of your records will be printed using the form layout.

MICROSOFT FRONTPAGE TIPS

WEBBOTS: INCLUDE

The Include WebBot allows you to merge content from other web pages to your page. You can think of it as a "dynamic" link to other web pages. This will save you time by not having to write up the same code. Also, it will allow you to use less space on the server since you will not be duplicating documents or files. This works best when you include parts of the web page (i.e. frames of the web page you are including) to your page. It is possible to include content from web pages that are not your own with this feature, but make sure that you have the proper authorization before doing so.

1. Click on the part of the page that you would like to include this WebBot.
2. From the toolbar, click on the WebBot button.
3. A window will appear asking you to select from the different WebBot components. Select INCLUDE and click on OK.
4. The INCLUDE window will appear. Enter the URL address of the page that you wish to include content from on the current page.
5. Click on OK.

The material of the URL address will appear on the page you are working on. If you are not connected to the web, the content of the URL you entered may not appear on the page. Instead, you may get a message indicating that the information is being retrieved.

Modifying the Content

You **cannot** modify the content from the current page. You must modify the page directly. It will then incorporate the changes into the page in which you used the INCLUDE WebBot. You can change the URL address by double clicking on the WebBot component from the EDIT view in FrontPage Express.

IMPORTANT NOTE

As with all other instances in which you use material from other web sites, make sure that you give credit to the page(s) that you borrow material from. More importantly, contact the webmaster of the page to ensure that you have the proper authorization and that you are not violating any copyright laws.

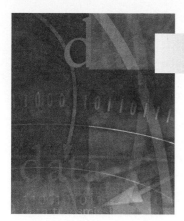

CHAPTER 10

COMPLEX DECISIONS AND ARTIFICIAL INTELLIGENCE
SMALL FRANCHISE INDUSTRY

Complex Decisions and Artificial Intelligence

Expert systems can assist in solving complex problems that require more sophisticated computer tools. Expert systems require the situation to be narrowed to a specific question or problem that can be analyzed by the computer through a set of questions. These types of systems can be built using layers. Each layer containing the rules involved in making the logical decisions. Techniques and tools such as pattern recognition, robotics and motion, and parallel computing have emerged to apply computing power to make decisions and perform tasks. While additional research will enhance these approaches, considerable progress has been made in the area of improving interaction between humans and machines. These areas include voice recognition, robotics, and artificial intelligence.

Expert Systems An expert system is a software program that structures a problem to enable the computer to methodologically step down the identified issues to a resolution. Usually built on an expert system shell, or platform, the application incorporates forward or backward chaining. Forward chaining begins with a problem and steps through its resolutions by making decisions about specific steps that could logically be followed. Backward chaining begins with the solution or present situation and steps backward through the process to determine how the issue started. Stepping to the "root cause" helps to analyze how the problem started and ultimately how it can be resolved. To be implemented, expert systems require an expert engine, a rule base, and an expert to moderate rules that are not accurate and make new rules to continue to be applied to new situations.

Artificial Intelligence Artificial intelligence is the effort to teach the computer to "think" using logical steps, if/then analysis, and specialized software. Programs like lisp or c are used in the analysis because loops are applied to the development effort. This means that the power of the computer is implemented in its ability to "learn" by listing and searching all the possible solutions that are available, or to use pattern matching to determine the sequence in which particular functions are followed.

Decision Support Systems Decision support systems outline, categorize, and weigh factors that need to be combined to develop a decision. They help users make a decision through the use of data, models, and presentations to map and solve general problems.

Artificial intelligence, expert systems, and decision support systems are most applicable to the following types of problems. This technology is applied to these developments because they are logical in their approach and the margins are substantial enough to justify and fund the research, programming, and expert time necessary for a successful expert system

Medical Diagnosis Diagnostic in approach, this is an example of backward chaining. The observable outcome of the problem or illness is clearly evident. This example provides a straightforward example of the ability to observe the symptoms of the illness or problem without the ability to see the cause. Often the cause must be deduced from the systems that are observable.

Legal Analysis Analytic in approach, this, too, is an example of backward chaining. The situation or difficulty is clearly at hand. An accident occurred, a contract was broken, or a crime was committed. To determine which laws apply or which cases take precedence, it is necessary to analyze the specific facts of the case, apply them to the situation at hand, then work backwards to the relevant legal statutes or case law.

Contract, Will, or Trust Generation Basic wills, contracts, and trusts can be standardized and written in a straightforward manner. This approach is used in many of the legal will and contract software that are now available on cd-rom or over the internet. This software provides an example of forward chaining. Information such as name, family situation, income, and property status is queried and then entered into the software. Based upon the standard approach that was used to generate the application, the software "fills in the spaces" and generates the forms based upon the standard rules that surround this straightforward area of the law.

From a business perspective, artificial intelligence assists with diagnosis because it is thorough, rapid, and consistent. The extensiveness of the database enables the application to incorporate all the questions, past recommendations, and rules into a proposed solution. Even after a recommendation is given, the computer can reapply the logic of the process to recheck and substantiate the recommendation. Given the ability of the computer to apply its processing speed to a repetitive task, a many-stepped process or more complex procedure can be carried to completion far faster than possible by even a group of individuals. One of the difficulties with diagnosis and evaluation is the ability to reach the same conclusion independent of who made it or when it was made. Artificial intelligence sets rules that can be applied consistently to the problem sets.

Building Expert Systems Many tools or shells exist today to build an expert system. An equally important component is the expert who understands the problem, can explain it, and can effectively communicate the reasoning process that needs to be incorporated into the expert system.

The basic steps to develop an expert system are to analyze the problem, recommend necessary data requirements and end results, quantify relationships between input data and the rules followed to make the decision, enter the data and rules into the expert system shell, and design the questions and responses. A knowledge engineer is usually hired to supervise the knowledge component of the process. Most expert systems are built using a knowledge base (basic data and a set of rules) that is processed or analyzed by an inference engine.

Limitations of Expert Systems Since expert systems are useful only for specific, narrowly defined problems, with logical solutions, complex problems with many rules are typically outside their reach. Issues can also arise with modifying the knowledge base once the problem changes

Word	W.1	Toolbars	Viewing Toolbars Placement of Toolbar Customizing the Toolbar What Do the Buttons Do? Saving Toolbar Settings
Excel	E.1	Formulas Additional Note	Entering the Formula
PowerPoint	P.1	Creating Master Slides Note	Adding a Logo to theMaster Slide Handout Master
Access	A.1	Queries Select Query Parameter Query CrossTab Query Action Queries	
Front Page	I.1	Word97 Documents on Your Web Site	Saving a Word97 Document as HTML Modifying The HTML Word97 Document

and modifications have been made to the system. This is particularly the case when expert systems apply hundreds of interrelated tools and data elements. Management issues with expert systems include the need for an expert person to be available to present the information and provide the required answer.

Problems with Artificial Intelligence Humans are significantly superior to computers in six areas: pattern recognition, performing multiple tasks at the same time, movement, speech recognition, vision, and language comprehension. While computer systems and tools have made great strides to close the gap between humans and computers in some of these areas, such as speech recognition, there are still significant gaps in performance in others.

Difference Between DSS, ES, and AI An inventory example of when an item should be reordered and the method used to accomplish it will further explain the differences between decision support systems, expert systems, and artificial intelligence. A decision support system would collect sales and cost data and automatically apply the chosen inventory searching method to monitor sales to send messages to suppliers when a reorder was needed using the chosen inventory reordering method. An expert system would help managers decide which inventory reordering method to use when asked for each product or store. An artificial intelligence system would determine the rules the expert system needs to make a decision. This would enable the manager to switch back and forth between inventory reordering methods whenever applicable.

Tests for Machine Intelligence There is currently a debate regarding the best way to determine if machines are "intelligent"; in other words, what tests should machines pass for somebody to deem them "smart"? Some propose using the Turing test, in which someone communicates with a machine, and then both communicate to a judge located elsewhere. If the judge cannot discern which communication came from a machine and which came from a human, the machine passes the test. Other proposed tests include the ability to beat players at chess, the ability to solve complex mathematical problems, tests that need a certain amount of creativity to solve (like composing music), and tests that specifically target areas in which computers are relatively "inferior" to humans.

Small Franchise Industry

DESCRIPTION OF THE INDUSTRY

Franchising is a system in which a producer or marketer of a product or service, the franchisor, sells others, the franchisees, the right to duplicate the concept and use the trade name while providing sales support in a specifically defined territory for an agreed length of time. The contract can involve the right to exclusivity. The amount of support varies from providing the product to resell to extensive sales training and control over business operations.

The first and simplest of the three types of franchises involves a contract between a supplier and a business owner. The latter agrees to only sell one version of a particular product, e.g., McDonald's only sells Coca-Cola soft drinks. The second type, product trade name franchising, accounts for 52 percent of all franchise sales and 33 percent of all the franchise units in the United States. This approach involves selling products to distributors who resell them. The third and last type of franchise is the fastest growing type and is the prototype or "package" franchise. In this method, the whole mode of business operations including the product or service, inventory system, sales and marketing methods, and record-keeping procedures are sold to the franchisee.

Package franchising has grown 10 times faster than product trade name franchising (11.1 versus 1.1 percent on average per year).

FINANCIAL ANALYSIS

The franchiser's revenues are in the form of a start-up fee, ranging from $10,000 to $600,000 depending on the size and market share of the franchise, the trade name, managerial training and support, and royalties that amount to 3 to 8 percent of gross sales.

For example, the start-up fees for McDonald's, Subway, and Domino's are $45,000, $10,000, and $1,300, respectively. There are also additional initial outlays, including rent, inventory, legal fees, equipment, insurance, and licenses. These can amount to 10 times the start-up fee and, in the case of McDonald's, can reach $500,000. The average initial cost is $330,000. Additional conditions may also apply. For example, franchisers can require that purchasers have experience in the particular franchise or in the business segment it represents.

Besides covering the costs needed to acquire a franchise, the buyer needs to commit to making the system work. Franchisees who fail have typically bypassed immersing themselves in the business and instead attempted to merely be managers. The training program for McDonald's, for example, can take months and require a degree from Hamburger University for completion.

Financially, the outlook for investing in a start-up franchise is modest profit and growth until market share increases. Due to substantial competition in low barrier-to-entry industries such as restaurants, cleaning services, and food delivery, franchise operators must keep prices competitive. Therefore, in order to be profitable and generate a considerable return on assets, a large volume of sales must be generated. Market penetration is the goal.

Fanchisees are not expected to immediately produce substantial returns. Because franchisees, as described earlier, face low-profit margins due to stiff competition, they often experience salary decreases. On the average, owner's salaries fall from $66,000 to $35,000 when moving from corporate America to a franchise operation. The workweek also increases.

Nevertheless, despite these statistics, franchising has continued to be a popular field making 170,000 new jobs in 1995. This can be attributed to the sense of autonomy franchisees attain, which contributes to their high level of job satisfaction. Additional components accounting for the popularity of owning a franchised business include recent corporate layoffs, which have left many qualified middle managers ready to undertake new challenges.

STOCK/INVESTMENT OUTLOOK

Franchise stocks enable the investor to choose the industry to invest in and a desired level of business maturity. The stocks can range from new businesses to established "graying" enterprises. Obviously, the risk and potential returns are higher on new ventures. Some of the risk is diversified away because the investment represents a stake in a multitude of independent stores located in different areas of the country. This means that unfavorable economic conditions in a specific area will not be detrimental to franchisers in different territories.

Franchise stockholders also need to be aware that sometimes when a franchise is successful and the franchisor raises sufficient capital, he may begin to repurchase some of the slower growth locations. Purchasing these locations for lower cost and bringing them to a higher level of production is a good way to increase the value of the franchise. This is one example of a long-term strategy for growing the franchise.

POTENTIAL/PROSPECTIVE FOR GROWTH

Currently 8,000,000 people are employed by franchises. Forty-one percent of retail sales are attributed to franchises. Franchising enables a business to grow rapidly and achieve higher market penetration than a sole proprietorship.

From the perspective of the franchisee, who is often an entrepreneur without the knowledge to start a business, franchising provides a business concept without starting from scratch. The franchisee also faces less risk in starting the business because the concept behind the franchise has already been proven to be profitable at another location. Hence, the five-year survival rate for franchises is much higher than that of start-up businesses (85.7 versus 23 percent).

COMPETITIVE STRUCTURE

Franchises can achieve higher efficiency than individual small businesses and small, single proprietor stores. Franchisees do not have to be concerned with internal competition because the franchise contract stipulates how many units can coexist within a particular area. Additionally, franchise owners who leave to open a related business are often precluded from opening one within a specified vicinity of their former operations.

One liability of this form of business occurs when franchisees find a more efficient way to manage their businesses in their particular markets or feel a slightly altered product mix would be more profitable. They are often unable to implement these ideas due to the restrictions imposed by the franchisor who has a commitment to standardization within the franchise.

The amount of control that a franchisor can exert is stipulated in the contract; most franchisees are required to submit monthly, quarterly, and annual financial reports to the franchisor while other owners may be required to purchase supplies from a select list of vendors.

ROLE OF RESEARCH AND DEVELOPMENT

Franchising has experienced considerable growth in the past two decades with 670,000 franchise units (5000 franchises) existing in the United States in 1995. A new franchise opens every 6.5 minutes per business day. According to the International Franchise Association, franchise sales are growing at 10 percent per year. Franchise sales are expected to reach $1 trillion by 2000.

The highest growth has been in the nonfood retail sectors such as lodging and services. One reason for this growth has been the ability of franchisors to adapt their businesses to most effectively service emerging market trends.

TECHNOLOGICAL INVESTMENT AND ANALYSIS

Technology has also impacted the growth of the franchise industry. Improvements in technology available to small business owners have been dramatic. They have included comprehensive systems to track inventories and sales. Better and more varied communication tools have made the transmission of information between owner and franchisor easier and more effective.

The wealth of information and services available to small business owners has also broadened rapidly. The Internet provides a means for small businesses to reach target customers regardless of location.

RECOMMENDATION FOR THE FUTURE

As many U.S. franchises, most notably in the food industry, have matured and reached market saturation, franchisors have expanded internationally. Besides international expansion continuing into the future, other key trends are predicted for the franchise industry. Steady growth is expected to continue; retail sales from franchising will go from 41 to 50 percent; sales are expected to reach $2.5 trillion by the year 2010. Franchises expected to thrive in the next 20 years are home service franchises such as cleaning, food delivery, and senior care services.

Although franchising is a risky business venture for the franchisor as well as the franchisee it has continued to expand. This can be attributed to the ability of franchisors to raise capital and replicate a business idea that has proven effective. Franchising has also benefited from international expansion, continuing to grow despite market saturation in certain industries. Finally,

technological advances have increased efficiency in the transfer of information. This contributes to franchise growth while changing demographics and the current political situation have made an offsetting impact upon the industry.

INDUSTRY WEB SITES

Small Franchise Industry

www.franchisesolutions.com/
www.entremKT.com/access/index.html
www.franchisedoc.com/
www.franchise1.com/
www.franchise.com/

BLOCKBUSTER ENTERTAINMENT

Executive Summary

Case Name:	Blockbuster Entertainment
Case Industry:	Entertainment
Major Technology Issue:	The best way to utilize their huge customer database
Major Financial Issue:	The effort to keep the profits and cash flow from continually decreasing
Major Strategic Issue:	How should Blockbuster react to a decreasing rental video market?
Major Players/Leaders:	Sumner Redstone, Viacom CEO; Bill Fields, former CEO of Blockbuster
Main Web Page:	www.blockbuster.com
Case Conclusion/Recommendation:	Blockbuster should not abandon its video market but should continue to diversify into different forms of transmission, including DVD. They should continue to emphasize international expansion and invest in technology.

CASE ANALYSIS

INTRODUCTORY STORY

On a typical night in America, if there is nothing to watch on regular television, people can simply switch among dozens of channels to watch a movie on cable or choose a pay-per-view movie, without having to leave their easy chair. Alternatively, improvements in video technology such as laser discs or digital videodiscs (DVDs) provide other options. Running to the local video store is less necessary than it used to be.

Yet, in today's society, going to the local video store to rent a movie with friends and family has been a source of entertainment. Video rental is still a relatively new technology. One of the pioneers in this key home entertainment industry is Blockbuster Entertainment Group.

SHORT DESCRIPTION OF THE COMPANY

Blockbuster is a video rental chain, with a national distribution system center in Dallas, Texas. Since its first store, Blockbuster has expanded domestically and in 27 countries. By 1996, Blockbuster was adding hundreds of stores per year through construction and acquisition.[1] Today, the stores register more than one million transactions per day. The Blockbuster Entertainment Group's earnings totaled $3.56 billion at the end of 1996.[2]

---

[1] www.blockbuster.com, June 20, 1997.
[2] Hoover's Online, www.hoovers.com, June 20, 1997.

SHORT HISTORY OF THE COMPANY

In 1985, H. Wayne Huizenga founded and opened Blockbuster Video in Dallas, Texas. The company mission statement focused on increasing the number of locations worldwide, entering into the various markets of entertainment, and producing cutting-edge technology. During the next four years, Blockbuster worked specifically on the first goal, expansion, by growing from 19 stores in 1986 to roughly 1,000 stores in 1989. This included new locations in the international markets of England and Canada.

By 1990, Blockbuster had built a solid foundation in the video industry and decided to begin integrating the second and third company goals through a series of acquisitions, mergers, and joint ventures. These were to complement Blockbuster's niche in the video market by placing the latest technology as well as various merchandise in all present and future locations.

Blockbuster's initial purchase came in 1990 with the acquisition of the third largest video retailer in the United States, Errol Video, Inc. The acquisition was critical for Blockbuster because the move enabled them to obtain a link in the distribution chain between the initial producer of the film, the studio, and the end retailer/renter, themselves. This eliminated the middle man and lowered the overall cost and expense of purchasing videos.

Blockbuster also continued to expand both domestically and internationally by opening locations in Australia, Chile, Japan, Mexico, Spain, Venezuela, and

Austria and operating over 2,000 stores by the end of 1991.

In 1992, Blockbuster continued to demonstrate a desire to enter the related fields of entertainment and utilize the newest technology in those areas by opening Blockbuster Music Stores. This was developed through the acquisition of the Sound Warehouse and Music Plus chains. The following year, Blockbuster entered a different share of the entertainment market by purchasing Spelling Entertainment Group, Inc. (Aaron Spelling is a producer of numerous successful television shows) and Super Club Entertainment Corporation (a leading video and music retailer in the southeastern United States).

By 1993, Blockbuster knew that it could not depend solely on renting videos. While the primary source of income for Blockbuster was still video rental, the Music Stores and Spelling Entertainment brought in revenue totaling $629 million. The acquisition of the Sound Warehouse and Music Plus chains in early 1993 and the Super Club chain in November 1993 made Blockbuster the fourth-largest music retailer in the United States.

These acquisitions were accompanied by the announcement of the first joint ventures with BET Holding (Black Entertainment Television) to produce and distribute black family-oriented films and with Sony Music Entertainment and PACE Entertainment Corporation to develop and operate amphitheaters in North America and Europe. Blockbuster opened another 1,700 locations in 1992 and 1993, reaching a total of 3,700 stores worldwide in 1993.

In 1994, a monumental moment in Blockbuster's history occurred when Blockbuster shareholders approved a merger with movie/television giant Viacom, Inc. Viacom desired Blockbuster's constant increases in profit over the previous nine years. Viacom needed to utilize the profit to eliminate its $7.5 billion debt from an earlier purchase of Paramount Productions.

Viacom is one of the largest and foremost communications and media conglomerates in the United States. The present form of the corporation dates from 1994 when Viacom acquired the entertainment and publishing giant Paramount Communications, Inc.[3] Viacom's merger with Blockbuster brought video rental and music retail operations to its considerable film, cable, television, and publishing holdings. This made it one of the most diversified entertainment companies in the world.[4]

For Blockbuster, the decision was based on the opportunity to complete the distribution link between beginning and end producer of the video spectrum, along with the opportunity to expand into the numerous areas of entertainment controlled by Viacom. The merger of Blockbuster and Viacom was the single largest event in Blockbuster's history and the main reason for their present status in the marketplace.

During 1995 and 1996, Blockbuster aligned itself with successful corporations in areas complementary to Blockbuster's style of business. These ventures included a Blockbuster Visa card, a monthly magazine titled *Blockbuster Entertainment Feature Magazine* published with the assistance of the New York Times Company, and an agreement for Coca-Cola distribution rights at all Blockbuster locations.

In an attempt to gain further market share, Blockbuster joined forces with Sears and Wal-Mart to place Blockbuster locations in their company stores throughout the United States. In a calculated maneuver to stay ahead of technology in the field, Blockbuster established a World Wide Web page to sell merchandise for themselves, MTV, and VH1 (Viacom subsidiaries). Blockbuster introduced Internet CD-ROM software with Sprint and purchased an interest in P.C. Upgrades, a company specializing in upgrading personal computers. They also finished 1997 with over 5,300 stores including locations in Brazil, Peru, Colombia, Germany, and Thailand.

In 1997, Blockbuster returned to Dallas from their headquarters in Fort Lauderdale, where they had originally moved from Dallas in 1987. Blockbuster opened a newly constructed corporate office building and innovative distribution center. Blockbuster's strategy of continual expansion, effective distribution, and new technology is evident from the number of stores, variety of business relationships, and continued retail and rental expansion throughout their numerous locations.

FINANCIAL AND PORTFOLIO ANALYSIS

In 1992, most of Blockbuster's revenue came from the video rental business. Revenue totaled $856 million. While revenue existed from product sales and franchise stores, renting videos was the core business.

In June 1994, Blockbuster had 2,829 company-owned stores and 926 franchise-owned stores operating in 49 states, Washington, D.C., Guam, Puerto Rico, and nine foreign countries. Blockbuster was larger than the next 375 largest domestic home video retailers combined. Yet Blockbuster's domestic market share was only 17 to 20 percent. The video, music, and programming businesses were earning revenues of $3,234 million with an operating income of $593 million. Blockbuster computer store sales were 13.1 percent.

---

[3] "Blockbuster Broadening Its Image Beyond Video Product," *Billboard,* January 25, 1997, v. 109, n. 4, p. 82(1).

[4] "Viacom Inc.," Encyclopedia Britannica Online, http://search.eb.com. Copyright © 1994–1999.

Both rental and sell-through businesses achieved double-digit comparisons during the first and second quarters of 1994. Revenue increased 37.3 percent during these quarters. Operating income was up 45.5 percent. Net income expanded 31.3 percent.

Blockbuster's decision to merge with Viacom resulted from their belief that a merger would bring many benefits. A strong cash flow from Viacom would provide Blockbuster with the resources to invest in opportunities outside of video rental. Another key component of their decision was ownership of movies. By owning the movies that Viacom's entertainment business produced, Blockbuster would have first access to movie rentals in their industry. In the case of digital delivery and technological advancements, Blockbuster would have access to the many entertainment properties owned by Viacom and Paramount, including movies, MTV, VH-1, home video, television shows, interactive multimedia, and books.

The merger between Viacom, Blockbuster Entertainment, and Paramount Communications offered many opportunities for television and video programming, distribution, and advertising. The diversification of program distribution lead advertisers to associate with a specific program, rather than a network. Video-on-demand services have grown. Television shopping has been enhanced by interactive software. Overall, the merger was beneficial for both parties, with each offering products and services the other could use.

These benefits did not make Blockbuster's merger with Viacom a smooth one. Cash flow for Viacom dropped 15 to 20 percent by the end of the first quarter of 1996. Blockbuster lost revenue from its once dominant video rental industry. By the end of 1996, Viacom needed to take a $100 million fourth quarter charge to pre-tax profit to cover the cost of closing about 50 Blockbuster Music stores, 10 percent of the chain's store count. The charge included the cost of the June 1997 move of Blockbuster Entertainment's headquarters from Fort Lauderdale, Florida, back to Dallas, Texas.

Blockbuster's CEO said in a statement, "The elimination of under-performing music stores, most of which were the result of past acquisitions, and the addition of an expanded array of entertainment products and services in all of our stores, will improve our current and long-term operating profile and help us reap benefits as the music retailing environment improves."[5]

In 1996 Blockbuster Video stores reported flat earnings and an operating loss for Blockbuster Music in the third quarter. For the 506 music stores, there was a negative cash flow (earnings before interest, taxes, amortization, and depreciation) of $4.1 million for the period, compared with a positive cash flow of $3.3 million in

[5] *Barron's,* April 28, 1997, v. 77, n. 17, p. 13(1).

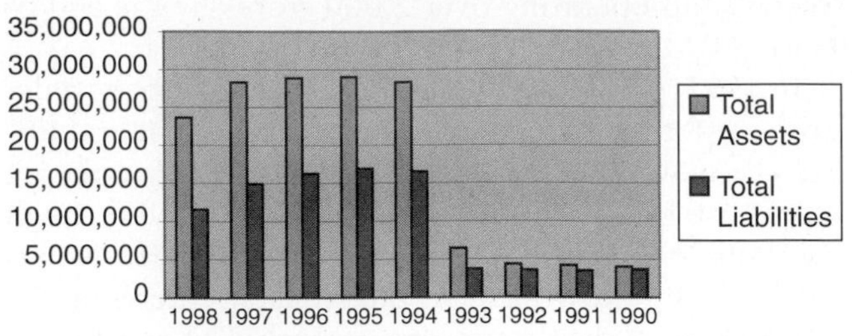

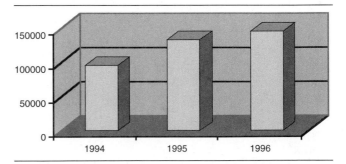

Figure 10.1 Blockbuster Video/Viacom assets to liabilities, 1990–1998.

1995. Music revenue rose 11.5 percent to $140.3 million from $125.8 million despite a reduction in the number of stores from 533 in 1995. Viacom had announced it would close up to 50 of the remaining music stores. In the fourth quarter, 1996, Blockbuster Video had cash flow of $193.9 million on $726.1 million in revenue, compared with $191.9 million in cash flow on revenue of $615.4 million in fourth quarter, 1995.[6]

According to Viacom's financial statements, short-term borrowings from banks increased, from $707,500 to $911,900 from the end of 1996 to the end of first quarter 1997, while long-term debt increased from $9,855,700 to $10,753,200 during the same period. Viacom took out loans to cover the decrease in cash flow. Revenues from the end of 1996 to the beginning of 1997 went up 1.1 percent. Expenses and costs also went up at the higher rate of 1.5 percent.

The assets to liabilities ratio in 1994 indicated both assets and liabilities would increase substantially due to the merger (Figure 10.1). However, there was still a lack of dramatic increase after 1994. Viacom and Blockbuster were both extremely large enterprises. Bringing together profitable companies such as these took time and commitment.

Net sales in relation to the number of employees within the two companies is important to consider (Figure 10.2). Whereas in some acquisitions or mergers,

Figure 10.2 Net sales to employees, 1994–1996.

[6] "Internet Access Comes Free At Blockbuster; Retailer Teaming With Sprint for Software Giveaway," *Billboard,* November 16, 1996, v. 108, n. 46, p. 62(1).

companies tend to downsize or cut costs by reducing the number of employees, Blockbuster and Viacom kept all employees and even expanded their workforce. By increasing their employee size, Blockbuster and Viacom incurred additional costs.

The annual statement for Viacom from 1997 indicated net income of $793,600,000 based upon income after Depreciation and Amortization of 752,800,000. Gross Profit was $4,342,800 based upon consolidation sales of 13,206,100. Cost of Goods Sold was $8,863,000. At the end of 1997, Total Assets for the company ran $28,288,700, with Total Liabilities of $14,905,100 and Total Equity of $13,383,600.

STOCK/INVESTMENT OUTLOOK

Viacom continued to consider the role of Blockbuster in its portfolio. This would be a step many on Wall Street would favor. On July 2, 1997, Standard & Poor's adjusted its ratings on Viacom Inc. and its units, based on concerns regarding the performance of Blockbuster.

Many analysts strongly doubt whether divestiture will rekindle Wall Street's fondness for Blockbuster, a favorite before the Viacom acquisition. The chain has not been "grossly mismanaged," one analyst said, "but I don't think investors' perceptions will improve."[7] On August 6, 1999, the stock price ran between 39⅞ and 41³⁄₁₆.

RISK ANALYSIS

One of Blockbuster's first problems was Bill Fields' resignation as chairman and chief executive of Blockbuster Entertainment Group. Regardless of whether Fields left of his own accord or was encouraged to do so, Blockbuster needed to repair a company with a serious negative cash flow. Cash flow reached below $800 million a year when Viacom purchased the company in 1994. Blockbuster's first quarter earnings in 1995 before interest, taxes, depreciation, and amortization were down 15 to 20 percent from 1994.[8]

At the same time it announced Fields' departure "by mutual agreement," Viacom outlined the initiation of a so-called "tracking stock." This enabled Viacom to sell shares in Blockbuster while retaining full financial control. Viacom chairman Sumner Redstone anticipated an offering early the next year, using the proceeds to lower the huge debt Viacom incurred to acquire Blockbuster and Paramount Communications.[9]

According to Josephthal Lyon & Ross analyst Dennis McAlpine,"They haven't got a lot of choices." Viacom attributed the poor first quarter in 1997 to the "inferior quality" of video releases and the cost of Blockbuster's move to Dallas from Fort Lauderdale. Both problems should have been ancient history by the fall/winter season. "If they don't look better in the third quarter, they are in a lot of deep petunias," McAlpine added.[10]

Fields recruited many high-ranking associates from Wal-Mart. Now their futures at Blockbuster were in question. Some would likely follow Fields to his next situation; the others would stay only if his replacement wants them to. A 25-year Wal-Mart veteran, Fields was a fish out of water in Fort Lauderdale. While taking credit for a strengthened Blockbuster, in his resignation statement Fields acknowledged that "general retailing is in my blood, and it is time for me to return to the industry where I spent my whole career."[11]

Fields was responsible for what many suppliers called the "Wal-Martization" of Blockbuster. He aggressively sought better terms from studios and music labels. In summer 1994, he removed video distributor ETD in Houston from the distribution chain in favor of direct delivery. The plan, which went into effect in 1995, should have saved $25 million to $30 million a year, according to earlier Wall Street estimates.[12]

Many abhorred the trend. Blockbuster, they maintained, had become increasingly difficult to deal with since Fields came on board. "That's good news," says one music executive of his departure. "I didn't like the Wal-Mart influence."[13] Fields' problem, related McAlpine, was that Blockbuster was not a mass merchandiser. "He had nothing like the same stroke he had at Wal-Mart."[14]

In July 1996, Blockbuster announced the acquisition of the 30-store Video Factory to signal the company's readiness to compete with other emerging video operations. Although the stock performance at Viacom was under scrutiny, Blockbuster Video purchased 175 to 200 stores in 1996. Meanwhile, other home video retail companies such as Hollywood Entertainment, Movies, and West Coast Entertainment increased their acquisition efforts as well.[15]

Viacom announced that second quarter earnings before interest, taxes, depreciation, and amortization

[7] "Big Changes Brewing At Blockbuster Top Executive Exits; Parent Viacom Sets Stock Sale," *Billboard*, May 3, 1997, v. 109, n. 18, p. 6(2).
[8] *Computer Retail Week*, October 13, 1997, v. 6, n. 186, p. 1(2)
[9] "Blockbuster Problems Cause $300 Million Write-Down," Broadcasting, July 7, 1997, v. 127, n. 28, p. 8.

[10] Ibid.
[11] "Blockbuster's New Script Doctor" *Business Week*, July 28, 1997, n. 3537, p. 101.
[12] Ibid.
[13] Mendel, Brett, "Mentor's Corner: The Price is Right for Blockbuster's Movie Kiosks," *InfoWorld*, May 31, 1999, v. 21, i. 22, p. 52.
[14] Harrington, Mark, "Blockbuster buys into Upgrades," *Computer Retail Week*, Oct. 21, 1996, v. 6, n. 151, p. 1(3).
[15] "Video Consolidation Continues Apace Blockbuster Purchase May Signal New Spree,"*Billboard*, August 10, 1996, v. 108, n. 32, p. 49(2).

(EBITDA) of Blockbuster would decline precipitously from the second quarter, 1996 performance. Blame was placed on industry weaknesses and disruptions from operational restructuring, among other things. Blockbuster accounted for more than 35 percent of Viacom's 1996 EBITDA; consequently, issues in the home video business as well as challenges specific to Blockbuster impacted the rating (Table 10.1).[16]

In June 1997, Blockbuster Video planned to expand domestically and internationally to keep its revenues healthy. They moved into new territories in Eastern Europe and Asia as part of global expansion plans. The chain's European operation now encompasses eight countries, with Ireland set to be added to the list with the acquisition of the 217-location Xtravision group.[17] Recently, Blockbuster signed a joint-venture agreement with Hong Kong-based Roly International for new stores in Taiwan, Hong Kong, China, Singapore, and Malaysia.

Based in the United Kingdom, the European operation has seen a year of rapid expansion. In addition to growth in Ireland, which was awaiting regulatory approval, the group opened five new outlets in Rome. Charlie McAuley, director of product for Europe, said, "We have a target of 2,000 stores by the year 2000, and our recent move into Ireland has contributed enormously to that. We aim to open more stores in Portugal this year. We are also expanding in Spain."[18]

Plans are still being finalized, but McAuley confirms that Blockbuster is eyeing new international areas. "We see the opportunity to expand into Eastern Europe, but I can't give any specific territories yet. And we are also looking at other Scandinavian territories. We want to develop the business from our base in Denmark and

will be looking to expand into Sweden, Norway, and Finland next year."[19]

So far, Italy has been Blockbuster's largest growth area. It currently has 38 stores in the country in a joint venture with the Standato retail group. "It is the largest center outside the U.K. that we have cracked, although that will change once the Xtravision deal is approved," McAuley adds. The current lineup of Blockbuster European locations is as follows:

UK	716
Italy	38
Spain	35
Denmark	32
Germany	18
Austria	10
Israel	4
Portugal	1

McAuley stressed that Blockbuster's European stores are not restricted to video. In the United Kingdom, the chain launched a number of member-only promotions highlighting its music products. About 220 of the chain's stores now carry top 20 music selections, through distributor/wholesaler Total Home Entertainment.

"For our regular U.K. customers, it is a way of getting their loyalty before Christmas and moving them toward the idea of Blockbuster as a home entertainment retailer," explains McAuley. "In other territories, the Blockbuster brand name takes on a different meaning because people recognize the name as an entertainment retailer, rather than just a rental store. We are certainly testing music promotions for members in the U.K. I think it will involve, and we may be able to offer, similar deals in other countries."[20]

Another U.K. feature that has been embraced in other territories is English-language videos. McAuley says that there is a demand in other markets for the original English-language versions of Hollywood films. Sections have been set up in a number of Blockbuster stores on the continent. Martin Rudolph, product manager at Blockbuster Germany, explains, "We had not expected this to be such a hit. Apart from the fact that it is now possible to hear the stars' original voices at last, there is a time advantage, since the films are launched much earlier than they traditionally have been made available in Germany."[21]

The German operation is a joint venture between Blockbuster and the Burda Print Publishing Group in Munich. It employs 180 people. Although video remains the core business, stores also stock the top 20 music CDs and the top 30 CD-ROMs and video games.

Table 10.1 Ratings Affirmed

Viacom Inc.

Corporate credit rating	BB+
Senior debt	BB+
Subordinated debt	BB−
Bank loan rating	BB+

Viacom International

Corporate credit rating	BB+
Subordinated debt	BB−
Bank loan rating	BB+

Blockbuster Entertainment Corp.

Senior debt	BB+

---

[16] "Blockbuster Is in a Free Fall," *Business Week*, May 5, 1997, n. 3525, p. 37.
[17] "Blockbuster Plots Shifts in Int'l Retail Course; Music Closures Planned," *Billboard*, October 19, 1996.
[18] "CBS, Viacom Make Media Monster," *Communications Today*, September 8, 1999, v. 5, i. 174, p. NA.
[19] Klein, Gideon, "Online music retail comes of age," *Interactive Content*, September 1996, v. 2, p. 6(1).

[20] Klein, Gideon, "Online music retail comes of age," *Interactive Content*, September 1996, v. 2, p. 6(1).
[21] Mendel, Brett, "Mentor's Corner: The price is right for Blockbuster's movie kiosks," *InfoWorld*, May 31, 1999, v. 21, i. 22, p. 52.

"We are continuously striving to gain new customers. We have extended our range, adding more titles and creating extra space in the individual stores. The aim is to show the customer that there is more to a video store than just video rental," said Rudolph.[22]

In Asia, the joint-venture company formed by Blockbuster and Roly International is called Asia Retail Development LDC. It is looking at retail opportunities in a variety of Asian territories. Roly International has 20 years of experience in merchandising and retail, owning an extensive network of stores in Hong Kong and manufacturing and distribution operations in mainland China.[23]

The video rental industry faces a variety of challenges, as consumers find other activities in addition to watching television, and as satellite dishes and cable television compete with a once dominant market share.[24] Video rental sales will continue to be lucrative internationally because many areas around the world do not have as many in-home entertainment options. The video rental industry, especially Blockbuster, must also develop digital strategies to keep up with the competition.

INDUSTRY AND MARKET ANALYSIS

The home video market is the single most important distribution medium for U.S. filmmakers. It provides 40 percent of the revenue and 50 percent of the profits to the motion picture industry. In the span of 16 years, the video industry's revenue has grown from $700 million in 1981 to $15 billion in 1997.

The industry declined in growth to a single-digit pace of 3 percent in 1990. The middle of 1995 was considered the video industry's lowest point since its beginning in 1981. Today, the video industry has been unable to reverse the 1990s trend and continues to maintain a relatively stable growth rate due to selling through videos and technology, using direct broadcast satellites and the Internet.

The impact of selling through videos on true video stores was most dramatic from 1990 through 1997. The sell-through portion of the video industry has jumped from 5 percent in 1990 to 12 percent in 1995, with a 20 percent increase in tape sales between 1994 and 1995. This increase in sales over rentals is the result of three influential factors related to a change in the distribution cost of the merchandise. First, a discount merchant is able to underprice video rental stores. Second, a motion picture studio favors selling the video rather than renting it; studios can generate a higher revenue with less production and distribute

costs for selling rather than rental. Studio revenues amount to only 25 percent of video rental compared to 40 percent of sell-through videos. In 1985, Disney made approximately $465 million by selling 30 million copies of the *Lion King*. To duplicate this dollar amount from rentals, Disney would have to sell 8.5 million tapes to the 14,000 video stores in the United States. This means over 600 tapes would have to be sold per store. Finally, parents have begun to purchase movies because the cost to rent combined with the number of times the tape is viewed is beginning to exceed the one-time purchase price in retail stores. Today a family will commonly view a movie more than five times. Sell-through videos have taken a large share of the home video industry away from the video rental stores. As a result, rental stores may not be able to prevent a substantial decrease in revenue from this change.

Technology is the second area reducing rental stores' market share in the home video industry. Direct broadcast satellites have been particularly effective in this market. The technology trend that video recorders introduced in the 1970s and 1980s is now forcing them out of the marketplace by the customer's desire and ability to utilize various methods to obtain information more efficiently and conveniently than traveling to the video store on a regular basis.

Statistics show that a frequent video rental customer owning a direct broadcast satellite will decrease his number of rentals by 30 percent. Households are being provided with an ever-widening variety of television entertainment without expending any more energy than using the remote control. The cost of the satellite, which will decrease in value over time, compares favorably to the cost a customer saves on the valuable resources of time, such as transportation, and actual cash output (rental fees, candy). While these benefits are uncontrollable by the rental industry, the convenience provided by a VCR and video rental does provide its own unique advantages to the rental customer. A person viewing a rented movie can pause or stop the movie to deal with distractions that may arise during the events of a day, such as answering the telephone or assisting a family member with a chore. A nonrented movie or one chosen by satellite cannot be stopped and a large portion of the movie may be missed. This advantage is not one the industry has a firm control over. Any available advantage must be utilized to its maximum potential before advancing technology eliminates it.

Although the home video industry is in a period of decline, video rental stores and companies can take numerous steps to ensure industry profitability in the future. The first step is focused on large video chains in the United States (Figure 10.3a). Video chains in the domestic video rental market compose only 25 percent of the market share, with Blockbuster controlling 22 percent (see Figure 10.3b) of an industry generating

---

[22] Leger, Jill, "Reel.com vs Blockbuster," *PC Magazine*, November 17, 1998, p. 148(1).
[23] *Billboard*, October 19, 1996.
[24] *Chain Store Age Executive with Shopping Center Age*, June 1997 v. 73, n. 6, p. 36(2).

Figure 10.3 (a) Home video industry analysis 1, and (b) home video industry analysis 2.

$15 billion in revenue. This leaves 75 percent of the market open for competition.

Second, video rental companies need to expand into international areas. At present, 70 percent of the world's VCRs are located outside the United States, with a majority of these countries having little to none of the in-home entertainment alternatives available in the United States. Market shares in foreign countries are readily available for any corporation willing to venture into the marketplace. This must be done before the technology boom is realized and the saturated domestic market depletes a company's ability to allocate profit for spending on expansion.

The home video industry has been on the decline for some time. However, the industry has numerous possibilities for companies to survive, profit, and grow.[25]

Customers are finding all sorts of ways to obtain infotainment more quickly than going to a video rental store. Once again, technology has been the key in the rise and fall of this multi-million dollar industry.

ROLE OF RESEARCH AND DEVELOPMENT

While technology has been the key to Blockbuster's success, technology can also be its downfall. Today there are many alternatives to home entertainment. To succeed, Blockbuster needs to make sure it has captured these opportunities.

TECHNOLOGICAL STORY

At the end of 1996, Blockbuster music and video stores offered customized Internet access software provided by Sprint Multimedia Group through 3,200 of its stores nationwide. This was Sprint's first distribution of its consumer Internet software through a mass-market outlet.[26] Blockbuster entered the market by offering 1.5 million free CD-ROMs with customized entertainment-oriented Internet access software called the Sprint Internet Passport—Blockbuster Edition. The software and 30 days of

free Internet access were available at no cost to consumers who rented a video or made a music purchase.[27]

The promotion, which started November 8, 1996, ran through December 31, 1996. The software provided users with direct access to a Blockbuster Entertainment web page where they could be linked to the latest news about entertainers, events, and products. It also enabled users to search the Internet for photos, art, videos, and music. A store locator helped them find the nearest Blockbuster video or music store. Consumers did not need to be Sprint long-distance subscribers to use the software. Once the promotion ended, customers were still able to get the software free at Blockbuster stores.[28]

TECHNOLOGICAL INVESTMENT AND ANALYSIS

A partnership between the Blockbuster Entertainment Group and Sony Electronics in Park Ridge, New Jersey, to promote and demonstrate the new digital videodisc technology may provide an example of how supermarkets can tie in to the product launch.

Select Blockbuster stores in major markets installed in-store demonstration kiosks with Sony DVD players in April 1997. Meanwhile, purchasers of the Sony hardware units received coupons for free DVD rentals at Blockbuster. According to Benjamin S. Feingold, president of Columbia TriStar Home Video, Culver City, California, similar demonstration programs would be made available to supermarkets.

"Over time I'm sure we will develop various types of promotional programs for various accounts in conjunction with Sony Electronics," he said. "But in the beginning, there may be inventory issues about how much hardware and software is available. Over time we would expect there would be promotional opportunities available for almost every class of trade that wants to be in the business."[29]

---

[25] *Forbes,* February 26, 1996, v. 157, n. 4, p. 46(2).
[26] *HFN, The Weekly Newspaper for the Home Furnishing Network,* November 11, 1996, v. 70, n. 46, p. 4(1).

[27] *HFN,* p. 4(1).
[28] Harrington, Mark, "Blockbuster exits PC business, closes stores," *Computer Retail Week,* October 13, 1997, v. 6, n. 186, p. 1(2).
[29] *Supermarket News,* Jan. 20, 1997, v. 47, n. 3, p. 76(1).

The Blockbuster/Sony partnership is noteworthy because Viacom's ownership of Paramount Pictures is in direct competition with Sony's Columbia and TriStar units. "Blockbuster is committed to being a leader in development of entertainment software experiences that exceed the expectations of our members," according to Tom Byrne, Blockbuster's vice chairman.[30]

John Briesch, president of Sony's Consumer A/V Group said, "We believe people already expect the latest in home video entertainment from Blockbuster, so it makes sense for them to be one of the first retailers in the country to demonstrate the incredible video and audio experiences only available from DVD. Once people have an opportunity to experience our new DVD video player, we believe they will immediately understand the excitement that DVD offers."[31]

TECHNOLOGICAL INNOVATIONS

TELECOMMUNICATIONS

Modern audiences demand technological impact on the movies, advertising, and television that they watch. All of these enhancements are expensive to develop and transmit. A company like KWCC, the special-effects house behind the films *Clear and Present Danger* and *Judge Dredd,* uses dedicated Silicon Graphics (SGI) workstations that cost hundreds of thousands of dollars. These companies charge $2,000 to $12,000 per second of screen time for performing their digital special effects. To make waves with digital photos, web graphics, or printed documents, eye-catching effects must be included. Everyday tasks look dull by comparison if some splash is not involved, whether it is adding color to e-mail, animations to a home page, or a personal touch to photos and videos.[32]

INTERNET

An agreement has been signed between General Electric's NBC and Intertainer Inc. to enable individuals to request, on-demand, rebroadcasts of NBC programming like "Late Night with Conan O'Brien" and "Dateline." NBC said it will partner with Intertainer Inc. to provide content from the programming it owns to Intertainer's on-demand broadband video entertainment and shopping service.

In the process, NBC and GE Capital's Equity Capital Group will pay $3 million in cash for 6 percent of the privately held Intertainer. NBC and GE Capital will also have the option to purchase up to 19 percent of the Santa Monica, California-based company for about

$75 million in 1998 and 1999. Details regarding the shows NBC will bring to the upcoming Intertainer service have not been immediately finalized. Intertainer's service will be delivered through a high-speed cable or phone line and will provide movies, music, television programming, shopping, and informational programming to a user's personal computer or television set.

The Intertainer service is based on the concept of on-demand video service. Customers are given the opportunity to watch what they want, when they want it. Intertainer's service is personalized through intelligent agent technology from Firefly Networks. The agent "reads" users' preferences and provides prompts and suggestions leading to personalized movie, music, television or interactive shopping program options.[33] Intertainer is available to consumers through their personal computers or televisions. It was initially distributed through channels provided by two of the original partners, Comcast and U S West.

Six mass media giants dominate the entertainment and information field. These companies are News Corp, Viacom, Seagram, Walt Disney, Time Warner, and Sony. April 1997 was a low point for Viacom and Sumner Redstone, its chairman. The stock price was down and the Blockbuster video retail chain was struggling. Since this time Redstone has engineered a turnaround that raised Viacom to new heights.

According to Redstone, Blockbuster is fixed because he cut deals with the Hollywood studios that enable more hit movies to be in his stores. Still, Viacom remains a work in progress. Its UPN Network is losing money. Redstone said he would still sell Blockbuster and Spelling Entertainment, and will likely make more acquisitions too. "But we will not re-leverage," he concluded quickly.[34]

Amid increasing concern at Viacom about reducing the company's $8 billion debt, rumors persist that Blockbuster Video will be sold. The success of *Titanic* helped increase revenues by 12 percent at Viacom for the last quarter of 1998. However, profits from continuing operations were down 83 percent, due to the continuing losses at Blockbuster.

Redstone sold half of USANetworks to Seagram for $1.7 billion. The money went toward reducing Viacom's debt. Yet Viacom's stock did not move from the low 30s.

The logic for selling Blockbuster revolves around the commitment by Viacom's Paramount film subsidiary to embrace Divx, a new home video format for digital videodiscs. The format requires users to buy an

[30] *Supermarket News,* Jan. 20, 1997, v. 47, n. 3, p. 76(1).
[31] Harrington, Mark, "Blockbuster buys into Upgrades," *Computer Retail Week,* October 21, 1996, v. 6, n. 151, p. 1(3).
[32] Pepper, Jon, and Alvarez, Cesar, "Hollywood Comes Home," *Computer Life,* July 1998, v. 5, n. 7, p. 58(1).

[33] "NBC: "Let Us Intertain You," *Newsbytes,* August 3, 1998, n. 67.
[34] Serwer, Andrew, "Viacom Wants an Oscar for Fixing Blockbuster," *Fortune,* April 27, 1998, v. 137, n. 8, p. 485(1).

encoded disc for about $5. After that, it is a pay-per-view deal. The disk player is linked to a phone line. The movie cannot be watched without dialing in. After a 48-hour viewing period, a charge is incurred for subsequent screenings. If the system catches on, the reduced likelihood that people will buy tapes will cut into rentals. Based upon an estimated $20 million advanced from the format's developers, Paramount is already licensing films for production in the Divx format.

COMPETITOR

The Hollywood Video rental chain paid $100 million to acquire the Internet-based video concern Reel.com Inc. Wall Street responded favorably to the Hollywood Video decision, increasing its stock price by 13.28 percent in one day of trading.[35] Hollywood Video is the second largest video store chain in the United States, with more than 1,000 superstores in 43 states. Each store carries about 10,000 titles and 16,000 videocassettes. Reel.com offers 85,000 VHS titles for sale, over 1,200 DVD titles for sale, and 35,000 video titles for rent. The cyberstore is also the leading video-only store on the Internet.

The acquisition enables Hollywood Video to leverage the base of 25 million members, industry knowledge, and studio relationships to a new and rapidly growing distribution channel. Because of the uniqueness of each person's taste in movies, the integration of the Internet with the PC's information processing capabilities should result in a substantial increase in movie consumption through focused marketing, collaborative filtering, and customized recommendations.[36]

RECOMMENDATION FOR THE FUTURE

One approach would be to steer Blockbuster away from "Blockbuster Video" and toward "Blockbuster Entertainment." By adding music, computer software, and other entertainment products to its stores, Blockbuster is attempting to expand its corporate image beyond video. The move to reinvent itself has triggered a $12 million, month-long drive during which the chain introduced the slogan "One World, One Word: Blockbuster." This was done with a series of television commercials. The new logo drops the words "video" and "music." As part of the campaign, customers are given a One World, One Word: Blockbuster FunCard. It is punched for every purchase worth $8.99 or more. After eight punches, customers receive a $5 discount from a rental or purchase.[37]

For more than a decade Blockbuster has been synonymous with video. Now the chain must broaden its image. According to Blockbuster spokesperson, Jonathan Baskin, "There is a change under way at our stores with the addition of books, music, and computer software. We want consumers to know that our stores are the local source for all kinds of entertainment products."[38] In the television ads, young people frolic on the beach and bungee-jump off bridges. No one is seen curling up on the couch to watch a video, listen to a CD, or play a video game.

Baskin said the point of the ads is to show consumers that Blockbuster means fun and entertainment. "It's not about showing a storefront, but a variety of images that convey the spirit and soul of Blockbuster." The single-word logo and all-encompassing entertainment theme will be carried into the store level during the coming months.[39]

The 500 to 600 stores scheduled to open in 1999 will each carry the new logo and a mix of video, music, computer, and other products that reflect the demographics of the particular neighborhood. In addition, 1,500 existing stores will be retrofitted with the new logo.[40]

According to Baskin, "The external signage crystallizes the growth of our business. It tells consumers if you want to know what's new in entertainment, come look at Blockbuster." Baskin adds that the chain will close 50 unprofitable music stores. Signage at existing Blockbuster Music and Blockbuster Video stores will not be impacted by the change. During 1998 and 1999, the chain began adding music departments to its video stores. Many of the music stores have sell-through video sections. Many of these music and video locations have carried computer software titles since 1991.[41]

In its quest to become the neighborhood source for entertainment, Blockbuster will use its extensive consumer database to select the product mix. "The goal is neighborhood retailing and the customization of each product for each store," said Baskin. "The key is to cater to the local market and service the local customer." Baskin says the chain has the "strategic advantage" of knowing the entertainment buying habits of half of the households in the United States. Managers at individual locations will have the most input on which products to stock. According to Baskin, "Having unmatched demographic information is a great guide, but it's not a silver bullet."[42]

[35] "Hollywood Video Reels Out $100Mil In Acquisition," *Newsbytes,* July 31, 1998, n. 152, p. NEW07310025.
[36] Johnson, Kelly, "Blockbuster now finds small stores to its liking," *Sacramento Business Journal,* July 23, 1999, v. 16, i. 19, p. 3(3).
[37] "Blockbuster Finally Gets it Right," *Business Week,* March 8, 1999, i. 3619, p. 64(1).

[38] "Blockbuster renews agreement with Time Warner," *The New York Times,* January 27, 1999, p. C4(L) col 1 (1 col in).
[39] Sweeting, Paul, "Blockbuster Makeover under Street Scrutiny," *Variety,* December 21, 1998, v. 373, i. 6, p. 19(1).
[40] "Blockbuster,'Titanic', Drive Viacom Earnings," *Supermarket News,* November 23, 1998, p. 42(1).
[41] Marcus, Ann M., "Four on a Match," *PC Entertainment,* March, 1996, v. 3, n. 3, p. 14(1).
[42] LaHood, Lila, "Dallas-Based Blockbuster Video Makes Quiet Market Entry," *Knight-Ridder/Tribune Business News,* August 12, 1999, p. OKRB9922408D.

In 1997, Blockbuster executives developed plans to add books to more than half of their 500 stores. They saw this move as "another step in the direction of becoming a total-entertainment store," according to Laura Fisher, book buyer for the chain. It took them just four months to open centrally controlled book sections in 276 of their largest music stores. This includes individually targeting local markets.[43]

Each Blockbuster Bookstore, as the book section is called, occupies approximately 1,000 square feet of space. The largest store carries 4,000 titles and 12,000 volumes, while smaller stores carry 3,200 titles and 8,000 volumes. The selection in each store covers a variety of genres, including entertainment, music, humor, self-help, science fiction, romance, and *The New York Times* bestsellers. According to Fisher, "We carry the best of the best in all of these categories. But in the areas that are particularly important to our customers—namely entertainment, music and humor—we carry a wide range of titles."[44]

Purchasing and display decisions for Blockbuster Bookstores are made at the chain's corporate office. All books are purchased through Charles Levy, a wholesaler in Chicago, who is the chain's only book buyer. Cover art, text, author, and title all enter in the decision on which books to stock.[45]

According to Fisher, all 276 stores display books in a similar manner. While 95 percent of the books are displayed in the book section, some are cross-merchandised in the music or video sections. All books in the store are displayed face-out. Beginning in February 1997, the corporate office tailored each store's book section to the area's demographics, where appropriate. Local sports and entertainment titles and books by local authors were added to the stores' selections. "It's a natural move," Fisher said.[46]

By expanding their business into other avenues, Blockbuster captured a market niche that they did not have previously. There are consumers who like to read books instead of watching movies, or like to read a book after watching its movie version. Blockbuster will now be able to take advantage of this market synergy.[47]

Blockbuster must continue to invest in technology. The demand for home entertainment will remain consistent. At this point in time, home entertainment includes television programming, movies, compact discs, and books. The technology that leads today will not necessarily determine what will be important in the next two, five, or seven years.[48]

Videocassettes may not be around for much longer. As long as videocassettes are making Blockbuster money, they should continue to rent and sell them. What Blockbuster must do is make sure that they have all the entertainment that consumers are looking for, including that technology which may be new to the consumer market. To expand in all the levels of technology that they carry in home entertainment, they must make sure that DVDs and laser discs are available in other sections of the store. Blockbuster must continue to develop an image in the consumer's mind that Blockbuster is where they need to go if they want to experience state-of-the-art technology in home entertainment.

Blockbuster must continue to focus more of its efforts on the international market. They need to take advantage of the market opportunity with its current product line, as well as keeping up and beating competitors to technological innovations. Significant portions of the company's net profits have come from the international marketplace. Blockbuster needs to continue to seize this opportunity.

[43] Parkes, Christopher, "Blockbuster Wins Back Customers," *The Financial Times*, May 19, 1998, p. 35(1).
[44] Gapper, John, "Viacom may sell video rent business," *The Financial Times*, June 22, 1998, p. 32(1).
[45] Kadlec, Daniel, "How Blockbuster changed the rules," *Time*, August 3, 1998, v. 152, n. 5, p. 48(2).

[46] Fabrikant, Geraldine, "Viacom's weak link grows a bit stronger; Blockbuster shows gains as parent proceeds with a strategy to shed it," *The New York Times*, October 5, 1998, v. 148, p. C1(N), p. C1(L), col 2 (43 col in).
[47] Vranica, Suzanne, "Blockbuster Moves," *The Wall Street Journal*, October 15, 1998, n. 206, p. B12(W), p. B12(E), col 5 (1 col in).
[48] Sweeting, Paul, "Video's Block Party," *Variety*, July 26, 1999, v. 375, i. 10, p. 11.

CASE QUESTIONS

Strategic Questions

1. What is the strategic direction of the corporation/organization?
2. Who or what forces are driving this direction?
3. What has been the catalyst for change?
4. What are the critical success factors for this corporation/organization?
5. What are the core competencies for this corporation/organization?

Technological Questions

6. What technologies has the corporation relied on?
7. What has caused a change in the use of technology in the corporation/organization?
8. How has this change been implemented?
9. Who has driven this change throughout the organization?
10. How successful has the technological change been?

Quantitative Questions

11. What does the corporation say about its financial ability to embark on a major technological program of advancement?

12. What conclusions can be reached from an analysis of the financial information to support or contradict this financial ability?

13. What analysis can be made by examining the following ratio groups?

    Quick/Current
    Debt
    Revenue
    Profit
    Asset Utilization

14. What conclusions can be reached by analyzing the financial trends? Are there long-term trends that seem to be problematic? Is the industry stable? Are there replacement products?

Internet Questions

15. What does the corporation's web page present about their business directives?

16. How does this compare to the conclusions reached by the Blockbuster case?

17. How does this compare to the conclusions reached by analyzing the financial information?

Industry Questions

18. What challenges and opportunities is the industry facing?

19. Is the industry oligopolistic or competitive?

20. Does the industry face a change in government regulation?

21. How will technology impact the industry?

Data Questions

22. What role do data play in the future of the corporation?

23. How important are data to the corporation's continued success?

24. How will the capture and maintenance of customer data impact the corporation's future?

MRS. FIELDS COOKIES

Executive Summary

Case Name:	Mrs. Fields Cookies
Case Industry:	Restaurant/eating places industry
Major Technology Issue:	Integrating all Mrs. Fields Cookies stores into the decision-making system of Mrs. Fields headquarters
Major Financial Issue:	Initially, funding for the company; recently, overcoming the cost of poorly researched store locations
Major Strategic Issue:	Extend growth of the company without sacrificing the quality of the product
Major Players/Leaders:	The Original Cookie Co., Keebler Cookie Co.
Main Web Page:	www.mrsfields.com
Case Conclusion/Recommendation:	Mrs. Fields needs to conduct more thorough market research before placing a store in locations that will not be profitable. Additionally, franchising the stores, rather than being company owned, would allow for greater and faster innovation.

CASE ANALYSIS

INTRODUCTORY STORY

The year is 1977. Randy Fields, Debbi's new husband, is at work giving financial advice to a client. Debbi has just returned home from a history class that she is taking at a local community college. She has been wondering what impact her life will make. She decides to make another batch of her relatively unknown chocolate chip cookies. Since she has been doing this so long, she knows she is good at baking cookies, and enjoys doing so. The light bulb in her head suddenly shines bright: "Why not open a small cookie shop where I can bake and sell my cookies?" Since Randy's clients like them so much, she is sure that many others will too. The first hurdle was to convince Randy that her idea would work.

SHORT DESCRIPTION OF THE COMPANY

Not too many people can pass up the smell of freshly baked cookies. In 1977 Debbi Fields was confident enough in her own baking skills to capitalize on them and start her own cookie retail business. Debbi experienced much success through the 1980s. In the early 1990s, economic and organizational problems with the business led to the beginning of a decline for Mrs. Fields Cookies.

Three factors played an important role in the story of Mrs. Fields Cookies: control, growth and technol-

ogy. Many times the foundation of a successful business is the way in which it is controlled, the rate and period of growth, and the company's effective use of technology.

SHORT HISTORY OF THE COMPANY

Mrs. Fields Chocolate Chippery started in 300 square feet leased from an old grocery market. Debbi bought all of the necessary equipment, from spoons and mixers to an industrial-sized oven. On a hot summer day in August, the store was opened. By the end of the day Debbi had sold $50 worth of cookies. Sales were up the second day by $25. From then on the bells of success rang unceasingly. Debbi did have standards for her business, such as selling only fresh cookies, meaning that they could not sit on the rack for more than two hours. Important details such as this added to the value and quality of her business.

The year 1988 marked a turning point in the story of Mrs. Fields Cookies. The management style that Debbi used was stifling the business; a change was necessary. Corporate headquarters consisted of a staff of 115. This included area sales managers, district sales managers, regional directors of operations, and a vice president of operations.[1] Debbi had formerly held the top managerial positions of chief financial officer and

---

[1] "Mrs. Fields Cookies," *The New York Times*, August 19, 1998, v. 14-1, p. C3(N), p. D3(L).

head of operations, but realized the importance of having professionals who specialized in these areas. Tim Pierce was hired from Price Waterhouse to be the CFO, and Paul Baird was hired from Godfather's Pizza as vice president of operations. Larry Holman was hired as senior vice president of corporate development.

With these three executives in place, many of the employees with whom Debbi previously interacted now reported directly to the new executives. This provided her with more time to read and respond to customer comments, visit stores, and talk with local managers. She once commented regarding the time when she controlled every aspect of the business, "those days are over . . . letting go has been hard."[2]

Along with new management approaches came new business opportunities. A license deal was completed in 1989 with Marriott to open stores in airports and highway travel plazas. In 1992, another deal with Ambrosia Chocolate allowed Mrs. Fields Semi-Sweet Chocolate Chips to be sold in supermarkets. With the acquisition of La Petite Boulangerie stores, a bakery-cafe concept was introduced where soups and sandwiches were sold, along with the signature cookie and brownie items.[3]

The reorganization of Mrs. Fields Cookies brought with it the concept of franchising. Debbi had stood firm on not using this method of expansion so she could maintain complete control over all her stores. In 1992, Debbi developed a program that allowed store managers who met outlined qualifications to purchase their stores from the company. In the early years this was unthinkable.

Financial problems continued to plague Debbi's business. In August 1996, *The Salt Lake City Tribune* reported that Mrs. Fields Cookies would be merging with its closest competitor, the Original Cookie Company. The combined company was called The Mrs. Fields Original Cookie Co.[4] Retired as chief executive officer of the business, Debbi now travels the country selling cookbooks containing recipes to many of her cookies.

FINANCIAL AND PORTFOLIO ANALYSIS

Mrs. Fields Cookies was never exempt from the rocky road with which most successful small businesses are challenged during their initial years. Issues such as expansion, reorganization, and market diversification all

kept Mrs. Fields management occupied throughout the 1980s and mid-1990s. The managers realized that financially one of the best ways to deal with all of these rapid changes and was to go public and issue stock.

In 1986, Debbi and her husband Randy tried putting the company on the public market to see if this would provide a better means of financing their business. The first market they tried was the London Stock Exchange. With a lack of knowledge and interest in the company, British stock buyers were slow to buy into the Fields plan. The next step was the issuance of more debt and increased reliance on their own cash flow.[5]

Mrs. Fields Cookies saw fast growth in the mid-1980s. Between 1985 and 1988 the number of stores reached the 225 mark.[6] In 1987, 543 stores were fully operational in six countries, with earnings of $18 million from $104 million in sales. Sales of the company's stock were increasing. Mrs. Fields holding company purchased La Petite Boulangerie, a national bakery chain formerly owned by PepsiCo.[7]

During this same time span, the company was facing increasing difficulties. In 1988, 97 stores were closed for various reasons, location being a leading factor. The year 1992 marked the peak in store closings with net losses progressing from $577,000 in 1985 to $19,900,000 in 1988.[8] Mrs. Fields Cookies borrowed $94 million. The obligations to this debt eventually resulted in the 1993 takeover of the company by the creditors.[9]

The current information systems were not serving the company's needs. Randy Fields made the point that "the problem of inconsistent performance throughout a company has been addressed by numerous corporate policies and procedures, large management staffs, and excessive reporting processes."[10] Financially, the company needed an answer to their operational cost problems. One improvement was made in the area of employment cost with the addition of "a time and attendance software package." This helped eliminate many of the errors made in the procedure of compiling and transmitting employee time reports. The new reporting system helped realize savings of $200,000 per year.[11] This was not enough

[2] Prendergast, Alan, "Learning to Let Go: Holding on Too Tight Almost Made the Cookie Crumble at Mrs. Fields," *Working Woman,* January 1992, p. 43.
[3] "One to Watch: Mrs. Fields—Legacy Brands Markets Ice-Cream Novelties," Dairy Record, p. 30. 1998, v. 99, n.8.
[4] Oberbeck, Steven, "Utah's Mrs. Fields Cookies to Merge with Original Cookie Co.," *The Salt Lake Tribune,* August 15, 1996, p. 8150219.

[5] Ibid., p. 5.
[6] Pogrebin, Robin, "What Went Wrong with Mrs. Fields?," *Working Woman,* July 1993, p. 9.
[7] Weisman, Katherine, "Succeeding by Failing," *Forbes,* June 25, 1990, p. 160.
[8] Oberbeck, Steven, "Utah's Mrs. Fields Cookies to Merge with Original Cookie Co.," *The Salt Lake Tribune,* August 15, 1996, p. 12.
[9] Pogrebin, Robin, "What Went Wrong with Mrs. Fields?," *Working Woman,* July 1993, p. 9.
[10] Fields, Randall, and Imparato, Nicholas, "Cost, Competition & Cookies," *Management Review,* April 1995, p. 57.
[11] Ibid., p. 59.

to make up for the large losses and problems that the company suffered, however.

STOCK/INVESTMENT OUTLOOK

Mrs. Fields Cookies took on many challenges and risks. They added a large and successful prepackaged cookie product. They decided not to franchise. Debbi assessed the overall market for the cookie business, looking for new places to expand, and evaluating the profitability of challenging any existing competitors with new business ventures. In the long term, Debbi's investment was lost due to overriding debt, high cost, and the poor choice of locations.

RISK ANALYSIS

Once the business plan for Mrs. Fields Cookies was in place, another issue had to be addressed. "In starting Mrs. Fields, the positive side was that I could bake like a champ; the negative side had to do with the bankers. You need two things to get a business going: an idea and a banker who'll believe in it."[12] Debbi knew that trying to find investors for the business was going to be a challenge because of her age. No one believed that a cookie business would be a practical investment. Bank of America's Ed Sullivan, a loan manager, really did not believe the cookie business was a good investment. He did believe that the Fields would pay back their debt if the business failed.[13]

Another major risk was the management structure of the business. As Mrs. Fields Cookies experienced success and needed more outlets, Debbi decided to make them all company stores. By 1981 the business expanded to northern California, Honolulu, Hawaii, and Salt Lake City, Utah, with 14 stores by 1981.[14]

Debbi did not want the other stores to conduct operations any differently than the way she had been doing them. She wanted to maintain control and oversee daily operations of each store as closely and often as possible. She determined not to franchise, perceiving this to be a loss of control. By 1987, there were nearly 500 company-owned stores in 37 states selling cookies with the same touch that Debbi had put into the cookies she originally baked for her husband's friends and clients.

Most people would expect to find the headquarters of a company of this size located in a high-rise building in the downtown area of a major metropolitan area. This was not the case with Mrs. Fields Cookies. In 1987, the headquarters staff consisted of 115 people lo-

cated in the town of its humble beginnings, Park City, Utah. To keep directly in touch with store managers, Debbi used a voice mail system called PhoneMail. Debbi maintained a close relationship with the stores instead of just delegating authority.

INDUSTRY AND MARKET ANALYSIS

Debbi Fields did extensive research when she decided to open up her cookie business, and continued to do so as she looked for the best way to efficiently expand. Along with an analysis of the "retail cookie" industry, she had to familiarize herself with the competitive struggles that she would encounter as she tried to make her own business successful.

In the late 1970s, the retail cookie industry was very small. Why pay money for someone else to do what "Dearest Mom" could definitely do much better? Mrs. Fields saw this opportunity, and wanted to capitalize on it. With ease of entry into the market, Mrs. Fields was one of the first players in the retail cookie industry.

The Original Cookie Company was the largest competitor, having started operations in 1976 in Cleveland, Ohio. Since they were in two separate regions of the United States, neither really competed with each other until increased expansion efforts by both companies started taking place.

Many large retail and restaurant businesses are always studying the market, spending a great deal of money to determine whether the general public will accept what the company has to offer. Market analysis at this level was available to Debbi, but she felt like a better way to get an accurate understanding of what people liked, in a specific market, was to open a store and observe firsthand what happened. This seemed to Debbi like the best market assessment. When a company executive approached her with the idea of expanding into an international market, she felt comfortable doing so.[15]

In 1982, Mrs. Fields International was started with target markets that included Japan, Hong Kong, and Australia.[16] Marketing the concept of stores that only sell cookies to a new demographic target group would be the next challenge, but Debbi was willing to do anything and everything that would help sell her cookies, with the exception of changing the cookie recipes.

Product expansion accompanied growth into the international arena. By 1988, 14 different types of Mrs. Fields Cookies were being sold. Soon brownies, muffins, candies, and ice cream were added. One factor that re-

[12] Ibid., p. 61.
[13] Ibid., pp. 63–64.
[14] Ostrofsky, Keri, "Mrs. Fields Cookies," Harvard Business School Case Study #9-189-056, September 14, 1993, p. 3.

[15] Fields, Randall, and Imparato, Nicholas, "Cost, Competition & Cookies," *Management Review,* April 1995, pp. 158–159.
[16] Ostrofsky, Keri, "Mrs. Fields Cookies," Harvard Business School Case Study #9-189-056, September 14, 1993, p. 3.

mained important to the sale of the cookies was to make sure they were always sold fresh. This meant that cookies that were not sold within two hours after coming out of the oven were discarded or given to a local charity organization.[17] Maintaining this freshness was important because of the competition in specialty stores, other cookie companies that began to blossom, and the sweet snack industry.

ROLE OF RESEARCH AND DEVELOPMENT

Randy Fields was instrumental in establishing a management system that would provide not only the control that Debbi wanted, but the business results as well. With the business world becoming technologically advanced at a rapid pace in the 1980s, he knew that for Mrs. Fields Cookies to stay on top, it would have to adapt to the times. Randy made no secret about his commitment to technology.

> *Technology—in the form of an action management system—helps to shatter the age-old dependence on high-cost controls in achieving corporate consistency because it replaces many of the costly vertical and horizontal controls that previously have been used to achieve uniform operations.*[18]

TECHNOLOGICAL STORY

"Good morning, San Francisco." The Mrs. Fields store manager hears this greeting of a local disc jockey on a foggy, cool Thursday morning in San Francisco. After starting a pot of coffee, he turns on a Tandy computer and enters specific data relating to his particular Mrs. Fields Cookie store for this particular day. After answering several questions dealing with issues such as the weather and results from the previous day, the system generates a report that forecasts the requirements needed to meet the sales projection for that day.

Following this procedure, the manager checks the PhoneMail messages to hear if Debbi has left any special messages for him. All the store manager has to do now is to make sure that his workers are in the store on time doing what has been outlined for them by the system-generated daily report, and focus on pleasing the customers as much as possible.[19]

It may seem as though the store manager does not have too much autonomy or authority to run the store as he wants. And this is exactly how Debbi Fields wants it to be. Randy Fields once said, "We felt that every store needed to run the way Debbi ran her first store. What we did was to take Debbi's operational ideas and embody them in a computer."[20] From the day that the very first store was opened, Debbi had been in complete control. She knew that the business was successful because of the way she ran her business, not the way someone else told her it should be run.

TECHNOLOGICAL INVESTMENT AND ANALYSIS

Trying a new management system that would continue to provide Debbi with the control she wanted, but would be more cost efficient, was necessary. Randy's philosophy was that the best management structure would be built as flat as possible. This meant not too many people would be involved with a great deal of paperwork.

The early years of Randy's management information systems department were full of basic implementations that were very useful. The use of PhoneMail enabled Debbi to leave personal messages with each of the store managers at all of the stores. The Form-Mail program was an "e-mail" system written by the MIS department to allow personal messages to be typed by store managers and sent to Debbi at corporate headquarters. Debbi personally promised a response to each message within 48 hours of her reading it. Now she was able to communicate with each of her stores without actually visiting them. Visiting was time intensive; Debbi logged about 350,000 commercial air miles in 1986.[21]

Improvements to the existing system included a corporate database that operated on IBM-computers. IBM compatible PCs, which soon interfaced with the cash registers, linked each store to corporate headquarters. The MIS group developed its own applications to perform various functions at the store level, such as production planning, staff scheduling, financial reporting, hiring practices, lease management, training, baking schedules, etc. This group of programs was labeled Retail Operations Intelligence (ROI). It was so successful within the company that the company decided to sell the software to other businesses.[22] The implementation of the ROI system gave Debbi the opportunity for the hands-on management that she wanted, allowing her to maintain control over individual store operations from one central office.

The ROI system simplified the role of the store managers to the point of being told what, where, how, and

---

[17] Ibid.
[18] Fields, Randall, and Imparato, Nicholas, "Cost, Competition & Cookies," *Management Review,* April 1995, pp. 158–159.
[19] "Richman, p. 66.

[20] Anonymous, "Mrs. Fields Automates the Way the Cookie Sells," *Chain Store Age Executive with Shopping Center Age,* April 1988, p. 73.
[21] "Richman, p. 66.
[22] McAllister, Celia F., "How Mrs. Fields Cookies Crunches Its Numbers," *Business Week (Industrial Edition),* February 5, 1990, p. 82.

when to do something. With the business focusing primarily on selling cookies, the new technology was able to tell a store manager how many cookies needed to be baked and sold at a certain time during the day. This helped to eliminate a great deal of waste, consequentially cutting costs. It provided store managers with more time to focus on customer needs and removed administrative details.

The main strategy of the MIS department at Mrs. Fields Cookies was to assist in solving any business problems the company faced. The problem with this strategy was that at the rate the business was expanding, problem solving would not be helpful in the prevention of new problems that would arise. Paul Quinn, the director of MIS, reported directly to Randy Fields. He was not concerned about problem prevention, but wanted to be aware of the issues dealing with cost efficiency and the benefits of any implementation of information systems coming from his department. Problem solving can be good for present situations. Analyzing the big picture and the possibilities for the future are just as important, especially when it involves a business the size and reputation of Mrs. Fields Cookies.

Quinn's definition of strategy for MIS had to do with anything that would promote sales and control food and labor costs.[23] Quinn wanted to know not only how a new technique would cut costs and save the business money, but also how it would develop new sales for the business and place the company in a better position to take advantage of opportunities.

Quinn implemented a Return on Investment System for the business as it moved into the 1990s. No longer was the company growing at a fast rate and trying to flood the market. Many viewed the ROI system to be an expert system (ES).

Randy Fields made the following statement about his belief in the use of Expert Systems at Mrs. Fields Cookies:

We couldn't run our business without information technology—not a single facet. Who we hire is determined by an expert system. What we make at each store is determined by an expert system. How we schedule our labor in each store is determined by an expert system. How we communicate internally is routed by an expert system. . . . What's left? At the store level, everything that the manager does that's related to control and administration has been "off-loaded" to a machine. So the manager's job is to think about people.[24]

With the implementation of the ROI applications, control by one person was eliminated at the store level. Implementation of these applications did take some of the burden off the shoulders of Debbi and placed the control into a more standardized format.

The ROI system included 12 applications, each with the purpose of decreasing the invested time and money spent on each function by the company. Four of the more important modules included Interview, Training and Testing, Automated Troubleshooting, and Form-Mail.[25] These were four applications that helped to decrease the time a manager needed to spend completing these tasks and not being able to assist customers with the best service.

The Interview application required the first part of a job applicant's interview process to take place on a computer. Basic questions were asked to give the company an understanding of the type of person applying. The computer program probed the intention of the applicant and the reason for applying to work at Mrs. Fields. It pinpointed inconsistencies of an applicant, such as a 17-year-old applicant who listed an educational background up to graduate school. The program produced a list of concerns about the candidate. Upon completion of the computer interview, it ranked the applicant against others in areas of education, honesty, and salesmanship. After the computer interview, the applicant was given the opportunity to "audition" as a performer in front of customers. The manager then decided if the applicant would be hired.

Each employee, from manager to baker, went through continuous training and evaluation by using the Training and Testing systems module. Again, the system asked several questions based on experience and performance to test and evaluate individual skills learned and to train in the development of new ones. Once an employee completed a training module, their records in human resources were updated automatically at corporate headquarters.

Automated Troubleshooting was a maintenance module used mainly by the store manager to deal with problems regarding faulty or broken store equipment. If the answers entered in the system did not lead to a solution for the problem, a function was added that requested an outside call for assistance. Each store had a file with the product service group at corporate headquarters, listing information about each piece of equipment at the store. This information was used to contact the product vendor to request any type of repair that was needed.

The Form-Mail application was used mainly by store managers to maintain communication with corporate

[23] Ostrofsky, Keri, "Mrs. Fields Cookies," *Harvard Business School Case Study* #9-189-056, September 14, 1993, p. 7.
[24] Anonymous, "Strategic Use of Expert Systems," *Chief Executive,* November/December 1990, p. 57.

[25] Schulman, Richard E., "Streamlining and Unifying Store-Level Decisions," *Supermarket Business,* May 1990, pp. 21–22.

headquarters. Debbi was also able to send memos to each of the stores with this application. It was a basic e-mail system developed in the early 1980s.

RECOMMENDATION FOR THE FUTURE

Many entrepreneurial endeavors experience fluctuation. These fluctuations can occur in the success of the company's various marketing campaigns, hiring practices, or overall management techniques. Inconsistencies in any part of the business can eventually impact

the entire business. In the case of Mrs. Fields Cookies, these fluctuations did not occur often, but the effects were observed by many. The biggest issues involve-management's strong control of the company, its rapid rate of expansion, and the too little–too late technological advances. Eventually, all of the changes took their toll. Nonetheless the business survives albeit as a consolidated company. To thrive the company must continue to stress quality, freshness, responsiveness and to respond to consumers' changing interests.

CASE QUESTIONS

Strategic Questions

1. What is the strategic direction of the corporation/organization?

2. Who or what forces are driving this direction?

3. What has been the catalyst for change?

4. What are the critical success factors for this corporation/organization?

5. What are the core competencies for this corporation/organization?

Technological Questions

6. What technologies has the corporation relied on?

7. What has caused a change in the use of technology in the corporation/organization?

8. How has this change been implemented?

9. Who has driven this change throughout the organization?

10. How successful has the technological change been?

Industry Questions

11. What challenges and opportunities is the industry facing?

12. Is the industry oligopolistic or competitive?

13. Does the industry face a change in government regulation?

14. How will technology impact the industry?

Data Questions

15. What role do data play in the future of the corporation?

16. How will the capture and maintenance of customer data impact the corporation's future?

TECHNOLOGY TIPS

MICROSOFT WORD TIPS

TOOLBARS

Toolbars allow you to have several commands at your fingertips by displaying them as graphical user interface (GUI) buttons on your screen. Word opens up with the standard toolbar on top, but you can customize the toolbar to show the commands or features that you use the most. The following is a general overview of how to view the different toolbars and how to customize your own.

Viewing Toolbars

1. Click on the toolbar with your right mouse button.
2. A drop-down menu will appear. The different toolbars that are available will appear by title.

3. Click on the toolbar that you would like to use.
4. The toolbar will automatically appear on your screen

Placement of Toolbar

1. You can integrate the toolbar to the top, bottom, or sides of your Word screen by clicking on the leftmost part of the toolbar (it will have two vertical bars) and dragging it to the section of the screen where you would like to place it. If the toolbar is not integrated to the screen already, click on "empty" space and then drag it.
2. A dotted outline will appear as you drag the toolbar around the screen. This outline will change shape depending on where you move the toolbar inside the screen.
3. Release the toolbar where you would like to display it.

Customizing the Toolbar

1. Click on any toolbar with your right mouse button.
2. From the drop-down menu click on CUSTOMIZE. . . .
3. The customize dialog box will appear with three tabs: TOOLBARS, COMMANDS, and OPTIONS.
4. Click on the COMMANDS tab. The command buttons on the right of the dialog box correspond to the toolbar selected from the left.
5. To add to the existing toolbar, click on one of the command buttons on the right and drag it onto the toolbar. This will automatically insert it onto your existing toolbar.
6. Click on CLOSE when you are done.

What Do the Buttons Do?

A brief explanation of what each command button does is given when you do the following:

1. From the customize dialog box click on the COMMANDS tab.
2. Click on the command button on the right side of the screen that you would like a description of.
3. Click on the DESCRIPTION button inside the dialog box. A small dialog box will appear with a brief description of the command button.

Saving Toolbar Settings

You can take your customized toolbar with you by saving it with your document. Whenever you open the document the customized toolbar will appear. This is helpful when you have to work with tables or drawings in certain documents and need to use these toolbars frequently.

1. After customizing your toolbar as explained above, click on the COMMANDS tab section in the dialog box.
2. Click on the SAVE IN drop-down box at the bottom of the dialog box.
3. Search for your document title in the box and click on it. Click on CLOSE.

MICROSOFT EXCEL TIPS

FORMULAS

One of the many advantages of working with Excel is the use of formulas in calculating data. Multiplication, division, addition, and subtraction can be used in the formulas you enter. The formulas will use cell addresses in order to calculate the results of your formula. The advantage of using cell addresses is that the result of any of the formulas containing the cell address will be recalculated to show the differences. This saves you time in updating information in different parts of the worksheet. There is an order of operations that Excel will follow when calculating your formulas if you have one or more operations (multiplication, division, etc.). The following section explains this topic further.

Entering the Formula

1. Click inside the cell in which you would like the result of your formula to appear.
2. Start the formula by typing the equal sign =. You MUST start all formulas with an equal sign to let Excel know

that a formula is being entered. The formula will appear in the formula bar as it is being typed. In the following example, cells B4, B5, and B6 have been added together, and the total for the month of October is shown in cell B8. Notice that the formula appears in the formula bar.

3. Copying and pasting the formula from cell B8 can enter the totals for the months of November and December. Another method would be to place the cursor on the bottom right corner of cell B8 and drag it to cell D8. Excel will automatically calculate the formulas for the same range of cells based on the formula entered in cell B8 for the months of November and October. The results are shown in the example.

ADDITIONAL NOTE

The formulas you enter can have several operations, and Excel will perform the operations in the following order:

1. Operations inside parentheses
2. Calculation of exponents
3. Multiplication and division, from left to right
4. Addition and subtraction, from left to right.

Operator	What it does	Example
+	Addition	=B5+B6
−	Subtraction	=B5−B6
*	Multiplication	=B5*B6
/	Division	=B5/B6
^	Exponents	=B5^3

MICROSOFT POWERPOINT TIPS

CREATING MASTER SLIDES

A master slide is a special slide or page on which you define formatting for all slides or pages in your presentation. Each presentation has a master for each key component (slides, title slides, speaker's notes, and audience handouts). If you have pictures, text, or special formatting you want to appear on every slide, title slide, notes page, or audience handout, add it to the corresponding master.

Adding a Logo to the Master Slide

The following is an example of what can be done with the master slide. This will save you time if you want all the slides in your presentation to have a uniform look.

1. With your presentation open click on VIEW, then MASTER, and finally SLIDE MASTER.
2. The master slide will appear with different areas available for you to fill out. If you have a logo or picture that you would like to insert in each slide click on INSERT, then PICTURE and FROM FILE.

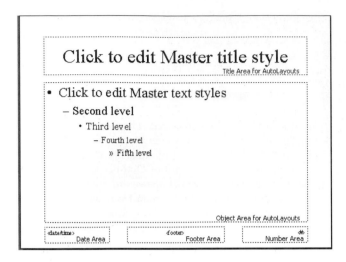

3. Locate the file that contains your picture and click on INSERT.

4. The picture will appear on your slide. Resize the picture and place it within the slide. Be aware that the picture will appear on each slide.

5. Once you have placed the picture in your master slide and are finished with any other modifications, click on VIEW and SLIDE to go back to your presentation.

Handout Master

If you plan to distribute handouts during your presentation, you can add information in the header and footer area. The date and other pertinent information can also be included.

1. With your presentation open click on VIEW, then MASTER, and finally HANDOUT MASTER.

2. The handout master slide will appear. The pop-up toolbar (shown on the right) will appear. Click on the type of handout format you will be using (two slides, three slides, six slides, outline).

3. Enter the appropriate information in the spaces provided.

4. Once you have completed your modifications and want to return to the presentation, click on VIEW, then SLIDE.

NOTE

All the slides in the presentation will have whatever modifications you made to the master slide. If you wish to change the master slide, you must go back into the master slide view and make the modifications there. You will not have access to them from slide view.

MICROSOFT ACCESS TIPS

QUERIES

Queries are rules and procedures you set that will search through data in tables and display the information you want in a format that you create. There are a number of different types of queries available and their uses vary. You may not use all of the queries and, depending on what you are trying to accomplish, one type of query may be more appropriate than others. This chapter will discuss the types of queries,

and in the following chapter a simple select query will be done.

SELECT QUERY

A select query is the most common type of query. It retrieves data from one or more tables and displays the results in a data sheet where you can update the records (with some restrictions). You can also use a select query to group records and calculate sums, counts, averages, and other types of totals.

PARAMETER QUERY

A parameter query displays its own dialog box prompting you for information, such as criteria for retrieving records or a value you want to insert in a field. You can design the query to prompt you for more than one piece of information; for example, you can design it to prompt you for two dates. Access can then retrieve all records that fall between those two dates.

Parameter queries are also handy when used as the basis for forms and reports. For example, you can create a monthly earnings report based on a parameter query. When you print the report, Access displays a dialog box asking for the month that you want the report to cover. You enter a month, and Access prints the appropriate report.

You can also create a custom form or dialog box that prompts for a query's parameters instead of using the parameter query's dialog box.

CROSSTAB QUERY

A crosstab query displays summarized values (sums, counts, and averages) from one field in a table and groups them by one set of facts listed down the left side of the data sheet and another set of facts listed across the top of the data sheet.

ACTION QUERIES

An action query makes changes to many records in just one operation. There are four types of action queries: delete, update, append, and make-table. The delete, update, and append query will be discussed. More information on queries can be found by asking the Office Assistant.

Delete query deletes a group of records from one or more tables. For example, you could use a delete query to remove products that are discontinued or for which there are no orders. With delete queries, you always delete entire records, not just selected fields within records.

Update query makes global changes to a group of records in one or more tables. For example, you can raise prices by 10 percent for all dairy products, or you can raise salaries by 5 percent for the people within a certain job category. With an update query, you can change data in existing tables.

Append query adds a group of records from one or more tables to the end of one or more tables. For example, suppose that you acquire some new customers and a database containing a table of information on those customers. To avoid typing all this information in, you'd like to append it to your Customers table. Append queries are also helpful for appending fields based on criteria. For example, you might want to append only the names and addresses of customers with outstanding orders.

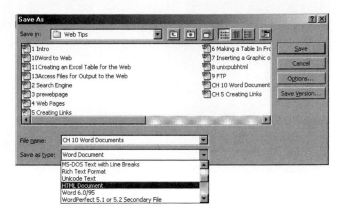

MICROSOFT FRONTPAGE TIPS

WORD97 DOCUMENTS ON YOUR WEB SITE

You may have a document that you wrote using Word97 that you wish to put on your web page. Word97 will convert your document to HTML format, but you may loose some formatting and graphics. Another option may be to have the document available for download for visitors to your web site. Either way, Word97 takes you step by step through the process.

Saving a Word97 Document as HTML
1. Open your Word document
2. Click on FILE from the menu bar and select SAVE AS. . . from the drop-down menu
3. The SAVE AS dialog box will appear. Type in the name of the FILE NAME field
4. Click on the down arrow from the SAVE AS TYPE field and scroll down till you see HTML document. Click on it.
5. Now click on SAVE.

Modifying the HTML Word97 Document
Once you have converted the document to HTML, you can use FrontPage Express or Word97 to modify it. You will notice that the document will not look the same way it did when it was in Word. HTML is different and not all formatting is brought over from Word. If you want to make any adjustments, open the document from the FrontPage Express program and make the necessary changes there.

1. From FrontPage Express, click on FILE from the top menu bar.
2. Select OPEN from the drop-down menu.
3. When the OPEN FILE dialog box appears, click on the BROWSE button and locate the Word document you saved.
4. Select the document and click on OPEN. The document will open in FrontPage and will be ready for you to make any changes.

CHAPTER 11

STRATEGIC ANALYSIS
TRAVEL RESERVATIONS INDUSTRY

Strategic Analysis

Information systems not only help cut costs; they can also be used to gain competitive advantage. An example of this is the ability to gain control over distribution channels using electronically linked suppliers and customers. The application of information systems can result in greater efficiencies, which can improve the quality of the product, expand the market, or differentiate the company from the competition. Michael Porter's five external forces model can help identify competitive advantages for the business. Strategies in research, engineering and design, lower manufacturing costs, improved logistics, and the identification of customer desires are also important. In service-oriented businesses, information flows can be refined through better decision tools for managers.

Pitfalls exist in the application of information systems to strategic purposes. Strategic information systems can be expensive, difficult to build, and easily imitated. Your strategic moves could change the industry itself. That change could negatively impact your organization. Government regulations, such as antitrust legislation, can also impact strategic initiatives.

Strategic Direction and Information Systems Using technology to execute strategies is an important part of defining and capitalizing on a company's competitive strength. The application of strategic systems requires a thorough understanding of the company, including its internal and external environment. It is important to note how interested parties react with the company. A common strategy is to improve communication with consumers and suppliers. The most difficult aspect is the decision to pursue ideas that will give the firm a competitive advantage, especially those with a reasonable cost.

Competitive Environment Today's increased media presence has enabled competition to increase dramatically. Large chains put pressures on small stores by negotiating lower prices from suppliers and offering a wider selection. International trends, such as cost cutting and decreasing trade barriers, are helping increase competition.

External Agents Entities such as suppliers, customers, rivals, potential rivals, substitute products, and the government are external agents that can be used to gain competitive advantages. Porter's five forces model portrays the relationship between a company and the external agents. Each of the external agents affects the company, yet is outside a company's control. Information systems can be used to improve ties to and information about each of these agents, improving the competitive position of the firm. For example, offering electronic payment options to customers can improve sales and customer satisfaction. Another example is the electronic integration of suppliers and business customers, making it easier to order, track shipments, and monitor quality. Rivals, potential rivals, and substitute products all present companies with competitive pressures that can be reduced by the intelligent use of technology. The United States government requires firms to file increasing numbers of financial reports electronically. This leads to the further standardization and competitiveness of the reporting process.

Competitive Advantage Competitive advantage can be gained by increasing the barriers to entry, increasing the costs or difficulties associated with switching to a competitor, lowering production costs, improving product differentiation, controlling distribution channels, and investing in innovation and quality control. Information systems can be used to take advantage of each of these techniques. For example, by propagating the installation of ATMs, banks have increased the barrier to entry into the banking industry. Another example is the use of computer systems to enable FedEx to track individual shipments, further differentiating its product.

Value Chain A value chain illustrates the essential operations of a business. The main operations of an organization and the processes that support the operations are listed to determine where value is added. Strategic benefits can be derived by studying a value chain and exploiting the portions of the chain that provide greater value to the company.

IT and Innovation One way to gain strategic advantage is to use IT to administer process innovation within an organization. One method to organize the search for processes that could be improved is to examine the basic processes of the firm, such as research (supported by information technology through analysis and modeling), engineering and design (CAD/CAM), manufacturing (mass customization), logistics and supply (forecasts), marketing (multimedia promotion), sales and order management (laptop computers for field sales reps), and service (phone support).

Pitfalls and Costs of Strategies Developing and implementing new strategies can be exciting and expensive. Customers may not support the new direction or procedures of a company. Competitors may be able to match an invention without investing in research and development. The industry may change and leave the new strategy useless. The government may decide that the strategy "restricts free trade" and therefore violates antitrust regulations. For example, the strategy of differentiation carries the risk of costing too much and competitors imitating it. Imitation from competitors is also a risk with the strategy of cost leadership. In another example, developing customer–supplier links could result in security threats.

In conclusion, computer systems can provide value beyond cost cutting; strategic gains are often temporary and can be surpassed or copied. The decision when to invest in new technology is critical.

Travel Reservations Industry

DESCRIPTION OF THE INDUSTRY

The travel and tourism industry is growing rapidly. This is due to social factors that have increased demands for travel and technological advances that make travel possible and less expensive. The swelling of the middle class in developing countries, years of prosperity in the United States, and lower prices have increased the demand for travel significantly.

While it is difficult to determine the economic impact of tourism, the World Travel and Tourism Council, an industry lobby group, placed total demand at $3.6 trillion in 1996. This is about 10 percent of the world's gross product. Important growth segments include package tours and cruises. Average tourist spending is expected to grow by 8 percent annually through 2005, according to *The Economist*. This has led groups such as the World Travel and Tourism Council and local and

Word	W.1	Formatting Your Document into Columns Additional Note	Only One Section of the Document How Will Text Appear in the Columns? Dividing the Columns with a Line
Excel	E.1	Copying Formulas: Relative References	Using Cell Addresses from Other Worksheets Getting Errors
PowerPoint	P.1	Inserting Graphs	Creating a Graph Inserting a Graph from Excel
Access	A.1	Creating a Query Modifying a Query	
Front Page	I.1	Converting Excel to HTML Format Note	Converting to HTML

national governments to spend money on improving infrastructures that will support tourism. Some countries, such as Canada, have responded by increasing their spending on tourism dramatically.

With this fast growth, the hotel business has matured. Hotels, once mostly independent businesses, are quickly joining chains. They are, in effect, being branded. Information technology, such as the Internet and electronic ticketing, is also altering tourism by changing the way tourism is being sold. Nothing has impacted the globalization of travel and tourism more than cheap airline tickets, however. Technology has made the biggest impact in this area.

Even with all these factors and trends, there are great risks. Hotels and airplanes are still large investments that can be expensive failures. Also, the tourism part of travel, as opposed to business travel, a small but very profitable segment of the travel and hospitality industry, is basically a luxury. This means that a recession, especially if it impacts a large geographic area such as the one experienced by Asia in 1998, can be devastating to the travel industry.

Surprisingly, the recession in the industrialized countries in the early 1990s slowed the growth of tourism, but did not stop it. Tourism is also sensitive to external shocks. The Caribbean islands can be a paradise one day. A hurricane can turn away tourists very quickly. Another example is the attacks suffered by European tourists in Miami in 1992. This kept Europeans from visiting South Florida for many years.

One way to combat external dangers and to address the issue of depleting or destroying natural attractions is to develop the tour environment from scratch. Theme parks are such places. These destinations are custom built to entertain and delight visitors. As technology advances and popular destinations become more crowded, these artificial worlds may increase their market share.

STOCK/INVESTMENT OUTLOOK

The outlook for companies in the travel and tourism industry is good. Companies positioned to take advantage of current trends in this industry will be star performers.

Airlines that are forming code-sharing alliances, which allow them to book travel on their partner's routes, seem to be the best long-term investment. Code-sharing allows airlines to cover more territories by banding together. Thus, American Airlines' impending partnership with British Airways and other airlines seems to bode well for them; just like United Airlines' partnership with a handful of international airlines seems like a good strategic direction.[1]

Mergers and acquisitions in the hotel industry occur frequently. Branding helps hotels smooth out demand. The recent increase in hotel mergers, especially internationally, where hotels are less likely to be part of a chain, is the result of hotel overbuilding during the 1980's and technological improvements that make economies of scale more significant.

Cruise ship companies are also good investments, in light of their increasing popularity. Carnival Cruise Lines and Royal Caribbean, the two largest cruise companies, are both expanding and building larger ships to accommodate and take advantage of this boom in cruising.

POTENTIAL/PROSPECTIVE FOR GROWTH

With the next few years projected to be positive for the travel and tourism industry, the potential for growth ranges from moderate to high, depending on the market segment. The growth in the cruise ship segment is good, assuming the cruise companies remain focused on why many people choose cruises: They are relatively inexpensive (usually everything except liquor and gambling is included) and they provide a relaxing atmosphere with entertainment. Cruise ship operations are more predictable than hotel operations, with generally high occupancy rates, a captive audience, and more predictable costs.[2]

The growth in the airline industry is projected to be moderate. While airline travel is expected to continue to increase, the market is saturated and mature in some areas, such as domestic travel within the United States. Newly formed alliances, deregulation abroad, and foreign governments freeing up their air space, mean changes, challenges, and opportunities. Those airlines forming alliances with international airlines are the ones with the most to gain. The American–British Airways alliance is an example. Business travelers provide additional incentives to airlines.[3]

Hotels are also expected to grow. Hotels not part of major chains will need to identify specific niches to do well in an era of branding, buyouts, mergers, and consolidation. There are many aspects an independent hotel or small hotel chain can offer to lure travelers, as long as they market this difference properly.

COMPETITIVE STRUCTURE

For many reasons, most of the tourism and travel industry used to be fragmented. The airline industry was fragmented due to government regulations, the difficulty of growing in a less advanced technological age, and less powerful planes. The hotel industry was fragmented due to difficulties operating geographically dispersed properties in an efficient and consistent manner. The cruise industry was first injured by the long-haul passenger jet, which all but replaced the cruises-to-Europe a few decades ago. Once shorter term and more

---

[1] Klein, Stephen, "Industry Surveys: Airlines," *Standard and Poor's*, May 14, 1998.

[2] Roberts, Mark, "Dream Factories: A Survey of Travel and Tourism," *The Economist*, suppl., January 10, 1998.
[3] Klein, Stephen, "Industry Surveys: Airlines," *Standard and Poor's*, May 14, 1998.

affordable cruises were offered to the Caribbean from South Florida, the industry revived.[4]

As the entire travel and tourism industry grows and matures, the competitive structure is moving toward an imperfect oligopoly. A few major players enjoy leadership in each segment of the travel and tourism industry. A large number of small players fight for the rest of the market. The major players offer competitive prices for their services, while the smaller players focus on particular niche markets. This process can be slower in segments where government intervention is a significant factor, such as international flights.

ROLE OF RESEARCH AND DEVELOPMENT

Research and development is an important component of this industry. R&D affects some segments more than others. Research and development has led to the realization by airlines that business travelers are less price sensitive than leisure travelers. Airlines have devised elaborate pricing strategies for available seats. R&D has led to technological advances like the jet airplane, hotel and airline reservation systems, jumbo cruise ships, and multiple kinds of rides in theme parks.

Airlines have used research to develop things such as frequent flyer programs to develop loyalty, "weekend getaway" fares to sell tickets on poorly sold routes, "Saturday night requirements" to differentiate passengers, and more fuel efficient and safer planes.

By branding themselves, hotels can give a customer a familiar setting and a perception of quality, no matter where the location. Even the same hotel chain might offer a range of hotels and brands. Each one is positioned to appeal to a specific type of traveler from the person looking only for the bare necessities who is very price sensitive to the "extended-stay" business traveler who may be on a multi-month assignment outside his or her home town. Another hotel innovation is the use of time shares, for vacation properties. This is slowly gaining acceptance.

TECHNOLOGICAL INVESTMENT AND ANALYSIS

Without technological advancement, the travel and tourism industry would still be mostly for the rich. The driving force behind industry growth has been the refinement of the jet airplane. Before the jet, most vacations were either close to home or required one of two things most people did not have or were not willing to part with: a lot of money or a lot of time. The jet airplane allowed prices to come down for flying, making far destinations more affordable for middle-class consumers. The newest revolution in technology with regards to tourism is the Internet.

Information technology is changing the way tourism is sold. Travel agents find cheap tickets and package

tours on their computer screens through one of the two major airline and tour reservation systems: SABRE or Galileo. SABRE has expanded beyond its core users of travel agents and has set up its own web site for retail customers: http://www.travelocity.com. Galileo, meanwhile, has taken a different approach, concentrating on serving its main group of users: the travel agents that book most travel. Using the Internet, customers can make their own searches and purchases directly through the computer, not only with Travelocity, but also with a myriad of online travel agents. Sophisticated computer reservation systems help hotels track their customers' spending and preferences over time, giving the company a better idea of the lifetime value of the customer to a particular hotel chain.[5]

The airlines use a yield management formula to differentiate ticket prices for the same flight, providing what they hope will be the greatest amount of revenue for each flight. Without computers, calculating this in an efficient manner on a nationwide level would be impossible.

Theme parks are another development that would be impossible without the application of technology. These wonderlands of artificial reality are developed solely for entertainment and leisure. Customers come back more than once because of new attractions. Technology is used to find more and different ways to entertain and delight crowds. Technological advancements provide an avenue to develop new sources for revenues and profits.

RECOMMENDATION FOR THE FUTURE

To remain competitive, companies in the travel and tourism industry must look at current trends while focusing on the future. When the industry was highly fragmented, it was more difficult for travelers to obtain complete information. This sheltered many businesses from competition. Those days are gone. Technology is now available to take advantage of location, services, convenience, and value. An unaffiliated business with no apparent advantage is best served by affiliating itself with a chain. For example, a nondescript hotel in North Miami Beach, in an area where hotel rooms are plentiful and many new ones are being built, will have difficulty thriving in the future. Even if the hotel doesn't become part of a chain, it must at least develop a web page, list itself in as many search engines and web directories as possible, and advertise in nontraditional, as well as traditional, channels where there is less competition.

INDUSTRY WEB SITE

Travel Reservations Industry
www.travel.yahoo.com/
www.ossn.com/
www.kenpubs.co.uk/watanetwork/
www.naita.com.au/

[4] Roberts, Mark, "Dream Factories: A Survey of Travel and Tourism," *The Economist*, suppl., January 10, 1998.

[5] Palmeri, Christopher, "This Might Not Fly," *Forbes*, April 20, 1998, p. 200.

Executive Summary

Case Name:	American Express
Case Industry:	Travel Industry
Major Technology Issue:	Developing smart card and internet travel service technologies and new products such as CustomExtras (a one-to-one marketing venture)
Major Financial Issue:	Increasing the acceptance of the American Express card and name worldwide
Major Strategic Issue:	Increasing the size of the travel agency with acquisitions; increasing global credit card business from $14 billion to $30 billion
Major Players/Leaders:	Harvey Golub, CEO; Kenneth Chenault, president of American Express
Main Web Page:	www.americanexpress.com
Case Conclusion/Recommendation:	Emphasis on growth in the corporate card market must be made. Greater cross-selling across Amex customer bases must be attempted.

CASE ANALYSIS

INTRODUCTORY STORY

American Express has long been the recognized leader in the worldwide travel and corporate financial services arena. Until 1992, American Express relied on its strong brand name to maintain its position in the industry. The reality was that the company had been losing market share in the credit card business to Visa and MasterCard over the past 10 years, and had over-expanded into corporate divisions that did not work well together.

With the appointment of Harvey Golub as CEO of American Express in 1992, a series of major restructuring projects began. The objectives were to strengthen the company's capital position and refocus toward its core businesses to improve efficiency and produce higher returns. Golub eliminated the brokerage, investment banking, and life insurance units and focused on the company's three principal operating divisions.

SHORT DESCRIPTION OF THE COMPANY

Travel Related Services (charge and credit cards, travelers' checks), American Express Financial Advisors (financial planning, insurance, and investment products), and American Express Bank (international banking) are the three main operating divisions of American Express.

The company operates the largest travel agency in the world with 1,700 Travel Services offices in over 130 countries. It is the largest global marketer in travelers' checks and the largest global issuer of corporate cards and of charge cards in terms of charge volume. Its strength in these markets well-positions American Express to reach its corporate goal to increase revenue from foreign operations from 30 to 50 percent of total revenue within a decade. Plans are to accomplish this through increased sales of its products and services.

Recently, the company has made significant strategic changes to increase its share of the United States card market. American Express now offers 35 different consumer and business cards, up from just 5 cards in 1987. It introduced more credit and charge card products from 1996–97 than it did in the 1980s. For the first time in its elitist history, the company has begun to share space on the face of its cards with cobranding partners, including banks outside the United States such as The National Westminster Bank in London and with corporations such as Hilton Hotels, Delta Air Lines, and United Airlines. Many of these arrangements offer discount and incentive programs to cardholders, such as the Membership Rewards program, which encourages increased card usage and promotes loyalty to the American Express brand. The results are more revenue for both American Express and the cobranding partner. The introduction of smart cards is the latest product line and is one that more fully utilizes technology.

American Express is also focused on improving merchant relationships and enlisting merchants in new industries such as supermarkets, telecommunications, and health care. Their goal in this segment is to capture a larger portion of card member spending on personal purchases. The company has lowered its discount rate slightly and offered marketing assistance to merchants. This has increased the number of participant merchants that accept its cards by 20 percent from 1992–1997. Much of this effort has centered on enabling merchants to access information from American Express's customer database for more effective marketing, and on extending other technological tools to merchants, such as a Windows-based software product designed to improve the way merchants do business with American Express. Web storefronts are also being developed to expedite electronic commerce with web merchants.

In achieving these results, one of the key elements of the restructuring has been to apply technology to improve customer service and efficiency. To support its global network of products and services, American Express realized it was critical to remain continually at the forefront of the financial services industry in terms of technology and innovation. To that end, American Express has teamed with Microsoft to develop an interactive system on the web for corporate use in booking travel arrangements and tracking business expenses.

The company maintains corporate service relationships with 70 percent of the Fortune 500 companies. American Express must continue to offer superior technological tools in their products and services to preserve its standing as an industry leader in both the corporate and overseas markets.

SHORT HISTORY OF THE COMPANY

In 1992, American Express reached a high mark in revenues of $27 billion on assets of $176 billion. Its net income was only $653 million. During the late 1980s and early 1990s, American Express increased revenue annually, along with increasing assets and long-term debt. Their net profit margin never exceeded 5 percent annually. Earnings per share were generally stagnant.

James Robinson III, the CEO at the time, had turned the company into an unwieldy financial jack-of-all-trades, extending it into periphery business units that did not complement one another. The acquisition and development of more businesses accounted for increased revenues; American Express was not actually growing; it was simply expanding. The company was not operating efficiently. Unknown to them, higher costs were negating any profits derived from the new assets.

While attention was diverted to new ventures, American Express was losing market share and revenue in its traditional charge card business. With the proliferation of free Visa and MasterCard bank cards in the market, more than 2 million American Express cardholders dropped their cards in the early 1990s. Despite this occurrence, American Express did not change its corporate and individual green charge cards. The board of directors and Robinson initially agreed on a separation in 1992 for his overexpansion of the company and for his failure to react to the changes in the industry.

Harvey Golub was appointed CEO in 1992 and immediately began restructuring the company; he initially slashed $2.3 billion out of a $13.4 billion cost structure; 12,000 jobs have been eliminated since 1991. Noncore businesses were eliminated. This reduced total assets but also eliminated the associated extra costs. Under Golub, the company stepped down from its pedestal as the imperial issuer of yesteryear and became more responsive to its market segments. American Express followed industry trends and cobranded its cards with other companies. It allowed foreign banks to issue American Express cards. The slogan "Membership Has Its Privileges" became "You Can Do More with American Express" as the company improved its product line by offering new credit card products designed to capture more personal spending beyond the standard business and travel and entertainment expenditures.[1]

FINANCIAL AND PORTFOLIO ANALYSIS

The latest step for American Express is the pursuit of revenue opportunities elsewhere in the financial services arena. The American Express Financial Advisors division sells mutual funds, certificates of deposit, insurance, and other services through almost 8,400 financial planners. Under Golub's direction, the Financial Advisors division has expanded its operation and is reporting increased revenues annually. This provides a third revenue stream beyond the card and travel operations. This revenue and earnings growth has benefited from the higher fee revenues due to yearly increases in managed assets, as indicated:

American Express Financial Advisors (assets owned or managed, in $billions)

1991	66
1992	83
1993	100
1994	106
1995	130
1996	149

(*Source*: American Express Annual Report 1997.)

[1] American Express Annual Report 1997.

The Financial Advisors and the card divisions operate independently: Financial Advisors has 2 million clients. American Express has 20.5 million United States cardholders. There are only 250,000 overlapping relationships. American Express is branching out to test whether a card and travel company can successfully sell other financial services to its customers. The Financial Direct division was launched in 1996 with the intention of providing many of the same general services offered by Financial Advisors to cardholders. American Express has an excellent cardholder database from which to extract high probability members as potential clients. This move by the company is a well-conceived effort to develop growth in other areas and meet consumer demand for a variety of financial products.

The financial data since 1992 illustrates that Golub's restructuring of the company into a competitive player in the financial services industry has been successful. Revenue has increased annually since the downsizing. Costs have been substantially reduced. Expenses are being kept in line with sales growth. Net income as a percentage of revenue is averaging 10 percent. Net income is actually higher now than when American Express held 25 percent more assets.

Since 1992, the company had five straight years of increasing revenues, net income, and earnings per share. The year 1997 produced American Express's third straight year of record profits, with net income of $1.99 billion (14 percent higher than 1996). After years of decline in the number of cards in the market, American Express finally showed an increase in its share of the $469 billion general-purpose card volume in the first half of 1997 from 18.3 to 18.9 percent. Industry leader Visa slipped slightly during the same period. This has translated into a steadily climbing stock price that reached a historical high of $91.50 late in 1997.[2]

The following financial details provide a closer analysis regarding this impressive turnaround and resulting growth.

Percent Net Income of Revenues Since Harvey Golub became CEO in 1992 and began restructuring American Express, the percent of net income to revenue has increased threefold, from 3 to over 10 percent annually. Much of this is attributable to the $2.3 billion in cost savings that occurred in 1992. The fact that the company has not yet reached its revenue target indicates that there is potential for both revenue and net income to continue increasing at the current rates.

Current Ratio A ratio of 2.0 or higher is desirable. In the case of American Express, the current ratio has declined steadily from 2.26 in 1993 to 1.74 in 1996 and 1.50 in 1998. Both assets and liabilities have declined during that period; assets have declined at a faster rate.

Percent Return on Assets American Express has improved its return on assets threefold in the past four years, from an average return of 0.55 to an average return of 1.6. This indicates that the company is making more efficient use of its assets. This higher return was also achieved by the company selling less profitable divisions during its restructuring.

Percent LT Debt to Capital Generally, the greater the proportion of debt to equity, the greater the risk to the stockholder. With American Express averaging around 50 percent of their capital structure as debt, it would appear to fall into the category of greater risk. However, if the company is in a finance-oriented business, as American Express is, the higher debt-to-equity ratio is less significant. In addition, it is a positive sign that American Express has been steadily reducing its percentage of long-term debt from 68.4 to 43.4 percent during its turnaround in the 1990s. This would support the proposition that the company is not using new debt to support capital growth.

Percent Return on Equity Return on equity averaged 20 percent from 1993–97. This is attractive to investors, illustrating the success of American Express in cutting costs and increasing revenue since 1992.

SPS Sales per share showed positive growth from 1994–97. This occurred after a significant drop from 1992 to 1993 as the result of the reduction in total assets leading to reduced total revenue.

EPS EPS provided steady annual growth averaging 16 percent from 1993–97. This is a significant improvement over the inconsistent (and lower) EPS that existed prior to 1994.

Stock Price American Express has been a very strong growth stock since 1994, with its price more than tripling in that time. The growth ratio has substantially exceeded that of the overall market. Significantly, American Express's high stock price of $91.50 in 1997 was more than double its average high stock price from 1987–97.

P/E Ratio American Express is averaging a high P/E ratio of 15.92 and a low P/E ratio of 10.35. The 1997 average P/E ratio of 17.44 was roughly one-third higher than the median P/E of 12.0 for the company. A current P/E that is greater than the median P/E could mean that the stock is overvalued; in this case, the company's strong fundamentals prove otherwise.

Relative P/E Ratio American Express's average relative P/E ratio of 0.75 is below 1.00, meaning that the stock sold at a discount of around 25 percent to the market his-

---

[2] Ibid.

torically. For 1997, however, American Express's relative P/E ratio was almost equivalent to the S&P 500 P/E ratio. This indicates that the market began to realize during 1997 that the stock rated a strong buy. It began bidding the price up. Given the strong growth from 1993–97, many feel the P/E ratio for the stock should be higher. This indicates that the market's expectations for the stock are not as high as anticipated, given the strong growth rate for American Express.

The restructuring since 1992 has positioned American Express to reap the benefits of increased revenues and EPS. The company has seen increases in revenue through its new products and services. American Express has set long-term targets of 12 to 15 percent annual growth in EPS, a minimum of 8 percent annual revenue growth, and a continued return on equity of 18 to 20 percent.

As stated in their 1996 annual report, American Express wants to be known as a growth company, with the objective that at least two-thirds of their earnings improvement comes from higher revenues and the remaining third from lowered costs. In 1996, increased revenues accounted for less than half of the earnings growth. American Express has benefited from efforts to lower costs at the beginning of the recent growth period. They are under pressure from Wall Street to raise revenues, which have failed to increase in proportion to the economy after American Express initiated its cost-cutting measures.

STOCK/INVESTMENT OUTLOOK

The projected earnings and relative P/E ratio indicated that an estimated value for American Express stood ranging from a high of $72.51 to a low of $57.66. With American Express averaging annual EPS growth of 16 percent and ROE growth of 20 percent from 1993 through 1997, it seems unlikely that any significant drop in the price would make the stock a better value. Future earnings are forecast to exceed current growth rates, again supporting to the proposition that the stock is undervalued relative to the market.

RISK ANALYSIS

The company's position is that it has just begun its renaissance and will continue to grow. "We are by no means uncorking the champagne bottle," says Kenneth Chenault, president of American Express and Golub's heir apparent, "but we are very much in the game, which is a very different situation from 1992."[3]

With losses slowed in the credit card market, the company has restated its goal of increasing its global credit

card business from $14 to $30 billion through the year 2000. American Express will concentrate its proprietary businesses in 20 to 25 key markets, withdrawing from issuing cards directly to clients in the remainder of the 52 countries where it operates. The company is essentially moving away from its "lone ranger" policy of offering all services directly without using any intermediaries. This policy has been difficult to implement because it requires an extensive infrastructure.

American Express has enlisted banks in 19 countries, allowing them to issue an American Express card or their own proprietary card on the American Express global network. These arrangements enable the company to rapidly expand its card business into areas where setting up a proprietary operation would be difficult and expensive.

To combat competition for the larger, and more profitable, business travel operations, American Express has acquired the largest travel agencies in England and Brazil. It has a joint venture with France's largest travel agency and a cooperative agreement with a Chinese travel service. The company has made a heavy technology investment in its European corporate card business to enable it to offer expense management systems and record keeping for travel and entertainment budgets.

The success of these efforts remains to be seen. The overseas revenue goals are optimistic projections. Significantly increasingly merchant coverage overseas will be required. If overseas revenue fails to meet expectations, the stock price could suffer.

INDUSTRY AND MARKET ANALYSIS

In an increasingly sophisticated and concentrated marketplace, only four card issuers account for two-thirds of the industry's growth. With net charge-offs reaching historic levels due to an all-time high in personal bankruptcies, smaller companies cannot hold enough capital to absorb these losses.

To succeed in the financial services industry today, companies must bring innovative products and services to the market quickly. They must provide increasingly higher levels of quality and service to the customer. Corporate customers in particular are demanding more detailed transaction information on commercial card purchases and new products customized to meet their needs. The use of technology in business development to compete in this environment has become an even greater necessity. Investment in technology is projected to increase from $11.5 billion in 1996 to $14 billion in 2000.

ROLE OF RESEARCH AND DEVELOPMENT

While the company does much development in house, American Express makes it a point to pursue the best option for new systems development. According to Andrew

---

[3] Greenwald, John, "CHARGE!," *Time*, January 12, 1998, Business, p. 60(3).

Bartels, vice president of encrypted payments, "We rely on the vendor community for some emerging technologies, but not in a passive fashion."[4] American Express has recently formed partnerships with Microsoft, electronic-commerce vendor Mercantec, and Hewlett-Packard to develop software packages and web-based systems. The company does some "pure" outsourcing or purchasing of packaged software. Even when utilizing outside technology, American Express prefers to play an active role in its development through an alliance or partnership arrangement.

INTERNAL DEVELOPMENT

American Express developed a merchant workstation. This Windows-based software product provides merchants with access to electronic financial reporting and the processing of card member inquiries. It offers the ability to display data in graphic format so that merchants can analyze and compare business results in different ways.

OUTSOURCING

American Express discontinued development of its own internally developed expense reporter in January 1998 and contracted to market Portable's Xpense Management Solution (XMS) enterprise software instead. XMS will become a component of American Express's AXI system.

American Express has taken a leadership role in the industry with regard to technology. The results of a 1997 *InformationWeek* 500 survey of the top-ranking users of information technology reveal that American Express is second only to IBM in terms of having the largest information technology shop. The company makes a concerted effort to stay on the cutting edge of technological advances.

Part of the company's leadership is demonstrated in its ability to set a path for others to follow. American Express has been active in the initial establishment of industry standards for many of the new technologies impacting credit card services. A company-sponsored initiative in 1997 set technology and business practice standards for companies to buy goods and supplies over the Internet. This effort, through the Internet Purchasing Roundtable, announced OBI-1, the Open Buying on the Internet standard. This is a nonproprietary, vendor- and platform-neutral architecture for Internet purchasing.[5] The standard is aimed at streamlining business processes, reducing costs, and improving service levels. It represents the first serious attempt to develop an industry standard for online corporate procurement.

American Express is taking the lead in smart card technology. It was the first financial services company to join the Global Chipcard Alliance. Of even more significance was its announcement that it will license its smart card multiple function file structure to other companies. By being a leader in smart card technology, the company has placed itself in a position where it can encourage adoption of its file structure to achieve worldwide interoperability among smart cards. American Express plans to cooperatively adapt the file structure for various smart card platforms and to enhance and upgrade it on an ongoing basis.

TECHNOLOGICAL STORY

American Express is a relative newcomer to embracing technology as a means for achieving corporate goals. The company once prided itself on a decidedly non-technological service: the ability to return physical charge card receipts to its customers with their monthly billing statements. After recognizing the costs and slow processing time involved in performing this service, American Express utilized technology to expedite the billing process. It still provides cardholders with the technological equivalent of a physical receipt.

With this change in philosophy, and to support its global network, American Express realized the necessity to position itself at the industry forefront in terms of technology and innovation. In 1993, the company implemented a long-term technological upgrade in which seven different accounting systems were consolidated into one highly flexible system. This system provides front-end customer service and optimizes cross-selling opportunities while decreasing costs. American Express was able to leverage the benefits of this system to provide a better and higher level of service to its customers and merchants.

TECHNOLOGICAL INVESTMENT AND ANALYSIS

The primary goal for American Express is to build long-term relationships with its customers through products and services that offer superior service and value. This enhances the value of the American Express brand name. The company has been successful on several fronts in the development of new and innovative technologies that can be translated into legitimate products and services to upgrade the support and benefits given to customers. To a great extent, American Express has transcended beyond using technology to improve its operations and services to the point where technology itself has become a product for American Express to develop and market.

---

[4] Foley, John, "The Future Is Now—Leading-Edge IT Managers Tap into Vendor R&D Efforts," *Information Week*, August 25, 1997, p. 42.

[5] Chronister, Kristian, "Net-Based Buying Model Debuts," *Electronic Buyers' News*, June 16, 1997.

One driver for the company is to find ways to strengthen its relationships with merchants and to increase the number of merchants that accept its card. Technology furnishes American Express with a way to provide more assistance to merchants. This includes a low-cost way to set up web storefronts for merchants, enabling them to access card member spending information, and provide real-time authorization for American Express card purchases. Through these tools, American Express can offer a higher level of service to their merchants than they might receive from other vendors. It also justifies the company's discount rate, which is higher than the industry average.

The common theme is to leverage technology to establish a permanent link between the customer and American Express. Uniting customers with American Express systems and products prevents customers from developing their own systems or using those of a competitor.

American Express is funding its technology expenditures through a combination of new business development and improved margins through improved processes. The company has reduced costs and eliminated less profitable noncore divisions. Revenue has increased consistently over the past few years as a result of these and other efforts. The company is strongly capitalized and has the resources necessary to support technology spending. According to their annual report, American Express is committed to the goal of having a cost structure that allows freedom for company investment programs, product design, and pricing.

With the primary objective of increasing customer card business with the company, American Express measures its success based on levels of consumer spending using its card products. It can also measure the success of its one-to-one marketing strategy based on card member response rates to solicitations sent by the company.

The tremendous amount of data from the high-profile client base held by American Express gives the company the ability to develop more effective marketing strategies. This information is used both to market its own products and services and to increase card member spending. By utilizing their database and a closed-loop network, American Express is able to store and use this information to identify customer spending patterns, assist in budget planning, and increase efficiency. One primary use of the data is for target marketing, in which specific merchant offers are targeted to those customers most likely to take advantage of them, based on their previous spending behavior. American Express also makes customer purchase data available to merchants through a Windows-based software product designed by the company.

One of American Express's strategies has been to improve the technological support for its Financial Advisors division. The goal is to increase both productivity and the level of customer service. American Express provides advisors with laptops for remote access to client and product data. It previously took from 50 to 60 days for a financial plan to be delivered to a prospective client; better technological support has reduced that turnaround time to 24 hours. Prior to these improvements, 15 to 20 percent of customers did not act on the plan or take the plan's recommendations to other product providers. Once the technological improvements are completed, American Express can measure the number of customers accepting financial plans in the future to determine improvement in acceptance rates.

American Express, with Microsoft, has launched an online travel reservation system designed for corporate customers. Called American Express Interactive (AXI), the system is based primarily on Microsoft software, including the Internet Information Server, SQL Server, and Windows NT. The AXI software is aimed at companies that use American Express as their business travel agency. The software can be integrated with American Express's proprietary travel management software, which includes a low-fare search tool and an automated expense reporting system.

AXI enables corporate employees to negotiate and book air fares, car rental rates, and hotel rates from their desktops. It is designed to load data from computerized reservation systems through the Internet or corporate intranets. The system can be customized for each company to reflect its individual travel policies and procedures. With travel generally being the third-highest controllable expense for a firm, the ability to control costs and enforce compliance with corporate travel policy provides a significant benefit to customers. Chrysler is one of a half-dozen companies using AXI; they project a 50 percent savings in processing fees.

American Express is implementing an innovative marketing program called CustomExtras. This program is designed to treat each card member as a "market of one," in which personalized offers are made to selected customers. One-to-one marketing utilizes three technologies: customer databases, interactive media, and systems that support mass customization. Through the use of these technologies, American Express can learn specific details on customer spending patterns, form a closer relationship with those customers, and provide more customized products and services. Companies spend a great deal of time and money to acquire customers; one-to-one marketing protects that investment and more fully develops the amount of business that can be conducted with those customers.

A key use of data involves the American Express CustomExtras one-to-one marketing program. This program begins with the company's collection of all card member purchase records and other information, which is stored in a marketing database. Proprietary software selects merchant offerings and other American Express promotions that fit a customer's profile. Those offerings and promotions are then printed on the monthly bill. Through the use and evaluation of these stored data, American Express can tailor its marketing to the individual customer.

For the CustomExtras program, the company has deployed a second database, running on a mainframe with relational database software. This database draws data from the first database and uses it to track purchases, rewards, and promotions. It manages the printing of billing statements with customized offers and messages. As a follow-up, the American Express marketing database tracks customers activities regarding offers and promotions. Whenever a customer acts on an offer, American Express shares the results with the merchant.

American Express has an enhanced application for its corporate purchasing service. This enables customer purchasing data to be fed directly into their back-end SAP systems. The interface to American Express's AccountingLink application eliminates manual intervention. This is particularly important since large clients process more than 1 million purchasing documents a year.

The goal is to enable customers of American Express's purchasing service to outsource their accounts payable and purchasing operations. This business handled $4 billion in invoices and 15 million transactions in 1998 alone.

With the increasing recognition that mass marketing is an inefficient approach (a 3 percent response rate is considered good in the industry) the goal of one-to-one marketing is to make more selective, cost-efficient solicitations that generate a much higher response rate. Within the industry, the market for products and services that support one-to-one marketing is forecast to be one of the largest growth areas for technology in business.

The overall strategy for American Express through these initiatives is to maintain ideal customer relationships. "All this enables us to follow our customers as they move from phone or paper-based customer support or transactions to the use of the Internet to handle their travel activities to the use of smart cards,"[6] according to Andrew Bartels, vice president of encrypted payments at American Express.

At American Express's Smart Card Center of Excellence, the company is leveraging its technology and customer databases to develop stored value cards. The Company is forging alliances and partnerships with other companies to market the cards. Unlike other debit cards, the transactions on American Express

smart cards go through the company's central processing centers. This enables the company to collect its discount rate in exchange for transferring the credit risk from the merchant to American Express.

The Company has joined with American Express, Hilton Hotels, and IBM to test the use of smart card technology to support ticketless travel. Customer information, as well as hotel and travel preferences and loyalty programs, resides on a microchip. The chip enables the cardholder to use a machine at the airport to immediately register for a flight. Information contained in the card verifies the electronic reservation and confirms traveler identification. This eliminates the need for a boarding pass. The card can also be used to register for a hotel room by computer. Eventually, it will serve as the room key. It will be capable of carrying stored value in multiple currencies and has the potential to be coded with the user's fingerprints and even be used as a passport.[7]

By taking an early role in the development of smart cards, American Express has positioned itself to reap the revenue rewards once the smart card market becomes viable. According to David Boyles of American Express, "Our goal is to give value and convenience through globally operable, multifunctioning cards."[8]

American Express and Visa International have formed a joint venture to focus on developing applications for smart cards to encourage use of the technology in the United States. The companies hope that their smart card applications will become the standards for the electronic commerce industry, though their goal is to design open interfaces to support competitors' systems.

Banksys SA in Belgium and ERG Ltd. in Australia are also partners in the venture, called Proton World International. The company will continue to develop and license smart card applications that were originally developed by Banksys. This includes the Proton electronic purse application used by 30 million people worldwide.

Credit card companies have been reluctant to push multifunction smart cards because they were afraid that they would cannibalize the credit card company's brand by replacing traditional credit cards. American Express and Visa's commitment to this technology indicates that these firms believe they have more to gain than to lose with smart cards. "If you have a multifunction smart card, you can use it to gain entry to your office, take money out of the bank and ride mass transit,"

[6] Girishankar, Saroja, "American Express Online Travel Service Flies High," *Internet Week*, December 1, 1997, p. 15(1).

[7] "Internet–American Express Offers an Internet-Based Business Travel Planning Service," Communications News, 1998, v. 35, n. 11, p.82.
[8] Block, Valerie, "Amex to Test Smart Cards with Hilton and IBM," *American Banker*, May 29, 1997, p. 1.

according to Jim Balderston, an analyst at Zona Research, Inc., in Redwood City, California.[9]

In contrast, MasterCard International, Inc., supports the Mondex electronic purse system, which follows a different verification structure.

Rather than simply relying on its own proprietary distribution systems, American Express utilizes many other types of distribution networks, including brokerage, direct marketing, and online systems to attract and service its customers. American Express utilizes a worldwide electronic network. This enables the company to increase charge volume, reduce fraud, and minimize bad debt. This network provides the infrastructure to access a multitude of markets, many of which provide opportunities for expansion.

American Express has two goals for its information technology: Reengineer the company and develop new products. According to American Express CIO Allan Loren, "We're changing distribution channels." The Internet helps to distribute new products and expand the transactional capabilities of the company.[10] The overall intent for technology is to better service the customer and maintain a solid position in a highly competitive business environment.

The most recent data for American Express identifies its allocation of IT expenditures as follows:

- Reengineering and new product development (50 percent)
- Maintenance of existing technology (40 percent)
- Determining new directions for the company (10 percent)

American Express uses a closed-loop network to collect and use customer information for target marketing. Point-of-sale transactions feed a massive parallel database for use across the organization.

Teamed with Hewlett-Packard, American Express has introduced a new electronic commerce program (ExpressVault) designed to enable merchants to conduct business over the Internet quickly and securely. It combines HP's computing and security technologies with American Express's payment processing system. ExpressVault enables merchants to add online commerce features to web sites, protects transaction, database, and web site information against unauthorized access, and provides real-time processing for American Express card transactions.

At the core of the American Express Company financial services business, the IDS division employs 8,500 "advisors" who sell a broad range of financial products and services. They work out of remote field and home offices to service clients throughout North America. Financial planning is an increasingly lucrative business for American Express. Its advisors work with individuals and families to develop long-range financial goals for retirement, education, illness, disability, and estate planning.

Financial planning has historically been a paper-intensive business. Advisors met with prospective clients, typically at the client's home or business location. They gathered relevant data on client assets, liabilities, and goals, and then reported back to the local regional office. At the regional office a clerk entered information and uploaded it to the legacy mainframe-based application in Minneapolis. Weeks later, a rudimentary financial plan would be mailed to the advisor, who would make an appointment with the client, go back to deliver the plan and meet with him/her to tailor the plan to their precise needs. Depending on the client, this could go on for three or four iterations.

AdvisorLink[11] has changed all of this. This remote application encompasses a wide range of applications specifically designed for field advisors. New functionality is added through in-house development projects or software purchased from third parties. AdvisorLink brings together internal "best practice" processes and technology that American Express believes will provide its advisors with a significant competitive edge over other financial services firms.

The AdvisorLink software is written in Smalltalk, an IBM proprietary language. It resides on advisors' laptops and processes client plans locally. Although client data are still uploaded to legacy systems, the turn-around time for completing sophisticated financial plans has been cut from weeks to hours.

The advisor directs the initial data gathering of goals, income, assets, and debt from the client. The client then uses the new software to develop customized plans that specifically tie the client's long- and short-term goals to existing and future assets. Rather than rely on the boiler-plate results that came from the previous legacy application, the new software gives the advisor the opportunity to tailor a plan more precisely. When the plan is complete, the advisor meets with the client, validates the results, and conducts "what if" scenarios to ensure that the client is satisfied with the results. At any time, the client can request adjustments and the advisor can make them on the spot. This has shortened dramatically the processing time for sophisticated financial plans.[12]

[9] Cole-Gomolski, Barb, "Amex-Visa Deal tp Push Smart-Card Technology," *Computerworld*, August 3, 1998, v. 32, n. 31, p. 6(1).
[10] Gupta, Udayan, "Sharing Data to Get an Edge," *Information Week 500*, September 9, 1996, p. 132(3).

[11] LaPlante, Alice, "Commanding a Mobile Army," *Computerworld*, July 20, 1998, v. 32, n. 29, p. 55(1).
[12] Ibid.

INTERNET

On the consumer side, American Express promotes travel, dining, and entertainment. To do so, it has entered an investment and joint marketing agreement with CitySearch Inc., the developer of online city guides. CitySearch supplies maps and information for 16 cities including New York, Portland, Oregon, San Francisco, Washington, D.C., Chicago, Sydney, and Toronto. In doing so, it covers news about sports, the arts, entertainment, community activities, shopping, recreation and weather. CitySearch also helps small and medium-sized businesses develop web sites. It then hosts these sites. It gathers this information from its newspaper partners in each city.

Security

On May 31, 1997, Visa International, MasterCard, American Express, and most of the major players in electronic commerce and internetworking, unveiled the Secure Electronic Transactions (SET) standard. SET was established to standardize online transactions and make the Internet safe for electronic commerce. Unfortunately, the implementation of this technology has moved more slowly than expected. The difficulties have included both business and technical reasons.

The goal of SET is to increase consumer confidence in the security of online transactions. Both credit card holders and merchants are issued digital certificates, which are verified by a certificate authority to make a transaction. Neither the merchant nor the consumer can be anyone else other than they purport to be. This reduces the threat of impersonation fraud.

The difficulty comes in the requirement that merchants using SET install expensive new software and build their businesses around a complex transaction infrastructure. Current online merchants have hesitated to join the SET standard. Its largest shortcoming is the client channel. Vendors like VeriFone and IBM have developed SET plug-ins for the popular web browsers. Yet, Internet users do not favor external plug-ins.

In the meantime, electronic commerce continues to grow on the Internet, protected by Secure Sockets Layer encryption. While not as secure as SET, it provides enough security to satisfy many consumers.

Free Internet E-Mail

American Express introduced a free Internet e-mail service, AmExMail, in April 1998. The service, available only to American Express customers, was developed with the help of the Colorado Springs, Colorado-based electronic messaging firm, USA.Net. The new e-mail system uses USA.Net's e-mail engine architecture. This purchase makes American Express the first major business outside the Internet industry to offer free e-mail. Services such as AmExMail have become more common among companies seeking to build close ties to their customers. This is an important way for a credit card company, such as American Express, to keep its customers active and in the information flow. In April 1997, American Express announced the purchase of a minority interest in USA.net, which is privately held.

Other free e-mail services such as Four11, Hotmail, and WhoWhere have been partnering with or purchased by larger companies, including Yahoo, Microsoft, and Qualcomm, respectively. These partnerships have linked free e-mail to already existing Internet products or services.

American Express Interactive

American Express Interactive is a web-based travel solution that integrates a company's travel policies and directives with the reservations system. Reservations that do not comply with policy directives are marked. "Preferred supplier" services are emphasized. AXI's linkage to Microsoft's Expedia software means users can take advantage of added features such as airline seat maps for seat selection and access to international destination information. The travel system can operate in multiple environments, with multiple computer reservations systems and an Internet, intranet, or extranet connection.

American Express Travel Online provides an easy-to-use reservation system, access to vacation and last-minute travel specials, and excellent customer service. As such, the service is good for travelers without special needs. It does not offer the more specialized ability to book flights using frequent-flier miles or to book more than five legs of a business trip.

The American Express reservations system is driven by Internet Travel Network (ITN). All reservations are sent to American Express Travel Related Services. This provides several advantages, including options to purchase tickets. American Express provides the ability to change an itinerary worldwide through its offices or its toll-free number. Ticketing is available 24 hours a day; customer service is available on a more limited basis.

To use the system, each user must register and establish a profile identical to the ITN profile which is stored in the system. For security reasons, the credit card number cannot be stored from one session to another.

The site's vacation packages, including those from certified suppliers and vendors are guaranteed to be at the lowest prices available. The drawback of the vacation packages is that the prices quoted are for fixed tours; fares increase drastically if changes are made.

American Express Retirement Services

American Express Retirement Services has instituted natural language query software on its ExpressLink extranet to eliminate the requirement that retirement planners and benefits administrators learn basic query software. The query tool, which required users to download some data to a desktop and to point and click on the desired data elements, frightened some users away. In its place, the natural language software returns an answer for queries typed in plain English or suggests alternatives that can help users find what they need. Some users accustomed to the older querying tools found the new option slow and awkward. However, they felt it would be most beneficial to those users who had never previously used any query tools. The ExpressLink service costs $2,500 plus a $1,500 annual support fee.

American Express used English Wizard, a natural language tool from Linguistic Technology Corporation in Littleton, Massachusetts, to develop the ExpressLink extranet. The extranet went live in spring of 1999 and is used by approximately 60 external users. Many individuals use ExpressLink to work on their 401(k) plans. In addition to the query tool, ExpressLink provides users with monthly reports, the ability to check call center statistics, and access to send electronic mail to their account managers.

SoftCart

American Express is working with Mercantec, an electronic commerce vendor, to offer companies economical web-based storefronts. The companies use Mercantec's SoftCart payment and virtual shopping software. American Express handles the back-end processing and offers financial and marketing expertise. SoftCart provides companies with a way to explore a web store without making a major financial commitment. The partnership with Mercantec offers American Express a good entry point to offer web services. American Express uses SoftCart and a network of payment gateways to provide web merchants with authorization for American Express and bank card purchases.

Unlike many companies that act as web commerce enablers, American Express already has strong relationships with both merchants and consumers. In comparison, Visa and MasterCard work through affiliate banks. Many of these have faltered in the area of electronic commerce.

SoftCart features a relatively low-cost entry point for web merchants, with a one-time licensing fee of $1,800. Monthly licensing is also available. Merchants can purchase a solution directly from American Express, or work with integration partners, including ISPs, that will implement the software on their networks.

RECOMMENDATION FOR THE FUTURE

It is critical for American Express to meet the demands of their corporate customers if they are to continue to grow in this lucrative market. Industry observers expect the number of commercial cards and charge volume to grow as much as 50 percent through 2005. Some of that growth is anticipated to result from small businesses, which have limited technology to monitor and control expenses in house. The ability of American Express to develop an Internet system to purchase cards ahead of its competition is essential to capturing a large share of the small business market.

As commercial card products become more sophisticated, corporations see more cost savings. The more money corporations can save through the use of these products, the more they will be used. This translates into increased transactions and more revenue for the card issuers.

American Express has a premier client base of customers who average twice the amount of annual card expenditures as Visa. Yet, American Express does not receive as high a percentage of their customer's spending for personal purchases. While the company has been working to remedy this through increased advertising, the fact remains that 5 million merchants worldwide accept American Express versus 14 million merchants that accept Visa. To increase the number of merchants that accept the American Express card, the company must successfully leverage technology to better serve its retail partners.

Technology is enabling American Express to sell additional financial services to its card members. Of American Express's 20.5 million customers, only 250,000 have accounts with American Express Financial Advisors. The company should continue to develop its customer database to evaluate marketing strategies to enlist additional cardholders for other financial services offered by American Express.

Given the intense competition in the industry, American Express must continue to implement technology to remain at the forefront of meeting customer needs. In recognition of this fact, management must continue to leverage technology to improve customer service and efficiency.

CASE QUESTIONS

Strategic Questions

1. What is the strategic direction of the corporation/organization?

2. Who or what forces are driving this direction?

3. What has been the catalyst for change?

4. What are the critical success factors for this corporation/organization?

5. What are the core competencies for this corporation/organization?

Technological Questions

6. What technologies does the corporation rely on?

7. What has caused a change in the use of technology in the corporation/organization?

8. How successful has the technological change been?

Quantitative Questions

9. What does the corporation say about its financial ability to embark on a major technological program of advancement?

10. What conclusions can be reached from an analysis of the financial information to support or contradict this financial ability?

11. What analysis can be made by examining the following ratio groups?

    Current
    Debt
    % Return on equity

12. What conclusions can be reached by analyzing the financial trends? Are there long-term trends that seem to be problematic? Are there replacement products?

Internet Questions

13. What does the corporation's web page present about their business directives?

14. Is the web site designed adequately?

Industry Questions

15. What challenges and opportunities is the industry facing?

16. Is the industry oligopolistic or competitive?

17. Does the industry face a change in government regulation?

18. How will technology impact the industry?

Data Questions

19. What role do data play in the future of the corporation?

20. How important are data to the corporation's continued success?

Executive Summary

Case Name:	The SABRE Group
Case Industry:	Service industry
Major Technology Issue:	SABRE has to continuously invest in their technology in order to keep it at a level above the competition and prepare itself for the international arena that it will soon be trying to service in full.
Major Financial Issue:	There are no major financial issues facing SABRE. They have a healthy source of revenue that has continued to grow through the years.
Major Strategic Issue:	Keeping its competitive advantage by staying ahead of the competition through superior products and services
Major Players/Leaders:	Max Hopper, former CIO; Terrell B. Jones, current CIO
Main Web Page:	http://www.sabre.com/
Case Conclusion/Recommendation:	SABRE should continue to improve its system while building relationships with key players within the hotel/motel industry and the auto rental industry in order to expand its services to its customers.

CASE ANALYSIS

INTRODUCTORY STORY

The headquarters for the SABRE Secure Computer Center is an underground complex in Tulsa, Oklahoma. Constructed of reinforced concrete surrounded by cement walls four feet thick, it is fireproof, earthquake-proof, flood-proof, and blackout-proof. The roof is composed of three and a half feet of reinforced concrete covered by five feet of hard packed dirt. The facility can operate for up to three days without outside electricity or water.[1] SABRE is one of the largest real-time computer systems in the world. Its importance in the airline industry warrants this level of secured facility.

SHORT DESCRIPTION OF THE COMPANY

SABRE is a reservation system that averages more than 150 million transactions a day. It handles about one-quarter of the world's airline reservations, one-fifth of the world's hotel bookings, and four-fifths of U.S. automobile rental bookings. Travel agents are able to access 50 million different available airfares through SABRE.

Beside reservation services, SABRE tracks 80 million passengers, 4,400 flights, and 200,000 meals every day. It inventories 28,000 parts on more than 600 different aircraft. In doing so, it serves approximately 28,000 travel agencies across the world.[2] SABRE's market share is represented by the number 2 in Figure 11.1.

SHORT HISTORY OF THE COMPANY

SABRE's data processing services and transaction processing depend upon the central computer operations and information processing facility located in the Data Center. The Data Center contains over 120,000 square feet of space. It is home to 15 mainframes with 12,639 gigabytes of storage and 3,371 MIPS of processing power.[3]

The SABRE system is connected to over 120,000 computer access terminals and operates continuously throughout the year. It maintains over 50 million air fares, which are updated several times each business day. SABRE receives an average of 93 million requests for information per day. In July, 1996, it processed a record 4,969 requests for information per second.[4]

---

[1] "Let's See the Numbers," http://www.travelocity.com/si/numbers.html.

[2] "What Is SABRE Computer Services," http://www.amr-corp.com/sabr_grp/scs/scs.htm.

[3] Form 424B1 Report, http://www/sec/gov/Archives/ edgar/data/1020265/0000950134-96-005342.txt.

[4] Ibid.

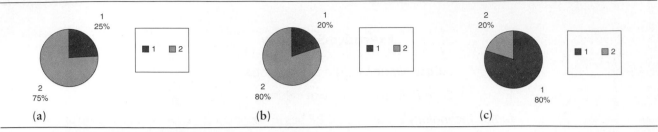

Figure 11.1 The SABRE System: light gray is the percentage of (a) Airline reservations worldwide. (b) Hotel bookings worldwide. (c) Car reservations nationwide.

In addition to the main Data Center, the company maintains a computer center in one of its office buildings in Fort Worth, Texas. At the Fort Worth Center, the company operates processors and computer systems as well as server- and client/server-based distributed systems.

SABRE began with a "request and reply" system in the 1930s. A reservations agent would phone a central control point where the inventory of airline seats was maintained. The reply was returned by teletype.

In the 1940s, the system became more complex and slightly more efficient. In this system, a small group of employees sat around a "Lazy Susan,"[5] which contained dozens of colored index cards, each representing a different flight. A quick count of the check marks on a card (each card representing a different flight) enabled a clerk at the reservations center to give an affirmative or negative reply to a request for a seat. In spite of this improvement over the original system, this was still an extremely time-consuming process. It was intensely dependent on manual labor.[6]

In 1946, the Availability Reservisor was implemented. It was the first electrical/mechanical device to control seat inventory.[7] Despite some flaws, it improved the airline reservation system dramatically. Basic computer file technology was applied to the task of tracking American Airlines' seats and flights; however, the system was not able to sell the seat or cancel a reservation.

More significant improvements were made in 1952. A random access memory drum and arithmetic capabilities were added to the Availability Reservisor. This enabled an agent to check seat availability and automatically sell or cancel seats. Nonetheless, the system still relied almost completely on the work of humans.

The major breakthrough in the development of SABRE came in 1953 when C.R. Smith, American Airlines' president and R. Blair Smith, a senior sales representative for IBM met by chance on a cross-country flight. From their meeting came the 1959 announcement of the Semi-Automated Business Research Environment (SABRE).

American's initial contribution to the project was $40 million—at that time the cost of four Boeing 707s.[8] Only five years after SABRE's announcement, the network extended from coast to coast. In 1976 the first SABRE unit was installed in a travel agency. By the end of 1979, SABRE was used in more than 1,000 travel agencies.

As illustrated by its history, SABRE was originally an advanced system for tracking seat availability and was used only by travel agents. Since its founding, it has grown to a huge electronic service available to any consumer through easySABRE and Travelocity. SABRE has been likened to an electronic supermarket for the airlines, hotels, and car rental agencies and other travel services. Consumers can "shop" the system for flights on a multitude of different airlines and book reservations with a large number of hotels and car rental agencies.[9]

SABRE's competitive strengths give it a leadership position in its markets and a foundation from which to pursue further growth. During the last 20 years, the firm has developed core competencies to include:

1. Comprehensive knowledge of all aspects of the travel industry.
2. Expertise in the application of operations research, information technology, and industrial engineering to solve complex operations problems.
3. The capability to perform high-volume, high-reliability, real-time transactions processing.[10]

These core competencies provide SABRE with the ability to develop an efficient electronic marketplace for the sale and purchase of travel services and to offer a broad array of technological solutions to the travel industry.

FINANCIAL AND PORTFOLIO ANALYSIS

SABRE's financial statements demonstrate consistent annual revenue growth, from $1,097 million in 1991 to

---

[5] "The SABRE Story," http://www.amrcorp.com/sabr_grp/sabstory.htm.
[6] Ibid.
[7] Ibid.

[8] Hopper, Max, "Rattling SABRE," *Harvard Business Review*, May, 1990, v. 168, pp. 118–125.
[9] "Travel Apps. Branch Out to Internet," *Internet Week*, April 20, 1998, n. 711, p. 23(1).
[10] Form 424B1 Report.

$1,530 million in 1995, and operating earnings growth, from $220 million in 1991 to $380 million in 1995.

A majority of the company's revenues, 59.1 percent, is attributable to bookings made by travel agents using SABRE. This is based upon long-standing relationships with most of the travel agency subscribers. Approximately 97 percent of the travel agency locations that were SABRE subscribers at the beginning of 1995 were still SABRE subscribers at the end of 1995.[11]

Based upon the stability of its customer base, SABRE can be queried to make relatively accurate predictions about future earnings. A significant portion of SABRE's revenues, 24.2 percent in 1995, is derived from information technology solutions provided to American Airlines and its affiliates.[12] SABRE is diversifying its services to maintain stability in the marketplace.

According to Form 424B1 filed with the SEC, "The Company's non-affiliated customer revenues grew at a 13.5% compound annual rate to $982 million in 1995, and grew from 53.9% of total revenues in 1991 to 64.2% in 1995."[13] This form predicted that the proportion of SABRE's revenues represented by nonaffiliated customer revenues will continue to increase.

Since competition has increased during the past decade with the entrance of a number of other computer reservations systems into the market, it is important to note that SABRE has maintained its dominance in the market. Robert Crandall, chairman of American Airlines, said that "if he had to choose between unloading the airline or its SABRE reservations system, he would dump the airline without hesitation because the reservation system makes more money and has potential for greater growth."[14]

STOCK/INVESTMENT OUTLOOK

The AMR Corporation, the parent company of American Airlines, announced its intention to offer stock in the SABRE Group in late 1996.[15] AMR's expectation before the initial public offering was that the stock would generate somewhere in the order of $434 million with the first issue (20.2 million shares at around $20 to $23 a share). The proceeds were committed to repaying the debt to AMR and to financing operations and expansion of SABRE.[16] Table 11.1 illustrates the

Table 11.1 IPO for SABRE Group

	Initial Public Offering Price	Underwriting Discount	Proceeds to Company
Per share	$27.00	$1.49	$25.51
Total	$545,400,000	$30,098,000	$515,302,000

actual figures from the initial public offering, which was underwritten by Goldman, Sachs.

According to Dana Canedy, an airline analyst, SABRE's main attraction is unique among initial public offerings—the company dominates the market with more than 40 percent of all airline bookings through travel agents in the United States going through SABRE. SABRE's dominance shows up on the company's bottom line. Between 1994 and 1995 the company's annual earnings grew by 15 percent. SABRE's size will continue to provide an advantage as it embarks on its plans to expand into Asia and to increase its presence in Europe and Latin America.[17]

RISK ANALYSIS

Because SABRE is a subsidiary of AMR, it has often been argued that SABRE gives on-screen preference to American Airlines, providing it with a marketing advantage. This contention, however, is considered to be groundless by the SABRE Group because the government mandated elimination of such biases in 1984.

AMR does not deny the importance of SABRE to its economic well-being; however, AMR takes a different stance on why SABRE is so important to American Airlines. According to Hopper:

> SABRE's real importance to American Airlines was that it prevented an erosion of market share. American began marketing SABRE to travel agents only after United pulled out of an industry consortium established to explore a shared reservation system to be financed and used by carriers and travel retailers. The way American was positioned as an airline—we had no hubs, our routes were regulated, and we were essentially a long-haul carrier—meant that we would have lost market share in a biased reservation system controlled by a competitor. SABRE was less important to us as a biased distribution channel than as a vehicle to force neutral and comprehensive displays into the travel agency market.[18]

Hopper also expressed other concerns about the way that analysts view SABRE. He argued that SABRE

---

[11] *Internet Week*, p. 23(1).
[12] Cronin, Mary J., "The Travel Agents Dilemma: American Airlines SABRE is Designing Websites That Protect Travel Agents," *Fortune*, May 11, 1998, p. 163(2).
[13] *Internet Week*, p. 23(1).
[14] Ziemba, Stanley, "Feds Wonder if All's Fair in the Air," *Chicago Tribune*, March 29, 1992, Sec. 76, p. 1.
[15] Canedy, Dana, "For Sabre Group, Some Long-Term Reservations," *The New York Times*, October 6, 1996, Sec. 3, p. 6.
[16] Ibid.

[17] Maxon, Terry, "Texas-Based Tech Services Firm SABRE Vies for Global Business," *Knight-Ridder/Tribune Business News*, March 29, 1999, p. OKRB990881A5.
[18] Hopper, Max, "Rattling SABRE," *Harvard Business Review*, May 1990, v. 168, n. 3, pp. 118–125.

has grown through four distinct stages. He asserted that critics of SABRE were focused only on the CRS distribution stage. Hopper explained the four stages as follows[19]:

First Stage
SABRE was developed in response to a need to inventory available seats and make reservations. Although this was a relatively high-tech tool in the early 1960s, it was really just an inventory management tool.

Second Stage
By the mid-1970s, SABRE expanded to track more than just inventory. It was responsible for generating flight plans, tracking maintenance parts, and scheduling airline crews. Essentially, SABRE had become the control center for American Airlines.

Third Stage
In 1976, the first SABRE terminal was installed in a travel agency. In the subsequent years, additional services were added to the basic function of making airline reservations, including car rentals and hotel reservations. As a consequence of this introduction, travel agents are now responsible for booking almost 80 percent of all airline reservations, compared with 40 percent before the implementation of computer reservations systems. In subsequent articles, Hopper asserted that SABRE and its CRS rivals revolutionized the marketing and distribution of airline services.

Fourth Stage
According to Hopper, "Today, SABRE is neither a proprietary competitive weapon for American Airlines nor a general distribution system for the airline industry. It is an electronic travel supermarket, a computerized middleman linking suppliers of travel and related services."

Hopper contends that all 2,000 employees of the SABRE Travel Information Network, the system's marketing division, would agree that American Airlines is treated materially the same as any of the other hundreds of airlines whose schedules and fares are on the system. American pays the same booking fees to SABRE as do the other airlines.

Hopper admitted that limited performance differences remain since SABRE was originally an in-house reservations system. He asserts that the SABRE programmers are doing their best to overcome these problems to put all airlines on equal footing.[20] The one advantage that American Airlines does receive from SABRE, without a doubt, is the revenue generated by

the computer reservations system. This, however, cannot be considered to be an unfair advantage. No travel agency is required to use the SABRE Reservations System. Travel agencies are able to choose any computer reservation system available.[21] Now that a number of different computer reservation systems are available to consumers, including Apollo, DATAS II, and System I, each must fight for consumers' business by providing unbiased all-encompassing listings.

Although distribution through travel agents continues to be the primary method of travel distribution, new channels are in place for direct distribution to businesses and consumers through the Internet, computer online services, and private networks. SABRE faces competition in these channels not only from its current competitors but also from travel providers and possible new entrants in the sale of travel products. For example, American Express and Microsoft are continuing to refine an online travel booking service for corporations.[22] SABRE expects that this online travel service, while still in the developmental stage, will eventually directly compete with BTS, SABRE's business travel system. Furthermore, SABRE is now facing stiff competition from the Internet, which gives consumers direct access to travel providers. This eliminates the need for both traditional travel agents and global distribution systems such as SABRE. Although the company has positioned its BTS, Travelocity, and easySABRE products to compete in these emerging distribution channels, there can be no assurance that the company's products will compete. Despite SABRE's current dominance, it must prepare to face even greater competition in the very near future.

ROLE OF RESEARCH AND DEVELOPMENT
SABRE has focused its research and development attention on tapping resources available from outside suppliers. SABRE realizes that computer systems are becoming too large and expensive for one company to develop and own. Consequently, joint ventures and shared access will become the rule rather than the exception when it comes to updating and expanding technological equipment.[23]

TECHNOLOGICAL STORY
Recent developments by SABRE indicate the company is focused upon finding ways to make the usage of its services easier. Turbo SABRE, for example, is an advanced point-of-sale interface that enables screen customization and reservations sales process structuring and eliminates the difficult-to-learn SABRE-specific

---

[19] Ibid.
[20] Foley, John, "SABRE's Challenge," *Information Week*, August 18, 1997, n. 644, p. 83(3).

[21] Ziemba, "Feds Wonder if All's Fair in the Air," p. 1.
[22] Form 424B1 Report.
[23] Hopper, "Rattling SABRE," *Harvard Business Review*, May 1990, v. 168, n. 3, pp. 118–125.

commands. This reduces keystrokes and training requirements for high-volume travel agencies. Turbo SABRE provides access to data sources other than SABRE, including LAN databases.[24]

Planet SABRE, introduced in 1997, is still undergoing improvement.[25] Planet SABRE provides a graphical interface that enables the user to move to any function with a mouse. It includes a customizer feature. This allows travel agencies to adapt Planet SABRE to meet their own specific needs. Planet SABRE also provides a tutorial, online help, a place to store notes about clients, destinations, procedures, and a suggestion system.

Planet SABRE transforms SABRE from a complex command-oriented system to an all-graphic interface with continued access to the SABRE host system and its many features.[26] In doing so, SABRE has made its system more user friendly. The developers hope this will generate increased customer loyalty and satisfaction among the travel agencies.

TECHNOLOGICAL INVESTMENT AND ANALYSIS

SABRE recently installed IBM's new System/390 Parallel Enterprise Server. Its many features make this high performing computer cost efficient. According to Terrell B. Jones, the CIO of the SABRE Group, the group was attracted to the new server because it is environmentally friendly—it is air instead of water cooled, and because it uses considerably less power than previous units.[27]

According to Dennis Erkine, managing director of distribution planning for Holiday Inn, in his experience, "replacing a water-cooled 9021-900 with a new eight-way S/390 G3Enterprise Server can reduce energy bills by 97%, while increasing capacity by 10 to 15%. At the same time, the R84 takes 94% less floor space than the 9021-900 and can cost 70% less to maintain."[28] This placed the server's price–performance ratio in the range that the people at SABRE were searching for.[29]

The new system is advantageous because it is much more compact than the systems that SABRE had been using previously. The transition to the new system was relatively easy. In less than 24 hours the new system was in place and functioning correctly. The users did not even notice that the transition had been made. According to Jones, "since it was an unannounced prod-

uct, we never told anyone it was there. It performed so well that no one ever knew it was there—which is exactly the result we wanted."[30]

Since more than 4,000 S/390 CMOS processors are installed worldwide, repairs and maintenance are easier than if the system were a unique, in-house system developed specifically for SABRE.[31]

Because SABRE has become available on the Internet, the IBM S/390 uses powerful servers for network computing and is specifically designed for client/server environments. It has new features such as the cryptographic coprocessor and the full duplex Open System Adapter (OSA). These deliver secure connections to ATM, Ethernet, token ring, and FDDI local-area networks. These features, when used with facilities such as the Internet Connection Secure Server for OS/390 and native gateways for CICS™, DB2®, IMS™, and the MQSeries™ products, enable the S/390 platform to serve new and existing applications over the Internet.[32]

TECHNOLOGICAL INNOVATIONS

TELECOMMUNICATIONS

The SABRE Group developed Travelocity, the web-based travel agency. Travelocity uses a three-tiered architecture. The first tier are the site's web servers, including Silicon Graphics' Origin 200 servers running Netscape Enterprise Server. These servers handle the static HTML pages. The second tier consists of transaction processing servers. These handle the dynamically generated HTML pages that provide the reservation information. These SGI Origin 2000 servers run proprietary software to access the third tier, the company's immense SABRE Reservations System. This is a seven-terabyte database that runs on eight IBM S1360 mainframes and is affectionately referred to as Mother Sabre. The SABRE Reservation System, which runs a proprietary transaction protocol, provides a three-second response time anywhere in the world.

Although bandwidth has not been the bottleneck, Travelocity added a new Internet connection in 1998. This is a T-3 (45 Mbps) from Uunet Technologies. The site was running a 2Mbps link from Sprint and a 10Mbps connection from MCI.

DATA

SABRE Technology was one of the first companies to adopt Informix's object relational database for its

---

[24] Form 424B1 Report.
[25] "Planet SABRE," http://www.amrcorp.com/sabr_grp/stin/planet_sabre.htm.
[26] Form 424B1 Report.
[27] "American Airlines SABRE Group Soars on IBM's New System/390 Parallel Enterprise Server," http://www.ibm.com//Features/AAirlines/AAirlines.html.
[28] "IBM S/390 Parallel Enterprise Server—Generation 3™," http://www.S390.ibm.com/stories/gen3/g2214221.html.
[29] "SABRE Outsourcing Deal Flies," *PC Week*, January 18, 1999, v. 16, i. 3, p. 80(1).

[30] Madden, John, "SABRE rattles its own cage in restructuring," *PC Week*, April 5, 1999, v. 16, i. 14, p. 64(1).
[31] "Boeing and SABRE Join XML Standards Group Oasis," *Computergram International*, June 7, 1999, i. 3676, p. NA.
[32] Cohen, Emily, "On the Road Again," *PC Magazine*, March 10, 1998, v. 17, n. 5, p. 40(1).

data warehouse. Object relational technology speeds execution times for complex queries and makes the system easier to program. SABRE chose the Informix system because its DataBlade modules can execute in parallel and process many sources simultaneously. Its warehouse will eventually pull information from 80 sources ranging from passenger reservation to ticketing systems and will house up to eight terabytes of data. Thirty developers are writing logic to clean the data and load it correctly.

The warehouse promises to be commercially significant for SABRE and its customers. By knowing who is flying where, when, and for how much money, SABRE can gather valuable data to sell to airlines and other businesses, such as travel agencies, hotels, and real estate firms. The new relational database will enable SABRE to find who is flying to a specific city in the next three weeks. This information could be very valuable to all kinds of associated industries like hotels and entertainment companies.

SABRE intends to consolidate on a single database for both transactional and warehouse purposes. The cost of maintaining two databases is prohibitive. The existing four-terabyte TPF database has the capacity to handle more than 1 billion transactions daily.

RECOMMENDATION FOR THE FUTURE

Several opportunities for future revenue growth exist. These include increasing the use of SABRE in foreign countries, offering new products in emerging distribution channels, such as corporate direct distribution and the Internet, expanding participation of travel providers in SABRE, and providing technology solutions products and services more broadly.

SABRE's market recognition is not as well developed in foreign markets as in the United States. As a result, the company feels this is where its greatest potential for growth exists. A number of trade barriers erected by foreign travel providers—often government owned—have hindered the company's ability to gain market share abroad. These providers have occasionally prevented SABRE from offering its full line of products and services. This has reduced the attractiveness of SABRE's product to travel agencies in those markets. Some international markets are served by other global distribution systems that have substantially greater market presence than SABRE or have developed long-standing relationships with travel agency subscribers.

The statistics indicate that penetration into the international marketplace is possible. SABRE's revenues from its travel distribution products outside the United States grew at a compound annual rate of 29.8 percent from 1990–95, with $250 million in revenues posted for 1995.[33] SABRE is committed to increasing the visibility in its already established European and Latin American markets while at the same time building market presence in Asia.

SABRE believes that the market for associate participation in the SABRE system should be expanded through the addition of nonairline associates and an upgrade to higher levels of functionality in SABRE. When advertising SABRE's services to associates, the company highlights its global distribution capabilities, the ability of associates to display information at no charge until a booking is made, and SABRE's extensive subscriber network.[34]

In terms of enhancing technology and operating capabilities, SABRE has budgeted approximately $100 million through the year 2000 to enhance SABRE's core operating capabilities.[35] According to the company, "The goals of this development effort are to accelerate new product development, increase flexibility, power, and functionality for subscribers and associates, improve data management capabilities, raise capacity levels, and lower operating costs."[36]

SABRE is continuing to make the process of reserving a room or a car easier.[37] According to a recent article, "SABRE travel agencies worldwide with clients requesting a stay at Motel 6 can now reserve the room electronically at one of the motel chain's more than 200 properties. The agreement between SABRE and Motel 6 marks the first time the motel chain has used a global distribution system to make reservations. Motel 6, which owns, operates, and is affiliated with more than 700 hotels in North America, plans to add additional properties to SABRE in the coming year."[38] "Direct Request for Hotels" properties are listed in SABRE and give agencies the ability to access and request information regarding participating locations while using pre-existing formats. When a customer requests a room reservation, SABRE sends a fax message with all the booking information to the appropriate hotel. SABRE then electronically reads information from the hotel's file and updates the reservation automatically.

Overall SABRE is doing well financially, and has many plans for improvements and expansion in the future. Competition will require SABRE to enhance its current services and offer new products to supplement those currently in existence.

[33] Form 424B1 Report.
[34] Carr, David F., "How Travelocity Gives Consumers Rock-Bottom Airfares," *Internet World*, May 17, 1999, v. 5, i. 19, p. 19(1).
[35] Maddox, Kate, "Travel, Web-site style," *Communications-Week*, May 13, 1996, n. 610, p. S1A1(2).
[36] "SABRE savors online sales," *PC Week*, June 29, 1998, v. 15, n. 26, p. 86(1).
[37] "Travelocity Portal Intros Best Fare Search Facility." *Newsbytes*, April 23, 1999.
[38] "Motel 6 and SABRE Now Leave the Light on for Agencies," http://www.amrcorp.com/amr/mar1097b.htm.

CASE QUESTIONS

Strategic Questions

1. What is the strategic direction of the corporation/organization?

2. Who or what forces are driving this direction?

3. What has been the catalyst for change?

4. What are the critical success factors for this corporation/organization?

5. What are the core competencies for this corporation/organization?

Technological Questions

6. What technologies has the corporation relied on?

7. What has caused a change in the use of technology in the corporation/organization?

8. How has this change been implemented?

9. How successful has the technological change been?

Quantitative Questions

10. What does the corporation say about its financial ability to embark on a major technological program of advancement?

11. What conclusions can be reached from an analysis of the financial information to support or contradict this financial ability?

12. What analysis can be made by examining the following ratio groups?

    Revenue
    Asset Utilization

13. What conclusions can be reached by analyzing the financial trends? Are there long-term trends that seem to be problematic? Is the industry stable? Are there replacement products?

Internet Questions

14. What does the corporation's web page present about their business directives?

15. How effective is the web page in drawing the viewer in?

Industry Questions

16. What challenges and opportunities is the industry facing?

17. Is the industry oligopolistic or competitive?

18. Does the industry face a change in government regulation?

19. How will technology impact the industry?

Data Questions

20. What role do data play in the future of the corporation?

21. How important are data to the corporation's continued success?

22. How will the capture and maintenance of customer data impact the corporation's future?

TECHNOLOGY TIPS

MICROSOFT WORD TIPS

FORMATTING YOUR DOCUMENT INTO COLUMNS

There may be times you want to write part of your document in columns. One reason would be to show the pros and cons between two arguments for a particular cause. Another use for columns may be to write a newsletter. You can format the columns to resemble those of any national newspaper. Whatever reasons you may have to use columns, the following section will allow you to make use of this feature.

1. From the toolbar click on FORMAT.
2. A drop-down menu will appear. Click on COLUMNS. . . .
3. The columns dialog box will appear. Study your options from this dialog box and make the appropriate selections for the type of document you are writing.
4. When you are satisfied with your choices click on OK.

When you return to the document after pressing OK, you will notice that the ruler displays the column divisions. If you cannot see the ruler, click on VIEW, then click on RULER. This will allow you to manipulate the width of the column by clicking and dragging the slider markers on the ruler.

Only One Section of the Document?

A section is defined according to the breaks that you have inserted in the document. If you only want the section that you are preparing to write in column format, indicate so in the AP-PLY TO: section of the column dialog box. THIS SECTION will format the whole page and all pages after. FROM THIS POINT FORWARD will format the document from the cursor on down and all pages after. If you wish to write a general paragraph and then start your columns, pick the latter option.

How Will Text Appear in the Columns?

The text or data that you enter in your document will be "pushed" down and over to the other column as shown in the figure on the right. If you *do not* want the text you enter to move in this way you must insert a column break.

Dividing the Columns with a Line

To insert a line between your columns, do the following:

1. If you have made your columns already, place the cursor anywhere within the two columns.
2. From the toolbar click on FORMAT.
3. A drop-down menu will appear. Click on COLUMNS. . . .
4. The columns dialog box will appear. Click on the LINE BETWEEN check box.
5. Click on OK.

ADDITIONAL NOTE

To have columns on only one page and to learn how to insert a column break, refer to Inserting Breaks in Chapter 12.

MICROSOFT EXCEL TIPS

COPYING FORMULAS: RELATIVE REFERENCES

Copying formulas is made easy by using the Copy and Paste command buttons, but this method allows only for relative cell references. Relative cell references are usually based upon their position relative to the cell that contains the formula. If the data entered in the cells may change from time to time (i.e., estimates that need to be updated), relative cell references are suitable for the task since the copied formulas will be automatically updated when the values in the cells change. The following example will show how relative cell references work.

In the following example, cell C11 contains the formula =B10; Excel finds the value one cell above and one cell to the left of C11 (the value in cell B10 is what will be displayed on the worksheet).

	B	C
9		
10	500	
11	200	=B10
12		

When you copy and paste the formula from C11 to C12 the formula will refer to B11 (the value in cell B11 is what will be displayed on the worksheet).

	B	C
9		
10	500	
11	200	=B10
12		=B11
13		

Using Cell Addresses from Other Worksheets

If the data you wish to use is located in another worksheet you can still use the data. This would be used when you have a separate sheet for variables or you wish to total data located in different worksheets. The cell address will simply have the following format: WORSHEET NAME!CELL ADDRESS (i.e., Invoice!B72) in the formula. The following steps guide you through the process:

1. Click on the worksheet tab that will contain the formula. Click inside the cell in which the formula will be entered.
2. Enter the equal sign (=) in the activated cell.
3. Click on the sheet tab that you wish to have the formula refer to, then click on the cell that you wish to enter into the formula (you can also type the name of the sheet inside the formula along with the cell address). Excel will enter the sheet name and the cell address that you clicked on. Notice the exclamation point between the sheet name and cell address. The exclamation point is necessary for the formula to recognize that the cell is located in another worksheet.
4. After the first cell address is entered, type in an operand (+, −, ×, ÷) or use one of the functions provided by Excel (i.e., SUM, AVERAGE, etc.) from the function bar.
5. Enter the next cell address by clicking on a different cell on the current sheet or repeating step 3 to enter cell addresses from other worksheets.
6. After you have completed entering all of the cell addresses into the formula press ENTER. The formula will be entered in the cell and the result of your function will show up in the cell.

In the example shown below a formula has been entered in the *Invoice* worksheet using a cell address from the *Variables* worksheet and *Invoice worksheet*.

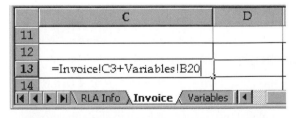

	C	D
11		
12		
13	=Invoice!C3+Variables!B20	
14		

RLA Info \ **Invoice** \ Variables

	A	B	C
20	unit price	$ 30.00	
21	15day disc. rate	0.2	
22	30day disc. Rate	0.1	
23			

Down Info \ **Variables** \ Invoice

Getting Errors?

The function will not work properly if you enter the wrong information in the formula. Review your formula and ensure that the cell addresses have compatible data and the cell exists. The following are just a few of the common errors found. Further assistance can be found using the Office Assistant or help files.

#VALUE!   The #VALUE error occurs when the wrong type of argument or operand is used, or there is incompatible data in the formula (numbers and text).

The numeric value is too large for the cell. Resize the column in order to display the value.

#REF!   The cell reference used in the formula is not valid. Make sure that you are using compatible data (text and numbers do not work).

MICROSOFT POWERPOINT TIPS

INSERTING GRAPHS

Graphs can be inserted or created in PowerPoint slides. If you have graphs that were created in other programs, you can import them. In the following chapter, you will learn how to have "real time" links between your presentation graph and the source in order to keep the presentation updated.

Creating a Graph

If you want to insert a graph into an existing slide do the following:

1. While on the slide into which you want to insert the new slide, click on INSERT, then click on CHART from the drop-down menu.

2. A graph will appear on your slide along with a table to input information. The toolbar will change to the graph toolbar.

3. Input your data into the table. The graph will change to show the data that you input.

4. Once you have completed entering data into the table, click outside of the graph and you will revert back to the slide.

5. To make changes to the data, double click on the graph to activate it.

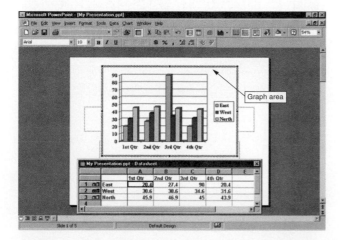

If you are starting with a new slide:

1. Click on CTRL + M or click on the NEW SLIDE button from the top toolbar.

2. The NEW SLIDE dialog box will appear. Double click on one of the three choices available for slides with graphs:
   - Text & chart
   - Chart & text
   - Chart

3. The new slide will appear on your screen. Double click on the chart icon and follow steps 3 through 5 above to fill out the chart.

Inserting a Graph from Excel

If you have created a graph in an Excel spreadsheet and would like to include it in your presentation, do the following:

1. Open the presentation to the slide into which you want to insert the graph.

2. Open the Excel spreadsheet to the sheet that contains the graph.

3. Right click in the graph area (the area immediately surrounding the graph) to highlight the graph. The outer edges of the graph will be highlighted. *Note:* If you click on the graph itself, only the graph will be highlighted.

4. Select COPY from the pop-up menu.

5. Go back to the slide in your PowerPoint presentation and click on EDIT. From the drop-down menu select PASTE SPECIAL . . . .

6. The Paste Special dialog box will appear. Select the Microsoft Excel Chart Object from the menu and then click on OK.

7. The chart will appear on your slide.

8. Modify it as you wish by double clicking in the chart area. Note that when you double click on the graph this time the Excel spreadsheet program will be activated within PowerPoint.

MICROSOFT ACCESS TIPS

CREATING A QUERY

This chapter will walk you through the procedure of creating a simple query using the Simple Query Wizard. If you want, the wizard can also sum, count, and average values for groups of records or all records, and it can calculate the minimum or maximum value in a field.

1. In the Database window, click the Queries tab, and then click New.

2. In the New Query dialog box, click Simple Query Wizard and click OK.

3. Click the name of the table or query you want to base your query on, and then select the fields whose data you want to retrieve. You can select an additional table or query and then select the fields you want to use from it. Once you have all the fields you need, click on the NEXT button.

4. Depending on the type of fields selected, the next window may allow you to select a summary of the query or to show all the fields. Click on summary and then the SUMMARY OPTIONS button. A small table will appear with choices as to how you can have the query appear. This is

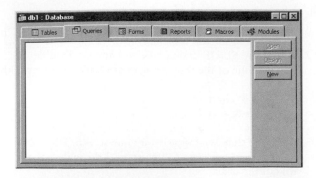

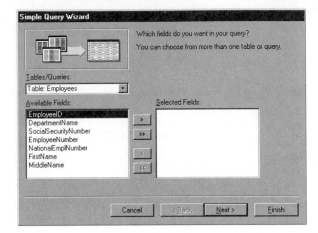

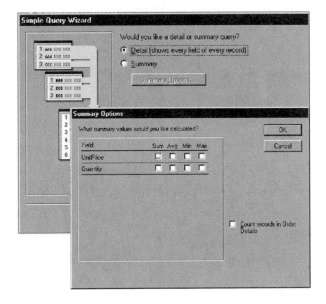

optional. Click on the CANCEL button to back out. Once you have made your selections, click on the NEXT button

5. In the last dialog box, click on the FINISH button and your query will appear as a table with the fields you selected.

Once you have run a query you can view it by clicking on the query tab of the database window, selecting the query, and clicking on the open button.

MODIFYING A QUERY

You can modify a query by clicking on the design view button. You will have an ample range of modifications to make in this window that will help you fine-tune your query and better understand it.

MICROSOFT FRONTPAGE TIPS

CONVERTING EXCEL TO HTML FORMAT

Just as with your Word document, you will also be able to convert your Excel document to HTML format. This may be useful if you want to share data that you have already compiled or want to avoid creating tables. No matter what reason you have to convert your Excel spreadsheet over to HTML, the steps are rather easy.

Converting to HTML

1. With your Excel file open, click on FILE from the top menu bar.
2. Select SAVE AS HTML from the drop-down menu
3. The Internet Assistant Wizard dialog box (below) will appear.
4. The wizard will walk you through all of the necessary steps to get your Excel file saved in HTML format.

NOTE

If the SAVE AS HTML does not appear or is not active, you may have to add this feature to the Excel program. Click on TOOLS from the menu bar in Excel and select ADD INS. . . . Look for the Internet Assistant Wizard from the list. Check it off and then click on OK. If the Internet Assistant Wizard is not available on the list you may have to use the Office setup to have it installed.

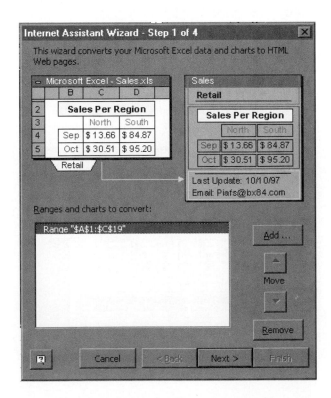

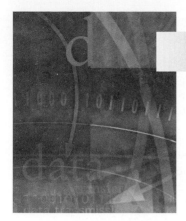

CHAPTER 12

SYSTEMS DEVELOPMENT
GOVERNMENT INDUSTRY

Systems Development

Systems development is always difficult. Most projects that are deemed failures either cost too much or did not produce useful systems. Large projects are especially difficult. To deal with these difficulties and provide some control over the process, a systems development life cycle (SDLC) has been developed. This system analysis technique breaks projects into manageable pieces. Software tools display interrelationships and integrate modules. Modules have inputs, processing steps, controls, and outputs. The prototyping approach is iterative, as opposed to the rigidity of the SDLC method, and provides an early version of the system. This contains the design of the final version. The early version is then developed into a fully working system.

Another way to build systems is to ask end users to develop their own systems using more user-friendly fourth-generation tools such as database management systems (DBMS) or spreadsheets. This last approach carries the risks of lack of testing, incompatibilities, and duplication.

All of the methods mentioned have the same five basic stages: feasibility and planning, systems analysis, design, implementation, and maintenance. Systems designers need to remember that working systems must be maintained and modified as business needs arise.

Systems Development Life Cycle The SDLC is one of the most formalized techniques used to develop computer systems. There are different versions of this technique, but all have the goal to build computer systems by analyzing the process it should replicate and breaking the process into smaller, more manageable, pieces. This approach avoids problems such as duplicated efforts, incompatible portions of programs, and runaway costs due to situations such as programmer turnover and shifting directions.

A *feasibility study* is a quick examination of the benefits, goals, costs, and problems of the proposed system solution. The objective of this stage is to decide whether a system is the right procedure to solve the situation.

Planning consists of developing a schedule for the project, appointing team leaders, and laying out a plan.

System analysis determines present system procedures and problems and breaks the current system into pieces. It uses diagrams, such as a visual table of contents (VTOC), which shows the relationship between the modules of a system.

System design describes the new system on paper, including a detailed description of its modules and interrelationships. It then translates this description into workable code.

Systems implementation is the most difficult step. It consists of installing the new system, training end users, making adjustments, and converting from the old system. An important element of this stage is final testing. The final testing and quality control of the new system before it is presented to the end users can uncover problems that can be resolved before multiple end users replicate the problem in production.

Involving end users in the design, education and training is important because it programs system flexibility, recognizes the impact of the new system on the business, and reduces the resistance to change from the end users to the new system.

Maintenance, provides a method to address changing hardware and software requirements, problems not found during testing, end users who request additional features from the software, and changes to the program that may come from changes in the industry.

Evaluation, the last phase, is important for future projects. The effectiveness of the new system, with regard to reliability, speed, ease of use, and cost, are all important criteria with which to judge the new system.

Prototyping Prototyping is a systems-building technique that uses more advanced building blocks. The main objective is to construct a working version as quickly as possible, even if the initial working system does not have all of the necessary details. This technique works best when the necessary systems are not too complex and the number of users are limited. Advantages include users which have more input into the final system, a final system that is more flexible, and a working version of the system that is much faster than using SDLC methodology. Rapid application development (RAD) is similar to prototyping.

End-User Development End-User Development occurs when the final user of a computer program develops the program using advanced development tools. Any systems development effort is potentially expensive and

hard to implement. Two trends causing this technique to become more popular are the backlog of projects and maintenance in most companies' IT departments, and the proliferation of powerful and user-friendly software tools.

Pseudocode This method was an early technique to help programmers outline the system. Pseudocode describes the logic of a program. It provides an overview of the program written in "plain" English, without the computer syntax.

Top-Down Design Using this approach, the design of a new computer system begins by looking at the big picture, or the company as a whole. A bottom-up design starts with building computer systems as the need arises and responding quickly to management demands.

Computer-Aided Software Engineering (CASE) CASE tools are new software tools that assist with systems and software development. CASE tools are typically used for either software development or the maintenance of existing systems. They can speed the development process, accomplishing such tasks as writing the computer code and drawing system development diagrams. For the maintenance of existing systems, some CASE tools can perform reverse engineering. They can

Word	W.1	Inserting Breaks Additional Note	Page Break Using Insert from the Toolbar Column Break Between Columns Column Break Between Pages Having Coumns on Only One Section of the Page
Excel	E.1	Absolute References and Using the Fill Handle	Making Absolute References Using the Fill Handle to Copy Formulas
PowerPoint	P.1	Object Linking and Embedding	Linking Objects Embedding Objects Break a Connection to a Linked Object
Access	A.1	Creating Reports Using Report Wizard Using Report Wizard	
Front Page	I.1	Saving PowerPoint as HTML	Preparing Your Presentation for the Web

take the older software/system and update it by rewriting the program. These tools can be expensive. The IS personnel must be knowledgeable in the CASE methodology and technology aspects of the program.

Joint Application Development This technique was developed to speed the design stage. The main system is designed in an intense workshop lasting several days. All levels of the involved parties, from users to system analysts, participate in the intense meetings. This approach limits the time-consuming task of going back and forth between users and designers when designing a system. The drawback is the need for all parties to commit the time and energy to this intense process.

Three Levels of Developing Systems Vessey and Sravanapudi identified three levels of tasks in system design and development. Level 1 tasks cannot be shared. Level 2 tasks require the sharing of work products. These are teamwork tasks where the output of one task is needed to finish the other. Level 3 tasks represent group sharing tasks.

Object-Oriented Development A technique similar to SDLC for developing computer systems is object-oriented development. The ultimate goal is to build a set of reusable objects and procedures. Objects have a set of characteristics or attributes. The object comes first, with properties of that object being inherited. Ideally, new systems can be developed, or old ones modified, by reusing an existing object or implementing a new module. This technique results in a set of information systems building blocks.

Government Industry

DESCRIPTION OF THE INDUSTRY

The U.S. federal government consists of three major branches: executive, judicial, and legislative. It is the job of these groups, as stated in the Constitution's preamble, "to form a more perfect union, establish justice, insure domestic tranquillity, provide for the common defense, promote the general welfare, and secure the blessings of liberty." These goals are achieved through laws passed by elected officials to Congress, with the approval of the president. The president can veto laws Congress submits. With a majority vote, Congress can override a presidential veto. All laws are subject to the interpretation of the courts. The federal government is structured this way to provide checks and balances; the purpose of electing officials is to have a government that is a "representation of the people" or a democracy.

Currently, two political parties, the Democrats and the Republicans, dominate the U.S. government. These two parties maintain different platforms. Changes in control change the general direction of government initiatives. The election cycle is such that every two to four years a major turnover in political power is possible.

The government can raise money by levying taxes, instituting fees, or raising debt. The amount of money brought in by taxes is directly related to the well-being of the economy.

The people elected to government are not necessarily the most qualified or skilled. The mission of the federal government is not profit maximization. Ideally, the government should be run like a business but its political nature can get in the way. This is significant since Congress, the president, and the judicial branch have hundreds of committees and agencies at their disposal. The federal government employs 2.25 percent of the U.S. workforce. It spends over $1.5 trillion annually.

FINANCIAL ANALYSIS

In the first half of the 1990s, government revenues increased by 16.6 percent and expenditures by 10 percent (Figure 12.1). Unfortunately, on an average, expenditures were ranging 16 to 23 percent over revenues. This pushed the deficit to a little over 2 percent of the GDP;

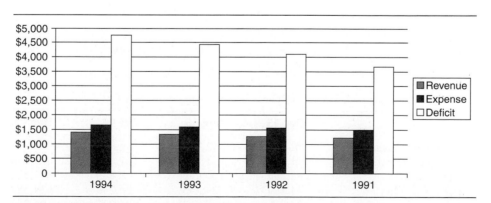

Figure 12.1 Government financials in billions of dollars.

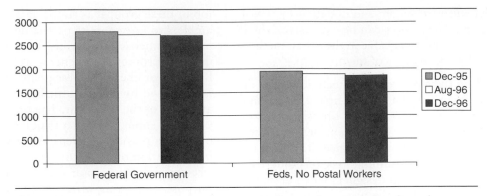

Figure 12.2 Federal government employment, in thousands, seasonally adjusted.

a 28 percent increase in the first half of the decade. The situation is not as bleak as it sounds. The European Community, in comparison, maintains a deficit averaging 5 percent of its GDP.

Other financial points of interest are:

- The economy has been growing at a general rate of 3 percent.
- Government expenditures will be 21 percent higher by 2002, growing at a rate that is slightly faster than the projected rate of inflation.
- The public is pushing the government to hold and/or lower taxes.
- Medicare's trust fund is facing bankruptcy by 2002.
- By the year 2029, Social Security will exhaust its surplus and taxes will cover only 75 percent of the promised benefits. To ensure solvency for the next 75 years, Congress must act by either increasing the 12.4 payroll tax, or cutting benefits, or both.

STOCK/INVESTMENT OUTLOOK

Citizens and institutions of other countries hold most of the United States' debt. According to a *Wall Street Journal* article in December 1996, there was concern that a recent drop in global financial markets would cause Japanese institutions to stop buying U.S. bonds, "which might force up U.S. interest rates and thus push stocks off a cliff." This is not the situation today. Interest rates are so low in Japan that the Japanese put

money in overseas investments, especially blue-chip securities like U.S. Treasury bonds. In general, the U.S. government strongly supports free markets and encourages foreign investors to buy government securities.

The U.S. Treasury is promoting an "inflation-indexed" bond. This bond will provide variable returns pegged to the officially reported rate of inflation. The January 1997 launch of this type of bond was postponed, however.

POTENTIAL/PROSPECTIVE FOR GROWTH

The government must be funded to continue operating. A certain amount of this growth is dependent upon taxes. The amount of taxes that are raised is dependent on the economy. A report released by the Labor Department in early January 1997 showed an economy that was steadily growing. Unemployment rates were at a low of 5.3 percent. There was a 6 percent gain in average hourly earnings to $12.05. On average, weekly earnings increased 1.4 percent to $419.34. The average workweek for service, production, and manufacturing jobs rose 0.3 hours.

In contrast, the actual size of the government is shrinking (Figure 12.2). The number of elected officials remains constant but the rest of the federal government is downsizing. Federal government employment peaked in May 1992 and since has fallen by 322,000 jobs. A review of employment figures shows that, in 1996, private sector jobs grew by almost 2.5 percent while federal government jobs fell by 0.05 percent (Table 12.1).

Table 12.1 Employment Figures, in Thousands, Seasonally Adjusted

	Dec 95	**Aug 96**	**Oct 96**	**Dec 96**
Federal government	2,790	2,739	2,731	2,720
Feds, no postal workers	1,939	1,888	1,878	1,864
All private	98,789	100,446	100,803	101,184
Goods producing	24,160	24,298	24,284	24,384
Service producing	93,976	95,793	96,027	96,352

COMPETITIVE STRUCTURE

Although at an all time low, voter turnout might be viewed as an indicator of public attitude toward government. The U.S. federal government has no fear of being replaced. It has no competition as a government. However, in the area of investments, the government competes for dollars against the private sector. Among the major developed countries of the world, the United States has one of the lowest rates of gross savings, so the competition for investment dollars is strong.

The other type of competition the government faces is from within. The two major political parties are constantly competing for electoral votes and the ability to control the government. The 1990s have seen the reemergence of independent and "third-party" movements. They have not made a significant impact.

ROLE OF RESEARCH AND DEVELOPMENT

The government is heavily involved in research. One agency focused on research and development in the area of technology at the Congress's disposal. This section is the Office of Technology Assessment. Founded in 1972, the primary task of this agency is to identify the impact of technology on society.

The Information Technology Management Reform Act of 1996 also promotes technological research. Through the Information Technology Acquisition Pilot Program, the administrator of the Federal Procurement Policy (FPP) is authorized to "conduct pilot programs to test alternative approaches for the acquisition of information technology." Here are the program parameters:

- Each pilot program is limited to five years.
- Each agency conducting a pilot program must establish measurable criteria for evaluation.
- The FPP administrator must submit a detailed test plan to Congress before implementation.
- Each program's findings must be reported to the director of the Office of Management and Budget (OMB) and to the Congress.
- The OMD director will submit to Congress recommendations for legislation if the pilot program results show this type of action is needed.
- The FPP administrator can authorize a pilot program in which a private contractor "provides the Federal Government with an information technology alternative process."

TECHNOLOGY INVESTMENT AND ANALYSIS

On July 16, 1996, the President's Executive Order on Federal Information Technology was issued. It begins as follows:

Figure 12.3 NPR's 1993 recommendations for implementation by 1996.

A Government that works better and costs less requires efficient and effective information systems. The Paperwork Reduction Act of 1995 and the Information Technology Management Reform Act of 1996 provide the opportunity to improve significantly the way the Federal Government acquires and manages information technology. (Executive Order 13011)

The White House is "Reinventing Government" according to their web page.[1] Their solution involves information systems. Each agency is to have a chief information officer who designs, develops, and implements information systems. The CIO's goal is "to use information technology to improve the productivity of Federal programs and to promote a coordinated, secure, and shared government-wide infrastructure that is provided and supported by a diversity of private sector suppliers and a well-trained corps of information technology professionals" (Executive Order 13011). These systems are supposed to pay for themselves through their savings. They are intended to streamline and downsize government.

There is bipartisan support for technology implementation. A report issued by the National Performance Review (NPR) on September 7, 1993, outlined 130 major recommendations pertaining to government management systems like budget, procurement, financial management, and personnel (Figure 12.3). In 1994, Congress shifted from being dominated by the Democrats to the Republicans. Even with this turnover in party, 38 percent of the NPR recommendations were accomplished by 1996. Additionally, 49 percent of the initiatives are still in progress and only 13 percent are on hold or not making expected progress.

RECOMMENDATION FOR THE FUTURE

The U.S. government must find ways to promote a higher savings rate in the country. Although foreign direct investment is high, an increase in the U.S. savings rate would lower the cost of capital. This would encourage economic growth, thus increasing tax revenues.

---

[1] www.whitehouse.gov.

In addition, the government must find ways to cut costs so the deficit can be reduced. Programs to streamline the Social Security and Medicare database and payment systems must be constantly reevaluated with regard to their impact.

INDUSTRY WEB SITES

Government Industry

www.whitehouse.gov/WH/Welcome.html
www.senate.gov/
www.house.gov/
www.thomas.loc.gov/
www.jurist.law.pitt.edu/clerk.html

DENVER INTERNATIONAL AIRPORT

Executive Summary

Case Name:	Denver International Airport (DIA)
Case Industry:	Airports
Major Technology Issue:	Making the automated baggage system operate as intended.
Major Financial Issue:	Construction cost overruns that now leave debt service accounting for over two-thirds of the annual operating budget; debt stands at $5.3 billion
Major Strategic Issue:	Need to attract passenger and cargo traffic to use fixed assets at 100 percent
Major Players/Leaders:	Frederico Pena, former mayor of Denver, former transportation secretary; Wellington Webb, present mayor of Denver
Main Web Page:	infodenver.denver.co.us:80/~aviation/index.html
Case Conclusion/Recommendation:	DIA should remain competitive. It has new technology, ample space at present, and room to expand. World air traffic is increasing 5 to 6 percent per year.

CASE ANALYSIS

INTRODUCTORY STORY

Heralded as the "Airport for the 21st Century," by former Denver Mayor and U.S. Transportation Secretary Frederico Pena, the Denver International Airport (DIA) is the first airport totally designed, built, and operated using computers. It is the first entirely new airport in the United States in over 20 years and is the world's largest airport, encompassing an area of 53 square miles. DIA was designed to face issues of expansion, delays, and forecasts of increasing demand that its 66-year-old predecessor, Stapleton International Airport (SIA), could not. DIA is the most technologically advanced airport in the world.

SHORT DESCRIPTION OF THE COMPANY

On February 28, 1995, Denver International Airport (DIA) opened. This was after 16 months of highly publicized delays which included gross mismanagement, exorbitant cost overruns, and a troubled baggage handling system that shredded baggage like a cheese grater. DIA's opening has made way for numerous lawsuits, investigations, and further questions about the progress of this megaproject.

The airport serves the Denver regional area, as the Stapleton Airport did. It is located 24 miles from downtown Denver, compared to SIA's distance of 7 miles. The airport occupies 53 square miles, twice the area of Manhattan.

SHORT HISTORY OF THE COMPANY

The City of Denver's airport history began in 1929 with the opening of Stapleton International Airport (SIA). SIA underwent periodic expansions to accommodate increased air traffic since its opening. In the 1970s, local planners realized that SIA, which had become one of the 10 busiest airports in the world, had to be expanded again to meet projected future demand. SIA had both pairs of runways located so close together that during bad weather, only one could be used. This increased delays at SIA and consequently other airports across the nation.

One of the options was to expand onto a U.S. Army arsenal property north of SIA. This expansion option was pursued even with the knowledge that the arsenal was one of the most contaminated parcels of land in the country. Cleanup costs were estimated at $6 billion in 1982. During mayoral campaign speeches, soon-to-be mayor Frederico Pena strongly criticized the prospect of building a new airport. It was not until 1985 that the arsenal expansion option was considered inferior to a new regional airport. The agreement to build a new airport was met with mixed reactions.

The decision to annex land for the new airport was voted upon at a May 16, 1989, election. The vote was 63 percent in favor of annexing land for a new airport. With this local endorsement, Washington, D.C., responded with $500 million in funding. The FAA followed with approval of the final environmental impact statement. The groundbreaking of the new airport occurred on September 28, 1989.[1]

One of the major tenant demands from United Airlines was the installation of a fully automated baggage system that would use a system of tunnels to move passenger luggage rapidly between the terminal and its concourse. United believed an automated baggage system could give them the ability to turn around their planes in less than 35 minutes. This was not possible using conventional tug-and-cart baggage handling methods.

The city decided that, rather than have a separate baggage system for each airline, the automated system should be extended to the entire airport. In the end, the automated baggage system was a major, if not the main, reason why the opening of the DIA was delayed four times. The delays caused the bonds sold to finance the airport to be downgraded several levels. On February 28, 1995, DIA opened. The automated baggage system was partially used. The city redesigned the airport with baggage tunnels that could handle running a conventional baggage system.[2]

In its short operating existence, the DIA has operated efficiently and profitably. Specifically, DIA has significantly reduced the delays that plagued SIA. DIA has done this at an astounding cost and without all of the projected tenants.

FINANCIAL AND PORTFOLIO ANALYSIS

The major portion of the funding, eventually totaling more than $4 billion, came from the sale of bonds. The bonds sold with the understanding that the airport had to secure two major hub airlines with signed agreements for significant gate utilization. Continental and United Airlines both reached agreements with the City of Denver in exchange for numerous design modifications and demands. United's demands would eventually have a profound impact on the project's implementation. At $5.3 billion, Denver International Airport represents one of the United States' largest publicly financed projects of all times.

RISK ANALYSIS

There is still significant financial risk for DIA. The biggest hurdle was to become operational; further hurdles remain. DIA is heavily dependent on Continental and United Airlines traffic. Risks to these airlines represent risk to DIA. There is also the economic risk that

Denver might fade as a business or pleasure/resort destination. Reasons may include bad weather, political and legislative obstacles, and the attractiveness of the business climate in Denver.

TECHNOLOGICAL STORY

Elrey B. Jeppesen Terminal is named for the businessman and aviation pioneer whose navigational maps and charts are standard equipment in every commercial airline cockpit around the world. The terminal, at 1,200 feet in length, is longer than Chicago's Sears Tower is tall. It covers 3.5 million square feet over seven levels, the equivalent of 35 football fields. Most notable are the 34 masts, 25 miles of support steel, and 15 acres of Teflon-coated fiberglass used to make the peaks and roof of the terminal. These peaks have been described as "snow-topped mountains, Indian tepees on the plains, or as a spiny covered caterpillar with a sheet draped over it."[3]

The floor of the main terminal consists of six types of colorful granite, which were cut from quarries around the world: North America, South America, Europe, Africa, and Asia. They are laid in a sweeping V design. These tiles have proven costly and troublesome. The city surveyed the floors after DIA opened and found cracks in 1.35 percent of the tiles examined. Reports in Denver newspapers put the percent of tiles with cracks well above 5 percent.

Connected to the terminal are three concourses that have a total of 94 gates, of which 84 are used on a regular basis by over 20 airlines. The airport has the ability to expand to over 200 gates with additions to the three existing concourses and additional new concourses when needed. Concourse B is served almost entirely by United Airlines, which carries more passengers than any other airline in the world, and has its second largest connecting hub located at DIA. The concourses are linked by an underground train. Passengers can also access concourse A by walking to the terminal through a glass-enclosed bridge named Lorenzo's Bridge. The 350-foot bridge was built because during the construction process Continental Airlines insisted that a bridge be built in case the subway malfunctioned. It is the only bridge crossing an active airport taxiway in the world. It is sufficiently high that Boeing 737 aircraft can pass underneath.[4]

Throughout the terminal, concourses, and subway tunnels are displays of art and artifacts that complement the airport's contemporary architecture. DIA's public art

[1] Blaha, Bill, "Concrete Goliath," *Concrete Products*, March 1994, v. 97, n. 3, p. 16.
[2] Knill, Bernie, "Denver International Airport Carries Its Own Baggage," *Material Handling Engineer*, December 1994, v. 49, n. 13, p. 7.

[3] "A Meeting of the Minds at Denver International Airport," *Buildings*, July 1993, v. 87, n. 7, p. 50.
[4] Blaha, Bill, "Concrete Goliath," *Concrete Products*, March 1994, v. 97, n. 3, p. 16.

program was assigned a budget of $7.5 million by a city ordinance. At the terminal atrium's focal point is a cactus and palm tree garden installed by workers from Denver's Botanic Gardens. In the subway tunnel, artists Antonette Rosato and William Maxwell installed a "kinetic light air curtain" which consists of 5,280 metal propellers embedded in one subway tunnel wall. Air currents generated by the subway train turn the propellers. Much positive and negative press have followed about the quality and value of the artwork displayed.

The airport has 130,000 square feet of leased space for food/beverage, retail, and service companies. Prices must be no more than 110 percent of prices found elsewhere in the city.

TECHNOLOGICAL INVESTMENT AND ANALYSIS

DIA's underground train system, the Automated Guideway Transit System (AGTS), was designed and built by AEG Westinghouse. At the opening of DIA there were five two-car trains that could take 6,000 passengers per hour from the terminal to each of the concourses every two minutes at 30 miles per hour. The fully automated rail system consists of two parallel guideway tunnels that run north and south through the center of the terminal and the concourses. Each train car holds 80 passengers and runs on rubber tires following a center guide beam that carries electric current to power the cars' motors. Traveling one way from the terminal to the farthest concourse takes less than 5 minutes. Since the opening, train cars have been added to the system.

There are 5 runways, each 12,000 feet long and 150 feet wide. These runways replaced SIA's 4 commercial air strips. During inclement weather FAA regulations forced the closing of all but two of the SIA runways. This caused a chain reaction of delays throughout the country. DIA's runways are arranged in a unique pinwheel configuration so that none of the runways crosses each other. This greatly increases the safety and movement of air traffic. The runways are spaced more than 4,300 feet apart. In the future, the airport has the ability to increase to 12 runways.

DIA's 33-story air traffic control tower is the world's highest and is essential for viewing the world's largest airfield. The 327-foot tower is designed to sway no more than 0.5 inch in an 86 mile per hour wind. Each panel of distortion-free glass in the tower weighs 11,000 pounds. On a clear day it is possible to see Wyoming and New Mexico from the tower.

DIA has two airline support areas. These include maintenance hangar complexes and flight kitchens. To the north is the North Business Complex. Its proximity makes it ideally situated for aviation-related support facilities. A cargo area includes a joint-use cargo build-ing for combination passenger/cargo carriers, exclusive-use facilities for FedEx, Airborne Express, and the U.S. Postal Service. The Airport Gateway has been exclusively planned for business development with a system of high-pressure water mains and other utilities.

TECHNOLOGICAL INNOVATION

DATABASE

For airports and other installations where maps play a very important role, spatial data have become an integral component of information systems. This approach improves current applications focused on mapping or delivery. As it migrates into the IS mainstream it will continue to be integrated into the standard business processes.

The visual display of data as a map or drawing conveys an additional level of information to the user. Reusing the visual display as an input mechanism enhances its value and reduces the time and effort required for data input and query specifications.

Once strictly in the province of geographic information systems (GISs), spatial information is moving into the mainstream of enterprise databases and applications. Increasingly, database products incorporate the data structures and functionality needed to support these new types of information.

Spatial information systems are based on four types of computer graphic systems: GISs, computer-aided design (CAD), automated mapping/facility management (AM/FM), and computer-aided facilities management (CAFM). Current spatial information systems are associated with data types, operations, and integrity constraints. In construction, they follow business processes and are constructed over spatial information systems. In the past, users had to choose one of these software packages to accomplish the task at hand. To design water pipes inside a building, the engineer used a CAD package. After construction, the building owner used a CAFM product to schedule maintenance. Outside the building, the utility company used an AM/FM package to model the water-pipe network. A GIS product might be used to keep track of the land easements in which the pipe is buried. But if a water main were to break, which system could be best suited to identify the pipe in question?[5]

Spatial information provides a significant benefit to traditional nonspatial applications. Progress in standardization and database vendor support for spatial data management at the database level helps overcome

---

[5] Tiboni, Frank, "NASA Develops Software to Assist Nation's Air Traffic Controllers," *Government Computer News,* October 12, 1998, p. 13(1).

many of the issues that previously prevented spatial information from proliferating in traditional information systems.

RECOMMENDATION FOR THE FUTURE

DIA must concentrate on efficient handling of the bond debt. They must consider if and when refinancing might prove worthwhile. If service to DIA should decrease, steps would need to be taken to ensure that revenue could be generated to cover bond interest payments. Technology can help identify and control costs throughout the airport.

CASE QUESTIONS

Strategic Questions

1. What is the strategic direction of the organization?

2. What forces are driving this direction?

3. What has been the catalyst for change?

4. What are the critical success factors for this corporation/organization?

5. What are the core competencies for this corporation/organization?

Technological Questions

6. What technologies has DIA relied on?

7. How successful has the technological change been?

Quantitative Questions

8. Will DIA be able to service its debt?

9. Are there long-term risks to the financial health of DIA?

Internet Questions

10. Does the DIA web page reflect DIA's strategic mission?

11. Who is the DIA web site geared to serve?

Industry Questions

12. What challenges and opportunities is the industry facing?

13. Is DIA oligopolistic or monopolistic or competitive?

14. Does the industry face a change in government regulation?

FEDERAL AVIATION ADMINISTRATION

Executive Summary

Case Name:	Federal Aviation Administration
Case Industry:	Government
Major Technology Issue:	Implementing the type of technology that will handle the growing air traffic safely
Major Financial Issue:	Keeping the costs of the restructuring at bay
Major Strategic Issue:	Making sure that the technology used to solve today's problems can handle the demand that it will face in the future
Major Player/Leaders:	FAA Administrator David R. Hiason
	FAA PICS-21 Program Manager Jeff Yarnell
Main Web Page:	www.faa.gov
Case Conclusion/Recommendation:	The agency should begin to act more like a business in devising solutions for the issues it faces. Performance criteria should be set and required to be met by the different private contractors. Furthermore, the agency could vastly improve the performance of its systems by going digital.

CASE ANALYSIS

INTRODUCTORY STORY

"Doctors said no one could have lived through the collision that turned the two aircraft into twin fireballs, incinerating the planes before they hit the ground near this town of 50,000 residents. Wreckage and baggage were strewn across six miles. Wearing handkerchiefs and mufflers around their noses, searchers walked shoulder-to-shoulder across the fields."[1] These were just a few of the sights and sounds of the aftermath of a tragic crash in New Delhi, India, in November 1996. Two planes collided in midair, killing 349 passengers.

What causes two planes to collide in midair? All planes are required to fly at least 300 meters apart. Somewhere there was an error. The United States depends on the Federal Aviation Administration to "provide a safe, secure, and efficient global aviation system that contributes to national security and the promotion of U.S. aviation."[2] If the FAA is efficient and does its job, such accidents should not occur in the United States.

SHORT DESCRIPTION OF THE COMPANY

The following is a list of the areas on which the FAA focuses[3]:

Air Navigation and Air Traffic Control This is historically the primary function of the FAA. Employing people in a large variety of specialties, the FAA has developed various navigational aids as well as an air traffic control system. Crucial to civil aviation, this air traffic control system keeps planes at a safe distance from one another while in flight. The FAA is responsible for maintaining several facilities as well as sophisticated computers, radars, and communication equipment for the ever-increasing amount of air travel.

Certification, Regulation, and Compliance The agency sets standards for all facets of the air travel industry including certification and training for pilots, maintenance workers, air traffic controllers, and flight service specialists; standards for aircraft manufacturers, carriers, and airports; and continued improvement and maintenance standards for all aircraft. Aircraft are subject to periodic inspections and "airworthiness directives" to ensure that they are continually maintained in a safe condition.

---

[1] "Judicial Inquiry Called to Investigate New Delhi Crash," *Associated Press*, November 12, 1996.

[2] "Agency Mission, Vision, and Values," *Federal Information Exchange*, November 8, 1994, p. 2.

[3] "FAA Advisor," *Flying*, March 10, 1999, v. 126, n. 3, p. 59.

Aviation Security The FAA regulates aviation security to maintain a safe air travel environment. The agency has many security policies for airport safety, sets standards, and approves potential security plans for airports. The FAA acts as a partner with law enforcement officials to prevent criminal activity and to investigate both in the United States and overseas.

Environment, Growth, and Support for Aviation The agency is continually making progress toward safer and more environmentally sound air travel. This includes sound as well as air pollution. The FAA also provides development grants to state and local governments for installation of navigation aids, purchase of rescue equipment, and acquisition of land for alternative airport sites to reduce noise. The agency works closely with the International Civil Aviation Organization (ICAO) to establish worldwide safety standards and exchange information on current technology and strategy.

Research and Development Programs The FAA has developed the National Airspace System (NAS) plan to maintain its world leadership. NAS works to improve facilities, terminal control systems, and ground-to-air surveillance and communication. The agency is also taking a step forward using computer simulation to analyze and reduce delays and increase safety given the higher volume of traffic. FAA's research includes studies into airborne windshear detection systems and new ground-based radar technology that warns pilots of meteorological hazards.

SHORT HISTORY OF THE ORGANIZATION

As long ago as 1926, the U.S. government took responsibility for regulating and controlling civil aviation. Throughout this century, the FAA has faced many obstacles ranging from a turbulent aviation industry to governmental stalemate and budgetary concerns. To better understand the FAA and its functions, it is important to look at an historical overview, [4] the environment in which the agency operates,[5] and current issues and reform affecting the FAA. Refer to Figure 12.4 as you read the following paragraphs.

In May 1926, the Air Commerce Act authorized the first federal regulation of civil aviation. Originally, the secretary of commerce was given the responsibility of controlling air commerce, certifying pilots and aircraft, establishing airways, and investigating accidents. To carry out the mandate, the Secretary of Commerce es-

tablished a new Aeronautics Branch. In 1934 the Branch was renamed the Bureau of Air Commerce to carry out these duties. In December 1935, the airlines began to establish air traffic control centers. By July, 1936 the bureau took over control of these centers. It was not until 1938 that the bureau, renamed the Civil Aeronautics Authority, began to regulate the economics of the airlines. At this point, the federal government took control and established itself in its role of influential player in the aviation industry.

After the reorganization and formation of smaller agencies, the Federal Aviation Act of 1958 called for the establishment of the Federal Aviation Agency. The FAA was to be an independent agent giving sole responsibility for all aviation industry functions including civil and military navigation and air traffic control. The FAA took over all of the duties of the Civil Aeronautics Administration and the safety rulemaking duties of the Civil Aeronautics Board. In 1996, the Department of Transportation Act authorized establishment of the Department of Transportation. This Department pulled together 31 different agencies in the transportation segment. The FAA became part of this alliance, renaming itself the Federal Aviation Administration.

The political environment plays a huge role in where the FAA is today and how it will progress and succeed in the future. The technical advances in the industry are the primary driving forces for current and future FAA products. The 1990s have brought larger planes to the skies. This calls for improved runways, larger gates, and better flow of passengers through terminals. New aircraft are also much faster and fly at a higher altitude than the old. These enhancements place greater pressure on the air traffic control system. Aviation advances guide the direction of the FAA.

In addition to the increased variety of aircraft, the financial environment also factors into FAA activity. In recent years, the airline industry has suffered. Although the FAA does not have direct influence on the business cycle, its decisions can greatly affect industry costs and consequently impact the type and quality of the services provided. With the reorganization of much of the airline industry, the United States has seen many mergers. By 1994, most small carriers were victims of bankruptcy and had virtually collapsed. Changes in the market greatly impacted the services the FAA provided. Industry volatility constantly challenged the FAA to stay ahead of the needs of their present stakeholders.

In addition to market concerns, a major influence on the industry is international and political unrest. Major events around the world like the Gulf War have a huge impact on the economy and, in turn, on the aviation industry. Political upheaval causes many challenges in terms of security. With technologically and chemically advanced weapons, terrorists have made air security a

---

[4] Information regarding the historical overview was found as a part of the *Federal Information Exchange,* March 29, 1994, on the World Wide Web.
[5] Information regarding the aviation industry environment was found on the *Federal Information Exchange,* April 24, 1996.

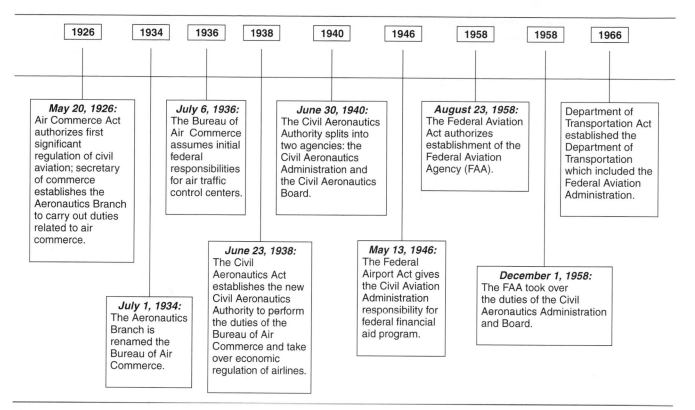

Figure 12.4 The Federal Aviation Administration historical time line.

huge issue. The FAA is forced to predict and address any weaknesses in airport and airplane security.

FINANCIAL AND PORTFOLIO ANALYSIS

The FAA has many responsibilities; the most important is the air traffic control and navigation function. A recurring theme when under media scrutiny is the inadequacy of the FAA's technology. When considering investments in technology, the largest concern is financing. Budget uncertainties have made it difficult for the FAA to accomplish long-term planning.

Larry West, a spokesperson for the FAA, was quoted as saying, "As you have a steadier financing package, it's easier. Every year, we have to go back to Congress, propose a budget, then wait to see what kind of money we get. That makes it hard to carry out a system as large and complex as the air traffic control system."[6]

According to FAA management, the procurement process is the reason why a much-needed air traffic control modernization project has been significantly delayed. In 1995, Congress passed a reform bill that freed the FAA of its old regulations and procurement policies. The FAA is now financed by user fees while continuing to be under the jurisdiction of the Trans-

portation Department.[7] The FAA believes that this reform will provide more budgetary stability and help the agency advance faster technologically.

Senator William V. Roth (R–Del.) said that the General Accounting Office "found the FAA's problems are not the procurement or personnel laws, but a lack of adequate management."[8] When the proposal for the bill was presented to Congress, it was not widely accepted. Throughout the discussions of the reform bill, one issue was always debated: Is the procurement process causing financial difficulties for the FAA, or is it simply a function of poor management and planning?

The reform bill was originally drafted as two separate bills. The Senate bill ultimately passed in August 1995 with some argument from a small group of senior senators. Nevertheless, it was passed by the Senate. In October 1995, the amendment to the Transportation Department Appropriations Bill was accepted by the House. The amendment required the FAA to develop a new buying and personnel strategy by December 31, 1995 and implement it by April 1, 1996. This amendment gave the FAA power to control its own acquisition

---

[6] "Congress Weighs FAA Reform Options," Government Computer News, October 16, 1995, 14, n. 22, p. 63(1).

[7] "FAA Freed from Constraints on Buying, Hiring," *Government Computer News*, November 13, 1995, v. 14, n. 24, p. 3(2).

[8] "Senate Would Free FAA from Pesky Rules," *Government Computer News*, August 21, 1995, v. 14, n. 17, p. 80(1).

spending. Under the plan, the acquisition funding will come primarily from charging a fee to users of FAA services.

The FAA has pioneered two major projects that have been detrimental to their financial stability. The first is the Advanced Automation System (AAS). By 1995, AAS was five years behind schedule and $3 billion over budget.[9] This project received a lot of attention because there were publicized equipment failures due largely to an aging air traffic control system.

Another project that has become grossly expensive is the security system in the nation's airports. Because the air traffic industry was in such a hurry to implement highly effective security systems, each airport developed its systems independently with almost no duplication in hardware or software. These systems are incompatible with one another. The FAA must continue to upgrade, maintain, and replace a number of systems. This project was expected to cost $211 million, but will end up costing more than $654 million. This amount will be shared by the FAA, airports, and airlines. Projects like these were neither analyzed for cost effectiveness or run through pilot programs.

Many FAA representatives believe the amendment will solve the problems; however, there are still those who believe that there are more serious issues within the agency that need attention. George L. Donohue, procurement chief of the FAA, said, "We're not going to be so naive as to think that if we just remove the federal acquisition laws, everything will be all right with the FAA. What we have is an acquisition problem, not a procurement law problem."[10] Donohue blames the problem on the institutional behavior of the agency. The FAA has responded to the critics by identifying a model upon which to base its modernization program.

In 1995, the FAA ran a $34.5 million pilot project that provided them with feedback for a new approach to the bidding process. The FAA instituted a competitive environment using a contractor prequalification process and heavily weighing past performance as a means to reduce the number of bidders. The FAA called the plan their "Acquisition Management System."[11] The new procurement system heavily incorporates the ideas and reform goals from Vice President Gore's National Performance Review to make the federal government buy products the same way private businesses do.

The FAA went from making huge billion dollar purchases at one time to making small incremental purchases as needed. Specifically in regard to technology, the new system included "open architecture, module design, standard interfaces, and portable software."[12] This system attempted to standardize all the technology within the agency. The agency formed teams called "Integrated Product Teams" (IPTs).[13] When the FAA accepts a bidder for a project, the IPT assembled for the project is placed in charge of every aspect of the project. The IPT decides the scope and method of the procurement, how the goods will be purchased, the source for selection, and the type and importance of the evaluation criteria. When the IPT decides to make a purchase, it will make a public announcement, probably over the Internet. The IPT will also issue a "screening information requirement" (SIR).[14]

Risk Analysis

Mehler has developed a list of common risk factors[15] that often plague technology implementation. These risk factors can be used to outline some of the FAA's weaknesses and help identify suggestions for improvement.

Complex Business Change The FAA has been in the midst of complex business change in recent years. Besides being in a dynamic industry, the FAA has experienced more change in management operations in the last two years than any other period in its history. Given its position as a federal agency, the FAA should consider its turbulent environment as a major risk factor.

Contractors (Hidden Failures) The FAA has many large dollar contracts in place. Implementing technology is a time-consuming and costly process for any business. The FAA began a spending surge after being released from the federal procurement process. The dollar amounts of the contracts as well as the number of different contractors the agency is currently employing should be considered a risk factor for the FAA. The FAA should develop a process to funnel projects so that one contractor can provide many services. This will eliminate the learning curve from taking on new contractors.

Inexperienced Staff Air traffic controllers are highly qualified professionals as are the pilots that they control. Just like any other business, cost cutting can be troublesome. As the FAA continues to rely on system-based controls, they should consider the quality of personnel. This does not pose a present risk; it could be a problem as operations continue to change.

[9] "FAA Procurement Chief Says Exemption Is No Panacea," *Governmental Computer News*, December 11, 1995, v. 14, n. 26, p. 56(1).
[10] Ibid.
[11] "FAA Creates Teams to Manage Procurements," *Small Business Press*, March 25, 1996, v. 4, n. 6.

[12] Ibid.
[13] Ibid.
[14] Ibid.
[15] Mehler, M., "Reining in Runaway Systems," *Information Week*, December 16, 1991, v. 351, pp. 30–34.

Leading Technology Despite the plans the FAA has as a result of its new Acquisition Management System, the current technology is archaic. While implementation is in effect, the current system must continue to carry and control air traffic. This should be considered a risk factor. The FAA needs to keep its systems updated on an ongoing rather than a need-to-change basis.

Insufficient User Involvement In a recent GAO report,[16] researchers presented a study of the efforts to integrate human factors research into the FAA's activities. The study concluded that human error contributed to about 80 percent of all air crashes. The study of human factors as it relates to the FAA aims to reduce human errors in aviation accidents. It will concentrate on different types of training as well as on how well systems designed around human factors can decrease the likelihood of fatal air accidents. When an organization designs systems, it is essential that the end users of the system feel comfortable using them.

Setting Goals The FAA has improved over the last year in updating its goals and objectives to include deadlines and realistic timetables. The first stage of AAS was originally targeted for 1996. The project has been changed, reorganized, unfunded, and refunded. This is common with FAA projects. Large projects in any bureaucratic organization can be very difficult. The FAA has aggressive timetables for every project. By setting attainable goals and using committees, like the IPT teams working on acquisitions, the FAA can get a better handle on expenses. The FAA should consider making its goals for completion and action steps public. This will motivate its project teams to meet its time deadline. It will also develop a sense of accountability for those participating in the project teams.

Lack of Senior Management Oversight With the use of so many contractors in the modernization project, it is essential that there be management oversight through every phase. The FAA could possibly set up incentive plans or other types of recognition programs to reward executives. The agency should implement best practices to oversee projects and integrate many different contractors.

ROLE OF RESEARCH AND DEVELOPMENT

In today's world, society is heavily dependent on technology to improve productivity and safety. Technology difficulties have become the major risk factor in the air traffic control system.

Outdated technology poses huge risks for air traffic control. To ensure safe air travel, the FAA needs to develop technological products that have the capacity to support new aircraft, increased traffic, and more sophisticated weapons detection equipment. The FAA is currently running out-of-date systems. These systems have caused a risk in their traffic environment.

TECHNOLOGICAL STORY

The FAA systems are generally considered to be outdated and unsafe. Gary Duffy, overseer of computing for the Chicago Air Route Traffic Control Center, says the present 9020E computer is old and needs to be replaced. Yet, he claims it is still safe.[17]

Some of the most amazing changes in airline technology have impacted cockpit operations. Air-to-ground communication, including both position and other relevant data, was transmitted through radio reports. The pilot told the control tower the information over the radio. The message would have to travel through four transmission systems before reaching the air traffic controller.

Today, communication technology is based upon digital interface. Presently, planes have about 400 different sensors that report the status of everything including oil pressure, engine temperature, position of control structures, and tail structure on the aircraft.

TECHNOLOGICAL INVESTMENT AND ANALYSIS

According to a *Government Computer News* article in August 1995, "The Federal Aviation Administration will spend $65 million on Band-Aids."[18] The truth of the matter is that the FAA has had big plans to overhaul its air traffic control system. Its largest project so far has been the Advanced Automation System (AAS). AAS is the FAA's air traffic modernization project that ideally would address all air traffic control difficulties from the en route segment to digital tower control.

The first stage of AAS was scheduled to be implemented in 1996. The project remains years behind schedule and over budget. AAS is being designed to integrate all air traffic control data onto a single workstation for the controllers. Currently air traffic controllers are using a mix of manual and automated plane and weather tracking systems. This makes the process extremely labor intensive and cumbersome.

Because the AAS is delayed, the FAA has not been able to implement new technology fast enough to prevent breakdowns. Air traffic controllers are currently operating on IBM 9020E machines to process radar

---

[16] "Human Factors—Status of Efforts to Integrate Research on Human Factors into FAA's Activities," GAO Report, June 1, 1996, p. 49.

[17] "Data Takes Flight," *LAN Magazine,* March 1996, v. 11, n. 3, p. 107(5).

[18] "FAA to Spend $65m on Stopgap Replacements for Old Computers," *Government Computer News,* August 7, 1995, v. 14, n. 16, p. 3(1).

data from the aircraft. These machines, as well as most of the other air traffic systems, are more than 30 years old. Several of the FAA's machines are run on vacuum tubes and punch cards.

Many risks are involved with using these outdated systems. The controllers are well trained on these systems. As volume continues to increase, system failure becomes a greater concern. The FAA has faced serious outages in major markets with these systems. These outages often occur when the Display Channel Complex (DCC), the center's mainframe computer that processes data into images displayed on a screen, shuts down.[19] An outage can occur when any of the systems in the long line of processors malfunctions.

According to the FAA, outages simply cause the controllers to depend on backup systems. Safety is never an issue.[20] However, outages cause long fight delays as well as air traffic difficulties. The longer these systems are in use, the more frequent the outages will be and the longer it will take to repair them. These are serious problems facing the FAA that must be addressed as soon as possible.

A second technology issue is airport/aircraft security. Due to bad planning and panic, implementation of airport security processes has proven to be costly and inefficient. Following the crash of Pan Am Flight 103, the industry was in a hurry to enhance airport security. The result was many different independent systems developed haphazardly by the airports. These included features such as electronic screening of passengers and crew, secured doors with electronic ID card readers, video monitoring, and various computer systems to track employee security clearances.[21] Because these functions were independently generated, most of the systems (hardware and software) were incompatible with one another.

Because of the sense of urgency following Pan Am 103's crash, the FAA was unable to run pilot programs to test cost effectiveness. Maintaining these expensive systems, which many experts feel are not performing effectively, continues to be the responsibility of the FAA. These cost concerns are a major issue for the FAA, given continuous financial difficulties and delays in advancing their technology. The FAA will be forced to upgrade/maintain these systems while new ones are being developed.

The FAA does have a current plan to deal with risk management. The FAA is developing a sophisticated risk management plan using Akela's Security Analysis Support System (Sassy).[22] This software uses customized parameters to fit a particular organization. It is applied in other federal government agencies. Akela is currently compiling information based on area expertise and knowledge to develop a product that will aid the FAA to assess risk areas in all types of security operations. The software can help to develop new strategies, evaluate possible options, and simulate potential threats. With the implementation of this software, the FAA can identify risks and formulate plans to address these risks in a timely and cost-effective manner.

A few key systems are instrumental in transmitting information from aircraft to controllers on the ground.

Aircraft Monitoring System (ACMS) The function of ACMS is to compile all the data from the various sensors on the aircraft and transmit them to the pilot. ACMS reads present conditions as well as giving the pilot historical data. The pilot can use the historical data to evaluate relative measurements and spot trends. The monitor is also extremely sensitive and can detect engine vibrations undetectable to humans. The information that is collected about the aircraft and the flight is interfaced with the systems in place at the ground stations. This ground system is called ACARS.

Aircraft Communication Addressing and Reporting System (ACARS) ACARS was introduced in 1976. It was intended to cut down the use of spoken radio messages to transmit information to the ground. It was thought that if the crew could save time by using data to transmit information to the ground, they could spend more time concentrating on flying the plane. ACARS directly interfaces with ACMS and also gives and receives messages directly to/from the pilot. The pilot punches in a message, such as flight plans, in an alphanumeric keypad or touch screen. This message is then relayed to the ground. The ground can also send messages like weather conditions, estimated times of arrival, and assignment updates to the aircraft through ACARS. The tie between ACMS and ACARS is very important, yet there is still another system that connects the airlines, ARINC.

Aeronautical Radio, Inc. (ARINC) ARINC is a system commonly owned by all the domestic airlines that is used to keep in touch with one another. Because all airliners have the ACARS system, ARINC interfaces with this system and transmits messages from the individual ACARS Management Unit on each plane through VHF (radio waves) or satellite to ARINC headquarters. From there the message is received by ARINC's Datalink Ser-

---

[19] "Air Traffic Control—Good Progress on Interim Replacement for Outage-Plagued System, But Risks Can Be Further Reduced," GAO Report, October 17, 1996.

[20] Ibid.

[21] "GAO Finds Spending Out of Control for FAA-Mandated Airport Security," *Government Computer News*, August 7, 1995, v. 14, n. 16, p. 3(1).

[22] "Human Expertise at Heart of Aviation Security System," *Federal Computer Week*, December 18, 1995, v. 9, n. 36, p. 19(2).

vice Processor, which processes and controls the message on the ground. ARINC then searches for which antenna offers the best reception and communication begins. This entire system operates much like a LAN network.

For example, if United Airlines wanted to send a message to any plane, on the ground or in the air, it can enter its message through its ACARS system. The message then goes through the United Airlines host system. It is then transmitted to the ARINC headquarters. ARINC can locate the plane, wherever it is, and send the message to the appropriate ground station. All information must be formatted for ground-to-air transmittal since ARINC must transmit via radio or satellite. The intergration of these systems gives pilots and controllers quick access to almost any data.

The conversion to a completely new system must be done in a way that permits real-time operation. Shutdowns of the air traffic control system are not an option; there must be a system in place to take control while the switchover is made.

The importance of keeping these systems running cannot be underestimated. When a 9020E shuts down, controllers are able to see their air space sectors. They are not able to automatically transfer aircraft to other controllers in control of other air sectors. These transfers must be made manually. The controllers have to write the information on a piece of paper and hand it to another controller.

TECHNOLOGICAL INNOVATIONS

NETWORK

The FAA replaced its system for acquisition management with a distributed architecture. The present system runs on 1980s-era minicomputers at 12 centers nationwide and processes more than 200,000 purchases per year. It was not updated for more than three years and was not year 2000 compliant. Mounting problems in the old system led many FAA officials to revert to paper to track agency purchases.

The new system is called Acquire. It will use Oracle Corporation's Alert software and Discoverer/2000 querying tool. The FAA must also use Oracle Federal Purchasing software to get Acquire to run on a network that links headquarters to regional offices and field centers.[23]

TELECOMMUNICATIONS

The FAA is preparing a communications system overhaul aimed at readying the agency's infrastructure for the 21st century. The FAA Integrated Communications Systems for the 21st century (FICS-21) program will cost an estimated $2.75 billion. FICS-21 will provide ground-to-ground transmission switching and network management control for voice, data, and video communications. The new initiative will replace at least 11 major programs, including FAA-owned networks and leased ones. FAA FICS-21 Program Manager Jeff Yarnell says it is a good time to rebuild the FAA's telecommunications infrastructure because many telecommunications contracts will expire around the year 2000.[24]

RECOMMENDATION FOR THE FUTURE

The goal of the FAA is to make operations a digital system. The air traffic control community wants to use and expand the capabilities of ACARS. The current system is the Automated Terminal Information System (ATIS).[25] All pilots must listen to this broadcast before taking off or landing. The broadcast is a tape that tells the pilot about wind direction and speed, visibility, runways in use, and other information that affects airport operations.

This broadcast was originally on an audio loop tape that the pilot would listen to prior to takeoff and landing. The minute just before landing, however, is busy in the cockpit. Listening to the ATIS can be distracting. By moving the information to a digital format, the pilot can down load it into the ACARS system and then study it when there is more time to concentrate on it.

Expanding the role of ACARS is one of the many stepping stones to the future for the FAA. Currently, due to the new acquisition plan, the FAA has many contracts out for new technologies. Discussion of some of the high-priced contracts/projects the FAA currently has in place includes:

GLOBAL POSITIONING SYSTEM (GPS)

GPS is a satellite-based navigation system that was developed by the Pentagon and previously only available for use in connection with military air travel.[26] GPS allows pilots to navigate based on satellite signals instead of radar signals. It allows real-time flight planning for pilots. As more use of satellite technology becomes available, the integration of air traffic information as well as weather information and other data communication will become a necessary technological step.[27] Four-dimensional GPS readings—longitude, latitude, altitude, and time—allow an aircraft to come within 50 feet of any given target. Encryption technology is currently in place to protect security in the transmission of the satellite messages.

[23] "FAA to Finish Y2K Tests Soon," *Government Computer News,* June 14, 1999, v. 18, i. 17, p. 20.

[24] "Agency Takes Long View on IT," *Government Computer News,* June 14, 1999, v. 18, i. 17, p. 20.
[25] "Data Takes Flight," *LAN Magazine,* March 1996, v. 11, n. 3, p. 111(5).
[26] "Clinton Approves Commercial Use of GPS," *Newsbytes,* April 1, 1996, p. NEW04010028.

STANDARD TERMINAL AUTOMATION REPLACEMENT SYSTEM (STARS)

"STARS is the next big step in the FAA's comprehensive effort to upgrade air traffic control facilities across the nation. The new system will provide the platform for improvements to handle the ever-growing volume of air traffic safely and efficiently well into the 21st century," said FAA administrator David R. Hinson.[28] STARS will standardize all air traffic control equipment at up to 172 FAA facilities as well as 199 Department of Defense facilities. STARS will supply new hardware and software to these facilities. The program will provide complete replacement for the aging systems currently in use. Display transmission will be the most important feature of the STARS program.

ARTS, the system currently in place, was developed in the 1970s and 1980s. The FAA believes that interim programs can extend ARTS life somewhat in the short term. It is generally accepted that this system does not have the capabilities to take air traffic into the next century. ARTS software contains various versions and languages that are very labor intensive as well as expensive to support.

The STARS program consists of a commercial standard system that the FAA believes will be much cheaper and easier to maintain. A key feature of the system is that one can extend the capacity of the system without engineering basic architecture. By essentially relying on commercially available software and hardware, the time to acquire the software will be cut down significantly while maintenance costs should also be much lower than those of ARTS.[29]

COMPUTED TOMOGRAPHY DETECTION SYSTEM (INVISION CTX5000SP)

This new technology[30] is designed to detect explosives in checked baggage. Existing technology is designed to spot objects that people may bring on the plane that are obviously threatening like guns or knives. Currently, checked baggage is not even scanned. CTX5000SP is an automated x-ray system that uses the CAT scan technology from the medical field. CTX5000SP first does a prescan of the object and points out areas of interest. It then takes slices from the identified area as well as some random slices and makes a three-dimensional view of the slices. It can also display a full three-dimensional image. The console fits the slices together and alerts the operator, projecting the image and location of the object in the luggage by highlighting it in red. CTX5000SP was developed in response to the crash of TWA Flight 800 in Summer, 1998.

The FAA awarded this contract to InVision Technologies for $52.2 million. InVision will supply from 54 to 100 explosive detection systems set to be installed later in 1997.[31]

WIDE-AREA AUGMENTATION SYSTEM (WAAS)

WAAS is a system that is used in conjunction with GPS.[32] Using a network of 36 ground stations to "distill" satellite GPS signals, WAAS will enable commercial aircraft to pinpoint a location within seven meters. With the use of WAAS/GPS, the FAA hopes to close many of its ground control centers and allow pilots to fly more direct routes. These mechanisms are all a part of the vision of "free flight."[33]

FREE FLIGHT

Free flight is an ideal that the FAA is working to make a reality in the near future.[34] Free flight would enable pilots to control their own navigation procedures like never before. Pilots would use the WAAS and GPS systems for navigational purposes and choose their own routes, speed, and altitude. Ground support will be kept to a minimum. Pilot flexibility will be hindered only when flights are in congested airport areas, when flights approach restricted air space, or if safety is at stake.

Two principles that drive the free flight plan are the protected and alert air space zones. The sizes of these zones are determined based on aircraft speed, performance characteristics, and communications, navigation, and surveillance equipment. The protected zone is the zone closest to the aircraft. No aircraft should meet the protected zone of another aircraft. The alert zone is one that extends far from an aircraft's protected zone. The distance between planes will be monitored closely. If an instance occurs when a plane touches another plane's protected zone, the pilots and the air traffic controllers will determine if course corrections are needed. Under the free flight system, no interference will occur until alert zones collide.

---

[27] "The Sky's the Limit," *Federal Computer Week,* December 4, 1995, v. 9, n. 35, p. S14(4).

[28] "FAA Selects Raytheon for Next-Generation Air Traffic Control System Upgrade," FDCH Federal Department and Agency Documents, September 16, 1996, p. 16.

[29] "FAA Is Set to Begin Initial Phase of STARS Rollout," Government Computer News, June 14, 1999, v. 18, i. 17, p. 22.

[30] "InVision CTX5000SP," *Business Wire,* December 26, 1996, p. 41.

[31] "Airports to Beef Up Bomb Detection; It's Unknown Where Devices Will be Installed," *Sun-Sentinel,* Fort Lauderdale, FL, December 28, 1996, p. 19C.

[32] "FAA Confirms Wilcox as $475M WAAS Winner," *Federal Computer Week,* August 7, 1995, v. 9, n. 22, p. 3(1).

[33] Sweetman, Bill, "Free Flight—The Future of US Air Traffic Control," *Interavia,* October 1, 1995, v. 50, n. 594, p.39.

[34] "FAA Ready for Free Flight," *Advanced Transportation Technology News,* April 1996, v. 2, n. 12.

CASE QUESTIONS

Strategic Questions

1. What is the strategic direction of the organization?

2. Who or what forces are driving this direction?

3. What has been the catalyst for change?

4. What are the critical success factors for this organization?

Technological Questions

5. What technologies has the organization relied on?

6. What has caused a change in the use of technology in the organization?

7. How has this change been implemented?

8. How successful has the technological change been?

Quantitative Questions

9. What does the agency say about its financial ability to embark on a major technological program of advancement?

Internet Questions

10. What does the agency's web page present about their directives?

11. How does this compare to what is actually being done by the FAA?

12. How does this compare to the conclusions reached by analyzing the financial information?

Industry Questions

13. What challenges and opportunities is the industry facing?

14. What type of environment does the agency have to operate in?

15. Does the industry face a change in government regulation?

16. How will technology impact the industry?

Data Questions

17. What role do data play in the future of the agency?

18. How will the capture and maintenance of customer data impact the FAA?

TECHNOLOGY TIPS

MICROSOFT WORD TIPS

INSERTING BREAKS

Changes that you make in one section of your document will affect the whole document. Margin adjustments, column settings, fonts, line spacing, or almost any other setting can be limited to one section of the document by inserting a break. Insert the breaks at the beginning and end of the section to which you to want to limit the settings.

Page Break

A page break may be useful when you want to start a new segment, such as a chapter, at the top of the next page. This can be done by placing the cursor at the end of the page that you want to insert the page break and press CONTROL + ENTER.

Using Insert from the Toolbar

There are different types of breaks available. The insert break dialog box from the toolbar will give you a brief explanation of each and allow you to apply them. For an explanation of a particular break, click on it with the right mouse button while in the dialog box.

Column Break Between Columns

1. Place the cursor where you would like to insert a break.
2. From the toolbar click on INSERT. Now click on BREAK . . . from the drop-down menu.
3. A dialog box will appear. To stop a column from continuing to the next column, click on COLUMN BREAK, then click on OK.

Column Break Between Pages

1. Place the cursor at the end of the rightmost column.
2. From the toolbar click on INSERT. Now click on BREAK . . . from the drop-down menu.
3. From the dialog box click on PAGE BREAK. Then click on OK.

ADDITIONAL NOTE

Having Columns on Only One Section of the Page

If you want to format only one section of your page in the column format, you must insert a CONTINUOS break at the beginning and end of the columns. If you already have your columns formatted, just insert a CONTINUOS break at the end of the rightmost column. The columns format that you used for the previous section will still be in effect for the new section. However, to remove these presets use the COLUMNS dialog box for a new format.

MICROSOFT EXCEL TIPS

ABSOLUTE REFERENCES AND USING THE FILL HANDLE

As demonstrated in the previous chapter, copying formulas is simply a matter of copy and paste. However, if you do not want references to change when you copy a formula to a different cell, use an absolute reference. Absolute reference cells are helpful when you have several formulas located through-out your worksheet or workbook that need to use the same variable. An example of a variable can be unit price, feet per second, cost per unit, or discount rate. By creating a separate worksheet that contains all these important variables, and using absolute references to these cells, you can update the formulas for an entire worksheet from one location. The alternative is to locate all the formulas and update them individually.

Making Absolute References

There is only one thing that makes absolute references different: a dollar sign ($). Placing a dollar sign in front of the section of the cell address that you do not want to change is all it takes to make it a permanent part of the function. Simply write your formula as explained in the previous chapter and insert the dollar sign ($) in front of the cell address that you would like to make an absolute reference. In the following example the function in the Sales worksheet has a dollar sign in front of the column *and* row number for the cell address in the Variables worksheet. Whenever this formula is copied the 'Variables!B20' section of the formula will not change. Only the first part of the formula will change since it is using a relative cell reference.

	A
1	=Sales!B34*Variables!B$20
2	

`|◀ ◀ ▶ ▶|  Variables ⟍ Sales ⟋ Sheet5`

Using the Fill Handle to Copy Formulas

The copy and paste function works fine for copying formulas, but there is an additional feature that will allow you to quickly copy a formula to adjacent cells that have related data: the fill handle. The fill handle was briefly introduced in Chapter 2 to copy data. This section will demonstrate how the fill handle can be used to copy formulas.

1. Click on the cell that contains the formula to be copied
2. Notice that the lower right corner of the cell contains a small black box. This is the fill handle

Fill handle

3. Place the mouse cursor on the fill handle and notice how it changes to a cross when the cursor is held over the fill handle. To make use of the fill handle click on it and drag the handle to the cells you wish to copy the formula to.

4. The cells that will have the formula copied into them will be framed. Release the handle once you have highlighted all the cells that you wish to copy the formula into.

You will notice that the formulas copied into the other cells will have relative references according to the way you moved the fill handle. In the example shown the fill handle was dragged down and all cells under cell B34 from the Sales worksheet were used in the formula. Also, notice that the cell used from the Variable worksheet remains the same in all the formulas. This is because of the dollar sign used to make it an absolute reference in the formula above.

	A	B
18		
19		
20	unit price	$ 30.00
21	15day disc. rate	0.2
22	30day disc. Rate	0.1
23		
24		

`|◀ ◀ ▶ ▶|  Variables ⟍ Sales ⟋`

	A	B
33		
34		45
35		35
36		34
37		33
38		21
39		

`|◀ ◀ ▶ ▶|  Variables ⟍ Sales ⟋`

	A	B
1	$ 1,350.00	
2	$ 1,050.00	
3	$ 1,020.00	
4	$ 990.00	
5	$ 630.00	
6		
7		

`|◀ ◀ ▶ ▶|  Variables ⟍ Sales ⟋`

Microsoft PowerPoint Tips

Object Linking and Embedding

Use a linked object or an embedded object to add all or part of a file created in an Office program, or in any program that supports linked and embedded objects, to another file. If the file you want to use was created in a program that does not support linked and embedded objects, you can still copy and paste information from the file to share the information between programs.

The main differences between linked objects and embedded objects are where the data is stored and how it is updated after you place it in the destination file. With a linked object, information is updated only if you modify the source file (i.e., graph in Excel). Linked data is stored in the source file. The destination file (i.e., graph in PowerPoint copied from Excel) stores only the location of the source file and displays a representation of the linked data. Use linked objects if file size is a consideration.

With an embedded object, information in the destination file does not change if you modify the source file. Embedded objects become part of the destination file and, once inserted, are no longer part of the source file. Double-click the embedded object to open it in the source program.

Why would you link objects? Linking objects will allow you to update information in all files that are linked to the source file (i.e., Excel spreadsheet). This provides you with the latest information in your linked files and saves you time from updating each linked file.

Note: Both the source file and the destination file must be accessible while working on them in order for the updating to take place. For example, if you copied from the source file located on the hard drive to a diskette and then work on the destination file (diskette) on a different computer, your files will **not** be updated.

Linking Objects

Whenever you copy something from another file and you want to link it, do the following:

1. After copying the object (i.e., graph, spreadsheet, word document), go back to the slide in the presentation.
2. Click on EDIT and select PASTE SPECIAL from the drop-down menu. The paste special dialog box on the right will appear.
3. If the object supports linking you will be able to choose from PASTE or PASTE LINK. Select PASTE LINK and the file you want to insert into your presentation.
4. Click on OK. The object will appear on your presentation. Whenever you update your source file the object in your presentation will be automatically updated.

Embedding Objects

Follow the above steps, but select PASTE in step three instead of PASTE LINK. This will allow you to insert the object without a link.

Break a Connection to a Linked Object

1. Click on EDIT and select LINKS from the drop-down menu.

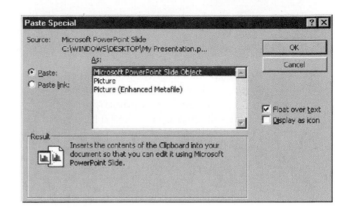

2. In the LINKS box, click the linked object you want to break the connection to. To select multiple linked objects, hold down the CTRL key and click each linked object.
3. Click on BREAK LINK.

Note: After you break the connection to a linked object, you must insert the linked object into your document again to reconnect the link.

Microsoft Access Tips

Creating Reports Using Report Wizard

By now you should be familiar with how the wizards operate by working with them in the other chapters. Reports can also be created using the wizards, and they will help you in presenting your information about the database to others. Think about who will be reading your reports and how the tables are linked when creating your report. Several reports can be prepared and will be ready for your use in the database window.

Using Report Wizard

1. From the database window click on the REPORT tab.
2. Click on the NEW button and from the pop-up menu click on REPORT WIZARD. Choose table or a query from which you will create your report. Click on the drop-down arrow and select the table or query. Click on OK when you have completed your selection.
3. The following window (not shown) allows you to pick which fields from different tables you would like to include in your report. Once you are done selecting the fields that you would like to appear on your report, click on the NEXT button.
4. In the following dialog box (next dialog box down), you can determine the levels in which you would like to display your data. If you decide to break the report down in levels, click on the field that you would like to group by and click on the right arrow button. Notice that the layout of the form will change depending on the fields you have selected. To further determine how you would like to sort the data click on the GROUPING ORDER button. Click on the NEXT button when you have finished organizing the levels.
5. The next dialog box will depend on the choices made in the previous window. If you elected to show your report in levels, you will be prompted by a dialog box that will

allow you to determine the layout of your report. Otherwise, the dialog box that will appear will be the one at the bottom of the page, which allows you to set the order in which the records will appear on the reports. Click on the NEXT button when you are satisfied with the order.

6. The rest of the windows involve the appearance of the report. Click on the different options that you want, name the report, and click on the FINISH button to generate the report. The report will appear in the print preview window of the dialog box on the right.

The report will be available to you in the database window under the REPORTS tab. Select the report you want to see and click on the PREVIEW button. To print out the report just click on the print button while the report is being viewed in the print preview window.

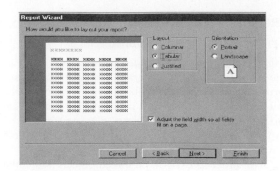

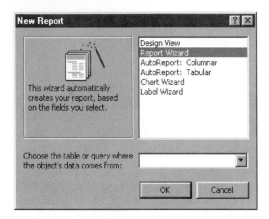

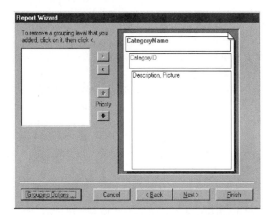

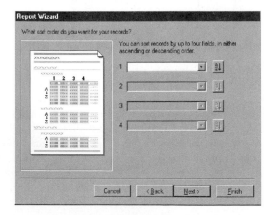

MICOSOFT FRONT PAGE TIPS

SAVING POWERPOINT AS HTML

As you may have already guessed, converting a PowerPoint presentation over to HTML is also handled by a step-by-step process. However, you will have some more input when saving a PowerPoint presentation.

Preparing Your Presentation for the Web

1. With your presentation open, click on FILE from the menu bar.
2. Click on SAVE AS HTML from the drop-down menu.
3. The SAVE AS HTML dialog box will appear. Click on the NEXT button to begin the process.
4. Make your selections at the different steps and continue to click on NEXT. You can always click on the BACK button to make changes in the previous window.
5. Once you have reached the final window, just click on FINISH and your presentation will be converted for you.

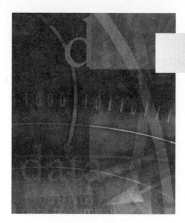

CHAPTER 13

ORGANIZING INFORMATION SYSTEMS RESOURCES
FINANCIAL SERVICES INDUSTRY

Organizing Information Systems Resources

The never-ending struggle between centralization and decentralization has not bypassed MIS. In the past few years, the trend toward decentralization has been more pronounced. This trend has placed additional work on MIS departments built on legacy systems in highly centralized companies. MIS decentralization can occur in areas such as personnel, hardware, software, and data. Due to the increased affordability of personal computers (PCs), many companies have moved to a client/server approach. This approach applies PCs to bridge the gap between centralization and decentralization while capturing the benefits of both. Advantages of centralization include economies of scale (in hardware), easier upgrades and compatibility (in software), increased control over access and sharing (in data), and easier training and hiring of specialists (in personnel). Advantages of decentralization include low prices of PCs (in hardware), increased flexibility (in software), easier access and personal control (in data), and faster and more personal response time for users (in personnel).

Some companies find it better to outsource part or all of their computer function. While this can have benefits such as access to computer specialists and enables a company to focus on its primary business, it may not be the best route for companies facing complex market structures or where there is a great need for specialized talent or extremely high security requirements.

Hardware Since PCs cost substantially less than main frames (about 1000 times less per processing second), they provide substantial cost advantage in the work environment.

Centralization Advantages: Centralization makes it easier to share hardware, software, and data. It also makes it easier to control access to data with less duplication.

Decentralization Advantages: Decentralization diminishes the chance for a total breakdown. Equipment can be personalized and the hardware is usually much cheaper.

Client/Server Advantage: In a client/server environment, the hardware is the most distinctive feature. The benefits of each extreme can be realized, such as centralized concurrency and security controls of data. Peripherals can be more personalized by residing in the "client" or PC.

Software Each setup has advantages.

Centralization Advantages: Centralization results in cheaper cost on a per-user basis, with fewer compatibility problems.

Decentralization Advantages: Decentralization provides more flexibility for end users in what software they use and faster access to software residing on the individual workstation. Support and configuration software applications can be integrated.

Client/Server Advantages: This arrangement can provide advantages by maintaining some software on the server and some on the individual "clients" (PCs).

Data

Centralization Advantages: These include the ability to easily share data with all users, control access to the data, and make a backup file.

Decentralization Advantages: Users have better and faster access to the data. They know where and how the data are organized. Control over the data is important.

Client/Server Advantages: Shared data resides on the server, while more personal data, such as electronic mail or documents, can be sent to the client.

MIS Personnel This aspect of MIS can also be centralized or decentralized.

Centralization Advantages: Working together with other MIS workers can lead to team efforts and faster solutions to complicated problems. This also provides more diversified career path opportunities.

Decentralization Advantages: The MIS worker is closer to the end users and more familiar with a group's particular needs. This approach, however, is usually more expensive.

Client/Server Advantages: A comparable approach would be to have an MIS staff take care of the servers and the issues that surround them. Placing IT personnel throughout the organization assists the "client" end users. The "scattered" employees can also help develop new client solutions for a group's or individual user's particular needs. Another approach is to implement a Help Desk. Users call a central number for all computer problems. A technician is dispatched to that location if the problem cannot be resolved over the phone.

Peer-to-Peer System Another method of balancing centralization and decentralization approaches is the peer-to-peer system. With PCs becoming increasingly more powerful, this approach follows the viewpoint that any computer can be a server, a client, or both. PCs can be linked to allow for this. This method gives more flexibility in storing and accessing data. It can also become cumbersome in terms of management and difficult to make a backup.

Object Orientation While decentralization works well with an object-oriented approach, it also becomes much harder to manage objects in a decentralized or distributed environment. The object orientation approach has occurred much more in PCs and the UNIX platform. Developing graphical user interfaces and finding distributed or decentralized data is easier if the data are stored in objects. Problems often occur when object definitions are different across computers.

Outsourcing and Organization of Information Systems
Many companies are outsourcing their computer operations. This usually means the firm sells their computers to third parties, who take over responsibilities for all of the information technology in a company. Companies adopt this approach for many reasons, including the desire to change to a client/server approach when the company does not have the resources or expertise to move into this area, the temporary cash flow from the sale of their systems, the ability to concentrate on the strategic focus of the business if the IT function is outsourced, and lower operating costs. Outsourcing is not for every company. Even if outsourcing is viable for a company, it must be carefully analyzed, both financially, managerially, and strategically.

Financial Services Industry

DESCRIPTION OF THE INDUSTRY

The financial services industry is typically divided into banking and nonbanking organizations. Services overlap between these divisions in many different ways. Some of the services offered include, but are not limited to:

- Consumer loans such as home mortgages, home equity loans, auto loans
- Personal and business lines of credit, especially profitable "sub-prime" credit risks
- Credit card and related credit card loss and life insurance
- Purchase warranties and service guarantees generally offered with appliances and home electronics
- Equipment leases
- Investment management services
- Mutual fund management
- Multiple-line insurance
- Financial planning, including tax preparation and related services.

FINANCIAL ANALYSIS

The financial services industry has witnessed a stunning 18.8 percent median sales growth from 1992 through 1996. The year 1996 ended with an 18.4 percent increase over 1995. Profitability figures for 1996 reflected a median return on equity of 21.6 percent, compared to the overall United States industrial return of 13.0 percent. Median net income for financial service companies in 1996 amounted to $265 million per company. The United States industrial return overall was $86 million per firm.

The returns for the industry in 1996 were due to a steady interest rate environment, low inflation, and respectable gains in personal income. Lending spreads to sub-prime customers increased, also increasing income.

Even though credit card delinquencies and bankruptcies have been rising, many finance companies have witnessed a 50 percent increase in credit loans. Typically, sub-prime loans offer stronger growth opportunities and are more profitable than traditional loans or mortgages. Disposable income increases ranging between 4 to 6 percent annually have continued to bolster the industry.

Personal bankruptcies have reached more than 1 million annually; reserves have been increased industry-wide (Figure 13.1). Though delinquent credit cards have reached as high as 3.66 percent, industry insiders expect this to be reduced with better management of credit card portfolios.

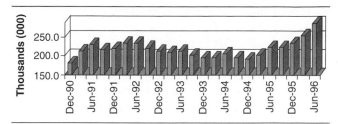

Figure 13.1 Personal bankruptcy filings (Chapters 7, 11, 13). (*Source:* Administrative Office of U.S. Courts.)

STOCK/INVESTMENT OUTLOOK

The financial services industry outperformed broad market averages from 1990 through 1998. The years 1997 and 1998 have been most stellar. For 1996, EPS grew by 21.5 percent, compared to the entire U.S. industry of 6.4 percent.

Although trailing price-to-earnings ratios average about 15, industry analysts cannot find anything to be skeptical about as long as the economy remains robust, propelled by strong loan growth. In 1996, eight consumer finance companies went public. Their stock prices rose an average of 40 percent after doing so.

The financial services industry tends to have many high-risk firms. Beta coefficients are higher than market averages. It is certainly a risk if lower creditworthy borrowers fall on hard times. In a sinking economy, financial firms, especially those specializing in uncollateralized loans such as credit cards and personal lines of credit, may suffer. If the economic downturn of the late 1980s in the real estate market was an indicator, highly leveraged finance companies could also be crippled by an extreme housing slump.

POTENTIAL/PROSPECTIVE FOR GROWTH

As previously mentioned, the favorable interest rate environment and low inflationary pressures have positioned the financial services industry well for the beginning of the new millenium. Although credit concerns could hurt some highly leveraged companies such as mortgage or credit card specialists, sizable spreads

Word	W.1	Envelopes and Labels Additional Notes	Creating a Label Envelopes Creating a Mailing List for Labels and Envelopes
Excel	E.1	Functions	What are Functions Exactly? Selecting Functions
PowerPoint	P.1		WordArt Modifying WordArt
Access	A.1	Saving Forms as Reports Reports Out of Forms	
Front Page	I.1	Saving FrontPage Files for Output to the Web Additional Note About Static and Dynamic HTML Format	Export a Data Sheet to Static HTML Format

built into such sub-prime businesses make disastrous losses less likely.

Additionally, this industry is known for consistently developing new and innovative products. The GM Card made its debut in 1993. It offered rebates on the purchase of GM cars based on levels of credit card use. It proved to be a successful innovation in a crowded credit card industry.

COMPETITIVE STRUCTURE

The financial services industry is highly fragmented and very competitive. Recently, there has been significant bank merger activity. Consolidation is a means of increasing efficiency, service levels, and product depth. It is also a way to spread back office costs over a larger product base. Not only do the money center banks compete with the growing super-regional and other large commercial banks, they also compete with non-bank institutions providing financial services.

The industry's innovations have threatened traditional banks, yet banks are far from relinquishing their market share to finance companies. With the banking industry whittling away at the Glass-Steagall Act, an act which restricts banking activity, banks will soon be muscling into industries such as brokerage and insurance. Some banks already sell insurance with certain restrictions. Banks are increasing their focus on credit card affiliations with airlines and other high-profile industries.

ROLE OF RESEARCH AND DEVELOPMENT

Research in the financial services industry is focused on product innovation and marketing. By looking for new ways to market products, credit card issuers attempt to increase market share and develop new market niches. Many retail stores entering into the credit card business utilize co-branding to help increase market share. Co-branding strategies allow smaller issuers to team up with larger organizations to obtain a competitive advantage.

Another marketing technique for the future involves the Internet. Due to the high costs of current mass marketing campaigns, Internet marketing will become a higher profile medium for advertising and financial services marketing. The challenge for banks in this new distribution channel is to be innovative, effective, and targeted.

TECHNOLOGICAL INVESTMENT AND ANALYSIS

Strategic advances in this customer service-oriented industry are propelled by technological innovation. Tech-

nological improvements have aided banks in their efforts to control expenses while providing better customer service. Electronic banking through phone lines, automated teller machines (ATMs), and personal computers gives customers improved levels of service by offering 24-hour banking at convenient locations.

Many financial services firms have utilized enormous phone banks to provide customer service. The customer service representatives often have instantaneous access to large customer databases with the ability to provide credit approval, status, balances, and the maintenance of accounts.

RECOMMENDATION FOR THE FUTURE

To take a lead in the competitive financial services industry, financial institutions must focus on leveraging technology and seizing opportunities that arise from regulation changes. It will also be important to consider strategies for a global market and for the consolidation and integration going on in the industry. There is no doubt that the financial services industry will continue to outperform other industries. The ones that strive to reduce their administrative costs will be the most successful.

Technological and regulatory forces are pushing the industry toward greater consolidation and product integration. Critical to the financial success of firms will be their level of investment in technology and the ability to achieve cost savings. Finance is increasingly becoming a global rather than a national industry. The reliability of instantaneous telecommunications and the convergence of economies around the world increases the importance of a global focus for successful financial services firms.

INDUSTRY WEB SITES

Financial Services Industry
www.aba.com/aba/About ABA/homepage.asp
www.bankers.asn.au/
www.cba.ca/
www.cbanet.org/
www.e-banking.org/
www.takecreditcards.com
www.napainc.org/

AMERICAN NATIONAL BANK

Executive Summary

Case Name:	American National Bank (ANB)
Case Industry:	Financial services
Major Technology Issue:	Choosing the technologies that will allow ANB to cut costs
Major Financial Issue:	How to increase profit margins
Major Strategic Issue:	Which newly unregulated opportunities to explore
Major Players/Leaders:	William Elliot, chief information & technology officer
Main Web Page:	www.anbchicago.com
Case Conclusion/Recommendation:	ANB needs to cut costs in its noncore functions and outsource more of its information systems functions.

CASE ANALYSIS

INTRODUCTORY STORY

First Chicago Corporation acquired American National Bank and Trust Company in May 1984. This acquisition was the result of First Chicago Corporation's growth strategy. First Chicago was committed to diversifying both sides of its balance sheet, with particular emphasis on the consumer and middle markets, largely in the Midwest. At this point, First Chicago Corporation was the 12th largest bank holding company in the United States, and the largest in Illinois and the Midwest.

American National Bank and Trust Company of Chicago has been quite successful over the years. The bank's primary customers consist of midsized middle market retail corporations with yearly sales between $5 and $150 million. American National Bank has distinguished itself by focusing on its customers better than its competitors, which include Bank of America and the Northern Trust Company.

SHORT DESCRIPTION OF THE COMPANY

American National Bank is a subsidiary of First Chicago NBD. It has historically been a middle market bank catering to smaller business customers. Its operations are presently being merged into the parent company's systems. It would appear that the name of the bank will be merged into its parent as well.

SHORT HISTORY OF THE COMPANY

The year 1933 was a year of turmoil. That year the U.S. president declared a bank holiday, Hitler came to power in Germany, and the world was in the grip of an economic contraction. On December 4, 1933, American National Bank opened for business at LaSalle and Washington Streets in Chicago with capital funds of $1,400,000 and deposits totaling approximately $13,000,000.

The company showed a consistent growth in deposits and capital funds (Figure 13.2) at a time when the nation was recovering from the great depression and the people in the nation were actively involved in the war raging in Western Europe. By 1942, deposits exceeded $100 million for the first time. Noteworthy was the formation of the American National Safe Deposit Company, organized in February 1943 to purchase the vaults from the Trust Company of Chicago.

In 1945, the bank saw a greater expansion in deposits than in any 12-month period. Deposits were over the $200 million level, totaling $228,346,328 at year end, a $49 million increase over the preceding year. During this year, ANB management looked bravely toward a future world where trade between nations would once again be possible. It organized an International Banking Department.

Postwar conditions brought many imbalances to the economy. Industries moved from around-the-clock munitions and armament production to the manufacture of capital and consumer goods. Savings were high because few consumer goods were available during World War II. As appliances, automobiles, clothing, and homes became available, individuals spent accumulated savings and saved at lower rates than previously. During 1946, 1947, and 1948 there was no growth at American National, in accordance with the banking industry as a whole.

Since that time American National Bank continued to grow in every area of operations. The company had tremendous growth in customers, employees, services offered, income, and deposits. Along with the growth came the development of new departments and procedures to support the organization.

Year	Deposits	Capital Funds
1933	$13,000,000	$1,400,000
1935	$35,530,804	$2,402,569
1938	$57,000,000	$2,968,343
1941	$91,000,000	$4,365,142
1950	$277,377,324	$10,699,941
1954	$326,360,899	$13,414,878
1958	$400,000,000	$18,193,416
1960	$443,770,389	$22,235,745

(*Note:* 1938, 1941, and 1958 total deposit figures are an approximation.)

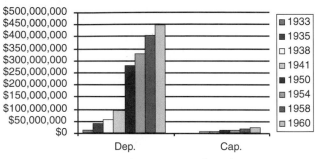

(*Notes:* Dep. = Deposits and Cap. = Capital Funds.)

Figure 13.2 (a) top (b) bottom Total year-end deposits and capital funds for selected years at American National Bank.

One of the improvements the company made was the adaptation of an electronic means to handle millions of checks and deposits. In 1961, an electronic data processing center was developed in the newly purchased ninth floor. In 1962, the entire check handling operation was converted to an automated, electronic system. The conversion was not without its problems. By year-end, the program was working smoothly. No staff were terminated because of this conversion. A number of individuals were transferred to other departments, and still more were extensively retrained to operate effectively in the data processing field.

By December 31, 1962, American National's deposits had grown to $513,699,262. This was mainly because government regulations increased the legal limit banks had to pay on savings deposits to 4 percent per year. As a result, customers increased their savings account deposits at American National Bank. In 1963, an additional computer was ordered to handle an increase in check volume. In August 1966, the bank purchased Tel-A-Data Corporation, a data processing center providing modern online customer account service for correspondent banks and savings and loans associations.

During 1968, the bank joined the growing network of bank credit card issuers through its entry into the

MasterCharge system. In the mid-1970s overseas expansion continued with offices established in the Cayman Islands, Hong Kong, West Germany, Canada Columbia, Peru, Mexico City, Holland, Brazil, and Singapore. The bank's Trust Department commanded worldwide attention and recognition, with its innovative investment strategy techniques, its pioneering concept of indexing, and its practical use of modern investment portfolio theory.

Critical to American National's success has been the following factors:

- Knowledgeable, personalized service
- Stable, long-term relationships
- Credit availability
- Convenience, offering most services customers need when and where they need them
- A dedication to customer service, both external and internal
- Providing customers with high-quality services and products

Over the years, the company's main logo has been "We serve thousands of people, but we serve them one at a time." With this theme, the bank allocates certain officers for customers. The officers deal with customers on an individual basis to meet specific needs.

Critical to American National Bank's success has been its location in downtown Chicago. This location put the company in a position to conveniently offer its services to midsize corporations in a wide range of industries. This helped American serve a diversified marketplace.

FINANCIAL AND PORTFOLIO ANALYSIS

American National Bank derives its income from several sources. One generator is fees on products and services. Establishing the proper fee to charge customers for products and services is vital to the profitability of American National Bank. ANB also derives income from interest received on loans, time deposits, funds sold, trading account assets, and investment securities.

As a subsidiary of First Chicago NBD, ANB is positioned to increase its middle market share. As First Chicago continues to merge with other midwest banks, the parent company increases its consumer products volume and at the same time increases American National's midsize business accounts volume.

In July 1996, First Chicago moved 30,000 consumer and small business accounts from American National Bank to First Chicago. Following this move, First Chicago NBD also moved midsized business accounts from National Bank of Detroit and the community Bank Group to American National Bank so that ANB could focus on its specialty area.

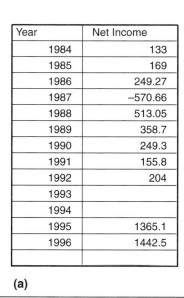

Year	Net Income
1984	133
1985	169
1986	249.27
1987	−570.66
1988	513.05
1989	358.7
1990	249.3
1991	155.8
1992	204
1993	
1994	
1995	1365.1
1996	1442.5

(a)

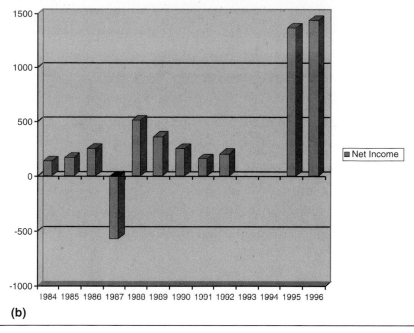

(b)

Figure 13.3 Spreadsheet analysis of First Chicago NBD net income in million of dollars.

A close look at net income for First Chicago NBD (parent company of ANB) reveals that the company has experienced a steady increase in net income (Figure 13.3). The plunge in 1987 and first quarter 1988's net income was the result of a $1.1 billion write-off and associated tax benefits. The great increase in net income in 1995 and 1996 was the result of the merger between First Chicago and the National Bank of Detroit.

The quick, current, and receivable turnover ratios have held steady (Figure 13.4). Although First Chicago has been able to increase its market share through mergers, the corporation has not been able to collect on outstanding loans at a faster rate.

Table 13.1 shows First Chicago NBD Corporation's ranking position among 37 Midwest banks in 1995. Looking at the ranking of First Chicago for 1995 within its region, it is clear that the corporation ranks highest in revenues, deposits, and assets. Furthermore, the corporation also ranks very high in net income and net loans. However, the corporation does not rank high in return on assets, profit margin, and price-to-earnings ratio.

The corporation's high ranking in revenue, deposits, and assets is due to the recent mergers. The low ranking in return on assets and profit margin indicates that while the corporation has substantial assets at its disposal, it is not utilizing its resources to their fullest potential to generate income. It is also clear that the corporation is not profiting from its operations compared to other banks within the region.

STOCK/INVESTMENT OUTLOOK

In recent years, the banking industry has experienced an increase in mergers between large and small banks. The banking industry today does not allow small banks to compete effectively with larger banks. This is because the smaller banks do not have the capital resources to penetrate the market as easily as larger banks, which have capital resources to spend on technology.

The merger of First Chicago and smaller banks such as American National Bank is an example. Based on the changing nature of the banking industry, the driving force in the near future will be the convenience that a particular bank offers.

Table 13.1 First Chicago's Rank

Performance Base	Rank
Revenues	1
Deposits	1
Total assets	1
Net income	2
Net loans	2
Yield	9
12-Month price score	18
Return on equity	20
7-Year price trend	25
Return on assets	30
Profit margin	32

Key Annual Financial Ratios	12/31/96	12/31/95	12/31/94
Quick ratio	1.11	1.11	1.11
Current ratio	1.11	1.11	1.11
Sales/cash	0.34	0.23	0.17
Receivable turnover	0.16	0.17	0.16
Net sales/working capital	0.84	0.95	0.87
Net sales/property & equip.	7.15	7.51	6.59
Net sales/current assets	0.11	0.1	0.08
Net sales/total assets	0.1	0.09	0.08
Total liab./total assets	0.91	0.93	0.93
Total liab./common equity	11.17	14.26	14.58
Net inc./net sales	0.14	0.11	0.14
Net inc./total assest	0.01	0.01	0.01
Net inc./investment capital	0.08	0.07	0.08
Net inc./common equity	0.17	0.14	0.17

(a)

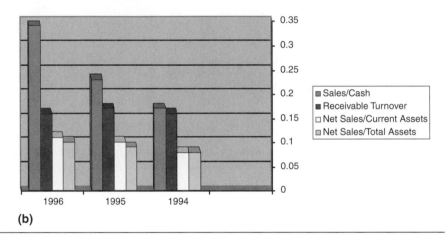

(b)

Figure 13.4 Key ratios for First Chicago.

Bank stocks are predicted to grow but at a slow and gradual rate, excepting mergers.

RISK ANALYSIS

For many years, the Federal Reserve has been concerned about payment system risk. It has recently taken action to reduce that risk by charging for daylight overdrafts. Banks recognize four basic types of payment system risk.

1. *Operational.* Operational risk is the risk of sustaining a loss as a result of errors, omissions, or a catastrophic occurrence.
2. *Fraud.* Fraud risk is the risk of loss from altered transactions or other acts perpetrated by individuals for fraudulent reasons.
3. *Credit.* Credit risk is the risk of loss from the inability of a party to a transaction to settle for the transaction.
4. *Systematic.* Systematic risk is the risk that the inability of a member of a settlement system to settle a transaction will cause others banks of the system

to fail. Payment system risk must be addressed and dealt with by bank management. Failure to take preventive measures today could result in substantial losses in the future.

INDUSTRY AND MARKET ANALYSIS

The banking industry system in the United States has developed over the past 200 years. Generally, the industry has been slow to change. Major developments in the banking system have come about as a result of reaction to crisis. The industry has gone from a totally decentralized and unregulated system to one of the most regulated and controlled segments of the economy.

The Federal Reserve Act of 1913 was passed to address the weaknesses of the National Bank Act. This Act established the Federal Reserve System and solved problems like pyramiding of reserves and the lack of a check collecting system. Twelve Federal Reserve districts were formed to establish a nationwide check collection system. Reserves were maintained in the Federal Reserve banks. The inflexible currency problem was solved by the distribution of the Federal Reserve note, which still constitutes the nation's basic currency.

During the depression, banks were allowed to underwrite securities issues and pay interest on demand deposits. In 1933 Congress passed the Glass-Steagall Act, which established significant controls on banks. The Act prohibited the payment of interest on demand deposits, and did not allow banks to underwrite stocks or invest in common stock. It authorized the federal government to control bank loans for securities and established the Federal Deposit Insurance Corporation (FDIC).

The restrictions on the banking industry continued to tighten from 1933 until 1980. Then Congress passed the Depository Institutions Deregulation and Monetary Control Act. The act allowed banks to compete more evenly with nonbank competitors by lifting some restrictions. The Garn-St. Germain Act was passed in 1982 with the intention of allowing banks to be more competitive in the area of additional mutual funds.

The decrease in government regulation and the recession in the early 1980s caused additional banking problems. Savings and loan organizations (S&Ls) entered the commercial banking business. S&L's inexperience with nonmortgage loans led to significant write-offs and ultimately widespread failure of many S&Ls.

In 1989 Congress stepped in to avert a total disaster by passing the Financial Institution Reform, Recovery and Enforcement Act (FIRREA). FIRREA completely restructured the S&L insurance and regulatory agencies by reforming and consolidating the federal savings and loan insurance system. In 1991, Congress fine tuned FIRREA by passing the Federal Deposit Insurance Corporation Improvement Act (FDICIA). FDICIA provided additional funds for failed banks and S&Ls and changed the direction from deregulation toward regulation.

As a result of the FDICIA, financial institutions are required to meet new safety and soundness standards, including operational and managerial standards, officer and director standards, and compensation standards. Financial institutions must perform assessments to determine their credit exposure to correspondent banks. Restrictions are also placed on state-chartered banks by prohibiting them from engaging in activities that are not allowed by national banks. The FDICIA includes consumer provisions that require financial institutions to comply with new truth-in-savings laws limiting brokered deposits activity. These limitations have further restricted competition in this industry.

The National Bank Act allows banks in towns of fewer than 5,000 people to sell insurance products. Taking advantage of this provision, some banks have attempted to offer insurance products on a nationwide basis. They have met resistance from the insurance industry. The United States Supreme Court has ruled that the National Bank Act provision authorizing the sale of insurance in towns of fewer than 5,000 people is still valid today. However, the Court has not addressed the issue of whether a bank located in a town of fewer than 5,000 residents may sell insurance in a town of more than 5,000. The federal district courts have reached different conclusions on the issue. Until the Supreme Court examines the issue, the conflict will remain. In the meantime, financial institutions may sell credit life and health insurance incidental to making loans.

Changes in banking technology allow banks to offer new products and services and help them streamline their operations. Imaging technology decreases processing time. This provides banks with the opportunity to significantly change the way they process work. File folder imaging enables banks to eliminate a great deal of paper. It also provides bank employees instant access to information. Image Proof of Deposit (POD) reduces some of the labor-intensive aspects of processing checks. It may ultimately reduce reliance on the physical transactions around check processing.[1]

The financial service industry is further limited when it comes to making investments in technology. Technology investments need to be supported by high margin products; however, for the most part, the products from financial institutions have low margin returns compared to most other industries.

ROLE OF RESEARCH AND DEVELOPMENT

American National Bank is presently taking a great interest in technology, particularly as it relates to finding and serving the customers it has targeted.

TECHNOLOGICAL STORY

ANB implemented the Vector digitized systems (Vector-Kite and Vector-Signature) to improve its ability to detect and address customer fraud.

When the Vector-Kite system was acquired, the hope was that the kite[2] system would enable the bank to pinpoint those customers who intended to defraud the bank. So far, the system has not been able to pinpoint customers with the full intent to defraud the bank. Rather, the system shows that most customers of the

---

[1] Davis, Beth, "'Shared Vision' Makes IT Pay Off—Banks Increasingly Rely on IT for Customer Service and in Company Communications—So Planning Is Key," *Information Week*, September 14, 1998, n. 700, p. 93(1).

[2] Kiting is the process of attempting to draw against uncollected or nonexisting funds for fraudulent purposes. A depositor issues a check, overdrawing an account at one bank, and deposits into that account a check drawn on insufficient or uncollected funds at another bank.

bank are kiting suspects. This is because the system is limited in its ability to evaluate the float[3] time involved in a check traveling through the banking system.

The Vector-Signature system was acquired with the intent to decrease the time required to verify checks and detect fraudulent activity. This goal has not been completely achieved. One benefit is that the bank no longer uses huge rolodexes of signature cards. Since these signature cards are in the Vector system, staff members can get signature images from their PCs through the Vector system. Although this system does save time, it is also problematic. The software application shuts down frequently when making the transition from one signature image to another.

Meanwhile, the support staff for the software have moved to other projects which include CIS ECIS/DDA, SAP, intranet applications, and year 2000 compliance. As a result, the Vector system has not provided as much efficiency and effectiveness as was expected. Staff members within the unit did not have to undergo training sessions since the software is easy to use.

TECHNOLOGICAL INVESTMENT AND ANALYSIS

Over the years, American National Bank has not been a pioneer in making technological changes in the banking industry, preferring to remain in the background of technology advancement in the banking industry. The acquisition by First Chicago gave American National Bank additional expertise to tap for technological solutions. The company now adopts technology advancements from its parent company. The company has implemented a new mainframe application. It distributes information across the bank through local area networks.

In February 1996, a group of people representing the newly merged corporation (First Chicago NBD) convened to assess the implementation of a customer information system and a consolidated deposits application. They determined that a relationship-based customer information system was critical to maximizing market penetration and customer profitability. Additionally, most of the existing deposit systems within the merged corporation were determined to not meet year 2000 compliance requirements.

As a result, First Chicago NBD selected both the Hogan DB2 Customer Information System for enterprise-wide use and the Hogan Demand Deposit Accounting System for use in the Corporate and Institutional Banking Area and at American National Bank. Since the Hogan software was already used

within the bank's retail and middle market environments, it was easier to implement on a broader scale.

The Information Systems Department at First Chicago NBD is currently working on the following projects:

1. Systems Application Products (SAP) implementation. SAP is a purchased system that is used for general ledger reconciliation processes. Staff members in these units were given workstations with the application and three to seven full-day sessions to learn how to use the SAP system.
2. Windows-Based Standard. The corporate goal was to make Windows the bank-wide standard by the end of 1997. In conjunction with this, the IS unit set up training schedules to train employees on the best way to obtain the most benefit from Windows applications.

The Information Systems Department at American National Bank is divided into subunits according to projects being worked on, divisions in the bank which they support, and the type of programs being developed. For the most part, staffing is flexible. This allows staff members to rotate and move from old projects onto new ones.

During the last six months of 1999, the information systems department concentrated on making its computer programs year 2000 compliant. The recent mergers of NBD and First Chicago have also set priorities in terms of working on programs that will facilitate lines of communication across the whole organization. The corporation has increased the number of staff members in the Information Systems Department to meet these two goals. Because of the significance of these changes, they are being overseen by a corporate Implementation Team. Figure 13.5 shows the flowchart for the Implementation Team.[4]

Note also that William Elliott, CIO at First Chicago NBD, is also chairman of a steering committee for the implementation team. Table 13.2 lists the members of the steering committee.

The sheer size of the systems at First Chicago has resulted in outsourcing not being embraced by either American National Bank or its parent corporation. However, American National Bank has outsourced some of its operations. When the corporation decided to upgrade and update its Deposit Accounting Department, it purchased software packages required to accomplish this task rather than build the application in house. In addition, when the company was ready to scan signature images into the signature system, it outsourced this function.

---

[3] Float is the dollar amount of deposited cash items that have been given immediate, provisional credit but are in the process of collection from a drawee bank. Float is also called uncollected funds.

[4] Cole-Gomolski, Barb, and Fusaroand, Roberta, "Lessons Learned the Hard Way: Customer Service Requires Integrated Systems, *Computerworld*, December 21, 1998, p. 20(1).

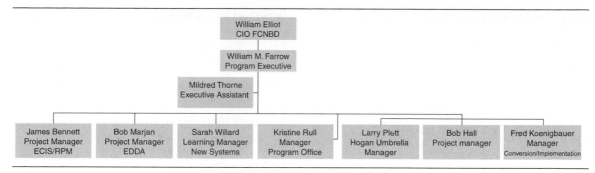

Figure 13.5 Technology implementation team.

Table 13.2 Members of Steering Committee

Members	Position
William Elliott (chair)	Chief Information & Technology Officer
Fred Adams	Head of Retail Banking Services
Dave Bolger	Head, Illinois Regional Banking
Marty Bronstein	Chief Systems Officer (C&IB)
Susan Moody	Head, C&IB Domestic Markets
Bill Valpey	Head, Michigan Regional banking
Judy Feldman	Head of Global Treasury Management (C&IB)
Alan S. Adams	Head of Systems and Operations (ANB)
Jim McCord	Head of Operations
Bob Lee	Head of Banking Products and Services (ANB)
John Skubik	Chief Systems Officer (Retail)
Andy Paine	Head, Indiana Regional Banking

RECOMMENDATION FOR THE FUTURE

American National Bank has grown through acquiring accounts from the parent company after the parent merges with other banks. The corporation has concentrated on mergers. Mergers between First Chicago NBD and other banks increased the assets, market share, and revenue of the organization. In conjunction with this focus on mergers, First Chicago consolidated its operations department with that of American National Bank in December 1998. American National Bank consolidated its vault operation with that of First Chicago in December 1997. As First Chicago integrates its operations, it must continue to focus on cutting costs and efficiently serving the customer in all core and noncore functions.[5]

[5] Caldwell, Bruce, "Cost-Reduction Tactic Now Seen As Strategic Weapon—Outsourcing Mission: Manage, Not Avoid, Change," *Computer Reseller News*, October 12, 1998, n. 811, p. 50(1).

CASE QUESTIONS

Strategic Questions

1. What is the strategic direction of the corporation/organization?

2. Who or what forces are driving this direction?

3. What has been the catalyst for change?

4. What are the critical success factors for this corporation/organization?

5. What are the core competencies for this corporation/organization?

Technological Questions

6. What technologies has the corporation relied on?

7. What has caused a change in the use of technology in the corporation/organization?

8. How has this change been implemented?

9. Who has driven this change throughout the organization?

10. How successful has the technological change been?

Quantitative Questions

11. What does the corporation say about its financial ability to embark on a major technological program of advancement?

12. What conclusions can be reached from an analysis of the financial information to support or contradict this financial ability?

13. What analysis can be made by examining the following ratio groups?

    Revenue
    Profit

14. What conclusions can be reached by analyzing the financial trends? Are there long-term trends that seem to be problematic? Is the industry stable? Are there replacement products?

Internet Questions

15. What does the corporation's web page present about their business directives?

16. How does this compare to the conclusions reached by the case?

17. How does this compare to the conclusions reached by analyzing the financial information?

Industry Questions

18. What challenges and opportunities is the industry facing?

19. Is the industry oligopolistic or competitive?

20. Does the industry face a change in government regulation?

21. How will technology impact the industry?

Data Questions

22. What role do data play in the future of the corporation?

23. How important are data to the corporation's continued success?

24. How will the capture and maintenance of customer data impact the corporation's future?

FIDELITY INVESTMENTS

Executive Summary

Case Name:	Fidelity Investments
Case Industry:	Financial services
Major Technology Issue:	How to use the latest technology to improve customer service, provide a competitive advantage, and cut costs
Major Financial Issue:	Fidelity needs to regain lost investment money flowing out.
Major Strategic Issue:	Should the company cater to the retail or 401(k) market?
Major Players/Leaders:	Edward Crosby Johnson III, Chairman
Main Web Page:	www.fidelity.com
Case Conclusion/Recommendation:	As the size of Fidelity's funds make it difficult to compete aggressively, Fidelity must leverage its customer service and marketing skills to capture the 401(k) market.

CASE ANALYSIS

INTRODUCTORY STORY

Edward Crosby Johnson III walked to 82 Devonshire with more on his mind than usual. It was the first day of winter in Boston, and he was evaluating his company's performance for the year. As the chairman of Fidelity Investments, the company was "his" because of his formal position of authority. It was also his because the Johnsons owned most of the privately held company, worth billions.

Most of all, Fidelity was Ned Johnson's because he had made the right decisions for Fidelity with remarkable regularity, building the firm into the world's largest mutual fund company, with over $400 billion in managed assets. It seemed fitting that Ned walked to work; it reflected his puritanical background and hatred of waste. Even though he had known wealth his whole life, a Brahmin sense of stewardship guided his behavior at all times, even when he managed other people's money.

The headlines from throughout the year passed through his head again and again. "Magellan Had Near $1 Billion Outflow in July," "Lagging Fidelity Investments Launches Customer-Service Tour," "Fidelity after the Earthquake," "The $400 Billion Behemoth from Boston Has Started to Slip," "Can Ned Johnson's Famous Money Machine Get Back into High Gear?" In a banner year for the stock market, Fidelity's funds had consistently underperformed. There was of course the public relations problem with former Magellan manager Jeffrey Vinik, who had been accused of manipulating stock prices, not to mention competition from hungrier, more agile competitors making a bid

for the number one spot. It had not been a stellar year at Fidelity.

As Ned made his way to the office, he began to think practically. What were the issues facing Fidelity over the long term? Observers were correct to remark that "Johnson is 'a sucker for a good idea.' Fidelity's hottest new idea was to leverage its massive technology infrastructure."[1] Johnson's primary goal was to serve the customer, through high returns on their investment, quick access to information, and efficient administration of their accounts. Technology was an important tool, perhaps *the* tool, for establishing a service edge over the competition. It was not an end in itself. As the president of Fidelity Systems, Albert Aiello asserted that system objectives must flow from business objectives.[2]

Ned quietly entered 82 Devonshire, flashing a forced smile to fund managers as he made his way to his office in the corner of the top floor. He passed rooms full of young analysts and continuous streams of stock quotes, thinking about the weak performance of the past year. Ned was reminded of the unpredictability of investments. There was no widget-making flowchart that could guarantee Fidelity a good product in the investment sense. For Ned, the essential question became, how can we satisfy and grow our customer base in the face of volatile financial markets?

---

[1] Collins, James, "The Money Machine," *Time,* September 30, 1996, v. 148, p. 46.

[2] Rao, Srikumar S., "Network Assets Value: The Fine Art of Continually Upgrading Aging Computer Systems," *Financial World,* December 5, 1995, pp. 75–77.

SHORT DESCRIPTION OF THE COMPANY

Fidelity Investments is a mutual fund powerhouse. It sells mutual funds for nearly every sector of the stock and bond markets. It offers other complimentary products like 401(k) plans and some of its proprietary technology.

SHORT HISTORY OF THE COMPANY

The history of mutual funds is one of frequent innovation. Pinpointing their birth is made difficult because mutual funds have developed over time. The first identifiable strain of today's mutual fund is most likely the British investment trust. Begun in the early 1870s, these trusts were marked with early difficulties. Intended to pool several investors' money in order to enter the stock market, trust managers frequently deceived the public and hoarded profits for themselves.[3]

Investment trusts operated like any other company, except their business was trading securities instead of manufacturing lamps or selling food or distributing car parts. They sold common stock that had a market-determined value, unlike today's mutual funds. As an investment vehicle, they had the same appeal as stock and not much more; although they provided diversification, the benefits did not flow through directly to shareholders.

British-type investment trusts and various related companies had some success in the United States in the early part of the century. It was not until Edward Leffler sold the idea to the Boston brokerage firm of Learoyd, Foster & Company in 1924 that the first American-style mutual fund was established. Leffler's Massachusetts Investment Trust was intended to be "a pooled investment vehicle that was professionally managed, that was diversified to reduce risk, that kept its costs 'within tolerable limits,' and that would redeem its customers' shares at any time."[4] It was on this formula that the Johnsons built their Fidelity empire.

The history of Fidelity and the Johnson family are tightly intertwined. The Johnsons were associated with the town of Milton, Massachusetts, which today "remains an enclave of wealth and privilege, whose leading residents hold by birthright a lofty place in the caste system of nearby Boston."[5] Although they were Mayflower descendants, the Johnson clan originally made their fortune in retailing, as opposed to being professionals. This paved the way for Edward Crosby Johnson II, born around the turn of the century, to take the family into a new field of business.

Around the time he finished at Harvard, "There were a number of bright, creative young men working on State Street who were fascinated by the possibilities of 'prudent speculation' in common stocks and by the challenge of offering safe ways for average Americans to participate."[6] Beginning as a corporate lawyer, Johnson was familiar with investing only because of the large wealth his family held. He became involved with an investment company called Incorporated Investments in the early 1930s.

In 1943, after leaving his position as an attorney, Edward took over a portfolio called the "Fidelity Fund," ostensibly for the purpose of managing his family's holdings. He quickly opened the fund to the public, focusing on a personalized approach and value investing over the long term. The fund was a modest success, relating mostly to general postwar prosperity and an increasing interest in investing by the average American. As the company grew, investment managers became more aggressive.

While Edward was the quintessential investor, his son Ned was an inventor. Beginning his leadership in the early 1970s, Ned "tinkered endlessly with the company's people and its entire approach to selling funds to the public."[7] Part of Ned's approach was to surround himself with the best people and allow them to initiate new ideas. Unlike the automobile or TV manufacturing industries, in the financial services industry new products can be designed solely through good ideas. For example, Ned had a stroke of brilliance in attaching a check-writing ability to money market funds, which soon boomed.

By the mid-1970s, Fidelity made a foray into toll-free customer service lines and spent millions on computer systems. Fidelity even pulled all bookkeeping functions in house from banks, because Ned "always hated to rely on anyone outside his command."[8] At the same time, Fidelity reached high visibility because of two of their star managers, Gerald Tsai and Peter Lynch. Fidelity cultivated an image as a company "known for its arrogance and aggressiveness," a place that "prefers cocky young managers and gives them independence."[9] It was an attitude that produced consistently high returns.

The 1980s proved to be boom years for Fidelity. By 1986, the entire mutual fund industry was bursting at the seams.[10] Fidelity was at the top of this phenomenal growth, for at least three reasons: (1) The company had a broadly diversified product line, including mutual

[3] Henriques, Frank, *Money's Long History*, Random House, 1989, p. 50.
[4] Ibid., p. 54.
[5] Ibid., p. 37.
[6] Ibid., p. 50.
[7] Ibid., p. 186.
[8] Ibid., p. 270.
[9] Collins, "The Money Machine."
[10] Henriques, Frank, *Money's Long History*, Random House, 1989, p. 271.

funds for almost every sector of the bond and equity markets. (2) Anticipating the importance of computer systems, Fidelity designed a "bullet-proof, completely fail-safe system" to better serve customers.[11] Their technology-driven service, which included the ability to switch investments between funds over the phone, was second to none. (3) Fidelity stopped marketing individual products and started focusing on the Fidelity brand name itself. Some argue that Ned made marketing the heart of Fidelity.[12] In following Fidelity's lead a competitor described the approach: "We're doing what packaged-goods companies do, creating a brand consumers can relate to, understand and identify."

FINANCIAL AND PORTFOLIO ANALYSIS

Although thousands of mutual funds are offered by a wide variety of companies, a few large firms dominate the market. In 1995, Fidelity vastly outsold the competition, bringing in a full 15.7 percent of all sales dollars in the mutual fund industry for the year. The nearest competitor, Vanguard, trailed at 7.9 percent, with the field quickly dropping off after Putnam, American Funds, and Oppenheimer.

By late 1996, Fidelity's dominance had begun to wane. Vanguard broke through to the number one position in the industry for attracting new cash: a leap up to 11.2 percent, followed closely by Fidelity at 10.6 percent. Among its largest competitors, Fidelity had a ten-year return on investment second only to Twentieth Century. The number two spot was maintained on five-year returns as well. From 1994–1996, Fidelity's returns slipped to being third in the business. When just 1996 was examined, Fidelity dropped to number five. This trendline signaled a deteriorating advantage in relation to the competition.

Another means for measuring success is to compare fund performance not against competitors but against the market. From 1994 through 1996 only four of 34 diversified Fidelity U.S. stock funds beat the S&P 500, according to Morningstar; by June, 1997, only one was ahead.[13] Of course, one-year returns could just be a minor fluctuation, which is exactly what Fidelity suggested. Fidelity still manages to be the largest investment fund in the industry by dollars invested by a healthy margin.[14]

An important response to waning fortunes was the reduction of management fees for Magellan. As a sign of good faith, the fee declined from 0.73 percent of managed assets to 0.47 percent. Fidelity spokesman Scott Beyerl justified this linkage between fund performance and management fees. "We think that makes sense for our shareholders. This way our interests are aligned with theirs."[15]

STOCK/INVESTMENT OUTLOOK

Fidelity Investments is privately owned.

RISK ANALYSIS

No matter how good customer service is, a company that manages investments must usually produce respectable returns to maintain its customers' business. Particularly in 1996, as the stock market boomed, Fidelity showed surprisingly weak returns. One trouble spot particularly indicative of the company's underperformance was the weak showing of its largest fund, Magellan. With $50 billion in managed assets, the performance of the Magellan fund is watched closely by many investment sectors.

In an excellent year for stock growth, Magellan returned an annual 9.9 percent compared to a phenomenal 21 percent for the Standard & Poor's 500.[16] In July 1996 alone, nearly $1 billion was withdrawn by investors.[17] In October 1996, investors' withdrawals pushed the available cash in the fund down to a possibly dangerous 1.2 percent of assets. Clearly something was wrong with Magellan, and Fidelity was affected by the bad press: "[A]gainst the backdrop of mammoth Magellan's recent underperformance, more than a few investors were spooked by Fidelity's big funds."[18]

Perhaps the most visible and controversial aspect of Fidelity's reaction to its relatively poor performance was a major reshuffling of fund managers within the firm. Ned Johnson removed 26 equity fund managers from their positions in March 1996, trailing a bond fund manager shakeup nine months earlier. Although reorganizing Fidelity's fund management team was considered to be "one of the most important changes in its history" by some,[19] Fidelity again downplayed its significance.

One of the more significant changes was the departure of Jeffrey Vinik from the helm of Magellan amid

---

[11] Ibid., p. 270.

[12] Ibid., p. 349.

[13] Whitford, David, and Nocera, Joseph, "Has Fidelity Lost It?," *Fortune*, June 9, 1997, p. 58.

[14] Gasparino, Charles, "Vanguard Edges Past Fidelity in Attracting New Cash," *The Wall Street Journal*, October 31, 1996, p. C1+.

[15] Stein, Charles, "Fidelity Reduces Management Fee Charged to Investors in Magellan Fund," *Knight-Ridder/Tribune Business News,* December 12, 1996.

[16] Hirsch, James S., "Magellan's Stansky Put More Money in Stocks," *The Wall Street Journal*, November 13, 1996, p. C1+.

[17] McGough, Robert, "Magellan Had Near $1 Billion Outflow in July," *The Wall Street Journal*, August 13, 1996, p. C1+.

[18] McGough, p. C1+.

[19] Collins, "The Money Machine," p. 46.

bad publicity regarding allegations that he manipulated stock prices. Vinik was considered to be the hottest fund manager at Fidelity before he took over at Magellan in 1992. Vinik "was always looking to catch big market trends" and "was also consumed by arcane technical factors," both downplayed strategies in the investing heyday of Peter Lynch.[20]

Although his differences with Fidelity's traditional trading philosophy were considerable, Vinik's personal trading habits drew the most attention. Fidelity had long accepted that managers would play the market on their own accounts; it was assumed that this activity was indicative of a manager's personal passion for investing. After an SEC tightening of restrictions on personal trading in 1994, Vinik continued to make nearly 500 transactions a year. With regard to personal trading, Fidelity management "never came out and said you can't do it; they just put on more and more restrictions that made it not worth it."[21] As the culture grew more conservative at Fidelity, some saw Vinik's trading as a conflict of interest or a needless side distraction. In the fall of 1995, Vinik publicly praised Micron Technologies, while at the same time selling Magellan's Micron shares.

Charges of unethical behavior began to surface because of this incident, but Vinik's troubles extended beyond his allegedly manipulative practices. In anticipation of a correction in the stock market, Vinik had attempted to move Magellan into bonds to provide a hedge against the volatility of the stock market, especially in the face of the loss of principal. Instead, the stock market boomed in 1996, and Vinik was proven wrong. He was soon replaced by a more predictable Robert Stansky, who slowly moved Fidelity out of bonds. The Vinik episode was another black mark on Fidelity's public relations for the year.

In April 1996 Fidelity removed J. Gary Burkhead from his role as president and CEO of Fidelity Management and Research Company. The company replaced him with Robert Pozen, a lawyer with no investment management experience. Pozen initiated several changes for fund managers. Further, he has removed the administrative aspects from fund managers' jobs so they can focus on investing. He is putting more emphasis on research and expanding the managers' stock ownership program.

Pozen is also forcing managers to invest within the boundaries of their fund's description, a weak point previously exploited by the competition. One of Fidelity's biggest competitors is Putnam, a Boston rival who rolled out an advertising campaign attacking Fidelity's allegedly brazen disregard for fund charters. Fidelity's penchant for allowing fund managers to run their portfolio as a private fiefdom led to most funds being run as equity growth funds, to which Putnam responded, "There are stricter labeling laws for a $2 container of cottage cheese than a $2 billion mutual fund."[22]

The addition of Pozen was intended to look like a response to Fidelity's public relations issues. However, "in typically secretive Fidelity style, everything was assiduously downplayed. Johnson brushed away suggestions that the changes were aimed at stanching the blood before things got any worse."[23]

Despite Johnson's denials, Fidelity remained anxious about its recent apparent decline. Another very visible strategy for regaining the confidence of investors and stemming the outflow of those nervous about Fidelity's performance has been to take the company on the road. In January 1997, Paul Hondros, president of Fidelity's Individual Investors' Group, and Burkhead attempted to comfort investors in New York, Atlanta, Dallas, San Francisco, Chicago, and Boston on a two-week damage control mission. Referring to Fidelity's flagging funds as "problem children,"[24] Hondros argued that the success of the stock market was tightly focused on the top 30 companies; thus Fidelity's diversified funds were not favored for the year.[25]

Some have sensed desperation in this cross-country scramble to rein in doubtful investors. As one expert argued, "Fidelity is part of the issue. They have to come to the recognition that investors are clients and they can choose to do business with them or with someone else."[26] Coinciding with this road show, Fidelity introduced three new ultra-diversified index funds that basically follow the performance of the stock or bond market over time. Competitor Vanguard was successful in this niche; Fidelity conservatively decided to follow suit. One attendee passed off the road show as "just a Public Relations program."[27] Fidelity has decided to run these programs on a regular basis to remain in touch with the investing public.

Fidelity became the premier mutual fund firm by posting consistently high returns. They maintained the brightest investment managers and gave them free

---

[20] Whitford and Nocera, "Has Fidelity Lost It?" p. 66.

[21] Whitford, David, "Is Fidelity Losing It?," *Fortune*, January 13, 1997, v. 135, n. 1, pp. 20–21.

[22] Norton, Leslie P., "Trying Harder: Boston's No. 2 Mutual Fund Firm Makes a Name for Itself," *Barron's*, January 6, 1997, p. F3+.

[23] Whitford and Nocera. "Has Fidelity Lost It?," p. 59–60.

[24] Samuel, Terence, "Lagging Fidelity Investments Launches Customer-Service Tour," *Knight-Ridder/Tribune Business News*, January 28, 1997, pp. 2–3.

[25] Schmeltzer, John, "Fidelity on the Road: The Mutual Fund Company's Troupe Hits Chicago, Hoping to Smooth Over the Lackluster Performance of Some of Its Stars," *The Chicago Tribune*, January 29, 1997, Sec. 3:1.

[26] Ibid, p. 2.

[27] Ibid, p. 2.

reign. Fidelity's claim to supremacy in these areas has justifiably been questioned recently. Fidelity has also distinguished itself in customer service and marketing, with forward-thinking technology decisions.

Ned Johnson has steadily implemented emerging information technology into the service of customers. Johnson "is a techno-junkie who pours more than $500 million a year into making Fidelity a state-of-the-art operation."[28] Other financial firms have even suggested that Fidelity's practice of highly compensating their IT personnel has actually placed an undue burden on competition, because they are scrambling to pay their professionals comparable salaries.[29]

While critics focus on the negative aspects of Fidelity's size, the company derives benefits from this fact as well. When Fidelity is a customer, suppliers have no choice but to be cooperative. Several brokerage houses learned this last year when Fidelity demanded to receive research immediately upon completion. Generally, Wall Street firms do financial research on companies and provide the printed information to their clients, for whom they execute trades. Fidelity saw a chance to pull their significant weight and gain an advantage over competitors: "What Fidelity will do is to try to push the envelope to get some kind of competitive advantage."[30] Fidelity is the largest commission payer and the largest impact player in the stock market. When they want to provide a service, they will do what they can to provide it.

To analyze securities, Fidelity asked Merrill Lynch, Goldman Sachs, Smith Barney, Morgan Stanley, and Donaldson, Lufkin, & Jenrette to enable them to be wired into these securities firms' proprietary modeling systems. Fidelity not only wanted instant analysis, which would provide a basis for portfolio managers to make trades, they also wanted to see how these firms arrived at their analyses. They could best accomplish this by examining the assumptions these firms made in their own models.

Furthermore, Fidelity wanted to interact with these models and to develop their own analyses through the securities firms' own proprietary software. Jack Rivkin, former head of Smith Barney's equity research department, noted that some analysts were uneasy about sharing their secrets with Fidelity employees who would probably not be at Fidelity forever. Ironically, this demand from Fidelity pulls brokerage firms in two directions. On the one hand, they desire to serve their top commission-paying clients with quick access to in-

formation; on the other hand, firms like Merrill Lynch remain in direct competition with Fidelity in the selling of mutual funds.

ROLE OF RESEARCH AND DEVELOPMENT

Like corporations in every other industry, "financial firms feel compelled to market themselves on the internet because all their competitors are going there."[31] In fact, "every one of the top 50 brokerage firms is making some use of the Internet."[32] The most visible sign of Fidelity's commitment to technology is their Internet web site launched in February 1995 (www.fidelity.com). The web page is focused on the approximately 30 percent, and rapidly growing, portion of their clients who own home PCs with modems.[33]

TECHNOLOGICAL STORY

Fidelity's Internet approach was meant to be "more than simply putting out education, but to actually have actionable solutions that investors can use."[34] Fidelity's web page was originally fairly convoluted, with excessive amounts of information presented at the difficult points and more links than the user could handle.

Even the name of the page, the "Online Investment Center," was more hopeful than realistic. Fidelity jumped into the Internet without understanding how it might be useful to their business. Fidelity went into the Internet because they knew everyone else was developing a presence. Ironically, users could not make a single transaction through the Online Investment Center. What was available was reams of information which detailed how to contact people at Fidelity, through old-fashioned means like the telephone, United States mail, and walk-in investment centers.

TECHNOLOGICAL INVESTMENT AND ANALYSIS

INTERNET

In the span of a few months, during 1997, Fidelity completely revamped its Internet service. In doing so, it moved the site from being a confusing information provider to a place where "actionable solutions" could take place. Today Fidelity's web page has become remarkably simplified, yet it seems to provide more information at the same time. Most importantly, investors can now trade online.

---

[28] Wilder, Clinton, "The Money Machine," *Information-Week,* January 8, 1996, n. 561, p. 28(6).
[29] Coffey, Brendan, "Tech Wars: Recruiting and Retaining IT Personnel on Wall Street," *Wall Street & Technology,* December 1996, v. 14, n. 12, pp. 42–44.
[30] McGeehan, Patrick, "Fidelity Asks Firms for 'Instant' Research," *The Wall Street Journal,* August 30, 1996, p. C1+.

[31] Mulqueen, John T., "Financial firms go for 'Net.," *CommunicationsWeek,* June 30, 1997, n. 670, p. 53(1).
[32] Liebmann, Lenny, "Building the Internetwork," *VARbusiness,* March 1, 1997, v. 13, n. 3, p. S9(7).
[33] "Internet Market Strategies: An Invisible Revolution?," *Computer Reseller News,* December 18, 1995, v. 663, p. 134.
[34] "Fidelity Emphasizes Web," *Computerworld,* August 18, 1997, p. 8(1).

From the user's perspective, online trading is relatively simple. First, assuming one is already a Fidelity customer, one obtains a PIN number through a toll-free call. Second, customers must have suitable software, which means a browser that supports 128-bit encryption. This software is available online directly from Fidelity. The company has quickly progressed from having a token presence on the net to operating a viable information and trading tool.

One option of Fidelity's Internet service is real-time access to fund prices, a service also available over the telephone. The $9 million client/server system that provides this service takes a significant step beyond its predecessor. Until 1993, Fidelity used a system that now seems very involved. A Fidelity customer service representative would answer a customer's phone call and pull up the customer's account on a personal terminal. If the customer asked for a quote on the price of a fund or stock, representatives would wait their turn to use a Lazy Susan-like terminal shared by five representatives. Often representatives would have to wait five minutes or more. Once the representative had the use of the terminal, he needed to translate the name of the fund or stock into its abbreviated code through a paper list of codes. Other financial information was halfway across the room.

Fidelity's "Maxxess" system, which replaced the old technology, is considered to be the most sophisticated customer service approach in the industry.[35] According to Fidelity Investment Systems Senior Vice-President Don Sundue, "If we went out and bought someone else's system off the shelf, we could get a reasonable facsimile of what we do here. But we wouldn't get to control our own destiny."[36]

Based on Microsoft Word, the new system corrects the deficiencies of the former system. Integration is the key. Phone representatives can access all the information they need through one terminal. The system integrated information on a retail basis from diverse sources, including stock markets, news services, and analysts. These data are integrated with the customer's individual portfolio information. Technologically, levels of servers feed seamlessly into the representatives terminals. The local and regional servers maintain only the most requested information for that area. When unusual data are requested, the representative is automatically transferred to the national server.

Maxxess has saved Fidelity $20.5 million that formerly went to a third party. Maxxess is actually generating new revenue since the program is now being sold to outsiders who need real-time price quotes. Viewed as

an investment, Fidelity delivered a 62.8 percent return on its technology expenditure investment from 1992 to 1997. In doing so, Fidelity has looked beyond a temporary fix, employing a long-term technology strategy that directly and quickly benefits the company while adding value for the customers and distinguishing Fidelity from its competitors.

While Fidelity has improved access to phone representatives, it has ironically made efforts to phase them out. Actual speaking calls, numbering 70,000 to 90,000 daily, represent only a quarter of total phone-ins. The rest are answered by touch-tone systems; this is a huge savings for Fidelity. The cost per speaking call is $11. Each phone interaction with a computer costs $0.70.[37]

Another aspect of Fidelity's customer service/technological dominance is its Covington, Kentucky, mail distribution center. Unlike its rivals, Fidelity treats the mundane activity of processing mail as a core part of its business. It gives "every ounce of its energy" to bettering rivals in this service-oriented end of the business. This investment is made because "Consistent operations can help comfort customers amid volatile market swings, or, recently at Fidelity, mediocre investment results."[38] Fidelity is attempting to add as much predictability and efficiency as possible to its necessarily volatile business environment. High investment returns cannot be achieved every year, but sending out a prospectus or a statement on time is possible.

Fidelity's commitment to consistent service has not been cheap. The Kentucky operation cost $100 million, including a self-imposed testament to Fidelity's good corporate citizenship. The construction of the rural plant caused significant excavation, requiring Fidelity to rebuild hills surrounding their buildings to blend the 24-hour operation into the countryside. For instance, "a bundle was spent on an earth-tone, multi-story garage, sloped to fit into the countryside so parking lots full of cars wouldn't sully the bucolic views."[39] This innovative facility broke new ground in mail distribution plants. It incorporated ideas like the heavy use of robotics from manufacturing. Suppliers such as Bell & Howell and Cisco-Eagle collaborated with Fidelity to develop sophisticated materials moving and sorting products.

The attention to detail in the mailing process says a great deal about Fidelity's concern for customer service. The center ships over 140 million pieces of mail a year,

[35] Wilder, Clinton, "The Money Machine," *Information-Week*, January 8, 1996, n. 561, p. 28(6).
[36] Bresnahan, Jennifer, "Semper Fidelity," *CIO*, February 1, 1997, v. 10, n. 8, pp. 62–66.
[37] Ibid., p. 64.
[38] Hirsch, James S., "Stamp of Approval: A High-Tech System for Sending the Mail Unfolds at Fidelity; Robots at 'Kentucky Farm' Boost Output, Invigorate Back-Office Operations; Rolling Hills of Red Balloons," *The Wall Street Journal*, March 20, 1996, p. A1.
[39] Ibid., p. A5.

in about 3,000 separate formats or "kits." These include prospectuses, promotional material, and personal statements. One extreme example of Fidelity's passion for detail is the type of paper on which the statements are printed. Prior to construction of the new facility, Fidelity was plagued with paper that retained high amounts of moisture. This caused statements to curl and smudge easily. In consultation with paper producers, Fidelity experimented with drying the paper before printing, fine-tuning their method until the answer was discovered. The paper was dried in a 70°F room for two days, with humidity levels between 45 and 55 percent. This supports Director of Operations Christopher D. Cramer's claim that "paper and print are a strategic advantage."[40]

The Covington, Kentucky, center incorporates a sophisticated system in which conveyor belts and rotating carousels, run by software unique to Fidelity, haul materials through cavernous, concrete rooms. Computers coordinate movements through nonstop gabfests with each other. This all occurs under one 256,000 square foot roof. The automated storage and retrieval system designed by ESKAY Corporation enables Fidelity to support the claim that when a customer makes a request for information, it will be in the mail the next day.

DATABASES

Customer names and addresses are pulled from a database and printed directly on the paper materials, which are then metered, bar coded, and sent across the country without seeing the inside of a U.S. postal facility. A least-cost routing system ensures that the lowest priced shipping company is used for larger orders. Fidelity has even integrated this new plant with a "massively parallel" system from AT&T Global Information Solutions that quickly analyzes and sorts a customer database to determine which product offerings should be advertised by mail. This makes printing and mailing initiatives even more cost effective.[41] Competitors see shipping as a necessary but uninteresting side note to the investment business. Fidelity focuses upon customer service, even in the shipping details.

Another area in which Fidelity has been distinguishing itself through technological service is with 401(k) plans. "The critical characteristic of a successful 401(k) plan or any financial service provider is technology. This is a factor Fidelity has historically emphasized."[42]

Previously, Fidelity's 401(k) operations were spread throughout the company. In 1989, Fidelity formed Fidelity Institutional Retirement Services (FIRS) to focus the energies of the disorganized, unwieldy department. The business objectives of FIRS were to "set the industry standard in customer service, sustain double-digit annual growth, and continue to achieve profitability in all segments of the business."[43] Today, when an FIRS employee walks into the office, "they have one mission, and that mission is 401(k)."[44]

To accomplish this change, FIRS invested 20 percent of its $2 billion annual revenue on technology. When one of its two million customers calls, they reach a telephone representative whose computer accesses the on-line, continuously updated portfolio of the caller. The departmental integration has enabled FIRS to branch out to every conceivable product distribution network. Only half of its revenues come from direct marketing from Fidelity. The rest are sold through banks or other financial institutions.

FIRS views 401(k) plans as essentially a record-keeping business. Fidelity plans to maintain the best-kept records in the business. While other companies may possess the same technology as Fidelity, no one has made such a long-standing commitment to continual change. Additionally, Fidelity plans to organize all benefits administration around the same 800 number. This will provide a one-stop shopping center for defined contributions, defined benefit plans, and health plans.

FIRS asserts that it puts its employees first to maintain its outstanding service for customers. This is based upon the assumption that "a staff of loyal, satisfied employees drives customer satisfaction and loyalty. This in turn drives profit and growth."[45] FIRS has developed a well-organized, sequential program named Service Delivery University to ensure that employees have opportunities for professional growth and development.

TELECOMMUNICATIONS

Analysts were impressed when Fidelity moved to wireless trading in October 1998. Fidelity rolled out InstantBroker, which lets its most frequent customers track their investments via pager, e-mail, fax, or personal digital assistants, such as 3Com Palm III.

Of more interest to analysts, two-way pager users were able to use their pagers to trade stocks and options starting in January 1999. While Fidelity is not the first financial services firm to offer wireless updates, being

[40] Ibid., p. A5.
[41] Goldberg, Michael, "Powerful Processing," *Computerworld*, July 3, 1995, v. 29, n. 27, p. 28.
[42] Rohrer, Julie, "The Fidelity Factor: Technology Has Helped Fidelity Leap So Far Ahead of the 401(k) Pack That It's Doubtful Anyone Can Catch Up," *Institutional Investor*, October 1994, pp. 227–228.

[43] McColgan, Ellyn A., "How Fidelity Invests in Service Professionals," *Harvard Business Review*, January–February 1997, v. 75, n. 1, pp. 137–143.
[44] Rohrer, "The Fidelity Factor," p. 227.
[45] McColgan, "How Fidelity Invests," *Harvard Business Review*, January–February 1997, v. 75, n. 1, p. 137.

able to get account updates and request stock positions wirelessly is new enough that Fidelity should be able to differentiate itself from its major competitors. Fidelity's size made this move significant for the technology. "When Fidelity or Schwab does something, other people follow suit. It gives this technology some credibility and gives people something to monitor as far as the [technology's] success rate goes."

InstantBroker is available free of charge to the 55,000 Fidelity investors who trade at least 36 times a year. The service uses encryption technology to protect investments, though the company has not indicated what level of encryption was being used. A Fidelity spokesman, James Griffin, said the firm has not decided whether it will offer the service to its other customers, even for a fee. Griffin added that the company had not worked out a commission structure for two-way trading. Griffin said Fidelity added the wireless trading service because customers indicated that they need to get information more frequently if they are not near a computer or a phone. Fidelity expects a significant number of the 55,000 eligible users to register for the service. "It will appeal to an awful lot of people, but you won't find pager sales increase 5 percent next year because of this. Two-way paging has a bright future ahead of it, but the killer two-way messaging application is a consumer one—communicating with friends and family," said Craig Mathias, principal at the FarPoint Group in Ashland, Massachusetts. Mathias noted that two-way paging can be done from handheld devices, such as the PalmPilot and Palm III, and from telephone-based short-messaging services. As part of the same announcement, Fidelity said it will enhance its Fidelity Automated Service Telephone (FAST) by adding speech recognition.[46]

NETWORKS

In 1997, the only way to uncover a problem on Fidelity Investments' online trading network was to wait for customers to complain. Then management issued an edict. Be ready for the next trading frenzy, or else. Management soon approved an elaborate war room to track web activity from a variety of angles, including real-time monitoring of rival site operators Charles Schwab & Company, E*Trade Securities Inc., and DLJdirect.[47]

The Internet Operations Center, a circular room that resembles the bridge on the Starship Enterprise, went live in June 1997. When all the automation features were added by the end of 1998, the system was able to identify trouble in real time and respond immediately—with little human intervention. "We were in a situation

where customers were finding problems before we were; there were complaints every day," said Bruce Ferland, the executive vice president who supervised development of the IOC. Although there were never major outages, "we'd have slowdowns, we'd have application servers down, we'd have database problems."

It didn't help that Fidelity, one of the top three online brokerages, had to contend with massive growth—from 30,000 online accounts in January 1997 to 1.5 million in December 1998. Like its competitors, Fidelity's outages were routine. Capacity had to be expanded continually. Fidelity needed a way to monitor in real time the many factors that could handicap customer service. These included the performance of its private Sonet ring, numerous Internet services, and content and transaction-oriented applications.

To reach the goal of providing the reliability and redundancy of Fidelity's famed call center, Ferland brought in Christopher McLellan from the customer service telephone facility. McLellan is now director of Internet operations at Fidelity. Automated call distributors (ACDs) and phone centers are now at the point where we are able to trend, forecast, look at how customers were reacting, dynamically load balance, and redistribute calls. This is inherently what we want to apply to the Internet," McLellan said.

The Internet Operations Center (IOC) has more than a dozen network management systems and an even larger number of consoles and views that serve as windows into virutally all web operations from a central location. Officials would not commit to a dollar amount but said investments totaled less than $1 million.

By December 1998, Fidelity deployed Atreve Software's WebSpective Traffic Manager. This tool automatically routes web traffic to available servers and balances the load to maximize performance. The iteration of the software now in use simply monitors activity and recommends how traffic should be routed. A person is required to make manual changes.

SiteScope from Fresh Water Software monitors the web servers by continually performing transactions over different types of connections and posting warnings of error conditions. To complement this, Fidelity developed an internal system called the Competitive Analysis Tool (CAT). This application gathers statistics from SiteScope and competitive web sites. This enables authorized Fidelity officials to generate their own customized charts and reports. The interest in competitors' sites is to be informed of any potential problem that could negatively affect Fidelity. The company believes it is important to be informed regarding what competitors are doing with technology. If they have a problem in their environment, it could have a domino effect.

The IOC has numerous other tools. Keynote Systems sends requests to web sites from 27 locations and

[46] "Finance," *InfoWorld,* March 8, 1999, v. 21, i. 10, p. 92.
[47] Barnett, Megan, "The Street Plugs Into New Trading Network," *Network World,* July 26, 1999, p. UA.

records the response rates. IBM's NetView TME10 provides real-time monitoring of every node on Fidelity's wide area network. This provides performance, utilization, and collision statistics. The internally developed Electronic Trading Statistics monitors trades, new and canceled orders, and other transaction-oriented events. The trends are logged into an Oracle database and made accessible to business managers on an Intranet. All problems and resolutions are stored in Tracker, a Lotus Notes-based knowledge base.

Fidelity's web architecture consists of three geographically dispersed servers. All of the servers run Netscape Enterprise Server on Sun SPARCstations. They are connected by multiple T3 lines in a Sonet ring through Cisco's 7513 routers. At peak traffic loads, they are at 9 percent utilization. Transactions are performed using IBM's Encina transaction monitor linked to CICS on RS/6000 servers.

RECOMMENDATION FOR THE FUTURE

Although Fidelity processes paper better than anyone else in the business, the need to process paper may not be so important in the future. Fidelity has applied technology to the plant in Covington, Kentucky, in an area that may only be relevant in the short term. The ability to use the Internet to download prospectuses and other information about the company is already possible. Customers also may prefer to see their accounts electronically. Sending paper information may become less important.

Fidelity's Internet presence, although impressive, is similar to other Internet discount brokers. There is a low barrier to entry for an Internet presence. The extent to which Internet discount brokers will present a threat to larger, more established companies remains to be seen.

When Edward Johnson II was at the helm, Fidelity was a successful but undistinguished mutual fund company. When Ned Johnson III took over, Fidelity made its name in customer service and technology. It became known as an investment powerhouse with a culture that bred brash, risk-taking managers whose investments always seemed to show the best returns. Today, Fidelity is undergoing significant change. Although growth has been dramatic over the past few years, returns have faltered.

Today, Fidelity is targeting the 401(k) retirement planning market segment. Fidelity emphasizes its historical returns, slick marketing, and widespread name recognition. To maintain its customers, Fidelity efficiently administers record keeping and services customer accounts. Investment returns are important. However, many individuals saving for retirement do not track or watch closely money they cannot access.

Whether it was true in the past, Fidelity now recognizes the importance of retirement money. The company manages 15 percent of the entire 401(k) market. More significantly, 54 percent of Fidelity's assets under management constitute retirement funds. This represents a major change in Fidelity's customer base.

Today, "Fidelity's most important customer is a corporate administrator charged with choosing a 401(k) retirement plan for company employees."[48]

As Fidelity has shifted to the retirement market, the culture of the company has fundamentally changed. "The 401(k) market runs on a different set of assumptions than the retail market. Corporate administrators are not nearly as interested in out-of-the-park returns as they are in predictability; after all, they have a fiduciary responsibility to company employees."[49] Fidelity must focus its efforts on this market segment to be successful.

---

[48] Whitford and Nocera, "Has Fidelity Lost It?," p. 61. op. cit.
[49] Ibid., p. 62.

CASE QUESTIONS

Strategic Questions

1. What is the strategic direction of the corporation/organization?

2. Who or what forces are driving this direction?

3. What has been the catalyst for change?

4. What are the critical success factors for this corporation/organization?

5. What are the core competencies for this corporation/organization?

Technological Questions

6. What technologies has the corporation relied on?

7. What has caused the intensive use of technology in the corporation/organization?

8. How has this change been implemented?

9. Who has driven this change throughout the organization?

10. How successful has the use of technology been?

Quantitative Questions

11. What does the corporation say about its financial ability to embark on a major technological program of advancement?

12. What conclusions can be reached from an analysis of the financial information to support or contradict this financial ability?

13. What analysis can be made by examining the following ratio groups?

    Quick/current
    Debt
    Revenue
    Profit
    Asset utilization

14. What conclusions can be reached by analyzing the financial trends? Are there long-term trends that seem to be problematic? Is the industry stable? Are there replacement products?

Internet Questions

15. What does the corporation's web page present about their business directives?

16. How does this compare to the conclusions reached by the case?

17. How does this compare to the conclusions reached by analyzing the financial information?

Industry Questions

18. What challenges and opportunities is the industry facing?

19. Is the industry oligopolistic or competitive?

20. Does the industry face a change in government regulation?

21. How will technology impact the industry?

Data Questions

22. What role do data play in the future of the corporation?

23. How important are data to the corporation's continued success?

24. How will the capture and maintenance of customer data impact the corporation's future?

MASTERCARD

Executive Summary

Case Name:	MasterCard
Case Industry:	Financial services
Major Technology Issue:	Enabling a "virtual private network" to unite old and new computer infrastructure in an efficient manner
Major Financial Issue:	Keeping transaction costs and technology costs under control
Major Strategic Issue:	Marketing a payment system for internet commerce
Major Players/Leaders:	H. Eugene Lockhart, president
Main Web Page:	www.mastercard.com
Case Conclusion/Recommendation:	MasterCard must develop new products with its data. MasterCard must develop brand recognition and growth overseas. MasterCard must continue to market and refine its Internet commerce payment system.

CASE ANALYSIS

INTRODUCTORY STORY

Money, is "something generally accepted as a medium of exchange, a measure of value, or a means of payment."[1] To most people, money means cash or checks. But imagine for a moment a world without cash or checks. Sound unlikely? Impossible? Like something from the Jetson's? Believe it or not, a world without cash or checks is not far from reality. Just as cash and checks replaced the barter system of exchanging objects of like value, virtual money (credit, debit, and electronic cash products) is rapidly replacing cash and checks. Although the definition of money has not changed, money transactions are becoming more flexible, timely, and convenient.[2]

SHORT DESCRIPTION OF THE COMPANY

MasterCard is one of the companies leading the trend toward more flexible money transactions. MasterCard facilitates transactions between those who use Master-Card products, those who accept MasterCard, and the 23,000 member financial institutions that manage the relationships of these groups.

MasterCard's core competencies are credit and debit products. The company offers a variety of products to meet the needs of both consumers and businesses. Consumer products consist of six offerings: Maestro®,

MasterCard®, Gold MasterCard®, Platinum Class MasterCard®, Cirrus®, and MasterMoney™. The flexible and comprehensive product mix has been successful. MasterCard has experienced an average of over 20 percent annual growth in its 30-year history. MasterCard has 400 million credit and debit cards that are accepted at more than 14 million merchant, cash, and ATM locations worldwide. It generated a gross dollar volume of more than $650 billion in 1998.[3]

SHORT HISTORY OF THE COMPANY

For the past 30 years, MasterCard International Inc. has been a leading innovator in the global payments industry. A list of MasterCard's "firsts" includes:

- 1981: First gold card
- 1983: First laser hologram as an antifraud device
- 1987: First payment card issued in the Republic of China
- 1989: First tamper-resistant signature panel
- 1990: Implementation of a co-branding strategy
- 1991: First global online debit program, Maestro®, with Europay International
- 1992: First coast-to-coast national online debit transaction in the United States.[4]

MasterCard continues to lead the industry in the development of smart cards and in the area of electronic commerce. Smart cards are payment cards with microchips that store electronic cash. Electronic commerce

---

[1] Britannica Online, http://www.britannica.com, August 9, 1999.

[2] MasterCard International Incorporated, *Annual Report*, March 1997.

[3] Ibid.

[4] http://www.mastercard.com/about.

on the Internet is now safer and easier because Master-Card helped to set the industry standard for secure credit card transactions over the Internet.[5]

FINANCIAL AND PORTFOLIO ANALYSIS

Both Visa and MasterCard have experienced annual growth in excess of 20 percent for many years. The growth in this industry is attributed to the consumer's demand for convenience.[6] Companies that might otherwise be only competitors for each other's share of the market are collaborating on projects. This collaboration is intended to increase the market itself.

The global payments industry has experienced a great deal of success, prompting one Wall Street analyst to comment that "the credit card business has been one of the most attractive in the financial services sector."[7]

Operating margins have also grown significantly from 1994 through 1996. MasterCard has increased its operating income as a percentage of total revenue from 3.12 percent in 1994 to 5.58 percent in 1996. In comparison, American Express has seen similar growth in operating margins. Operating income was 13.6 percent of revenue in 1994 and 14.78 percent in 1996. Over the same period of time, as shown in Table 13.3, return on equity also increased.

STOCK/INVESTMENT OUTLOOK

MasterCard is owned by its member banks and is not publicly traded. It has been very profitable for its owners.

RISK ANALYSIS

The global payments industry is most like an oligopoly. A few companies control most of the market. The top five competitors in the industry are Visa, MasterCard, American Express, Discover and Diner's Club. Collectively, Visa, MasterCard, and American Express hold 73 percent of the market share.[8] The companies in the industry compete through product differentiation and advertising but cooperate in attempts to expand the market.

Although there is some product differentiation in the marketplace, there is also a good deal of convergence in product offerings. Most credit card companies offer

Table 13.3 Returns on Equity

Company	1998	1997	1996
MasterCard	33.9%	30.2%	75.4%*
Visa	N/A	N/A	N/A
American Express	27.8	25.1%	25.6%

*Includes gain on sale of MasterCard automated point-of-sale program.
N/A, not applicable.

similar products but focus on different aspects or areas of the market. American Express concentrates a large part of its business on travel and entertainment. Many merchants were reluctant to use American Express credit cards because of their high discount rates. As a result, American Express introduced the Optima card, which closely resembles the Visa and MasterCard credit cards.[9]

In an industry with similar credit and debit services, global payments companies must use other methods to establish product differentiation. The single most important method to differentiate credit and debit services is through brand recognition and loyalty. Brand perception is integral; the advertising budgets in the global payments industry reflect the intensity with which these companies compete in this area.

American Express is the advertising leader, spending $127.5 million in the first six months of 1996. Visa was second, spending $91.9 million, and MasterCard and Discover spent $57.2 million and $26.3 million, respectively.[10] In 1998, MasterCard spent $483.5 million on advertising which represents 38.5 percent of total revenue for 1998.[11]

Other methods for establishing brand loyalty include co-branding and attaching other services to credit card services. MasterCard uses co-branding to differentiate its credit cards. Associating with companies such as AT&T, General Motors, Wal-Mart, and Sears, MasterCard can tailor its services to specific segments of the market.[12] Visa is well known for linking its credit services with frequent flyer incentives. Travel enthusiasts are less likely to switch products when they are earning frequent flyer miles every time they purchase goods and services with their Visa cards.

Although they are serious competitors, evidence suggests that these companies are not in an all-out share battle. When it comes to expanding the global payments market, Visa, MasterCard, and American Express have shown the ability to put competitive differences aside. High growth has focused the three

[5] http://www.mastercard.com/newways.
[6] Meece, Mickey, "Visa, MasterCard Posted Big Volume Gains in 2Q," *American Banker*, September 19, 1995, v. 160, n. 180, p. 22(1).
[7] Brown, T.K., "Donaldson, Lufkin & Jenrette Securities Report," Banks Specialty Financials/Credit Card-Industry Report, *Investext*, July 8, 1996, pp. 1–17.
[8] Coulton, Antoinette, "Where Cardholders Want to Be: Still Visa, by Far, Survey Finds," *American Banker*, January 2, 1997, v. 162, n. 1, p. 1(2).

[9] Ibid.
[10] Ibid.
[11] *Annual Report*.
[12] Coulton, "Where Cardholders Want to Be," p. 2.

companies on growing the entire market as well as competing for a larger share of the existing one.

MasterCard and Visa have formed a cooperative relationship. When a merchant accepts one card, they accept the other. MasterCard and Visa logos are frequently seen together. More importantly, MasterCard and Visa have developed a uniform standard to conduct safe credit card transactions over the Internet. American Express is supporting this standard as well.[13]

Market share is important but it is not the only thing on which companies are focusing. Visa has been the winner of the brand recognition and brand loyalty battle. MasterCard holds a definitive second. A recent survey of credit cardholders by *American Banker* "reveals that Visa is by far the most popular card, being used more often than any other credit card, by 44% of the survey respondents. MasterCard, American Express/Optima and Discover had survey shares of 21%, 8%, and 7%, respectively"[14] (Figure 13.6). The most remarkable result of the study shows that Visa had an impressive lead "in every age and income category."[15] In addition, 71 percent of those surveyed had at least one Visa card, 53 percent had at least one MasterCard, 30 percent had a Discover card, 27 percent had an American Express card, and 3 percent had a Diner's Club card.

Although Visa dominates in all areas of the market, American Express has an impressive loyalty among those 55 and older and the upper class. MasterCard, on the other hand, has a strong presence among the middle class. It is also competitive among the 55 and older group. In terms of market share, Visa held 39 percent of the $879 billion market in 1995, MasterCard held 23 percent, and American Express 13 percent.[16]

Rather than challenge Visa's number one spot, MasterCard is focusing on "systems and service quality, brand strength, and co-branding innovations."[17] MasterCard is also pushing to broaden acceptance in places where only cash and checks are used as well as establishing new products, such as the smart card, and new markets, such as the Internet. Examples of broader acceptance include taxis, doctor's offices, fast-food restaurants, toll booths, buses, commuter trains, and post offices.[18]

INDUSTRY AND MARKET ANALYSIS

An analysis of the industry indicates significant barriers to entry, moderate competition between companies,

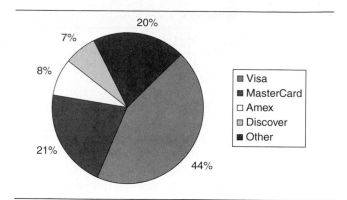

Figure 13.6 Card usage.

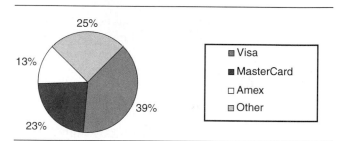

Figure 13.7 Market share.

and a lack of bargaining power on the part of consumers and merchants.

The global payments industry is difficult to enter. New companies find it difficult to break into this market because success requires the economies of scale made possible by the low transaction costs. To achieve economies of scale, a potential entrant must make large capital investments and gain widespread access to distribution channels.

Any company attempting to break into this market must make a significant investment in its technological infrastructure. Significant support must be provided to ensure that the systems continue to run, even during peak times. A retailer that is processing a credit card sale needs to communicate with the merchant to authorize the transaction. Large-scale computers are required to handle a significant volume of transactions. Transactions require instantaneous authorization and communication between consumer, retailer, and merchant.

MasterCard has an entire corporate function devoted to network and technology processing and services. In addition, many of its new products are technology based. With the movement toward electronic commerce on the Internet, additional investments will be required to handle and monitor transactions.

Large capital requirements are not the only barrier to entry. Access to distribution channels is also problematic.

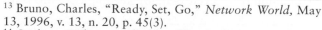

[13] Bruno, Charles, "Ready, Set, Go," *Network World,* May 13, 1996, v. 13, n. 20, p. 45(3).
[14] Coulton, "Where Cardholders Want to Be," op.cit., p. 2.
[15] Ibid.
[16] Ibid.
[17] Hoffman, Thomas, "MasterCard, Amex Push Online Tracking; Corporate customers to get Net Access to Track Spending," *Computerworld,* April 5, 1999 p. 4(1).
[18] *MasterCard Annual Report,* 1998.

Table 13.4 Fixed Costs

Operating Leverage 1998	MasterCard	American Express	Visa
Fixed costs as a percent of total costs	52%	56%	N/A
Fixed costs as a percent of total revenue	49%	54%	N/A

N/A, not applicable.

In the global payments industry this refers to merchants who accept credit cards and consumers who use the cards. Without a substantial number of merchants and consumers, a potential entrant will not have the required volume of transactions to remain a going concern.

As Table 13.4 shows, fixed costs account for nearly 52 percent of total costs and total revenue. A company needs high transaction volume to spread those fixed costs over more units. It would be difficult for a company to enter an industry with an unknown brand and build the needed transactions volume quickly. Many merchants would be unwilling to affiliate with an unknown brand. Brand identity inspires consumer confidence. The creditworthiness of a start-up would also be called into question.

ROLE OF RESEARCH AND DEVELOPMENT

MasterCard's technology office was the first department to complete its Team Excellence implementation to increase morale and employee retention. This department added at least 100 employees to the 850 at headquarters. The importance of growth in the technology staffing reflects the new status of technology at MasterCard. The company is moving toward a Sun/UNIX open platform to enable it to take advantage of Internet technology. This new technology is considered "critical to becoming the world's best and most preferred way to pay."[19] "The fact we have more people in St. Louis says we are in the technology business; technology is the fiber that supports the brand, the marketing, the administration,"[20] according to M. Elhatton.

TECHNOLOGICAL STORY

In the 1970s, MasterCard installed a state-of-the-art IBM Series 1 computer system.[21] This system was designed to authorize transactions from anywhere in the world. For nearly 20 years it supported the company's core competencies, debit and credit card products. Like many companies during this time, information technology (IT) was not very highly regarded within the

company. IT was not located near the New York headquarters but was in St. Louis. Few upgrades were ever made to the system. IT's role was to maintain or fix the existing system.

In the 1980s, IBM stopped manufacturing the Series 1 computers. By the early 1990s, it was clear that MasterCard needed an extensive upgrade of its global telecommunications network called Banknet®. In 1991, MasterCard announced its intention to replace "the card association's 300 aging IBM Series 1 computer systems with new computer systems by the end of 1992."[22] This project was expected to cost $65 million. Politics, high management turnover, and a lack of focus caused extensive delays on the project. By mid-1993, "only two of the new systems, from NCR, had been installed. The card organization decided to keep much of its existing technology."[23]

From the beginning, management turnover plagued the project. Each year, the lead manager departed and a new one took his place. The old IBM computers were supposed to be replaced by NCR computers using the UNIX operating system and running new authorization software. Only 30 of the 300 systems, however, were in place by the end of 1993. As a result, MasterCard decided to rewrite the old authorization software from the IBM computers to run on IBM personal computers. MasterCard never revealed how many NCR systems it installed. Both the NCR and IBM systems continued to be used and supported.[24]

TECHNOLOGICAL INVESTMENT AND ANALYSIS

With the turmoil surrounding system upgrades, it is not surprising that MasterCard would investigate outsourcing its data processing and communications operations. Negotiations with IBM, DEC, and AT&T began when the company estimated it could save $20 million over five years through outsourcing.[25]

In 1992, MasterCard cut off negotiations when further research determined that the company would save $50 million over seven years by keeping operations in-

[19] Kutler, Jeffrey, "Determined to Put MasterCard's Back Office in Front," *American Banker,* January 8, 1997, v. 162, n. 5, p. 12(2).

[20] Ibid.

[21] Iida, Jeanne, "MasterCard Pulls Back from $65 Million Plan to Upgrade Computers," *American Banker,* May 14, 1993, v. 158, n. 92, p. 3(1).

[22] Ibid.

[23] Ibid.

[24] "IBM & MasterCard Team to Push New ECML Wallet," *Computergram International,* September 15, 1999, i. 3747, p. NA.

[25] "Out with Outsourcing," *American Banker,* September 9, 1992, v. 157, n. 174, p. 2(1)

house.[26] This is the position MasterCard has maintained ever since. Instead of outsourcing, MasterCard cut the number of suppliers and renegotiated deals with its remaining suppliers to lower its in-house operating costs. In addition, AT&T became MasterCard's primary vendor for telecommunications.[27]

The technology office focused on four major areas: virtual private networks (VPN), MasterCard Online, smart cards, and Secure Electronic Transaction (SET) standards.

NETWORKS

MasterCard's global telecommunications network, Banknet®, authorizes millions of transactions a day, with a 99.999 percent success rate.[28] The network enables MasterCard to "handle increased speed, volume, and geographic diversity, while reducing fraud."[29] It only supports core MasterCard services, including debit and credit products. As a result, MasterCard is upgrading its system to ensure it has the strength and flexibility to support emerging products and services such as smart cards and Internet commerce.[30]

MasterCard is moving toward a virtual private network, which is a "cheaper way than private networks to link LANs or connect field employees to the company's database via the Internet. Together with encryption and encapsulation, this technology, called tunneling, provides a private virtual communication passage."[31] The virtual private network will enhance the current Banknet system. MasterCard implemented VPN from 1996 to 1998.

VPN will provide "faster access and transport speeds, support for emerging products and services, and enhanced security."[32] Most remarkable, however, is that VPN can be implemented on the existing infrastructure, eliminating the capital cost of building a new infrastructure. In addition, VPN will improve flexibility and be able to "integrate newer, faster technologies as they become available."[33] This will enable MasterCard to bring new products to the market faster.

TELECOMMUNICATIONS

MasterCard Online is an information system for its members[34] The information system uses Oracle database technology to provide value-added services to MasterCard's membership. The initial phase of MasterCard Online enabled banks to track performance of credit card co-branding programs. It will soon address information such as fraud, authorizations, and quarterly statistical reports. The system requires one terabyte of data to store the information on MasterCard's daily 8.5 million cardholder transactions. Visa International was the first company to provide a service like this. MasterCard's is likely to be better. It provides online, desktop access to data for the previous 13 months and has graphics capability. More importantly, the service helps members understand customer usage patterns so they can better promote their products.[35]

SMART CARDS

A smart card is an ATM or credit card with a built-in computer chip. This chip stores up to $100 and is reloadable when all of the stored money is spent. Eventually, the computer chip will replace the magnetic strip on all its cards.[36] Computer chips introduce more flexibility into the credit card market than the magnetic strip is capable of. The magnetic strip limits cards to certain financial transactions and is able to store only small amounts of information. The smart card is capable of many different financial transactions, including arranging "a ticketless airline flight and buying merchandise from a vending machine."[37]

The smart card technology is supported by a UNIX system running an Oracle database. It has moved from AT&T hardware to a Sun Microsystems high-end server. The system "performs transaction processing, clearing and settlement, customer service, lost or stolen card recovery, and generates reports regarding fraud."[38]

By 2000, MasterCard expects to convert all its products and terminals to support this technology. Its advantages include savings of $3 billion "from fraud reduction and lower processing costs over a seven-year period."[39] In addition, since the smart cards will actually store cash, the authorization process is eliminated. This relieves pressure from transaction processing systems.

INTERNET

Since the popularization and commercialization of the Internet, consumers and merchants have been excited

[26] Ibid.

[27] Ibid.

[28] *Annual Report.*

[29] Ibid.

[30] Ibid.

[31] Fisher, Susan E., "VPNs Use Tunneling to Build Private Business Links," *Datamation,* June 1, 1996, v. 42, n. 11, p. 66(4).

[32] *Annual Report.*

[33] Ibid.

[34] Block, Valerie, "MasterCard, Like Visa, Starts Building Huge Information System for Members," *American Banker,* July 31, 1995, v. 160, n. 145, p. 1(2).

[35] Ibid.

[36] Daguio, Betty B., "MasterCard Tests a Smart Way to Trash Cash," *Computerworld,* July 15, 1996, v. 30, n. 29, p. 79(1).

[37] Harvey, David A., "Cash in Your Chips: Smart Cards to Put Digital Dollars in Consumer Wallets," *Computer Shopper,* July 1996, v. 16, n. 7, p. 74(1).

[38] Daguio, "MasterCard Tests."

[39] Kutler, Jeffrey, "MasterCard Makes It Official: Business Future Is in Chips," *American Banker,* July 22, 1994, v. 159, n. 140, p. 11(1).

about the possibilities of online commerce. The Internet promises an entirely new way to market to consumers with unprecedented speed, convenience, and flexibility. Nonetheless, online commerce has been slow to develop. Consumer and merchant acceptance, security issues, and the lengthy development of a standard for a safe, secure payment system all contribute to the slow growth of commerce on the Internet.

"Before online commerce really takes off, a broader base of consumers needs to become more experienced Internet users."[40] Fortunately, the U.S. is now starting to see an explosion of users. In 1996, 19 percent of U.S. consumers claimed they had accessed the Internet, and "another 12 percent said they planned to access it for the first time in the next year." Of those currently using the Internet, 84 percent said they were somewhat likely to purchase items over the Internet. Computer software/hardware, information, flower delivery services, and travel agencies are seen as the biggest prospects for growth.

Consumers are now ready for online commerce. They recognize the advantage of 24-hour shopping at home, time savings, privacy, and easy comparison shopping. Security issues continue to prevent consumers and merchants from taking full advantage of these benefits.

Analysts have identified the ability to build trust for conducting secure electronic payments as the biggest factor or deterrent to successful online commerce for most merchants.[41] To accomplish this, the web needs to be marketed more aggressively as a safe, effective means to purchase products.[42] Many merchants have been unwilling to risk accepting credit cards online out of fear that their consumers will view the process as unsafe.

TECHNOLOGICAL INNOVATIONS

TELECOMMUNICATIONS

The key to overcoming hesitancy on the part of consumers and merchants alike is to establish a safe, secure standard for transmitting credit card information over the Internet. The standard will be more successful if it is established by a well-respected company or group of companies in which the public has trust. As a result, MasterCard, Netscape, Visa, and Microsoft are collaborating on the Secure Electronic Transaction (SET) project. MasterCard is driving the process. The public recognizes these companies as strong institutions. According to one CyberTrust director, "MasterCard can offer services under strong brands that denote trust and

reliability, permitting many participants to 'take the plunge' in electronic commerce right away."[43]

The development of the SET standard had a rocky beginning. Initially, competitors in the global payments and the software development industries were working on separate standards development projects. Each was racing to be the first to finish. Visa had joined with Microsoft to work on SET. MasterCard and Netscape, on the other hand, were developing a secure Electronic Payment Protocol. The fact that Visa and MasterCard were competing on this project was of great concern to many observers on many levels. Major electronic commerce companies opposed the Visa/Microsoft standard because the code would not be made public. This required competitors to license the code from them. MasterCard and Netscape, on the other hand, were promoting an open standard.[44] Many observers were concerned that competing standards "would confuse consumers and slow the growth of electronic commerce."[45] It would also be very "confusing to both banks and merchants" by causing them to have "more than one electronic bank card transaction system."[46]

Historically, it was unusual for Visa and MasterCard not to cooperate on a project that would clearly extend opportunities for both businesses. The blame for the competition was placed at the feet of Microsoft and Netscape, both of which were vying for market share and knew "first-hand the benefits of owning industry standard technology."[47]

Fortunately, all the companies came together to support one standard, recognizing that a common specification is critical to advance electronic commerce on the Internet.[49] The new standard (SET) would be an open one and would use "electronic certificates" to simplify the process of making purchases over the Internet. Essentially, "users would be issued the certificate electronically once their credit-card numbers were authorized by an approved agency. Once the authoriza-

[40] "New Study on Retailing on the Internet Released," *HFN—The Weekly Newspaper for the Home Furnishing Network,* March 4, 1996, v. 70, n. 10, p. 63(1).
[41] Shein, Esther, "The Virtual Storefronts." *PC Week,* September 23, 1996, v. 13, n. 38, p. E1(3).
[42] "New Study," p. 63(1).

[43] "E-Commerce: MasterCard and GTE to Offer Digital Signatures for Secure Electronic Commerce in Fourth Quarter 1996," *EDGE, On & About AT&T,* July 29, 1996, v. 11, p. 13(1).
[44] Markoff, John, "Microsoft Joins Visa to Propose a Standard for Online Paying", *The New York Times,* September 28, 1995, v. 145, p. C1.
[45] Ibid.
[46] Karpinski, Richard, "Net Security Agreement Disintegrates," *Communications Week,* October 2, 1995, n. 578, p. 1(2).
[47] Joachim, David, "Visa, MasterCard Spar Over 'Net Payment,'" *Communications Week,* October 9, 1995, n. 579, p. 5(1).
[48] Moeller, Michael, "SAP, Banks Seek to Cash in on Electronic Commerce: MasterCard, Visa Squabble Over Spec," *PC Week,* December 18, 1995, v. 12, n. 50, p. 1(2).
[49] Ibid.

tion is received, the certificate is attached to users' browsers and acts as an electronic credit card for all future purchases."[50]

The SET standard was published in February 1997. Tests of the protocol occurred throughout the year. Banks across the United States were interested in the trials and were particularly excited about the protocol design, which could be easily integrated into the existing global financial backbone.[51]

MasterCard's investment in the SET standard appears to be paying off. Software companies are already writing SET standards into their software programs. Many merchants and retailers are also integrating this standard into their businesses as quickly as possible.

This project, however, was a risky one for MasterCard and all of the other companies involved. Consumers, retailers, and merchants had to support the concept that the SET standard would become the standard that everyone would adopt. If it failed, a whole new marketplace could be lost or at least set back indefinitely.

DATABASES

MasterCard International launched a new subsidiary in early 1999 that uses MasterCard's huge warehouse of credit-card transaction data to sell information on consumer buying habits to retailers. Transactional Data Solutions, a joint venture of MasterCard and market research firm Symmetrical Resources Inc., offered its first service, Merchant Advisor, in the first quarter of 1999. Merchant Advisor provides aggregate consumer buying information based on credit card transactions and other data. To protect privacy, the reports do not include customer-specific information such as names, addresses, phone numbers, and e-mail addresses, says Bill Engel, CEO of Transactional Data Solutions. Reports will draw on data from MasterCard's 7-terabyte Oracle data warehouse in St. Louis, as well as from other sources. The new service is unrelated to an online data service MasterCard offers its member banks.

Merchant Advisor is designed to help retailers boost sales and attract customers with more cost effective marketing and advertising. It compares retailers' and competitors' performance over a period of time and in different stores. "Macy's knows what's going on in its own stores, but it does not know what's going on among the competition," says Greg Mazzanobile, TDS's chief operating officer and former director of alliances and new ventures at MasterCard.

Age, income, buying habits, and other data will be provided in clusters, such as women aged 35 to 45 with incomes of $80,000 to $100,000. With data from Symmetrical, the reports will also tell retailers which media sources the shoppers prefer to watch.

Customer profiling is a high priority for retailers as they try to improve their ability to stock the merchandise customers want, plan better locations for stores, and detect buying patterns, says Tom Friedman, president of the research firm Retail Systems Alert Group. Merchant Advisor reports will be provided quarterly for $75,000 to $150,000 a year, depending on the size of the retailer. Monthly reports will be available in the year 2000. National and local versions of the service will be available for apparel, automotive, grocery, home furnishing, and other specific industries.[52]

RECOMMENDATION FOR THE FUTURE

MasterCard continues to drive the industry and has added another "first" to its list—the accepted standard for conducting secure electronic payments over the Internet. MasterCard's investment in the technology needed to introduce the industry's newest products, smart cards and electronic commerce, has positioned the company to address the marketing needs in the near future.

MasterCard should consider the possibilities of its immense log of customers and transactions as information products. The data warehouse that MasterCard possesses by default could be turned into valuable products for marketers. This would require data mining and other tools to extract useful knowledge from this information.

MasterCard should also continue to push its brand overseas. Market saturation is still low internationally. This represents tremendous opportunities.

---

[50] "Twenty Million Merchants Can't All Be Wrong," *HP Professional,* January 1997, v. 11, n. 1, p. 13(1).
[51] Violino, Bob, "Venture Taps Mastercard Warehouse—Consumer Data to Be Sold to Retailers," 1999 CMP Publications, Inc.

[52] Reynolds, Jonathan, "Retailing on the Net," *International Journal of Retail & Distribution Management*, September, 1998, v. 26, i. 9, p. 377.

CASE QUESTIONS

Strategic Questions

1. What is the strategic direction of the corporation/organization?

2. Who or what forces are driving this direction?

3. What has been the catalyst for change?

4. What are the critical success factors for this corporation/organization?

5. What are the core competencies for this corporation/organization?

Technological Questions

6. What technologies has the corporation relied on?

7. What has caused a change in the use of technology in the corporation/organization?

8. How has this change been implemented?

9. How successful has the technological change been?

Quantitative Questions

10. What does the corporation say about its financial ability to embark on a major technological program of advancement?

11. What conclusions can be reached from an analysis of the financial information to support or contradict this financial ability?

12. What analysis can be made by examining the following ratio groups?

    Fixed costs/total costs
    Fixed costs/total revenue
    ROE
    Operating income/total revenue

Internet Questions

13. What does the corporation's web page present about their business directives?

Industry Questions

14. What challenges and opportunities is the industry facing?

15. Is the industry oligopolistic or competitive?

16. Does the industry face a change in government regulation?

17. How will technology impact the industry?

Data Questions

18. What role do data play in the future of the corporation?

19. How important are data to the corporation's continued success?

20. How will the capture and maintenance of customer data impact the corporation's future?

Executive Summary

Case Name:	Charles Schwab & Co.
Case Industry:	Financial services
Major Technology Issue:	Developing additional computer system capacity and contingency planning for computer failure
Major Financial Issue:	Keeping margins intact in the face of price competition
Major Strategic Issue:	Creating products to gather financial assets
Major Players/Leaders:	Charles Schwab, founder; David S. Pottruck, president and COO
Main Web Page:	www.schwab.com
Case Conclusion/Recommendation:	Schwab should focus on acquiring new clients and revenue sources, with a new focus on 401(k) plans. Schwab must continue to develop new products, particularly those dependent upon technology for dissemination.

CASE ANALYSIS

INTRODUCTORY STORY

The days of the ticker tape are over. Today, anyone with a personal computer and a modem can obtain a stock quote, conduct company research, place a trade, or check the status of a portfolio. There is no need to speak with a stockbroker. In 1996, estimates indicated that 14 percent of computer users who had Internet access obtained investment information or traded securities online.[1]

Discount brokers, firms that offer order execution for low prices, have benefited from technological innovation. These firms are gaining market share, currently receiving 13.6 percent of all retail commission revenues, up from 10.4 percent in 1990 and 5.4 percent in 1985,[2] as illustrated in Figure 13.8. The growth in discount brokerage, the breadth of new financial products, and the increasing numbers of personal computers in homes are changing today's retail brokerage industry.[3]

SHORT DESCRIPTION OF THE COMPANY

Charles Schwab & Co. is the largest discount brokerage firm in the United States. While its core business as a discount broker is transacting trades for clients who make their own investment decisions, Schwab offers a wide range of financial services to its customers. Its customer base includes individuals, investment managers, retirement plans, and institutions. Schwab services are provided at a discount, compared to full-service firms such as Merrill Lynch and Paine Webber. The company serves over 4 million active customer accounts, with total assets reaching $253 billion at the end of 1996.[4]

Schwab aggressively pursues growth and is considered an industry leader in developing new products.[5] Schwab has distinguished itself from its competitors by providing value-added services and through development of new distribution channels for products. The company has built its reputation as a discount broker by being an aggressive user of technology to cut costs and then passing the savings on to the clients.

In addition to discount brokerage through traditional distribution channels of telephone brokerage services or in-person office transactions, Schwab provides its customers with online trading services. The services are provided through the Internet or dial-up software

[1] Lewison, John E., Bernstein, Phyllis, and Zarowin, Stanley, "Cyberspace Investing," *Journal of Accountancy,* July 1996, v. 182, n. 1, p. 63.
[2] Standard and Poor's, Investment Services Industry Survey, January 2, 1997, p. 8
[3] "Survey: National Study Finds On-Line Services are Changing the Nature of the Brokerage Industry," IAC (SM) Newsletter Database, Edge Publishing, November 13, 1995.

[4] Charles Schwab Corporation, *Annual Report,* 1997.
[5] S&P, Investment Services Industry Survey, p. 22.

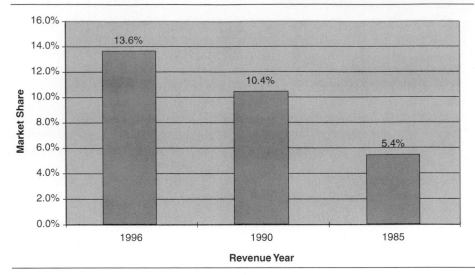

Figure 13.8 Discount brokerage firm growth.

systems, a mutual fund supermarket, educational materials, cash management accounts, free stock quotes, touch-tone phone trading system, flat-fee for Internet trade execution, and various software offerings.

SHORT HISTORY OF THE COMPANY

Charles Schwab and Company, Inc., founded in 1971 by Charles Schwab,[6] was initially a full-service brokerage. The firm entered the discount brokerage field in 1975, after the Securities and Exchange Commission deregulated fixed commissions. The company was sold to BankAmerica in 1983. Federal regulations prohibited banks from acting as brokerages, limiting Schwab's expansion into mutual funds and telephone trading.[7] In 1987, Charles Schwab bought the company back from BankAmerica and took it public.

In 1989, Schwab bought discount competitor Rose & Company from Chase Manhattan Corporation. Rose had been the fifth-largest discount broker. This acquisition provided Schwab with an increased customer base of 200,000 new accounts without an increase in overhead. It eliminated a competitor and provided Schwab with a larger market share in the Midwest.[8]

Historically, Schwab has been an innovator of low-cost investing and technology in the investment services industry. As Schwab President and COO David S. Potruck commented in 1996, "investors have come to rely on Schwab's leadership and aggressive use of technology to lower costs."[9] Schwab's development of distribution channels utilizing technology includes the following:[10]

1980:   First to offer 24-hour quote service
1982:   First to offer 24-hour, 7-day-a-week order entry and quote service
1985:   The Equalizer for DOS—computer trading software
1989:   Telebroker—trade execution on a push-button telephone
1992:   First to offer no transaction fee mutual funds, OneSource; dividend reinvestment service for any U.S. public stock in any type of account
1993:   StreetSmart for Windows—a proprietary software package enabling customers to dial in to the brokerage directly and conduct trades at 10 percent off regular commission[11]
1994:   StreetSmart for Macintosh
1996:   e.Schwab—software product providing online trade execution via direct dial into Schwab computers over telephone lines; similar to StreetSmart but geared to the investor requiring minimum personal

---

[6] Schwab began his business career as a door-to-door salesman at the age of 12. He first sold eggs and chicken manure fertilizer. He graduated from Stanford University. (*Source:* Adler, Frederick, and Shaykin, Leonard, "The Wall Street," *Financial World,* June 28, 1988, p. 44.
[7] Hoover's Database, 1997, The Charles Schwab Corporation.
[8] Wayne, Leslie, "For Charles Schwab, A Time to Tinker," *The New York Times,* May 7, 1989, Sec. 3, p. 8.

[9] "Schwab Electronic Trading Growth Drives New Cost Savings for Investors," *PR Newswire,* July 1, 1996.
[10] Ibid.
[11] Harbert, Tam, and Bort, Julie, "Have Computer, Will Trade," *Computerworld,* June 24, 1996, p. 127.

service[12]; Internet trading—providing online trading via the World Wide Web, no proprietary software needed[13]; and StreetSmart Pro

1997:   MarketBuzz—a web site offering up-to-the minute market highlights from various news sources[14]

Schwab commands the on-line trading market with a 47 percent market share.[15] However, it still offers face-to-face contact at its 226 offices.

After the close of trading on May 30, 1997, Schwab was added to the Standard & Poor's 500 Index, replacing Morgan Stanley & Co. Until May 30, 1997, Schwab had been included in the Standard and Poor's MidCap 400 Index.[16] Schwab's move from the S&P MidCap to the S&P 500 reflects its position as a major competitor in the investment services industry and also recognizes the increased importance of discount brokers in this industry sector.

Schwab's business strategy involves three elements: innovation, diversification, and technology. Schwab's overarching business goals of asset-gathering, increased sales, and increased net income are achieved by a combination of these factors. The firm, while having a history of implementing technology to enhance its products, does not let technology drive its business decisions. Schwab determines its business goal and then determines how it will achieve this target.

This is fully illustrated by Schwab's mutual fund supermarket, OneSource. With OneSource, Schwab saw an opportunity to gather assets and increase the profit potential. The fact that technology enabled the development of this innovative product line was secondary to the firm's goal of asset gathering through a new channel of distribution.

Due to innovation, Schwab has steadily grown over its more than 20-year history. Schwab's 1975 transition from a full-service brokerage to discount brokerage was one of its first innovations. Schwab responded to deregulation and price competition by dropping prices, rather than increasing commissions, which was the response of many full-service firms. Schwab followed this innovation with many more changes.

Schwab's innovation as a discount broker went further. Schwab recognized that customers worried that by choosing low price they lost service reliability. Schwab responded by investing in computer technology, which made it possible to provide customers with nearly immediate confirmation of orders by telephone. This was a value-added service that, at the time, even Merrill Lynch could not provide.[17] Schwab is recognized for having one of the most technologically advanced back offices, with the ability to confirm most orders in 90 seconds. Most trades are handled without Schwab employees filling out a single sheet of paper.[18]

Schwab also provided confidence for its customers through investment name recognition and retail office space. Initially, establishment of retail office space was considered unnecessary and costly for a discount brokerage. When Charles Schwab's uncle was looking for a business to run, Schwab responded by opening an office for him in Sacramento, California. Schwab's Sacramento operation significantly outperformed other cities where no office was established.

While there was no obvious explanation for this, research determined that retail sales offices provided the firm with advantages. The main advantage was that a physical sales office provided a source for customer leads through walk-in traffic. It also provided a sense of security to customers, many of whom had concerns about trusting a broker that they could not see. As a result of the success of the Sacramento office, Schwab expanded their retail network, an innovation in the discount brokerage business.[19]

Schwab has continued to diversify its product line and attract a broader base of customers with its offerings of a mutual fund supermarket, online trading, Internet trading, and other value-added services. Schwab's history of innovation can be partially traced to the 1987 market crash. Charles Schwab had just bought his company back from BankAmerica, when the stock market crashed and trading volume dropped nearly 50 percent. Schwab recognized a need for diversification, and began offering new fee-based services to adjust for the drop in commissions. In addition, Schwab expanded the growth of "customer payables" such as margin lending and invested the credit balances in customer brokerage accounts.[20]

During the post-crash market slump from 1987 to 1989, customer payables at Schwab grew nearly 75 percent. In 1988, when customers sold stock and stayed

[12] Wagner, Mitch, "Schwab Woos On-Line Home Traders," *Computerworld,* January 8, 1996, v. 30. n. 2, p. 20(1).

[13] Harbert and Bort, "Have Computer, Will Trade."

[14] "Charles Schwab Launches One-Stop Site for Online Investment Information," *PR Newswire,* February 19, 1997.

[15] Hoover's Database, Charles Schwab Corporation.

[16] "Charles Schwab Added to S & P 500 Index," Reuters, May 27, 1997.

[17] Stalk, George, Jr., Pecaut, David K., and Burnett, Benjamin, "Breaking Compromises, Breakaway Growth," *Harvard Business Review,* September, 1996, p. 131.

[18] Wayne, "For Charles Schwab, A Time to Tinker," p. 8.

[19] Stalk et al., "Breaking Compromises, Breakaway Growth," *Harvard Business Review,* September–October 1996, v. 74, n. 5, p. 131(9).

[20] Wayne, "For Charles Schwab, A Time to Tinker," p. 9.

out of the market, their cash sat in their brokerage accounts. Schwab paid them 6.75 percent interest. The firm earned 7.65 percent on these funds. At the same time, Schwab charged 9.55 percent for margin lending. Schwab's expanded diversification into customer payables resulted in a powerful asset-gathering tool, realizing revenue of $42.4 million in 1988.[21]

Schwab has successfully developed innovative packaging of services by combining people and technology in new ways. Such innovation has provided the firm with additional diversification. The firm has focused on financial planners as a target expansion market, offering them information services to help them deal with their clients.[22] In addition, Schwab has expanded offerings to financial advisors to include special services and discounts.[23] Uniting information technology and financial planners has been so successful for Schwab that other major industry members, such as Merrill Lynch, have developed competing systems.[24]

Further diversification at Schwab has included expansion of its customer base to include development of 401(k) management.[25] Schwab is erasing the traditional borders between banking and brokerage services by using technology to offer money market accounts and other products.[26]

Schwab's business strategy of innovation and diversification is carried out most fully through its use of technology. Schwab estimates that two-thirds of its customers own PCs and that 28 percent of its trades are conducted online.[27] Schwab has cultivated online trading as an additional distribution channel for its services, expanding access to online trading beyond modem interface with its proprietary computer to include access to trade execution through the Internet.

Schwab and other members of the investment service industry have embraced online investing primarily for increased profits. Cost savings are realized through a reduced paper trail and incentive tie-ins to other services provided by the firm.[28] The same holds true for Schwab's innovative new distribution channel for mutual funds: OneSource. Schwab has also embraced this mutual fund supermarket concept for increased profitability. Schwab receives a fee of 0.25 to 0.40 percent of the assets it manages under OneSource.[29]

FINANCIAL AND PORTFOLIO ANALYSIS

Schwab's ability to be innovative, provide new channels of distribution, and present value-added services to its customers has resulted in continuous growth during the past 10 years. The firm has remained focused on its business objectives of asset gathering, increased sales, and increased net income. Schwab has utilized technology to achieve these goals. Analysis of Schwab's financial data confirms this to be a growth company.

Sales for year ending December 31, 1996, were $1.851 billion, as compared to $0.354 billion for year ending December 31, 1987 (Figure 13.9). In each interim year during this 10-year period, Schwab sales increased from the prior year. Similarly, during this same 10-year period net income also consistently increased annually, growing from $8.235 million in 1987 to $233.803 million in 1996.

This consistent growth is attributable to a product line and market base that included not only individual investors, but also financial advisors and 401(k) administrators. The phenomenal sales growth that Schwab realized from 1987 to 1996 was the basis for the firm's selection as a component S&P 500 Index, moving from the midsize firm index, S&P MidCap.

A review of Schwab's key financial ratios for the three years 1994 to 1996 reflects that, despite the fact that both net sales and net income have increased, they have increased proportionately, as the ratio of net income to net sales has remained level within the range of 0.12 to 0.13. Net sales to employees decreased from 1994 to 1995, reflecting the 40 percent increase in staffing levels that occurred between the fourth quarter of 1995 and the first quarter of 1996.[30] Despite this increased staffing, net sales per employee rose during the fiscal year. This increase in net sales per employee is consistent with the growth attributed to OneSource.

Schwab's ability to use current dollars to meet debt was consistent from 1994 to 1996. It ranged from 1.05 to 1.04, as determined by the quick ratio. The ratio of net sales to plant and equipment has dropped significantly from its 1994 level of 8.25 to the 1996 level of 5.87. This again reflects the phenomenal sales growth that Schwab has experienced. Even though Schwab has increased its long-term debt in each of the past 10 years, much of this increase is attributable to the firm's investment in technology. Sales have grown at a proportionately greater rate. This reduced the ratio of net sales to plant and equipment.

[21] Ibid.
[22] Crane, Dwight B., and Bodie, Zvi, "Form Follows Function: The Transformation of Banking," *Harvard Business Review,* March 1996/April 1996, p. 109.
[23] Wayne, "For Charles Schwab, A Time to Tinker," p. 9.
[24] Crane and Bodie, "Form Follows Function."
[25] Hoover's Database, Charles Schwab Corporation.
[26] Corrigan, Tracy, and Authers, John, "Internet Use in Financial Services to Soar," *Financial Times,* June 6, 1997, p. 24.
[27] Prins, Ruth, "On-Line Trading Takes Off," *U.S. Banker,* May 1997, p. 81.
[28] Ibid.

[29] S&P, Investment Services Industry Survey, p. 10.
[30] Ibid., p. 20.

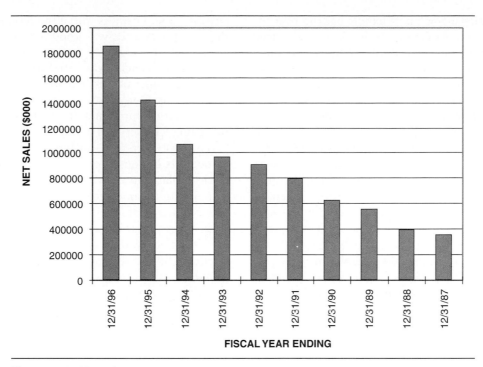

Figure 13.9 Net sales.

While Schwab has continually increased its long-term debt over the past 10 years, the ratio of long-term debt to equity decreased between 1995 and 1996. It experienced only a modest 0.02 gain between 1994 and 1995. This reflects the firm's income growth. Schwab's ratio of total liabilities to total assets has remained a constant 0.94, reflecting the firm's consistent ability to meet its liabilities.

Inventory turnover decreased from 1994 to 1995 but increased again in 1996. It did not return to 1994 levels. Conversely, inventories to days sales was up from 1994 to 1995, moving from 20.37 to 28.78. It decreased to 24.87 from 1995 to 1996.

The profitability of the firm is further reflected in the consistent rise in earnings per share (EPS). EPS has increased annually from 0.45 in 1992 to 1.3 in 1996.

STOCK/INVESTMENT OUTLOOK

Schwab's long history of increased sales, net income, and EPS underscores its success in finding and serving market demand. The firm's long-term history of investing in technology can be credited with its ability to increase its net income, even in years when other industry members have experienced downturns in revenue.

Schwab is the leader in its field, the full-service broker among the discount brokers. The stock has done well and should continue to perform. Broadly speaking, the financial services industry is gathering assets and seeking market share. Schwab should continue to outperform in this business measure. With the added influx of assets from baby boomers, Schwab is likely to prosper.[31]

RISK ANALYSIS

Schwab's business goals have been achieved by a combination of innovation, diversification, and technology. While the firm's success is directly linked to technology, the company's business decisions are not driven by technology. Rather, Schwab sets its business goals and then determines the best way to achieve them. The firm's ability to utilize technology in its overarching business strategy has provided both value-added services and new channels of distribution to its customers. In this manner, technology has directly contributed to the profitability of the firm.

To continue its record of excellence, Schwab must continue to vigilantly focus on its business objectives of asset gathering, increased sales, and increased net income. The plan for Schwab's future encompasses four areas: system capacity, technology, revenue loss, and growth. Each of these areas has its positive attributes; each also has inherent risks.

Schwab and other brokers that provide online brokerage services to their clients must begin addressing system capacity issues. Firms must be prepared to handle high capacity and must have the technology capabilities

---

[31] Stedman, Craig, and Vijayan, Jaikumar, "Schwab Acts," *Computerworld*, June 21, 1999, p. 113(1).

to do so. A contingency plan to handle backup over the telephone or other means must be in place.[32] The need for capacity and contingency planning is becoming more apparent as demand pressures are placed on Schwab's technical systems.

On July 2, and again on July 11, 1997, Schwab customers were left wondering if their trades had been completed, because the firm's computers were not working properly. This followed other technology difficulties such as the one on July 16, 1996, when e.Schwab's computers went down for about 15 minutes. Bob Franz, senior partner at Booz, Allen & Hamilton Inc., who specializes in technology issues at financial service companies, commented, "This is not a trivial matter, especially in a world where you have broad-based usage by customers directly through technology and the Internet. The issues of reliability and security are at the forefront of everyone's mind."[33]

Historically, Schwab has determined its business direction and then utilized technology to move toward its goal. If Schwab fails to address system capacity issues, technology decisions may begin to drive its business. Where capacity issues are concerned, it would be a matter of technology limiting the ability of the firm to address new business.

While Schwab has been successful in developing revenue sources through implementation of technology, the firm has also taken some financial "hits" from it. As recently as last year, the firm typically received $5.00 for each company research report it provided. Today there are competitors on the web who provide this service for less. MarketEdge's web financial service provides 25 company research reports per month for a monthly fee of $7.95.[34]

Increased competition among investment service firms is placing pressure on the revenues these firms can realize. This competition, coupled with technological innovation, has led to more efficient ways for investment service firms to package their services. With the right mix of products, providing value-added benefits to customers, and new distribution channels, Schwab is in a position to benefit and grow in the changing investment services industry.

Schwab used OneSource to convince mutual fund companies to share the names and addresses of their customers. Fund companies who allied with OneSource determined that control of the proprietary aspect of their customer base was of less value than their revenue stream. The business the fund companies received through OneSource was good for them. It was not as good as the business the fund company originated for itself, but it did add to the fund companies' cash flow.[35]

The customer names and addresses Schwab acquires in operating OneSource provide the firm with a customer relationship which it can use to build growth in other financial services areas.

The customer relationships Schwab has developed through its brokerage and mutual fund business are an obvious platform on which to build a banking relationship. If banks can offer investment services, the reverse service pattern of investment firms providing bank services is a reasonable business development. Schwab has an identified customer base, many of whom already conduct financial transactions through touch-tone phones, online computer systems, or the Internet. Simultaneously, the banking industry is expanding into online transactions.

Schwab could easily build a banking relationship with its current customers, without increased retail office space. Business growth in this area would require expansion of the current capacity of Schwab's technology systems and minimal increase in customer service personnel. Furthermore, expansion into banking could provide new jobs for customer service staff who are no longer needed because of the savings from the implementation of the automated VoiceBroker.

A merger of a discount, technologically innovative firm, such as Schwab, with a full-service firm would also be a marketing coup for demographic reasons. Currently, the majority of wealth holders are older non-technologically savvy investors. The transfer of wealth will be to younger technologically informed investors. A firm that is able to service both types of investor will be able to attract and retain investment funds as they shift from one generation to the next. A similar merger occurred in December 1996, when Dean Witter Discover & Co., the third-largest full service investment industry member, acquired deep discounter Lombard Brokerage Inc.

Another growth area Schwab should consider is management of 401(k) funds. Schwab has begun to address this market but not in an aggressive manner. Schwab needs to expand its services and handling capacity in this expansion area.

Schwab needs to be attentive to this market segment for two reasons. First, as baby boomers amass 401(k) funds for retirement, they will seek the convenience of a single management facility for their investments. This situation would be analogous to the supermarket concept provided for mutual funds through OneSource.

[32] "Putting Money Where Our Mouse Is," *Los Angeles Times,* April 29, 1997, Sec. D, p. 5.
[33] "Computer Problems Hit Schwab Again," *Bloomberg News,* as reported in *Los Angeles Times,* July 4, 1997.
[34] Ruply, Sebastian, "Web-Wise Investment Wisdom," *PC Magazine,* June 11, 1995, v. 15, n. 11, p. 66(1).
[35] Smith, Carrie R., "The Golden Touch," *Wall Street & Technology,* July 1994, v. 12, n. 1, p. 24(6).

Table 13.5 Securities Industry Composition

	Number of Companies	Percent of Total Industry Profits
Full-service firms (national)	6	38
Large investment banks	9	33
Regional firms	63	14
New York City-based firms	75	10
Discounters	16	5

Schwab has begun offering products and distribution channels for this type of product. However, there is still room for expansion and further development of services with this product line.

Second, with the potential of future privatization of Social Security, the public will need private investment management for Social Security contributions. When this happens, the public will look for investment firms that have a proven track record in managing 401(k) accounts. Schwab must have a recognized presence in this market niche to be in a position to benefit from a change in Social Security laws.

INDUSTRY AND MARKET ANALYSIS

The Securities Industry Association segmented the 169 firms comprising the brokerage industry at the end of 1995 as shown in Table 13.5.[36] As stated earlier, discounters are gaining market share, accounting for 13.6 percent of retail commission revenues in 1996. This reflects an increase from 1990 levels of 10.4 percent and 1985 levels of 5.4 percent. To gain a larger percent of total industry profits, discount brokers will have to expand their product offerings. The growth of discounters can be attributed to the individual investor. The typical customer for a discount broker is a white male in his mid-40s who owns a home, makes between $75,000 and $250,000 annually, and has approximately 4.5 years of college. These clients are attracted to discount brokers by the savings on commission.[37] Typically, these customers are from two-income families. They are pressed for time, desire information, and make their own investment decisions.[38]

The January 2, 1997, Standard and Poor's Industry Survey credits discount brokers with being aggressive marketers, opening retail offices in well-traveled areas, advertising extensively, and installing state-of-the-art telecommunications equipment to improve customer service.[39] Interestingly, this recent industry survey omits

mention of the impact the Internet has had on discounters. This omission reflects how recent the impact of the Internet has been on the industry. Brokerage firms first used the Internet solely for home page postings. In 1996, the first major industry member used the Internet for trading.

Steven Wallman, commissioner of the Securities and Exchange Commission, compares the growth of Internet trading to the rise of discount brokers in the 1980s. It is changing the landscape for small investors. Internet trading allows these investors to execute trades without paying for advice they do not want.[40]

Schwab's 1996 launch of web-based trading engendered many imitators. Other discounters, such as Quick and Reilly, entered the Internet trading market with the rest of the discounters following. Internet trading is also being explored by full service firms such as Merrill Lynch and Smith Barney. Due to the low barriers to entry, web-based trading is bringing further competition to the industry through new players, electronic brokerages, such as Portfolio Accounting World-Wide (PAWW), the Financial Network, and E*Trade.

Internet trading is very low cost and does not have to reach the level of profitability required by a traditional "brick and mortar" brokerage firm.[41] Electronic brokerage firms provide investors with account information 24 hours a day and offer substantially lower trading fees than even discount brokerages. These firms face the greatest competition from big discount brokers, such as Schwab, that have sufficiently deep pockets to finance investment in technology and offer proven ability in trade execution.[42]

Discounters have embraced the Internet more quickly than other industry players, possibly because the "do-it-yourself" nature of the Internet complements the characteristics of the investor who uses a discount

[36] S&P, Investment Services Industry Survey, p. 7.
[37] Ibid.
[38] Eaton, Leslie, "Wall Street Without Walls," *The New York Times,* November 11, 1996, Sec. A, p. 1.
[39] S&P, Investment Services Industry Survey, p. 9.

[40] Bransten, Lisa, "Comment & Analysis: A Share Deal in Cyberspace," *Financial Times,* May 21, 1996, p. 18.
[41] Lux, Hal, "The Cyberspace Threat; Will the Internet Do to Wall Street what Wall Street Did to the Banks?," *Investment Dealer's Digest,* June 3, 1996, p. S4.
[42] Bransten, "Comment & Analysis," p. 18.

brokerage firm.[43] Clients of discount brokerage firms already follow a do-it-yourself ethic by making their own investment decisions, unlike clients of full-service brokerage firms.

Wall Street and its customers' concerns regarding the security of web-based trading seem to be eroding quickly. This is attributed to large firms, such as Schwab, making account information or trading available through the Internet. Brokerage firm clients do not believe they would be offering this service if security was inadequate. A major security breach in online trading could adversely affect consumers' interest in online trading.[44]

Keeping security issues in perspective, K. Blake Darcy, chief executive of PC Financial Network, a service of Donaldson, Lufkin and Jenrette Securities, commented in 1997: "I'm sure every broker is using encryption to transmit anything that's at all sensitive. What I get a kick out of is that everyone goes to a restaurant and hands someone their credit card. It goes into a back room, and they could have a little printing press there, putting out additional credit cards with their name and their number on them. But they don't lie awake thinking about that."[45]

Security remains a concern for all investment firms, even though there has been no reported tampering with investment accounts or diversion of funds. Four necessities for securing Internet transactions are available today. Encryption insures data are not altered as they proceed through the World Wide Web. Private–public key cryptograph provides authentication of the origin and the destination of data. Verification of authentication entered the market in 1996,[46] and it insures the information is accurate in its statements.

Full-service Wall Street views Internet investing as dangerous. It eliminates Wall Street as the middleman and provides the individual investor with the same benefits previously available only to large institutional investors. Full-service firms have not yet offered online trading to their individual customers. In 1997, all 33 firms offering online trading were discount brokerages, according to the American Association of Individual Investors.[47] Full-service firms, while protective of their stockbrokers, were slower to accept the Internet. In 1996 Merrill Lynch introduced an online service providing customers with access to their accounts. Customers have the capability to execute transactions electronically. The firm hopes the Internet will link its customers more closely to its brokers.[48]

Full-service investment firms rely on their past resilience during periods of transition to prove that they will survive the changes imposed by online trading. These firms survived the 1975 doomsday predictions that surfaced when discount brokerages changed the distribution channels in the industry. Full-service firm clientele tend to be long-term investors who use the Internet for information. They also want advice, portfolio management, or a consultant with whom they can have a quick conversation regarding their investments. Most importantly, the full-service brokers' clients have the most assets.[49]

Ultimately, demographics will impact online trading. Most assets are held by older investors, while younger investors have superior computer skills. Presumably the demand for online trading will increase as the transfer of wealth occurs between these generations.[50] John Sherman, president and chief executive officer of the regional full-service firm Scott & Stringfellow, commented, "In 10 or 15 years, when the technologically proficient generation gets into a huge earning power position, it will cause a giant change."[51] By then, the full-service market will be repositioned to provide its clients with online trading options.

The full-service market's ability to retain customers in the face of increasing pressure from competitors who provide Internet or other online trading services is important in view of the growth of discount brokers. These low-cost brokers acknowledge that they are not going to grow if their customer base does not expand beyond current discount clientele. Discount brokerage firms are competing for customers who currently use full-service brokers and are considering investment on their own.[52]

Schwab's 1992 launch of OneSource provided investors with a new distribution channel for mutual funds. OneSource, through the application of technology, united Schwab with mutual fund providers and diversified Schwab's product line.[53] From the view that imitation is the most sincere form of flattery, OneSource's success caused both discount and full-service competitors to develop and implement similar programs.

While investors have been able to trade stocks on the web since early 1996, Internet trading of mutual funds

[43] Lux, "The Cyberspace Threat," p. S4.
[44] Ibid.
[45] "Putting Money Where Our Mouse Is."
[46] Lewison, et al., "Cyberspace Investing."
[47] Harrigan, Susan, "Online Trading Boom. Shop Wisely for Electronic Broker," *Newsday,* April 6, 1997, p. F10.

[48] Eaton, "Wall Street Without Walls," p. 1.
[49] Rule, Bruce, "The Future of On-Line Trading," *Investment Dealers' Digest,* December 16, 1996, p. 14.
[50] Ibid.
[51] Ibid.
[52] "Putting Money Where Our Mouse Is."
[53] Wilson, Walter P., "Why You Need a Digital Strategy—Today," *Electrical World,* July 1996, v. 210, n. 7, p. 54.

Table 13.6 Industry Comparison of Net Income

Firm	1991	1992	1993	1994	1995
Alex Brown, Inc.	52.0	58.6	89.2	70.9	95.6
Bear Stearns Cos.	143.0	295.0	362.0	387.0	241.0
Edwards (AG), Inc.	106.0	119.0	155.0	124.0	171.0
Inter-Regional Fin. Group	21.1	34.5	47.6	25.5	35.9
Legg Mason, Inc.	21.1	30.2	36.0	16.3	37.9
Merrill Lynch	696.0	952.0	1394.0	1017.0	1114.0
Morgan Stanley Group	475.0	510.0	786.0	395.0	600.0
Paine Webber Group	151.0	213.0	246.0	32.0	80.8
Piper Jaffray Cos.	19.3	37.5	41.0	25.3	−14.1
Quick & Reilly Group	22.7	28.7	42.5	41.5	69.4
Raymond James Financial	26.7	41.0	49.3	42.1	46.1
Salomon, Inc.	507.0	550.0	864.0	−398.	457.0
Schwab (Charles), Corp.	49.5	81.5	124.0	135.0	173.0

was a problem. Difficulties resulted from regulations, settlement systems, and the multiple classes of shares in the same fund. By late 1996, several firms, including Schwab and Jack White & Co., provided trading for mutual funds on the web. Limitations were placed on clients at the Schwab site. They either had to be existing clients or had to telephone the firm to obtain an account name and password. As with its Internet equity trading system, Schwab conducts off-line verification of security issues for OneSource clients.[54]

Only Schwab and Bear Stearns experienced an increase in net income in 1994. While Schwab increased its income in 1995, Bear Stearns net income declined 37.72 percent. A five-year comparison of Schwab with the 12 principle market participants, summarized in Table 13.6, indicates that Schwab was the only industry member to experience continued growth in net income from 1991 to 1995.[55] As the industry leader, Schwab has provided value-added services to its customers through products such as OneSource.

In further comparing industry participants, an important financial ratio for investment services firms is Return On Equity (ROE). This is a measure of profitability derived from net income divided by average shareholder's equity. ROE is not used to analyze investment service firms because broker balance sheets include matched fund assets. Many product areas do not have these associated assets. The 1995 ROE for full-service brokers was 20.3 percent, 11.5 percent for large investment banks, 33.8 percent for regional brokers, and 38.8 percent for discounters.[56] Schwab realized an ROE of 31.4 percent in 1995.

ROLE OF RESEARCH AND DEVELOPMENT

Schwab must remain in the forefront of technology applications in the investment services industry. Remaining current with technology and service is critical to Schwab's vision for the future. Due to the fast pace of change in the industry and the associated technology systems, Schwab risks losing market share if it does not continue to use technology to achieve its business goals.

TECHNOLOGICAL STORY

Schwab's latest business strategy involves computer telephony integration (CTI) technology. Schwab's VoiceBroker provides computerized voice recognition. Unlike earlier technology, CTI does not require a learning process. With CTI, IT managers can link their phone systems with databases.[57] VoiceBroker enables customers to verbally request stock and mutual fund quotes and market information. When a client calls Schwab for a quote, the call is answered by a computer. The computer provides the requested information. Developed by Schwab in conjunction with Nuance Communications, Voice-Broker has one of the largest vocabularies of any voice recognition system on the market. The database for the system contains more than 13,000 stocks.[58] VoiceBroker was installed to respond to the more than 30 million calls Schwab receives annually for price quotes. The system has achieved 95 percent accuracy.[59]

Schwab's director of voice technology, Andrea Smart, advised, "the motivation for developing the system [VoiceBroker] is clear. Nationwide our [customer

[54] Whelan, John, "In the Shadow of the Internet," *Financial Planning*, November, 1996, p. 177.
[55] S&P, Investment Services Industry Survey, p. 30.
[56] Ibid., p. 21

[57] McCarthy, Vance, "CTI Lets You Coddle Customers at Lower Cost," *Datamation*, December 1996, v. 42, n. 18, p. 46(4).
[58] Tomasula, Dean, "On the Cutting Edge," *Wall Street & Technology*, December 1996, v. 14; n. 12; p. 36.
[59] Ibid.

service] representatives take hundreds of thousands of calls a day. Anything we can do to shift that work to technology will help us maintain good customer service."[60] VoiceBroker has increased the productivity of Schwab's customer support staff, as well as cut the costs associated with staffing the telephone response lines.

Smart does not intend to let this latest Schwab innovation remain unimproved. Schwab engineers are working to push the CTI of VoiceBroker beyond simply getting a stock quote. Smart and her staff are expanding the system so customers can enter buy or sell transactions. [61]

TECHNOLOGICAL INVESTMENT AND ANALYSIS

Schwab's technology utilization can be seen to foreshadow the future. Ernst & Young reported in the June 6, 1997, edition of *Financial Times,* that the number of financial service firms using the Internet is spiraling upward. Internationally, the information technology budgets of financial services firms grew 4 to 6 percent from 1995 to 1996.[62]

OneSource collects approximately 600 mutual funds from 70 fund families in one product, making Schwab one of the top three mutual fund distributors.[63] OneSource developers Tom Seip and John Coghlan claimed to have invented the mutual fund supermarket. "We knew that this was how we wanted to buy mutual funds, and we figured there were millions of other people who did too."[64]

Until 1992, each mutual fund company serviced its own accounts. It was difficult for consumers to achieve both diversification and high performance in a single fund family. Consumers dealt with different firms, statements, rules, and sales representatives.[65] OneSource united Schwab with mutual fund providers to expand and diversify Schwab's product line.[66] It changed the mutual fund business by providing consumers with a choice of funds from a variety of fund providers. Their funds were summarized in a single account with one monthly statement to track all their funds. No transaction fees are incurred on OneSource accounts. Customers could shift money to different fund families without charge. Schwab is remunerated for OneSource directly by the funds, receiving between 0.25 and 0.40 percent for every $100 of fund shares held in the supermarket accounts.[67]

Sophisticated technology and software applications enable funds to be consolidated and a single summary statement of client fund holdings to be printed. In 1994, two years after OneSource was started, Charles Schwab commented, "Technology is at the core of OneSource. The forces of technology have enabled us to introduce a far-flung set of funds in one package. It is only because of this [technology] that we are able to integrate all of these funds together into OneSource."[68]

Schwab's sentiments were echoed by John Philip Coghlan, executive vice president of Schwab Institutional. "We are very much a technology company. Before, we had a fairly monolithic system that would have made this approach into these different markets impossible."[69] To implement OneSource, Schwab revamped their technology to a client/server platform. This system provides clients with the ability to download information on a daily basis for portfolio valuation.[70] Technology also provides Schwab customers with a variety of methods in which to conduct OneSource business. Customers can contact a broker on an 800 line available 24-hours per day, a touch-tone phone, or through the Internet.[71]

The impact of the OneSource innovation is reflected in Schwab's sales. In the first half of 1996, Schwab's sales of mutual funds through OneSource increased 70 percent over sales during the last half of 1995. This was considerably faster than the industry's growth rate.[72] OneSource has proven to be a forceful asset-gathering tool for Schwab. It accumulated $60 billion in customer accounts in 1996.[73]

OneSource's impact on the industry is also reflected in the fact that full service broker-dealers have amended their policies regarding brokers selling outside funds. Firms such as Smith Barney now offer investors a wide range of fund choices, partly in response to the competition posed by fund supermarkets such as OneSource and partly to demonstrate to customers that they want to provide the best products for each investor.[74]

The success of OneSource is further underscored by Schwab's recent policy of charging new funds $12,000

[60] Ibid.

[61] Ibid.

[62] Corrigan and Authers, "Internet Use in Financial Services to Soar."

[63] Stalk, et al., "Breaking Compromises, Breakaway Growth."

[64] Whitford, David, "The Mutual Fund Revolution: Is it Good for You?," *Fortune,* February 3, 1997, v. 135, n. 2, p. 136(4).

[65] Stalk, et al., "Breaking Compromises, Breakaway Growth."

[66] Wilson, "Why You Need a Digital Strategy—Today."

[67] Whitford, "The Mutual Fund Revolution."

[68] Smith, "The Golden Touch."

[69] Ibid.

[70] Ibid.

[71] McLean, Bethany, "A Better Way to Buy No-Load Mutual Funds," *Fortune,* December 25, 1995, v. 132, n. 13, p. 150(3).

[72] S&P, Investment Services Industry Survey, p. 8.

[73] Stalk, et al., "Breaking Compromises, Breakaway Growth."

[74] S&P, Investment Services Industry Survey, p. 10.

to join the network. Schwab now collects fees from each fund ranging from 0.25 to 0.40 percent for shares held in the supermarket account plus a "membership fee" directly from the fund to allow the fund to be distributed through OneSource.[75] Fee generation on the $60 billion Schwab held in account in 1996, at a minimum, totaled $150 million.

In 1994, the Internet was not discussed at the Securities Industry Association's annual technology show. In 1995, the topic received substantial interest. In 1996, the annual show had an entire section devoted to it. Such developments are reflective of the manner in which the Internet grew from an interesting new addition in the technology market to a primary channel of distribution for the investment industry.[76] A 1996 study by Business Communications Company identified that the U.S. electronic trading market in 1995 was almost $1.4 billion. It was predicted to grow at an 11.9 percent average annual growth rate and reach a level of $2.3 billion by 2000.[77]

Schwab was the first major brokerage to permit online trading through the World Wide Web. Schwab built its reputation as a discount broker as an aggressive user of new technology to cut costs. It passed the savings on to clients. It was not surprising that it was the first major security industry member to implement Internet trading. What is noteworthy is that Schwab considered the web sufficiently secure to become one of the first to risk putting customer accounts online.[78]

At the beginning of 1996, Schwab estimated that 15 percent of its customers were trading online through the firm's computer network.[79] After determining that the web provided sufficient security to allow trading, Schwab initiated a pilot program for web-based online trading in March 1996. Schwab's Internet trading started only one year after the firm first established its web home page (www.schwab.com). Members of the pilot group who executed trades through the e.Schwab system were charged $39.00 per trade while non-e.Schwab customers received a 10 percent discount off the firm's regular commission schedule.[80]

The success realized from the Internet pilot program resulted in Schwab offering Internet trading to all cus-

tomers in May 1996. In addition, the cost savings Schwab realized from the increased percentage of trades executed electronically were passed on to its customers. Effective July 9, 1996, Schwab reduced its flat fee on all stock transactions up to 1,000 shares executed through e.Schwab to $29.95 and 3 cents for each additional share, a 23 percent reduction from the $39.00 fee imposed in March of the same year.[81] This $29.95 rate is compared with Schwab's $70 rate for phone trades.

In January, 1997, Schwab launched a dedicated web site for the mutual fund marketplace (www.schwab.com/funds).[82]

Schwab's advance into the Internet underscores its belief that online investing is the future of the brokerage business. Beth Sawi, vice president with Schwab, commented "all investors will be managing their investments through their PC." Sawi advised that prior to launching its online service, Schwab explore whether it would be taking business from its existing market. As a result of this research, Schwab determined that if it did not provide an Internet distribution channel, someone else would.[83]

The technology Schwab implemented for its Internet trading was developed in house. Schwab believed the knowledge it had gained from other trading software, such as StreetSmart and e.Schwab, provided the ability to build a system with Internet-based transaction capabilities.[84] Schwab provided Internet trading by linking its web site to its proprietary mainframe system. The system was enhanced with a custom code for menu-driven customer options.[85]

Schwab utilized Netscape's Secure Socket Layer technology. This approach includes encryption and is considered the industry standard for security technology.[86] By providing online trading through the Internet, Schwab implied that the net is secure ground for transmitting customer account information. Schwab extended security measures by prohibiting customers from changing an address, withdrawing money, or liquidating an account through the Internet.[87]

Schwab's web-based trading was built in only eight weeks. This quick response is credited to several factors, including planning ahead, working with small

[75] Whitford, "The Mutual Fund Revolution."

[76] Lux, "The Cyberspace Threat."

[77] "Bullish Future for Electronic Trading," *Economic Trends*, February 1996, v. 23, n. 10; Lexis-Nexis, accessed July 1, 1997.

[78] Smith, Laura B., "Putting Safety Net to the Test: Schwab to Offer Trading via World-Wide Web," *PC Week*, March 11, 1996, v. 13, n. 10, p. 1(2).

[79] Lux, "The Cyberspace Threat."

[80] Weisul, Kimberly, "Schwab Gives Go-Ahead for Trading on Internet; Brokerage Launches Pilot Program This Month," *Investment Dealers' Digest*, March 18, 1996, p. 12.

[81] "Schwab Electronic Trading Growth Drives New Cost Savings for Investors," *PR Newswire*, July 1, 1996.

[82] "Schwab Launches OneSource Web Site," *PR Newswire*, January 15, 1997.

[83] Lorek, L. A., "Firms Take Stock On-Line; Accounts Allow Customers to Buy from Home," *Sun-Sentinel*, November 13, 1996, p. 1D.

[84] Weisul, "Schwab Gives Go-Ahead."

[85] Smith, "Putting Safety Net to the Test."

[86] Weisul, "Schwab Gives Go-Ahead."

[87] Smith, "Putting Safety Net to the Test."

development teams, using internal staff, sticking to a short development cycle, and, while concerned about security, not letting security concerns cripple development. Schwab successfully balanced results with the need to build an infrastructure.[88]

Schwab has realized great success from its Internet experience. Trading on the Internet provides Schwab clients with fast trades, easy access to real-time information, including portfolio accounting services, electronic news and quote services, and cheaper brokerage commission.[89] In March 1997, Schwab reported reaching $50 billion in online customer assets, both Internet traded and other online trading venues, in 700,000 active accounts. The figures shown on Table 13.7 reflect continued growth in Schwab's online business.[90]

Through online accounts, individuals manage approximately $100 billion in assets. That figure could jump to $525 billion by the turn of the century.[91] If Schwab's market share remains at 47 percent,[92] it will have access to nearly $247 billion dollars of investment assets in the year 2000. Whatever the percent of online traded assets Schwab ultimately administers for its clients, online trading, including Internet trading, will add up to a powerful asset-gathering tool.

Schwab does not intend to abandon its retail office or telecommunications presence. Randy Goldman, vice president of electronic brokerage marketing at Schwab, commented in 1996, "In the world of electronics, when you really don't know who's on the other side of a trade, its nice to have the Schwab name out there."[93]

Schwab decided not to sacrifice its retail office operations. A 1996 study by SRI Consulting estimated that by the year 2000 no more than 8 percent of all U.S. households will regularly use online brokerage services. However, that 8 percent of households represents 15 percent of all investors. Additional research identifies these users as prime customers who are financially competent and well informed. They are the type of client that financial institutions would want to attract.[94]

Table 13.7 Growth of Schwab Online Business

Date	Number of Active Online Accounts	Assets In Billion $
December 1995	336,600	$23.3
June 1996	467,000	$31.5
December 1996	617,000	$41.7
January 1997	669,000	$46.5
February 1997	712,000	$50.0

TECHNOLOGICAL INNOVATIONS

NETWORK

Schwab has implemented a customized web-based analysis reporting application that helps the company locate and fix trading errors. It also helps identify market trends and track changes in tax law and other regulations. The application is code-named Schwab Metric and Analysis Reporting Tool (SMART).

SMART generates significant payback by automatically collecting information for audits on Schwab's finance controls and risk assessment systems in one-sixth of the time previously required. It also lets Schwab capture trading errors proactively instead of reactively, reducing the time required for a correction from days to hours. SMART helps ICAD users be more productive and informed.

DATA

Schwab has an intranet, called the Schweb. It is being used to help marketers better understand customer trends by using data. If a customer opens an account with $10,000, Schwab wants to know if that customer also has significant additional funds available to invest. To get this information Schwab has installed Epiphany's Clarity, a web package that can extract information from numerous sources, both legacy systems and external repositories.

Steve Blank, Epiphany's founder and executive vice president of marketing, said Schwab had two choices: install an online analytical processing (OLAP) server and a variety of data extraction and mining tools along with a web application server; or install a shrink-wrapped product. Schwab chose Epiphany's product.[95]

RECOMMENDATION FOR THE FUTURE

The financial services industry is being transformed by information technology, whether by development of

[88] Comaford, Christine, "Schwab: Faster Than a Speeding Web Site," *PC Week,* April 29, 1996, v. 13, n. 17, p. 59(1).

[89] Gianturco, Michael, "Software for Hard Choices," *Forbes,* August 26, 1996, v. 158, n. 5, p. S33(2).

[90] "Schwab Reaches Milestones in Online Business," *Business Wire,* March 17, 1997.

[91] Hannon, Kerry, "Click Buy, Click Sell," *Working Woman,* February 1997, v. 22, n. 2, pp. 58–60.

[92] Hoover's Database, Charles Schwab Corporation.

[93] Lux, "The Cyberspace Threat."

[94] "The Potential of Online Investing," *Industries in Transition,* March 1997, v. 24, n. 11.

[95] Schwartz, Jeffrey, "Schwab Gets Serious About Backup," *InternetWeek,* June 21, 1999, p. 12.

value-added services for customers or new channels of distribution for its products.

For a firm like Charles Schwab, the changes occurring in the financial industry are an opportunity. The firm will have to continue its policy of setting its business goal(s) and determining how it will best achieve its desired targets. Technology has been an important part of Schwab's success, enabling product innovations and new channels of distribution such as OneSource and Internet trading.

These technology-enabled products have helped Schwab achieve its business goals, but did not drive the firm's business decisions. To remain successful, Schwab will have to plan and prepare to address the changing landscape of the investment industry. Schwab must be ready to move on several issues or risk losing its market share.

First, Schwab must be constantly aware that its credibility is on the line for every trade it makes. If unable to maintain its credibility, customers will conduct business with Schwab's competitors. The firm must address the system capacity issues that it has been experiencing. Schwab's technology systems have to be prepared to handle unexpected high-capacity trading.

Second, Schwab must continue to be an innovator in implementing technology in the investment service industry. Schwab has been successful due to its ability to address consumers' needs and product demands in a quick and cost-efficient manner. It is too early to tell if Internet trading or VoiceBroker will have the same effect on the firm's bottom line as OneSource had. Regardless, Schwab must continue pursuing excellence in providing products and distribution channels that ad-

dress clients' needs. Technology has been a partner in Schwab's success and can be expected to continue being an ally in the firm reaching its future business goals.

Next, Schwab will have to continue monitoring areas of revenue loss. The competition within the industry will continue to place pressure on revenue margins. In the past, Schwab has been able to diversify and provide innovative products that bridge these areas of revenue loss. This is a business strategy that the firm must continue to pursue if it expects to continue to grow.

Finally, Schwab has to look outside its traditional customer base to acquire new clients and new revenue sources that will enable the firm to grow. Schwab should consider entering new product areas such as banking and insurance. Additionally, Schwab should consider merging with a full-service competitor and expanding its capacity in 401(k) management offerings. By expanding its customer base, as well as services offered, Schwab will not only increase its sales and profits, but also its percent of profits within its industry segment.

The investment services industry is growing, thanks in part to aging baby boomers who are investing more and building up savings for retirement. Schwab is in a position to seize this opportunity. With continued planning and preparation, Schwab will succeed in its business objectives of asset gathering, increased sales, and increased net income. Technology will continue to be an important component of this success.[96]

---

[96] Serwer, Andrew, "Online and Off, Schwab's the One," *Fortune,* May 10, 1999, v. 139, i. 9, p. 181(1).

CASE QUESTIONS

Strategic Questions

1. What is the strategic direction of the corporation?

2. Who or what forces are driving this direction?

3. What has been the catalyst for change?

4. What are the critical success factors for this corporation?

5. What are the core competencies for this corporation?

Technological Questions

6. What technologies has the corporation relied on?

7. What has caused a change in the use of technology in the corporation?

8. How has this change been implemented?

9. How successful has the technological change been?

Quantitative Questions

10. What does the corporation say about its financial ability to embark on a major technological program of advancement?

11. What conclusions can be reached from an analysis of the financial information to support or contradict this financial ability?

12. What analysis can be made by examining the following ratio groups?

   Net income/net sales
   Net sales/no. of employees

Quick ratio
Net sales/plant and equipment

13. What conclusions can be reached by analyzing the financial trends?

Internet Questions

14. What does the corporation's web page present about their business?

15. Is the corporation's web page a good use of corporate resources?

Industry Questions

16. What challenges and opportunities is the industry facing?

17. Is the industry oligopolistic or competitive?

18. Does the industry face a change in government regulation?

19. How will technology impact the industry?

Data Questions

20. What role do data play in the future of the corporation?

21. How important are data to the corporation's continued success?

22. How will the capture and maintenance of customer data impact the corporation's future?

TECHNOLOGY TIPS

MICROSOFT WORD TIPS

ENVELOPES AND LABELS

Writing on an envelope may not be professional when sending your resume to a company. You may want your printer to do this for you. How about writing the addresses of every member of your organization on the envelopes? This can be time consuming, but with the labels feature this does not have to be the case. The following will allow you to tackle these two tasks.

Before you can proceed with the following, ensure that you have labels that are compatible with Microsoft Word97 and that you have the product ID number of your labels.

Creating a Label

1. With WORD97 already open, click on FILE. From the drop-down menu, click on NEW.
2. A dialog box will appear. Click on the LETTERS AND FAXES tab.
3. Double-click on the MAILING LABEL WIZARD
4. The office assistant will appear. Click on CREATE ONE LABEL. . . .
5. Click on the LABELS tab. Type the address or anything you would like in the address section.
6. Make sure that the product ID number of the labels you are using matches the one in the product ID label section. If it does not, click on the label area in order to bring up the LABEL OPTIONS dialog box. This will allow you to select the type of labels that you have. NOTE: *the printer will automatically use the manual feed tray when printing your labels and envelopes. You may change this by selecting from the TRAY options in the LABEL OPTIONS dialog box.*
7. When you have completed selecting your label and have typed in the information, select from the print option. You may select a full page of labels or just one label.
8. Click on PRINT when you are done.

Envelopes

1. With WORD97 already open, click on FILE. From the drop-down menu, click on NEW.
2. A dialog box will appear. Click on the LETTERS AND FAXES tab.
3. Double-click on the ENVELOPE WIZARD icon.
4. The office assistant will appear. Click on CREAT ONE LABEL. . . .
5. Type in the return and delivery address in the appropriate boxes.
6. The wizard is set to print on Size 10 envelopes (standard business size). If you have a different sized envelope, click on the envelope icon. The envelope options will appear. You can select which envelope size you are using, or customize the size of the envelope, by entering the dimensions. In addition, you can select which tray in the printer you are going to feed the printer the envelope and how you are going to feed the envelope from the printing options tab.
7. Once you have completed your selections, you can either print the envelope or save it to the active document. Saving it to the active document will allow you to print the envelope with the document and have the envelope available at all times. NOTE: *The envelope will always print out with the document unless you select the pages that you want printed when you use the ADD TO DOCUMENT option.*

ADDITIONAL NOTES

Creating a Mailing List for Labels and Envelopes

If you have an Access database with the addresses of the persons/companies, you can create labels and envelopes for each one. Just click on TOOLS and then MAIL MERGE. . . . Just follow the steps in order to set up the mailing list. The Access section will go into more detail as to how labels can be created from databases.

MICROSOFT EXCEL TIPS

FUNCTIONS

If you forgot how to perform a certain computation, Excel may be able to help with over 200 built-in formulas called functions. Not all functions can be covered here. Instead, we will concentrate on the use of functions and how to use them.

What Are Functions Exactly?

Functions are predefined formulas that perform calculations by using specific values, called arguments, in a particular order, called the syntax. For example, the SUM function adds values or ranges of cells. Arguments can be numbers, text, logical values such as TRUE or FALSE, arrays, error values such as #N/A, or cell references. The argument you designate must produce a valid value for that argument. Arguments can also be constants, formulas, or other functions.

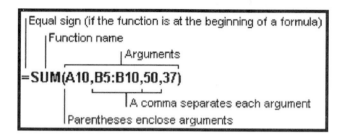

The syntax of a function begins with the function name, followed by an opening parenthesis, the arguments for the function separated by commas, and a closing parenthesis. If the function starts a formula, type an equal sign (=) before the function name. As you create a formula that contains a function, the Formula Palette will assist you.

Selecting Functions

1. To make use of a function, click the cell in which you want to enter the function.

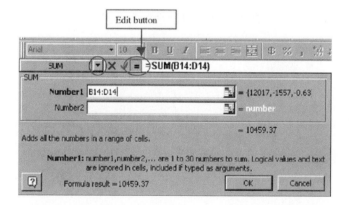

2. Click on the Edit Formula button in the formula bar.
3. Click the down arrow key next to the Functions box. Click on the function you would like to use from the drop-down list. Click on More Functions to make the Paste Function dialog box appear and display all of the available functions.

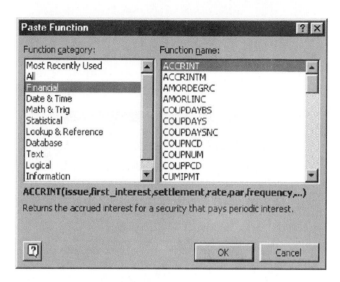

4. Enter the arguments by clicking on individual cells, selecting a range, or entering a range name. In the window shown on the right, the function will add values in cells B14 through D14.
5. When you complete the formula, press Enter or click on OK.

Function Example	Description
=SUM(S15:S28)	This function adds all values in cells S:14 through S:28
=AVERAGE(C4:G9)	This function calculates the mean average of the values in cells C4 through G9
=MIN(SALES)	This function looks for the minimum value in the range named SALES

6. The result of the formula will appear in the cell in which the formula was entered.

MICROSOFT POWERPOINT TIPS

You can create special effects on your text WordArt tool on the Drawing toolbar. WordArt objects are actually drawing objects and aren't treated as text. You can use tools on the WordArt and Drawing toolbars to change a WordArt object in the same way you change a drawing object. For example, you can change its fill, line style, shadow, or 3-D effect. However, you can't see the WordArt object in outline view or check its spelling.

WordArt

1. If the drawing toolbar is not displayed, right click on the top toolbar and select DRAWING from the drop-down menu.

2. Click on the WordArt button.
3. The WordArt gallery below will appear. Select the WordArt style that you would like to use and click on OK.

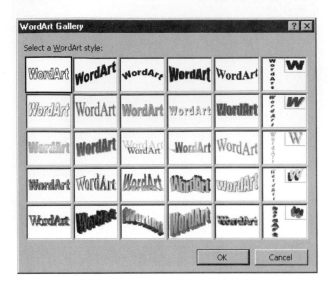

4. Type in the text that you would like to convert to WordArt. Select the font size and style from the EDIT WordArt TEXT dialog box. Click on OK when you are finished.
5. The WordArt will appear on your slide along with its toolbar.

Modifying WordArt

Use the WordArt toolbar to:

* Edit text
* View the WordArt gallery
* Format WordArt
* Change the WordArt shape
* Rotate WordArt
* Make all letters in WordArt the same size
* Put WordArt into a vertical alignment
* Set the alignment
* Adjust the spacing between the letters

MICROSOFT ACCESS TIPS

SAVING FORMS AS REPORTS

Creating a report to present certain information about the database is not always necessary. Your forms may suffice if you just want to show a customer's record, information on a product, or the status on an order. Forms may be easier for others to read since they are normally used to enter data and do not have the cluttered look that tables have. The following steps will demonstrate how to create a report from an existing form.

REPORTS OUT OF FORMS

1. From the database window click on the FORMS tab and click on a form that you would like to create a report from. In the figure below we have clicked on the Mailing List Form.

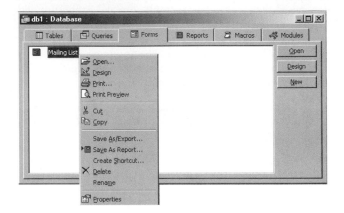

2. Now right click on the form so the pop-up menu appears. Select SAVE AS REPORT.
3. A dialog box will appear asking you to assign a name to the report. You can leave the report with the same name as the form or enter a different one. Click on OK when you are done.
4. Your form will be saved under the reports tab of the database window. To view your report, click on the REPORTS tab.
5. Click on the report you just converted from a form and then click on the PREVIEW button located inside the database window.

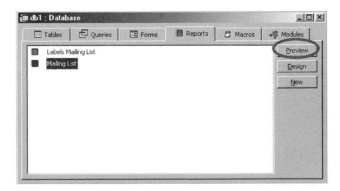

A preview of your Report will appear in a separate window. You can either print it out or close the window and use the report later.

MICROSOFT FRONTPAGE TIPS

SAVING FRONTPAGE FILES FOR OUTPUT TO THE WEB

If you have an Access database that you would like to put out on the web, you can simply click on a couple of buttons and everything will be converted to HTML. There are different ways to save an Access database (static, dynamic, dynamic ASP). In this chapter we will concentrate on the simplest way of saving the database, which is the static HTML format. Static web pages are easier to create, yet they lack the power, timeliness, and accuracy of dynamic web pages.

Export a Data Sheet to Static HTML Format

1. With the database you wish to save as HTML open, click on FILE from the menu bar in Access.

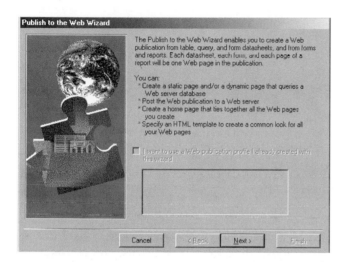

2. The Publish to Web Wizard dialog box will appear. Click on the NEXT button.
3. The wizard will provide step by step instructions on how to save the database in HTML format and allow you to select which parts you would like to convert in HTML.

4. In the fifth window you will be asked if you want to create a home page that will serve as an index page for all of the Access documents that you save as HTML from the current database.

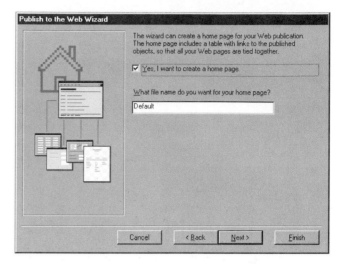

5. Continue with the rest of the steps and click FINISH at the end. The database will be converted to HTML format and will be ready for you to publish on your web page.

ADDITIONAL NOTE ABOUT STATIC AND DYNAMIC HTML FORMAT

You determine which HTML file format to use based on your application needs. Use static HTML format when your data does not change frequently and your World Wide Web application does not require a form. Use dynamic format when your data changes frequently and your web application needs to store and retrieve live data from your Microsoft Access database using a form.

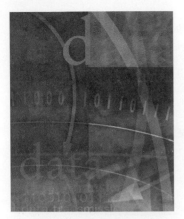

CHAPTER 14

INFORMATION MANAGEMENT AND SOCIETY
HEALTH CARE INDUSTRY

Information Management and Society

The increased use of information systems impacts almost everyone and everything, from individuals to society as a whole. Businesses must be very careful to protect their data, its integrity and privacy, and the way it is used. While technology is presumed to increase employment in general, those workers displaced by technology must be retrained. They must learn new skills to find a new position or to operate the technology that now performs their old job.

Governments have long been involved in collecting large amounts of data. Technology has enabled them to collect and operate on this data more efficiently. Lower prices, improved capabilities, and more user-friendly features have made technology available to many more people. An important social issue is providing access to technology for everyone. Increasing dependence on technology brings new issues and risks to an organization and a society. These include data control issues from workers, consultants, and business partners. Ways to minimize data threats include training, oversight committees, audits, and the separation of duties.

Threats also come from the outside. These can be minimized by software and hardware techniques including the encryption of data, dial-back modems, or access controls.

Working in today's technological environment brings business ethics increasingly to the forefront, not only for companies as a whole, but also for individual workers. People's lives can be impacted by technology mishaps such as inaccurate data, the abuse of information, or defective or poorly designed software or hardware.

Effect of Technology on the Privacy of Individuals The ease with which information regarding individuals can be acquired is astonishing. Basic and statistical data can be purchased from sources such as the government, universities, clubs, mail-order firms, and the Internet. Laws in the United States protecting what private organizations can do with data makes data even more available. In the federal government, strict laws regulate what can and cannot be divulged.

Employee privacy is another issue. Computers can be used to monitor employees and what they do while they are working on the computer. Some employers read their employees' electronic mail or evaluate their performance using the computer. Ways to protect yourself include asking the company not to distribute your personal data, why they need the data, and what data are optional to give. You can also ask the company not to distribute your personal data. You have the right to check any data that refers to you and to ask to have it changed if you feel the data is inaccurate. Some people find the increased use of technology dehumanizing, since companies can know increasing amounts of information about their employees and their work habits.

Jobs It is generally believed that technology increases jobs overall and improves the standard of living. However, as technology replaces more jobs of less skilled workers, those workers will have a more difficult time finding other jobs unless they are retrained. The new jobs provided by technology tend to be better paying, physically safer, and less repetitive. To remain competitive, everyone must continuously learn new skills to stay ahead in a rapidly changing marketplace. It is important to carefully study technology trends to predict correctly in which skills to invest for the future. Technology offers people with disabilities the opportunity to work in ways never previously thought possible.

Telecommuting As the percentage of service versus manufacturing jobs increases, the opportunities to telecommute, or work from home, increase. Service jobs tend to be less dependent on a worker's physical location. Cities with long commute times such as New York are experimenting with telecommuting. The organization gains because of decreased costs for office space and flexibility in hiring additional workers. Evaluating and managing telecommuting employees are difficult tasks, however. The worker gains the time and expense of commuting to work, but loses because of a loss of personal contact, decreased motivation, and a home environment that can be more comfortable and more distracting.

Education The effects of technology on education have not been as marked as in other areas of society. Some Internet teaching is occurring, but this phenomenon is not widespread due to the high cost of development and lack of interaction. Problems with using technology to educate include its expense, the fact that developing lessons through technology is time intensive, and the limited evidence that teaching through technology is the same or better than traditional methods.

Governments While governments can be slow to use new technology due to limited budgets, long procurement cycles, and smaller IS staffs, there is much to gain from applying technology. The federal government has used the Internet and bulletin board systems to provide information and responses, including the filing of tax forms. Politicians are likely to use more technology during campaigns to target voters, write letters, solicit contributions, and announce meetings.

Access to Technology The gap between the haves and the have-nots can easily be widened through the abuse of technology. This occurs most readily through the control of access to technology. Many suggest that as companies get new hardware and software, the old equipment should be donated to poor schools or poor countries. Although this technology might be completely outdated, the recipients might otherwise not have received anything. On the other hand, rapid advances in technology and decreasing costs of hardware

sometimes cost the nonprofit organization more than the outdated equipment is worth.

Legal Liability The legal system is a paper-based world. Laws and court decisions about electronic media are still being shaped. If an electronic media provider exercises control over its output, such as altering or deleting messages from users, they may be sued for tampering with the output from its customers.

Digital Cash Digital cash refers to a method of payment used in transactions over electronic networks. Buyers and sellers connect through a third trusted party, such as a bank, to exchange payment. Digital cash can insure buyers are legitimate to make purchases and sellers are able to receive payment and provide the product.

Threats to Information The biggest threat to information comes from authorized users who make mistakes such as deleting wanted data, designing flaws into programs, or who input the wrong information. Through careful design, testing, and training, some of these problems can be minimized internally.

As technology changes, external threats change and so do the criminals. For example, robbers are now more likely to hold up customers at an ATM rather than trying to hold up a bank. Threats to information can come from such places as employees and consultants, outside hackers, links to business partners, and viruses.

Threats from Employees While a company must trust its employees, it also faces a threat from them. Careful screening and monitoring of potential and current employees can minimize risks. Especially complicated issues can arise with IS employees. Since these employees provide programs and support, they must be given greater access to technology than other employees. This access provides them with a greater capability to harm information. There are also ways to diminish this risk, such as the separation of duties. Teamwork in technological endeavors can help to keep workers honest without impinging on their individual privacy. Consultants can also provide input on employee honesty.

Personal Computers and Viruses Personal computers have limited security capabilities. In a client/server computing environment, they can pose a large security threat to companies. Especially dangerous are viruses. These are small pieces of code in a program that copy themselves to other files in the computer when the original program is used. By making the virus inactive for a period of time, it can be copied to multiple files. The virus can then be programmed to delete files or copy sensitive information. While most viruses come from outside sources, a few of them have come from commercially purchased software. Antivirus software can disable most viruses. Maintaining a regular program to backup the data is also important.

Computer Security Three major security issues are unauthorized disclosure of information, modification of information, and withholding of information. The protection of electronic documents and information is critical since this information is so easy to be copied and taken elsewhere.

Backup protection: It is very important to have a regular backup program. Most large businesses back up their data at least once a day. Local-area networks make backups of individual user machines in a client/server setting. Backup tapes must be stored in a separate and secure location. They must be erased if they are discarded. A company should also plan for hardware backup in case the computer has a physical disaster, such as a flood, fire, or electrical problem.

User identification: Different methods exist to identify authorized users when using computers. The most popular method is the password. Passwords present a small problem: People often choose easy words so they can remember the password. Others can then easily guess simple passwords, such as an immediate family member's name. Two rules apply to passwords. Change them often, make the alpha numerical, and do not write them down. The problem for users is the proliferation of passwords and the need to remember them all.

Access control: Once a user is identified, control over each file or group of files must be established. Usually this control includes read, write, modify, copy, execute, or delete.

Alternative security measures: Audits are used to locate mistakes and prevent fraud. The pressure of technology audits may help users abide by the rules. Of course, there are costs and risks associated with audits. Physical access to the computers, such as the mainframes, should be restricted to only those who have need for it. Call-back modems call back authorized users at home so that even a criminal with a user's name and password will not be able to break into the computer. Monitoring access and data usage and carefully hiring, screening, and monitoring employees can also help maintain computer security.

Encryption: Encryption is the process of applying code to modify the original information so that it can be read only if the user knows the decryption key. Encryption is used most often to transmit data and keep it from being intercepted by an unwanted audience. Encryption is also used when storing files. Two basic types of encryption exist.

Most methods follow the Data Encryption Standard (DES) and use a single "key" to both encrypt and decrypt a message. The other method follows the Rivest-Shamir-Adelman (RSA) algorithm. This uses a private and public key. Whichever key is used to encrypt the data, the other key must be used to decrypt it. Many people will know your public key, but only you will know your private key. Not surprisingly, governments are at the forefront in the development of encryption algorithms.

Responsibility and Ethics

Users engage in software piracy when they illegally copy software. This takes money away from the legal owners of the software and reduces the incentive to continue development. If the original software was company-purchased, employers are at risk. This provides an illegal advantage over the competition. Companies have the responsibility to guard a customer's data and provide access to that data to only those who need it. Companies must provide training and monitoring for employees, while giving them a reasonable amount of privacy.

Governments must continue to update their laws to incorporate new technology and to provide compensation to those unfairly injured. The federal government did not begin to pass laws regarding computer crime until the 1980s.

Legislation has clearly fallen behind technology. Enforcement and judicial interpretation are also behind the current technological direction.

Health Care Industry

DESCRIPTION OF THE INDUSTRY

The United States is the global leader in the production of medical equipment and supplies. In 1996, the United States had 47 percent of the $130 billion global market for medical devices. The health care business is mature; it is also constantly changing. It is not subject to economic cycles to the same degree as other industries.

The health care industry consists of public, private, and nonprofit institutions. These institutions are hospitals; offices and clinics of medical doctors; nursing homes; and other specialized health care facilities. Managed care programs consist of prepaid plans such as health care facilities, health maintenance organizations (HMOs), preferred provider organizations (PPOs), and independent practice associations (IPAs).

Health care is different from other consumer purchases. Individuals must be prepared for, but often do not know when they need health care. Most of the time consumers have very little to say about what type of services they receive. America's complex health care system is a leader in the use of sophisticated and expensive technology.

Pressure for change in this industry stems from large employers, intermediaries, managed care companies, and individual payers who are looking to cut health care costs. These customers are demanding more efficient, more responsive, and lower cost alternatives. This demand has led to the restructuring of the health care industry, which has shifted much of its focus to a managed care model.

According to one survey, some form of managed care accounts for 74 percent of private sector medical insurance. Medicaid enrollment in managed care has also continued to grow rapidly, with further plans under way in several states. Medicare enrollments in managed care have also increased. The pace has remained well below that for Medicaid or private coverage.

FINANCIAL ANALYSIS

The health care industry in the United States is very large. In 1989, 12 percent of the United States' GNP was spent on health care. This totaled $670 billion, compared to $4 billion in 1940. Health care expenditures are projected to increase to $1.5 trillion by the year 2000. The cost of the nation's health care rose

Table 14.1 National Health Care Expenditures

Year	Per Capita ($)	As Percent of GNP	Total ($ Billions)
1950	80	4.4	12.7
1955	101	4.4	17.7
1960	142	5.2	26.9
1965	205	5.9	41.9
1970	349	7.4	75
1975	591	8.3	132.7
1980	1054	9.1	248.1
1985	1710	10.6	422.6
1986	1837	10.9	458.2
1987	1973	11.2	497

about 19 percent in 1996 to reach an estimated $1,360 billion, or about $4,600 per capita. As health care expenditures have risen, their composition has changed (Table 14.1). Public sector spending on health care has risen faster than private sector spending. Private sector health care expenditures represented about 52 percent of total health care spending in 1995, down from 59 percent in 1980. Medicaid programs accounted for most of the 6 percent increase in public sector spending.

Despite the 1.2 percent decline in the U.S. economy from 1990 to 1991, the Census Bureau estimated revenue from health care services rose 9.5 percent from

Word	W.1	Linking Documents and Creating Links to the WWW	Linking Documents Creating Links to the Web Creating a Link Using an Image
Excel	E.1	Printing Worksheets Additional Note	To Reach the Page Setup Dialog Box Size Adjustment Fit to Headers and Footers Gridlines Page Order
PowerPoint	P.1	Running Slide Shows—Presentations	Presented by a Speaker Browsed by an Individual Browsed at a Kiosk
Access	A.1	Creating Labels	
Front Page	I.1	Further Developing Your Web Page	HTML Tutorials Advanced HTML General HTML and Web Development Pages

$521.7 billion to $571.3 billion. The highest revenue growth occurred in home health care services (19.2 percent), specialty outpatient facilities (17.4 percent), and nursing and personal care facilities (15.7 percent). Hospitals realized a 10.8 percent increase, while offices and clinics grew 7.2 percent during that period. Hospitals accounted for 58 percent of all revenues for the health services industries in 1995.

Medical products company margins are in the 25 to 30 percent range. In 1996 net profit margins for medical products producers were 11.3 percent, and for drugmakers, 17.8 percent. In comparison, in 1996, the profit margins for companies in the Standard and Poor's 500 was 5.7 percent.

STOCK/INVESTMENT OUTLOOK

Since the 1980s, large amounts of capital have been invested in health care facilities. The industry's profits and stocks are doing well. Health care costs continue to rise. The prospect of aging baby boomers increases expectations for future profits in the industry.

The outlook for health care stocks looks bright. The next century will provide improved pricing conditions, greater penetration of developing overseas markets, and rising contributions from new drugs and medical products. In 1992, talk of national price controls weighed heavily on the pharmaceutical industry. Wall Street's worries were not realized. The 10 largest U.S. pharmaceutical companies posted close to $22 billion in profits on $127 billion in sales for 1997, up 51 and 31 percent, respectively, from 1994.

Drugmakers are selling many new products. An important new drug is Warner-Lambert's cholesterol-lowering Lipitor with $450 million in sales in its first year. Eli Lilly's schizophrenia drug Zyprexa is useful, but also expensive. A one-year prescription costs about $2,150.

Improved regulatory conditions for both pharmaceutical and medical device industries have also helped their stocks. Under political pressure, the FDA has made its new drug review procedures more efficient. Approval times are now expedited. New drug therapies for life-threatening conditions such as AIDS have been approved.

Rapid growth of HMOs and other managed care organizations is also viewed as a positive for the industry. In spite of substantial discounts extended to these providers, they rely on cost-effective pharmaceuticals and other medical products that might prevent illness. The growing influence of managed care, which now represents over 50 percent of the medical products market, is expected to spur growth in the sales of drugs and medical products in the years ahead.

POTENTIAL/PROSPECTIVE FOR GROWTH

As the average age increases so does the prospect for growth in this industry. Almost 80 percent of people over the age of 65 have at least one form of chronic illness. This causes demand. Additionally, drug firms are constantly developing new products and therapies.

Health care organizations are reexamining their business practices. Every health care organization today is implementing, or at least contemplating, some form of change or reengineering process designed to make it more flexible and competitive.

The annual cost of health care for a family in the United States may reach $14,000 by the year 2000. In 1992, average per capita spending for health care in the United States totaled $3,160 a year, up from $1,000 in 1980. The United States spends twice as much on health care as the average for the 24 industrialized countries in Europe and North America. There is speculation that the economic drain on the United States economy posed by rising health care costs threatens to jeopardize the United States' competitive position in international trade.

COMPETITIVE STRUCTURE

Competition occurs throughout the health care system. The intensity of the competition varies in different sectors of the market. Companies playing a role include those selling pharmaceuticals, product supplies, insurance, and HMOs. Medicaid and Medicare are two federal programs that are not immune to market forces. However, they are not quick to adapt and be cost effective.

ROLE OF RESEARCH AND DEVELOPMENT

Telemedicine began more than 30 years ago with the development of two-way closed-circuit television. It is now becoming workable as a new technology with potential cost savings. Forty percent of existing telemedicine programs have been in operation for a year or less. Telemedicine can be useful for practitioners in places far from major medical centers. Telemedicine is particularly effective in the monitoring of cardiac and kidney dialysis patients. There is also a growing acceptance in the fields of psychiatry, dermatology, and education.

TECHNOLOGICAL INVESTMENT AND ANALYSIS

Millions of dollars are spent each year for new health technology and procedures. The advances in technology bring better diagnosis, more accurate EKGs, and less invasive microscopic and laser surgeries.

Technology growth that emphasizes quality improvement may increase costs. Other improvements to productivity may decrease costs. The continued shift in insurance coverage to lower cost forms of managed care, primarily HMOs, will increase downward pressure on health care expenditures by improving cost-containment efforts.

RECOMMENDATION FOR THE FUTURE

Managed care continues to have a major impact on the health care market. It is a major reason for very low price inflation for many health care products in recent years. Certainly the federal government's threat to regulate health care has also kept medical price inflation lower than it might have been otherwise. Different systems and organizations are continuing to be examined to achieve low-cost health care delivery.

INDUSTRY WEB SITES

Health Care Industry
www.healthquality.org/
www.aahp.org/menus/index.cfm
www.ahqa.org/
www.ashrm.org/

Executive Summary

Case Name:	Eli Lilly
Case Industry:	Health care
Major Technology Issue:	Automating and standardizing data collection and regulatory reporting must be made cost effective
Major Financial Issue:	Overall margins have decreased due to the purchase of PCS Health Systems, creating larger revenues in a lower margin business. Prozac goes off patent in 2001.
Major Strategic Issue:	The best mix of cost-effective product research from various sources such as internal laboratories, collaborative efforts, university laboratories, and contract laboratories must be found.
Major Players/Leaders:	Tom Trainer, CIO
Main Web Page:	www.elililly.com
Case Conclusion/Recommendation:	Research and new products should be targeted to the baby boomer generation.

CASE ANALYSIS

INTRODUCTORY STORY

Eli Lilly performed well during the early 1990s. This was in large part due to the success of its best-selling drug, Prozac. People suffering from depression have a chronic condition requiring a daily regiment of maintenance therapy. Prozac is the world's most widely prescribed brand name antidepressant. It is used by more than 24 million people worldwide.

Competition has come in the form of SmithKline Beecham's Paxil, a direct competitor. It has also come from the Canadian government, which forced a price cut of 42 percent due to an expired patent. The threat of this competition, which is a threat to the company's cash flow, has forced Lilly to strategically position itself for a future without patent protected profits from the sales of Prozac. Lilly's strategic positioning has involved two major steps: increasing its presence in rapidly growing new markets and aggressively introducing new drugs.

SHORT DESCRIPTION OF THE COMPANY

Based in Indianapolis, Indiana, Eli Lilly is a pharmaceutical company with more than 26,000 employees worldwide. The company conducts and sponsors research, development, and manufacturing of health care products for human and animal consumption.

Lilly is the sole owner of several subsidiary companies which provide services to the pharmaceutical industry.

PCS Health Systems provides managed pharmaceutical care for over 56 million U.S. residents. Lilly's 1995 acquisition of Integrated Medical Systems (IMS), a provider of community medical information networks, has enabled PCS to extend interactive information systems into physicians' offices. With the aid of this technology, PCS provides disease management services, medical claims processing, and disease prevention services.

Elanco Animal Health is a Lilly subsidiary specializing in the international marketing of animal health products to cattle, dairy, poultry, and swine producers. Additionally, Sphinx Pharmaceuticals is a semi-independent division of Lilly Research Laboratories. This organization provides Lilly with an emerging methodology for the discovery of promising pharmaceutical compounds through the use of combinatorial chemistry library generation and screening.

The most visible star in Eli Lilly's constellation of drugs and drug-related products is Prozac. Due in large part to the success of this drug since its introduction in 1986, Lilly ranks among the top 10 companies in the pharmaceutical industry. Additional products include antibiotics (Ceclor and Keflex), insulin, growth hormones, anti-ulcer agents, cardiovascular therapy medications, sedatives, vitamins, and cancer drugs (Oncovin and Gemzar). Lilly also makes antibiotics, feed additives, and other products for livestock and poultry.

The company is currently focusing resources on five disease categories that it feels represent critical unmet needs. These categories include central nervous system

Figure 14.1 Eli Lilly, grandson of Colonel Eli Lilly.

diseases, endocrine diseases (diabetes and osteoporosis), infectious diseases, cancer, and cardiovascular diseases. One particular developing product, Raloxifene, holds great potential for the treatment of osteoporosis in the rapidly expanding market of aging baby boomers. A second product, Humalog insulin, is being marketed globally in an attempt to strengthen Lilly's international position. Lilly claims to possess a rich product pipeline for the cancer market through the recent release of Gemzar. This marked the company's first new cancer drug in over 25 years.[1]

SHORT HISTORY OF THE COMPANY

In 1876, in the wake of the Civil War, a Union officer and pharmacist by the name of Colonel Eli Lilly invested $1,300 in a small company in Indianapolis, Indiana. The colonel was frustrated by the poorly prepared and often ineffective medicines used during the war. In the early years of the business, the colonel developed a successful process of coating pills with gelatin.

In 1898, the colonel died. The company was run by his son and two grandsons until 1953. It was the colonel's grandson who turned the company into the industrial giant it is today (Figure 14.1). During the 1920s, Lilly pushed the company into the industrialized era by installing modern equipment and stressing biomedical research. Investment in research paid off for

Lilly in the form of insulin, a product which, in those days, required the pancreas glands of either 6,000 cattle or 24,000 hogs to yield a single ounce.

Lilly introduced new products in the 1920s and 1930s. These included an antiseptic called Merthiolate, a sedative called Seconal, and treatments for pernicious anemia and heart disease. In 1952, Lilly researchers isolated the antibiotic erythromycin from a species of mold found in the Philippines. The 1950s saw Lilly capture 60 percent of the Salk vaccine market as a result of this discovery to prevent polio.

In the 1970s, Lilly introduced a drug called Darvon, which was targeted to the analgesic market. Darvon succeeded in capturing an 80 percent share of the market. An increase in R&D spending yielded several new antibiotics including Ceclor in 1979. Until recently, Ceclor remained a major source of revenue for Lilly. The 1970s saw the company diversify through the purchase of a cosmetics company, Elizabeth Arden, and a medical instrument manufacturer, IVAC.

Lilly became the first company to market a biotechnology product in 1982 by introducing a substitute human insulin called Humulin, which it licensed from Genentech. Three years later, Lilly introduced Prozac, which would prove to be a major source of revenue for at least the next 10 years. It also proved to be its last major success for a long while. During 1986, Lilly acquired Hybritech, a biotechnology company. In 1987, it sold Elizabeth Arden.

President Clinton's proposed reforms caused turmoil in the health care industry from 1992 to 1994. Eli Lilly responded by embarking on a course of restructuring and reengineering. The implementation of these plans involved manufacturing facility consolidations and closures, streamlining of manufacturing processes, and work force reductions. The restructuring plans did not, however, discourage additional acquisitions. In 1992, Lilly purchased two companies: German drug maker Beiesdorf GmbH and surgical products maker Origin Medsystems.

In 1994, Lilly merged five of its medical device and diagnostics businesses to form Guidant Corporation, which it subsequently sold. Also during the same year, in an attempt to increase its presence in the growing managed care market, Lilly purchased PCS Health Systems from McKesson for $4 billion. The second acquisition during 1994 was Sphinx Pharmaceuticals, a company proficient in state-of-the-art drug discovery and development. The following year Lilly purchased medical communications network developer Integrated Medical Systems to strengthen its ties with the health care community. In 1995, Lilly sold Hybritech, the biotech company it acquired in 1986, for a price estimated to be less than $10 million, well below the purchase price of $300 million.

[1] Bricknell, David, "Guilding the Lilly," *Computer Weekly*, October 1, 1998, p. 34(1).

With regard to new drugs, a revived R&D effort produced several promising new drugs in the mid-1990s. These included Zyprexa, a treatment for schizophrenia; Humalog, an insulin product; ReoPro, a blood thinning agent; and Gemzar, the first new drug in decades for the treatment of pancreatic cancer.

Though Lilly has hesitated to make a notable presence in the rapidly expanding generic market, it has recently collaborated with American Home Products. As a result, AHP is currently marketing Lilly's anti-ulcer drug Axid in an over the counter format under the brand name Axid AR. This collaboration did not yield profits for Lilly until 1998.

FINANCIAL AND PORTFOLIO ANALYSIS

From a financial perspective, Lilly is typical of companies in the pharmaceutical industry. Lilly operates with high profit margins. Its cost of sales is escalating as subsidiary PCS generates a larger portion of the total revenue. This results from health care management revenues having lower margins than pharmaceuticals. Specifically, Lilly's sales revenue, net income, and income as a percentage of sales for the 1991 through 1997 period are given in Table 14.2. While the numbers shown in the table are impressive relative to companies in general, they must be compared to competitors in the pharmaceutical industry to provide a more accurate picture.

With regard to sales revenue generated during the last decade, Lilly has consistently generated revenues that have placed it in a number three position compared to its peers. This comparison uses Merck, Pharmacia & UpJohn, Pfizer, and Schering-Plough. Recent years have seen Lilly drop to the number four position in terms of sales revenue generated as sales of Prozac wane in the face of increased competition.

In terms of compound growth rate in sales/operating revenues, Lilly displayed 7.5 percent growth in the decade between 1985 and 1995, and a 5.4 percent rate between 1990 and 1995. This growth is the lowest relative to its peers. During these same periods, Merck, the industry leader, exhibited a 16.7 percent compound growth rate during the 1985 to 1995 decade and a 16.8 percent rate for the five years ending in 1995.

An examination of Lilly's sales growth rate data as broken down by major products appears as in Table 14.3 In all cases the numbers show a reduced sales growth rate. While Lilly's newer drugs (those introduced in 1996 such as Zyprexa and ReoPro) are not represented due to a lack of historical data, the slumping sales growth rates of the company's major margin producers reflect a need for innovative new products.

Examination of the international market shows that the percentage of Lilly's total sales that have been generated abroad has remained fairly constant, fluctuating

Table 14.2 Lilly Sales Revenue, Net Income, and Income, 1991–1997

Year	Sales Revenue ($ million)	Net Income ($ million)	Income as percent of Sales	Profit Margin (%)	Net (%)
*1997	8,315.0	1,686.0	20.2		20.3
1996	7,347.0	1,524.0	20.7		19.7
1995	6,763.8	1,306.6	33.9		18.3
1994	5,711.6	1,185.1	22.5		22.4
1993	6,452.4	491.1	7.6		N/A
1992	6,167.3	827.6	13.4		N/A
1991	5,725.7	1,314.7	23.0		N/A

*Estimates made by Donaldson, Lufkin & Jenrette.
N/A, not applicable.

only four percent in the three years between 1993 and 1995. Relative to the 10 other major U.S. drug companies, Lilly has consistently ranked ninth.

During 1996, several factors impacted the reduced growth rate of foreign sales as seen in Table 14.3. The first factor involves a Prozac price cut required by the Canadian government. This reduction came as the result of a patent expiration that will not affect other markets until the year 2001. The second issue that damaged Lilly's sales growth rate abroad was a decline in Japanese sales of 21 percent. The 21 percent drop was primarily the result of an industry-wide price reduction brought about by the Japanese government. To further complicate matters in both Japan and Europe, the dramatic appreciation of the U.S. dollar relative to other major currencies combined with other factors to produce a reduced sales growth rate. In Europe, a 13 percent volume growth rate was reduced to a 5 percent gain in dollars due to this appreciation.

STOCK/INVESTMENT OUTLOOK

Eli Lilly's stock price, as of May 1997, was approximately $92 per share. The corresponding EPS value was 2.78 (a value currently below the estimated 1997 EPS reported in Table 14.4) with a current yield of 1.5. The number of outstanding shares is 552,823,000. The 1991 through 1997 year-end earnings per share values, high-low values, and return on equity percentiles appear in Table 14.4. The 1997 values were estimates based on data provided by Donaldson, Lufkin & Jenrette. As of the first quarter of 1997, the actual EPS value was 0.71.

The 1996 data presented in Table 14.4 are somewhat confusing as a 6 percent decline in the number of outstanding shares produced a 17 percent increase in earnings during the second quarter. This drop in the number of outstanding shares was the result of the divestiture of medical device subsidiary Guidant.

Table 14.3 Lilly Sales Growth

| Drug | Percent Change | | | | | |
| | Domestic | | International | | Total | |
	96*/95	95/94	96*/95	95/94	96*/95	95/94
Prozac	15	22	8	29	13	24
Darvon	−5	6	−5	5	−5	6
Ceclor	−73	−42	−1	18	−24	−11
Lorabid	−11	29	5	56	−9	32
Humulin	6	16	16	26	9	19
Axid	6	12	−9	15	2	13
Total	11	17	8	22	9	19

*1996 data reflect numbers partially estimated sales values.

Relative to the competition in the pharmaceutical industry, Lilly's EPS numbers have consistently placed it in a fourth or fifth position throughout the comparison period between 1992 and 1995. In 1991, however, when most of the industry was suffering from a number of problems resulting from President Clinton's very vocal plans to reduce health care costs, Lilly captured the number one seat. This landslide was primarily the result of the success of the antidepressant, Prozac.

As for return on equity, the numbers displayed in Table 14.4 place Lilly in a fourth or fifth position relative to the four industry peers (Merck, Pharmacia & UpJohn, Pfizer, and Schering-Plough). The data are furnished by Standard & Poor's.

Looking into the future to discern Lilly's long-term growth prospects, consideration must be given to the company's promising new products. The drugs Zyprexa, ReoPro, Humalog, and Gemzar are all exhibiting massive sales growth. This trend is expected to continue. Sales of Zyprexa were expected to grow approximately 250 percent domestically and 300 percent internationally through the year 2000. Forecasts are similar for the other new drugs: 300 percent overall growth for Humalog, 50 percent domestic and 200 percent international growth for ReoPro, and 100 percent overall growth for Gemzar. These numbers, though only estimates, indicate the massive potential for Lilly's stock value to increase in the future.

RISK ANALYSIS

The pharmaceutical industry is characterized by fierce competition, mergers, and the formation of strategic alliances. The already high level of competition is further raised in intensity by the growing dominance of the generic drug market. In the decade between 1986 and 1996, generics rose from 23 to 40 percent of the total prescription volume. Furthermore, 86 percent of HMOs use generic substitution. This eliminates coverage for higher profit brand name drugs when a generic drug exists. Though most major drug companies have generic drug-producing subsidiaries, the generic industry undermines profit potential by eliminating innovator drug profits and engaging in cutthroat pricing.

Pharmaceutical companies also face competitive threats from knock-off drugs. Due to lax or ignored patent protection laws in many foreign countries, drug manufacturers lose $1 for every $3 exported due to illegal copies of their products.

Intense competition in the industry has also led to a reduction in the amount of time that a manufacturer is the sole producer of a drug in a therapeutic class. Examination of data provided by PhRMA illustrates a decline in this time period from six years in the late 1970s to less than a year in 1992 for certain types of drugs. Fierce competition compounded with regulatory changes in the 1980s have conspired to increase competition in the pharmaceutical industry and reduce profit earning opportunities. In 1984, passage of the Hatch-Waxman act permitted the FDA to expedite approvals for generic copies of brand name drugs. This reduced the time between patent expiration and entry into the market of generic competition to zero.

Faced with cost-constrained drug reimbursement and competitive pricing pressures in nearly all world markets, pharmaceutical companies are pooling their

Table 14.4 Lilly Year-End Figures, 1991–1997

Year	Earnings per Share	Share Price (High–Low)	Return on Equity (%)
1997*	3.10	N/A	N/A
1996	2.78	80.38–49.38	25.0
1995	2.30	57.00–31.25	24.2
1994	2.05	33.13–23.56	23.9
1993	0.84	31.00–21.81	10.4
1992	1.41	43.88–28.88	16.8
1991	2.25	42.56–33.75	31.4

*Denotes estimates made by Donaldson, Lufkin & Jenrette.
N/A, not applicable.

resources to compete more effectively. This has led to a growing number of mergers and strategic alliances. Mergers have typically taken place among companies whose principal drugs have lost or are about to lose patent protection or between manufacturers and pharmacy benefit management firms (PBMs). Alliances have been common between pharmaceutical and biotech companies or between pharmaceutical companies with differing expertise. These tactics have produced significant cost savings and efficiencies in manufacturing, marketing, and R&D.

INDUSTRY AND MARKET ANALYSIS

The pharmaceutical industry involves the development, manufacture, and sale of pharmaceutical drugs. While the industry's roots date back to ancient times when plants and minerals were used with medicinal intent, the industry as it exists today was born in the 1920s with the discovery of penicillin and other antibiotics. The industry experienced massive growth in the years during World War II and has continued to expand in the years since, although the early 1990s saw a reduction in the rate of expansion.

The pharmaceutical industry is, for the most part, immune to the economic cycles that afflict most other industries. In the United States the growth in the demand for drugs has remained fairly constant for years. The industry suffered significantly, however, from reduced sales growth rates in in the early 1990s as a result of President Clinton's plan to reform the nation's health care system. The public exposure brought about by this campaign revealed long-term industry trends for hyperinflation and a large discrepancy between United States prices and those abroad. The rise to power of the Republican leadership in Congress removed the fear of government price controls, however. The industry is currently experiencing a more friendly political climate.

The goodwill the industry is currently experiencing from the government is further underscored by reforms made to the FDA and the adoption of GATT. The reforms in the FDA have resulted in more expedient new drug approvals. This enables the industry to gain quicker access to patent protected profits. The approval of GATT in late 1994 also helped the industry by extending the patent lives of many drugs.

The pharmaceutical industry is currently rebounding from a period of intense political scrutiny and regulatory threat. During 1992–1994, when President Clinton was most vocal about his plans for reform, the industry suffered a sales rate growth drop from the double digits to a low of 1.0 percent domestically. The industry is currently experiencing healthy sales growth rates as shown by the data in Table 14.5.

The outlook for the pharmaceutical industry is favorable. Several factors encourage investing in the industry today. The first is that the difficult period in the early 1990s appears to have ended. The three factors contributing to this period of reduced growth rates were the rapid expansion of the managed care business, the political pressure to reduce hyperinflated drug pricing, and European regulations enacted to reduce health care costs. These issues contributed to a 45 percent industry decline in the United States stock market from 1991 to 1994. This threefold threat appears to be reduced since managed care organizations have lost much of their threat. The Republican Congress is not threatening to regulate drug prices.

The second encouraging factor is that today's pharmaceutical industry is characterized by initiatives to improve margins. These initiatives include downsizing, corporate realignment, restructuring, and plant closures. Ultimately, these changes will impact profit margins by reducing the overall costs.

The third factor is the promising profit potential for new drugs. A cursory look at some of the important new drugs to be approved reveals these possibilities: a

Table 14.5 Pharmaceutical Industry Growth, 1990–1997

Year	Net Domestic U.S. Sales ($ million)	Annual Change (%)	Sales Abroad ($ million)	Annual Change (%)	Total ($ million)	Annual Change (%)
1997*	66,063.7	5.5	39,793.5	9.5	105,857.2	7.0
1996*	62,611.8	9.6	36,345.6	7.2	98,957.4	8.7
1995	57,145.5	12.6	33,893.5	†	91,039.0	†
1994	50,740.4	4.4	26,870.7	1.5	77,611.1	3.4
1993	48,590.9	0.0	26,467.3	2.8	75,058.2	1.7
1992	48,095.5	8.6	25,744.2	15.8	73,839.7	11.0
1991	44,304.5	15.1	22,231.1	12.1	66,535.6	14.1
1990	38,486.7	17.7	19,838.3	18.0	58,325.0	17.8

*Denotes estimated values.
†Indicates data affected by mergers and acquisitions.

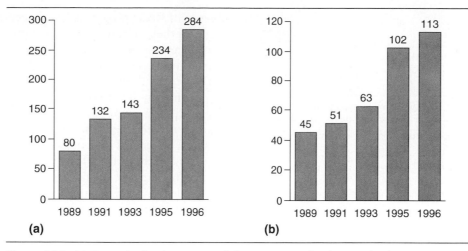

Figure 14.2 (a) Drugs in development and (b) companies developing the drugs.

drug for osteoporosis, which could be taken by some 20 million women; a new treatment for prostate cancer, which kills more than 40,000 in the United States alone each year; and a vaccine for chicken pox with an unlimited potential for consumption.

The pharmaceutical industry appears to be continuing a long-term trend of above average growth relative to other industries. This growth rate is due to several factors, including the aging of the baby boomer generation. The elderly age of such a large demographic segment will result in a vast market for the industry's products.

Further indication of the industry's potential for growth is the number of new drugs currently in development and the number of companies participating in this development. As illustrated by Figure 14.2, the number of drugs being developed has tripled since 1989. The number of companies participating in this development has more than doubled since 1989.

Research and development growth is a key indicator of industry growth as a whole. A majority of drug companies' profits are produced by so-called "innovator" drugs. An innovator drug is one discovered and patented by a given company. Prior to the expiration of the patent on this drug, the company is able to use its monopolistic position to set prices. The profits gained in this manner enable the company to continue R&D for new drugs to replace older ones with aging and expiring patents.

Another avenue of growth for the pharmaceutical industry is the booming market for generic and over-the-counter (OTC) drugs. The large number of innovator products losing patent protection in the near future will foster robust growth in the generic industry. Similarly, the OTC drug market is projected to increase from a $9.6 billion market in 1995 to $14 billion by 2000. This growth is attributed to the increased willingness of consumers to self-medicate and the large

(>50) number of prescription drugs expected to be approved for conversion to OTC drugs.

The only aspect of the pharmaceutical industry that is not producing increased growth is employment. In an effort to cut costs, many firms are downsizing and restructuring. This has resulted in the first decline in annual employment growth in 22 years. Between 1994 and 1995, employment in the industry declined by 1.7 percent after 10 years of 2.9 percent average growth.

R&D is the primary source of growth in the pharmaceutical industry. Over the past 15 years, the percentage of domestic United States sales allocated to R&D has increased from 11 to 21.2 percent, while the average R&D to sales ratio for all United States industries remains less than 4 percent. The total R&D expenditures for research-based pharmaceutical companies are projected to reach $18.9 billion in 1997, an increase of 11.5 percent over 1996. Figure 14.3 displays this industry-wide growth in R&D spending. To examine these numbers further, companies allocate over 84 percent of their R&D budgets toward new products and 16 percent to improvements or modification of existing products. Additionally, FDA testing requirements consume 35 percent of R&D budgets while nearly 10 percent is necessary to accommodate stringent manufacturing standards.

A major technological investment in the pharmaceutical industry is in the area of biotechnology and advanced screening methods. Advances in this area are enabling drug companies to improve and expedite their research and development. One important advancement is a state-of-the-art screening method utilizing combinatorial libraries. This procedure facilitates the discovery of new drugs by actuating the rapid synthesis of millions of different compounds. Researchers are able to scan these libraries for combinations of compounds that possess

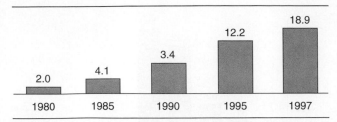

Figure 14.3 R&D expenditures for the pharmaceutical industry by year (in $ millions).

potential therapeutic benefits. An additional trend is for companies to avoid costly investments in research facilities by either purchasing or forming alliances with other companies with expertise in key areas.

The future of the pharmaceutical industry is one of vast potential. Three means of capitalizing on this potential include (1) investing in cost-reducing technological systems, (2) targeting key markets, and (3) expanding offered services.

In addition to investing in technology, pharmaceutical companies must target markets in which there is a high need and demand for drugs. The top three markets are central nervous system drugs (especially antidepressants), gastrointestinal drugs, and anti-infectives with cardiovasculars and cholesterol reducing agents, or antilipemics, representing rapidly expanding markets. The first four of these markets accounted for 64 percent of the overall U.S. prescription market in 1994. This number emphasizes the importance that must be placed on key market segments. Drug companies must gain or maintain position in these markets to remain competitive and profitable. Positions can be established by either R&D expenditures or through mergers or alliances with companies specializing in these areas.

A final course of action for the pharmaceutical industry is to expand the pharmaceutical services sector. Two new services offer potential. The first, referred to as disease management, involves the focusing of R&D and marketing efforts on specific ailments and the subsequent offering of comprehensive treatment packages for that ailment. The second service is outcomes research. This service evaluates the effectiveness of medical procedures, devices, or drugs in curing a targeted medical condition. The service also considers the relative cost of each therapy and ranks products and services for selection by managed care organizations. Pharmaceutical companies that enter this market will gain the twofold advantage of improving their products and increasing the likelihood of their selection by managed care organizations.

ROLE OF RESEARCH AND DEVELOPMENT

No debate exists regarding the importance of research and development to a pharmaceutical company. The in-

fluence of R&D programs has shaped the drug companies and their cultures. The major pharmaceutical companies are large enough to absorb the high R&D expenditures. The most successful companies are those with a steady flow of new drugs.

A company has two options in the pursuit of new drug research. One is to hire scientists and fund the research; in other words, to accomplish the work in house. The second is to outsource the research process through collaborative efforts or licensing agreements.

The discovery of profitable and successful new drugs has eluded Eli Lilly for the better part of a decade. Recent introductions aside, the newest successful product discovered by Lilly's research staff was Prozac which was made available for prescription use in 1986 and was discovered years earlier.

From 1993 to 1996, the company consistently spent approximately 15 percent of its sales on research and development. Examination of data for the first quarter of 1997 shows that Lilly spent $301.2 million on R&D versus sales of $1,953 million. This is a percentage of sales invested of 15.4 percent. Leading drugmakers in the industry spend from 14 to 18 percent of their sales on R&D. While Lilly may be on the lower end of this spectrum, it is certainly within the industry average.

In terms of actual dollars spent funding research and development, Lilly spent $755 million in 1993, $838.9 million in 1994, $1,042 million in 1995, $1,190 million in 1996, and $301.2 million during the first quarter of 1997. These numbers correspond to a percent of sales value of 15 percent, which is average for the industry. In terms of actual dollars spent, Lilly has ranked ninth or tenth among 13 of its peers in the industry for most of the 1990s.

More recently, Lilly's R&D spending has yielded results. The discovery and subsequent production of Zyprexa, ReoPro, Humalog, and Gemzar have begun to be quite profitable. Several other promising new drugs are currently under development.[2]

TECHNOLOGICAL STORY

How does a company increase its presence in the explosive PBM (pharmaceuticals-by-mail) market? If the company were paying attention to industry trends, the answer would be through acquisition. Increased presence is exactly what Eli Lilly achieved after purchasing the nation's largest PBM, PCS Health Systems. The subsequent purchase of IMS strengthened Lilly's position by combining the resources of an information system provider with the services of a PBM.

This combination of resources has enabled Lilly to develop an interactive information system networking

---

[2] Ross, Philip E., "Pills Against Cancer," *Forbes*, May 31, 1999, p. 238(1).

physician's offices to PCS offices and providing online drug benefit management services. The network specializes in areas for which Lilly has products. These acquisitions have not only provided Lilly with a low-margin, highly profitable subsidiary, they have established a brand loyal consumer base for its products.

TECHNOLOGICAL INVESTMENT AND ANALYSIS

"Elvis is alive and well," reads a Lilly press release regarding the deployment of a new corporate intranet. Eli Lilly Virtual Information Service, ELVIS for short, has transformed the Internet from a novelty into a critical resource for Lilly's 25,000 plus employees. The information system is an intranet run on Microsoft Windows NT servers and Netscape Communications servers running on Silicon Graphics computers. The system is accessed and utilized through the Netscape Navigator web browser, which was installed on every corporate desktop during 1996.

ELVIS provides employees access to corporate news bulletins, job postings, stock prices, and daily news on the pharmaceutical industry. Senior management is provided with an executive tracking system that maintains schedules, similar to a web-based version of Microsoft Project, and an executive corporate information database. The most valuable features are provided to the brand marketing teams and individual sales representatives. The intranet provides these employees with the means to access updated product information, market research, competitive analysis, customer lists, and sales leads from any location in the world, at any time, day or night. This feature further serves to synchronize sales information and pricing worldwide.

Portions of ELVIS are interactive form-based pages. For example, a number of these pages enable users to order promotional material directly online from third-party distributors, while allowing Lilly to track the orders. Since the intranet's inception, it has undergone almost constant updates and modifications.

The second major investment made by Lilly in the area of computer-related technology is the purchase of two software products from BBN Domain Corporation. These products are intended to aid Lilly's R&D staff by automating and standardizing the data collection and regulatory reporting associated with the discoveries of new drugs. Clintrace is used to simplify the process of adverse event reporting during the testing of new drugs. Clintrial is used to standardize the process of clinical trial data collection. Clintrial is intended to accelerate a new product's time-to-market by collecting, organizing, and managing data within regulatory guidelines. The software will be run on a client/server architecture networked to offices in over 30 countries that was constructed by Lilly specifically for this purpose. By utilizing these two products, Lilly plans to gain a competitive advantage by standardizing clinical trial data collection and management procedures throughout its worldwide facilities. As a result, it hopes to get new medicines to market more quickly.

These two expenditures on technology represent different directions toward increased productivity. On the one hand, ELVIS provides an information link and forum for employees and develops a virtual corporate culture. On the other hand, the BBN Domain products provide a mechanism to enhance R&D productivity.

Strategically, Lilly has adapted third-party packages for many of its horizontal business functions. Development is focused only on applications that support the most important business functions. In particular, Lilly builds 90% of the software used in its research and development efforts. This includes everything from molecular discovery and product testing to the various processes required to get a new drug approved by the Food and Drug Administration.

Since, according to Tom Trainer, CIO, "R&D is the name of the game, it is vital that we have software that meets our very special needs." Trainer explains that commercial software does not meet Lilly's aggressive R&D processes. He believes that part of the market edge comes from building its own software solutions. "Our custom software plays a very important part in our business."[3]

Trainer came to Lilly as CIO in 1994, following terms at SmithKline Beecham, Seagram, and Reebok. He joined Lilly soon after the company bought one of the PCS Health Systems, a firm that links thousands of chemists and processes claims.

When he arrived, Trainer described Lilly as having extensive IT operations. However, rather than being tentacles that supported the business, the operation more closely resembled spaghetti, with 17 different divisions doing their own thing. There was no unified IT structure serving core business requirements such as managing costs and cutting product development time. This was also the time frame for Lilly in which margins came under increasing pressure from health care organizations trying to cut costs.

Trainer's first goal was to get a handle on Lilly's IT costs, then set targets. He emphasized the need to categorize costs. This included the cost of supporting desktops, the performance of the help desk, and expenditures for telecommunications. In addition, he wanted to support the accumulation of data collected during the pharmaceutical development process.

Trainer implemented processes under which information technology executives could make decisions for

---

[3] "Strategic Applications: Companies Are Forging a Unique Blend of Custom and Commercial Software to Gain a Competitive Advantage," *InformationWeek*, November 23, 1998, p. 63.

the organization. According to Trainer, "They had not come together as a group in the past. We had to set common goals. You can always figure out the techy stuff, but it is the people that make things work. You have to set appropriate goals taking into account what you have to work with, and managing the expectations of colleagues."[4]

To accomplish this change, Trainer set up an organization tailored to the fact that Lilly defined the business in value cycle terms. This included the appointment of "information officers" who supported the company's four key processes: discovery science, commercialization, manufacturing supply and demand, and global business unit support.[5] Four IT councils focused on the key areas of applications, data technology including R&D and methods and tools, and organizational effectiveness.

Trainer focused on cutting the cost of drug development by looking for applications to assist in the processing of huge volumes of data. In the chemistry labs, 3-D mathematical modeling tools were used to analyze the behavior of molecules in new medicines. This significantly cut the time necessary to formulate a new drug.[6]

Trainer has rationalized the number of suppliers to the company. The move was adopted to slash Lilly's business costs. From using more than 100 IT service providers, Lilly now only uses nine. "We can crank the process to consider taking competitive bids from suppliers for products and services," says Trainer.[7]

The same pragmatic approach is used to ensure Lilly has the appropriate IT skills in place, including flexible supply channels. Alliances are developed to achieve the required core competencies, data mining enables choices to be made internally, and in-sourcing provides other skill sets.

To support his approach, Trainer adopted the charge, "Information without boundaries; execution without excuses."[8]

TECHNOLOGICAL INNOVATIONS

DATA

"One of the most important things for us is the whole notion of helping discovery researchers cope with more data—and more complex data—than they've ever had before," says Thomas Trainer, Eli Lilly's VP and CIO. The alliance between the Indianapolis company's IT

staff and researchers is so important that in 1997 the two groups set up shop down the hall from each other. "Lilly Research Laboratories and IT are literally hand-in-hand," says Tom Bumol, executive director of research technology and proteins.

Eli Lilly is focusing on the emerging field of bioinformatics. This field uses specialized algorithms and databases to analyze the structure of genes. The analysis helps identify proteins that cause disease. Bioinformatics is accelerating the pharmaceuticals industry beyond what technology does for businesses in general. At Eli Lilly, the IS staff and researchers are correlating data in several databases into a single relational database structure.

Lilly subscribes to a database of gene-sequencing information from Incyte Pharmaceuticals Inc. They co-own a database generated by Millennium BioTherapeutics Inc. and generate their own gene sequencing information internally. In addition, the company downloads information nightly from public databases on the Internet, such as the federal government's Human Genome Project. All data are stored in Oracle databases that run on Sun Microsystems servers.

EXPERT SYSTEMS

Lilly has not only put knowledge management into practice; it has also found a way to measure the approach's business value. Lilly has developed several Lotus Notes-based applications, some still in pilot phase, designed to enable drug development teams worldwide to trade information.

The projects have been under way for two years and involve both business and information technology staffs. The Lotus Notes-based applications offer researchers, chemists, marketers, and business managers updated access to product information, best practices, costs, and time lines.

But even more important, the projects are rated to assess Lilly's knowledge management efforts. Rebecca Field-Perez, manager of IT and planning operations at Lilly, said the projects are scored subjectively from 1 to 10 in each of five characteristics: technology, profit, context, people, and content. According to analysts, the biggest obstacle to more widespread adoption of knowledge management is that people do not understand what it is and how to measure it.[9]

Many corporations have realized that their intranets have morphed into massive, uncontrollable beasts that require new data management strategies. One such approach is that taken by Eli Lilly, which defined and implemented web page authoring policies and guidelines at the onset. The guidelines address such issues as how many hops to a web page, thumbnail size images, and

---

[4] "Gilding the Lilly," *Computer Weekly*, October 1, 1998, p. 34(1).
[5] Ibid.
[6] "Strategic Applications: Companies are Forging a Unique Blend of Custom and Commercial Software to Gain a Competitive Advantage," *InformationWeek*, November 23, 1998.
[7] "Gilding the Lilly," *Computer Weekly*, October 1, 1998, pg. 34(1).
[8] Ibid.

[9] Fusaro, Roberta, "Rating Intangibles No Easy Task," *Computerworld*, November 30, 1998, p. 8(1).

other account performance concerns. While the responsibility for updating information on a web site falls on the content owner, some companies assign their IS staff to educate employees regarding web standards for accessing and publishing pages.[10]

The firm's adoption of Internet technologies has been measured. Lilly has invested in a high level of electronic data interchange activities in the past. They are very careful how they present information on products to customers.

Lilly has successfully established an intranet directed toward simplifying the scheduling of clinical trials and submissions for new drugs in 120 countries. The company also offers an information exchange and help facility for those suffering with specific diseases or medical conditions.

Lilly has integrated BusinessObjects, decision-support software for reporting and analytical applications, and WebIntelligence, which governs access to the data warehouse. According to Brent Houk, BusinessObjects coordinator at Eli Lilly, the functionality in WebIntellingence, which is mainframe based, has not caught up to that of BusinessObjects, which is client-server based. When and if it does, Houk plans to switch to a completely Web business intelligence infrastructure. "Maintaining everything on one server saves a lot of headaches," according to Houk.[11]

These applications provide Lilly with features such as a searchable report catalog that organizes reports by categories; the ability to schedule report updates; automatic updates that alert users to refreshed reports; and viewers that apply ActiveX or HTML technology to optimize reports for browser environments.[12]

Edward Tunstall, Information Officer for Enterprise Information Systems, reduces costs in web proliferation by standardization. Individuals requesting an IP address must have the right version of NT, the right version of Office, and the right amount of backup. Tunstall believes that is the best way to make sure that anyone in the organization can share information and that the unit costs for PC support remain low.[13]

NETWORKS

Pharmaceutical maker Eli Lilly & Co. has given the management of its ambitious online health care network to EDS, conceding that a technology company is better suited for the effort. A new joint venture, called Kinetra, now directs Lilly's Integrated Medical Systems Unit. Kinetra now operates a private data network that links 70,000 physicians to hospitals.

Lilly spent over $4 billion in 1996 to acquire IMS and PCS Health Systems Inc., a pharmacy benefits manager. The plan was for physicians using PCS services to tap into the IMS network to process claims and write prescriptions electronically. Lilly's goal is to wire 100,000 physicians' offices into the network. Although Lilly is keeping PCS, it is transferring IMS to Kinetra to expand the network to hundreds of thousands of physicians, pharmacies, hospitals, and health care payers. These will include state Blue Cross/Blue Shield organizations and Medicare systems. According to Kinetra CEO Tim Hargarten, formerly VP of pharmaceuticals marketing at EDS, "EDS brings to the table relationships with payers, such as Blue Cross/Blue Shield in 17 states. It also brings technical assets and expertise that Eli Lilly recognized it did not have."[14]

Kinetra will continue to service IMS and PCS customers. One of Kinetra's other goals, Hargarten says, will be to establish relationships with Lilly's pharmaceutical competitors, such as the pharmacy benefits-management companies of Merck and SmithKline Beecham.[15]

RECOMMENDATION FOR THE FUTURE

Lilly is on the crest of reaping rewards from a new series of pharmaceuticals. As Lilly continues to research and distribute new products, it must continue to develop a LAN and Internet-based distribution system for its products and the related information.

---

[10] Cummings, Joanne, "Taming the Web Data Beast," *Network World*, February 17, 1997, v. 14, n. 7, p. 518(4).
[11] Davis, Beth, "Updated Decision Support—Business Objects Adds Web Support," *InformationWeek*, May 17, 1999, p. 87(1).
[12] Ibid.
[13] "Centralization's New Twist: Corporate IT Takes Center Stage as Companies use the Web to Recentralize," *InternetWeek*, January 18, 1999, p. 35(1).

[14] Dalton, Gregory, "Small World—A Global Economy Mandates a Global IT Strategy," *Information Week*, August 10, 1998, n. 695, p. 38(1).
[15] Kolbasuk McGee, Marianne, and Dalton, Gregory, "Lilly Outsources to EDS," *Information Week*, February 23, 1998, n. 607, p. 34(1).

CASE QUESTIONS

Strategic Questions

1. What is the strategic direction of the corporation/organization?

2. Who or what forces are driving this direction?

3. What are the critical success factors for this corporation/organization?

4. What are the core competencies for this corporation/organization?

Technological Questions

5. What has caused a change in the use of technology in the corporation/organization?

6. Has productivity been improved with technology?

7. How successful has the technology change been?

Quantitative Questions

8. What does the corporation say about its financial ability to embark on a major technological program of advancement?

9. Are there trends that are problematic?

10. Is the industry stable?

Industry Questions

11. What challenges and opportunities is the industry facing?

12. Is the industry oligopolistic or competitive?

13. Does the industry face a change in government regulation?

Data Questions

14. What role do data play in the future of the corporation?

15. How important are data to the corporation's continued success?

OWENS & MINOR

Executive Summary

Case Name:	Owens & Minor
Case Industry:	Health care
Major Technology Issue:	Centralization of the warehouse computer system
Major Financial Issue:	Refocusing on revenue creation instead of cost reduction
Major Strategic Issue:	Establishing strong partnerships with customers
Major Players/Leaders:	G. Gilmer Minor, Chairman and CEO; Don Stoller, Director of Decision Services
Main Web Page:	www.owens-minor.com
Case Conclusion/Recommendation:	Owens & Minor must continue to invest in technology, particularly in the area of distribution of products and information.

CASE ANALYSIS

INTRODUCTORY STORY

Since money is expected every time an item of business is handled, Owens & Minor (O&M) developed ways to simplify the receipt and storage of materials and to exploit state-of-the-art technology every step of the way. O&M's goal is to replenish supplies directly to the point of use, bypassing the customer's warehouse and storeroom and the attendant paperwork.

SHORT DESCRIPTION OF THE COMPANY

Owens & Minor is the second largest wholesale distributor of medical and surgical supplies after Baxter International. The company carries over 163,000 products from approximately 3,000 different manufacturers and operates 53 distribution centers.

Due to the 1994 acquisition of Stuart Medical, Inc., the third largest distributor, O&M now has a presence in all 50 states. The company recently discontinued its involvement in the distribution of pharmaceuticals and other products to chain drug stores and independent pharmacies in Southern Florida.

O&M services hospitals, nursing homes, integrated health care systems, physicians offices, and surgical centers. The majority of its sales come from hospitals. This emphasis on hospitals, which is estimated to account for 60 percent of medical equipment industry sales, reflects O&M's belief that hospitals will remain the primary focus of the health care industry.

SHORT HISTORY OF THE COMPANY

Founded in 1882, Owens & Minor began in Richmond, Virginia, as a wholesale drug company. In 1966, they entered medical/surgical distribution. In 1992, they sold the wholesale drug and specialty pharmaceutical packaging divisions to focus on becoming the country's highest quality distributor of health care products.

In May 1994, Owens & Minor completed the merger with Stuart Medical. This strengthened their national distribution capabilities. The products distributed by Owens & Minor, such as needles, syringes, dressings, surgical packs, gowns, and intravenous products, are disposable and typically ordered in high volume.

FINANCIAL AND PORTFOLIO ANALYSIS

Growth was significant in 1994 as a result of the acquisition of Stuart Medical, soaring from $1.4 billion in 1993 to $2.4 billion. This acquisition was not cheap, however. The company incurred restructuring expenses of $12.1 million and $29.3 million in 1994 and 1995, respectively. This compared to an eight-year prior average of $4.1 million due to the acquisition as well as a decision to outsource the management and operation of its mainframe computer system.

Sales for O&M in 1995 rose 24 percent to $2.98 billion, from $2.40 billion a year before (Figure 14.4). Compared to a net income of $18.5 million in 1993, a net income of $7.9 million was realized in 1994 versus a net loss of $11.3 million in 1995. Earnings per share in years 1993 to 1995 were $0.60, $0.15, and ($0.53), respectively. This compared to the medical supplies industry (MSI) average of $0.91. O&M paid dividends of $0.19 and $0.18 in 1994 and 1995, up from $0.14 in 1993. This was quite low compared to the MSI average of $0.34.

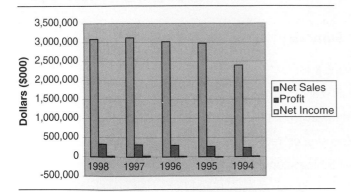

Figure 14.4 Owens & Minor's revenues.

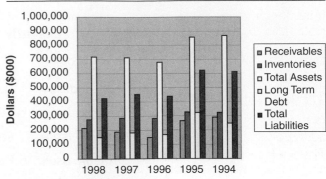

Figure 14.5 O&M total assets.

STOCK/INVESTMENT OUTLOOK

Owens & Minor's common shares are traded on the New York Stock Exchange under the symbol OMI. As of December 31, 1996, there were approximately 17,000 common shareholders. O&M's five-year high was $18.18 and its five-year low was $4.15. Given the recent acquisition of Stuart Medical, the competitive edge that O&M enjoyed through its financial health has diminished due to restructuring costs.

Once O&M fully assimilates the cultures and facilities, converts the entire information system, and begins to realize its synergies with Stuart Medical, SG&A is projected to return to preacquisition levels. O&M should once again experience its competitive edge (Figure 14.5).

INDUSTRY AND MARKET ANALYSIS

Owens & Minor operates in a highly competitive, extremely dynamic industry riddled with the anticipation of government regulation which, in turn, could have a significant impact on the industry (Figure 14.6). Other players in the distribution market include Johnson & Johnson, Baxter International, Abbott Laboratories, Becton, Dickinson, C.R. Bard, and St. Jude Medical.[1]

Survival depends upon obtaining and maintaining very strong relationships with customers, by guaranteeing and delivering high-quality service while minimizing inventory and handling costs. O&M's product lines are usually disposable and manufactured in high volumes. Because profit margins are low for most of these products, they must be sold in high volumes. Focusing on large hospitals, health care conglomerates, and alternative-care institutions as potential customers has been successful to increase profitability.

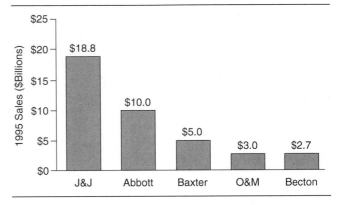

Figure 14.6 Sales for major medical supplier companies, 1995.

ROLE OF RESEARCH AND DEVELOPMENT

Producers of drugs and medical products have experienced a high commercial success rate from their R&D efforts. This results in even more substantial investment in new medical technology. Government agencies such as the National Institutes of Health (NIH) are the primary funders of basic research in the health care industry. NIH's annual budget exceeds $7 billion, although a substantial portion of these funds is aimed at research in general medical science and the evaluation of the application of that research to the treatment of diseases.[2]

R&D has led to a large number of breakthrough medical products and procedures. Technology has contributed to these successes, but high tech does not always mean low cost. Since the growing influence of managed care has placed the emphasis on cost-efficiency, there is a new and challenging standard in the health care industry today. How does a company deliver a high-quality, low-cost product while maintaining a competitive R&D budget? The answer seems to lie in the implementation of

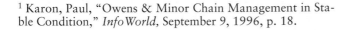

[1] Karon, Paul, "Owens & Minor Chain Management in Stable Condition," *InfoWorld*, September 9, 1996, p. 18.

[2] Ibid.

information technology to obtain greater economies of scale. This should in turn boost margins. Increased margins will then enable companies to maintain a healthy R&D budget.[3]

TECHNOLOGICAL STORY

O&M relies heavily on computer technology in warehouses and reaps large rewards in terms of efficiency. The newest warehouse management system is a distributed network that provides each customer with the most flexible, custom-tailored information services to date. The technology insures the item is where it is supposed to be when it is supposed to be, even if it is off-site.[4]

TECHNOLOGICAL INVESTMENT AND ANALYSIS

O&M, like Baxter International and other medical supply companies, understands the importance of information technology as the primary method to achieve cost savings. Some of the value-added services O&M offers customers include inventory management, electronic data interchange, logistical support, and an online order entry system. These services save customers time and money by providing the customers with direct access to O&M databases. The customer can check O&M's inventory levels and scheduling for the actual delivery schedule.

Another example of O&M's utilization of information technology was the upgrading of its warehouse computer system. Warehouse operations were consolidated at a cost of $25 million. The centralization of warehouse operations will provide O&M with more control over inventory and scheduling. This will make the ordering and delivery process more efficient. Again, through technology upgrades, O&M continues to actively cut costs and deliver savings to the balance sheet and to customers.[5]

In addition to basic distribution services, O&M offers CostTrack Supply Chain Management (SCM). This is the industry-leading initiative in activity-based management. CostTrack SCM enables customers to realize operational efficiencies, and ongoing cost savings through integrative programs in logistics, information technology, asset management, and product mix management.[6] CostTrack identifies and tracks the cost-drivers in a company's distribution activities. It provides products and services in logistics, information management, asset management, and product mix management to help

these customers cut costs, drive workflow efficiencies, and raise employee productivity.[7]

SOME OF O&M'S CostTrack SCM PROGRAMS

BusinessIntelligence™, an information technology tool, enables O&M to compile account-specific information that helps customers make well-informed business decisions about product standardization, contract compliance, and cost saving opportunities.[8]

WISDOM, the Internet-based version of BusinessIntelligence, gives customers and suppliers online, password-protected access to their account information through their own personal computers. According to G. Gilmer Minor, III, chairman & CEO of Owens & Minor, "WISDOM is the first e-business intelligence application of its kind within our industry. We have made a serious and long-term investment in developing Web technologies that will provide our customers a competitive edge in turning information into knowledge. In today's demanding healthcare market, our customers count on us to deliver not only product and customer service but powerful business tools to help them make well-informed decisions that impact their bottom lines." WISDOM connects Owens & Minor's subscribing customers to its comprehensive, industry data warehouse and offers them web access to in-depth account information about their medical/surgical product purchases, inventory and usage, contract compliance and other customized data.[9]

PANDAC® provides customized data to help customers better manage their wound closure inventory, including suture and endoscopic equipment, by reducing their asset investment and reassessing their ordering/stocking patterns.

FOCUS is the partnership program with suppliers that helps customers reduce their supply expenses through product standardization, consolidation and utilization.[10]

DATABASES

Owens & Minor reduced its inventory investment and increased customer service after installing a client/server system. The company formerly relied on a mainframe that provided inaccurate forecasting and was not flexible enough to let the company set separate goals for different products. The mainframe was also unsuited to the company's distributed nature, in which each office

[3] Hammond, Mark, "Cashing In on Warehouses," *PC Week* August 31, 1999.
[4] Ibid.
[5] Hammond, Mark, "Cashing In on Warehouses," *PC Week*, August 31, 1998, v. 15, n. 35, p. 45(1).
[6] http://www.owens-minor.com/.

[7] Owens & Minor Company Press Release, "Owens & Minor Delivers WISDOM On Line to Customer Desktops," Richmond, Va., June 23, 1996.
[8] http://www.owens-minor.com/.
[9] Owens & Minor Company Press Release, "Owens & Minor Delivers WISDOM On Line to Customer Desktops," Richmond, Va., June 23, 1996.
[10] http://www.owens-minor.com/.

satisfies local needs according to its own standards. The client/server system lets each division customize the new chain management software to suit a specific market segment. The software tracks the inventory replenishment cycle, helping the company decide when to order new products, and verifies that products are available to fill customer orders. The new client/server system automates most of the processes, alerting managers only to unusual situations. Even before completing the new installation, Owens & Minor reduced their inventory by $44 million.[11]

In the development of its data warehouse[12] and WISDOM, Owens & Minor partnered with Business Objects, the world's leading provider of integrated enterprise decision support tools. This partnership has provided innovative decision support applications to help companies save money, operate more efficiently, and win new customers.[13]

In 1998, the first phase of an enterprisewide data warehouse project was finished. For the first time, sales professionals were able to access all information on customers and suppliers, from initial contact to final invoice. The initial plans were to finish the sales piece and move quickly on to other functional areas, including marketing, finance, and distribution.

According to Don Stoller, Director of Decision Services, "We simply did not anticipate the user enthusiasm."[14] With the goal of maintaining the enthusiasm, he scaled back new development of other subject areas to keep up with user-suggested enhancements to the warehouse. Stoller set up steering committees to help set priorities. He meets with his immediate staff, which includes technologists and business users, on a weekly basis. Every other month there is a senior management meeting to assess progress and decide on larger scheduling issues.[15]

The company supports field salespeople with WebIntelligence, BusinessObjects' Web front end. This Java applet is downloaded to the browser at runtime. The salespeople are away from the office but need to pound a distant server with queries. "A lot of them have laptops so they log on through a modem, which futher slows their ability to work."[16] says Stoller. The Java applet puts the onus on the server to do the work and maximizes the rate at which field users can manipulate data. By quickly getting access to current customer sales and purchasing patterns, customer history, and inventory management, salespeople can keep O&M competitive while increasing sales. In 1998, O&M won 15% more business from one group of hospitals because of its speed of delivery.

O&M is simplifying ongoing user support by letting users take charge. People in the business areas have become the gurus for their area. "It's a role that listens to the users to figure out how we can better help them to deploy decision support to help the company."[17] O&M is also incrementally building a data warehouse. Since a warehouse was necessary for BusinessObjects, O&M started with a data warehouse that made the first subject area sales. New subject areas are being added about every three or four months, including inventory, customer account, balances, and supplier data. Companies continue to find a wealth of benefits from the query and reporting tools, which can boost communications and access to information between customers and providers.[18]

INTERNET

BusinessObjects, based in San Jose, California, delivered WebIntelligence 2.0 during the fall of 1997. The product governs access to O&M's data warehouse. WebIntelligence 2.0 offers a new OLAP module, and advanced features for extranet deployments. This enables companies to take advantage of emerging e-business intelligence opportunities by accessing databases in other companies.

O&M wants to sell its suppliers portions of the data in its 90GB warehouse. This includes information on how the suppliers' products are selling to hospitals and doctors. "Our suppliers can get information to see what's moving and not moving and alter their manufacturing process to lower their costs," said Don Stoller, director of decision services at Owens & Minor.[19]

NETWORKS

The impact of supplier networks on independent hospitals is demonstrated by an example from Community Hospitals of Central California (CHCC). CHCC hired a pharmacy manager to streamline its supply organization and installed computer systems to record and analyze supply information. CHCC uses a "TracePak" to receive supplies from different places. CHCC orders a specific procedure-based TracePak from DeRoyal, who fills the Pak with the products that DeRoyal can furnish at the lowest cost. The TracePak is then sent to CHCC's distributor, Owens & Minor, where more supplies are added. The ability of distributors to add supplies to the TracePak is an important component of the system. This allows hospitals to cut supply costs on products from multiple

---

[11] Karon, Paul, "Owens & Minor Chain Management in Stable Condition," *InfoWorld*, September 9, 1996, p. 32.
[12] Hammond, Mark, "Cashing In on Warehouses," *PC Week* August 31, 1999, p. 83.
[13] Owens & Minor Company Press Release, "Owens & Minor Delivers WISDOM On Line to Customer Desktops," Richmond, Va., June 23, 1996.
[14] "The Eternal Project," *Computerworld*, July 13, 1998, p. 71.
[15] Ibid.
[16] "Ready for Web Query Tools," *Software Magazine*, July, 1998, p. 120.

[17] Ibid.
[18] Ibid.
[19] Lattig, Michael, "WebIntelligence Gives Single Point of Entry," *InfoWorld*, May 10, 1999, v. 21, i. 19, p. 35(1).

manufacturers. These are purchased under national contracts through purchasing cooperatives, such as CHCC's affiliation with Dallas-based VHA.[20] Finally, reusable components and physician preference items are added to the TracePak in the sterile processing department within the hospital. The completed TracePak is custom configured to the hospital's or physician's specifications.

As supplies are used, exact usage is tallied and sent through electronic data interchange (EDI) to DeRoyal. Unused supplies are sent back to DeRoyal and CHCC's account is credited. Supply utilization is then sharpened through increases or decreases in the TracePak contents. EDI links between CHCC, DeRoyal, and Owens & Minor provide for electronic configuration, inventory, and reordering.

When using the TraceCart, CHCC's supply cost per total hip replacement was $503.91. This dropped to $406.03 when CHCC switched to the TracePak system. This resulted in a total supply cost savings of 19.35 percent. Similarly, CHCC's supply cost for a total knee replacement was $381.46 with the TraceCart system. The same procedure's supply cost dropped to $307.30 with the use of the TracePak system, a savings of 19.4 percent.[21]

RECOMMENDATIONS FOR THE FUTURE

Mergers, acquisitions, and strategic alliances among key customers, manufacturers, and suppliers are rapidly changing the medical supplies industry. Realizing this, O&M acquired Lyons Physician Supply in 1993, Emery Medical Supply in 1994, and Stuart Medical, Inc., also in 1994.

Strategic partnerships are also crucial to O&M's growth. With this understanding, O&M has entered alliances with some of its major customers including Columbia/HCA Healthcare Corporation, the University Hospital Consortium, and VHA Inc. Its major suppliers are 3M, Kimberly-Clark, and Johnson & Johnson. These alliances accounted for approximately 19 percent of 1994 revenues.

Despite the cost-consciousness of providers of medical care, and the threat of cuts in Medicare, which represents approximately two-fifths of hospital industry revenues, medical suppliers should experience an acceleration of both revenues and earnings in the years to come. In addition to the increased cost and time efficiencies that result from computerization, the industry is driven by factors such as the graying of the baby boomers, an increase in foreign market demand, and a continuous flow of innovative diagnostic and therapeutic products.

Owens & Minor must continue to invest in technology to remain competitive in this fast-paced, unpredictable industry. With many products becoming commodities, the pressure for companies to differentiate themselves is greater than ever.

Product differentiation may come through lower costs, better service, or increased convenience through customer-accessible information. Owens & Minor must stay one step ahead of the needs of its customers through differentiation, quality management, and cost control.

---

[20] Braly, Damon, "Pharmacist Fills Order to Cut Supply Costs with I/T," *Health Management Technology,* April 1, 1996, p. 93.
[21] Ibid.

CASE QUESTIONS

Strategic Questions

1. What is the strategic direction of the corporation/organization?

2. Who or what forces are driving this direction?

3. What has been the catalyst for change?

4. What are the core competencies for this corporation?

Technological Questions

5. What technologies has the corporation relied on?

6. What has caused a change in the use of technology in the corporation/organization?

7. How has this change been implemented?

8. How successful has the technological change been?

Quantitative Questions

9. What does the corporation say about its financial ability to embark on a major technological program of advancement?

10. What conclusions can be reached from an analysis of the financial information to support or contradict this financial ability?

11. What analysis can be made by examining the following ratio groups?

    Debt
    Revenue
    Net income

12. What conclusions can be reached by analyzing the financial trends? Are there long-term trends that seem to be problematic? Is the industry stable?

Internet Questions

13. What does the corporation's web page present about their business directives?

14. What type of web site does the company have (promotional/transactional/informative)?

Industry Questions

15. What challenges and opportunities is the industry facing?

16. Is the industry oligopolistic or competitive?

17. Does the industry face a change in government regulation?

18. How will technology impact the industry?

Data Questions

19. What role do data play in the future of the corporation?

20. How important are data to the corporation's continued success?

TECHNOLOGY TIPS

MICROSOFT WORD TIPS

LINKING DOCUMENTS AND CREATING LINKS TO THE WWW

If you are creating a report that includes PowerPoint, Access, and/or Excel, you can create links to these documents from your Word document. Links allow the reader of your document to see other sections of the report, such as an Excel worksheet, by simply clicking on the link that you create. Links can also be created to the World Wide Web (WWW). A direct link to the web source used in your report would allow the reader to go directly to the web site if they wish to explore the topic further. This is especially helpful if you decide to publish your document on the web.

Linking Documents

1. Highlight the text in which you wish to create a link with your mouse.
2. From the tool bar, click on the INSERT HYPERLINK icon.
3. You will be prompted to save your document before creating the link. Save it.
4. The Insert Hyperlink dialog box will appear. Enter the name of the file you wish to link your document to in the LINK TO FILE OR URL box. Use the BROWSE button to help you in finding the file, i.e., A:\FILENAME.DOC.
5. Click on OK when you are done.
6. The text that you highlighted will appear blue on your screen. This allows the text to stand out and distinguish it as hyperlink. Whenever you click on it, your screen will change and open that file for you.

Creating Links to the Web

1. Highlight the text in which you wish to create a link with your mouse.
2. From the tool bar, click on the INSERT HYPERLINK icon.
3. You will be prompted to save your document before creating the link. Save it.

4. The Insert Hyperlink dialog box will appear. Enter the URL of the site you wish to link your document to. Make sure that the URL is correct. Otherwise, the link will not work and an error message will appear.
5. Click on OK when you are done.
6. Just as before, the text will appear blue on your screen. When the reader clicks on the link their web browser will automatically start and take them to the URL that was entered. They must be connected to the Internet in order for this feature to work.

Creating a Link Using an Image

You can also create links for a picture, graphic, clipart, etc. This might be helpful if you have a company logo, or a graph that may need further explanation.

1. Click on the image that you wish to create the link with.
2. From the tool bar click on the INSERT HYPERLINK icon.
3. You will be prompted to save your document before creating the link. Save it.
4. Depending on whether you wish to create a link to a document or a web site, enter the appropriate information as explained in the prior sections.
5. Click on OK when you are done.

The cursor will change appearance whenever it is placed above the image. This is to indicate that a link exists. When clicked upon, the link will transport the reader to the document or web site.

MICROSOFT EXCEL TIPS

PRINTING WORKSHEETS

Printing worksheets is simply a matter of clicking on the Print command button from the standard toolbar. However, if you need to print the worksheets with headers, adjust the size, etc., you can use the page setup to make these selections.

To Reach the Page Setup Dialog Box

1. With the Excel worksheet already open, click on FILE from the Menu bar and select PAGE SETUP from the drop-down menu.
2. The Page Setup dialog box will appear.

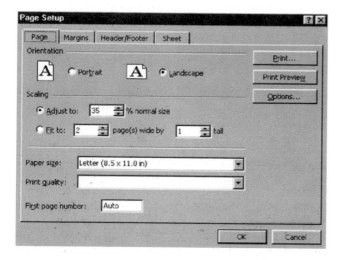

Size Adjustment

1. Click on the PAGE tab from the dialog box.
2. In order to shrink the worksheets to a certain percentage or enlarge them, click on the up or down arrows located next to the ADJUST TO: portion. You can preview the effect of the percentage dialed in by clicking on Print Preview.

Fit To

1. Click on the PAGE tab from the dialog box.
2. In order to have Excel adjust the printout of sheets to a number of pages you choose, use the FIT TO section of the Page Tab. Excel will prompt you if it is possible or not to fulfill your request of pages selected for printout.

Headers and Footers

1. Click on the HEADER/FOOTER tab of the dialog box.
2. The list-down arrows provide a number of choices to select from to appear on the printouts. Simply click on the arrow to make the choices appear similar to the ones shown.

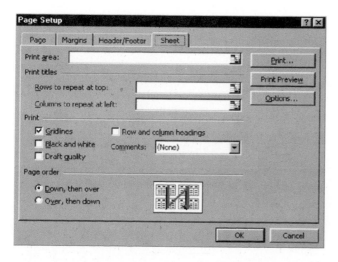

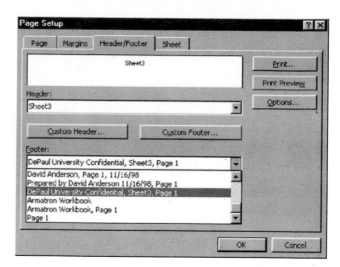

3. If the selections provided do not have what is required, click on the CUSTOM HEADER or CUSTOM FOOTER buttons located in the middle of the dialog box in order to create your own.

Gridlines

1. Click on the SHEET tab of the dialog box.
2. Gridlines can be eliminated from the printout by deselecting the gridlines check box.

Page Order

1. Click on the SHEET tab of the dialog box.
2. The order in which the worksheet will printout to the different pages is at the user's discretion. If the worksheet is rather large take into consideration how the data will be used since it will be printed out in a series of pages.

ADDITIONAL NOTE

There are several ways that you can printout the Excel worksheets. Explore the different sections of the Page Setup dialog box to discover the possibilities and do not be afraid to click on the Options button for more choices.

MICROSOFT POWERPOINT TIPS

RUNNING SLIDE SHOWS—PRESENTATIONS

Depending on your needs, you can run a slide show three different ways. The following options are available when you click SET UP SHOW from the SLIDE SHOW menu. To run the show, click on VIEW and then SLIDE SHOW.

Presented by a Speaker

Click this option to run a full-screen presentation. This is the most common method, usually with a speaker who directs the show. The presenter has complete control of the show and can run it automatically or manually, stop it to add meeting minutes or action items, and even record narration as the show progresses. You also use this mode when you want to project a slide show on a larger screen or use presentation conferencing.

Browsed by an Individual

Click this option to run a smaller-screen presentation. That is, one that may be browsed by an individual over a company

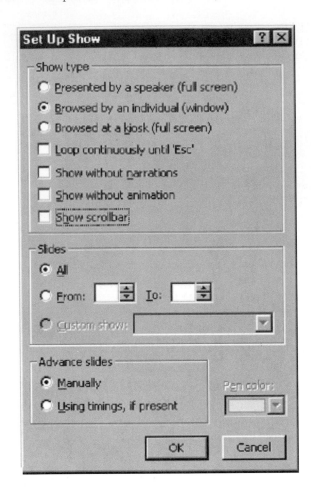

network. The presentation appears in a smaller window, with commands available for moving through the show and for editing, copying, and printing slides. In this mode, you move from slide to slide by using the scroll bar, and you can have another program open at the same time. You can also display the web toolbar so you can browse through other presentations and Office documents.

Browsed at a Kiosk

Click this option to run a self-running presentation. This method is helpful at a trade show or convention. If you have a booth, kiosk, or other location where you want to run an unattended slide show, you can set up the show to run with most menus and commands unavailable, and to restart automatically after each showing. Make sure that you include timings with each slide and you select USING TIMINGS . . . option from the SET UP SHOW dialog box.

MICROSOFT ACCESS TIPS

CREATING LABELS

Labels can be created using the data that you have entered in the tables. Whether it is mailing addresses or the compact disk information of your CD collection, Access can create labels rather quickly. Once you select the labels you want to use, make sure you have a style number. This will aid in selecting the labels from the list that Access contains. Access is

set up to use Avery brand labels, but you can also customize the labels for Access.

1. From the database window, click on the REPORTS tab, then click on the NEW button.
2. Click on LABEL WIZARD and select a table from which the information will be used to create the labels. A list of tables available will appear when you click on the drop-down arrow. Click on the OK button once you have selected a table.

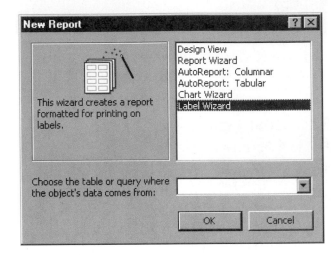

3. In the next dialog box, select the Avery number from the scroll window or click on the CUSTOMIZE button to make your own labels. Different style numbers will appear when you click on the unit of measure options or label type. Click on the NEXT button when you have made your selections.

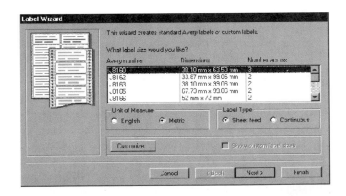

4. The next window allows you to choose font settings. Click on the NEXT button when you have made your selections.
5. The next window is used to select the fields that you would like to appear on the labels. Click on the NEXT button when you are done.
6. The next window allows you to select how the labels will be sorted. Click on the NEXT button to proceed to the last window.
7. In the final window, name the report and click on the FINISH button. If you want to make any modifications before printing, click on the MODIFY THE LABEL DESIGN button, then click on the finish button.

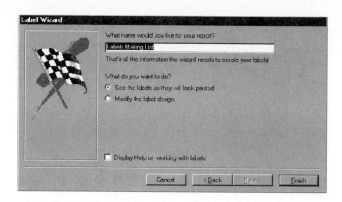

8. The labels will appear in the print preview window. If the labels are in order, make sure that the labels are in the printer and click on the PRINT button.

MICROSOFT FRONTPAGE TIPS

FURTHER DEVELOPING YOUR WEB PAGE

It is quite obvious that FrontPage express has limitations, but it helps in getting your web page started quickly and with little or no knowledge of HTML language. However, to further develop your web page, it will be to your advantage to learn HTML. If you think that HTML is too difficult, you can always purchase an HTML editor (FrontPage, AceExpert HTML Editor, etc.) that will write the HTML in the background. Listed below are some sites that provide tutorials on HTML and talk about other web development issues.

HTML Tutorials

WDVL.com
http://www.wdvl.com/Authoring/HTML/

A Beginners Guide to HTML
http://www.ncsa.uiuc.edu/General/Internet/WWW/HTMLPrimer.html

Learn HTML Lesson by Lesson
http://www.merlin.met.au/html hlp/index.html

Advanced HTML

Advanced HTML Tips
http://www.merlin.net.au/htm help/index.html

HTML 4.0
http://www.w3.org/TR/REC-html40/

General HTML and Web Development Pages

HTML Goodies
http://www.htmlgoodies.com/

About.com
http://html.miningco.com/

Spotlight on HTML
http://builder.cnet.com/Authoring/Html/

HTML Station
http://www.december.com/html/

BIBLIOGRAPHY

PREFACES

Combs, Martin. *Information Systems for Business Management*. London: Pitman, 1995.

Davis, Gordon B. *The Blackwell Encyclopedic Dictionary of Management Information Systems*. Cambridge, Mass.: Blackwell Business, 1997.

Davis, William S. *Management, Information, and Systems: An Introduction to Business Information Systems*. Minncapolis/St. Paul: West Publishing Co., 1995.

Gordon, Steven R., and Judith R. Gordon. *Information Systems: A Management Approach*. Fort Worth: Dryden Press, 1996.

McLeod, Raymond. *Management Information Systems: A Study of Computer Based Information Systems*. Englewood Cliffs, N.J.: Prentice Hall, 1995.

O'Brien, James A., *Introduction to Information Systems: An End User/Enterprise Perspective*. Chicago: Irwin, 1995.

Taylor, Allan, and Stephen Farrell. *Information Management for Business*. Metuchen, N.J.: Scarecrow Press, 1995.

Varughese, Roy T. *Strategic Enterprise Management: An IT Manager's Desk Reference*. Boston: International Thomson Computer Press, 1997.

Wilson, Martin. *The Information Edge: Successful Management Using Information Technology*. Washington, D.C.: Pitman, 1997.

CHAPTER 1

Coleman, Kevin G. *Reengineering MIS: Aligning Information Technology and Business Operations*. Harrisburg, Pa.: Idea Group, 1996.

Currid, Cheryl & Company. *Computing Strategies for Reengineering your Organization*. Rocklin, CA: Prima, 1996.

Fong, Joseph, and Shi-Ming Huang. *Information Systems Reengineering*. Berlin; New York: Springer, 1997.

Lucas, Henry C. *Information Technology for Management*. New York: McGraw-Hill, 1997.

Martin, Merle P. *Analysis and Design of Business Information Systems*. Englewood Cliffs, N.J.: Prentice- Hall, 1995.

Minoli, Daniel, *Analyzing Outsourcing: Reengineering Information and Communication Systems*. New York: McGraw-Hill, 1995.

Stair, Ralph M. *An Introduction to Information Systems*. Cambridge, MA: Course Technology, 1997.

CHAPTER 2

Keen, Peter G. W. *Business Multimedia Explained: A Manager's Guide to Key Terms and Concepts*. Boston: Harvard Business School Press, 1997.

CHAPTER 3

Österle, Hubert. *Business in the Information Age: Heading for New Processes*. New York: Springer, 1995.

CHAPTER 4

David, Werner. *Managing Company-wide Communication*. New York: Chapman & Hall, 1995.

Gupta, Uma G. *Management Information Systems: A Managerial Perspective*. Minneapolis/St. Paul: West, 1996.

Jablonski, Stefan, and Christoph Bussler. *Workflow Management: Modeling Concepts, Architecture and Implementation*. Boston: International Thomson Computer Press, 1996.

Schultheis, Robert A., Mary Sumner, Douglas Bock. *Management Information Systems: The Manager's View*. Burr Ridge, IL: Irwin, 1995.

Vitalari, Nicholas P., and James C. Wetherbe. *Cases in Systems Analysis and Design, Best Practices*. Minneapolis/St. Paul: West, 1995.

Wigand, Rolf T., Arnold Picot, Ralf Reichwald. *Information, Organization, and Management: Expanding Markets and Corporate Boundaries*. New York: Wiley, 1997.

CHAPTER 5

Adam, Nabil R., and Aryya Gangopadhyay. *Database Issues in Geographic Information Systems*. Boston: Kluwer Academic Publishers, 1997.

Inmon, William H., Claudia Imhoff, Greg Battas. *Building the Operational Data Store*. New York: Wiley, 1996.

Inmon, William H., John A Zachman, Jonathan G. Geiger. *Data Stores, Data Warehousing, and the Zachman Framework: Managing Enterprise Knowledge*. New York: McGraw-Hill, 1997.

Korfhage, Robert R. *Information Storage and Retrieval*. New York: Wiley Computer Pub., 1997.

Kowalski, Gerald. *Information Retrieval Systems: Theory and Implementation*. Boston: Kluwer Academic Publishers, 1997.

Simon, Alan R. *Strategic Database Technology: Management for the Year 2000*. San Francisco: Morgan Kaufmann Publishers, Inc., 1995.

Watson, Richard Thomas. *Data Management: An Organizational Perspective*. New York: Wiley, 1996.

CHAPTER 6

Koenig, W. (ed.). *Distributed Information Systems in Business*. Berlin; New York: Springer-Verlag, 1996.

Martin, James, Kathleen Kavanagh Chapman, Joe Leben. *Enterprise Networking: Strategies and Transport Protocols*. Upper Saddle River, N.J.: Prentice Hall PTR, 1996.

O'Brien, James A., *Management Information Systems: Managing Information Technology in the Networked Enterprise*. Chicago: Irwin, 1996.

Rhodes, Peter D. *Building a Network: How to Specify, Design, Procure, and Install a Corporate LAN*. New York: McGraw-Hill, 1996.

CHAPTER 7

Benesko, Gary G., *Inter-corporate Business Engineering: Streamlining the Business Cycle from End to End*. Cary, N.C.: Research Triangle Consultants, 1997.

Cook, Melissa A. *Building Enterprise Information Architectures: Reengineering Information Systems*. Upper Saddle River, N.J.: Prentice Hall PTR, 1996.

Johnson, James H. *Investigation of Alternatives to an Equipment Assembly Structure for a MAMC/MAXIMO Data Base*. Champaign, Ill.: Construction Engineering Research Laboratory, 1996.

Wiederhold, Gio. *Intelligent Integration of Information*. Boston: Kluwer, 1996.

CHAPTER 8

Dhar, Vasant, and Roger Stein. *Intelligent Decision Support Methods: the Science of Knowledge Work*. Upper Saddle River, NJ: Prentice-Hall, 1997.

Scholz-Reiter, Bernd, and Eberhard Stickel (eds.). *Business Process Modelling*. New York: Springer, 1996.

Sprague, Ralph H., and Hugh J. Watson. *Decision Support for Management*. Upper Saddle River, N.J.: Prentice-Hall, 1996.

CHAPTER 9

Frants, V., Jacob Shapiro, Vladimir G. Voiskunskii. *Automated Information Retrieval: Theory and Methods*. San Diego, Calif.: Academic Press, 1997.

CHAPTER 10

Albert, Steven, and Keith Bradley. *Managing Knowledge: Experts, Agencies and Organizations*. New York: Cambridge University Press, 1997.

Davenport, Thomas H. *Information Ecology: Mastering the Information and Knowledge Environment*. New York: Oxford University Press, 1997.

Liebowitz, Jay, and Lyle C. Wilcox (eds.). Knowledge Management and Its Integrative Elements. Boca Raton, Fla.: CRC Press, 1997.

Moutinho, Luiz, Bruce Curry, Paulo Rita. *Expert Systems in Tourism Marketing*. New York: Routledge, 1996.

Rowe, Alan J., and Sue Anne Davis. *Intelligent Information Systems: Meeting the Challenge of the Knowledge Era*. Westport, Conn.: Quorum Books, 1996.

CHAPTER 11

Applegage, Lynda M., F. Warren McFarlan, James L. McKenney. *Corporate Information Systems Management*. Chicago: Irwin, 1996.

Chan, Yolande E. (ed.). *Business Strategic Orientation, Information Systems Strategic Management, and Strategic Alignment*. Cambridge, Mass.: Marketing Science Institute, 1996.

Hope, Jeremy, and Tony Hope. *Competing in the Third Wave: The Ten Key Management Issues of the Information Age*. Boston: Harvard Business School Press, 1997.

McKeen, James D. amd Heather A. Smith. *Management Challenges in IS: Successful Strategies and Appropriate Action*. New York: Wiley, 1996.

Tozer, E. E. *Strategic IS/IT Planning*. Boston: Butterworth-Heinemann, 1996.

Ward, John, and Pat Griffiths. *Strategic Planning for Information Systems*. New York: Wiley, 1996.

CHAPTER 12

Core competencies for financial system analysis in the federal government [microform]. Washington, D.C.: The Office; Gaithersburg, MD (P.O. Box 6015, Gaithersburg 20884-6015): The Office [distributor, 1997].

Crawford, I. M. *Marketing Research and Information Systems*. Rome: Food and Agriculture Organization of the United Nations, 1997.

United States Congress. Senate Committee on Governmental Affairs. Subcommittee on Oversight of Government Management and the District of Columbia. Implementation of the Information Technology Management Reform Act of 1996: hearing before the subcommittee and the District of Columbia. One Hundred Fourth Congress, second session,

July 17, 1996. Washington: U.S. G.P.O.: For sale by the U.S. G.P.O., Supt. of Docs., Congressional Sales Office, 1996.

CHAPTER 13

Remenyi, Dan, Michael Sherwood-Smith, Terry White. *Achieving Maximum Value from Information Systems: A Process Approach*. New York: J. Wiley & Sons, 1997.

CHAPTER 14

Ankrapp, Betty (ed.). *Health Care Software Sourcebook*. Gaithersburg, Md.: Aspen Publishers, 1996.

Austin, Charles J., Stuart B. Boxerman, Tee H. Hiett. *Quantitative Analysis for Health Services Administration*. Arlington, VA: AUPHA Press, 1995.

Ball, Marion J. (ed.). *Healthcare Information Management Systems: A Practical Guide*. New York: Springer-Verlag, 1995.

Deans, Candace amd Jaak Jurison. *Information Technology in a Global Business Environment: Readings and Cases*. Danvers, MA: Boyd & Fraser, 1996.

Itoh, Toshio. *Technology in the 21st Century: Future Readings for an Information-oriented Society*. Tokyo: Ohmsha, 1996.

Kreider, Nancy A., and Becky J. Haselton (eds.). *The Systems Challenge: Getting the Clinical Information Support You Need to Improve Patient Care*. Chicago: American Hospital Pub., 1997.

Lorenzi, Nancy M. (ed.). *Transforming Health Care Through Information: Case Studies*. New York: Springer-Verlag, 1995.

Tan, Joseph K. H. *Health Management Information Systems: Theories, Methods, and Applications*. Gaithersburg, Md.: Aspen Publishers, 1995.

Worthley, John Abbott, and Philip S. DiSalvio. *Managing Computers in Health Care: A Guide for Professionals*. Ann Arbor, Mich.: Health Administration Press, 1995.

INDEX